ANCIENT MONUMENTS

OF

THE MISSISSIPPI VALLEY

ANCIENT MONUMENTS

OF

THE MISSISSIPPI VALLEY

EPHRAIM G. SQUIER AND EDWIN H. DAVIS

EDITED AND WITH AN INTRODUCTION BY
DAVID J. MELTZER

SMITHSONIAN INSTITUTION PRESS
WASHINGTON AND LONDON

The volume editor and the Press are profoundly grateful to Susan and Claude C. Albritton III for their generous support of this publication, given in memory of Claude C. Albritton Jr., who so highly valued the history of science and recognized its vital importance to contemporary scholars.

New material for this edition edited by Jan McInroy

Library of Congress Cataloging-in-Publication Data
Squier, E. G. (Ephraim George), 1821–1888.
    Ancient monuments of the Mississippi Valley : comprising the results of extensive original surveys and explorations / by E. G. Squier and E. H. Davis.
      p.   cm.
    ISBN 1-56098-873-8 (hardcover : alk. paper) — ISBN 1-56098-898-3 (pbk. : alk. paper)
    1. Indians of North America—Mississippi Valley—Antiquities. 2. Mounds—Mississippi Valley. 3. Mississippi Valley—Antiquities.   I. Davis, E. H. (Edwin Hamilton), 1811–1888.   II. Title.
E78.M75S64   1998
976.2′01—dc21   98-24831

British Library Cataloging-in-Publication Data available

Manufactured in the United States of America
05 04 03 02 01 00 99 98 5 4 3 2 1

♾ The paper used in this publication meets the minimum requirements of the American National Standard for Information Sciences—Permanence of Paper for Printed Library Materials, ANSI Z39.48-1984.

This 150th anniversary reissue of
Ancient Monuments of the Mississippi Valley
is dedicated to the memory of
James B. Griffin, 1905–1997

CONTENTS.

INTRODUCTION:

EPHRAIM SQUIER, EDWIN DAVIS, AND THE MAKING OF AN AMERICAN ARCHAEOLOGICAL CLASSIC.

David J. Meltzer

Ancient Monuments of the Mississippi Valley, by Ephraim Squier and Edwin Davis, was the first publication ever issued by the Smithsonian Institution—in any subject. As such, much was riding on it. The fledgling institution's first publication, in 1848, would send a clear signal to Congress, the scientific community (here and abroad), and especially the Smithsonian's Board of Regents, all of whom were watching closely to see how Joseph Henry (the institution's first secretary) would choose to interpret James Smithson's generous but "enigmatic behest" that the institution he endowed have as its object "the increase and diffusion of knowledge."[1]

On *Ancient Monuments* Henry (1797–1878) staked his vision for the Smithsonian's future, for that book would, inevitably, set a scholarly and scientific precedent for the institution, launch its Contributions to Knowledge series, and thus help (or hinder) his efforts to establish the Smithsonian's credibility on the national and international scientific scene. *Ancient Monuments* would also be the first major work in the still-undisciplined disciplines of anthropology and archaeology, and thus unavoidably a landmark in those fields—and, for that matter, in American science in general (which was then often viewed as the poor stepchild of European science).[2]

All this was riding on a book devoted to the questions of the origin, antiquity, and identity of the moundbuilders. Those questions had surfaced after the Revolutionary War, as emigrant trains began streaming over the Appalachian and Allegheny Mountains into the lowlands of the Ohio and Mississippi valleys (then the American West) and settlers came upon vast numbers of abandoned mounds and earthworks. By then, local Native Americans had been mostly decimated or dispersed by "spirituous liquors, the small-pox, war and an abridgment of territory," as Jefferson put it; remaining individuals had neither recollections nor legends of building the earthworks, and their numbers seemed too few to account for the extensive construction that had obviously taken place.[3] The result was that mound construction was widely and popularly attributed to a race of moundbuilders, who either no longer existed or at least no longer existed where and as they had earlier.

There was no single moundbuilder story, but many, and in the first half of the nineteenth century these took a variety of mythic, romantic, and scholarly forms and thrived in a literature of fantasy, bad poetry, antiquarian studies, and best-selling romantic novels with racist undertones (it was naturally assumed that the people who had created these great empires of mounds were white). The moundbuilder myth also, arguably, spawned a religion. There was considerable speculation, among antiquarians no less than others, about who the moundbuilders were, where they had come from and when, and where they had disappeared to. Some of that speculation was informed, much of it was not, but rarely did it incorporate a significant measure of archaeological data.[4]

Nor was it clear how the moundbuilders related to living Native Americans: Were they linked as ancestors and descendants? Was one civilized, the other savage? If so, what caused the apparent tumble from the "demi-civilized" state of the moundbuilders to the "savagery" of the Indians? Was one vanquished and the other the conqueror? How did the moundbuilders relate to the comparably advanced civilizations of Central and South America? Were those the places where the moundbuilders originated, or were they the refuges of the moundbuilders flight from the encroaching Indians? And how, ultimately, did these distinctive American races relate to the peoples of the Old World?[5]

These were loaded questions to a new nation being swept along in an undirected and uncontrolled social experiment mixing three different races, one "savage," another enslaved, the third certain of its racial superiority but hamstrung by an Enlightenment belief in the common humanity of all. The queries also sparked sharp political repercussions in a nation that was expanding westward and that often perceived Indians as brutal, warlike, and savage obstacles to settlement. The idea that Indians themselves drove off or killed the glorious moundbuilders made it easier to rationalize their inevitable demise as a form of historic justice.[6]

These questions were also deeply discomforting to a nation that viewed the past through a biblical lens, yet was confronted with the realization that neither the moundbuilders nor the American Indians were easily identified in the chronicles of Moses. On the presumption of monogenesis—the idea that "all the varieties of the human race were descended from a single pair, and that after the Flood the earth was indebted solely to the ark of Noah for the replenishment of man and beast"—American origins were sought among historically known or imagined groups, among them the Egyptians, Phoenicians, Mongols, Welsh, "Hindoos," and Atlanteans. But all these claims, and even the perennial favorite—that the American races were descendants of the Ten Lost Tribes of Israel (a claim with two great virtues: It explained who the Indians were *and* where the Israelites had been lost all those years)—failed to withstand close scrutiny. Making matters even more uncomfortable were the polygenists, who through the 1830s and 1840s were arguing with increasing intensity and seemingly insurmountable evidence that the Bible was utterly irrelevant to the question of the origins of the American race (moundbuilder or Indian), for the *races* of humanity were, in fact, separately created *species*—Genesis notwithstanding. As Curtis M. Hinsley argues, the search for human origins had deep religious import.[7]

So it was that the moundbuilder question, a straightforward archaeological issue on its face, at times hovered dangerously close to the raw nerves of religion and racism. Surely, launching the Contributions to Knowledge series with a volume devoted to, say, meteorology, ornithology, or even agricultural chemistry would have been safer. Yet Henry deliberately elected to lead off his brand-new series with a volume on the moundbuilders, written by two avocationalists working in a field that hardly existed (or at the very least had few rules or standards to follow), and on a subject that could easily become hopelessly entangled in divisive issues that Henry desperately wished to keep out of the realm of scientific discourse—and even farther away from his institution.[8] No wonder he was nervous.

But in the end, Squier and Davis proved to be talented observers, surveyors, collectors, and writers, and Henry proved to be a skilled scientific adviser and political tactician, although a slightly clumsy administrator and a heavy-handed editor. The result was that *Ancient Monuments of the Mississippi Valley* quickly became an archaeological classic and remains so to this day. It is a classic for all the usual reasons: for its pioneering methods, its broad scope, its record of data and a way of thinking about the past that is now long gone, and—arguably—for its status as a key step in the formation of the modern discipline of American archaeology. For nearly half a century, *Ancient Monuments* was the centerpiece of American archaeology, and as Joseph Henry had assured Squier and Davis, the volume would win "a permanent and enviable reputation and lead you to fame if not to fortune."[9]

Which makes the volume's triumph all the more remarkable, for it came almost in spite of, and not because of, its authors. By the time *Ancient Monuments* was heading into proof sheets, in the fall and winter of 1847, Squier and Davis were deeply in the midst of a bitter proprietary dispute over authorship—among other things. By the time the volume appeared, in the fall of 1848, they had ceased speaking altogether, were threatening each other with lawsuits, and had taken to actions against each other that skated uncomfortably close to burglary. Joseph Henry was caught up in the middle of their increasingly ugly brawl and had to appease not just the warring parties but also the Smithsonian's Board of Regents, who were understandably concerned that the institution's inaugural volume was taking so long to publish and that the cost was spiraling far beyond Henry's initial estimates. At the same time, he had to allay the fears of several correspondents around the country, who felt certain that their hard-earned field data and results—which they had freely shared with Squier and Davis—were being used in *Ancient Monuments* without due credit to them.

Over the last 150 years, *Ancient Monuments* has been an enduring classic. Its lavish illustrations and detailed accounts of an archaeological record that has now been mostly lost have provided for successive generations a look at a bygone era of archaeology, archaeological data, and archaeological interpretation. But Joseph Henry did his job well: The volume gives very few hints of the controversies swirling around the issues raised by Squier and Davis, and hardly any indication at all of the birth pangs of its production.

AN ARCHAEOLOGICAL PARTNERSHIP

Forever wedded in the archaeological literature by virtue of their joint work, Squier and Davis actually had very little in common before they came together to produce *Ancient Monuments*. They collaborated on but one project—this one. They grew to despise one another, and their intense and lifelong dislike was fueled by a resentment for each other's claims of credit for the book's success. After *Ancient Monuments* they went on to very different careers. Squier found the literary and scientific celebrity he so desperately sought and left behind a wealth of published and unpublished materials to ensure that his name would outlive him. Davis, on the other hand, retreated to the quieter life that he had enjoyed before the Squier whirlwind had blown through and left a family rich in memories but few more tangible traces. So it is that in most historical studies of their work, this one included, Squier gains the lion's share of the attention—but then, he would have it no other way.

They were altogether two very different individuals who led very separate lives— save for the time when their paths crossed in Chillicothe, Ohio, and they discovered a mutual interest in archaeology.

EPHRAIM GEORGE SQUIER

Ephraim Squier (1821–88) was the younger of the pair (by ten years). He aggressively sought fame, occasionally found notoriety, led a peripatetic life of hard work, travel, and writing—including an extensive correspondence with scholars, scientists, and politicians in this country, Latin America, and Europe—and had highly productive careers in archaeology and journalism, with brief stints in state and national politics. During his productive lifetime, he published nearly a dozen books, many more articles, and countless newspaper pieces. He was honored by learned societies here and abroad, and he represented the United States in archaeological and diplomatic circles. He was lively, energetic, flamboyant at some times, grievously insensitive at others, and as a contemporary recorded, "one of the most audacious spirits I have known." Yet, in the early 1870s, after his personal life took a series of bizarre and sordid turns and began to unravel, his emotional volatility spilled over into deep mental illness. Finally, at the request of a younger brother and on the advice of a neurologist, a New York Supreme Court justice ordered that Squier be placed in an insane asylum, where he spent most of the last fourteen years of his life.[10]

Squier was born in Bethlehem, New York (Albany County), on June 17, 1821, the son of a Methodist minister (Joel Squier) and the descendant of a line that reached back to the Englishman Samuel Squier (a friend and first lieutenant of Oliver Cromwell) and included a grandfather (Ephraim) who served with distinction in the Revolutionary War—at times directly under General George Washington. Although a distinguished family, it was not a wealthy one, and Squier's formal schooling was necessarily limited. As was customary in those days, he earned his own education, by working on local farms in the summer and teaching younger children in the winter.[11]

Showing an early aptitude for mathematics and geometry, Squier also began a study of civil engineering, with hopes of catching on as a surveyor or engineer, but the economic panic that began in 1837 (triggered largely by overdevelopment in what was then the western states) and continued through 1839 sharply limited his employment opportunities. It was evident to him that he needed to pursue other career paths. Teaching was the profession recommended by his father, and at age eighteen (in 1839) Squier enrolled in the Troy Conference Academy in West Poultney, Vermont, for formal training. His heart wasn't in it, however. As he wrote later to his

Ephraim George Squier. Courtesy of the National Anthropological Archives, Smithsonian Institution

parents, he saw no future in leading the life of a "dispised [*sic*] and miserable peda-gogue—the most illy paid and thankless of all employments." Besides, teaching was not the route to fame or fortune for a restless free spirit like Squier, and he wanted both. He wanted, as he explained to his parents, to leave "a NAME to the world."[12]

Having a knack for writing, he decided to abandon teaching for journalism, or possibly a literary career. In 1841 he moved to Albany "without money and without friends" and found a job as a writer and editor for the *New York State Mechanic*, the paper of the prison reform party in the state. The *Mechanic* gave Squier a job, a cause, and a platform, and he reveled in them. He became one of the paper's more aggressive writers, crafted reports on the prisons to the state government, and actively organized branches of the Mechanics' Association across the state. Doing so gave him a taste for politics, and he soon set his sights on larger targets; he became active in the Whig Party, publishing newspaper articles and letters that championed Whig causes. On the side, he wrote for monthly magazines, tried his hand at poetry (he had a strong romantic streak), and even undertook publishing, but his *Poet's Magazine: A Repository of Original and Selected American Poetry,* failed after two issues. All the while, as one overwrought (auto?)biography put it, he "struggled with every degree of poverty and privation."[13]

Though he was not able to launch a career as a poet, his frenetic activity paid off in 1843, when the *New York State Mechanic* folded (its mission of prison reform complete) and he found himself out of work. Whig activists in Connecticut had heard of Squier (who came with a recommendation from Horace Greeley) and asked him to join a pro-Whig newspaper in Hartford. The first number of the *Hartford Journal* appeared in November 1843, and through the elections in the spring of 1844, Squier actively campaigned for the party of Henry Clay, attacked Van Buren's Democrats with his sharp editorial claws, and organized rallies and Clay Clubs around the state. He did his work well. The Whigs carried Connecticut, but they lost the national election. On the heels of that bad news, Squier learned that the *Journal* had been sold (it folded in 1845), and he was again unemployed.[14]

A job offer came from Baltimore, but Squier refused to "live where there are slaves." Instead, in April 1845 he headed west to Chillicothe, Ohio, apparently tempted by the opportunity to see the mounds and earthworks of the region close-up and, more pragmatically, by the offer to become the editor of the weekly *Scioto Gazette*.[15] On arriving in Chillicothe, Squier encountered some of the most spectacular mounds and earthworks of the American West.

Editing a weekly gave him plenty of time to explore these monuments, and in doing so he found a calling. As he later wrote,

Before going to Ohio in 1844 [*sic*], I had primed myself of all the information I could acquire [about] our aboriginal monuments and the third day after my arrival there found me in the field examining their character. I was at once struck with the extremely incorrect and imperfect nature of the accounts which had been presented to the public respecting them, and immediately resolved, with the simple view of informing myself on the subject, to devote my leisure time to their investigation. I had not proceeded far before I became satisfied that it was hopeless to enquire of residents for facts respecting them, and finally that the only mode of acquiring information was to take the compass and chain in one hand and the mattock and spade in the other and go into the field in person.

From that time on, he diligently attended to his archaeological pursuits—and apparently little else. A fellow editor at the *Scioto Gazette* later publicly grumbled, "All of Mr. Squier's several 'vocations,' while a resident of Ohio, were made secondary to his antiquarian researches."[16]

But the work would not be done alone. Soon after arriving, Squier met a local Chillicothe physician who already had considerable interest in the subject and had started a collection of artifacts.

EDWIN HAMILTON DAVIS

Edwin Davis (1811–88) spent the first half of his life in and around Chillicothe, Ohio. He was trained as a physician, practiced in the state for a dozen years, then moved (in 1850) to New York City, where he taught in the New York Medical College for ten years. On the East Coast he also realized a few modest dividends from the publication of *Ancient Monuments,* delivering a course of lectures on archaeology at the Lowell Institute in Boston. After teaching, he returned to private practice in New York, where he spent the remainder of his years. By contemporary accounts, Davis was quiet and thoughtful—somewhat diffident—and a soft touch for patients who could barely afford medical fees. He lacked Squier's ambition and drive, and over his lifetime he published only a smattering of papers in scientific and medical journals.[17]

Davis was born on January 22, 1811, in Hillsboro, Ohio, just a short distance down the road from Chillicothe and the extraordinarily rich mound and earthwork complexes of southern Ohio and the Scioto River Valley—many of which would later figure prominently in *Ancient Monuments*. He was born to a Dartmouth-educated merchant and banker, but overall, little is known of his early years or much more of his ancestry and background. His generation of the family proved to be an accomplished one: Davis and two younger brothers all graduated from Kenyon College in Ohio—Edwin in 1833—and all of them attained some prominence—in medicine, politics, law, or, in Edwin Davis's case, archaeology.[18]

Growing up where he did sparked a lifelong interest in mounds and earthworks, but it was an interest not easily pursued at a time when careers in archaeology did not exist. As a student at Kenyon in the early 1830s, Davis explored the mounds of the Scioto Valley and read a paper on them before a local learned society (the Philomathesian Society). He subsequently revised that paper and delivered it at his Kenyon College commencement (under the title "Antiquities of Ohio"). The paper was heard by a visiting Daniel Webster, who was then touring the western states. Webster was an early member of the American Antiquarian Society, in Worcester, Massachusetts, and he had an abiding interest in archaeological subjects. After the talk, he urged Davis to continue his research into mounds and earthworks.

Davis did so, first from the town of Bainbridge, Ohio, to which he moved after graduation and where he was a daily witness to the construction of the Milford-to-Chillicothe turnpike and the consequent destruction of many of the mounds in Paint Creek Valley. As those mounds were dissected or removed, Davis scrutinized their

Edwin Hamilton Davis. Courtesy of the National Anthropological Archives, Smithsonian Institution

structure and stratification and collected artifacts from them. During his time in Bainbridge (1835–39), he also attended the Cincinnati Medical College, from which he graduated in 1837/38. Afterward, he settled in Chillicothe, married Lucy Woodbridge (in 1841), and set up a medical practice.[19]

In his free time over the next decade or so, Davis explored many of the mounds and earthworks in the area and amassed a substantial collection of artifacts from them. By 1845 he was corresponding with several major figures in anthropology, including Samuel George Morton (1799–1851) at Philadelphia's Academy of Natural Sciences, and John Russell Bartlett (1805–86), a New York bookseller and printer who was a prime mover in New York's American Ethnological Society (AES).

TAKING TO THE FIELD

To hear Squier tell it, when he met Davis in Chillicothe, the latter had been collecting for years, but over that time had made "no surveys, had no maps or plans, nor had he ever opened a mound, or if he had certainly could tell nothing of their construction or content." Of course, Squier said all of this three years after their initial meeting, when he was in the midst of battling Davis over credit for authoring *Ancient Monuments*, arguing with Joseph Henry over what the Smithsonian owed him in money and copies of *Ancient Monuments* (and how that remuneration would be divided with Davis), and trying to convince a powerful member of the Smithsonian's Board of Regents to take his side. His recollections were more than a little self-serving. Still, even then Squier admitted to being pleased to have found "a man who manifest any interest in the subject, and I felt gratified when he consented to accompany me in a visit to some of the more remarkable works of the neighborhood."[20]

Davis, for his part, was pleased to have a "junior partner" with a ready pen and a knowledge of surveying, and he was soon writing Morton and others to say that Squier was now assisting him with his fieldwork. Squier's infectious energy and grand visions entranced Davis and opened his eyes to the broader interest and value of the work. And if he occasionally felt pressured by the overly ambitious and hard-charging younger man, he was at least bemused by him as well: "My friend, Mr. Squier, is so enthusiastic upon this subject, that he goes off half-cocked sometimes (as the Western phrase is)."[21]

Precisely when and under what terms they agreed to collaborate on their research is uncertain. Without question, by the summer of 1845 they were spending considerable time together in field explorations (Davis's participation mostly depending on when he could break away from his medical duties). By Squier's recollection, which in this instance seems reliable enough, their initial intent was merely to build their "cabinets" (private artifact collections). At some time over the winter of 1845–46, however, a broader design of research and results took hold in their minds, and in the spring of 1846, armed with introductions from Davis, Squier headed east to announce their presence and activities and to try and drum up financial support for a large-scale archaeological project. That he went east is no surprise: That was where the established learned societies, interest, prestige, and money were.[22]

MEETING THE ISSUES

Squier's travels took him across Ohio, to Baltimore, Washington, Philadelphia, New York, Boston, and finally to Worcester, Massachusetts. Davis was partly able to track his progress through the newspapers, for Squier was carrying with him many of the artifacts recovered from their work in 1845 and the arrival of the collection was a newsworthy event in many places. In Philadelphia, Squier met Morton, quickly developed a rapport with him, and asked for his help in those "branches of science" (notably cranial and skeletal anatomy) in which Squier keenly felt his own lack of knowledge. Morton was delighted to do what he could, and he proved just as eager as Squier to obtain skeletal material from the mounds, but for reasons that Squier may not have fully appreciated at the time.[23]

Morton, the patriarch of the American polygenists (and a man whose gentle demeanor belied his scientific ferocity), was on the lookout for scientific evidence and arguments to refute the biblically anchored idea of the unity of the human race (monogenesis). Since the 1820s he had been amassing a collection of human skulls that by the time of his death in 1851 numbered more than one thousand specimens— the "American Golgotha," his contemporaries called it. Morton's studies of the skulls began as a classroom exercise to furnish his anatomy lectures at Pennsylvania Medical College. Yet as he examined and measured the skulls of Native Americans, Africans, and Caucasians, he began to detect differences among them, especially in cranial volume, which seemed to correlate neatly with their respective races.[24] Cranial capacity, it appeared, was a distinctive marker of race, each race being quite separate from others and yet homogeneous within itself.

Morton announced that discovery in *Crania Americana* in 1839, along with the more startling observation that those racial differences reached back in time. At least, sculptures from ancient Luxor and Karnak in Egypt implied as much: They depicted "the Caucasian and Negro races . . . as perfectly distinct in that country upwards of three thousand years ago as they are now." As there had been no changes in the races since then and was no apparent reason to believe they could have physically diverged from a common ancestor in just the preceding thousand years (between Noah's Flood and Egyptian civilization), Morton could only conclude that the physical and (by extension) the intellectual characteristics of each race were present at the beginning and were otherwise unaffected by environmental factors.[25]

To Morton the American race was distinct from those of the Old World, and though there was variation among the Indians, on the whole they were much alike: "He who has seen one tribe of Indians," Morton often intoned, "has seen all." Morton found it difficult to credit the civilizations of Mexico and Peru, and the "demi-civilization" of the mounds, to the "barbarous" Indians. Their "intellectual faculties" seemed too limited, and they had failed to improve on that score despite two centuries of proximity to Europeans (clear testimony, in Morton's mind, that the Indian's "inferior" intellect was hardwired at Creation, and not the result of environmental cause or historical circumstance). So he split the American race into two families, based on their cultural attainments: the intellectually superior and cranially distinct *Toltecans*, which included the moundbuilders and the inhabitants of

Mexico and Peru; and, below them the *Barbarous* Indians, "the numberless hordes which have inhabited the American continent."[26]

That distinction proved uncomfortably awkward when the mean cranial volume for Toltecans came to a mere 75 cubic inches, far *less* than the 84 cubic inches for the skulls of the barbarous Indians. Worse, the Toltecans "possessed a brain no larger than the Hottentot or New Hollander." Were Toltecans an exception to the phrenological "law" that brain size measured intellect? Phrenologists thought not, asserting that both of the American families had comparable "intellectual lobes" but that in the barbarous Indians the intellect was overpowered by "animal propensities and passions." That moundbuilders apparently predated the Indians testified to the degeneration of intellect and cultural accomplishment and the resurgence of animal propensities.[27]

At the time he met Squier, Morton had just updated his argument that "all the American nations, excepting the Eskimaux [whom he linked with Asians], are of one race, and this race is peculiar and distinct from all others."[28] At that moment, Morton wasn't *publicly* claiming that the races were separately created or separate species. His belief in the permanence of racial types and his vigorous denial that climate could modify the human form brought him to the brink of doing so, but there he stopped: The union of the races, as everyone in America well knew, produced fertile offspring. How could such races be separate *species*? The answer, it seemed, lay in changing the definition of a species.[29]

The summer Squier visited, Morton was hard at work on a paper on "hybridity in animals," the singular aim of which was to show that the traditional criteria by which species were recognized—the ability to produce viable offspring—was flawed. Different species, Morton would argue, *could* produce fertile progeny. Consequently, the fact that the different human races produced fertile offspring was *not* proof that they were the same species. That argument was, in the eyes of the polygenists, a powerful one, but they believed it could not stand alone. As Josiah Nott (1804–73), a Mobile, Alabama, physician and one of Morton's closest colleagues, put it, the issue of *chronology* was where "the matter is to be clinched—we may put forth the facts of Natural History as much as we please, but the *crowd* will not be convinced until it is shown that the chronologies of nations are irreconcilable with the common readings of Moses."[30]

Here is where Squier and Davis's work could be useful to the polygenist cause. It seemed to Morton that there was no more resemblance between Indians and Asians "than exists between any other two distinct races [species] of mankind." But to prove that Indians had not descended from Asian or Old World groups who had migrated to America required showing that their distinctive physical characteristics were present even among the most ancient Americans. Yet Morton's collection was woefully short on craniums from the western mounds—craniums that should be among the oldest on the American continent.[31] If Squier and Davis could discover more specimens, they could help to prove that the American race was ancient and distinct and thus round out the polygenists' arsenal for their attack on the Bible's version of the Creation and the idea of the unity of the human race.

Davis, while he may not have accepted the full implications of Morton's arguments, nonetheless found his claims about the distinctiveness of the American race "quite conclusive." For his part, Squier was only too happy to oblige, for the minister's son was impious at the very least and had promised his father earlier that spring "to show [him] some things" he never dreamed of "in [his] philosophy."[32] He would easily tumble under the heretical influence of the polygenists, but that was for the future. For now, Squier was thrilled to win the personal approbation of Morton and the promise of help.

From Philadelphia, it was on to New York, where Squier encountered a very different perspective on the history of the American race. There he attended a meeting of the American Ethnological Society, at the home of its "venerable President" and founder, Albert Gallatin (1761–1849). Economist, diplomat, and statesman, Gallatin had been Thomas Jefferson's secretary of the treasury, served as minister to France and England, and then retired from government service to finish a career in banking and pursue his interests in science—particularly ethnology.[33]

In his ethnology, as in his economics, Gallatin was conservative, carrying from his younger days the staunch Enlightenment belief that human progress was propelled by environmental, not racial, factors. Gallatin was not so enlightened, however, that he thought Indians were civilized (he didn't), but then neither was he so conservative that he would argue that Indians were doomed as a race to forever being primitive (he wouldn't). Rather, he firmly believed in their *capacity* for progress up the developmental ladder from savagery to civilization, environmental circumstances permitting or demanding.[34]

That Indians were still at the level of savagery was evident to Gallatin from their languages. Despite the great number of their languages (more than in Asia and Africa combined), they apparently shared the same grammatical construction from the Arctic to Cape Horn. Peter Duponceau had labeled it *polysynthetic*, and that structure ostensibly reflected their inability to conceive abstract terms and the necessity of stringing together in a single word the characteristics of several "thoughts or observations" to convey an idea.[35]

That common structure, in turn, bespoke a common origin—and a great antiquity, for a long time must have elapsed to produce from that single ancestral tongue the many American languages now being spoken. How long? It seemed to Gallatin that "this continent received its first inhabitants at a very remote epoch, probably not much posterior to that of the dispersion of mankind."[36] Gallatin chose his words carefully here, however. The dispersion he had in mind was the one following Noah's Flood. His "remote epoch" fit easily within the biblical chronology. He guessed that America was first occupied within a thousand years of Noah's beaching the Ark.

Staunch monogenist that he was, Gallatin was willing to concede that the American Indians (not including the Eskimo) were a discrete *variety* who developed over the course of a long separation from the world's other populations, but he held firm that all Native Americans were ultimately related to Asians. The Eskimo were the most recent of those arrivals from Asia, shared the same polysynthetic language structure, and seemed to differ physically (if at all), largely because of the "excessive severity of the climate" in which they lived. So far as Gallatin was concerned, unless one supposed ("which we have no right to do"), a "second miraculous interposition of

Providence in America," philology and ethnology confirmed the common origin and essential unity and equality of the human race.[37]

It was a distressing blow, then, when Gallatin learned in 1846—from a paper that Morton sent to the AES—the polygenist direction in which Morton was heading. The blow was hardly softened when several members of the society (which was otherwise dominantly monogenist) took up Morton's side and challenged Gallatin on the issues there in his own home.[38] The elderly Jeffersonian, infirm and unable to write, dictated a letter, asking Morton whether the Eskimo (and, by extension, Asians) were truly anatomically distinct from the American Indian. Their languages suggested otherwise, he reminded Morton, and wasn't it possible that they were a part of the same family and that "climate, habits or local causes might not produce a material change in the physical characteristics of a people rendering them as different as the Esquimaux and the N. American Indians"? Morton doubted it, and he even doubted the relevance of the linguistic similarities, which seemed themselves contingent on local circumstances. Physical characteristics, on the other hand, were permanent. The precision of craniology was a far superior tool for tracing human relations than the blunt instrument of philology.[39] Morton dismissed the old man's pleas.

On the matter of the mounds, however, Gallatin and Morton were of closer minds. Gallatin did not believe that any of the "remnants" of the mounds indicated "a much more advanced state of civilization than that of the present inhabitants" of the region. Yet the origin of the mounds was "entirely unknown" to them, and Gallatin was unwilling to attribute their construction to the "savage tribes" (his term). His reasons were straightforward enough. While moundbuilding was itself not beyond the capabilities of the American Indians, moundbuilding on such a vast scale was.

> [I]t may be inferred from their number and size that they [the mounds] were the work of a more populous nation than any now existing; and if the inference is correct, it would necessarily imply a state of society in which greater progress had been made in agriculture. For wherever satisfactory evidence of a greater population is found this could not have existed without adequate means of subsistence, greater than can be supplied by the chase alone.

Gallatin's idea that moundbuilding required an agricultural base, and that Indians were "hunters" and not farmers, would persist over the next half century at the very least.[40]

Ever the believer in the human capacity for progress, Gallatin refused to accept the view (held by Morton, among many others) that the developmental gap between the moundbuilders and the Indians was evidence of degeneration from one to the other. Rather, they must represent different and unrelated groups. Not surprisingly, he detected in the mounds "a strong family likeness to the Mexican pyramids" (where, of course, groups had acquired agriculture and begun marching toward civilization). Perhaps the moundbuilders "were a colony from Mexico; or some of the savage tribes must by conquest, or by some other means unknown to us, have converted themselves into an agricultural nation." In either case, it seemed to him, they were not strong enough to hold their position and were "exterminated or driven away by the savage tribes that surrounded them."[41]

In expressing the idea that the construction of mounds required large sedentary, agricultural populations (quite in keeping with his more general canon that agriculture was a vital first step toward any level of civilization), Gallatin was being more conservative than most. Others would bestow on the moundbuilders a knowledge of geometry and astronomy, complex religious and political systems, and such skills as metallurgy. Gallatin would not go that far, but he still insisted that moundbuilding entailed a degree of civilization (or at the very least, a subsistence strategy) that he—and most other early nineteenth-century writers—thought was lacking among the American Indians north of the tropics. They were, rather, nomadic hunters who lived "by the chase," whose artifacts were crude and humble, and who had neither the time nor the capacity to construct mounds.[42]

Those themes would reappear in Squier's own writings, and though he followed Gallatin's lead on many issues, he would never quite appreciate (let alone accept) the depth of Gallatin's commitment to monogenesis. For his part, Gallatin took an immediate liking to Squier on meeting him that summer of 1846 and provided strong and welcome encouragement. And why not? Here was an opportunity to shed light on a possible connection between the mounds of the Mississippi Valley and the pyramids of Mexico. Better still from Squier's vantage, Gallatin provided "something more substantial than mere praise"—he proposed to help finance the publication of a work in the AES *Transactions* on the mounds, "with a view of directing attention at home and abroad to the subject."[43]

Davis was glad to hear it, approved the plan of publication, but then raised a point that, given the subsequent history of their troubles, seems ominously prescient: "Upon reflection, Mr. E.G.S., I am convinced that our papers should appear under our joint signatures, the authors name first. This will be no more than justice to each, as we expect to conduct the work matters jointly."[44] At the time it seemed a minor concern, hardly worth dwelling on. Davis reiterated his delight at the reception Squier was receiving, promoted him to "Gen'l. S." for so successfully storming the eastern bastions, and asked only that the "General" not forget his friend at home: "Mete out to him equal credit, and a due share of the honors." He also sent Squier money with which to purchase books. After all, as Davis put it, if they were to write about the history, "yea, the natural history, not only of this region, but those of Mexico, Central, and South America," they should have all of the best works bearing on the subject of this grandly unfolding scheme.[45]

IN SEARCH OF MONEY AND METHOD

Yet, even in their heady exuberance to tackle the prehistory of the entire Western Hemisphere, they remained sober enough to realize that such an undertaking would require substantial resources, resources that they did not possess. Squier headed north in search of money: first to Boston, to solicit funds from the American Academy of Arts and Sciences (where he made his pitch to John Warren [1778–1856]), then on to Worcester and the American Antiquarian Society. His primary target was the endowment fund of the latter, and he arrived in Worcester armed with a letter of introduction and an endorsement of his plea for funds from Bartlett to Samuel Foster Haven (1806–81), the antiquarian and librarian of the AAS.[46]

Haven listened to Squier's proposal, saw the artifacts and sketches, and was interested but not quite prepared to recommend that the society open its coffers. Instead, he asked Squier for a written proposal. A day or so later, on the road in Hartford, Connecticut, Squier put one together. That proposal reveals much about how he conceived—in the summer of 1846—an ideal archaeological investigation.

Up until that point, archaeological investigations of the archaeological monuments of the western states (now the Midwest) had been the work of scattered individuals, whose efforts were made on their own time and using their own money, with their only reward being the possibility (but by no means the certainty) of publication. There was hardly hope of realizing financial gain—let alone compensation. There was rarely any institutional support, for the United States was still a nation of dispersed, geographically isolated rural communities. The growing towns of the region often formed historical and antiquarian societies, partly to assert their intellectual independence from the more established learned societies of the east. But these local societies generally lacked the critical mass to provide significant financial or intellectual support for research efforts (or even to sustain themselves for more than half a dozen years). Furthermore, since archaeology was in its infancy, with few rules or guidelines, there was little coherence in the effort or in the results of its widely scattered practitioners. Everything was done informally, and Squier and others could see that such a practice would not be very successful in the long term or on a large scale.[47]

The way Squier saw it, progress in archaeology and on the moundbuilder question required a large-scale attack on the problem. That could be accomplished by harnessing the energies of "gentlemen of high attainments, scattered through the West" who were interested in antiquities but who otherwise lacked the time, money, or incentive to pursue that interest. If the *eastern* learned societies (which had the necessary resources) would be willing to reimburse their expenses, and possibly provide a small remuneration for their time and trouble, those individuals would "be ready to lend a hearty aid in making a complete and thorough exploration of the antiquities in their vicinity." Their efforts would be coordinated by individuals such as Squier, who envisioned himself as the central node in the network of correspondents. He would send them each "a letter of Instructions, based upon the investigations and developments thus far made, with respect to the method of procedure, and directing *special attention* to those points upon which information is esteemed more desirable." In return, he would amass and collate the information and arrange its publication. The result would be "a more desirable and complete survey and examination of our Western monuments." This was just the strategy, Squier assured Haven, that was used by the "General Government, in collecting information for specific objects," and he was right. Such a program was neatly suited to a sparsely populated continent where instruments in the hands of a conscientious observer could provide valuable baseline data for, say, the weather.[48]

But while recording temperature was one thing, gathering archaeological data was quite another. Squier's proposal was woefully vague about what his instructions, methods, and procedures might be, even by forgiving mid-nineteenth-century standards. What he had in mind was extensive surveying and occasional excavation, and he promised Haven and the others that they would have a close watch over the details. They realized, however, that the success of the effort they were being asked to bankroll was completely dependent on a far-flung collection of individuals of uneven talent and reliability, over which they had little direct control. It was not a very attractive proposition. Edwin Davis, back in Chillicothe, quickly saw through to the essential flaw in the proposal. It would be difficult to "get men to work without our superintendence," and lacking that oversight,

> My God! You might as well expect information from the moon by addressing the man there, as to get anything of value from most correspondents. As a general rule, you know they will not work for love nor money. But suffice, some might attempt it, they require a years experience before their observations would be of any use to us—so that I think it would be futile to undertake it upon this plan. Not only that, one year is too short to get up a work of such magnitude, even with all the advantageous circumstances that might be brought to bear upon this subject. I should say not less than 5 years will be required to get up such a work as would do justice to the subject, ourselves, and the Country.

Davis urged Squier to try a different tactic: Try to solicit support for just *their* fieldwork, and from just a single society. Then, if they succeeded, they could expand their field operations under and call on the "united energies" and patronage of several societies. Squier admitted there was "some sense in that."[49]

It was too late. By then his proposals were out of his hands, and there was nothing to do but continue the trip. He passed through New Haven, where he met Benjamin Silliman (1779–1864), the editor of the *American Journal of Science,* who urged Squier to write for the journal. He then started back for Ohio, stopping in Philadelphia (where Morton gave him papers, drawings, and other materials he had collected on mounds and earthworks) and touring various mound sites, including the "celebrated Grave Creek Mound" (the condition of which appalled him).[50]

Once back in Chillicothe in late July, Squier wrote Haven to remind him of all he'd done in the Scioto Valley and of how much more needed to be done there and elsewhere. Plaintively confessing that the American Antiquarian Society seemed by then to be the only hope for funding, Squier let his anxiety show through:

> Pray tell me, has the Ant. Soc. taken any action on the suggestions which I submitted, or in any way in relation to further researches? And what in your estimation is the prospect, so far as the Society is concerned? . . . So far as we are concerned, active investigations must soon be suspended, for we cannot afford to continue them at their present scale, much less enlarge our operations, as it would become necessary to do, if we prosecuted the work.[51]

Perhaps to sweeten the pot, Squier assured Haven that four years and five thousand dollars might be enough to make a thorough examination of the earthworks of the Ohio valley, the Upper Mississippi and Missouri, and the Lower Mississippi and Gulf region. Davis, who thought five years would be required for the Ohio Valley alone, would have been troubled by such a rash promise.

No matter. Squier's proposal and promises failed to convince the council of the

American Antiquarian Society. Haven wrote with his regrets. A few days later, so did John Warren—the American Academy of Arts and Science was "quite unable to contribute anything" to the project.[52] Both professed support for the work, but each thought Squier and Davis should first put out some of their results—in published form, or at the very least on the lecture circuit. Bartlett had been urging that strategy all along: "You must push ahead with your article for the Ethn. [AES] Transactions which will be the best feeler we can throw out. It will show the world that we have antiquarian treasures among us, not surpassed in the world for their interest. With this we can come forward and ask for aid in the larger work." Squier, discouraged that his efforts had failed to produce any funds, nevertheless appreciated the need to produce "*our* publication"[53]—especially as there now appeared to be competition in the field.

APPROACHING RIVALS

A few months after Squier's triumphant visit to the East Coast, Montroville Wilson Dickeson (1810–82), a Philadelphia physician and antiquarian, and sometime resident of Natchez, Mississippi (best known for his discovery the previous year in Natchez of a human pelvis associated with the bones of the Pleistocene ground sloth, *Megalonyx*), arrived in New York, bringing with him artifacts and drawings of collections and discoveries he had made in mounds in Florida, Mississippi, Louisiana, and Texas. He presented his material to an appreciative audience at the annual meeting of the Association of American Geologists and Naturalists, which included John Bartlett. It made quite an impression. Bartlett gushed to Squier that

> [Dickeson] has opened upwards of 200 mounds. On one of them he employed 50 Negroes for a week, so immense was its size. His collection of antiquities is of course very large, for as the contents of his mounds do not appear to have been subject to the action of fire, the various objects discovered are perfect. In his collection are 16,000 arrow & spear heads (whole), the specimens shown me surpass in execution anything I ever saw. . . . also 150 vases and articles in pottery, *all perfect*, of every form and size—many curious articles, the use of which we cannot tell—but no articles of copper or other metals. He also has several pieces of rude statuary and images; and in the *crania* he has been very successful, having succeeded in obtaining about 60 tolerably perfect skulls. In one mound there were supposed to [be] 3500 skeletons.[54]

The news of this treasure trove of material, which apparently eclipsed in quantity alone anything Squier and Davis had been able to muster, came close on the heels of Squier's own visit and badly wounded his pride.

After all, they'd made "desperate" efforts to get just a single skull. Bartlett's assurance that Dickeson had heard of him and was pleased by the work he was doing didn't improve the bad taste in Squier's mouth. He petulantly wondered whether Dickeson had erred in guessing the age of his material—perhaps it wasn't from the moundbuilders at all but from a more recent group of Indians: "Dr. Dickeson . . . seems to have accomplished a great deal, though the 16,000 arrowheads don't amount to much. I will agree to take a contract to supply an indefinite number. A hundred specimens illustrating their various forms is just as good as a wagon load. His pottery I should like very much to see. . . . Is it possible Dr. D. has got upon the depositions of the Natches?"[55] Squier planted these doubts but then quickly backpedaled lest he appear too petty: "But I will offer no conjectures, for the very excellent reason that I know very little of the character of the southern works." He was equally guarded when Morton wrote him a few months later praising Dickeson's work, merely pointing out that the southern mounds (Dickeson's) might be larger, but the northern mounds (his and Davis's) yielded copper, silver, and lead, and were likely older as well.[56]

Dickeson heard as much of Squier and Davis as they of him, and in late December 1846 he came out to Chillicothe to see them and the mounds and earthworks of Ohio. Squier had recently been elected clerk of the Ohio State House of Representatives and was now in Columbus, busy with the affairs of the legislature. Davis played host to Dickeson in Chillicothe, and after his visitor left, he reported to Squier that he "has accomplished much more than we had given him credit for." He knew more of "osteology than mounds" but overall was an unassuming and "very intelligent man."[57]

Squier, who had heard enough fawning over Dickeson from Bartlett and Morton, was in no mood to hear it from his collaborator too and snapped back that there had to be less to Dickeson than met the eye. Duly provoked, Davis's next letter admitted:

> The great difficulty with the Doctor is that he is extending his observations over too large a field and expending his energies on too many subjects for his special attention—Geology, Mineralogy, Paleontology, Conchology, Osteology, with a dozen more besides *Moundology*. . . . His manner of collecting facts is too loose, and not always to be relied upon—for instance, he sets down too many hearsay facts—and secondly, his mode of opening the mounds is not calculated to furnish the most accurate scientific knowledge. He hears of a planter who has a group of tumuli on his estate, he writes him a polite note for permission to explore them, and also to know when his Negroes will be disengaged, that he may obtain their assistance. The answer is generally, "You are welcome to examine any work that may be upon my estate and also to command from 10 to 50 Negroes if you want them;" so he makes a picnic. He and his friends quarter upon the planter for a week—the Negroes dig & he sketches. 1st. A view of the whole group. 2nd. the mounds opened. 3rd. Sections vertical & horizontal. 4th. Articles found in the mounds. etc. etc. etc. At night he sets down every thing that has transpired through the day.

In the end, Davis sniffed, "This is all [a] very cozy, and not very expensive pastime, which may furnish considerable information for a journalist. But there is none of that close measurement and accurate investigation which characterizes *our labours*."[58] That was what Squier wanted to hear.

Then there was Caleb Atwater (1778–1867), whose *Descriptions of the Antiquities Discovered in the State of Ohio and Other Western States,* published twenty-six years earlier by the American Antiquarian Society, had been the first serious attempt at a survey of the antiquities of a single region. In the late summer of 1846, perhaps after learning what Squier and Davis were up to, Atwater attempted to publish by subscription a volume of his writings that would include his earlier monograph—the only one, he claimed, "ever published from actual surveys"—along with materials that would render it "almost a new work."[59] But Squier wasn't worried:

> I very much doubt whether Mr. Atwater ever made a survey in person, or assisted in making any, except, perhaps, of the single work at Circleville. His own work, for the most part, derived from persons not greatly interested in the subject, and [who were] not among the closest observers. His investigations in the mounds . . . were entirely insignificant and without results. Probably no memoir of equal length and pretenses was ever written upon any subject, with so slight a *sub-stratum* of well attested facts, as the paper of Mr. Atwater's.

Squier insisted to Haven that he had "no intention of disparaging or undervaluing Mr. A.'s labors, such as they were," but he was only fooling himself.[60]

He and Davis (who had already used his commencement address at Kenyon the decade before to criticize aspects of Atwater's work), viewed their own methods as superior, their results as more meaningful and comprehensive, and their predecessors and contemporaries as second-rate. A friend would later caution them not to be "too hard upon the poor devils (the antiquarians) that have gone before us, as we may have followers too," but that was advice easily ignored. After Squier had examined what had been written on the subject of American antiquities, it seemed to him that "nothing has, as yet, been done towards developing the truth respecting them."[61] Squier and Davis would develop the truth.

TO THE BUSINESS AT HAND

There was nothing to be done with Dickeson, except hope that he would sink out of sight—which was a good possibility, given his indifference to publishing.[62] The odds were against Atwater's proposed volume getting off the ground (it never did). So Squier and Davis simply kept at their work through the fall and winter of 1846. They did fieldwork as weather permitted and hosted visiting dignitaries, including the Reverend Edward Robinson (1794–1863), a philologist and biblical scholar at Union Theological Seminary in New York and an influential member of the AES.

Mostly their efforts were devoted to the archaeological remains in Chillicothe and the immediate surrounding area, but occasionally they ventured farther afield. One such excursion took them nearly 100 miles southeast, across the Ohio River and up the Guyandotte, in Cabell County, Virginia (now West Virginia). While out in the field they wrote Bartlett a cheery letter that conveys the nature of fieldwork in those days and captures the warm tones of what was still a friendly and good-humored relationship:

> Here we are, in the most infernal country the Lord ever made, on the Guyandotte River, in Virginia. What for? To see the sculptured rocks on this interesting stream. And we *have* seen them, much to our gratification, and to the future illumination of the World. The rocks are 12 miles above this point, over the awfulest hills and through the

gloomiest ravines extant. We heard of but one, but found five, of all of which we have made fruitful sketches. They will prove quite as interesting, no doubt, to the Denmark antiquarians as the Dighton rock. There will be no difficulty in making German, or Runic, or Latin or Chuckchi out of them.

There are some others which we shall visit before going home, making drawings of the same, That is to say, *if* we don't break our necks meantime . . . [we took] a tumble, horse & rider, this afternoon. . . . [But] a sprained ankle is the only memento of the feat which I happen to carry—but that's nothing, the neck being sound.

The Doctor is "snoozing" on the floor, just enough awake to send his best respects, which I enclose together with my own. You shall hear from us more when we return to civilization once more. The Dr. is up now, so I'll make him speak for himself. So adieu, E. Geo. Squier

p.s. The major [Squier] has said everything that is necessary, so I will close by sending my best respects to you—and my prayers above that I may get out of this country safe. Yours etc. E. H. Davis[63]

By the winter of 1846, Squier and Davis could report that they had excavated nearly 150 mounds, some of them of large size, and surveyed about 100 earthworks. They were pleased with their efforts: "So far as this immediate section of country is concerned," Squier crowed, "I have the vanity to suppose that little more remains to be learned."[64] It still rankled Squier that they had been "I regret to say, entirely unsuccessful in all our attempts to recover an indisputable skull of the mound builders. We opened several of the Sepulchral Mounds for that purpose, but in every instance the skull was too much decayed to be of the slightest value, or completely crushed and flattened out by the weight of the superincumbent mass of earth." The best they could do was a couple of jaws (not surprisingly, given that their attention was mostly on the mounds of Ohio Hopewell groups, who tended to cremate their dead). Squier confessed his disappointment to Morton that there seemed to be "nothing to be deduced from them, except that the people, when meat they ground, had flat and wide faces!" But, he supposed, "[e]ven *that* is something." Morton let him down easy: "I thank you for the drawings . . . but I confess that in these I see nothing that has not been long familiar to me in our aboriginal heads." Perhaps they would have better luck in the spring.[65]

PUBLISHING ANCIENT MONUMENTS

All of Squier and Davis's efforts, of course, were self-supported. Davis shouldered most of the financial burden (more than five thousand dollars, by his estimate), though they shared the materials recovered. Yet, as Davis was more often tied to his duties in Chillicothe, Squier took the lead in the surveying and excavation, while Davis assumed the greater responsibility for the cleaning, restoration, and analysis of the collections recovered. The writing was left mostly to Squier.[66]

Compiling the material and writing the text for what would become *Ancient Monuments* went slowly over the winter of 1846 owing to Squier's duties at the legislature and the demands of Davis's medical practice. Progress was being made, however, and by late January 1847, Squier reported to Bartlett (who was nominally responsible for the American Ethnological Society's publications) that the book would run more than three hundred and perhaps reach four hundred pages.[67] But in doing so it had outgrown the ability and the funds of the AES to publish it in the *Transactions,* as had been the original intent.

THE SMITHSONIAN STEPS IN

It would appear that Bartlett began shopping the memoir around, possibly mentioning it to George P. Marsh (1801–82), a member of the AES and a Vermont congressman who would soon be on the Smithsonian's Board of Regents. Marsh passed the word along to Joseph Henry about Squier and Davis's efforts, and in late February 1847, he was asked by Henry to write Squier to inquire what the cost of his collection of "American antiquities" might be and whether he would be willing to "offer the results of your investigations to that body for publication."[68] Squier quickly said yes.

That Henry was interested must have been a surprise to Squier. A physical scientist by training and experience, Henry had previously paid no attention to archaeology. Now that he was secretary of the Smithsonian, however, he was savvy enough (perhaps helped by Marsh's counsel), to realize that he needed to make a bold statement with the first volume in the Contributions to Knowledge series. Squier and Davis's work would serve that purpose in several useful ways, not the least of which was the "general interest that is felt on the subject" of the mounds, the testimony it would provide of the Smithsonian's intention to nurture aspiring disciplines, and—perhaps most important tactically—the proof this would give that the Smithsonian's "object is not exclusively the promotion of physical knowledge [Henry's specialty] but . . . every branch of human thought susceptible of increase proper incouragement [*sic*]."[69]

Squier soon heard back from Marsh that Henry was "much interested in your investigations, and desires me to say to you that the Smithsonian Institution will publish your essay in the best style both of letter press and illustration, provided it can be done within reasonable limits of expense & will make liberal pecuniary arrangements with you in respect to it." And they were liberal arrangements. Henry assured Squier that the institution would pick up the costs of the engravings and illustrations; ensure a widespread distribution of the book to libraries and learned societies in this country and abroad; provide him a "sufficient number" of extra copies of the book; and, perhaps most important, give him free use of the book's illustrations in case he later wanted to reprint the volume for profit.[70] The last was especially generous, given the high cost of preparing the sixty lithographic plates and two hundred woodcuts that were anticipated for *Ancient Monuments.*

Henry was quite prepared to absorb those costs. He had already asked the Smithsonian Board of Regents for a thousand dollars to launch the series, and they had approved the expense. This would be a major commitment on the part of the institution (*any* institution), for at that time few learned societies or organizations in America could even consider scientific publication on the scale envisioned by Henry. It was simply too expensive. The result, Henry explained, was that "[t]he geologists, naturalists and ethnologists of the United States cannot give to the world many of their labors, because the expense of illustrations is too great to be encountered by any bookseller, or by ordinary scientific journals, and cannot be borne by the individuals themselves." The Smithsonian, however, had the wherewithal, and more: publishing with "a respectable Institution," Henry assured Squier, would make his research "favorably known to all engaged in the same persuit [*sic*] throughout the civilized world."[71]

Only, there were a couple of strings attached. Henry's assurances notwithstanding, the Smithsonian wasn't yet a fully "respectable" institution. It had had an auspicious beginning, to be sure, but to that point it had done no more to earn a reputation than hire Henry—though that act alone did much to establish its serious scientific intent. A successful launch of the Contributions to Knowledge series was vital to the institution, but ultimately its success (and the justification of its expense), Henry knew, rested in establishing the series' scientific credibility. He therefore wanted a work of "cautious inductive research." Squier would oblige. The "sole purpose of the publication," he assured Henry, was "to present facts; without indulging in speculations." Theirs was not to be like, say, Atwater's book, "a congeries of hearsays, many of them improbable and few well attested."[72] Perhaps not. But Henry wasn't going to leave the judgment of what constituted facts as opposed to speculation to Squier and Davis alone. He would exercise tight editorial control over the product—assuming, that is, that the manuscript was accepted for publication.

And here was the second string: Marsh was instructed to tell Squier that in accordance with the rules of the institution (which, of course, Henry was making up as he went along), "all manuscripts offered for publication are subject to the decision of a proper committee." But Marsh quickly added that he thought this a mere formality and assured Squier that he had "no reason to fear an unfavorable result in respect to your labours." Henry echoed that assurance, which must have been especially comforting, as he would choose the reviewers for the manuscript.[73]

The manuscript, of course, first had to be completed—or at least taken far enough along that it could be sent to reviewers. By early April, Squier guessed he might have it ready to bring east by May, though it was becoming an even "more bulky volume" than he had anticipated at the start.[74] In early June, the manuscript was in Henry's possession, and he turned to the problem of having it reviewed.

In those years, there wasn't much of a pool of reviewers to choose from. Few individuals in the country were qualified to review such a work. Those who were would be found mostly among the members of either the American Antiquarian Society or the American Ethnological Society, many of whom were already very familiar with (and supportive of) Squier and Davis's work. The obvious choice to oversee the review—in terms of knowledge, experience and the reputation he would bring to the task—was Albert Gallatin. He would certainly be able to judge the manuscript's merits, or at the very least to find suitable reviewers for it among the members of the AES, and it was to Gallatin that Henry turned. That it was also Gallatin who suggested to Squier in the first instance that they publish the work, and who had advanced some of the funds to do it, was also known to Henry.[75] Henry wanted to go through the motions of a formal review, but given that the manuscript came highly recommended (by the very individuals who would now judge its merits), he well knew that the process was a mere formality.

Henry sent the manuscript and a number of the illustrations on to Gallatin, who in turn gave it to a committee of the AES that included John Bartlett, Edward Robinson, and philologist W. W. Turner (1810–59). Supplementary reviews were sought from two other AES members: Marsh and Samuel Morton. Henry had told Squier and Davis that he intended to mask their identities from the reviewers, but if he really believed that this pretense of anonymity would work, he was the only one. All the reviewers certainly knew better. More than likely, Henry was simply establishing a precedent for future works in the series for which anonymity might be possible.[76] So it was that the official version of Henry's letter to Gallatin that was published in *Ancient Monuments* requesting the review omitted the names of the authors.

The AES received the manuscript the first week of June 1847, and the review committee worked fast. No surprise there. Just two weeks later Gallatin sent their *Report* to Henry, entirely approving its "resolutions and recommendations," which heaped praise upon the research on which the volume was based and urged its publication. Separate letters were submitted by Morton and Marsh, echoing the high praise of the *Report*.[77]

Morton had particular reason to be pleased. Just two months earlier, Squier and Davis had finally found what they had all been looking and hoping for. Squier could hardly contain himself:

> Eureka; My Dear Doctor! Give us joy! We have uncovered one genuine skull of the Mound Builders at last! I enclose you four views of it with the measurements, from which I presume you will be able to form a very good conception of its character. . . . This is the *only* skull we have found, which we regard as belonging to the mound era . . . and both the skull and the circumstances attending it, are very remarkable. Did you ever observe a more *compact* head? The vertical diameter is greater than I have [seen] in any skull, falling under my attention. . . . Pray let us hear your opinion *of our skull*.

Morton rejoiced in their discovery "of a truly *aboriginal skull*. Nothing of the kind was ever found more characteristic than this relic." It seemed to him

> a *perfect type* of the race to which it belongs; that race which is indigenous to the American continent, having been planted here by the hand of Omnipotence, & which, in all its . . . localities, conforms with more or less precision, and for the most part with amazing exactness in its cranial proportions to the skull you have . . . discovered.

Every new observation, Morton added immodestly, only seemed to confirm his previous conclusions, "that our Indian populations, of all epochs, have belonged to a single homogenous race."[78]

PROBLEMS WITH PEER REVIEW

Everything appeared to be well and good on its face, but there were words and phrases in the *Report* that Henry objected to, and that would ultimately trigger a bitter rivalry between Squier and Davis. Henry's objections to the original *Report* were straightforward enough. It spoke of the Smithsonian as a government agency, and as Henry had fought desperately to keep the institution from becoming entangled in the federal budget or governance (a battle that he had not yet fully won), he wanted not a hint that his position might be weakening. In addition, the AES committee had crowed that this was "eminently an American work," and Henry was loathe to color it in those terms. This was not just because the Smithsonian endowment came from a foreigner, but more because it implied a scientific provincialism that he fervently wished to avoid. The manuscript would be accepted on the merits of the research, not the authors' citizenship or where they'd done the work. Henry outlined his objections to Bartlett and asked for changes. Bartlett consented.[79]

But then there was another, more awkward matter that Henry privately broached only with Squier. The *Report* seemed to imply that the AES had volunteered the manuscript to the Smithsonian with AES approval for its publication (which, in essence, is what had happened) and that even prior to receiving the manuscript the Smithsonian had already agreed to publish it (which was also true). This put Henry in a tight spot in terms of establishing precedent, as he feared it would lead to his being overwhelmed with manuscripts coming in from around the country with the approval of societies (learned and not) and the expectation that they would be published by the Smithsonian. That would not do and would damage the very credibility he sought to build. So far as Henry was concerned, it was better to leave the public "in the dark" as to how *Ancient Monuments* had actually come to be published. It was best if it appeared that the manuscript had been submitted for publication, then sent for review to the AES, approved, then (and only then) accepted for publication by the Smithsonian.[80]

Of course, that was not what had happened, but Henry thought it could be made to appear that way in the published version of the *Report* "by a little management" on the part of the parties involved, so long as none were "disposed to stand too much on etiquette." Squier wasn't. He quickly proposed a scheme whereby he and Henry would backdate some letters, fabricate others, and generally concoct a fictional chronology of events. Henry liked the plan, the AES reviewers had "no scruples on the subject," and the changes were quietly made. By the late summer he proclaimed the revised *Report* "completely satisfactory."[81] For him, perhaps. But within just two months, the revised *Report* would ignite an explosion that would drive a deep and lasting wedge between Squier and Davis and, for a few unhappy months over the winter of 1847, threaten the very appearance of *Ancient Monuments*.

GIVING CREDIT WHERE CREDIT WAS DUE[82]

Henry had given Squier a copy of the revised *Report;* in late September 1847, the *Report* also found its way into *Literary World*. Squier sent a copy on to Davis.[83]

Davis had not seen it before, and when he did he was furious. For the *Report* ended with two resolutions, the second of which read:

> Resolved—that we regard the work prepared *by Mr. Squier* upon this subject as an object of general interest, and as intensely worthey [*sic*] to be adopted for publication by the Smithsonian Institution, both as resting on original researches and as affording remarkable illustrations of the Ante Columbian history of the American continent.[84]

It appeared to Davis that he was not getting credit for their joint effort, and he fired off an angry letter to Squier:

> I was not only disappointed, but grieved to find they [the writers of the *Report*] had stepped out of their way to inflict a severe injury upon my character. I was not aware before, that the *comte.* [committee] was appointed to settle who was the author of the manuscript, placed in their hands for a different purpose, but it would seem from their second resolution that this question was also forced upon them. . . . To say the least, I must consider it a breach of our *private understanding* (an arrangement of your-own proposing, as your letters show) and that too, without the slightest cause on my part to justify the course. . . . I can't conceive that you desire to appropriate the whole credit of the work, as the resolution does, to yourself: nor will I as yet permit myself to believe it was intended—I should regret very much the occurrence of any thing that should disturb that friendship which has sprung from several years of constant intercourse.[85]

Davis demanded a prompt reply and an explanation. Distrusting Squier, he also asked for a copy of the title page. He wanted to see for himself how the names appeared on the manuscript.

Squier was broadsided by Davis's letter and resented it: "I am much surprised at the *tone* of your letter, which I would fair believe you mailed without due consideration. There are several paragraphs which it would not be the part of friendship to believe were designed to be personally offensive, and which require all the palliatives which friendship can suggest to be regarded in any other light." He insisted he was blameless for the content of the *Report:*

> All I have to say is, that with the report of the Ethnol. Soc. Committee I had no more to do than yourself. I suggested nothing, asked nothing, knew nothing of it, until it was presented to the Society. . . . If the Committee transcended their duties, it is no fault of mine, nor do I consider myself as punishable for their acts or language. . . . If you told them, any one of them, who was or who was not the author of the [manuscript] you did more than I did. I do not remember having mentioned to any person anything about the authorship, and so far from appropriating it to myself, I have always, publicly and privately, alluded to it only as containing the results of our joint labours, without exploring the part that each has performed in the preparation.

Still, consciously or not, he twisted the knife in Davis's wounded pride a little deeper by wondering aloud whether Davis was perhaps overreacting: "I was very far from suspecting the existence of anything offensive to you in the Report which I sent to

Cincinnati Gazette published an angry letter on behalf of James McBride (1788–1859), whose generous contribution of material to Squier and Davis was also not fully acknowledged in Squier's *Transactions* piece. This was becoming an all too familiar and disturbing complaint to Henry, and by now the damage could no longer be easily contained. The issue was aired before the Smithsonian's Board of Regents at its December meeting.[95]

The Regents were not pleased by either the delay in the publication or by the unseemly and embarrassingly public misbehavior of the participants (not surprising, given the amount of money and prestige riding on this work), and they let Henry know they held *him* accountable. A testy Henry, his anger barely in check, promptly wrote Squier to announce that he did not care to suffer the "odium and abuse" that would befall him if the book was not published in due time or if "it is not found to do justice to the subject or to previous explorers." Henry wasn't going down without Squier, either, for the problems clearly could be laid right at the latter's doorstep: "I regret on the whole for more reasons than one that your paper in the transactions of the ethnological society was published just at this time and under your own name since it has given rise to considerable enquiry on the part of some of the members of the Board." So far as Henry was concerned, Squier should immediately suspend all his other research and writing activities and fully devote his attention to completing the memoir.[96]

Squier was furious. He dashed off a reply, thought better of it, waited a few days to cool off, then wrote another. The waiting didn't sweeten his mood any, and he unleashed a barrage of accumulated resentment. It was Henry who had reneged on their arrangements. He (Squier) was free to publish under his own name wherever and whenever he pleased. Davis was getting far more credit than he deserved. And it was "unfounded and ungenerous" to imply that Squier wasn't working hard on finishing the volume.[97]

Squier's outburst may have come as a surprise, but only if one hadn't been paying attention. What made it especially caustic was that this was not just about names, or sharing credit, or publishing deadlines. It was about money.

THE ROOT OF ALL EVIL

When Henry and Squier entered the agreement to publish, neither had a clear sense of the time, effort, or expense of a venture on this scale. As the months wore on, amendments (verbal and written) were made to their arrangement, Henry apparently agreeing (or so Squier thought) to give Squier a lump sum payment for the manuscript (in lieu of providing copies of the book) and to pay Squier's expenses while he was in New York supervising the production of the illustrations. Squier badly needed the money. Unlike Davis, who could always count on income from his medical practice, Squier was limited to the income that he might make through his freelance writing—and what Henry promised to provide. That promise, along with unanticipated increases in production costs (which came despite Henry's watchful eye on expenses), pushed the bill for the publication far beyond Henry's original estimates, and in December he had to ask the Regents for an additional $3,500 for publication.[98]

So far as Squier could learn, however, not only had the Regents failed to make an appropriation for the money due him but Henry had not even asked for one. Granted, Squier complained, any payment the Smithsonian might offer would hardly recoup a quarter of the funds he had put into the research, and yet he was surely owed something—particularly since the promise of providing him the plates and engravings to issue his own edition was looking to be a hollow one. The Smithsonian planned to distribute *Ancient Monuments* free to public institutions, learned societies, and libraries of this country and Europe. That would undercut the only dependable market Squier had for the sale of a private edition. Now he would have to rely on selling his edition to individuals—and why would they pay for a copy when they could consult one in their public library?

To add insult to injury, Squier continued, the hundred dollars advanced to cover his expenses in New York, and the additional fifty dollars that he received in December, hardly covered half of his costs. Yet it seemed to him that Henry begrudged him even that pittance, or perhaps he (Squier) was just being thankless. Yes, that was it, Squier sneered: "I shall therefore take the earliest possible opportunity of returning the [fifty dollars] to the Treasury of the Inst[itution], for I fear I am not sufficiently grateful for the alms thus bestowed."[99] Perhaps, Squier informed Henry, it would be better if they stopped production on *Ancient Monuments* right then, until they could talk these matters over in person. Squier had just crossed the line. Henry agreed to go to New York.

Squier wasn't going to let the resolution of this matter rest with Henry. He diligently lobbied his one ally on the Board of Regents. George Marsh was sympathetic—to a point. He assured Squier that the board and Henry would make a reasonable settlement. But Squier had by then also upped the ante and was now claiming he should be sole author of *Ancient Monuments*. Marsh called his bluff: "I cannot say that you are wrong in insisting that your name alone should appear on the title page, but the title which you at first proposed to give certainly implied joint authorship, as well as joint investigation." He urged Squier to be generous, for in the end "the harvest of honor that you will reap will be so abundant that you can well afford to spare a crumb to those who have occupied a humbler rank than yourself in the field of labour." Squier conceded the argument, but made sure Marsh knew exactly what the division of labor had been. So far as he was concerned, Davis had done nothing more than the tasks "capable of being performed by any boy in the country."[100]

Henry came to New York in mid-January, and though they failed to fully resolve the problems, after he left Squier admitted to Marsh there was a "better, but far from a clear or satisfactory arrangement of our affairs." That would be the best they could do, for the problems they faced were structural. Squier desperately wanted wealth and fame, but Henry couldn't provide both, and he couldn't let Squier steal the fame. This was a unique opportunity for Squier, but it all had to be on Henry's terms, not his own—and that was a source of immense frustration (for both of them—

Henry had been warned that he would have difficulty "keeping [Squier] in the traces," and it had come to pass).

Davis also came in for the meeting, and at the request of Henry and the Regents he stayed on in New York to help with the production of the book (a residence that he would later estimate cost him a year's lost income from his medical practice—he never asked Henry to reimburse that, or to repay his expenses in New York). It was Squier and Davis's first encounter since the fall, and the cold tension between the two thawed ever so slightly: "Dr. Davis . . . has, so far, explained some portions of his conduct as to induce me to recede somewhat from the position which I felt myself forced to take with respect to him." Even so, Squier wasn't about to let the matter drop. He decided to insist on a careful and detailed explanation in the book's preface "of our relative positions etc. in reference to the work."[101]

AN UNEASY ALLIANCE

In late January, the Smithsonian signed a contract for the printing of *Ancient Monuments* (under the tentative title "Archaeological Researches, an Inquiry into the Origin and Purposes of the Aboriginal Monuments of the United States").[102] Henry returned to Washington, and Squier and Davis got down to the business of overseeing the production of the volume.

Squier also continued his efforts to interest a major publisher (Harper and Brothers or D. Appleton and Company) in bringing out a private edition of *Ancient Monuments,* but, as he had feared, they balked at the idea of competing with the Smithsonian's free edition. There was always the gamble of issuing a book by subscription, but paper and printing cost something, and "[g]etting subscribers on empty pockets is a prospect not the most delightful to contemplate, and I fear my note of hand would not command a heavy premium in Wall St." Squier resigned himself to his fate: "I suppose I shall have the felicity of working hard and—*starving.*" Only the rich could afford patrons like the Smithsonian.[103]

Over the next few months, all eyes turned to checking proofs, a task made all the more laborious by the fact that this was Henry's first opportunity to see the work in full and wield his editorial knife. Naturally, he proved to have a far different take than Squier on what was acceptable science and what constituted unacceptable speculation and theory. Squier had been struck, for example, by the recurrence of the serpent symbol in artifacts and mounds (e.g., Serpent Mound) in Ohio and around the world. It had led him to probe the symbol's possible cross-cultural significance in the ethereal realm of myth and superstition. Henry would have none of that nonsense. He insisted that Squier cut the discussion of these "analogies" and save it for a separate memoir—which, of course, someone else would have to publish. Just to make sure that Squier got the message, Henry reminded him that he, and the AES committee, would have final approval of the work. Not Squier. Squier snapped back that he considered himself "quite as competent to judge of what is pertinent and proper as the Sect. of the Smithsonian" and might himself insist on keeping some of the offending parts. But it was a false bravado, and its very shrillness and insulting tone made it all too evident that Squier knew perfectly well who had the upper hand.[104]

The tense and occasionally angry haggling over the details of the publication thrust into stark relief the fact that this was largely untrod ground for all parties. Henry was creeping cautiously along, well aware (as he frequently reminded Squier) that what he did with this first volume to appear under the Smithsonian's imprint would set precedents and establish a pattern that could prove difficult to alter in the years to come. The difficulties were magnified since, at a more general level, Henry was working without a net. He was groping for standards in a discipline that still hadn't defined its own, a discipline with which he had, at most, only a passing acquaintance. And he was having to do so under unblinking scrutiny—not just from the Regents but from across the scientific community and squarely in the public eye. Some, like *Scientific American,* were already grumbling: "Smithson left his fortune for the express purpose of advancing *knowledge,* and the appropriation of any part of this money to foster a useless and ambiguous science like Archaeology, is a malappropriation of Smithson's sacred bequest." Ultimately, Henry had to make decisions based on what he felt was best for American science in general, and the Smithsonian in particular.[105] Not on what might be best for Squier and Davis.

For their part, Squier and Davis (but mostly Squier) were facing the challenge of finding and defining the edges of their field, at a time when those edges were fluid and ill-defined, and then asserting their right to decide what constituted legitimate archaeological inquiry and knowledge. They, and not Henry, knew what passed in archaeology, and they felt it their prerogative to steer research in ways they judged to be the most productive. This was their opportunity to define archaeology, but they would have to do it to Henry's liking, and for an individual with as much ambition as Squier, this created an extraordinarily frustrating situation. Not that Henry found the role of judge any easier in the face of Squier's growing sense of self-importance: "The attention which Squire [*sic*] has received from some of the great men in Boston and New York has nearly turned his head and caused him to give me considerable trouble."[106] Squier's frustrations and his deep financial worries kept the tension festering, and he fired a steady barrage of complaints at Henry, Marsh, and Bartlett. Davis stayed in New York through the spring, helping out with the production of the book, serving as a constant reminder to Squier of perceived injustice: "Dr. D. is here, for what object I know not. He has done nothing, will do nothing, *can* do nothing, and I cannot discover the value [of him being in New York] until the work is out."[107]

Henry went back to New York in early April, regretting by then not only the inconvenience of using a printer in New York but also that he had put Squier in charge of supervising the engraving and printing—a task for which he proved "wholly unworthy of the trust."[108] At Squier's urging Marsh had been pushing Henry to resolve the financial dispute, and when Marsh learned that Henry was heading to New York he wrote ahead to Squier, advising him that "unless Mr. Henry is false, and the Board shamefully dishonest," Squier could rely on receiving adequate remuneration for his expenses, and two hundred copies of the book (the latter to split with Davis). Marsh tipped Henry's hand partly to defuse Squier and partly, it would appear, because he didn't entirely trust Henry to resolve such problems. As he explained to Bartlett in a confidential letter that same day:

I have no doubt that Squier has been ill used. He is a little hasty perhaps, but from my observation of Mr. Henry's manner of transacting business, I presume S. is in the right of the controversy. In all matter of business, Prof. H. is as imbecile a person as I ever met, & a man more utterly unfit for his place could hardly be found. Still the aid of the Institution is important to S. & I hope your influence with him may prevent an outbreak between him & Prof. H. I shall write him by this mail & refer him to you. It was expressly understood between Prof. H. & me that S. was to have 200 copies of the book, & such funds as were necessary in the progress of the work for his support etc. & I really don't know where the disagreement between them consists, although I can easily understand that it must be very difficult for a person of common sense, & reasonable acquaintance with men, to agree with Prof. H. in anything.[109]

The meeting (on April 5, 1848) seemed to go well enough. Squier and Davis reached an agreement on how best to share all the artifacts and materials between them and their respective credit for the work. They also made a last-minute change to the title—from *Aboriginal Monuments* to *Ancient Monuments*. While this was a change that Squier and Davis requested (perhaps to distinguish the book from Squier's *Transactions* paper), it was one that Henry readily accepted, as the term "aboriginal" seemed to "express more than is known."[110] By that, perhaps, he meant that "aboriginal" implied a connection between the archaeological remains and the present Native Americans, a connection that he may not have felt was then warranted (for that matter, neither did Squier and Davis).

DOWN THE HOME STRETCH

Over the next several months, Henry, Squier, Davis, and now Marsh read proof sheets of *Ancient Monuments*. Despite the slowdown caused by having to send the proofs on this circuit, and an occasional delay at the printers, over the late spring and summer of 1848 the finishing touches were put on the publication and the final sheets began to take shape.[111] Everything was going about as smoothly as one could expect, and a slightly bemused (if not surprised) Henry could even report that he found "Squier in good spirits & Dr. Daves [*sic*] likewise" when he visited New York in July.

Henry had helped in that regard. Ever mindful of the small details, in June he saw to it that Squier was awarded an honorary A.M. degree from the College of New Jersey (now Princeton University), which Squier was urged to place after his name on the title page. The degree came with a friendly challenge from Henry that it should stimulate a person "of properly balanced mind . . . to new exertions in the way of intellectual and moral attainment." A proud Squier crowed to his parents that the awarding of the degree "was entirely spontaneous, and . . . without suggestion or application on my part." That was true enough, except it was not a wholly spontaneous or altruistic gesture by Henry. He had arranged for the degree, as he confided privately to a friend, "to adjust the titles of the two gentlemen on the title page" (Davis being an M.D.). That it would also enhance the credentials of those who published with the Smithsonian was merely an incidental benefit.[112]

In August 1848, the printer reported to Henry that the last pages of the memoir had been put in press, and it was time to finish the front matter—the Advertisement (which gives a brief history of the Smithsonian and the laundered version of the review process) and the author's preface. Henry read over what Squier had written, suggested some final revisions, and proposed that it be backdated to correspond to his manufactured letter of May 15, 1847 (this, presumably, to fit it into the fictional sequence of letters in the Advertisement). Squier did so and along the way had one more prepublication scuffle with Davis over the wording of the preface describing who had been responsible for what, and then it was done.[113]

Yet, just as the long haul was over, one final major battle took place that forever killed any chances for a reconciliation between Squier and Davis.

THE LAST STRAW

In late September Davis went to Squier's room at the Judson Hotel in New York to retrieve some of his artifacts (or at least what he thought were his artifacts)—that were in Squier's possession while he was illustrating them for *Ancient Monuments*. Squier wasn't there when Davis arrived, so he waited. But soon his car man came, and Davis could wait no longer. He scratched a hurried note to Squier telling him that he'd been there and taken "some of the relics" to his rooms "to repair & arrange them." Squier returned and was furious:

> The note which you left at my rooms yesterday afternoon when you made an unauthorized entrance into them in my absence removing some property in which you had a claim and some in which you had none at all, was a superfluous piece of hypocrisy. Had your intentions been honorable, you [would] have mentioned the matter to me, when you met me an hour before. You have all along deceived yourself in supposing that your machinations and . . . maneuvers—the piebald offspring of a morbid jealousy and cowardly hypocrisy—were unknown to me. I have not noticed them in the hope that our connections will soon terminate. In this hope I was induced under Mr. Henry's suggestions to commit to a lie in your favor in the Preface to the memoir just printed. But the events of yesterday have precipitated matters, and brought to an abrupt end [a condition] which I had hoped would have terminated without [such unpleasantness]. Henceforth I dissolve all connection with you; this dissolves *privately* if you please, *publicly* if you wish.

As Squier wrote he began to cool off, and his draft ended on an almost (but not quite) nostalgic note, remembering their happier times together. Those memories must have made him think better of sending what he'd just written, or perhaps he simply wanted to cover any sign of weakness, and so he instead sent an emissary with a stiffly worded note announcing that he wished the errant property "placed in the hands of an impartial third party, to be disposed of for our mutual benefit. The bearer of this is authorized to receive your decision, and will govern himself accordingly. You will see the necessity of an immediate answer accordingly."[114]

In the event that Davis was not forthcoming, or perhaps to strengthen his hand in case there was haggling over who was the rightful owner of the artifacts, or perhaps just for sheer spite, Squier plotted a retaliatory strike. The day after he wrote Davis demanding the return of the material, he sent a letter to a Milton Clark in Chillicothe—a friend whose ethics were plainly on the questionable side. Exactly what Squier asked of Clark is not known, but what Clark tried to do on Squier's behalf is clear enough:

> I at once called upon Mr. Chas. Woodbridge [an in-law of Davis's], and delivered your request. He informed me that the office of Dr. Davis was locked up & that the key was lost, adding however that he would make a search & find it if possible. Today I called upon him again & he said he had not been able to find it & further that *even if it was found* he would not like to go into & send from Dr. D's shop anything that might be therein, as the Doctor had the shop sealed & locked up, further adding that he would be pleased to accommodate you but that he did not think it would be right in doing so unless he should be so directed by Dr. Davis by letter or otherwise.[115]

Clark's attempt to break into Davis's office and remove some of the artifacts was foiled by a key lost—or perhaps a conscience found. Ultimately, the matter would not be resolved by breaking and entering, though Squier apparently tried again after Clark's aborted attempt. John Bartlett stepped into the dispute, and tried—without much success—to maneuver the parties into arbitration. Squier wouldn't budge. Bartlett could just tell Davis and his "jackass lawyer" to "go to the devil. I won't be bothered with their nonsense," Squier snarled. "I am only sorry that I permitted myself to be persuaded to parlay with them. Hereafter I shall act towards dogs as dogs." And were it necessary, Squier insisted, he was quite prepared to take Davis to court to recover the $2,500 he was owed "for services etc. rendered."[116]

So in the end it came down to this: poisoned arbitration, the threat of lawsuits, and a bitterness and enmity that would last a lifetime. All surfacing just as *Ancient Monuments* appeared—the moment they should have shared as their greatest triumph. All because of a few ill-timed words—"prepared by Mr. Squier"—that appeared in the second resolution of the AES *Report*. And all the more ironic, since those words did not actually appear in the original AES *Report*.

WORDS NEVER SPOKEN

Squier and Davis had fought angrily and bitterly over why the AES committee had singly credited Squier for the effort. What Davis didn't know was that it hadn't. Davis had read only a revised version of the *Report*, not the original. That original still exists (easily identifiable by its signatures), in an obscure corner of the Squier Papers at the Library of Congress. It is quite different from the revised (*Literary World*) version in significant ways and, for that matter, from the final version published in *Ancient Monuments*. But perhaps the most significant difference of them all was in the second resolution. In the *original* it reads:

> 2. *Resolved*, That we regard the publication of the work proposed upon the subject an object of national interest, and worthy to be adopted by the Smithsonian Institution;

both as being in itself eminently an American work, and as affording remarkable illustrations of the history of the American continent.[117]

The AES committee had made no mention of Squier.

So who inserted Squier's name into the second resolution of the revised version? The answer to that has been long lost to history. It was certainly not one of the revisions Henry requested (or even a revision Henry would have requested). One possibility is that after the original *Report* was submitted to the Smithsonian in June 1847, it was recopied and amended to address Henry's concerns (as noted above). Perhaps in the process of the rewriting, a part of the language used earlier in the document was mistakenly carried down into the second resolution, so that the revised version inadvertently gave credit to Squier.

Other possibilities exist, the darkest being that Squier himself made the change. But that scenario demands a disingenuousness and mean-spiritedness on Squier's part that, whatever his ambitions and faults (and they were many), seems unlikely. It is not beyond the realm of possibility, however. Both the original and this revised version of the *Report* are in the Squier Papers. That he, and not Henry, would have them is not itself surprising. Henry only wanted to keep the final, published version, not any of the earlier versions, and especially not the original *Report*. As Marc Rothenberg observes, "Officially, as far as the Smithsonian was concerned, the original *Report* never existed."[118]

More to the point, it was Squier who sent the offending copy to Davis (or to *Literary World*). To do so he would have had to copy one of the versions in his possession, and he must have seen (or added) the offending phrase to the second resolution, even if he couldn't or wouldn't see that it might cause offense. In the blistering heat of Davis's accusations that September of 1847, did Squier simply forget what the original resolution said? Or did he choose to ignore it, in order to send Davis the none-too-subtle message that he felt the lion's share of the credit was due him?

A century and a half after the fact, it's likely that we will never know the answers, but no matter. One can draw from this painful episode the inescapable conclusion that the history of publishing *Ancient Monuments*, and the relationships among all of the parties involved, would likely have been very different if the error in transcribing the *Report* (if an error it was) had never happened.

ANCIENT MONUMENTS OF THE MISSISSIPPI VALLEY

When the first of the Smithsonian's Contributions to Knowledge finally appeared in late September 1848, it weighed in at just over 300 pages, with 48 lithographed maps and plates, and some 207 wood engravings. Henry thought *Ancient Monuments* would "make one of the most beautiful books ever published in this country," and he was right.[119] *Literary World* proclaimed it a work presented "in a form at once to attract and fix the attention," and well that it might. The mystery of the moundbuilders had long served "to quicken research and kindle the fancy," and *Ancient*

Monuments furnished "unquestionably the completest exposition we have of that strange old time."[120]

So it did, but as custom dictated, Squier and Davis were dutifully modest about their efforts: Their goal in *Ancient Monuments* was merely "to present facts in a clear and concise form, with such simple deductions and generalizations alone, as may follow from their careful consideration." It was a false modesty, however, and they knew it. After all, they reminded their readers, so much of what had come before them on the subject was "eminently unsatisfactory," the inevitable consequence of vague accounts, disconnected and casual observations, and presentations cluttered with "the crudest speculations and the wildest conjectures."[121] Naturally, they could do better.

In proclaiming that they had begun their research with "no hypothesis to combat or sustain,"[122] they were being especially modest—and not the least bit convincing. Squier and Davis had little doubt from the start that the moundbuilder race was separate and, in all ways, superior to that of the recent Indians of North America—even down to the sculpted nuances of stone pipes. Nothing in their research convinced them otherwise, and everything they saw confirmed the idea. The result is that *Ancient Monuments* is one long argument that the moundbuilders were a numerous, widespread, and homogeneous race of semi-civilized agriculturalists, deeply religious and of necessity militaristic, whose monuments, customs, symbols, artifacts, and cranial anatomy bore unmistakable traces of a deep historical connection to the semi-civilized peoples of Mexico and Peru. The mysterious race of moundbuilders lives on in *Ancient Monuments,* even if appreciably toned down and less glorious than its extravagant incarnation in the popular literature of the times. In fact, it was quite similar in overall theme and direction, though differing in the details, to the view of the moundbuilders held by Caleb Atwater—though Squier and Davis greatly tried to distance themselves from that earlier work (the points of contact between the two are noted below).[123]

That Squier and Davis could achieve all this under Henry's stern dictum that their "labours should be given to the world as free as possible from everything of a speculative nature"—and, indeed, their own insistence that they made every effort to avoid anything "like mere speculation"[124]—is testimony to the power of commonsense thinking and the persuasive grab bag of historic, ethnographic, and archaeological analogies that they invoked as a warrant for their inferences.[125] They could not see (nor, apparently, could Henry or their AES reviewers) how their discussions of facts and the generalizations that followed from them easily and imperceptibly slipped over the hazy line into conjecture. Cyrus Thomas (1825–1910), in his own more extensive report on the mounds nearly half a century later, would have to dispute many of their arguments (and to a lesser degree, their data)—testimony indeed to the effectiveness of their method and the persuasiveness of their conclusions.

But *Ancient Monuments* is much more than a paean to a lost race. The book provides a wealth of descriptive data on the size, shape, distinguishing attributes, topographic setting, construction, materials, associated features, artifacts, stratigraphy, geographic variation, age, and presumed function of hundreds of mounds and earthworks of the eastern United States, much of it compiled in a firsthand investigation of unprecedented scope and detail. Given the work's well-deserved status as a benchmark in American archaeology, it becomes useful to tour *Ancient Monuments*, albeit briefly and selectively (since the book does follow), to see how Squier and Davis gathered and used these data to address the "grand archaeological questions connected with the primitive history of the American continent [and] the origins, migrations, and early state of the American race."[126]

FROM DATA TO EVIDENCE

The discussions in *Ancient Monuments*, as the subtitle promised, ranged widely over the Mississippi Valley. Its core of descriptive data, however, came mostly from Squier and Davis's firsthand surveys and explorations of the mounds and earthworks in Ross and a few other Ohio counties, supplemented by reports that they obtained from others, among them James McBride, whose surveys covered western and southwestern Ohio; John Locke, who provided data of the effigy mounds of Wisconsin; and Charles Whittlesey, who, as noted, sent plans of the Newark and Marietta monuments and many of mounds and earthworks from northern Ohio. For other parts of the Mississippi Valley, they simply had to rely on the few (and often unsatisfactory) reports of others, such as Dickeson and Constantin Rafinesque (1783–1840).[127]

They would blame their limited field data on the shortsightedness of the eastern learned societies from which they sought funds for more-extensive fieldwork, for they knew one had to attack those "grand questions" on an appropriately large scale. But if their study area was not as extensive as they had hoped it would be, it was nonetheless extraordinarily rich in archaeological remains. Ross County alone, they estimated, contained one hundred enclosures and five hundred mounds, and here and in nearby areas were many now justly famous sites, including Fort Ancient, Hopewell, Mound City, Seip, Harness, Tremper, the Newark Earthworks, and Serpent Mound, all detailed (some for the first time) in *Ancient Monuments*.[128] So dense was the archaeological record of this area of Ohio, in fact, that Squier and Davis considered it "one of the centres of ancient populations."[129] As such, they would come to see it as broadly representative of the archaeology of the moundbuilders.

ESTABLISHING METHOD

If, that is, it could be demonstrated that their fieldwork provided an accurate and reliable picture of the archaeological record. Squier and Davis were quick to assure readers of *Ancient Monuments* that it did. They had taken great care, they insisted, to "secure perfect fidelity in all essential particulars" in their maps and plans of the earthworks, and each of these was based on "actual and minute, and in most instances personal survey." Well they sounded that note, since those surveys had to support their startling claim that the earthworks were so precisely laid out that their builders must have possessed a knowledge of geometry and surveying that would challenge the abilities of even "the most skilful [sic] engineer" of the modern day.

Lest the readers of *Ancient Monuments* doubt them, they carefully outlined their method for mapping earthwork enclosures and explained why they were certain that many of these features were, indeed, perfect circles and squares.[130]

Squier and Davis's maps of earthworks—particularly the more elaborate enclosures—far surpass in number and generally exceed in quality any previously published. They include features that were not always recorded in earlier efforts—north arrows, for example, as well as scales, cross-sections, major landscape and archaeological features, and, insofar as they could portray within two-dimensional plan maps, hints of elevation differences and topographic variation. In case any of their readers failed to appreciate the quality of their work, they were equally quick to point out flaws in previously published surveys and maps—most of which, it seemed, Atwater had committed.[131]

Their own maps were not without flaws, of course, nor were they always accurate or even entirely factual. Squier (who drafted them) rarely hesitated to fill in gaps in the archaeological record. Walls and other earthwork features breached by erosion, roads, creeks and ravines, plowing, or other destructive processes were shown as being intact. That they were restored for illustration is no particular surprise—nor did Squier and Davis hide the fact. Earthen features laid out as precisely as these appeared to be were *expected* to have symmetry and completeness; forts were *supposed* to be fully enclosed by walls. Why not portray them as such, even if that wasn't their current condition?[132]

In sharp contrast to their carefully surveyed maps of earthworks and earthen enclosures, their illustrations of mounds (generally shown in cross-section) frequently lacked scales, did not always accurately portray relative proportions or internal stratigraphy, or reveal much of the form, location, and depth of the excavations. For that matter, their descriptions of excavation methods were brief and incomplete, even by modest mid-nineteenth-century standards. Often little more was revealed than the size and depth of the excavation units (which tended to be tunnels or shafts), with passing comments about the tools used and the difficulty of the work. Although it may be unnecessary to say so, the excavations were done without the benefit of precise horizontal or vertical control, and wholly without the use of excavation levels or screens.[133]

Their lack of interest in excavation and recovery techniques is understandable in light of the fact that the *product* of the excavation—the artifacts and features—was more important than the *process* by which that material was recovered. The mounds were merely overburden (not their term, of course), covering the burnt clay basins (which they took to be "sacrificial altars"), artifacts, and skeletons of the moundbuilders. There seemed no need to dwell on how the cover was lifted. There was little appreciation then (and for many decades thereafter) of how methods of recovery could influence what was recovered. The absence of that concern explains why they expended a proportionately greater effort in surveying the earthworks, for the form, shape, and size of the enclosures themselves were data, and their very definition depended on their being carefully delineated.

That said, Squier and Davis were nonetheless keen observers—if haphazard recorders—of the details of the mounds through which they tunneled. They were able to discern successive episodes of "altars" being fashioned, used, and remodeled; different construction and burning events; the faintly burned and stained traces of log tombs; postmolds; and the presence of exotic earth and stones used in mound construction.[134] Moreover, their careful observations of the strata within the mounds enabled them to determine construction sequences and recognize mounds that had been disturbed or that contained sequences of intrusive features or burials.[135]

They were especially concerned about the latter, for they came to be convinced—on both archaeological and ethnographic grounds—that there had been considerable secondary use of the mounds by later Indians. Thus, even though "[s]ilver crosses, gun-barrels, and French dial-plates, have been found with skeletons in the mounds; yet it is not to be concluded that the mound-builders were Catholics, or used fire-arms, or understood French."[136] They understood clearly—as many of their peers did not—the fundamental methodological point that material associated in the contemporary archaeological record had not necessarily been associated in the past. Without becoming entangled in the unproductive issue of whether Squier and Davis perceived stratigraphy as we do, we can say that their observations of the strata within the mounds show their grasp of that methodological point, which gave them a "means of determining, aside from the distinctive features of the articles themselves, which of the relics discovered in the mounds pertain to their builders, and which are of a later date."[137]

The ethnographic warrant that Indians buried their dead in the mounds and the archaeological observation that their graves tended to be shallow and cluttered with "rude implements" of bone, stone, and pottery (including material of European origin), while those of the moundbuilders were much deeper and differently positioned, led Squier and Davis to pronounce the "general rule, to which there are few exceptions, [that] the only authentic and undoubted remains of the mound-builders are found directly beneath the apex of the mound, on a level with the original surface of the earth; and it may be safely assumed, that whatever deposits occur near the surface of the mounds, are of a date subsequent to their erection."[138] Warren K. Moorehead (1866–1939) would later thank them for that conclusion (as explained below).

Accordingly, their excavations bypassed or ignored near-surface burials and burrowed deep into the center of the mounds, where experience had taught them to expect the moundbuilder remains. Not, it's worth adding, just *any* mounds, but altar/sacrificial mounds. The majority of the hundred mounds that they excavated were of this type, even though these did not represent a majority of mounds. They were, however, the "most interesting and productive in relics." Squier and Davis understood, albeit implicitly, that their sample of mounds lacked representativeness. No matter. They were well compensated by a rich collection of artifacts, and that had been one of their goals from the start.[139]

ARRANGING THE ARCHAEOLOGICAL RECORD

Squier and Davis had walked, surveyed, collected, and tunneled into enough of the large-scale monuments of Ohio to realize that they varied in form, arrangement, position, features, structure, and contents, however many "general points of resem-

blance" they shared. It was evident too from published and unpublished descriptions
that mounds and earthworks were scattered throughout the western states, and while
these were generally the same kinds as found in Ohio, they apparently differed in
their relative abundance and occasionally in specific attributes. Likewise, artifacts
appeared to vary in kind and quantity across the mounds of the Mississippi Valley.
That raised the possibility that the moundbuilder occupation was not a "single system of works," as Squier and Davis supposed, but might include different groups or
occupations at different times. Determining whether there was one or several
moundbuilder occupations required developing a classification scheme to help "bring
[a] system out of the disordered materials" and show just how varied these different
manifestations were.[140]

Their classification of the archaeological record was not without precedent (Atwater's work, for example), but it was without much established procedure. In these
early years, little of the archaeological record was known, and its variations—and,
for that matter, the dimensions of variability—were not well understood. Squier and
Davis did understand the importance of function and use, and that—along with
form and material—were the primary lines along which they sorted the phenomena
of the archaeological record. Because overall form was assumed to follow function,
their classification generally focused on objects or features (rather than on attributes
of those objects or features). And, because function was not always evident from the
form of the object/feature itself, they relied heavily on historic, ethnographic, and
archaeological analogies to fill in the details.

Squier and Davis initially divided the archaeological record of the moundbuilders
into several categories—large-scale monuments, "minor vestiges of art" (artifacts),
skeletal remains, and rock art. From there, they derived progressively smaller sub-
groups based mostly on their presumed function but also, to a lesser degree, on raw
material, morphology, and contents.

The large-scale monuments were divided into *earthworks* (walls, enclosures, embankments, lined causeways, and so on) and *mounds* ("used in this work in a technical sense, as synonymous with Tumulus or Barrow").[141] Earthworks were further sub-
divided into *defensive* and *sacred*, distinguished by their shape, topographic
position, and (most important) the location of the encircling ditch. The ditches on the
outside of the walls were obviously moats and served—as they did in medieval
fortresses—as a staunch line of defense against attack. If the ditch was within the enclosure, then the enclosure had to be sacred, for it was certainly not defensible. An
internal moat was a strategic "blunder which no people possessing the skill and judgment displayed in the defensive works of the mound-builders, would be apt to
commit."[142]

Mounds were divided into *sacrificial, sepulchral, temple,* and *observation,* by the
kind and variety of their contents, as well as their stratification, their proximity to
enclosures, and, especially, their presumed function. The effigy mounds of the north-
west (Wisconsin and the Dakota Territory) were more of a classificatory problem.
These mounds took the form of beasts, birds, reptiles, and humans, and were accompanied by small conical mounds and, occasionally, embankments. Squier and Davis
were at a loss as to where to put them in their functional scheme, since they hadn't

seen them firsthand and could only offer a few unsatisfactory guesses about their origins, purposes, distribution, and age. So different were they from effigies (like Serpent Mound) in Ohio, that Squier and Davis were "almost induced to assign them a different origin."[143]

Artifacts were sorted by raw material (pottery, metal, stone, bone, minerals, and so on) and then by their presumed function (form)—whether implements or ornaments, and of what kinds. Observations about manufacturing, technology, raw material sources, and wear patterns (especially burning, an important clue to the moundbuilders' sacrificial activities!) were frequently made in passing. These did not serve as classificatory criteria, except where the advanced skill and precision of the "workmanship" was used to distinguish moundbuilder artifacts from the more primitive forms of the Indians.[144]

The classification was hierarchical, ad hoc, often anecdotal (as, for example, their distinction between war arrows and peace arrows), and occasionally downright clumsy. Features and artifacts were shuffled into groups, but those groups were not defined analytically, left plenty of room for overlap and ambiguity, and were mutually exclusive only by virtue of which artifacts or features had been assigned to each and not because of the criteria by which they were defined. Not surprisingly, Squier and Davis admitted that at times the classification worked better in the "aggregate" than in specific cases.

This was especially true for mounds. While the two researchers brimmed with confidence that the "leading purposes of the [Ohio] mounds have been detected and settled," some of the mound sites resisted the best efforts to "determine the[ir] character." So stubborn was the resistance that they were compelled to create a separate formal group for those unwieldy cases—*anomalous* mounds, they called them.[145]

While their classification of mounds sometimes worked poorly, at other times it worked in circles. Sacrificial mounds, for example, were thus identified because they contained what appeared to be "altars," though the determination of the precise function of those features rested on little more than observations of their form and traces of burning—with a few ethnographic and archaeological parallels thrown in. From altars, it was but one small step to sacrifice—why else would they be covered with singular riches like mica or galena?—and from there on to *human* sacrifice, since bone fragments (presumed to be human) were occasionally intermingled with altar remains. All of that "seems to follow legitimately from the facts and circumstances," but lest this chain of reasoning fail to convince the skeptical, Squier and Davis played their trump card: Sacrificial mounds "are almost invariably found within enclosures, which . . . we are induced to believe were sacred in their origin." Naturally. What made those enclosures sacred was the presence of sacrificial mounds. That these features might not be altars, or might have a purpose other than human sacrifice, was never seriously considered.[146]

Squier and Davis encountered relatively fewer classificatory problems with artifacts and earthworks: artifacts, because many were still in use among the Indian tribes, and analogical warrants for their function were plentiful; earthworks, because there seemed little question about their purpose, even if fewer useful analogues were known. All of the large linear, geometric, and elaborate monuments and enclosures of the West, Squier and Davis declared, could have had only a military or a religious purpose. There was no classificatory middle ground between the two, for Squier and Davis could see no other factor(s) that would provide sufficient motivation for such burdensome and painstaking labor.[147] Earlier, Atwater had been even more emphatic. Responding to the suggestion that some of the earthworks had been used for sport, he replied, "I have always doubted whether any people of sane minds, would have ever performed quite so much labour in mere sport."[148]

Once defined, these classificatory groups organized the discussion in *Ancient Monuments*. The descriptions of individual mounds and features within them was generally qualitative rather than quantitative, and as such still stubbornly resists efforts by modern readers to tally, for a particular mound, just how much was found, where, and with what. Information on artifacts—whether their specific context, association, and/or quantities—was usually even more limited, or (as often) vague and indeterminate. For Squier and Davis, presence alone was more important than abundance.

For that matter, they valued certain elements of the archaeological record more than others. Thus the detailed description, illustration, and discussion of earthworks and mounds account for nearly two-thirds of *Ancient Monuments* and serve as the foundation on which rests the weight of their interpretations and conclusions about the moundbuilders. Artifacts, skeletal remains, and other scattered evidences play decidedly ancillary roles and are crowded together in the remaining third of the volume. That disparity must partly reflect their opinion on the relative information to be gained from each of these elements of the archaeological record, but perhaps also it indicates the greater amount of time and effort that they invested in surveying and exploring the large-scale monuments.

RECONSTRUCTING THE MOUNDBUILDERS

Armed with a battery of descriptive data and evidence, Squier and Davis crafted a richly textured reconstruction of moundbuilder life and death. Central to their reconstruction (as to their classification) was the use of analogy, although they insisted in their preface that "analogies, apparently capable of reflecting light upon many important questions connected with an enlarged view of the subject, have seldom been more than indicated." That is an odd disclaimer in a volume cluttered with references to ancient Britons, Celts, Danes, Greeks, Romans, Scandinavians, Laplanders, Africans, Asians, Egyptians, Siberians, "Hindoos," Chinese, Polynesians, Pacific Islanders, New Zealanders, Australians, ancient Peruvians and Mexicans, Aztecs, Mandan, "Rickarees," and "Eskimaux." But they are not being disingenuous; they are only making the point that *specific* analogies—say, to the symbolic role of the serpent—were not pursued, even if "fraught with the greatest interest."[149]

Of analogy *generally*, Squier and Davis and most of their archaeological peers here and abroad shared the belief, founded in the spectacular successes of early nineteenth-century paleontology in using comparative anatomy to reconstruct extinct animals, that comparative ethnology was essential to reconstructing extinct cultures. Their discussion of the moundbuilders invoked a series of ethnographic, archaeological, and historic comparisons drawn from around the world and back in time. It's no surprise that they had to reach so broadly, since the ethnographic record in those years was spotty and contained little enough information on groups that, so far as Squier and Davis could tell, were comparably as advanced as the moundbuilders (and thus could appropriately serve as analogues). What the record contained on American Indians was even more limited (they knew virtually nothing of the southwestern Pueblo groups, for example), heavily anecdotal, frequently pejorative, and painted in such broad brushstrokes as to be useful only for speaking in generalizations—as Squier and Davis mostly did when they commented on American Indians. Morton had said all Indians were alike, and they took him at his word.

Their purpose in using these comparative cases was twofold: first, to anchor inferences about the archaeologically invisible functions, uses, or activities represented by the otherwise silent monuments, features, and artifacts of the moundbuilders (an early, scattershot version of ethnographic analogy); and second, and no less important, to identify possible historical links between the moundbuilders and other known groups. In effect, these "analogies" were simultaneously pressed into service as homologies.

But only some of them. For Squier and Davis also believed that the appropriateness and significance of an analogy or parallel (they used the terms interchangeably) depended on where the parties to the comparison stood relative to each other and to the "law of harmonious development." The way they envisioned it, and this was decades before Lewis Henry Morgan (1818–81) codified the savagery-barbarism-civilization sequence, there was a ladder of progress from the most primitive to the most civilized of human societies. Advancement up that ladder was slow, steady, and involved simultaneously all the elements of the society (that was the "harmonious development" part—one element never leapfrogged over others). They began with, and never wavered from, the assumption that the moundbuilders were a "semi-civilized" nation—more advanced than the recent tribes of savage Indians but less so than the more complex civilizations.[150] On that point, of course, both Gallatin and Morton had agreed, and that assumption would guide Squier and Davis's expectations, inferences, and conclusions about who the moundbuilders were, how and when they lived, who they were related to, and where, in the end, they may have gone.

It certainly guided their selection of comparative cases, as careful readers of *Ancient Monuments* would have noticed. Old World analogues, both archaeological and ethnographic, appear frequently in the chapters on the mounds and earthworks and very infrequently in the chapters devoted to artifacts. In contrast, American Indian analogues are invoked regularly in the chapters on artifacts but rarely in the discussions of the large-scale monuments, and then mostly to emphasize that American Indians hardly ever constructed features of this kind. Yet throughout the work, analogies and parallels are drawn to the ancient Mexicans and Peruvians.

The reasoning behind that pattern was transparent enough. Analogies to Old World groups seemed the only ones appropriate for understanding the large-scale monuments of the moundbuilders, particularly their defensive enclosures, since for Squier and Davis the people of ancient and medieval Europe (and the tribes of the Pacific) were themselves barbarous or semi-civilized and thus provided the most di-

rect analogues for primitive warfare among the moundbuilders.[151] By that same ra-
tionale, warfare among the American Indians was considered irrelevant, since they
were less advanced in military science, were "averse to labor," and rarely constructed
fortifications on the scale that the moundbuilders had. Indeed, because of their apparent antipathy to labor, Indians rarely constructed any earthworks save the "rude"
stone heaps haphazardly piled up over time along the edges of well-worn trails.[152]
Little understanding of the moundbuilders could be gained by comparisons here, so
far as Squier and Davis were concerned.

That said, they freely invoked analogies to American Indian artifacts when discussing the "minor works of art" of the moundbuilders, particularly their stone
tools. That they did so was no concession that the two were at the same level of advancement (to use their terms), or even historically related, but rather it was the
recognition of what would later be termed *convergence*. As they put it, "the wants of
man have ever been the same, and have always suggested like forms to his implements, and similar modes of using them." Under the circumstances analogies were
appropriate, since there was little to distinguish the artifacts of the semi-civilized
moundbuilders from those of the savage Indians, save "the position in which they are
found, and the not entirely imaginary superiority of their workmanship."[153]

Although Squier and Davis were interested in who the ancestors and descendants
of the moundbuilders might be, they never considered the possibility that the analogies they were drawing to Old World groups or American Indians might also reflect
homologies. Atwater certainly had considered such an association, when he leaped to
the conclusion that similarities between Ohio mounds and those built by the "Hindoos or southern Tartars" suggested that the two were historically related.[154] Nor was
he alone in seeking Old World connections; most writers of the time did so, for most
were committed to monogenesis, which demanded as much. In fact, *Ancient Monuments* is *unusual* in showing virtually no interest in linking the moundbuilders to
any Old World groups. Squier and Davis's excuse for not doing so was that forging
any ancestral links to the Old World required analyzing worldwide religious beliefs
and symbol systems, for it was these elements that "mankind adhere[s] to with greatest tenacity" (in effect, cultural atavisms) and that should reveal the "elements common to all nations, far back in the traditional period." Making a connection between
the moundbuilders and Old World groups went far beyond the borders of acceptable
inquiry staked out by Joseph Henry. But that wasn't what stopped Squier. He had
by then already fallen under the polygenists' spell and was beginning to admit privately that the American race was independent of any Old World ancestry.[155]

For that matter, Squier and Davis didn't believe that the moundbuilders' descendants were living among the Indian tribes of North America. Neither did they believe that Indians had anything to do with constructing the mounds.

MOUNDBUILDERS AND INDIANS

It didn't take them very long to announce their intentions, either, as a glimpse at
the volume's frontispiece makes clear. Squier and Davis had selected a painting of
the mounds and earthworks at Marietta, Ohio, in which the complex is viewed from

the hills north of the site (to orient the view and identify the elements, compare the frontispiece with Plate XXVI). This is not a reconstruction but rather a representation of what the complex might have looked like sheared of trees but before the town of Marietta overgrew it. In the painting, the abandoned archaeological site is viewed from a distant hilltop by several Indians who have paused momentarily from their hunt. The only human figures in the scene, they are placed as far from the mounds and earthworks as possible. The artist's message, intentional or not, is unmistakable: The Indians are no more a part of the archaeological complex than the small log cabin in the foreground or Marietta's "Old Stockade" on the banks of the Muskingum River.[156] It was a message that would reverberate throughout *Ancient Monuments*.

Samuel Haven had seen it coming the summer before, when he tried to convince Squier that there was less to the "apparent superiority of the 'Mound builders' to the Eastern tribes" than met the eye. Haven wondered whether the apparent differences between the two were attributable to nothing more than differences in their respective environments:

> We know the difference that . . . locality, greater or lesser fertility of soil, and facility of supporting life, make among our own race. My wonder is less that the occupants of the rich valleys of the west should have left such remains behind there, than that they should have left no more, and none of the higher order, supposing them to have possessed permanent settlements in so temperate as well as so productive a region.

But if Haven wanted to draw the moundbuilders and Indians closer, Squier would go only partway with him. He agreed that "climate, position and general circumstances" did make a difference and that the inhabitants of America were "all of one stock" (here he appealed to the good authority of Morton). He was nonetheless convinced that the moundbuilders and the Indians—even if related by virtue of being members of the same (American) race—had developed along very different tracks, at very different times, and had achieved different levels of advancement.[157]

Ancient Monuments missed few opportunities to highlight the differences between the moundbuilders and the Indians, and it found many. The two differed in their artifacts—those of the moundbuilders were naturally more advanced and included the use of metals, sophisticated sculpture, and more (and more superior) forms than the relatively "rude" and depauperate remains of the Indians. They differed in their patterns of warfare and systems of defense—those of the Indians lacked walls and moats and had only the skimpiest of palisades.[158] They differed in their burial practices and in mound construction and use—Indian mounds were rare, distinct, and inferior to those of the moundbuilders, and it seemed to Squier and Davis that Indians preferred to bury their dead in moundbuilders' mounds.[159] Unlike the skeletal remains of Indians, those of moundbuilders were rare, deeply buried, and poorly preserved within mounds, as well as being physically distinct (though how well the cranial differences, presented in tabular form in *Ancient Monuments*, would withstand statistical scrutiny is an open question).[160] Finally, they differed in subsistence patterns—the Indians were hunters and the moundbuilders agriculturalists.[161]

The cumulative effect of those differences was telling, as Squier himself had long before asserted: "Nomadic tribes, hunters, never build works of this magnitude. Labor, especially unproductive labor, is utterly repugnant to them. This repugnance amounts to an indelible trait, a permanent characteristic. History furnishes no example of the construction of any great works by races having the characteristics of the Indians."[162]

The moundbuilders and the Indians, so far as Squier and Davis were concerned, could not have been one and the same people. On this, they recited the testimony of the Indians themselves, who, when pressed as to whether they had built the mounds or knew anything of their origins or builders could only reply, "They were never put up by our people."[163]

ALL ROADS LEAD TO MEXICO

Besides, it seemed obvious that the moundbuilders were related to the semi-civilized groups of Mexico and Peru, to whom, as noted, comparisons were drawn throughout *Ancient Monuments* (which comes as no surprise either, given that this was the closest comparably complex group that Squier and Davis and their contemporaries had reasonably complete knowledge of). Arguing for links with Mexico was nothing new. In 1820 Atwater looked south down an unbroken line of "ancient works [that] continue[d] all the way into Mexico." There, among the Aztec, he saw attributes (Teocalli [platform mounds], deities, mica mirrors, and human sacrifice) reminiscent of the Ohio moundbuilders. They must have left Ohio, drifted south around the "Mexican Gulph," and then settled in Mexico, having increased their populations, improved their arts, and generally "progressed" as they moved from north to south.[164]

Likewise, in 1845, Gallatin had linked the moundbuilders to Mexico, but he reversed the tide of migration. The domestication of plants—Gallatin's foundation for civilization (including that of the moundbuilders)—was indigenous to Mexico. If the moundbuilders were agriculturalists, as Gallatin insisted they must have been, then their agriculture must have been derived from Mexico, and thus they had moved from south to north.[165]

Squier and Davis weren't sure *which* way the moundbuilders had migrated.[166] They were not altogether convinced by Gallatin's arguments that agriculture had to have a tropical origin, or even that the Mexican civilizations predated those further north (as they should, were they the ancestral population). Wasn't it possible, they asked, that agriculture and civilization originated "among the builders of the ancient monuments on the banks of the great Mississippi river—the Nile and the Ganges of North America"?[167]

Perhaps. But one fact seemed certain. The connections between the moundbuilders and the Mexican civilization were broad and deep. It hadn't escaped Squier and Davis's notice that there were telltale differences in earthen monuments as one moved south. The large enclosures of Ohio became increasingly rare in the southern United States, while mounds—especially temple mounds—became more common: "No sooner do we arrive in the Southern States, than we find these Teocalli-shaped structures constituting the most numerous and important portion of the ancient remains." Defensive enclosures were correspondingly rare in the southern states (possibly a further clue about migration patterns, or at least about when and where hostilities ceased along that march), and those that did occur were at best "inferior" militarily and possessed none of the "requisites for resisting an enemy and . . . sustaining a protracted defense."[168]

So marked were these contrasts, Squier and Davis admitted, that many "regard them as the work not only of a different era, but of a different people." Or so it appeared, given the meager data at hand. But there was too much uncertainty in these secondhand accounts, and too little evidence on which to resolve how they were related to the mounds of the Ohio Valley and "whether the less imposing structures of the Ohio are the remains of a ruder and more warlike but progressive people, or the weaker efforts of a colony, pressed by foes and surrounded by difficulties."[169] No matter. The southern mounds so strongly resembled the Mexican Teocalli that they must be part of a "gradual transition, from the earthworks of the Mississippi to the more imposing structures of brick and stone of Mexico and Central America." Whichever direction the moundbuilders had migrated, they either began or ended "in the gorgeous semi-civilization of Mexico and Peru."[170]

Further historical links between the two areas could be seen in the respective defensive works (with allowances for the greater advances of the Mexicans in military skills); common symbols, deities, and religious ceremonialism; similar artifacts; and, more directly, in the obsidian used to manufacture some of the artifacts found in the mounds—obsidian that, so far as Squier and Davis knew, had "the nearest point of its occurrence [in] Mexico."[171] (The far western North American sources were then largely unknown.)

In fact, Squier and Davis recognized and sought to pinpoint the sources of all the unusual and exotic raw materials that had emerged from the mounds, such as copper, galena, mica, pipestone, silver, marine shells, pearls, and fossil shark's teeth.[172] "Accurate or approximate" identification of these sources, they believed, would "reflect light upon the grand archaeological questions of the origin, migration, and intercommunication of the race of the mounds." But it could also confound matters, for "side by side in the same mounds [were] native copper from Lake Superior, mica from the Alleghenies, shells from the Gulf, and obsidian (perhaps porphyry) from Mexico. This fact seems seriously to conflict with the hypothesis of a migration, either northward or southward."[173] How could one invoke a migration, when there appeared simultaneously so many and such scattered sources and destinations? But a migration it had to be, as far as Squier and Davis were concerned. So convinced were they that this was the primary mechanism for moving artifacts and cultural materials that they mention only in passing—and otherwise mostly ignore—the possibility that these materials were moved by exchange (or "intercommunication," as they put it).[174]

Besides, there were the stone pipe sculptures from the mounds, which "faithfully represent animals and birds peculiar to other latitudes," notably the "Lamantin or Manitus" (manatee), and the toucan—both tropical forms. Whoever had crafted these pipes, Squier and Davis confidently declared, depicted the animals so exactly that they had to be "well acquainted with the animal[s] and [their] habits." Manatees and toucans had to be seen to be carved, so either the moundbuilders extended over a vast territory and were in constant intercommunication or southern émigrés brought their memories of the manatee and toucan with them.[175] Squier and Davis admitted both possibilities but clearly favored the latter.

LIFE AND DEATH AMONG THE MOUNDBUILDERS

Regardless of which direction moundbuilder migrants had traveled the Mexican road, Squier and Davis felt they had a reasonably clear picture of the "character and condition" of the moundbuilders' world. It was, first and foremost, a very hostile place. Many of the earthen enclosures had "incontestably a military origin," as evidenced by their topographic position, walls, citadels, mazes and enfilades, alarm posts, blockhouses, bastions, palisades and gates (made of wood since eroded away—analogies provided the missing details), moats, and for times of siege, protected water reservoirs.[176]

These heavily fortified earthworks formed a vast "system of defences" that stretched from the headwaters of the Allegheny and Susquehanna in New York to the Wabash in the west. This was no temporary line hastily cobbled together in response to an unexpected invasion, but rather the entrenched response to grim, chronic warfare: "[T]he contest was a protracted one, and . . . the race of the mounds were for a long period constantly exposed to attack." Squier and Davis, themselves only a generation removed from the first settlement of the Ohio Valley, could easily conjure the image of the moundbuilder frontier: "We may suppose that a condition of things prevailed [among the moundbuilder forts] somewhat analogous to that which attended the advance of our pioneer population, when every settlement had its little fort, to which the people flocked in case of alarm or attack." This thin earthen line separated the moundbuilders from the "hostile savage hordes" to the north.[177] But did that border represent the final check of the northward advance of the moundbuilders or the onset of their retreat to the south in the face of the "incessant attacks . . . of exterminating cruelty"—a retreat that ultimately drove them into Mexico?[178] Either way, this prehistoric Maginot Line was no less than the demarcation between savagery and civilization.

Yet all was not violence and hostility in the moundbuilders' lives. *Ancient Monuments* paints a picture of an existence steeped in religion, rich in ceremonialism, accomplished in the arts, and skilled in the sciences. Moundbuilder society was governed by priests and chieftains, whose far-reaching powers (similar to those of the Aztec priests, naturally) exerted a "controlling influence" on the lives of their people. That ensured a uniformity in their customs and habits and explained the "extraordinary coincidences" in form among widely scattered mounds, earthworks, and artifacts—such as the perfectly squared and circular earthworks, many apparently of identical size and all testimony to the strong guiding hand of the moundbuilder priesthood, as well as a standard of measurement, a knowledge of geometry, and an ability to determine angles. One could hardly conclude that such "coincidences are the result of accident."[179]

Moundbuilder society was, in the eyes of Squier and Davis, highly stratified in death as well as in life. They recognized that burial in a mound was a rare privilege accorded the few—whom they took to be "the chieftains and priests [and] perhaps . . . the ashes of [their] distinguished families," along with the sacrificial victims who accompanied the revered dead ("in accordance with barbarian practice"). As to what became of the remains of moundbuilder commoners, Squier and Davis could only guess that they had been buried in undistinguished cemeteries long since eroded away.[180]

They—Squier especially—were intensely curious about what manner of religion the moundbuilders possessed, but the details were elusive. Idol worship, they were certain, was not part of it, but they suspected that the moundbuilders worshiped the moon and the sun (again, like the Aztecs) and guessed that their ceremonies included offerings and sacrifices from the "first fruits" of the harvest. If the details of their "superstitious rites" were beyond the pale, however, their many sacred enclosures and mounds, studded with sacrificial altars, topped by the platforms of temples long since degraded, and crossed by causeways through which the assemblies passed "in the solemn observances of a mysterious worship," testified to the "devotional fervor . . . superstitious zeal . . . and the predominance of the religious sentiment" among the moundbuilders. After all, human sacrifice was involved, and if that failed to affirm the moundbuilders' "devotional fervor," it at least provided a glimmer of the "magnitude of the calamity which that sacrifice was perhaps intended to avert."[181]

Whatever the nature of the calamity, Squier and Davis wouldn't say. If it was famine, they wouldn't know. *Ancient Monuments* is singularly uninterested in the details of moundbuilder subsistence, save that they must have been farmers, and good ones. The evidence, they declared, came "from a variety of facts and circumstances," but it was more circumstantial than factual, and there were only two circumstantial lines at that. First, their mounds and earthworks were found mostly in fertile valleys in "precisely the positions best adopted for agricultural purposes" (which also explained why moundbuilder sites were just where Euroamerican farmers settled).[182] Second, the labor demands of building—by hand with only "weak powers of transportation"—the many and vast mounds and earthworks of the Mississippi Valley were enormous, and only agriculturalists, they assumed, had the requisite spare time and necessarily large labor force available to build all these large-scale monuments. On that point, Squier and Davis could quote with approval Gallatin's opinion that

> There is not, and there was not in the 16th century, a single tribe of Indians (north of the semi-civilized nations) between the Atlantic and the Pacific, which had means of subsistence sufficient to enable them to apply, for such purposes, the unproductive labor necessary for the work [of constructing mounds]; nor was there any in such a social state as to compel the labor of the people to be thus applied.

As noted, they would not be the last to invoke the idea that hunter-gatherers hadn't the time or the wherewithal to build mounds.[183]

Beyond that, Squier and Davis did not seek direct evidence of subsistence, though they occasionally encountered possible food remains—such as the bones of deer and elk from several mounds. When they did, however, they were more interested in their use as tools than in their possible use as food, or in how they came to be at the site.[184]

ABOUT TIME

The moundbuilders—numerous, sedentary, agricultural, and "fixed" in their customs, laws, and religion—appeared to be broadly similar across space and likely synchronous in time.[185] But how long ago? By the 1840s there was a general suspicion that the moundbuilder occupation might be very old. That they were no longer extant suggested as much. So, too, did William Henry Harrison's growth-ring counts and observations on the successional sequence of trees growing atop the mounds and DeWitt Clinton's estimate of the time that must have elapsed for Lake Erie to recede eight miles from mounds that must once have stood along its shores.[186]

Squier and Davis hinted throughout *Ancient Monuments* that the moundbuilder occupation had a considerable antiquity, though they saved that argument for last—perhaps recognizing that here they were on slippery, if not hazardous, ground. If they were to push for great antiquity of the mounds, Marsh had warned Squier, they would have to do so with few firm chronological markers to guide the way, using what meager facts they could and avoiding speculation and "doubtful analogies" to other countries. Most of all, they would have to keep a careful eye on the biblical limits to human antiquity. But push they would, for the archaeological facts seemed to point toward a great antiquity. The several minor hints included the "accumulation of vegetable deposit" in the bottom of borrow pits, the drop in the channel to which the ramp at Marietta earthworks leads, the decay of the moundbuilder skeletal remains, and the absence of their cemeteries.[187]

More telling, however, was the topographic setting of the mounds and earthworks. While they were present on many river terraces, they were noticeably absent from one: "[I]t is a fact of much importance, and worthy of special note, that within the scope of a pretty extended observation, no work of any kind has been found occupying the first, or latest formed terrace. . . . [This fact] bears directly upon the question of their antiquity." Squier and Davis knew that the first and lowest terrace was periodically subject to flooding, but it didn't occur to them that that was the reason no mounds or earthworks were built there. Indeed, they could see no possible reason to avoid building on this terrace (or evidence that the moundbuilders had), save that this last terrace hadn't been formed at the time of the occupation. Since they believed that this last of the four terraces took longer to form than any of the preceding three (based on a simple and flawed fluvial model), a very long time must have elapsed "since the race of the mounds flourished."[188]

Corroboration on that point came from the huge trees and ancient-looking forests atop some of the mounds. Some of those trees possessed upwards of six hundred annual growth rings, but even six hundred years badly underestimated the potential age of mound constructions. Since one also had to "add the probable period intervening from the time of the building of the work to its abandonment, and the subsequent period up to its invasion by the forest, we are led irresistibly to the conclusion, that it has an antiquity of at least one thousand years." That conclusion assumes that the trees growing there now were the ones that originally colonized the sites, which seems unlikely, given the number of large trees found decaying on the sites, which suggested "an antiquity still more remote." Add up the time elapsed since the sites were built, abandoned, colonized by trees, and then subject to at least one long cycle of forest growth, and Squier and Davis were "compelled to assign [the mounds] no inconsiderable antiquity."[189]

The polygenists were quick to notice. Josiah Nott had been wondering just "how far back you [Squier] push the probable antiquity of the Mounds, for chronology to me is every thing. . . . I look to you to give the coup de grace to that venerable old braggart Moses."[190] Nott wouldn't be disappointed.

A MIRROR OF THE PAST

It has been said that Squier and Davis anticipated "in a degree, the modern method of formulating hypotheses and testing expectations." Perhaps, but there's little enough of that, and mostly it's lower-level tests of a specific artifact or mound function.[191] What they did anticipate fully was the use of accommodative arguments: Hardly a bit of data came their way that couldn't be fitted into their a priori belief that the mounds were the work of a superior group, farmers all, at a level of semi-civilization with skills in surveying and warfare (though obviously not skilled enough to beat back the savage hordes) and with ties that, literally and figuratively, snaked directly into Mexico. They were, moreover, extremely confident in their assertions, inferences, and conclusions: "[C]an hardly admit of doubt" and like assurances are given throughout *Ancient Monuments*.[192] These were accommodative arguments with an attitude.

It was a noble and inspiring vision, this image of the moundbuilders that emerges in *Ancient Monuments*. A courageous and deeply devout frontier people, capable of great works and superior in all respects to their savage neighbors. A people who had made a "heroic defense of homes and altars, and . . . daring achievement in siege and assault."[193] But a people who, in the end, were driven from their homes by wanton cruelty and destruction. That's quite an image for a volume ostensibly purged of anything "like mere speculation." Of course, from their vantage this wasn't speculation. Without putting too fine a point on it, for Squier and Davis the past was a set of self-evident facts, from which one could only draw irresistible conclusions. For them (no less than for Henry, perhaps) the moundbuilder occupation was just an exotic variant of a long-running story—one still being played out on the westward-moving American frontier, where even some of the players were still the same.

AFTER *ANCIENT MONUMENTS*

The Smithsonian's thousand copies of *Ancient Monuments* began circulating in late September of 1848. Squier and Davis, still feuding, each separately arranged another printing of the volume—Squier through Bartlett's bookstore in New York, Davis with friends in Cincinnati. Their books sold to subscribers for ten dollars each. Squier's copies (and presumably Davis's as well) sold quickly and earned their authors a nice profit.[194]

Recipients were enthusiastic in their praise. Even those who had provided field data and worried that they would not be properly credited for their contributions wrote to admit that they were satisfied (surprised, too, in some cases) with their treatment in the book, particularly by the generous acknowledgments in the preface. After all the unhappiness that had surfaced during the book's production over proprietary matters, Squier and Davis left no doubt—in the text, the plates, or the preface—just who had contributed what to the effort, and they effusively praised the work of all who provided survey data, collections, manuscripts, advice, drawings, descriptions, or critical editorial and production help. In fact, everyone who had anything to do with the project was thanked, it seems, except one: Joseph Henry, who had invested so much of his time, effort, and institutional and individual reputation in the project, was unmentioned. That, however, may have been his choice.[195]

As to the book itself, the great naturalist Alexander von Humboldt (1793–1864) reckoned it the "most valuable contribution ever made to the archaeology and ethnology of America," while Morton himself believed it "a monument that will immortalize its authors when marble itself has passed into disintegration." Squier could only grumble that the work had been "emasculated."[196]

Hyperbole aside, *Ancient Monuments* was instantly recognized as a milestone in American archaeology and, indeed, in American science. With the emphasis on "American." *Literary World*, reprinting highly laudatory comments from London's *Ethnological Journal*, couldn't resist crowing, "However slow our transatlantic neighbors may be to admit the claims of American literature, they have been ready (we will not say compelled) to recognize, and, in many instances, to defer to American Science."[197] Of course, Squier and Davis weren't out to make a patriotic statement (nor, as earlier noted, was Henry). Still, it couldn't be helped if in piercing the mystery of the moundbuilders they had achieved a more respectable standing for both American prehistory and American science. They just didn't want to say so themselves; but then, they didn't have to:

> After sitting down in silence under the reproach . . . of excessive modernness and newness of our country, which has been described over and over again by foreign and native journals as being bare of old associations as though it had been made by a journeyman potterer day before yesterday, we find we have here, what no other nation on the known globe, can claim: a perfect union of the past and present; the vigor of a nation just born walking over the hallowed ashes of a race whose history is too early for a record, and surrounded by the living forms of a people hovering between the two.[198]

If the comments in *Literary World* were unusual, it was only for their unabashed nationalism, not their heady praise of *Ancient Monuments*.[199]

Overall, there were few published reviews of *Ancient Monuments*. Quite simply, there were not enough scientific (let alone anthropological) journals to serve as a platform, and those that did exist—like the *American Journal of Science*—commonly published only book notices (as they did in this case), not book reviews. Even so, the volume received critical attention and acclaim in this country where it counted most: in the *North American Review*.[200]

Although by custom and tradition, pieces in the *North American Review* were anonymous, the author of the lengthy review of *Ancient Monuments* was no mystery to Squier. Charles Eliot Norton (1827–1908) first contacted Squier in early 1849 to say that he was preparing a "simple abstract" of *Ancient Monuments* for the *North American Review*. Only, there were a couple of points he wanted clarified. Careful reader that he was, Norton had noticed that Dickeson's work was slighted and wondered why that was so. And he was more troubled by the apparent antiquity of the mounds and wondered (as Cyrus Thomas would half a century later) whether a key bit of evidence for their great age hadn't been misinterpreted:

> You speak in your concluding chapter of the argument for the antiquity of the earthworks from the fact of their not being found on the lowest terrace of the Western Rivers. This fact has seemed to me . . . capable of being considered in another view. You mention that the . . . lowest terrace, is the only one, except in rare cases, liable to be overflowed. Why may we not then conceive the works of the mound-builders were not placed upon this terrace on account of the dangers of being inundated?[201]

Why not, indeed?

The Dickeson matter was easily managed. As to "how far Dr. D[ickeson] is regarded as reliable," Squier snorted, there are "many things which Dr. D. affirms to exist, [and] *may* exist,—but whether they *do* exist, is quite another question." Responding on the antiquity issue required more effort.

Squier prefaced his reply by explaining that *Ancient Monuments* was actually "little more than half the matter" originally prepared, much of which he chose to withdraw late in the book's production. "*My* work," Squier confessed, "has many deficiencies" and left several points unexplained, particularly in the concluding chapter. That said, he reminded Norton that even if the lowest terrace was occasionally flooded, it was hardly warrant to suppose that fear of flooding would have kept the moundbuilders from building on it—any more than it keeps modern inhabitants of the region from doing so. And since the moundbuilders had been as numerous as the modern inhabitants, and farmers too, they ought to have settled on this lowest and most fertile terrace—were it available to them. That none of their remains had been found on it confirmed—for Squier—that the terrace had not yet formed.[202]

Norton wasn't convinced by Squier's response, but that was no surprise. The possibility that the mounds could have great antiquity troubled the pious Norton and brought him to the only point in his review at which he directly criticized *Ancient Monuments* (he otherwise praised its "good judgment" and lack of "uncertain speculation" and completely accepted its interpretation of who the moundbuilders were and where they had come from). Norton's review repeated his suspicion that the moundbuilders avoided the lowest and latest terrace because they feared flooding, and he insisted (contra *Ancient Monuments*) that there was "no general rule" about the length of time it took for the western rivers to incise and form terraces.

Still, Norton didn't see that Squier and Davis's saying so had caused much harm. In the end, he applauded them for showing "no desire to enhance the interest attaching to these works by ascribing to them a very high antiquity." Ultimately, Norton believed, dating the mounds would have to be left to geologists, but he was confident that their age would only be "measured by many hundreds of years."[203]

Norton, obviously, had badly missed the point of *Ancient Monuments* when it said that the mounds and earthworks had "no inconsiderable antiquity." But polygenist Josiah Nott hadn't.

FUEL FOR THE POLYGENIST FIRES

Nott was thrilled that Squier had "the hardihood to assert that the Indians were making potato hills in [the] *Valley* before Eve was convicted & punished for stealing apples," but no less thrilled that Squier himself had become one of the "heathens."[204] The transformation had been quiet, and the early symptoms hardly visible during the production of *Ancient Monuments,* but in the end he'd become a heathen all the same. Partly it was Morton's influence, but mostly that of his disciples, Josiah Nott and George Gliddon (1809–57), who helped a willing Squier to see that his own hard-won evidence of an ancient and uniquely American race of moundbuilders forced an inescapable conclusion about the origins of humanity.

Gliddon was a British-born but onetime United States vice-consul in Cairo (it was he who provided the crania and revised dates of Egyptian history that Morton used in *Crania Americana* [1839]). Gliddon made his living traveling the cities and towns of America, hauling his "Grand Moving Transparent Panorama of the Nile, Egypt and Nubia," lecturing on the mystery and wonder of Egypt, and peddling the potent elixir that Egyptian hieroglyphics and history proved that whites and blacks were already distinct species at a time predating the Mosaic chronicles. But he never quite came right out and said that, or publicly explored its full, polygenist implications. For this self-proclaimed champion of truth and foe of humbug knew that in broad-casting the seeds of polygeny he had to be careful, lest he offend his more devout (and paying) audiences. And he was careful—even better, he was charming and in-gratiating. So good was he at disguising his infidelity that he was even asked to de-liver one of the prestigious Lowell Institute Lectures in Boston, which required every lecturer to declare a belief in divine revelation.[205] In private, however, the gloves came off: "Met several gentlemen at Morton's," Davis had reported to Squier when they were still speaking. "Gliddon was there as usual, 'knocking the Bible into a cocked hat.'" Gliddon was not completely hypocritical—he refused membership in the American Ethnological Society on the grounds that he found its religious faction unbearable.[206]

At Squier's request, Gliddon brought his wandering Egyptology show to Chilli-cothe in the spring of 1847, and he and Squier hit it off immediately. After Glid-don's talk, he summoned Squier to the stage and, in a scene that must have taken on something of the air of a witnessing in a Revivalist tent, Squier confessed for the first time publicly that the American race—like Gliddon's ancient Egyptians—may have been "created here"—though he hastily added that at the very least they arrived early during "the period of the dispersion."[207]

The next year, while lecturing throughout the South (where his message proved es-pecially popular), Gliddon made sure to alert "the right *Men*"—the physician Josiah Nott among them—of Squier's work. The imperious southerner's polygenist epiph-any had occurred in 1842, in reaction to the apparent observation in a Boston medical journal that mortality was highest amongst those of mixed race—far higher, apparently, than among "pure African" slaves or whites. Nott took this as proof that mulattos were hybrids, "degenerate, unnatural offspring" of distinct species. Proving that all the races were separately created, however, further required one to "blow up all chronologies, although it may not be very *politic* to do so in these days of Christian intolerance." Learning from Gliddon what Squier was up to, Nott kept a distant eye on his efforts, to see what they might yield of the antiquity of the American race. In the fall of 1848 he and Squier began to correspond.[208]

Squier's public conversion to polygenesis began almost immediately after *Ancient Monuments* was finished and he was beyond Joseph Henry's editorial reach. In a summary of American ethnology prepared in the spring of 1849, Squier denounced the "absurd and . . . impossible" hypotheses that sought to derive the American races from "a single pair on the banks of the Euphrates," via the Ten Lost Tribes of Israel. The Americans were not only physically separate and distinct, as Morton had proved, they were ancient as well—even Gallatin had testified to that (though it would have deeply pained the dying Gallatin to watch Squier twist his conclusion that American languages require "the very longest time which we are permitted to assume" into testimony that they predated those of the Old World. Gallatin never believed that. The great antiquity that he demanded fit well within the years the Bible allowed).[209]

Ancient Monuments, of course, had found no trace of the Lost Tribes (though it had plenty enough Old Testament fire and brimstone without them), nor any hint of migrations from the Old World. Indeed, any similarities between the peoples of the Old and New Worlds were perfunctorily dismissed as the result of "concurring conditions" (convergence) and the inherent commonalties in the "early stages of human development." There had been no migration of "vagrant tribes 'through deserts vast, and regions of eternal snow.'"[210] Squier could reach but one conclusion—the races had been separately created in their respective hemispheres. He knew it was not a popular conclusion:

> The doctrine of the diversity of origin in the human race, although gathering supporters daily [Squier among them] has yet so few open advocates, and is generally esteemed so radical a heresy, that investigators in this, as in many other departments of science, hesitate in pushing their researches to their ultimate results. The discussion of the question cannot, however, be long postponed, and it is not difficult to foresee in what manner it will be finally determined.[211]

Squier was right. Polygenesis was heresy, matters would soon come to a head, and it would be Nott and Gliddon who would be the cause. In 1852 Squier learned of their "big scheme," launched the year after Morton's death, to pull together the disparate threads of polygenesis—the natural history, chronology, history, and physical variation of humanity—as a lasting "literary cenotaph" to the memory of Morton. Besides, Nott admitted, "Gliddon wants money and thought he could make a book pay."

Nott went into the project with the righteousness of one who "knew the truth," and he agitated to "force the clergy & naturalists into open war." The way he saw it, "if a man wants to get on fast, he must kick up a dam'd fuss generally—a decent, civil,

competent, meritorious man may rot in obscurity—a man must get *notoriety* in some
way or the tide will run by him." The tide didn't run by Nott. Notoriety he had
plenty of, for even in the American antebellum South where racism was institutionalized, his particularly virulent strain of racism, infused with a venomous impious-
ness ("Parson-skinning," Gliddon called it), shocked many in his audiences: "delivered two lectures on Niggerology & knocked their eyes so wide open that I am told
some of the more godly have never slept since." Still, he was pleased to report "the
great mass of the people of the south at least have sustained me" and happily chirped
that the attention "doubled my [medical] practice."[212] Surprisingly enough, he was
reluctant to publish with Gliddon, for fear that *Gliddon* would "be too pugnacious.
He puts me in a mind of the character Mercure, in Moliere's *Amphitryon*, that . . .
has not hit anybody in so long that he feels immensely strong in the arm & is going
to hit him a hell of a lick."[213] He had reason to worry.

Over the next year they pulled together *Types of Mankind*. Standing firmly behind the "scientific" shield of Morton's unrivaled analysis, and scoring a major coup
by securing a chapter from Louis Agassiz (1807–73), *Types of Mankind* defended
polygenesis with ferocious biblical criticism (including a withering attack on the Mosaic chronologies) and raw racism.[214] Nott and Gliddon hooted at the idea that the
races were either anatomically or intellectually equal:

> a man must be blind not to be struck by similitudes between some of the lower races of
> mankind, viewed as connecting links in the animal kingdom; nor can it be rationally
> affirmed, that the Orang-Outan and Chimpanzee are more widely separated from cer-
> tain African and Oceanic Negroes than are the latter from the Teutonic or Palasgic
> types.[215]

These races were primitive and in ancient times already distinct, according to their
reading of ancient Egyptian and Roman histories. And Nott, with a cold political
eye and a deep belief that slavery was the natural place for an inferior race, was especially quick to proclaim that "Negro slavery" had been institutionalized in Egypt
by 1500 B.C.[216]

On the American race, their enthusiasm outran even Morton. So struck were they
by the disparity between the accomplishments of the Toltecs and the Barbarous family, they pounced on the possibility that the two had not sprung "from a single pair,
[but] originated in many." Regardless, one fact was certain: Just as "no single animal, bird, reptile, fish, or plant, was common to the Old and New Worlds," humans
were not "an exception to this general law." *Ancient Monuments* had given the skeletal proof of that, with its demonstration of the uniqueness of the skull of the oldest
American race. To them the Americans were as osteologically distinct from, say, the
Bushman, as a fossil hyena was from a prairie wolf.[217]

For Nott and Gliddon, Squier's investigations (they never mentioned Davis's
name—one time that Davis surely didn't mind getting no billing) proved not only
that the American race was wholly unlike any of the Old World races but also that it
was of comparable—if not greater—antiquity. *Types of Mankind* quotes from *Ancient Monuments* at length, as testifying that the *indigenous* aborigines of America

were present five thousand years ago, thus providing full "support of the contemporaneousness of American races with those first recorded on the monuments of the eastern world."[218] Granted, there may have been occasional, accidental migrations from the Old World to the New, but these were too rare and too trivial to be of any consequence. Like Squier and Davis, they saw no traces of the Old World in the New. Or vice versa.

Squier stood squarely with *Types of Mankind*. In a lengthy unsigned review for the *New York Herald* (mostly drafted by Gliddon),[219] he pronounced polygenesis no longer a "hypothesis to be sustained, but a result which is demonstrated." The races were separate *and* unequal: "The Indian proudly and sullenly recedes before the mental and moral vigor of the superior race, and the Negro holds, towards that same race, a position which must always belong to the inferior intelligence—a position of dependence." In demonstrating as much, he believed *Types of Mankind* exemplified "the advance which science has made in one of its noblest departments." It faced powerful opposition, however. Squier saw the contest between monogenesis and polygenesis as no less than a high-stakes struggle between orthodoxy and science: of vulgar chronologies and impossible claims, against reason and fact uncowed by "the lions of bigotry, superstition, and ignorance." Squier, running fast to keep up with his own (or Gliddon's) rhetorical leaps, cried out that the polygenist cause evoked no less a spirit than that of Galileo himself, facing the Vatican's Inquisition. *Types of Mankind*, regardless of what the latter-day orthodoxy may threaten, was "the most remarkable book which has yet appeared in America. . . . It is destined to exercise a great influence, and produce a profound and permanent impression on the public mind."[220]

Or so he hoped. Yet no matter how lavish his praise, *Types of Mankind* had deeply offended many, and though it sold astonishingly well (and over many printings), critical reaction to it was swift and often damning. The attacks that came in the secular and religious press aimed mostly at its infidelity, and less at its message of racial diversity and inequality. Still, even across the South secessionist hotheads steered clear of this superficially attractive defense of slavery. They could see all too clearly the theological costs in accepting it. When faced with choice between their Bibles and science, the southerners chose their Bibles—after all, the curse of Ham provided sufficient justification for slavery. Nott blamed the firestorm of criticism and controversy squarely on Gliddon's "very impolitic and undignified tone . . . [which had] done their cause great harm." But it was to Nott's everlasting disappointment that the book was largely dismissed in the scientific arena, for he badly hoped "men of science should think that the book, with all its imperfections, may assist in developing the truths involved in the discussion." They didn't, and it wouldn't. To be sure, this was no fringe document (not with contributions from Agassiz and Morton), but its sales may reflect more its notoriety than its scientific standing.[221]

Joseph Henry's reaction was perhaps typical. He staunchly defended the right of science and scientists to act "independent of revelation," but nonetheless angrily condemned those—like Nott and Gliddon—who "pride themselves on their infidelity and consider it a [mark] of superior intellect to reject all that their neighbors consider important truths." He was utterly appalled by *Types of Mankind*, which he considered "written in an improper spirit, or at least in very bad taste and regret, very much, that the name of my lamented friend Dr. Morton and that of Professor Agassiz should be mingled up with so much [puerility?] and sophistry as are to be found in this work."[222] A few years earlier, Henry had refused to permit Gliddon to use a Smithsonian lecture hall for his traveling Egyptology show (indeed, he was so painfully sensitive to entangling the Smithsonian in racial issues that he had forbidden abolitionist lectures as well). Now, the "vexed question of the unity of the races" was burning wildly, the nation (as Squier could see by the mid-1850s) was "trembling on the verge of Civil War," and the Smithsonian's first publication, which Henry had so carefully crafted as a model of neutral, inductive science, was suddenly ammunition in the arsenal of the racist polygenists.[223]

At the time, Henry was busy editing Samuel Haven's *Archaeology of the United States,* a forthcoming volume of the Smithsonian's Contributions to Knowledge series, and he urged Haven to give less attention to the "hypothesis of the diversity of origin." Then, thinking the matter over, he decided,

> [I]t would be safer for the Institution and better for the cause of science to omit as far as possible the discussion of the whole question. I say better for the cause of science because as a general rule men who possess the faculty of discovering and establishing new truths are averse to controversy and will abandon a line of research which may tend to place them in an unpleasant position.[224]

Davis would surely have agreed; by then Squier, just as surely, would not have.

DIVERGING TRACKS

By the mid-1850s, Squier and Davis had grown far apart in all ways. Their separation had begun in late 1848. They spent that fall tying up the loose ends from the publication of *Ancient Monuments,* not the least of which were the final skirmishes between Squier, Davis, and Henry—this time over the authors' copies of *Ancient Monuments.* By then, Henry and the Smithsonian Regents were reluctant to release those two hundred copies until they were certain that doing so wouldn't start yet another fight between the warring authors.[225] It didn't work, but then it didn't matter. Squier and Davis continued to snipe away at each other quite independently of the Smithsonian.

By year's end, Davis returned to the quiet of Chillicothe and his medical practice. Henry was busy overseeing the construction of the Smithsonian building and a myriad of other tasks (which included, over the next two decades, considerable support for archaeology).[226] Squier was at loose ends; having no particular place to go, or anything in particular to do, he spent his time casting about for new projects.

He was now residing in New York—the *Scioto Gazette* and Chillicothe but distant memories of a place (and a status) to which he would not return. His growing fame inflated his ego and brought even higher expectations and ambitions—not to mention the higher costs of a more suitable lifestyle. That fall, he entertained the idea of starting an "Archaeological and Ethnological Journal." Too often, Squier lamented, societies and journals were stymied by the prejudices of the "long visaged divines," who created a "Procrustean Bed upon which every thing comprehensive, bold and manly must suffer mutilation." Even the American Ethnological Society, though more liberal than most, still had "divers[e] and sundry D.D.'s [Doctors of Divinity] belonging to it, besides a number of individuals who really believe in a devil, that the world was made in six days of twenty four hours each, and that Moses wrote the Pentateuch!" There needed to be a "medium of expression of sound opinions and of Truth." Perhaps. But publishing a journal was hardly the way to achieve intellectual—let alone financial—independence. Morton listened to Squier's scheme, then quietly talked him out of it. There were already too many journals, he reminded Squier, and most of them proved "ephemeral."[227]

Of course, there was always archaeology. At the outset, Squier and Davis had envisioned a comprehensive survey of all the antiquities of North America. Although they had convinced themselves that such a survey could be done in a matter of half a dozen years, reality intervened, and they had to settle mostly for the Scioto Valley. Now was the chance to extend it elsewhere. Davis never would (at least not on any appreciable or visible scale), but Squier did. By the late spring of 1848 he was plotting new surveys and exploring sources of congressional support for the venture. His experiences with the Smithsonian (not to mention the several learned societies that had declined to support their work) had so soured him that he vowed to keep clean of all "entangling alliances" with institutions. "I have danced in fetters for the first and last time," he declared. Bold words, but in July he was once more on the doorstep of the American Antiquarian Society asking for funds. Once again the society turned him down—his solid achievement notwithstanding. It was back to Henry at the Smithsonian.[228] There was no point in letting pride get in the way of money.

Henry agreed to grant one hundred dollars for an exploration of the "Ancient Monuments in the northern part of the state of New York," provided that the results be given to the Smithsonian for publication in the Contributions to Knowledge series. Henry, who was almost certainly as happy to be done with *Ancient Monuments* and free of Squier as Squier was of Henry and the Smithsonian, was also obviously savvy enough to realize that however unpleasant their dealings could get (and with Squier they could get extraordinarily unpleasant), he could count on Squier to produce results. Besides, the difficulties in publishing *Ancient Monuments* would surely not be repeated, as there was now a precedent and a procedure firmly in place. Moreover, Henry himself saw this as an opportunity to expand the earlier work into a national survey—as he had intended the institution to ultimately carry out.[229]

The support from the Smithsonian was necessary, but hardly adequate. Squier went to John Bartlett in New York, who agreed to raise an additional hundred dollars. Armed with letters of introduction, he headed into the field in late October 1848. He was hampered by the weather at every turn, having to cope with "cold drenching 'Nor' Easters,'" an "old-fashioned" snowstorm, "oceans of mud," and the prospect of three to four times the work he had anticipated. When winter finally chased him out of the field in early December, the money was exhausted and the survey was unfinished.[230]

There were plenty of results, however, not the least significant of which was an observation that he had made early on in the fieldwork. To his surprise there were "no works . . . which I feel disposed or warranted to ascribe to the race of the Mounds." Instead, he credited them to the Iroquois. A year before, Squier had considered information on Indian groups to be utterly irrelevant to the mound studies. Now, he gratefully accepted Lewis Henry Morgan's unsolicited offer to provide him with an "Iroquois map of the state, including all the Indian trails . . . and Geographic Names," as well as the location of their villages.[231]

Squier would elaborate on the idea that the mounds might be related to the historically known Iroquois of New York in his subsequent monograph—written in 1849—for the next volume of the Smithsonian's Contributions to Knowledge. That same year, he would also bring together the known data on the mounds of Kentucky, an effort based not on his own fieldwork but on the "confused notes" of Constantin Rafinesque, from which "most of the facts were obtained."[232] But Squier was clearly losing interest, energy, or both, with the archaeology of North America. The New York monograph was two-thirds the size and had a fraction of the elaborately delineated maps and surveys of *Ancient Monuments*. The Kentucky "monograph" was a mere fourteen pages and had only two rather wretched maps. He needed new fields to conquer, and he began looking south. Not to the southern states, still the domain of his rival Dickeson, but to Central America.

The Whigs had won the presidential election in the fall of 1848 (with Zachary Taylor and Millard Fillmore on the ticket), and late that year Squier began quietly inquiring among his old Whig cronies about the chances of a diplomatic posting in Central or South America. Not that he had a burning interest in diplomacy. Rather, this would be a chance to pursue the "eminently suggestive" archaeological connections between these areas and the Mississippi Valley that he had first glimpsed while working on *Ancient Monuments,* to see how far each area served to "explain and illustrate each other." Through his political contacts he learned that the chargéship to Guatemala was open, and all the extraordinary enthusiasm and drive he'd once brought to bear on the Scioto Valley mounds was now concentrated on his influential friends, beseeching them to lobby hard for his appointment. "I pray you will avail yourself of it in my behalf," he wrote Morton, for "I *feel* this is a *turning point* in my life; I see on the one hand a prospect bright and promising—on the other a plodding, not uncomfortable, but very far from an illustrious career."[233]

His friends responded. Letters flooded Secretary of State John Clayton's office from a host of scientific and political luminaries, including Edward C. Everett, Samuel Morton, William Prescott, Jared Sparks, Benjamin Silliman, Washington Irving, Franz Lieber, George Marsh, J. L. Stephens, and his newfound New York friend Lewis Henry Morgan (who proved to have friends in high places, notably William Seward, onetime governor of New York and by 1849 a prominent Senate Whig). Even Josiah Nott offered to help from Mobile, so long as the Cabinet wasn't completely full of "Northerners & out of the range of my influence." All together, nearly fifty individuals wrote letters on Squier's behalf.[234] But the one whose endorsement mattered most was Joseph Henry.

Henry rode over to the State Department one day in late March of 1849, at the request of Clayton, presumably to talk over Squier's appointment. Whatever Henry said must have proved convincing, for when he returned to his office later that day he wrote Squier to come at once to Washington—but to say nothing to anyone. Squier did. Four days later, on April 2, 1849, President Taylor commissioned Squier chargé d'affaires to Guatemala. A month later, Squier left for Central America with several of the Smithsonian's meteorological instruments in tow and a promise to Henry to send the completed manuscript on the New York mounds.[235]

It was not a moment too soon, either, for Davis had just seen the first reviews of *Ancient Monuments* and all the barely healed wounds burst open. So far as Norton's *North American Review* was concerned, it was Squier's "enlightened zeal" and determination that drove the investigation: Squier who wrote *Ancient Monuments*, Squier who deserved the accolades, and Squier who ought to be encouraged to continue in this work for which he richly deserved the financial and intellectual support of the learned societies of America. In its thirty pages, Davis's name was mentioned but once, and then only in regard to the aid he'd given Squier. Burke's review in the *Ethnological Journal* likewise praised Squier, barely noticed Davis, and added the piercing observation that it was "obvious that Mr. Squier is the presiding genius of the whole undertaking." With this "one bound," Burke judged, Squier had "placed himself high in the ranks of science."[236]

Davis was apoplectic. "Have you seen the articles in the *North American Review,* and *Ethnological Journal of London?*" he screamed in a letter to Henry.

[T]hey are so outrageously *unjust* and *ex-parte* as to defeat their intentions—I console myself with the idea that no honest or unprejudiced mind could give such a review—Its whole character and peculiar markings are so unmistakably *Squirish* as to provoke a smile of derision and contempt from every one acquainted with the circumstances.

Davis was absolutely right about Squier's fingerprints being on the reviews, but that was at best a hollow victory. So too were the very few times when he turned the tables on Squier, or the outraged letters that his friends wrote to Ohio newspapers, condemning Squier's grab for credit.[237]

Henry clucked sympathetically, but there was little else he could do. Besides, he was having his own troubles with Squier and had finally concluded that Squier's "moral faculties, appear not to have been quite as fully developed as his intellectual." He did think to invite Davis to give a few lectures at the Smithsonian "to ofset [*sic*] the honors which have been paid to Squier," but that was small recompense indeed.[238]

Davis, only half jokingly, asked Henry who was serving as the United States representative to Peru. If that individual was "dissatisfied or would resign, then, as antiquarians are now in favor, might not I stand a chance to distinguish myself among the *huacas* of the *Incas?*" There was a hard edge to Davis's humor, however, and later that year he sent a friend into Bartlett's New York bookstore to snoop around about "all the particulars" of Squier's appointment. At least, Davis wrote Henry, he could take some solace from knowing that "Mr. S. cannot boast of your [Henry's] name among the list of worthies recommending him to office." Poor Henry didn't tell him the truth. It would have been too deeply painful for both of them.[239]

Davis spent the next few months—and, indeed, the next few years—bemoaning his lot for having so much of the credit for his many years of hard work in archaeology bestowed on another. Morton innocently asked whether he would continue pursuing archaeological questions, and Davis plaintively replied that he didn't see he had much of a choice: "I am convinced that I must do so, for the sake of my reputation, as a portion of what I have already done has been lost." He also pursued other interests, however, most notably in medicine, where he had been tracking for some years the incidence of "calculus disease" (gallstones, kidney stones) and whether the frequency of their occurrence was in any way influenced by the underlying geological formations (via the groundwater).[240] His archaeological activities and accomplishments never again rose to the level he had achieved when working with Squier.

Even so, he didn't easily forgive or forget the wrong he felt Squier had done him. A decade later he was still fuming, this time to Henry Rowe Schoolcraft (1793–1864):

> The time was, when many hereabouts considered Mr. S[quier] to be the only Ethnologist of the Country. But quite a change has taken place for he has now left but few worshippers besides himself. As an instance of his self-laudation I would refer you to the article prepared by him on American Antiquities in the last edition of the American Encyclopedia. The article, besides containing gross errors, is made use of to glorify himself—whilst ignoring most other writers and explorers. What would you think of the contemptible meanness of a man, who in citing a joint work quotes only his own name in connection with it?

Davis found a sympathetic ear in Schoolcraft, who despised Squier (the feeling was mutual) and his polygenist leanings, battled with him privately, and took obvious pleasure in humiliating him publicly (American anthropology could hardly accommodate two such large egos and volatile tempers as they possessed):

> I have been surprised that his [Squier's] poor qualifications & inflations should not have sooner exposed his shallowness & pretense. We could [find no better example] . . . than the absence of moral appreciation, to which you refer in relation to your joint work. I found this defect in 1848, and have since dropped him, as an unworthy correspondent, & [refuse] to reply to his . . . insane letters.

Schoolcraft was being uncharacteristically charitable. Just a few months earlier, he had referred to Squier as a "reptile."[241]

THE LAST DECADES

President Zachary Taylor died after just a year in office, and there was a shake-up in the State Department. In mid-September of 1850 Squier was recalled from his Central American post, having tried but failed to interest the U.S. government in building a canal between the Atlantic and the Pacific via Nicaragua. He cast about that fall for new diplomatic or overseas opportunities, especially ones that paid. Few came ready to hand, so Squier busied himself writing articles for newspapers and magazines, as well as a series of books that appeared irregularly over the next half dozen years.[242]

One, the *Serpent Symbol* (1851), scratched the chronic itch he'd had about the worldwide prevalence of the snake in artifacts and features and explored its meaning as a central symbol in the human psyche (and, incidentally, as testimony of polygenesis). It had a modest critical reception and, far worse (since he had printed the book at his own expense), proved to be a financial failure. His more general works on the people, natural history, and prehistory of Central America (including a pseudonymously published romantic novel) had better success and indeed created for him a prominent niche as the widely acknowledged expert on Central America.

Along the way, he also tried to interest a wary Joseph Henry in using some of the Smithsonian funds to establish an archaeological museum for the collections of the nation, including his own. Squier hinted that he himself would naturally be the most qualified to direct such an enterprise, but modestly declined to say so outright. Henry, who had grave misgivings about being in the museum business (and surely even graver misgivings about being Squier's employer), cautiously agreed in principle about the importance of an archaeological museum, but cautioned Squier that a museum "should be [only] of special objects and not an *omnium gatherum* of the ods [*sic*] and ends of creation." He printed Squier's letter in the Smithsonian's *Annual Report,* and nothing more came of it.[243]

Squier devoted much of his time in the mid-1850s to organizing the Honduras Interoceanic Railway Company (the canal idea having failed) and was able to hire his old friend George Gliddon to serve as an agent for the railroad. That was a good thing so far as Josiah Nott could see: "Glad to hear that you have Gliddon transported to a country where there are no printer types, though there may be Types enough of Mankind. For God's sakes make it a part of your bargain that he is never again to afflict suffering humanity with any more books, or even title pages." The cosmopolitan Gliddon, however, had difficulty adjusting to life in Central America and pleaded unhappily to return to New York, but then took ill in late 1857. In a delirium of tropical fever, he took an overdose of opium and died in November.[244]

Squier returned to New York, and in 1857 married Miriam Follin. She was fifteen years his junior and by all accounts (not just his) was beautiful, educated, multilingual, ambitious, and hungry for wealth and status. In brief, she was a perfect mirror and match for Squier. She had been briefly married once before and had toured for a time as an actress (under the name Minnie Montez). They married in Rhode Island—apparently to avoid "any unpleasant talk or trouble which might be brought up in New York"—though whether it was her past, his past, or *both* their pasts that they were hiding from is unclear. Miriam's uncle, who had known Squier in Honduras, sent his congratulations, ominously adding his wish that "past troubles may be compensated by future felicity." They weren't.[245]

The first few years of Squier's marriage were eventful: They featured the obligatory European tour in the summer of 1858 (which included a triumphant visit to the Society of Antiquaries in London), trips to Cuba, parties, plays and museum openings in New York, and writing—for both of them. Squier worked on his *Notes on Central America,* Miriam on a translation project, and together they edited a Spanish-language newspaper *El Noticioso de Nueva York.*[246]

In the early 1860s, however, Squier's business ventures were collapsing around him. The railway project failed and left him in debt, including 350 pounds to a London creditor. The *Noticioso* had a brief and undistinguished run. When publisher Frank Leslie invited Squier to write for *Frank Leslie's Illustrated Newspaper* he gratefully accepted. Leslie's paper had a weekly circulation of 200,000, gained largely because of its generous illustrations and its willingness to pander to—and even embrace—the lowest popular tastes. It was a large step down from the Smithsonian's Contributions to Knowledge series, but it appealed to Squier: He was good at the writing, and it provided a salary and a platform.

From his perch, he had a clear view of unfolding political events in the fall of 1860. Judging by his later appearance at Lincoln's inaugural, Squier had become a Republican and a Lincoln supporter. So was Josiah Nott, but hardly for the same reason: "By the by I am a Lincoln man—I want this thing to come to a fight. Kill all the dam'd fools north & south, stake a fresh start." With far less murderous designs, Nott the physician was busy using his considerable energy and drive to establish a medical school in Mobile, Alabama. He spent "$ 25,000 of other peoples money" and a great deal of his own in Europe in 1859, buying collections, instruction equipment, and museum materials for the new medical school.[247]

En route, he had visited Squier in New York, and he came away smarting from Squier's amusing himself over dinner by "ridiculing the 'dam'd grinning,' 'bluster,' 'bravado' & etc. of Southern people." Nott was especially irked that Squier thought Southerners "could not be kicked into resistance by black republicans & were incapable of any effort beyond grinning." Nott knew better and warned that the "northern politicians were gradually weaving a web" around the South, and it "ere long must result in a terrible upheaval." To what end? he asked Squier.

> Certainly you do not expect to conquer us & make us vassals! This idea is too absurd to be continued by any sane mind, that comprehends . . . the Saxon character. We have soldiers . . . to fight you 30 years . . . on our own soil. Our cotton crop is growing beautifully & Europe *will have it*. We have an abundant provision crop, for all our wants, growing, without the need of the West. More courage, more unanimity, more determination, did not exist at Thermopylae. Every man is brought up a horseman, a marksman, & to resist aggression. We have officers equal to any in the world, & the determination never to lay down the sword until we are *free*.

It was all for the "old spirit of '76. The Declaration of Independence is the chart by which the Anglo-Saxon race sails." So it was, William Stanton wryly observes, that when the cannons on the Charleston Battery boomed out across the harbor, there was Nott, "with no perception of the rich irony of the situation . . . standing firm on the Declaration of Independence."[248] All men are created equal, indeed.

Soon after the war came, Squier was appointed the editor of *Frank Leslie's Illustrated Newspaper*, and he spent the first two years of the conflict documenting the publisher's *Pictorial History of the American Civil War*. In 1863 he was sent to Peru by Lincoln's State Department to settle a financial dispute between the two countries over guano and silver, and while there he explored the country and its natural history and archaeology—which would provide the material for what would become his last book.

Back in New York, Davis—who had been in that city since moving there in 1850 to take the Chair of Materia Medica at New York Medical College—spent the Civil War in relative quiet. Shortly before the war he had established a private practice in the city, and although each of his brothers went into the service, he himself stayed close to home and tended to his medical duties.

In Washington, Henry and the Smithsonian were besieged—not militarily but by the many "interruptions and embarrassments" (some "perplexing") that war brought to the city.[249] Throughout, Henry tried to maintain a semblance of normalcy and continued to nourish interest in archaeology, publishing in his *Annual Reports* papers on American archaeology and the unfolding developments of European prehistory, along with George Gibbs's "Instructions for Archaeological Investigations in the United States." The "Instructions" were aimed at eliciting information from military officers, missionaries, Indian agents, and travelers and residents of the "Indian country." While they solicited information on the physical characteristics of the native peoples, they hardly asked for much, couched the request in the most innocuous of terms, and gave no hint of the controversy about the origin and antiquity of this and other races.[250]

After the war, Nott wasn't saying much about the topic either, for though he remained privately unrepentant, he was much chastened in defeat. In their first contact after four and a half years of war, Nott wrote Squier to say he "felt completely whipped after the Confederacy caved in, & so despairing of the future prospects of the South, that I had a serious notion of going off somewhere & actually wrote a friend in New York." And, irony of ironies,

> My pet (the Medical College in Mobile) has been taken over by the Freedman's Bureau for a Negro school. We have the finest building on the continent for the purpose. I paid my own expenses in traveling to Europe to expend $40,000 on a Museum & I confess it does not increase my love for the Government when I pass by every day or two & see two or three hundred Negroes racing through it & tearing every thing to pieces. . . . I have been petitioning for six months against such . . . but to no purpose.[251]

Unable and unwilling to witness what he saw as the desecration of his life's work, Nott fled the South for Baltimore, then moved on to New York, where he established a private medical practice. By then, he had no time for his ethnological writing. When Nott arrived in New York, Squier encouraged him to participate in the intellectual activities of his circle, but soon Squier had troubles enough of his own—mostly personal.

After Frank Leslie appointed Squier the editor of his newspaper, he (Leslie) separated from his wife, and Squier generously invited him to board in the spare bedroom in Squier's home. Inevitably, there was speculation in rival newspapers and gossip on city streets about the domestic arrangements in the Squier household, but all maintained a strict public decorum. The threesome worked together (Miriam was writing for *Frank Leslie's Monthly*, and in 1863 she was appointed its editor after it was renamed *Frank Leslie's Lady's Magazine*), lived under the same roof, and regularly traveled together. One of those trips marked the beginning of the end to this arrangement.

In early 1867, the Squiers and Frank Leslie sailed for Europe. Leslie had been appointed U.S. commissioner to the Paris Universal Exposition, Squier was a delegate to the first International Congress of Anthropology and Prehistoric Archaeology (representing the American Ethnological Society), and all were traveling to write stories about these events. At a stop en route, Frank Leslie—with dangerously privileged knowledge of Squier's precarious finances in regard to the ill-fated Honduras Railway—surreptitiously cabled ahead to one of Squier's English creditors to alert him that Squier was coming through England. When the boat docked at Liverpool (at Leslie's insistence—it was supposed to land in Southampton, far from Squier's creditors), Squier was promptly arrested as an "absconding debtor." He languished in prison for two weeks while a Liverpool solicitor and the Honduras Legation tried to free him. Meanwhile, his wife and Frank Leslie checked into a London hotel, took in plays and exhibitions, and dined around town. Just before they were scheduled to leave for Paris, Leslie went back to Liverpool and posted bail for Squier (money he'd had all along but had previously failed to produce). The trio proceeded on their way, as though nothing out of the ordinary had happened, and spent the next several months together in Paris.[252]

After returning to New York, the three continued to work and travel together (to England again in 1870). Over the next few years, Squier devoted increasingly less attention to anthropology or archaeology, though in the spring of 1870 he launched an effort to create the Anthropological Institute of New York, on the ashes of the old American Ethnological Society (which he had skillfully maneuvered out of existence the preceding fall). Squier modeled the new organization on Paul Broca's Institute of Anthropology in Paris, which he had visited in 1867, and enlisted the aid of Josiah Nott as his vice president. But Nott's health broke down, and he left New York to return to Mobile to die, and the Anthropological Institute published only one issue of its *Journal* before collapsing under the weight of massive indifference.[253]

Squier's personal life also began to collapse publicly in the spring of 1871. Frank Leslie's wife—who had until then resisted a divorce—took her estranged husband to court. She loudly accused him of adultery and named Miriam Squier as his mistress. Squier himself testified that the charges were false, and Miriam agreed (neither of them was particularly scrupulous about their marriage vows). All of this badly complicated matters for both Leslie and Miriam Squier, who evidently wanted to be shed of their current spouses, but on their own terms. Leslie was able to convince his wife to divorce him on the grounds of desertion. Miriam Squier took a more devious route.[254]

In a spectacular frame-up in the spring of 1873, she arranged for Squier to attend a dinner at a disreputable house and drink too much. He went, he did, and he ended up in a compromising position. Miriam had anticipated that he would, and had arranged in advance for two of *Frank Leslie's Illustrated Newspaper*'s artists to be on hand to sketch the whole sordid affair (renderings that would be useful in court and suitable for printing in one of Leslie's newspapers, if necessary). Shortly thereafter, Miriam sued for divorce on the grounds that Squier had committed adultery, brought in the two artists as witnesses, and within a month was granted a divorce (the court permitted her to remarry at any time but forbade Squier from remarrying until her death). On July 13, 1874, Miriam married Frank Leslie.[255]

Squier—his health and spirit broken—quickly descended into the darkness of mental illness. On August 11, 1874, his brother had him examined by the president of the Neurological Society. The diagnosis was grim. Squier was declared "a lunatic, not having lucid intervals, so that he was incapable of the government of himself or of the management of his goods and chattel." He was placed in an insane asylum by Charles Donahue, a justice of the New York Supreme Court. The city newspapers clucked over the "Eclipse of Genius" and the "Sad end of a journalist." What else could be expected, a contemporary wondered, of those "who followed such moneyless callings as writing poetry and studying archaeology?"[256]

Davis, a long-term resident of New York—they spent their last decades living within ten miles of each other, but there is not so much as a hint that they ever spoke—must have read the news. What he may have thought of it, and whether a twinge of regret for his onetime friend ever crossed his mind, is forever lost to history. Squier still had enough occasional moments of lucidity that he was able to see through to publication his volume on Peru, but beyond that his scholarly productivity came to an end. On his brother's orders, his library was auctioned off while he remained institutionalized.[257]

REQUIEM

On April 17, 1888, two months shy of his sixty-seventh birthday, Ephraim Squier died in Brooklyn at his brother's home. His death, the *New York Times* reported the next day, was not unexpected but the result of "a sickness of many years" standing. Scarcely a month later (on May 15, 1888), and just across the East River in New York City, Edwin Davis died at the age of seventy-seven. He, too, the *Times* reported, had been failing for some time, his death due to "general debility." Davis was buried in Chillicothe. Squier and Davis, joined briefly in life, were close in death as well. Squier, as usual, came first.

There were telling differences in their obituaries. Squier's (the longer of the two) made mention of *Ancient Monuments,* to be sure, but it was nearly crowded out by the many other details of a peripatetic life and an active publishing career. Davis's obituary talked of little besides *Ancient Monuments.* The aggressive and voluble Squier, who had resolved in Albany more than four decades earlier, to make "a NAME to the world," had mostly succeeded. He'd done so on sheer ambition, entrepreneurial spirit, and unbridled energy, but not without the deep frustration of trying to make a career in a field that couldn't offer one. The nineteenth-century history of American archaeology had many like him. Squier left behind no family, but with one eye on securing that hard-earned name for posterity, he left "a mass of correspondence and some manuscripts," much of which his brother turned over to the archives of the Library of Congress—a fitting place to help ensure immortality. In contrast—and typically the laconic Davis had left behind a family, four children of which were at his side when he died.[258]

The bulk of the archaeological collections acquired by Squier and Davis in their excavations had been sold in 1864 by Davis for ten thousand dollars (Squier was then in Peru). The buyer, William Blackmore of London, bought the material only after it had been for sale for several years, and the New York Historical Society and other American organizations (including, presumably, the Smithsonian) had proved unable or unwilling to meet the asking price. Blackmore originally intended to keep the material in the United States, but in 1867 he decided to establish a museum in his name in Salisbury, England, where the collection served as an "object of pilgrimage of American archaeologists." In 1924, the collection was purchased by the British Museum for the sum of four hundred pounds.[259] It remains there today.

The sale of that collection would, in later years, become a source of regret, and a lesson for American museums that they did not soon forget. In August of 1890, the acting secretary of the Smithsonian testified on Capitol Hill in favor of a bill to purchase for the United States National Museum a large collection of prehistoric copper implements from a Wisconsin collector, and in closing invoked the specter of that earlier loss:

> It would be a misfortune to American science, and in future years would undoubtedly be regarded as a reflection upon this country, if the collection in question should become the property of some foreign government. The transfer of the famous Squier and Davis collection of stone implements to England, some twenty years ago, has ever since been a great regret to Americans.[260]

Even more regretful was the loss of the many mounds and earthworks they had recorded. Throughout *Ancient Monuments* Squier and Davis repeatedly sounded the alarm about the relentless destruction of these features from environmental elements, shifting rivers and streams, the "leveling hand" of public improvements, and—worst of all—agriculture. Speaking of the Newark earthworks, they guessed that "[a] few years hence, the residents upon the spot will be compelled to resort to this map [in *Ancient Monuments*], to ascertain the character of the works which occupied the very ground upon which they stand."[261] They were correct, and though their words did not inspire widespread action to save these works, they did spur individual efforts. Henry, for one, picked up the preservation refrain and provided a portion of his funds annually to archaeological research on the disappearing monuments.[262]

It wasn't enough. Few of the mounds and earthworks that Squier and Davis saw 150 years ago now remain. Many of them were already badly mauled by century's end. Almost fifty years after first being surveyed by Squier and Davis, the "Clark's Work" on the North Fork of Paint Creek (Plate X) was visited by Warren K. Moorehead as part of the archaeological work of the 1893 World's Columbian Exposition. Moorehead was led there by *Ancient Monuments* and the expectation that he would find "one of the principal, if not actually the largest, settlement of the Scioto Valley moundbuilding tribe." The complex was still present, on what was then M. C. Hopewell's farm, but already the years of continuous farming since Squier and Davis had taken their toll. They had reduced the height and smeared the area of the largest mound on the site and obliterated portions of the earthworks of what would become known as the Hopewell site. As Griffin observed more than two decades ago, *Ancient Monuments* is the "primary source for many of the mounds and earthworks in the Ohio Valley and the eastern United States. For some of them it is the only remaining source."[263] *Ancient Monuments* as elegy.

As such, subsequent writers have criticized the data in *Ancient Monuments,* no less than the volume's interpretations, as being inaccurate or unusable. These later critics—mostly in the employ of the Bureau of Ethnology and writing around the turn of the century—took umbrage with Squier and Davis's claim that many of the mounds and earthworks were perfect circles and squares. A few—like the righteously irascible Gerard Fowke (1855–1933) and the stern Cyrus Thomas—didn't stop there but extended their criticisms to include the inaccuracies in *Ancient Monuments'* surveys and measurements, misleading observations about the mounds' contents, classification, and artifacts, the superficiality of their excavations and, not surprisingly, their errors of interpretation about just who the moundbuilders were. Fowke's stinging index entry for Squier and Davis is extreme but illustrative: "Squier and Davis, 'Ancient Monuments':—causes of their many errors, 58; credit due to, 58; falsity of their alleged proofs, 57; their test work wholly imaginary, 57–186; unfound claims of accuracy, 55."[264]

Still, even Fowke admitted that Squier and Davis's errors, as he saw them, were partly attributable to their being pioneers and being handicapped with limited surveying ability, rudimentary equipment, and meager resources (damning with faint praise, that). Kinder and gentler was Moorehead, who thought the errors were minor and was even *pleased* that Squier and Davis had been wrong about artifacts, features, and burials always being in the center of the mounds, for many a farmer bent on recovering them had acted on this instruction, thus saving at least some of the mounds' contents for later archaeologists.[265]

But in a very real sense Fowke's and Thomas's carping is beside the point. For one, they had their own particular axes to grind and were busy plotting their own version of the "New Archaeology" (as Thomas put it), for which *Ancient Monuments* was a convenient rhetorical foil against which their own work would and must be measured (much as Atwater's work had been a foil for Squier and Davis fifty years earlier). It remained for the coming generation, in the less polemical 1920s and 1930s, to fully appreciate the worth of *Ancient Monuments: "Ancient Monuments* is now a rare and highly sought literary and scientific treasure, the pride of any student of American Archaeology who is so fortunate as to possess a copy of the book."[266] That remains true today.

More to the point, there is a telling historical lesson here. It is not surprising or significant that Squier and Davis rounded numbers or squared corners to make the mounds and earthworks more perfect. Of far greater interest is what they stood to gain by doing so, and why they might have been inclined to emphasize the engineering artistry and symmetry of the mounds. The answer, of course, is that doing so opened wider the gap between the relatively rudimentary artifacts and architecture of the Indians and the complex and precise constructions of the more advanced moundbuilders. They knew, because Gallatin, Morton, and a host of others had told them, that there were or ought to be significant intellectual differences between these two families of the American race, and they duly found them in the archaeological record. In later decades, archaeologists like Cyrus Thomas, approaching the issue from precisely the opposite angle, would instead emphasize just how similar (indeed, identical) the Indians and the "moundbuilders" were. And so the pendulum swings.

EPILOGUE

Squier and Davis viewed the moundbuilders as one "grand system," a numerous, widespread, homogeneous population, whose mounds and earthworks were ancient and varied in space and in function (defensive, religious, and ceremonial), rather than through time. Indeed, beyond believing that the monuments were old in absolute terms, they had little sense of any temporal differences among them, except for the ones constructed in the historic period. They knew who had built them: a race of people now no longer extant in North America and unrelated to the American Indian (save for their both being members of the American race). The way they saw it, the "leading purposes of the mounds (of Ohio at least) have been detected and settled," and so too the essential questions of American archaeology were outlined and mainly answered. Mostly what remained was to fill in the details.[267]

Yet, within a decade Samuel Haven, taking a very different perspective on the record, reached a very different conclusion. Proceeding, as Haven insisted we must, "from the known to the unknown" and comparing the archaeological materials with the "habits, customs, and arts of the aborigines" led him inescapably to the conclusion that the mounds were built by Indians. Questions remained about the direction from which these groups entered this country, and whence their "arts were derived," but answers to those questions would have to come later. Haven thought these conclusions a "solid basis on which to build new theories."[268]

Perhaps, but then neither Haven—nor Squier and Davis—could see that archaeology would in a matter of just a few years become a profoundly different discipline than the one they had entered. In the late 1840s and 1850s, archaeology was still very much part of history—in both the disciplinary and the substantive senses. *Ancient Monuments* had spoken of the mounds as having "no inconsiderable antiquity,"[269] but at the time those words were written, only Squier and the polygenists even dreamed that meant they went beyond the comfortable Mosaic confines of *history*.

After 1859, such a phrase could scarcely mean anything else, for in Europe that year it was confirmed that human remains had been found in Pleistocene gravels. *Ancient Monuments* had ignored the claims of American ancestry among historically known Old World groups, but now suddenly their ancestry might lie deep in *prehistory*—a place it had never really imagined. Whether prehistory in the New World went back as far as it did in the Old, and whether ancestral Americans were comparable in age and evolutionary grade to the European Paleolithic, would emerge as the next great controversy of American archaeology.[270] But Squier and Davis's archaeology, focused as it was not on artifacts but on mounds and earthworks—which were now suddenly at the recent end of the prehistoric time scale (being far more advanced than the primitive Paleolithic materials)—would have little influence here.

And what of the "vexing question" of the unity of race and creation? Close on the heels of the demonstration of human antiquity in 1859 came Darwin's *On the Origin of Species*. The *Origin* had profound implications for humans, though the book itself only teased that "[l]ight will be thrown on the origin of man and his history."[271] But everyone knew what *that* meant. While in Europe in 1859, Josiah Nott picked up a copy of the *Origin,* read it carefully, then wrote Squier to report: "[T]he man [Darwin] is clearly crazy, but [the *Origin*] is a capital dig into the parsons—it stirs up Creation & much good comes out such thorough discussions."[272] Nott could also appreciate a good "Parson-skinning," but he also saw only too well that the Paleolithic and Darwin's evolution made polygenesis—and much of Morton's craniology—painfully irrelevant. Squier had warmly embraced polygenesis, but now there suddenly proved to be far less here than met the eye. Viewed in larger evolutionary terms, human races were no more than geologically temporary varieties of a species, and not separately created, nor fixed and unchanging.

Darwin himself thought that "when the principles of evolution are generally accepted, as they surely will be before long, the dispute between the monogenists and the polygenists will die a silent and unobserved death."[273] In America the issue did not go away quietly. At places like Shiloh, Antietam, and the Wilderness, hundreds of thousands would die—the sons of Haven, Morton, and Nott, among them—in the bloody dispute that was, in the end, all about the "vexed question" of race and human equality.

At Shiloh, near a sleepy crossroads church named for a biblical town (the same one that Atwater had long before used to draw an Old Testament analogy for the mounds), a young artillery engineer in Grant's command lost his right arm to a musket ball. But not before having poked into several local mounds, seen that they contained artifacts of European manufacture and, *Ancient Monuments* notwithstanding, jumped to the conclusion that the mounds must have been built by Indians in historic times.

John Wesley Powell (1834–1902) remembered that lesson decades later, when as director of the Smithsonian Institution's Bureau of Ethnology, he assigned Cyrus Thomas the task of resolving the moundbuilder question. In his own monumental effort Thomas would closely follow, though disagreeing with many a turn, the path blazed by Squier and Davis so many years before.[274]

NOTES

A NOTE ON ARCHIVAL SOURCES

Several archival collections were consulted in the course of this research and are identified in the notes by the acronyms that follow. Much of the original correspondence between Henry, Squier, and others relating to the production of *Ancient Monuments* that is cited as JHP/SIA is now available in the seventh volume of *The Papers of Joseph Henry* (Rothenberg et al. 1996).

BAE/NAA   Bureau of American Ethnology, National Anthropological Archives, Washington, D.C.
EGS/LC   Ephraim George Squier Papers, Library of Congress, Washington, D.C.

HRS/LC	Henry Rowe Schoolcraft Papers, Library of Congress, Washington, D.C.
JHP/SIA	Joseph Henry Papers, Smithsonian Institution Archives, Washington, D.C.
JRB/JCBL	John Russell Bartlett Papers, John Carter Brown Library, Brown University, Providence, Rhode Island.
SFH/AAS	American Antiquarian Society General Correspondence (Samuel Foster Haven letters), American Antiquarian Society, Worcester, Massachusetts.
SGM/LCP	Samuel George Morton Papers, Historical Society of Pennsylvania, Philadelphia, Pennsylvania.
WJR/SIA	William J. Rhees Collection, Subject Files, Smithsonian Institution Archives, Washington, D.C.

1. James Smithson's endowment was the then-munificent sum of $515,000—roughly equivalent to 1.5 percent of the entire United States annual budget at the time. It was a small investment for the return of immortality. Henry 1848:173; Rothenberg et al. 1996:xxii, 1.

2. Hinsley 1981:8; Rothenberg et al. 1996:xviii.

3. Jefferson 1787:Query XI; Haven (1856:22–27) details these early reports. He observes that Jefferson's *Notes on the State of Virginia* (written in the early 1780s) says little of the great earthworks of the west and south, making it a useful benchmark just predating the general knowledge of these features.

4. Silverberg 1968:82–96; Tax 1973:70. On the parallel rise of the moundbuilder myths and Mormonism, see Silverberg 1968:90–96, Tax 1973:74–77, Williams 1991:ch. 8. These sources also provide the most comprehensive treatments of the "moundbuilder myth."

5. Bieder 1986:109; Silverberg 1968:79–81; Tax 1973:70–71. For a contemporary look at these themes, see Haven 1856.

6. Gould 1981:42–43; Stanton 1960:2. As President Andrew Jackson explained in his December 7, 1830, message to Congress: "In the monuments and fortresses of an unknown people, spread over the extensive regions of the west, we behold the memorials of a once powerful race, which was exterminated, or has disappeared, to make room for the existing savage tribes. Nor is there anything in this, which, upon a comprehensive view of the general interests of the human race, is to be regretted" (Bieder 1986:112 n. 17). William Cullen Bryant summarized the prevailing view in *The Prairies* (1833):

The red man came—

The roaming hunter tribes, warlike and wild,

And the mound-builders vanished from the earth.

The solitude of centuries untold

Has settled where they dwelt.

7. Atwater 1820:205–6; Haven 1856:3; Hinsley 1981:22. The Ten Lost Tribes were scattered and exiled when the Assyrians conquered Israel in 722 B.C. An additional part of the appeal of this notion was that there appeared to be "corroboration in the customs and traditions of the Indians" (Haven 1856:5) with those of the ancient Israelites, although Robert Wauchope made the trenchant observation that the finding of such similarities should come as no surprise: In those early years Hebrew ethnology as described in the Old Testament "was about the only well-documented 'primitive' way of life known and therefore the first to occur to a seeker of Indian relationships" (Wauchope 1962:3). On the rise of polygenesis, see Gould 1981:42–43; Hinsley 1981:25–27; Stanton 1960:2, 82–89.

8. Hinsley 1981:16, 22, 34–37. This would prove no easy task, and one that grew increasingly complicated over the next decade, for early on in the Smithsonian's history slaves were still being sold in sight of the institution's buildings, and powerful senators like Jefferson Davis and Stephen Douglas sat on its Board of Regents.

9. Henry to Squier, November 24, 1847, JHP/SIA. Henry, much to Squier's dismay, was wrong about the fortune part.

10. The quote is from Howe 1889:442. Biographical information on Squier is available in Allibone 1870; *American Whig Review* 1850; Barnhart 1983, 1989; Hinsley 1981; Howe 1889; *New York Times* 1888a; Patterson and Stanton 1959; Seitz 1911; Stanton 1960; Stern 1953; Tax 1973, 1975; Williams 1935. Unfortunately, Barnhart's valuable dissertation (1989) became available to me only after this work was completed,

though I have shoehorned in a few references to it. It provides a particularly thorough history of Squier's early life, and interested readers are urged to consult this important work.

11. *American Whig Review* 1850:347; Seitz 1911:9–11.

12. *American Whig Review* 1850:347; Bieder 1986:105; Tax 1975:101–2; Squier to parents, December 30, 1841, quoted in Tax 1975:102.

13. *American Whig Review* 1850:347; Tax 1975:102. There is internal evidence to suggest that Squier himself was the author of the anonymous biography in the *American Review*.

14. *American Whig Review* 1850:348–49; Barnhart 1989:25–28; Bieder 1986:105; Seitz 1911:10–11. Squier put his forced unemployment to good use; he published his first book—on China (Squier 1843).

15. Squier to parents, January 1 and February 24, 1845; quoted in Tax 1975:102. Also *American Whig Review* 1850:349; Bieder 1986:105. According to an undated (but ca. 1849–50) news clipping from the *Scioto Gazette* in the Squier Papers at the Library of Congress, Squier was editor of that newspaper from April 1845 to December 10, 1847 (EGS/LC).

16. Squier to Marsh, January 8, 1848, EGS/LC. *Scioto Gazette,* ca. 1849–50, EGS/LC.

17. Biographical information on Davis is available in Allibone 1858; Barnhart 1983, 1989; Drake 1872; Hough 1930; Howe 1889; *New York Times* 1888b; Tax 1973, 1975. For his papers, see Davis 1847, 1850, 1860, and 1867.

18. Barnhart 1989:33–34. Hillsboro, where Davis spent his boyhood, is in Ross County, about midway between Cincinnati and Chillicothe, and is near several major mound groups, including Fort Ancient, Mound City, and Seip, portions of which still exist today. Edwin's younger brother, Joseph, studied and then practiced law, subsequently serving at various times as a judge, as mayor of Mount Vernon (Ohio), and as a paymaster for the U.S. Army in 1864–65. Another younger brother, Werter, like Edwin took a medical degree, practiced for a time, then became a minister, taught natural history and served as president at several small colleges in the Midwest, served as a U.S. Army chaplain on the front lines during the Civil War (rising to the rank of colonel), and then became a member of the Kansas state legislature (Appletons' 1887:95–96).

19. Information on Davis's early archaeological work comes from Davis to Rau, June 5, 1884, BAE/NAA (Record Group 7065). The Woodbridge family was well-to-do and prominent in Chillicothe, and Davis appears to have kept an office in one of their buildings. Drake (1872) puts Davis's graduation from medical school in 1837; Appletons' puts the date as 1838. Hough (1930), likely using those same sources, has Davis graduating in 1837 or 1838. However, Barnhart (1989:34) lists Davis's graduation as March 3, 1838. Also according to Barnhart, Davis assisted Charles Whittlesey in 1836 or 1837, during the latter's surveys of the Newark earthworks. Stephen Williams (personal communication, 1997) speculates that at Cincinnati Davis knew Daniel Drake (1785–1852), a pioneer archaeologist in that city.

20. Squier to Marsh, January 8, 1848, EGS/LC.

21. Davis to Morton, October 26, 1845, SGM/HSP; Davis to Bartlett, October 28, 1846, JRB/JCBL. Davis to Haven, SFH/AAS. Also, Barnhart 1989:81–82.

22. Davis to Morton, May 18, 1846, SGM/HSP; Davis to Bartlett, May 25, 1846, JRB/JCBL. Tax (1973:123–48) provides a useful discussion of the relative position and status of eastern and western scholars, institutions, and activities.

23. Newspapers of the day routinely carried reports of newcomers in town and their business—even to the point of listing those who had checked in at the local hotels. For someone to check in with artifacts from the mounds was an unusual occurrence and bound to attract attention. Davis to Squier, June 9, 1846, SGM/HSP; Davis to Bartlett, May 25, 1846, JRB/JCBL. For his reception in Philadelphia, see Morton to Squier, June 11, 1846, SGM/HSP.

24. The collection was gathered almost entirely by others, including government consuls and explorers worldwide, and collectors and army surgeons in remote western American outposts who sent Morton skulls from native graves and battlefield dead (Stanton 1960:27–28). Stanton makes the further point that Morton's interest in crania was not motivated by an interest in phrenology, which was then quite fashionable (1960:29). The differences Morton detected, Gould argues, have as much to do with his fudging of the data and finagling of the statistics as anything else (Gould 1981:54). The single best source on Morton's life and work remains Stanton's superb volume, *The Leopard's Spots* (1960), but see also Bieder (1986:ch. 3).

25. Morton 1839:1–3, 88. For a fuller discussion, see Gould 1981:52–53; Graymon 1989:150–60; Stanton 1960:30–31.

26. Morton 1844:4, 13, 1853:316. Also Bieder 1986:84–85.

27. Morton 1844:16, 1853:329–30. Also, Nott and Gliddon 1854:277–78; Phillips 1853:333–34.

28. Morton 1846:7; Morton had first published this conclusion in his *Crania Americana* (Morton 1839) but reiterated it in his 1846 paper in the *American Journal of Science*. The latter appeared in July of that year, just about the time Squier came to visit. It is more than likely that Squier received a copy on this occasion or on his return trip through Philadelphia a few weeks later when he received a number of papers from Morton (Squier to Bartlett, August 24, 1846, JRB/JCBL). Davis had previously been sent a copy of *Crania Americana* (Davis to Morton, May 18, 1846, SGM/HSP).

29. The following discussion is derived largely from Stanton 1960, especially pp. 43–44, 50, 80–81, 117–18.

30. Morton 1847; Nott to Morton, June 1, 1847, SGM/HSP. For biographical information on Nott, see Horsman 1987.

31. Morton 1844:28. Morton occasionally received specimens from the mounds from Samuel Hildreth in Ohio (whom Squier would "pump *dry*" for information on the mounds—see Squier to Bartlett, August 24, 1846, JRB/JCBL), Increase Lapham in Wisconsin, and even a specimen from the Grave Creek Mound (Morton 1839:221–24; Tax 1973:114).

32. Davis to Morton, October 26, 1845, SGM/HSP. Squier to parents, March 10, 1846, quoted in Tax 1975:104. There has been some discussion whether Squier was an atheist. Bieder (1986:131 n. 54) makes the point that although Squier as an adult was less religious than he was in his youth, he did not turn out to be an atheist—and here Bieder is responding specifically to Hinsley's (1981:28) assertion that Squier was. Tax (1975:104), however, also sees in Squier an "atheistic posture." The point obviously has some bearing on the degree to which one was inclined to accept monogenesis and the primacy of the biblical chronology. Squier was not inclined to accept either, and though his views on the subject did not assume the belligerent tone of Josiah Nott and George Gliddon on such matters, he was certainly in sympathy with them (Tax 1975:104; also Bieder 1986:133, on Squier's view of the negative influence of the Bible).

33. For a brief summary of Gallatin's career, see Bieder (1986:17–24). Gallatin's interest in ethnology began in his days in Washington, D.C., during Jefferson's administration; there he met visiting Indian delegations and sought information on the western tribes to prepare for the president a map of Indian territorial claims (Bieder 1975:92, 1986:20–21).

34. Haven 1856:62. Also Bieder 1986:32, 35, 41–42.

35. Gallatin 1836:5–6, 1845; Duponceau 1819; Haven 1856:59, 64. For a useful summary discussion, see Bieder 1986:27–34; Hinsley 1981:24–25. The polysynthetic tendency more specifically was attributed to the "want of general and abstract terms" among Native Americans, which would force them to have to string together in a term "the characteristics of every object of thought or observation" (Haven 1856:67–68; Hinsley 1981:24). Bancroft gave a more picturesque explanation, saying that the American Indian's "thoughts rush forth in a troop" (quoted in Haven 1856:70).

36. Gallatin 1836:6. In making this argument Gallatin was simply following the lead of Jefferson (among others), who believed that the degree of divergence from a common origin provided a gauge of elapsed time.

37. Gallatin 1845:179, in Haven 1856:63–64; Bieder 1975:95.

38. Bieder 1986:44; the membership included several clergymen who held influential positions in the society (Bieder and Tax 1976:14–17).

39. Bartlett to Morton, December 21, 1846, SGM/HSP; Morton to Bartlett, January 28, 1847, JRB/JCBL; Stanton 1960:97–98.

40. Gallatin 1836:146–47. That idea was not new with Gallatin, but he was the first to fully articulate it, and it proved central to his denying that the Indians had built the mounds. The idea was picked up and repeated by others, Squier and Davis included (*Ancient Monuments,* p. 302, and as discussed below). Cyrus Thomas, half a century later, knew he would have to refute it in order to build his own case for the Indians' having constructed the mounds. Thomas also saw that it was Gallatin, and not Squier and Davis, who mostly deserved the credit—or blame—for being the "father of the theory" (Thomas 1894:611–13).

41. As Gallatin put it, "it appears extremely improbable that . . . a people become agricultural should take such a retrograde step, as to degenerate again into the hunting or savage state" (Gallatin 1836:149, quoted in Bieder 1975:94). Also Gallatin 1845, quoted in Haven 1856:62, 64; Bieder 1986:33.

42. On Gallatin's views of agricultural as an engine of developmental advances, see Gallatin 1836:107–8, 145–51; Bieder 1986:36. For an early view of the moundbuilders, see, for example, Atwater 1820:111–12, 144. Gallatin, at least, held that Indians were capable of agriculture but hadn't adopted it owing to environmental circumstances or a lack of necessity (Bieder 1986:36–38). A few individuals did counter that the Indians possessed the skills, technology, and free time for mound construction, or at least would have before

the "decline in all domestic arts" following European contact (e.g., McCulloh 1829). But such voices were in the minority (for a fuller discussion, see Bieder 1986:110–11; Silverberg 1968:61–68; Tax 1973:71, 77–79). For a mid-nineteenth-century view of the matter, see Haven (1856:155). The alleged abilities and characteristics of the moundbuilders—and the apparent cultural depravity of the Indians—tended to be more exaggerated in the popular literature on the moundbuilders (see Silverberg 1968:88–89).

43. Squier to Morton, June 10, 1846, SGM/HSP.

44. Davis to Squier, June 9, 1846, EGS/LC.

45. Davis to Squier, June 14, 1846; with a letter the following day, Davis sent Squier the money, EGS/LC.

46. Bartlett to Haven, June 16, 1846, SFH/AAS. The American Antiquarian Society was a reasonable target for raising funds, as a portion of its endowment was earmarked for the support of archaeological research, and it had provided some support to Caleb Atwater two decades earlier (Tax 1973:131, 135).

47. Tax 1973:137–41, 1975:106. Squier and Davis themselves paid little attention to the few western societies, consistently seeking recognition and approbation for their work from the eastern societies (Tax 1973:181).

48. Squier to Haven, July 6, 1846, SFH/AAS; Hinsley 1981:34–35.

49. Davis to Squier, July 7, 1846, EGS/LC; Squier to Bartlett, July 16, 1846, EGS/LC.

50. Squier described his visit thus: "I visited also the celebrated Grave Creek Mound. . . . From what I could learn, both at Grave Creek and Wheeling, of the character of the younger Mr. Tomlinson who opened the mound, I am satisfied that very little reliance can be placed upon his word in matters when his *interest* is involved. He opened the mound, not through an enlightened, nor for that matter, unenlightened curiosity, but as a *speculation;* boarded it round, put on pad- locks, hung up his skeletons in horrible ghastliness, and sat down at the gate expecting that the universal Yankee native would come trooping to see it, at 'a quarter a head, children half-price.' He did not get *over 'fifty thousand'* quarters, and has now moved away, and the skeletons 'and things' are once more all heaped over, beyond hope of recovery" (Squier to Bartlett, August 24, 1846, JRB/JCBL).

51. Squier to Haven, August 17, 1846, SFH/AAS.

52. Haven to Squier, August 28, 1846; Warren to Squier, August 30, 1846, EGS/LC.

53. Bartlett to Squier, September 10, 1846, EGS/LC; Squier to Bartlett, August 24, 1846, JRB/JCBL, emphasis mine. Squier and Davis took Bartlett's advice, and over the next year produced a series of smaller reports, each under his own name (Davis 1847; Squier 1846a–c, 1847a).

54. Bartlett to Squier, September 10, 1846, EGS/LC.

55. Squier to Bartlett, September 21, 1846, JRB/JCBL.

56. Morton to Squier, December 8, 1846, EGS/LC; Squier to Morton, January 4, 1847, SGM/HSP.

57. Squier reported that his election was a surprise (Squier to Bartlett, December 9, 1846, JRB/JCBL). On Dickeson, see Davis to Squier, December 24, 1846, EGS/LC.

58. Davis to Squier, December 29, 1846, EGS/LC. Even those who worked with Dickeson in the field thought poorly of his excavation methods (Tax 1973:101), though to his credit he collected many artifacts and drew a map of his site locations (Williams 1991:43–44).

59. Atwater 1820; Atwater to Bartlett, August 28, 1846, JRB/JCBL. Biographical information and a sketch of Atwater's archaeological activity is in Tax 1973:130–32.

60. Squier to Haven, August 14, 1847, SFH/AAS; also Davis to Squier, December 24, 1846, EGS/LC, and Squier to Henry, March 24, 1847, JHP/SIA.

61. Davis to Rau, June 5, 1884, BAE/NAA (Record Group 7065); Squier to Haven, August 17, 1846, SFH/AAS. The advice was offered by a Mr. Clemson and conveyed via Davis to Squier, June 27, 1847, EGS/LC.

62. Dickeson scarcely published any of his results, but later (in the 1850s) he toured the country with a large panorama (320 feet long and 8 feet high, wound on two rollers and weighing about 100 pounds) depicting mounds and scenes of archaeological activities from Ohio to Mississippi. Admission to see the panorama was a quarter for adults, half price for children under twelve (Tax 1973:167–68, 170).

63. Squier and Davis to Bartlett, November 7, 1846, JRB/JCBL. The results of this excursion are in Davis 1847, and *Ancient Monuments*, pp. 293–300.

64. Squier to Morton (draft), January 16, 1847, EGS/LC. By the end, Squier and Davis had explored, surveyed, or excavated some two hundred mounds and earthworks in south central Ohio (*Ancient Monuments*, pp. xxi–xxii).

65. Squier to Morton, December 1, 1846, SGM/HSP; Morton to Squier, December 8, 1846, EGS/LC.

66. Davis's estimate of his financial commitment to the project is in Barnhart 1989:40. On the published (and agreed-upon) statement of their division of labor, *Ancient Monuments*, p. xxxviii. Also Squier to Marsh, January 8, 1848, EGS/LC, and Tax 1975:108.

67. Squier to Bartlett, January 24, 1847, JRB/JCBL; Davis to Squier, January 7, 1847; Hinsley 1981:36.

68. Marsh to Squier, February 24, EGS/LC.

69. Henry to Bache, June 25, 1847; Henry to Owen, August 7, 1847, JHP/SIA. See also the discussion in Tax 1973:225.

70. Marsh to Squier, February 24 and March 6, 1847, EGS/LC. Henry to Squier, April 3, 1847, JHP/SIA.

71. For Henry's view of the obstacles facing American scientists in their efforts to publish, see Henry to Preston, October 14, 1847, and Henry to Owen, August 7, 1847, JHP/SIA. See also Rothenberg et al. 1996:xviii, 78 n. 2. For his assurances to Squier, see Henry to Squier, April 3, 1847, JHP/SIA.

72. Henry to Bache, June 25, 1847, and Squier to Henry, March 24, 1847, JHP/SIA.

73. Marsh to Squier, March 6, 1847, EGS/LC; also Henry to Squier, April 28, 1847, JHP/SIA.

74. Squier to Morton, April 6, 1847, SGM/HSP.

75. Squier to Henry, March 24, 1847; Henry to Squier, April 28, 1847, JHP/SIA.

76. Henry to Squier, June 4 and July 5, 1847, JHP/SIA. Henry's insistence on rigorous and anonymous review paid dividends later; for example, when all aspects of the Smithsonian's operations, including its publications, were under congressional scrutiny in the mid-1850s, his careful review policy was offered in defense against the suspicion that the publication process was unfair (Rhees 1901:586). For the official letter requesting the review, see *Ancient Monuments*, p. viii. Morton, in fact, found out he was a reviewer when Davis came through Philadelphia and told him, and Squier was in New York when the AES committee made its report; see Davis to Squier, June 12, 1847, EGS/LC, and Squier to Henry, June 26, 1847, JHP/SIA.

77. See Gallatin to Henry, June 16, 1847, JHP/SIA; Marsh to Henry, June 19 and June 26, 1847, EGS/LC; and Morton to Bartlett, June 8, 1847 (copies in EGS/LC and JRB/JCBL). A much-laundered version of the *Report* and these letters (of which, more below) were published in *Ancient Monuments*, pp. viii–x, as well as in the Smithsonian Institution's *Annual Report* for 1847 (Henry 1848:185–88). Henry sought no more assessments of the manuscript beyond that provided by the AES, but later that year he heard a rumor that Samuel Haven was of the opinion that the work was not "as thorough or as accurate" as it might have been. Henry asked Haven directly for his opinion, but found out the rumor was unfounded (Henry to Haven, October 19, 1847, and Henry to Squier, November 4, 1847, JHP/SIA).

78. Squier to Morton, April 6, 1847, SGM/HSP, and Morton to Squier, April 10, 1847, EGS/LC.

79. The original version of the *Report* showing how it appeared before Henry's requested changes is in the Squier Papers at the Library of Congress (Microfilm Reel 14). On Henry's relationship to the federal government, see Henry 1848:178; Rothenberg et al. 1996:xxv–xxviii. His requested changes are laid out in Henry to Bartlett, June 23, 1847, JRB/JCBL. Henry's changes were made almost verbatim for the final version of the *Report*, published in the front matter of *Ancient Monuments*.

80. Henry to Squier, June 23, 1847, JHP/SIA. This would become the announced procedure for future publications in the series (Henry 1848:180–81, 1849:12).

81. Squier to Henry, June 26, 1847, and Henry to Squier, August 16, 1847, JHP/SIA. In a long letter to Bartlett, Turner reported having met Squier on the street in New York ("or rather he pounced upon me"), who explained the situation, Henry's discomfort, and his plan for resolving matters. Turner had no objection to the arrangements (Turner to Bartlett, July 7, 1847, JRB/JCBL).

82. It seems particularly appropriate at this juncture to note that Barnhart (1983, 1989) also treats this dispute, and in comparable detail. Our accounts were written wholly independently, but we cover much of the same ground, though naturally with different emphases. Readers interested in this catalytic dispute are urged to consult Barnhart's work (as I wish I had known to do before I wrote mine!). Again, I have been able to add only a few references to his work here.

83. In letter to Davis on September 30, Squier implies that he sent the *Report* to Davis. Davis does not mention where he got the copy, but even if he hadn't received it directly from Squier, the *Report* was published in *Literary World* on September 18, 1847 (*Literary World* 1847a), and parts of it were picked up by various newspapers.

84. *Literary World* 1847a:158, emphasis mine.

85. Davis to Squier, September 22, 1847; although copies of Squier's early letters to Davis do not apparently survive, Davis's letters to Squier indicate that theirs was to be a joint effort in the field and in publications; e.g., Davis to Squier, June 9 and 15, 1846, EGS/LC.

86. Squier to Davis, September 30, 1847, EGS/LC.

87. L. W. Davis to Squier, undated, but ca. October 1847, EGS/LC. (The term "ult." [*ultimo*] means "occurring in the month preceding the present.")

88. Davis to Haven, October 27, 1847, quoted in Barnhart 1983:66, 1989:81. Davis to Bartlett, November 18, 1847, JCB/JCBL. There is no direct evidence that Squier did send out five hundred copies of the *Report*. Of course, since it was published in *Literary World* (see above), he didn't have to.

89. Squier to Marsh, December 6, 1847, EGS/LC.

90. Squier 1847b. The references to Davis were relegated to an opening footnote and a passing reference on the third page of this seventy-page article.

91. Squier to Marsh, December 6, 1847, EGS/LC. Henry recorded the essence of their conversation in one of his notebooks. The actual entry is undated, and Rothenberg et al. (1996:137) place it in mid-July 1847. However, in mid-July the second resolution was not at issue, so it seems more likely that Henry's notes refer to his meeting with Squier in November 1847. Rothenberg agrees (personal communication, 1996).

92. Henry to Squier, November 24, 1847, JHP/SIA.

93. Squier to Marsh, draft copy, December 6, 1847, EGS/LC.

94. Henry to Squier, April 28, 1847, and November 4, 1847, JHP/SIA.

95. Squier had received detailed and quite accurate mound survey data from several individuals, notably McBride, John Locke (1792–1856), and Whittlesey, all of whom were highly adept, though only Locke and Whittlesey were formally trained and conducted their work as part of larger government geological or land surveys (see discussion in Tax 1973:100–121). Whittlesey provided data to Squier in his letters of July 9, October 4, and November 12, 1847; he voiced his unhappiness in Whittlesey to Squier, December 6, 1847, EGS/LC, portions of which are quoted in Rothenberg et al. 1996:250. For McBride's contributions to the effort, see the thorough discussion in Barnhart 1994, especially pp. 35–36. This problem was raised also in Henry to Squier, November 4, 1847, JHP/SIA; the complaints would continue over the next year (e.g., Locke to Henry, February 19, 1848, JHP/SIA; Marsh to Squier, January 7, 1848, EGS/LC). Henry thought the criticisms had the beneficial effect of convincing Squier that he was on the wrong track (Henry to Locke, February 29, 1848, JHP/SIA). Squier's take on the events, partly quoted above, is in Squier to Marsh, December 6, 1847, EGS/LC.

96. Henry to Squier, December 17/25, 1847, JHP/SIA. A number of the regents evidently disapproved of Squier's publishing the *Transactions*, though Marsh was not one of them (Marsh to Bartlett, January 10, 1848, JRB/JCBL). Henry would later claim that the publication of the paper did "good service in the way of calling forth som[e] pretty severe criticism and in convincing Mr. S that he was on the wrong track" (see Henry to Locke, February 29, 1848, JHP/SIA).

97. This summary of Squier's accumulated woes comes from Squier to Henry, undated and incomplete draft, ca. December 1847, EGS/LC, and the ever so slightly toned-down version in Squier to Henry, January 3, 1848, JHP/SIA.

98. The evolution of their agreement can be partly traced through Henry to Squier, August 16, 1847, JHP/SIA; Henry to Squier, December 29, 1847, EGS/LC; and Squier to Henry, January 3, 1848, JHP/SIA. On the budgeting for the publication, see Rothenberg et al. 1996:259 n. 14. Six months earlier, in June 1847, Henry had realized that the costs of producing the volume far exceeded his original estimates (see Henry to Bache, June 25, 1847, and Henry to Gray, January 10, 1848, JHP/SIA), though he continued to monitor the expenses closely and urged Squier to hold down the costs below what he had told the Regents (Henry to Squier, July 19 and August 16, 1847, JHP/SIA; April 11, 1848, EGS/LC). Both Henry and the board were willing to invest in the effort, not least because this was the inaugural volume in the Contributions to Knowledge series and they wanted it done well, but also because they had made a substantial commitment and investment already and had other papers waiting that could only be published after *Ancient Monuments* was completed.

99. Squier to Henry, January 3, 1848, JHP/SIA. According to Henry, however, the $150 was "double the sum you [Squier] stated would be required" (Henry to Squier, December 29, 1847, EGS/LC).

100. Squier to Henry, December 31, 1847; Marsh to Squier, January 7, 1848, and Squier to Marsh, January 8, 1848, EGS/LC. See also Barnhart 1989:80.

101. Davis to Rau, February 17, 1882, quoted in Barnhart 1989:79; Squier to Marsh (?), January 23, 1848, EGS/LC. It was the botanist John Torrey who—after but one meeting with Squier—took an immediate dislike to him and warned Henry that he would have trouble keeping Squier under control (Torrey to Henry, March 3, 1848, JHP/SIA). Also, Rothenberg et al. 1996:120; Tax 1975:120–21.

102. The contract called for a run of 1,000 copies of a volume of about 500 pages and about 200 cuts (illustrations), at the cost of no more than $0.68 per "token of eight pages" (a token was a unit of presswork from one form varying from 250 to 500 impressions). The charge for the editorial changes that Henry and others were making on the sheets was $0.25 per hour. Jenkins to Henry [signed by Drayton], January 20, 1848, WJR/SIA, copy courtesy of Frank Millikan, Joseph Henry Papers, Smithsonian Institution.

103. Squier to Bartlett, February 1, 1848, JRB/JCBL. Squier wasn't completely on his own: later that spring, Gallatin provided him with $350, half the funds necessary to bring out the private edition (Tax 1975:116).

104. Rothenberg et al. 1996:272 n. 4; Tax 1975:113–14. Perhaps in light of the difficulties he had had with Squier, Henry more explicitly staked his claim to have the final say about a volume's contents in his next *Annual Report* (Henry 1849:12). Most of the explicitly "theoretical" content of *Ancient Monuments* is contained in the relatively brief concluding chapter, pp. 301–6. On Henry's views, see Henry to Squier and Davis, February 16, 1848, and Squier to Henry, February 21, 1846, JHP/SIA. The parts of the serpent discussion that survived Henry's editorial knife appear in *Ancient Monuments*, pp. 97–98 and 304. Squier ultimately did publish a large memoir, *Serpent Symbol and the Worship of the Reciprocal Principles of Nature in America* (Squier 1851b), but by then he was using the "universality" of the serpent strictly as evidence of psychic unity, in order to bolster the polygenists' position (Bieder 1986:133–34).

105. Hinsley 1981:36–37; Rothenberg et al. 1996:280; *Scientific American* 1848.

106. Henry to Gray, January 10, 1848, JHP/SIA. Rothenberg et al. 1996:280.

107. Squier to Henry, February 21, 1848, JHP/SIA. Squier was even less charitable about Davis in writing to Bartlett (February 1, 1848, JRB/JCBL): "Mr. Davis is still here: for what purpose I cannot imagine—unless it is to *assist* in bringing out the—I mean *his* work. He looks *wise* when visitors call, and I have no doubt they are all properly *impressed* with his profundity. I intend to cultivate a busy visage, seeing it helps along so much."

108. Henry to Gray, May 23, 1848, JHP/SIA.

109. Marsh to Squier, March 31, 1848, EGS/LC; Marsh to Bartlett, March 31, 1848, JCB/JCBL (also JHP/SIA). Squier was not the only one having problems receiving promised payments; a few months later, Albert Gallatin called on Marsh to help in recovering from Henry the money he had advanced to support some of the engravings that ultimately were used in *Ancient Monuments* (Gallatin to Marsh, August 7, 1848, JHP/SIA). In Henry's defense, he was assuredly not dishonest—just badly distracted. In those years he had a tremendous administrative burden to carry and almost no staff to help him with it (Rothenberg et al. 1996:xxv). When Spencer Baird was hired as assistant secretary in 1850, one of his primary duties was to take on oversight of the Smithsonian's publications (Rivinus and Youssef 1992:57).

110. Squier to Bartlett, November 12, 1848, JCB/JCBL; Henry to Squier, April 6, 1848, EGS/LC.

111. Marsh did so at Squier's request; see Marsh to Squier, June 6, 16, and July 3, 20, 1848, EGS/LC. If by having Marsh examine the proofs Squier was hoping for an ally against Henry, he misjudged. Like Henry, Marsh objected to the "conjectural speculation," and "doubtful analogies" that Squier was drawing between earthworks in America and those in other countries. On the details regarding the circulation of the proof sheets and the occasional problems with the printer, see Henry to Jewett, May 19, 1848, and Henry to Squier, April 18 and May 13, 1848, JHP/SIA; also Henry to Squier, June 9, 1848, EGS/LC.

112. Henry to Squier, June 28, 1848, and Henry to Bache, July 4, 1848, JHP/SIA; Squier to Joel Squier, July 5, 1848, quoted in Rothenberg et al. 1996:346 n. 1).

113. Henry to Squier, August 18, 1848, JHP/SIA; Davis to Squier, undated letter, EGS/LC; Henry to Squier, May 13, 1848, JHP/SIA.

114. Davis to Squier, undated but by other evidence September 19, 1848, EGS/LC; Squier to Davis, draft, September 20, 1848, first and second drafts, EGS/LC.

115. Clark to Squier, October 5, 1848, EGS/LC, emphasis mine.

116. Squier's second effort at long-distance breaking and entering is recorded in Johnie [?] to Squier, October 19, 1848, EGS/LC. On the arbitration, Bartlett to Squier, October 25 and 28, 1848, EGS/LC; Squier to Bartlett, October 26, November 7 and 12, 1848, JCB/JCBL. It is unclear how Squier arrived at the figure of $2,500.

117. Robinson et al., June 12, 1847, from the *original* unpublished version of the AES *Report* with the Squier Papers, EGS/LC.

118. Rothenberg, personal communication, September 11, 1996.

119. Henry 1849:11; Henry to Gray, May 23, 1848, JHP/SIA. Massive as the volume is, it has virtually no production flaws and very few typographical errors (but see, for example, Plate IV and p. 210)—testimony to the extraordinary care that went into its production, and the many eyes reading the proofs.

120. *Literary World* 1848:768.

121. *Ancient Monuments*, pp. xxxiii and xxxviii.

122. *Ancient Monuments*, p. xxxviii.

123. The preface of *Ancient Monuments* (p. xxxiii) has a few kind words for Atwater's work, though the authors couldn't help but add that it contained "many errors" and later found it impossible to mention his work in the text without belittling it. Whether they appreciated it or not, much of their effort followed his lead. But they differed from Atwater and many contemporaries in one crucial respect—Squier and Davis did not invoke any Old World connections for the moundbuilders.

124. Henry to Squier and Davis, February 16, 1848, JHP/SIA. Also *Ancient Monuments*, pp. xxxviii, 80, 81, 89, 152, 181. Historians have echoed the assertion that Squier and Davis "refrained from speculation" (e.g., Bieder 1986:117; Hinsley 1981:37; Tax 1975:114), but *Ancient Monuments* proves otherwise. The long descriptive sections in *Ancient Monuments* often incorporated or were followed by interpretive flights (e.g., pp. 42–46, 101–3, 118–20), in which Squier and Davis made inferences—occasionally wildly speculative ones—based on their self-evident facts. For a sample of Cyrus Thomas's reaction, see Thomas 1894:27 and the discussion below.

125. For example, in order to buttress their case (in chapter 2) on the military strategies of the moundbuilders, Squier and Davis invoked analogies among the Polynesians, Australians, and New Zealanders (from modern groups), and the ancient Romans, Britons, Celts, Mexicans, and Peruvians (from among the archaeological ones) (*Ancient Monuments*, pp. 42–46). All of which on its face might have tested the limits of Henry's definition of what constituted reasonable interpretation, were it not for the fact that what they said made obvious intuitive sense, and who was Henry, a physical scientist, to question the reliability of any ethnographic accounts? Besides, Henry could hardly fail to appreciate the analogies they also drew from contemporary American frontier experience (*Ancient Monuments*, p. 44).

126. *Ancient Monuments*, pp. xxxiii–xxxiv. As many have realized, it would be invaluable to have an annotated edition of *Ancient Monuments*, which would update what has been learned of all of the sites discussed in the original and report on their present status. Unfortunately, that is far beyond the scope of this introduction, not to mention the competence of its author.

127. For illustrative comments on the scarcity of data from other areas, see pp. 104, 119. For biographical and historical information on Rafinesque, see Williams 1991, especially pp. 98–109.

128. Counts of the number of monuments in Ross County appear on page 4. Several of the larger and more noteworthy of those sites, including Fort Ancient, Hopewell, Marietta, and Newark, were earlier described and mapped by Atwater (Atwater 1820:126–89). Sites of note in *Ancient Monuments* include Fort Ancient, p. 18; Hopewell—then known as "Clark s Work; North Fork of Paint Creek," p. 26; Mound City, pp. 54, 149; Baum, pp. 57–58; Seip Mound, p. 58; Edwin Harness Mound, p. 56; the Newark Earthworks, p. 67; Tremper, pp. 83–84; Serpent Mound, pp. 96–98. Notable sites from other areas include Aztalan, p. 131; Grave Creek Mound, pp. 5, 168–69; and Cahokia and Monks Mound, pp. 5, 174. For a partial listing of the location and present status of some of these and other mounds and earthworks in Ohio, see Lepper 1995; Woodward and McDonald 1986.

129. *Ancient Monuments*, pp. xxxiv, 3.

130. *Ancient Monuments*, pp. xxxiv, 10, 57. The idea that there were perfectly laid out forms among the earthworks was not new with Squier and Davis; Atwater (1820:142, 144) had also claimed as much. For a contemporary discussion, see Kennedy 1994, especially pp. 16–17, 50–52, 267–71.

131. Atwater (1820) had provided maps of fewer than ten earthworks, but more than half of them prompted snide footnotes from Squier and Davis about their errors or poor quality (see the footnotes on pp. 26, 57, 73, 89 of *Ancient Monuments*). Their comments on Atwater's rendering of Fort Ancient are gentler, but then, Atwater had borrowed that map from an earlier work (*Ancient Monuments*, p. 18). They had an even lower opinion of Rafinesque, at least judging by the useless map of his that they reproduced as Figure 18, on p. 77. It was Atwater's and Rafinesque's everlasting misfortune to have been Squier and Davis's predecessors.

132. See, for example, the roads running through—and breaching the walls—at the Hopewell site (Plate X), and the Ancient Work, Liberty Township (Plate XX). Since Squier and Davis believed that the enclosure wall must have "extended uninterruptedly through," they drew it as such (*Ancient Monuments*, p. 27). The walls and other features of earthwork were normally shown as being of uniform thickness, although that mostly reflects the limitations of lithography. They themselves appreciated that wall thickness varied. Only occasionally did they admit of ambiguity, at least in regard to the form and features of earthworks. The Stone Work, near Bourneville, for example, was assumed to have an encircling wall, even though it was not regularly laid, was missing in some areas, and appeared at first glance to be the natural outcrop of the hilltop (*Ancient Monuments*, pp. 11–12). Generally, they were confident in their ability to tell the difference beween natural features and artificial ones (*Ancient Monuments*, p. 34).

133. It even requires a bit of sleuthing to determine just which hundred mounds they excavated. A small number of them are explicitly identified; the remainder are mentioned, if at all, only in passing (e.g., *Ancient Monuments*, p. 159). *Ancient Monuments*, pp. 139, 144, 150, 162, 179. For general remarks on the mound plans and sections, see p. 142. For a glimpse of the practice and problems of excavation, see p. 150, and the footnote on p. 179. Note: The term "drift," frequently used in the text, refers to an excavation trench or tunnel. The excavations were conducted under the direct supervision of Squier and Davis, though not always by them.

134. For examples of the degree of their observational detail, see *Ancient Monuments*, pp. 69, 99, 140, 150–52, 156–57, 166, 179–80.

135. On the internal stratigraphy of the mounds, see *Ancient Monuments*, pp. 60, 154, 164–65. Earlier, Atwater (1820) had made occasional reference to the stratification of the mounds, though he did not as well appreciate its significance. Davis later claimed that the stratification of the mounds was the first thing he noticed in them, and he did so in the context of refuting the claim that stratification within the mounds was evidence that they formed naturally under "aquatic" (alluvial) conditions; see Davis to Rau, May 30 and June 5, 1884, BAE/NAA (Record Group 7065). In regard to intrusive burials, see *Ancient Monuments*, pp. 37 n, 62, 64, 111, 134, 145–47, 148, 153, 166.

136. *Ancient Monuments*, p. 146 (for their evidence on the secondary use of the mounds by Indians, see p. 145, but also pp. 62, 64, 134, 288, 290). Squier and Davis report (p. 64) to being misled early in their excavations by skeletal material and artifacts high in the mounds, which they assumed belonged to the moundbuilders but were later convinced were intrusive. So pervasive did they come to believe was the practice of later Indians' burying their dead in the mounds that they doubted "whether any of the numerous skulls which have been sent abroad and exhibited as undoubted remains of the mound-builders, were really such" (p. 168). Thomas (1894:18) would later use historic artifacts in the mounds to mount a very different argument, notably that the mounds were indeed built by the Indians.

137. *Ancient Monuments*, pp. 186–87. They drew from this the further observation that if an artifact's recovery history and context were not known, any conclusions drawn from it "would necessarily be invested with painful uncertainty."

138. *Ancient Monuments*, pp. 145–46, 163. This rule codified an observation about the depth and position of the moundbuilder remains that Davis reportedly made while still a Kenyon student (Davis to Rau, June 5, 1884, BAE/NAA, Record Group 7065). Squier and Davis were not alone in proclaiming the fact that "modern Indians bury in shallow graves" (*Ancient Monuments*, p. 62). That truism dates back at least to Atwater, who believed that Indian graves were shallow, while those of the moundbuilders "were frequently found many feet below the surface" (Atwater 1820:125).

139. Their excavation procedure is described and illustrated in *Ancient Monuments*, pp. 147–50, 162–63. For their few comments on which mounds were selected for excavation, see p. 142. Shetrone (1930:201) would describe their excavations as "unpretentious and superficial; [but] nevertheless, their modest efforts were richly rewarded."

140. *Ancient Monuments*, p. 9. For summary comments on the variation in mounds and earthworks across the larger region, see pp. 2–3, 101–4, 124. They also detected variation in ceramics over that same area (see p. 190).

141. *Ancient Monuments*, p. 7 n. Their classification of the large-scale monuments follows—perhaps more closely than they themselves would care to admit—the scheme roughly laid out in Atwater (e.g., Atwater 1820:129, 142, 145, 163). Although they considered mounds and barrows as synonymous, they also understood that not all mounds were burial mounds.

142. *Ancient Monuments*, p. 72. The moundbuilders, Squier and Davis insisted, "understood perfectly the value of the external fosse" (moat). It was a very medieval view of moundbuilder warfare, and one shared by others (*Ancient Monuments*, pp. 8, 47–48; Atwater 1820:145).

143. *Sacrificial mounds* occurred within enclosures (though not all mounds within enclosures were sacrificial), were neatly stratified, and of course contained the "altars" on which the sacrifices were made (*Ancient Monuments*, pp. 142, 143, 151). *Sepulchral mounds* tended to be isolated and distant from the sacred enclosures, lacked altars and the neatly layered strata of the sacrificial mounds, but "invariably" covered a skeleton—usually a single skeleton buried in bark matting or a rude wooden "sarcophagus" (log tomb) along with a uniform scatter of "ornaments, utensils, and weapons"—the last being relatively uncommon (*Ancient Monuments*, pp. 161–62, 168; Grave Creek Mound was the exception to the rule of single burial, p. 168). *Temple mounds* had neither of the features of the other two, consisted chiefly of ramped and truncated pyramids or flat-topped mounds, which bore a "striking" likeness to the Teocalli of Mexico (*Ancient Monuments*, pp. 142, 172). *Mounds of observation* were on the hilltops that skirted the valleys, had evidence of fire, and lacked human remains. It seemed safe to liken them to the signal mounds of the Celts or the "primitive telegraphic system" of the Indians. But a few also contained human remains and were too far back from the brow of the hill to be effective as signal fires. Squier and Davis appreciated the difference between necessary and sufficient conditions, and they could only conclude that these mounds might have served several purposes; the fires atop them may have transmitted information, or perhaps been part of religious rites (see pp. 181–83). Squier and Davis were so puzzled by the northwestern effigy mounds that they were reluctant even to fall back on their familiar refrain that inexplicable works such as this must be religious. They granted that as a possibility but also thought that the mounds might be sepulchral (burial) or even erected as monuments of migrations long past (*Ancient Monuments*, pp. 124–25, 133, 135).

144. For examples of their observations of artifact wear patterns, see *Ancient Monuments*, pp. 205, 238; on material sources, see pp. 212, 214, 229, 278–79, 285–86; on technology, see pp. 195–96, 202–3, 216–17, 273; and on the relative superiority of the workmanship of moundbuilder artifacts, see the comments on pp. 189, 222, 228, 230, 242, 249, 272 (and elsewhere).

145. *Ancient Monuments*, pp. 142, 181. The *Anomalous mounds* wouldn't easily fit into the other categories, because they appeared to have either multiple purposes (and hence features of more than one group) or no discernible purpose at all. These were the features that stymied even Squier's normal enthusiasm for conjecture (pp. 142, 179–81).

146. *Ancient Monuments*, pp. 27, 99, 102–3, 159–60. Squier and Davis, of course, were not alone in imagining primeval scenes of human sacrifice on sacred altars (see also Atwater 1820:191).

147. As they confidently stated, the "purposes of the remains [artifacts] of the mounds generally are so apparent, that little doubt can exist as to the place which they should occupy in the simple classification here." Those few kinds that were "enigmatic" were "probably of not much importance" anyway (*Ancient Monuments*, pp. 231, 241). On their confidence in their classification of earthworks, see *Ancient Monuments*, p. 49. For examples of how they dealt with earthworks that did not fit well with the other sacred enclosures, see pp. 90–101.

148. Atwater 1820:157–58.

149. *Ancient Monuments*, p. xxxviii. On their reluctance to pursue the serpent analogy, see the discussion on pp. 96–98; but also see their hints of significance on p. 277. For an illustration of how they used analogy even to the point of demanding the presence of certain (otherwise absent) features of the archaeological record, see pp. 102–3.

150. Squier and Davis do not provide an explicit statement of the relative rankings of societies; however, throughout *Ancient Monuments* where artifacts or monuments of the Indians and moundbuilders are compared, the former are routinely described as "rude" or "savage," the latter as "more advanced" or "superior" (see, e.g., pp. 139, 186, 228, 230, 242, 249, 272, 273). On their "law of harmonious development," see p. 273. That "law" was why, for example, they dismissed the idea that the moundbuilders had writing; writing was an attribute of advanced civilizations, whereas the moundbuilders were only semi-civilized. Squier and Davis were not the first archaeologists to rank the moundbuilders above the Indians and among the semi-civilized—see also Atwater (1820:120).

151. *Ancient Monuments*, pp. 9, 25, 43.

152. *Ancient Monuments*, pp. 42, 45. On the stone heaps of the Indians, see pp. 184–85. Squier had held a low opinion of Indians for several years (e.g., Squier 1845).

153. *Ancient Monuments*, pp. 210, 215. For an early statement of Squier's belief that "like causes produce similar results," see his comments in the *Scioto Gazette* 1847. For examples of their use of analogies drawn from American Indians, see *Ancient Monuments*, pp. 205, 216, 219, 221–22, 224, 228–29.

154. Atwater fortified this conclusion with the startling claim that there were similarities between the moundbuilders and "Hindoos" in their customs and even in their "idols." On the latter, he perceived in effigy heads on the legs of a ceramic bottle from the Cumberland River valley a representation of the Indian gods "Brahma, Vishnoo, and Siva" (Atwater 1820:211–13; 240–41). So far as he was concerned, "If the coincidences between the worship of our people, and that of the Hindoos and southern Tartars, furnish no evidence of a common origin, then I am no judge of the nature and weight of testimony" (Atwater 1820:213).

155. *Ancient Monuments*, p. 304. In a newspaper account of his comments following a talk by polygenist George Gliddon in Ohio in the spring of 1847, Squier accepted the possibility that the American race was "created here" or, at the very least, arrived during "the period of the dispersion" (*Scioto Gazette* 1847). After his full-blown conversion to polygenesis, Squier would write in *Serpent Symbol* that it had been incorrectly assumed that the American Indians were "descendants of some one or more of the diversified nations to which earliest history refers." That they looked like Old World groups or possessed elements of their religious systems, he would attribute to convergence, or to the fact that all humans beings were alike in their "mental and moral constitutions"—the psychic unity of humankind (Squier 1851a:17–18; quoted and discussed in Bieder 1986:133).

156. All this isn't to imply that the painting was deliberately selected by Squier and Davis for its latent message and symbolism; they may have chosen it merely because it was available and/or suitable for a frontispiece. Still, the message is unmistakably there—and quite consistent with their text. It would be interesting to survey other contemporary illustrations of mounds, to see just how often Indians were included in the scenes and where they were placed. The frontispiece to *Ancient Monuments* may prove uncommon only in having Indians present (see, for example, the other mound-scenes that they included, on pp. 5, 69–70, 82, 88, 139, 141, 160–61, 169, 173, 177, and 185) but not in placing them on the margins and far from the ancient mounds and earthworks.

157. Haven to Squier, August 12, 1847, EGS/LC; Squier to Haven, August 14, 1847, SFH/AAS.

158. On the differences in their artifacts, see *Ancient Monuments*, pp. 188–89, 199, 228–30, 242, 246, 249, 259, 272; on the differences in patterns of warfare and defense, see pp. 42, 45.

159. *Ancient Monuments*, pp. 50, 62, 64, 145, 148, 153, 172, 184, 186, 288, 290. As noted, Squier and Davis were willing to concede that Indians occasionally built their own mounds (as opposed to their ostensibly more common practice of simply burying their dead in mounds constructed by the moundbuilders [pp. 145–46]), but these heaps of stone, perched alongside Indian trails, near Indian villages, and containing many humble and "rude" relics, and occasionally European trade wares, were not to be confused with the occasional stone mounds of the moundbuilders (p. 184). Otherwise, Indian burial grounds were not associated with the mounds or earthworks (p. 50).

160. On their physical differences, see *Ancient Monuments*, pp. 246–47 (which speaks to differences evident from their stone sculpture) and pp. 148, 153, 288–92 (moundbuilder skeletal remains). Because they believed that moundbuilder remains were so scarce and poorly preserved and that those of the Indians were so much more abundant and likely to occur in mounds as heretofore little-noticed intrusive burials, Squier and Davis were quick to question whether "any of the numerous skulls which have been sent abroad and exhibited as undoubted remains of the mound-builders were really such" (p. 168). They were puzzled by the scarcity of skeletal remains of the moundbuilders. Partly, they suspected, it was because many had been cremated (pp. 37, 172), and the cemeteries of the others—by virtue of their great antiquity and lack of protection beneath heaps of earth—had failed to preserve (pp. 171–72). Only the elite were buried in the mounds, where Squier and Davis thought conditions were at least potentially favorable to bone preservation, though in reality they often were not (p. 172).

161. *Ancient Monuments*, pp. 45, 196, 301–3.

162. Squier 1845.

163. At the time of the writing of *Ancient Monuments* (p. 46), it was assumed that this would be true of all the mounds of the United States, including those of New York. Squier would subsequently change his mind after fieldwork in New York (Squier 1851a:83). *Ancient Monuments* makes frequent reference to the Indians' disavowal of moundbuilding (pp. 108, 121, 123, 134, 233). It was "a fact well known," according to Squier and Davis, that Indians—though they knew nothing of the mounds—nonetheless regarded them with

"veneration" and often buried their dead within them. Just to be on the safe side, Squier and Davis made sure to point out that Hernando de Soto could not have built the mounds either (p. 112).

164. Atwater 1820:245–51. As the Ohio monuments were not as grand as those of Mexico, Atwater presumed that the Ohio mounds were older and that these emitters from the Ohio Valley reached Mexico around the year 648, which, according to Humboldt, was the year the "Aztecks" were reputed to have settled in Mexico (Atwater 1820:246).

165. Gallatin 1845, quoted in Haven 1856:64.

166. *Ancient Monuments*, pp. 119, 301.

167. *Ancient Monuments*, p. 303 (for the full argument, see the long footnote beginning on p. 302).

168. On the increase in temple mounds to the south, see *Ancient Monuments*, p. 176. These mounds were ramped and truncated pyramids, symmetrical in outline and constructed in a few cases by what were reported to be rude bricks. They were arranged carefully with respect to one another on broad terraces (plazas) and connected by "elevated passages and long avenues" (for fuller descriptions, see *Ancient Monuments*, pp. 104, 114, 118, and especially pp. 173–77). They were clearly describing Mississippian-age platform mounds. The decrease in defensive structures is noted in *Ancient Monuments*, pp. 104, 112, 118–19. Reservoirs, while they occurred with some of the southern earthworks, were interpreted to be merely convenient sources of water, not military necessities, as Squier and Davis believed they were further north [p. 114]).

169. The quotation comes from *Ancient Monuments*, p. 119. That they might suspect that the mounds were different ages is understandable, as it appears they were. Squier and Davis were generally comparing Early and Middle Woodland earthworks, with Mississippian features. Of course, they didn't know that (*Ancient Monuments*, p. 104). They blamed the meagerness of the data on the southern mounds on Dickeson, though without naming names. He was who they had in mind when they grumbled about investigations that had been conducted mostly with a view to "excite wonder" rather than to develop fact (*Ancient Monuments*, p. 119). At the opening of the chapter on the southern monuments they took a passing jab at Dickeson—this time by name—for not yet publishing his results (*Ancient Monuments*, p. 104 n).

170. Quotations from *Ancient Monuments*, pp. 104 and 119. For related notes, see also p. 118.

171. The comparisons and similarities are discussed in *Ancient Monuments* on pp. 45, 103, 159, 196, 198, 211–12, 214, 277, and 285–86. The quotation on obsidian is from p. 278.

172. E.g., *Ancient Monuments*, pp. 152, 214, 229, 265, 286 (on pipestone, which they sourced to the Coteau des Prairies of Minnesota); pp. 202, 279, 281 (copper and silver—to Lake Superior); pp. 212, 278, 285–86 (obsidian—to Mexico); p. 281 (galena—to Illinois); p. 282 (shark's teeth—to various localities, including the Lower Mississippi Valley); p. 283 (pearls—the tropical areas); p. 284 (marine shell—to the Gulf of Mexico); and p. 285 (mica—to points east, including the Schuylkill above Philadelphia).

173. *Ancient Monuments*, pp. 278, 306.

174. *Ancient Monuments*, p. 278; but see the comments on p. 254. Of course, long- distance exchange networks of precious materials would, a century later, come to be recognized as the very hallmark of Adena, and especially Hopewell occupations of Ohio.

175. *Ancient Monuments*, pp. 242, 251–54, 260, 266. Henshaw would later (1883:125–47) systematically refute Squier and Davis's identifications of these tropical animals.

176. *Ancient Monuments*, pp. 8–10, 12, 15–18, 20–21, 28, 30. Squier and Davis were never reluctant to appeal to authority, and what better authority on the defensive character of the earthworks than the late president—and military hero—William Henry Harrison, who had evoked images of the Acropolis of Athens to explain the fortified hill at the mouth of the Great Miami River (pp. 25–26).

177. *Ancient Monuments*, p. 44. Whittlesey offered a slightly different take on the evidence—he thought the line of fortified earthworks marked the advance front of a nation landing on the shores of Lake Erie poised to move south, or perhaps the invaders' defensive line to repel a southern invasion. Thus, the mounds and earthworks further south were not those of the same people, suggesting to Whittlesey that Ohio was then occupied by two nations, one warlike, the other peaceful—and that the peaceful one had been overcome (quoted in *Ancient Monuments*, pp. 41–42). Squier and Davis, as noted, saw all the mounds as having been built by the same group, in response to the hordes from the north. To them, Whittlesey's battle line was no more than the usual forts one could still see on the sparsely populated American frontier.

178. By the time the moundbuilders arrived in Mexico, Squier and Davis thought, they had learned from their experience and made considerable advances in the "art of defence" (*Ancient Monuments*, p. 45).

179. E.g., *Ancient Monuments*, pp. 47, 71, 168, 237, 301. They were particularly struck by the similari-

ties among the Newark (Plate XXV), Hopeton Works (Plate XVI), High Bank group (Plate XVII), and Marietta (Plate XXVI) earthworks. On the precision and standardization of the earthworks, see pp. 48–49, 57, 61, 66, 69. All this they attributed to the moundbuilders' religion: "Whatever may have been the divinity of their belief, order, symmetry, and design were among his attributes" (p. 82).

180. *Ancient Monuments*, pp. 170–72.

181. *Ancient Monuments*, pp. 49, 54, 62, 75, 155, 181. In arguing that the moundbuilders were not idol worshipers, Squier and Davis were directly contradicting Atwater (1820:240–41). They also dismissed another of Atwater's claims: that the monuments or their contents had astronomical or geographic alignments (cf. Atwater 1820:236–37 and Squier and Davis 1848:48, 66, 68, 172). On the moundbuilders' devotional fervor, see *Ancient Monuments*, pp. 158–59.

182. *Ancient Monuments*, pp. 6, 302–3.

183. *Ancient Monuments*, p. 302. Squier and Davis frequently mentioned the great amount of labor that must have gone into the construction of mounds and earthworks (e.g., *Ancient Monuments*, pp. 13, 16, 19, 29, 42, 22, 302), and they used that as a bridge to build an argument about the population and subsistence strategy of the moundbuilders. In regard to the labor requirements of moundbuilding, see pp. 5, 13, 16, 19, 29, 42, 44, and 302. Cahokia's great mound alone (Monk's Mound), they estimated, required the excavation, transport, and placement of 20 million cubic feet of earth. Even with "all the facilities and numerous mechanical appliances of the present day," they observed in wonder, the construction of even smaller works "would be no insignificant undertaking." Further, given how "comparatively rude" the means of the builders, the amount of labor that had to be invested becomes testimony to the "value" of the construction as well as the number and character of the people who would pull it off (p. 16).

184. *Ancient Monuments*, pp. 45, 196, 301–3. For their discussion of animal bones from the mounds, see pp. 220–21.

185. E.g., *Ancient Monuments*, pp. 1, 45, 63, 71, 87.

186. Clinton 1814:93; Harrison 1839. In *Ancient Monuments* (p. 306), Harrison's argument is quoted with obvious approval. See also Silverberg 1968:78–79; Tax 1973:79, 88.

187. Marsh to Squier, June 16, 1848, EGS/LC. *Ancient Monuments*, pp. 55, 75, 168, 172.

188. *Ancient Monuments*, p. 10, also pp. 59, 304–5. They flag the rare cases (such as the Seip Mound) where creeks might breach their banks and get close to earthworks, but they believe these do not "invalidate" their general conclusion that the earthworks never occur on the latest terrace (p. 59).

189. *Ancient Monuments*, pp. 16, 305.

190. Nott to Squier, August 19, 1848, EGS/LC.

191. Willey and Sabloff 1993:41; cf. *Ancient Monuments*, pp. 182, 205, 222, 238.

192. E.g., *Ancient Monuments*, pp. 9, 16, 17, 25, 29, 31, 36, 47, 62, 71, 146, 183.

193. *Ancient Monuments*, p. 29.

194. Tax (1975:115) puts the distribution of the work in July 1848, but Henry did not receive word in regard to the preface until August, and he was still getting last-minute advice on the content of his Advertisement section in early September (Bache to Henry, September 1, 1848, JHP/SIA). Morton, a recipient of one of the early copies, received his on September 23, 1848 (Morton to Squier, September 25, 1848, EGS/LC). On the private editions of the work, see Tax 1975:115–16. Bartlett and his partner took out full-page ads for the book two weeks running in *Literary World* (September 16 and 23, 1848); another notice was put in the September issue of *American Review*. They heralded the appearance on September 20 of this "Great American Work." Apparently the success of the private sale bothered Henry, as the higher price of these volumes prevented many people from obtaining a copy of the book, so he changed his policy, and afterward the Smithsonian simply printed extra copies, which were sold at cost. The authors could not do the same (Henry 1849:8; Tax 1973:208).

195. It is impossible to say whether the omission of Henry was the result of lingering bitterness on Squier's part, or Henry's editorial choice. For the full acknowledgments, see *Ancient Monuments*, pp. xxxv–xxxviii. The reactions are in Locke to Henry, November 23, 1848, JHP/SIA; Whittlesey to Squier, December 11, 1848, McBride to Squier, March 19, 1849, EGS/LC. McBride was pleased with the attribution of credit, but mostly wanted his field notes and drawings returned to him—a plea that he had made on previous occasions (e.g., McBride to Squier, October 22, 1848, EGS/LC). Some of McBride's meticulously detailed and useful field notes can still be seen today in the Squier Papers at the Library of Congress. McBride evidently never got them back.

196. Morton to Squier, September 25, 1848, EGS/LC; Squier to Morton, September 27, 1848, SGM/HSP;

Nott to Squier, February 14, 1849, EGS/LC; Whittlesey to Squier, December 11, 1848, EGS/LC; *Afternoon Express* 1848. Humboldt's opinion is recorded in Seitz 1911:12. There were one or two sour notes, as when, for example, George Marsh received his copy. He was "disappointed and mortified" to discover that his review letter approving the work, published in the Advertisement section (p. x), had not been changed as he had requested. There is no record in the correspondence to indicate just what that change was, but it might have involved using Davis's name, instead of referring to him as Squier's "associate" (Marsh to Squier, December 21, 1848, EGS/LC).

197. Burke 1848a:663. The comments on *Ancient Monuments* in the *Ethnological Journal* were part of a broad review of ethnology in the United States by the journal's editor, Luke Burke. The timing of Burke's review suggests that he must have seen proof sheets of *Ancient Monuments* rather than the completed volume. Squier thought he saw the "moving hands of our good friend Gliddon at the bottom of this" (Squier to Morton, September 27, 1848, SGM/HSP), which may explain how Burke obtained a set of proof sheets. See also Stanton 1960:87.

198. *Literary World* 1848:768.

199. Squier would himself later emphasize the uniqueness of the American contribution to anthropology (Squier 1849a:386).

200. Among the reviews were Burke 1848b and 1849, Norton 1849, and Woolsey 1849. Norton's was the most visible and comprehensive, Burke's the most partisan (he published it in the aggressively polygenist *Ethnological Journal,* of which he was editor).

201. Norton to Squier, February 5, 1849, EGS/LC. Also Thomas 1894:625–26. Norton would gain fame as an author, editor, and historian. At the time that he reviewed *Ancient Monuments,* he was a relatively new Harvard graduate, working in business and possessing connections to the literary and scholarly worlds through a friendship with the historian Francis Parkman—who was also a friend of Squier's. Norton had no particular expertise in archaeology; that he was selected to review the volume may have been the result of Parkman's influence. Parkman mentions in a letter to Squier written in early 1849, that "[a] friend of mine, a Mr. Charles Norton, who is going to review you in the next North American, is coming to New York and will call on you. He takes an interest in ethnology, and though I do not think your ideas and his are in all respects congenial—as his education has been rather of the strict and precise sort—yet you will find him a most capital fellow and well able to appreciate all that you have done" (Seitz 1911:19).

202. Squier to Norton, February 7, 1849, EGS/LC. By now, Squier had become highly possessive of *Ancient Monuments,* hence the reference to it as "my" work. Squier explained to Norton that the decision to *"peremptorily withdraw"* that large amount of material was driven by "entangling influences," which forced him, as a matter of "self-respect—not to say regard for my own reputation" to make the cuts. In regard to the terrace formation, Squier reported seeing direct evidence that sections of the terrace had formed since the construction of the mounds.

203. Norton 1849:492–494. Squier's letter, however, had the positive effect of prompting Norton to urge that Squier be given the opportunity to extend his research efforts (Norton 1849:475, 495–96). On the "rule" governing the downcutting of rivers, see *Ancient Monuments,* p. 305.

204. Nott to Squier, September 30, 1848, EGS/LC. Nott was particularly pleased to hear what Squier was claiming, as it came just in time to include in a series of lectures he was delivering in New Orleans on human race history (see Nott 1849:84).

205. So deft was Gliddon at his disguise that Massachusetts abolitionist senator Charles Sumner joined the subscribers' list to *Types of Mankind,* thus helping to support publication of a book whose message of human inequality he fiercely opposed (the subscription to *Types of Mankind* was five dollars—expensive in those days [Stanton 1960:146, 163]). Sumner was later viciously beaten on the floor of the Senate by a South Carolina congressman who devoutly believed that message. It happened following a lengthy speech ("The Crime against Kansas") on the Senate floor during the debate on whether Kansas would become a slave state. Sumner vigorously denounced slavery and personally attacked the absent South Carolina senator Andrew Butler. Two days later (May 22, 1856), Butler's cousin, Congressman Preston Brooks, violently beat Sumner over the head with a gold-topped cane—more than thirty blows, according to witnesses. Sumner survived. His beating galvanized northern abolitionists, made Brooks a hero throughout the South, and so enraged a demented Kansas abolitionist that he abducted five proslavery settlers and split their skulls with broadswords. John Brown was never punished for the massacre.

206. Stanton 1960:48–50. Davis to Squier, June 12, 1847, EGS/LC. The best biographical source on Gliddon is Stanton (1960). On Gliddon and the AES, see Bieder and Tax 1976:17. Gliddon warrants a footnote

in American history for another reason, beyond his staunch advocacy of polygenesis. It was he who hatched the idea of using camels for transport and hauling in the American West (Gliddon to Squier, March 7, 1854, EGS/LC).

207. Gliddon's visit to Chillicothe was arranged by Squier, who had "long cherished a desire to hear him"—see Squier to Bartlett, February 20, 1847, and Gliddon to Bartlett, March 9, 1847, JRB/JCBL; Gliddon to Squier, March 15, 1847, EGS/LC. For Squier's comments following Gliddon's lecture, see the *Scioto Gazette* 1847.

208. Stanton 1960:66–70; also Horsman 1987:108–9. Nott to Morton, October 15, 1844, SGM/HSP; Gliddon to Squier, April 29, 1848, Nott to Squier, August 18, 1848, and May 24, 1851, EGS/LC. Nott and Squier did not meet until 1851.

209. Squier 1849a:390–91. Gallatin was quite ill through the spring and summer of 1849; he passed away in August. Bieder (1986:139) believes Squier had constantly misread Gallatin and believed him to be a polygenist. That may well be, though it seems equally plausible that Squier was simply disingenuous.

210. Squier 1849a:388, 392, 394. The idea that all human groups were alike in their early stages and develop in a similar pattern, particularly when responding to like circumstances, would later be codified in the notion of the "psychic unity" of humankind.

211. Squier 1849a:392.

212. Gliddon to Squier, November 11, 1850, EGS/LC; Nott to Morton, February 20, 1845, SGM/HSP; Nott to Squier, February 14, 1849, and March 26, 1851, EGS/LC. Also Horsman 1987:171.

213. Nott to Squier, September 26, 1852, EGS/LC. As Nott later explained, "I am as bold in my opinions as anybody, but I have my own ideas about what a *gentleman* should do" (Nott to Squier, April 10, 1854, EGS/LC).

214. In writing *Types*, they had many of Morton's books and manuscripts, which were provided them by his widow. Agassiz was a devout creationist who had long insisted that each continent's flora and fauna had been separately created; it took little time or effort to convince him that human races followed the same plan (Gould 1981:42–50). For a history of the publication of *Types*, see Horsman 1987:172–79.

215. Nott and Gliddon 1854:457. For a summary of *Types of Mankind* and the reaction to it, see Stanton 1960:161–73.

216. Nott and Gliddon 1854:252, 255.

217. Nott and Gliddon 1854:274, 283, 289–92. Nott claimed that he could see the uniqueness of the American race just by walking the streets of Mobile, since it appeared to him that the heads of present-day Indians "strikingly contrast" with those of the "Anglo-Saxons, French, Spaniards and Negroes, among whom they were moving" (Nott and Gliddon 1854:290). Such claims were not atypical of the level of Nott's scientific "research" and were a point of weakness that his critics often targeted (Horsman 1987:199–200, 206–7).

218. Nott and Gliddon 1854:274, 288–89.

219. On Gliddon's role in the review, see Gliddon to Squier, April 9, 1854, EGS/LC, and Horsman 1987:179. After the review appeared, Gliddon—not one to miss an opportunity to pat himself on the back—wrote lavishly in its praise (Gliddon to Squier, April 30, 1854, EGS/LC).

220. Squier 1854; Squier to parents, October 20, 1856, quoted in Stanton 1960:193.

221. Gould 1981:70; Stanton 1960:162, 169–70, 174, 194; Gliddon to Squier, April 24, 1854, and Nott to Squier, April 30, 1854, EGS/LC. Horsman (1987:179) reports that within four months the book had sold 3,500 copies. It was destined to go through ten printings by 1871.

222. Henry to Haven, April 3, 1856, SFH/AAS.

223. Hinsley 1981:27–28. Squier's comments about the possibility of war are in Squier to parents, October 30, 1856, quoted in Stanton 1960:182. Henry's refusal to let Gliddon use the Smithsonian's lecture room led to an awkward encounter when they later bumped into each other in the halls of the Smithsonian. Gliddon smugly observed that Henry may have kept him from lecturing at the Smithsonian, but since his talk (given elsewhere) made front-page news, Henry couldn't avoid hearing about it at his own breakfast table (Gliddon to Squier, April 16, 1851, EGS/LC). Later, during the Civil War, Henry reluctantly permitted abolitionists such as Henry Ward Beecher and Horace Greeley to speak at the Smithsonian, but insisted that their lectures be preceded by the announcement that the institution was not responsible for the statements of the lecturers (Leech 1962:295).

224. Henry to Haven, December 8, 1855, and April 3, 1856, SFH/AAS. Also, Hinsley 1981:27, 37.

225. There were several angles to this latest skirmish: Henry and the board had decided to give Squier

and Davis two hundred copies of the book but no cash payment for their expenses (fearing the precedent that would be set by such a payment). They further stipulated that the books would not be turned over to Squier and Davis until they had settled their financial differences and could agree on how the books would be divided. Squier was still unhappy with the Smithsonian for not providing him with a financial remuneration, and though he and Davis were fighting over money and artifacts, he growled at the Regents that their dispute was irrelevant to the issue of the books, and none of the Regents' business. They agreed to split the two hundred copies evenly. The copies were released to them in February 1849 (Marsh to Squier, December 13 and 21, 1848; Henry to Squier, December 21, 1848, Squier to Smithsonian Institution Board of Regents, December 27, 1848, EGS/LC; Henry to Bartlett, December 16, 1848, JRB/JCBL; Henry to Squier, December 25, 1848, JHP/SIA. See also Rothenberg et al. 1996:441 nn. 2, 3, and Tax 1975:115.

226. Hinsley 1981:40–41; Tax 1973:233–63. Henry's support was both direct and tangible (funds, instruments, and a highly visible outlet for publications), as well as more subtle (he ensured a high profile for archaeology in the Smithsonian's publications, including the breaking discoveries in Europe confirming a deep human antiquity, and he subtly introduced standards into the discipline).

227. Morton to Squier, September 25, 1848, EGS/LC; Squier to Morton, September 27, 1848, SGM/HSP.

228. Marsh to Squier, January 7, 1848, Sparks to Squier, July 18, 1848, EGS/LC; Squier to Morton, September 27, 1848, SGM/HSP. Squier's efforts to solicit funds are discussed in Tax 1975:116.

229. Henry 1848:175, 182; Henry to Squier, September 30, 1848, JHP/SIA. As some measure of Henry's confidence, he promised the funds on his own responsibility and was prepared to pay them out of his own pocket if the Regents did not approve the expenditure. As a clear sign that Henry's management practices hadn't improved much in the intervening months, Squier again had to ask Marsh to intervene on his behalf to shake the promised money loose from Henry (see Marsh to Squier, December 13, 1848, EGS/LC; also Henry to Squier, December 16, 1848, JHP/SIA). The funds were actually put in Squier's hands on December 23, 1848 (Henry to Squier, December 21, 1848, EGS/LC).

230. Moore (New York Historical Society) to Squier, October 20, 1848, EGS/LC; Squier to Bartlett, October 26, November 7, 12, 1848, JRB/JCBL.

231. Morgan to Squier, December 22, 1848, EGS/LC. While Morgan and Squier kept up their correspondence, the map that Morgan offered ultimately was not published with Squier's report, but instead in Morgan's *League of the Iroquois* (Morgan 1851; see Tax 1973:210–11). Squier to Bartlett, November 7, 1848, JRB/JCBL.

232. Squier's New York monograph was accepted for publication by the Smithsonian in October 1849, but it did not appear until 1851 (Squier 1851a). Squier had received the papers of Rafinesque some two to three years earlier and published these notes (Squier 1849b) despite being "well aware of his [Rafinesque's] fanciful composition to attach any great degree of value to them, and sufficiently distrustful of his facts to avoid making any use of them, except in cases where I might be able to verify them" (Squier to Schoolcraft, February 5, 1849, HRS/LC). S. Williams, in Rafinesque's defense, notes that not everything Rafinesque "did or wrote was fraudulent" (personal communication, 1997). See also Williams 1991:ch. 5.

233. Squier to Morton, February 8, 1849, SGM/HSP. For an early inkling that Squier was looking toward Central America, see Squier to Morton, December 28, 1848, SGM/HSP.

234. Squier's efforts to win the post consumed virtually all of his energies and correspondence in February and March 1849, as the Squier Papers in the Library of Congress clearly illustrate. See Nott to Squier, March 8, 1849, EGS/LC; Squier to Henry, March 10, 1849, JHP/SIA; Tax 1973:212–13.

235. Henry to Squier, March 28, April 24, and October 30, 1849, Henry Desk Diary, May 1, 1849, JHP/SIA. Clayton to Squier, April 19, 1849, EGS/LC.

236. Burke 1848:288; Norton 1849:466. The ratio of Squier's name to Davis's name in Norton's review is about 30:1—in Burke's review, about 8:1. Squier's name or references directly to him occur on virtually every page of Norton's piece, and on some pages several times. Similarly, Burke spoke of the author of *Ancient Monuments* in the singular (Squier), not the plural. See also Rothenberg et al. 1996:525.

237. Davis to Henry, May 8, 1849, JHP/SIA. Davis had the satisfaction of a notice in the *New York Evening Express* of October 5, 1848, which lauded his fifteen years of effort, and the part-time assistance he had received from Squier. Squier wrote the reporter to give him the "true facts of the case" (Squier to the *New York Evening Express*, October 9, 1848, EGS/LC). Squier's letter was not intended for publication, and it does not appear that it was published.

238. Henry to Silliman, August 8, 1849, and Henry to Bache, May 11–12, 1849, JHP/SIA.

239. Davis to Henry, May 8, 1849, JHP/SIA. Bartlett to Squier, October 23, 1849, EGS/LC.

240. Davis to Morton, June 3, 1849, SGM/HSP. Davis had noticed that gallstones and kidney stones occurred in disproportionate numbers in the limestone bedrock areas of Ohio, as opposed to the areas of the state underlain by sandstone, slate, and coal. He attributed that difference to the excess amount of mineral bases in the limestone. The results of the calculus study appear in Davis 1850.

241. Davis to Schoolcraft, April 5, 1858, and Schoolcraft to Davis, April 8, 1858, HRS/LC. Squier and Schoolcraft clashed on several fronts; most important among them, they fundamentally disagreed on the relationship between the moundbuilders and the Indians (Schoolcraft thought them related), the unity of the human race (Schoolcraft was a staunch monogenist), and the direction and leadership of the American Ethnological Society in the wake of Gallatin's death (see Bieder 1986:129, 140; Bieder and Tax 1976:18; Tax 1975:121). In his multivolume *Historical and Statistical Information respecting the History, Condition, and Prospects of the Indian Tribes,* Schoolcraft frequently referred to Davis alone as the author of *Ancient Monuments* or to Squier as his assistant (e.g., Schoolcraft 1851:51–52, 1856:126). Schoolcraft's opinion that Squier was a "reptile" was prompted by a letter from Squier threatening a public reprisal for Schoolcraft's apparent "misstatements & perversions of fact, concerning myself, in your 'Historical Atlas on the History &c. of the Indian Tribes of N.A.'" (the offending passage appears in a footnote in Schoolcraft 1856:116), and vowing revenge by exposing Schoolcraft's "leech-like" hold on the public treasury, among other things. Squier's letter appeared anonymously in the *New York Herald* in January 1858, under the colorful title "Wasteful Extravagance in Public Printing—Costly Publication of Exploring Expeditions—Thousands of Dollars Squandered for Trash . . ." (Squier 1858a). Schoolcraft considered the letter "a piece of rude ribaldry" and unworthy of his notice (Squier to Schoolcraft, January 2, 1858, and note attached to same, dated January 17, 1858, HRS/LC).

242. As part of his efforts toward a canal, Squier had crafted an agreement with Nicaragua (Squier 1850). The agreement was never ratified by Congress, but it triggered the negotiations that eventually led to the Clayton Bulwer Treaty (Squier 1850; Williams 1935:489). Henry to Squier, October 3, 1850, EGS/LC. His books over this decade include Squier 1851b, 1852, 1855, 1856, 1858b.

243. On Henry's antipathy toward museums, see Hinsley 1981:64–65; Rothenberg et al. 1996:xxi. On Squier's efforts, see Tax 1973:120. Henry to Squier, December 5, 1850, EGS/LC.

244. Nott to Squier, July 1, 1857, EGS/LC; Stanton 1960:180; Stern 1953:33. Gliddon was destitute when he died, owing five hundred dollars to Nott and two thousand dollars to the publisher Lippincott and Company. Efforts to raise a subscription to relieve the financial hardship of his widow and child failed, largely because, Nott thought, Gliddon's books "have made him unpopular, as well all told him they must" (Nott to Squier, December 15 and 24, 1857, EGS/LC).

245. Stern 1953:25–27. I rely heavily here and below on Stern's important and fascinating biography of Miriam (Squier) Leslie.

246. Stern 1953:29–31.

247. Nott to Squier, August 22, 1860, EGS/LC. On Nott's efforts to establish the medical school, see Horsman 1987:237–45.

248. Nott to Squier, May 3, 1861, EGS/LC. Stanton 1960:183.

249. Henry's woes were many—income from the Smithsonian's investments in Tennessee and Virginia state bonds abruptly ceased, slicing his operating budget and forcing a sharp cutback in the popular winter lecture series. Abolitionists, politicians, inventors, and cranks (sometimes it was hard to tell the difference) daily demanded access to the Smithsonian's lecture hall (the largest in the city), testing Henry's fierce resolve to keep "political and sectarian subjects" from even appearing as though they were delivered under the institution's auspices. For a time the War Department threatened to take over Smithsonian rooms as temporary troop quarters, but it settled for using nearby fields as a firing range and a proving ground for Thaddeus Lowe's hot-air balloon. Henry laconically recorded Lowe's ascensions among the year's laboratory experiments. All of that happened in just 1861 (Henry 1862:13, 38, 47–48). Henry's *Annual Reports* over the next four years record many of the larger problems, but few of the thousands of minor ones that he faced. Leech (1941) paints an engaging portrait of Washington, D.C., during the Civil War.

250. Gibbs 1862. Also Hinsley 1981:51–55. Gibbs's "Instructions" were written between daily linguistic and natural history work and nightly guard duty at the Capitol (which was required in the months following the fall of Fort Sumter and until Union troops massed in Washington). The influence of *Ancient Monuments* was apparent in the "Instructions," particularly in the sections dealing with mounds and the importance of determining whether artifacts or physical remains found within them belonged to the moundbuilders or were later intrusions.

251. Nott to Squier, December 5, 1865, EGS/LC. The war years were hard on Nott, who served as a Confederate surgeon and medical inspector, lost two sons (at Shiloh and Chickamauga), and lived to read three of his own obituaries (Horsman 1987:276, 284–85; Stanton 1960:185, 187). The medical college did not return to its original use until 1868, after Nott had left Mobile (Horsman 1987:297).

252. Bieder 1986:142; Bieder and Tax 1976:15; Stern 1953:33, 47–49.

253. Bieder and Tax 1976:15–16; Squier 1871. Squier's *Circular* calling for the formation of the new society was sent out February 15, 1870; EGS/LC. On Nott's resignation, see Nott to Squier, October 28, 1872, EGS/LC.

254. Stern 1953:59–60, 62. Also Stanton 1960:184.

255. Stern 1953:63–65, 68. As Mrs. Frank Leslie, Miriam presided over lavish parties, entertaining governors, senators, U.S. presidents (Grant), and foreign dignitaries—including the occasional emperor. Her spending habits and taste for jewelry were legendary, but the social side of her personality should not mask her extraordinary abilities as a writer, editor, and, ultimately, publisher. The Leslie newspapers were financially crippled in the late 1870s, and after Frank died in 1880 Miriam inherited what remained, the debts included. Yet with the loan of fifty thousand dollars from a Brooklyn widow and with the timely help of some particularly gruesome news stories—the shooting and lingering death of President Garfield—she rebuilt the Leslie publishing empire. Over the next several decades, she presided over that empire, married twice more, and in the end left an estate valued at nearly two million dollars to Carrie Chapman Catt, "to the furtherance of the cause of women's suffrage" (Stern 1953:182).

256. Howe 1889:443.

257. Squier 1877; Stern 1953:69–70, 228. Squier had one final writing project in him. On July 14, 1878, a Nevada newspaper, the *Virginia City Territorial Enterprise*, incensed at Mrs. Leslie's comments about their city in a travel book she had just published, responded with a twenty-four-page pamphlet that reported, with excruciatingly malicious license, a detailed and very derogatory history of her marital infidelities, sordid divorces, and "life drama of crime and licentiousness" (Stern 1953:95–97). Frank Leslie hired a private detective to determine the source of the story, but the answer seems obvious. Ephraim Squier had come back from the dark recesses of his insanity, if only briefly, to write one more piece for publication. Curiously enough, Squier was not the only one of Miriam's husbands to go insane. Her first, David Charles Peacock, "died in a private asylum." As her biographer notes, Squier's wife "seemed to have a faculty for selecting gentlemen with unstable propensities, and a union with [her], whether brief or prolonged, was not calculated to increase the stamina of her husbands" (Stern 1953:17).

258. *New York Times*, 1888a, 1888b. Squier to parents, June 24, 1842, quoted in Tax 1975:102. Also Tax 1975:120–21.

259. Griffin 1973:vii. Given Henry's considerable antipathy toward and resistance to the idea of turning the Smithsonian into a museum, it is perhaps not surprising that the Smithsonian apparently made little significant effort (if any effort at all) to purchase Squier and Davis's collection. But Spencer Baird did chide Squier for not giving up some of his collection (Baird to Squier, June 9, 1873, EGS/LC). Materials that Squier collected in his travels across Latin America were purchased by the American Museum of Natural History in 1874. Davis presented plaster casts of some of his original collection to various U.S. museums (S. Williams, personal communication, 1997).

260. G. Brown Goode to Hon. William B. Allison, Chair, Senate Appropriations Committee, August 13, 1890, in Rhees 1901:1544.

261. *Ancient Monuments,* pp. xxxix and 71; also see pp. 30, 67 n, 69, 73, 75, and 135. Squier and Davis were certainly correct about Newark. Three pieces of it remain under the protection of the Ohio Historical Society in its Moundbuilders State Memorial, Octagon State Memorial, and Wright Earthworks State Memorial. Together these segments compose but a fraction of the original mound and earthwork complex (Bradley Lepper, personal communication, 1996).

262. Henry 1848:182.

263. Moorehead 1922:80–86; see also comments by Thomas 1898:133. Griffin 1973:viii; also Greber 1979:27; Kennedy 1994:239–41.

264. Fowke 1902:758; for specific errors, see e.g., Fowke 1902:55–58, 61, 86–87, 163, 168, 181, 184–86, 189, 193, 198, 202, 208, 215–17, etc. See also Henshaw 1883; Holmes 1892:368; Shetrone 1930:51, 201; Thomas 1894:27, 479, 562, 564, 566, 588, 602, 605, 625; and Thomas 1898:97, 131.

265. Moorehead 1892:11–12; 193. Shetrone, writing from the kinder vantage provided by history, better appreciated Squier and Davis's pioneering efforts (Shetrone 1930:200).

266. Thomas to Fowke, February 27, 1888, BAE/NAA. Shetrone 1930:23. Forty years later, Griffin repeated those words (1973), and they remain just as true today. Not surprisingly, an original edition of *Ancient Monuments* is now even harder to find than it was in 1930—and far more expensive.

267. *Ancient Monuments*, pp. 181, 301–2.

268. Haven 1856:141, 154–55, 158.

269. Squier and Davis 1848:305.

270. Grayson 1983; Meltzer 1983.

271. Darwin 1859:488.

272. Nott to Squier, August 22, 1860, EGS/LC. Nott had a much more favorable opinion of Spencer (Nott to Squier, September 27, 1868, EGS/LC).

273. Darwin 1871:I:235.

274. Thomas 1894.

REFERENCES

Afternoon Express
 1848 The first publication of the Smithsonian Institution. *Afternoon Express,* Monday, October 2, 1848. New York.

Allibone, S. A.
 1858 Davis, Edwin Hamilton. *A critical dictionary of English literature and British and American authors,* 1:483. Philadelphia: J. B. Lippincott.
 1870 Squier, Ephraim George. *A critical dictionary of English literature and British and American authors.* 2:2215–16. Philadelphia: J. B. Lippincott.

American Whig Review
 1850 Our foreign relations. Mr. E. G. Squier, Chargé d' affaires, Central America. N.s. 6:345–52.

Appletons' Cyclopaedia of American Biography
 1887 Davis, Edwin Hamilton. *Appleton's Cyclopaedia of American Biography.* New York: D. Appleton and Company.

Atwater, C.
 1820 Descriptions of the antiquities discovered in the State of Ohio and other western states. *Archaeologia Americana. Transactions and Collections of the American Antiquarian Society* 1:105–267.

Barnhart, T.
 1983 A question of authorship: The Ephraim George Squier–Edwin Hamilton Davis controversy. *Ohio History* 92:52–71.
 1989 Of mounds and men: The early anthropological career of Ephraim George Squier. Ph.D. diss., Department of History, Miami University, Oxford, Ohio.
 1994 James McBride: Historian and archaeologist of the Miami Valley. *Ohio History* 103:23–40.

Bieder, R. E.
 1975 Albert Gallatin and the survival of Enlightenment thought in nineteenth-century American anthropology. In *Toward a science of man: Essays in the history of anthropology,* edited by T. H. Thoresen, pp. 91–98. The Hague: Mouton.
 1986 *Science encounters the Indian, 1820–1880: The early years of American Ethnology.* Norman: University of Oklahoma Press.

Bieder, R. E., and T. G. Tax
 1976 From ethnologists to anthropologists: A brief history of the American Ethnological Society. In *American anthropology: The early years,* edited by J. V. Murra, pp. 11–22. St. Paul: West Publishing Co.

Bryant, W. C.
 1833 The prairies. *The Knickerbocker* 2:410–13.

Burke, L.
 1848a Progress of ethnology in the United States. *Ethnological Journal* 4:169–85. Reprinted in *Literary World* 3, no. 86 (September 23, 1848):663–65.

1848b Review of Ancient monuments of the Mississippi Valley, by E. G. Squier, A. M. and H. Davies [sic], M.D. *Ethnological Journal* 6:286–88.

1849 Ancient monuments of the Mississippi Valley. *Ethnological Journal* 8:376–88.

Clinton, D.

1814 Discourse delivered on the 6th of December, 1811. *Collections of the New York Historical Society* 2:37–116.

Darwin, C.

1859 *On the origin of species.* London: John Murray.

1871 *The descent of man.* London: John Murray.

Davis, E. H.

1847 Footprints and Indian sculpture. *American Journal of Science* 3:286–88.

1850 Report of the committee on the statistics of calculous disease in Ohio. *Transactions of the Ohio State Medical Society* [for 1850]:35–47.

1860 Exhibition of Indian relics and remarks upon them, before the American Ethnological Society, at two of its meetings, January 1859, and May 22, 1860. *Bulletin of the American Ethnological Society* 1.

1867 On ethnological research. *Smithsonian Institution Annual Report for 1866*:370–73.

Drake, F., ed.

1872 *Dictionary of American Biography.* Supplement. Boston: J. R. Osgood and Company.

Duponceau, P.

1819 Correspondence between Mr. Heckelwelder and Mr. Duponceau, on the language of the American Indian. *Transactions of the American Philosophical Society* 1:351–448.

Fowke, G.

1902 *Archaeological history of Ohio.* Columbus: Archaeological and Historical Society.

Gallatin, A.

1836 A synopsis of the Indian tribes of North America. *American Antiquarian Society Transactions and Collections* 2:1–422.

1845 Notes on the semi-civilized nations of Mexico, Yucatan, and Central America. *Transactions of the American Ethnological Society* 1:1–352.

Gibbs, G.

1862 Instructions for archaeological investigations in the U. States. *Smithsonian Institution Annual Report for 1861*:392–96.

Gould, S. J.

1981 *Mismeasure of man.* New York: W. W. Norton.

Grayson, D. K.

1983 *The establishment of human antiquity.* New York: Academic Press.

Greber, N.

1979 Comparative study of site morphology and burial patterns at Edwin Harness Mound and Seip Mounds 1 and 2. In *Hopewell archaeology: The Chillicothe conference,* edited by D. Brose and N. Greber, pp. 27–38. Kent State: Kent State University Press.

Griffin, J. B.

1973 Introduction to *Ancient monuments of the Mississippi Valley, comprising the results of extensive original surveys and explorations,* by E. G. Squier and E. H. Davis, pp. vii–ix. Cambridge, Mass.: AMS Press.

Harrison, W. H.

1839 A discourse on the aborigines of the Valley of Ohio. *Transactions of the Historical and Philosophical Society of Ohio* 1:217–67.

Haven, S. F.

1856 Archaeology of the United States. Smithsonian Contributions to Knowledge, vol. 8. Washington, D.C.: Smithsonian Institution.

Henry, J.

1848 Report of the Secretary of the Smithsonian Institution to the Board of Regents, December 8, 1847. *Smithsonian Institution Annual Report for 1847*:172–90.

1849 Report of the Secretary of the Smithsonian Institution to the Board of Regents, December 13, 1848. *Smithsonian Institution Annual Report for 1848*:10–21.

1862   Report of the Secretary. *Smithsonian Institution Annual Report for 1861:*13–48.

Henshaw, H. W.

1883   Animal carvings from mounds of the Mississippi Valley. *Bureau of Ethnology, Annual Report* 2:117–61.

Hinsley, C. M.

1981   *Savages and scientists. The Smithsonian Institution and the development of American anthropology, 1846–1910.* Washington, D.C.: Smithsonian Institution Press.

Holmes, W. H.

1892   Notes upon some geometric earthworks, with contour maps. *American Anthropologist* 5:363–73.

Horsman, R.

1987   *Josiah Nott of Mobile: Southerner, physician, and racial theorist.* Baton Rouge: Louisiana State University Press.

Hough, W.

1930   Davis, Edwin Hamilton. *Dictionary of American Biography* 5:113.

Howe, H.

1889   Some recollections of historic travel over New York, New Jersey, Virginia, and Ohio, in the seven years from 1840–1847. *Ohio Archaeological and Historical Quarterly* 2:419–49.

Jefferson, T.

1787   *Notes on the State of Virginia.* London: John Stockdale.

Kennedy, R.

1994   *Hidden cities: The discovery and loss of ancient North American civilization.* New York: Free Press.

Leech, M.

1941   *Reveille in Washington, 1860–1865.* New York: Harper and Row.

Lepper, B. T.

1995   *People of the mounds: Ohio's Hopewell culture.* Hopewell Culture National Historical Park, National Park Service.

Literary World

1847a   American archaeology. The first publication of the Smithsonian Institution. *Literary World* 2, no. 33:157–58 (September 18, 1847). Reprinted with the AES *Report* omitted in the *American Journal of Science* 4:438–39).

1847b   Recent publications. *Literary World* 2 (44):439 (December 4, 1847).

1848   The western mound builders. *Literary World* 3 (91):767–68 (October 28, 1848).

McCulloh, J. H.

1829   *Researches, philosophical and antiquarian, concerning the aboriginal history of America.* Baltimore: Fielding Lucas.

Meltzer, D. J.

1983   The antiquity of man and the development of American archaeology. In *Advances in archaeological method and theory,* edited by M. B. Schiffer, 6:1–51. New York: Academic Press.

Moorehead, W. K.

1892   *Primitive man in Ohio.* New York: G. P. Putnam's Sons.

1922   The Hopewell Mound group of Ohio. Field Museum of Natural History Publication 211, Anthropological Series, vol. 6, no. 5. Chicago: University of Chicago Press.

Morgan, L. H.

1851   *League of the Ho-de-no-sau-nee or Iroquois.* Rochester: Sage and Brothers.

Morton, S. G.

1839   *Crania Americana; or, a comparative view of the skulls of various aboriginal nations of North and South America, to which is prefixed an essay on the varieties of the human species.* Philadelphia: J. Dobson.

1844   *An inquiry into the distinctive characteristics of the aboriginal race of America.* 1842. 2d ed. Philadelphia: John Penington.

1846   Some observations on the ethnography and archaeology of the American aborigines. *American Journal of Science* 2:1–17.

1847   Hybridity in animals, considered in reference to the question of the unity of the human species. *American Journal of Science* 3:39–50, 203–12.

1853   Physical type of the American Indian. In *Historical and statistical information respecting the history, condition, and prospects of the Indian tribes of the United States,* by H. R. Schoolcraft, 2:315–31. Philadelphia: Lippincott, Grambo.

New York Evening Express

1848   The ethnological society. *New York Evening Express,* Thursday, October 5, 1848.

New York Times

1888a   Death of E. G. Squier. The close of the archaeologist's career after a long illness. April 18, 1888.

1888b   A loss to archaeology. Death of Edwin Hamilton Davis in this city. May 16, 1888.

Norton, C. E.

1849   Review of *Ancient monuments of the Mississippi Valley. North American Review* 67:466–96.

Nott, J. C.

1849   *Two lectures on the connection between the biblical and physical history of man.* New York: Bartlett and Welford.

Nott, J. C., and G. R. Gliddon

1854   *Types of mankind.* Philadelphia: Lippincott.

Patterson, J., and W. R. Stanton

1959   The Ephraim George Squier manuscripts in the Library of Congress: A checklist. *Papers of the Bibliographical Society of America* 53:309–26.

Phillips, J. S.

1853   Admeasurements of crania of the principal groups of Indians of the United States. In *Historical and statistical information respecting the history, condition, and prospects of the Indian tribes of the United States,* by H. R. Schoolcraft, 2:331–35. Philadelphia: Lippincott, Grambo.

Rhees, W. J.

1901   *The Smithsonian Institution. Documents relative to its origin and history, 1835–1899.* Washington, D.C.: Government Printing Office.

Rivinus, E. F. and E. M. Youssef

1992   *Spencer Baird of the Smithsonian.* Washington, D.C.: Smithsonian Institution Press.

Rothenberg, M., P. Theerman, K. Dorman, J. Rumm, and D. Yeffries

1996   *The Papers of Joseph Henry.* Vol. 7, January 1847–December 1849: The Smithsonian Years. Washington, D.C.: Smithsonian Institution Press.

Schoolcraft, H. R.

1851   *Historical and statistical information respecting the history, condition, and prospects of the Indian tribes of the United States.* Vol. 1. Philadelphia: Lippincott, Grambo.

1856   *Historical and statistical information respecting the history, condition, and prospects of the Indian tribes of the United States.* Vol. 4. Philadelphia: Lippincott, Grambo.

Scientfic American

1848   The Smithsonian Institute [sic]. *Scientific American* 3:157 (February 5, 1848).

Scioto Gazette

1847   Antiquities of the Old and New Worlds. May 10, 1847.

Seitz, D. C.

1911   *Letters from Francis Parkman to E. G. Squier.* Cedar Rapids, Iowa: Torch Press.

Shetrone, H. C.

1930   *The Mound-builders.* New York: D. Appleton and Company.

Silverberg, R.

1968   *Mound builders of Ancient America: The archaeology of a myth.* New York: Graphic Society.

Squier, E. G.

1843   *The Chinese as they are: Their moral and social character.* Albany: George Jones.

1845   American antiquities. *Scioto Gazette,* October 23, 1845, pp. 1–2.

1846a   On the discoidal stones of the Indian mounds. *American Journal of Science* 2:216–18.

1846b   Pipestone of the ancient pipes of the Indian mounds. *American Journal of Science* 2:287.

1846c   Discoidal stones. *American Journal of Science* 2:287–88.

1847a   Observations on the uses of the mounds of the west, with an attempt at their classification. *American Journal of Science* 3:237–48.

1847b   Observations on the aboriginal monuments of the Mississippi Valley. *Transactions of the American Ethnological Society* 2:131–207.

1849a　American ethnology: Being a summary of the results which have followed the investigation of this subject. *American Review* 9:385–98.

1849b　A monograph of the ancient monuments of the state of Kentucky. *American Journal of Science* 8:1–14.

1850　The Great Ship Canal question. England and Costa Rica *versus* the United States and Nicaragua. *American Whig Review* n.s. 6:441–55.

1851a　Aboriginal monuments of the state of New York. Smithsonian Contributions to Knowledge, vol. 2. Washington, D.C.: Smithsonian Institution.

1851b　*Serpent symbol and the worship of the reciprocal principles of nature in America.* American Archaeological Researches, vol. 1. New York: Putnam.

1852　*Nicaragua: Its people, scenery, monuments, and the proposed interoceanic canal.* 2 vols. New York: D. Appleton.

1854　Review of *Types of mankind,* by J. Nott and G. Gliddon. *New York Herald,* April 23, 1854.

1855　*Notes on Central America, particularly the states of Honduras and San Salvador: Their geography, topography, climate, population, resources, productions, etc. etc., and the proposed Honduras Interoceanic Railway.* New York: Harper and Brothers.

1856　*Waikna; or, adventures on the Mosquito shore.* London: Sampson Low, Son and Company.

1858a　Wasteful extravagance in public printing—Costly publication of exploring expeditions—Thousands of dollars squandered for trash—The cost of a parrot—Review of the publication of surveys and explorations. *New York Herald,* January 17, 1858.

1858b　*The states of Central America; their geography, topography, climate, population, resources, productions, commerce, political organization, aborigines, etc., etc.* [An enlarged edition of Squier 1855.] New York: Harper and Brothers.

1871　Proceedings preliminary to the organization of the Anthropological Institute of New York. *Journal of the Anthropological Institute of New York* 1:14–20.

1877　*Peru: Incidents of travel and exploration in the land of the Incas.* New York: Harper and Brothers.

Squier, E. G., and E. H. Davis

1848　Ancient monuments of the Mississippi Valley, comprising the results of extensive original surveys and explorations. Smithsonian Contributions to Knowledge, vol. 1. Washington, D.C.: Smithsonian Institution.

Stanton, W.

1960　*The leopard's spots: Scientific attitudes toward race in America, 1815–1859.* Chicago: University of Chicago Press.

Stern, Madeleine B.

1953　*Purple passage. The life of Mrs. Frank Leslie.* Norman: University of Oklahoma Press.

Tax, T. G.

1973　The development of American archaeology, 1800–1879. Ph.D. diss., Department of History, University of Chicago.

1975　E. G. Squier and the mounds. In *Toward a science of man: Essays in the history of anthropology,* edited by T. H. Thoresen, pp. 99–124. The Hague: Mouton.

Thomas, C.

1894　Report on the mound explorations of the Bureau of Ethnology. *Bureau of Ethnology, Annual Report* 12:1–735.

1898　Introduction to the study of North American archaeology. Cincinnati: Robert Clarke Company.

Wauchope, R.

1962　*Lost tribes and sunken continents.* Chicago: University of Chicago Press.

Willey, G. R., and J. A. Sabloff

1993　*A history of American archaeology.* 3d ed. New York: W. H. Freeman.

Williams, M. W.

1935　Squier, Ephraim George. *Dictionary of American Biography* 17:488–89.

Williams, S.

1991　*Fantastic archaeology.* Philadelphia: University of Pennsylvania Press.

Woodward, S. L., and J. N. McDonald
    1986   *Indian mounds of the Middle Ohio Valley: A guide to Adena and Ohio Hopewell sites.* Newark,
            Ohio: McDonald and Woodward Publishing Company.
Woolsey, T. D.
    1849   Monuments of the Mississippi Valley. *New Englander and Yale Review* 7:95–109.

ACKNOWLEDGMENTS.

MY good friend and colleague Smithsonian Institution archaeologist Bruce D. Smith originally planned to write this introduction, but then decided against it after hearing a paper of mine at the 1996 SAA meetings. He graciously insisted that I could do the job better, and though I didn't believe him, I appreciated the flattery.

Bruce's partner in arm-twisting was another good friend, Daniel Goodwin, former director of the Smithsonian Institution Press. Daniel—as he had already done twice before—cheerily dismissed my excuse that I couldn't possibly write this introduction until I'd finished my long-promised opus on the history of the human antiquity controversy. Daniel also has my thanks for helping me acquire key sources and for arranging my visit to essential archives—thereby putting me in Washington just in time for the Smithsonian Institution's 150th anniversary gala.

Others who provided references, ideas, and good advice were Alex Barker, Terry Barnhart, Robert C. Dunnell, Donald K. Grayson, Bradley T. Lepper, Marc Rothenberg, and Bruce Smith. Billie Stovall, of SMU's Interlibrary Loan office, Frank Millikan of the Joseph Henry Papers, and Bob Lockhart of the Smithsonian Institution Press tracked down many hard-to-acquire sources. This introduction benefited from thoughtful readings by Lepper, Smith, Stephen Williams, and the late James B. Griffin.

Griffin's comments, offered at a time when his health was failing, were helpful, incisive, witty, and wry, as was his custom. With his passing last year, we celebrate more than sixty years of contributions to American archaeology and mourn the loss of a living link to the past. For when Griffin was a young man, he walked the Fort Ancient site with Warren K. Moorehead. Moorehead, in turn, had been around the Ohio Historical Society with Henry Hyde, who had once stood on the banks of the Scioto, chatting with Squier and Davis while they engaged in the fieldwork that became *Ancient Monuments*.

I began work on this introduction in the field in Alaska, continued it in archives on the East Coast, and finished it here in Dallas. Along the way, the hospitality of friends and family eased the travel and the task: in geographic order, my thanks to Mike Kunz, Rick Reanier, the late Jean Siegel, Stephen and Florence Meltzer, Jeanne and Murray Halfond, and Peter and Anne Meltzer. Here in Dallas, Suzanne, Emily, and Ethan let me overwhelm the home office and computer with *Ancient*

Monuments. They have my thanks, given with the full knowledge that they are just as glad to be done with the undertaking as I am.

Research for this project was supported by a Research Fellowship Leave from SMU, the Southern Methodist University Fund for Faculty Excellence, and the Smithsonian Institution Press.

SMITHSONIAN

CONTRIBUTIONS TO KNOWLEDGE.

VOL. I.

EVERY MAN IS A VALUABLE MEMBER OF SOCIETY, WHO, BY HIS OBSERVATIONS, RESEARCHES, AND EXPERIMENTS, PROCURES KNOWLEDGE FOR MEN.—SMITHSON.

CITY OF WASHINGTON:

PUBLISHED BY THE SMITHSONIAN INSTITUTION.

MDCCCXLVIII.

ANCIENT WORKS, MARIETTA, OHIO,

Chas. Sullivan, del.

From an Original painting in possession of A. Nye Esq Marietta.

LITH. OF SARONY & MAJOR DIVISION ST. N.Y.

ADVERTISEMENT.

THIS volume is intended to form the first of a series of volumes, consisting of original memoirs on different branches of knowledge published at the expense, and under the direction of the Smithsonian Institution. The publication of this series forms part of a general plan adopted for carrying into effect the benevolent intentions of JAMES SMITHSON, Esq., of England. This gentleman left his property in trust to the United States of America, to found at Washington an institution which should bear his own name, and have for its objects "the *increase* and *diffusion* of knowledge among men." This trust was accepted by the Government of the United States, and an Act of Congress was passed August 10th, 1846, constituting the President and the other principal executive officers of the general government, the Chief Justice of the Supreme Court, the Mayor of Washington, and such other persons as they might elect honorary members, an establishment under the name of the "SMITHSONIAN INSTITUTION, FOR THE INCREASE AND DIFFUSION OF KNOWLEDGE AMONG MEN." The members and honorary members of this establishment are to hold stated and special meetings for the supervision of the affairs of the Institution, and for the advice and instruction of a Board of Regents, to whom the financial and other affairs are entrusted.

The Board of Regents consists of three members ex officio of the establishment, namely, the Vice President of the United States, the Chief Justice of the Supreme Court, and the Mayor of Washington, together with twelve other members, three of whom are appointed by the Senate from its own body, three by the House of Representatives from its members, and six citizens appointed by a joint resolution of both houses. To this board is given the power of electing a Secretary and other officers, for conducting the active operations of the Institution.

To carry into effect the purposes of the testator, the plan of organization should evidently embrace two objects,—one, the increase of knowledge by the addition of new truths to the existing stock ; the other, the diffusion of knowledge thus increased, among men. No restriction is made in favor of any kind of knowledge, and hence each branch is entitled to and should receive a share of attention.

The Act of Congress, establishing the Institution, directs, as a part of the plan of organization, the formation of a Library, a Museum, and a Gallery of Art, together with provisions for physical research and popular lectures, while it leaves to the Regents the power of adopting such other parts of an organization as they may deem best suited to promote the objects of the bequest.

After much deliberation, the Regents resolved to divide the annual income, thirty thousand nine hundred and fifty dollars, into two equal parts,—one part to be devoted to the increase and diffusion of knowledge by means of original research and publications,—the other half of the income to be applied in accordance with the requirements of the Act of Congress, to the gradual formation of a Library, a Museum, and a Gallery of Art.

The following are the details of the two parts of the general plan of organization provisionally adopted at the meeting of the Regents, Dec. 8th, 1847.

DETAILS OF THE FIRST PART OF THE PLAN.

I. To INCREASE KNOWLEDGE.—*It is proposed to stimulate research, by offering rewards, consisting of money, medals, etc., for original memoirs on all subjects of investigation.*

1. The memoirs thus obtained to be published in a series of volumes, in a quarto form, and entitled "Smithsonian Contributions to Knowledge."

2. No memoir, on subjects of physical science, to be accepted for publication, which does not furnish a positive addition to human knowledge, resting on original research; and all unverified speculations to be rejected.

3. Each memoir presented to the Institution to be submitted for examination to a commission of persons of reputation for learning in the branch to which the memoir pertains; and to be accepted for publication only in case the report of this commission is favorable.

4. The commission to be chosen by the officers of the Institution, and the name of the author, as far as practicable, concealed, unless a favorable decision be made.

5. The volumes of the memoirs to be exchanged for the Transactions of literary and scientific societies, and copies to be given to all the colleges, and principal libraries, in this country. One part of the remaining copies may be offered for sale; and the other carefully preserved, to form complete sets of the work, to supply the demand from new institutions.

6. An abstract, or popular account, of the contents of these memoirs to be given to the public through the annual report of the Regents to Congress.

II. To increase knowledge.—*It is also proposed to appropriate a portion of the income, annually, to special objects of research, under the direction of suitable persons.*

1. The objects, and the amount appropriated, to be recommended by counsellors of the Institution.

2. Appropriations in different years to different objects; so that in course of time, each branch of knowledge may receive a share.

3. The results obtained from these appropriations to be published, with the memoirs before mentioned, in the volumes of the Smithsonian Contributions to Knowledge.

4. Examples of objects for which appropriations may be made:

(1.) System of extended meteorological observations for solving the problem of American storms.

(2.) Explorations in descriptive natural history, and geological, magnetical, and topographical surveys, to collect materials for the formation of a Physical Atlas of the United States.

(3.) Solution of experimental problems, such as a new determination of the weight of the earth, of the velocity of electricity, and of light; chemical analyses of soils and plants; collection and publication of articles of science, accumulated in the offices of Government.

(4.) Institution of statistical inquiries with reference to physical, moral, and political subjects.

(5.) Historical researches, and accurate surveys of places celebrated in American history.

(6.) Ethnological researches, particularly with reference to the different races of men in North America; also explorations, and accurate surveys, of the mounds and other remains of the ancient people of our country.

I. To diffuse knowledge.—*It is proposed to publish a series of reports, giving an account of the new discoveries in science, and of the changes made from year to year in all branches of knowledge not strictly professional.*

1. Some of these reports may be published annually, others at longer intervals, as the income of the Institution or the changes in the branches of knowledge may indicate.

2. The reports are to be prepared by collaborators, eminent in the different branches of knowledge.

3. Each collaborator to be furnished with the journals and publications, domestic and foreign, necessary to the compilation of his report; to be paid a certain sum for his labors, and to be named on the title-page of the report.

4. The reports to be published in separate parts, so that persons interested in a particular branch, can procure the parts relating to it without purchasing the whole.

5. These reports may be presented to Congress, for partial distribution, the remaining copies to be given to literary and scientific institutions, and sold to individuals for a moderate price.

The following are some of the subjects which may be embraced in the reports:

I. PHYSICAL CLASS.

1. Physics, including astronomy, natural philosophy, chemistry, and meteorology.
2. Natural history, including botany, zoology, geology, &c.
3. Agriculture.
4. Application of science to arts.

II. MORAL AND POLITICAL CLASS.

5. Ethnology, including particular history, comparative philology, antiquities, &c.
6. Statistics and political economy.
7. Mental and moral philosophy.
8. A survey of the political events of the world; penal reform, &c.

III. LITERATURE AND THE FINE ARTS.

9. Modern literature.
10. The fine arts, and their application to the useful arts.
11. Bibliography.
12. Obituary notices of distinguished individuals.

II. To DIFFUSE KNOWLEDGE.—*It is proposed to publish occasionally separate treatises on subjects of general interest.*

1. These treatises may occasionally consist of valuable memoirs translated from foreign languages, or of articles prepared under the direction of the Institution, or procured by offering premiums for the best exposition of a given subject.

2. The treatises to be submitted to a commission of competent judges, previous to their publication.

DETAILS OF THE SECOND PART OF THE PLAN OF ORGANIZATION.

This part contemplates the formation of a Library, a Museum, and a Gallery of Art.

1. To carry out the plan before described, a library will be required, consisting, 1st, of a complete collection of the transactions and proceedings of all the learned societies in the world; 2d, of the more important current periodical publications, and other works necessary in preparing the periodical reports.

2. The Institution should make special collections, particularly of objects to verify its own publications. Also a collection of instruments of research in all branches of experimental science.

3. With reference to the collection of books, other than those mentioned above, catalogues of all the different libraries in the United States should be procured, in order that the valuable books first purchased may be such as are not to be found elsewhere in the United States.

4. Also catalogues of memoirs, and of books in foreign libraries, and other materials, should be collected for rendering the Institution a centre of bibliographical knowledge, whence the student may be directed to any work which he may require.

5. It is believed that the collections in natural history will increase by donation as rapidly as the income of the Institution can make provisions for their reception, and, therefore, it will seldom be necessary to purchase any articles of this kind.

6. Attempts should be made to procure for the gallery of art casts of the most celebrated articles of ancient and modern sculpture.

7. The arts may be encouraged by providing a room, free of expense, for the exhibition of the objects of the Art-Union and other similar societies.

8. A small appropriation should annually be made for models of antiquities, such as those of the remains of ancient temples, &c.

9. For the present, or until the building is fully completed, only one permanent assistant to the Secretary will be required, to act as librarian.

10. The Secretary and his assistants, during the session of Congress, will be required to illustrate new discoveries in science, and to exhibit new objects of art; distinguished individuals should also be invited to give lectures on subjects of general interest.

11. When the building is completed, and when, in accordance with the Act of Congress, the charge of the National Museum is given to the Smithsonian Institution, other assistants will be required.

――――

The first memoir of the proper character presented after the adoption of the foregoing plan of organization, was the one which occupies the present volume.

It was submitted in accordance with the rule adopted, to a commission of examination, consisting of a committee of the members of the American Ethnological Society, and on the favorable report of this committee and the responsibility of the Society, the memoir was accepted for publication.   The following is the correspondence which took place on the occasion.

CORRESPONDENCE, ETC.

CHILLICOTHE, OHIO, *May* 15, 1847.

DEAR SIR:—It is proposed in the recognized plan of organization of the Smithsonian Institution, of which you are the executive officer, to publish, under the title of " *Smithsonian Contributions to Knowledge,*" such original papers and memoirs " as shall constitute valuable additions to the sum of human knowledge."   Under the belief that it falls legitimately within the scope of the above plan, the undersigned herewith submit for acceptance and publication, subject to the prescribed rules of the Institution, a MS. memoir entitled " ANCIENT MONUMENTS OF THE MISSISSIPPI VALLEY, *comprising the results of Extensive Original Surveys and Explorations :* by E. G. SQUIER and E. H. DAVIS."   The extent of these investigations, and their general character, are sufficiently indicated in the prefatory remarks to the volume.   With high consideration, we are truly yours,   E. G. SQUIER,

" JOSEPH HENRY, ESQ., Secretary Smithsonian Institution.   E. H. DAVIS."

———

Princeton, June 2, 1847.

" DEAR SIR:—I am authorized by the Regents of the Smithsonian Institution, to publish, in the numbers of the ' *Smithsonian Contributions to Knowledge,*' any memoir which may be presented for this purpose, provided, that, on a careful examination by a commission of competent judges, the memoir shall be found to be a new and interesting addition to knowledge, resting on original research.   The accompanying memoir, entitled ' ANCIENT MONUMENTS OF THE MISSISSIPPI VALLEY,' etc. etc., having been presented for publication, I beg leave to refer the same, through you, to the American Ethnological Society, with the request that a committee of the members may be appointed to examine and report on the character of the work, with reference to the particulars above mentioned.   If the report of the committee be favorable, the memoir, without further consideration, will be accepted for publication ; full confidence being placed in the ability of the committee to judge of the article, and in their caution in making up their opinion.

" I have the honor to be, very respectfully,

" Your ob't servant,   JOSEPH HENRY,

" Secretary Smithsonian Inst.

" Hon. ALBERT GALLATIN, President American Ethnological Society."

———

" *New York,* June 12, 1847.

" DEAR SIR :—I have the honor to enclose a copy of the proceedings and resolutions of the New York Ethnological Society, upon the MS. work on American Antiquities, by Messrs. E. G. Squier and E. H. Davis, submitted with your letter of the 2d instant.

" I approve entirely of the resolutions and recommendations of the Society.   The publication of Mr. C. Atwater, in the first volume of the Transactions of the American Antiquarian Society of Worcester, which appeared twenty years ago, is as yet, so far as I know, the only general account of the antiquarian remains of the West, which is entitled to any credit.   Yet, many mistakes have been discovered in it, and it is very incomplete, and in no degree to be compared to the extensive researches of the gentlemen above mentioned.   What has particularly recommended their labors to me is their love of truth.

" Such are the combined effects of the fondness for the marvellous, of the illusions of the imagination, of credulity, thirst of notoriety and lack of discrimination, that, in many specific statements, and in almost all the general accounts of our Western antiquities, which I have seen, the most vague and fabulous reports (independent of most groundless theories), and even flagrant impositions, are so mixed with true accounts, as to render it almost impossible, even for the American reader, to make the proper discrimination, or arrive at a correct estimate of their extent or character.

" Whatever may be the intrinsic value of the remains of former times which are found in the United States, it is necessary that they should at least be correctly described, and that existing gross errors should be corrected ; and I repeat my conviction that, though ardent, Messrs. Squier and Davis are animated by that thorough love of truth, which renders their researches worthy of entire confidence.

" Late Ethnological researches have thrown such light on the History of Man, that it is unnecessary to dwell on their general utility. With respect to those which relate to the Indians of the United States, I am ready to acknowledge, the field is comparatively barren, and the results hitherto attained neither satisfactory nor refreshing. Still, with proper caution, important information may be acquired, on what man, insulated, and without intercourse with other nations, can, by his solitary efforts, accomplish. In order, however, to attain these results, considerations, foreign to the immediate object of this letter, are required, which may hereafter be made the subject of another communication.

" I have the honor to be, &c.

" ALBERT GALLATIN.

" Professor J. HENRY, Secretary Smithsonian Institution."

" At a regular meeting of the American Ethnological Society, held at the house of Hon. ALBERT GALLATIN, on the evening of the 4th of June, the President laid before the members a communication from Professor J. HENRY, Secretary of the Smithsonian Institution ; transmitting for the examination and opinion of the Society, a MS. work on the Ancient Monuments of the Mississippi Valley. On motion, the letter and accompanying MS. were referred to a committee, consisting of EDWARD ROBINSON, D.D., JOHN R. BARTLETT, Professor W. W. TURNER, SAMUEL G. MORTON, M.D., and Hon. GEORGE P. MARSH, to report upon the same. At a subsequent meeting of this Society, the committee submitted the following Report and Resolutions, which were unanimously accepted and adopted :—

"REPORT.

" The Committee of the American Ethnological Society, to which was referred the communication of the Secretary of the Smithsonian Institution, transmitting a manuscript work entitled ' ANCIENT MONUMENTS OF THE MISSISSIPPI VALLEY ; *comprising the Results of Extensive Original Surveys and Explorations,* by E. G. SQUIER and E. H. DAVIS,' beg leave to report that—

" They have examined the work in question, and regard it not only as a new and interesting, but an eminently valuable addition to our stock of knowledge on a subject little understood, but in which is felt a deep and constantly increasing interest, both in our country and abroad. In their judgment the work is worthy of the subject, and highly creditable to the authors. Its chief features are, a scientific arrangement, simplicity and directness of statement, and legitimate deduction of facts, while there is no attempt at mere speculation or theory. If published, it will be an enduring monument to connect the names of the investigators in honorable and lasting remembrance with the great subject of American Archæology.

" The existence and progress of these investigations were made known to the Society by correspondence, early in the year 1846 ; and in June of that year, specimens of the relics recovered, accompanied by numerous maps and plans of ancient Earthworks and Sectional Views of the Mounds from which the remains were taken, were laid before the Society by Mr. Squier in person. These excited deep interest and surprise in all who saw them ; and the Society immediately took measures to encourage further investigation, and secure the publication, under its own auspices, of the important results already obtained. A few months later, the chairman of the present committee, being in Ohio, was enabled, through the kindness of Messrs. Squier and Davis, to visit several of the more important monuments in the immediate vicinity of Chillicothe ; and among these ' Mound City,' so called, from which very many of the minor relics and specimens were procured. He was struck with the accuracy of the plans and drawings as well as of the accounts which had been laid before the Society ; and bears full testimony to the fidelity and integrity with which the process of investigation and delineation has been conducted.

" During the last and present season the researches of these gentlemen have been actively prosecuted and widely extended, and the above work, largely illustrated, comprising the results, has been prepared. These results are so numerous and important, and consequently such is the extent and magnitude of the work itself, as to put its publication beyond any means which the Society can command. Under these circumstances, your Committee learn with pleasure that preliminary arrangements have been made for its publication by the Smithsonian Institution, among its ' Contributions to Knowledge.' It can only be a matter of sincere gratification to this Society, to see that which it cannot itself accomplish for the history and antiquities of our country, taken up and carried out under such favorable auspices ; and they cannot but rejoice that an opportunity is thus afforded to that noble institution of opening its high career, by fostering scientific research into the interesting problems connected with the Ante-Columbian history and Ancient Monuments of our own country.

" In view of these facts, your Committee would recommend the adoption of the following resolutions by the Society :—

" *Resolved*, That this Society regard the researches of Messrs. Squier and Davis, as of very great importance in American Archæology, and as casting much light upon our Aboriginal Antiquities, especially upon the character and habits of the earliest races which had their seat in the Mississippi Valley.

" *Resolved*, That we regard the work prepared upon this subject, as one of great general interest, and as worthy to be adopted for publication by the Smithsonian Institution, both as resting on original researches, and as affording remarkable illustrations of the history of the American Continent.

" Your Committee would also append to this Report, the accompanying letters from Samuel G. Morton, M.D., of Philadelphia, and Hon. George P. Marsh, of Vermont, both members of this Society, and joint members of this Committee.

" All of which is respectfully submitted.   EDWARD ROBINSON,
                                                               JOHN R. BARTLETT,   } *Committee.*
" *New York*, June, 1847."   W. W. TURNER,

———

" *New-York.* June 9th, 1847.

" I have examined, with much interest and attention, the manuscripts, drawings, and ancient remains in the possession of Mr. E. G. SQUIER, and am happy to say that my previous impressions concerning the value of the researches of that gentleman and his associate, are fully confirmed. It is fortunate for the cause of American Archæology, that the systematic attempt at its elucidation should have been conceived and executed in so truly philosophical a spirit ; and, rich as this age already is in antiquarian lore, it has, I think, received few more important contributions than that which the enlightened and generous zeal of these two private gentlemen is about to confer upon it. The Smithsonian Collection could not begin with a more appropriate or creditable essay ; and I hope that every facility may be afforded to the investigators, in bringing before the public the results of their honorable labors, in as suitable a form and with as little delay as possible.   (Signed)   GEO. P. MARSH."

———

" *Philadelphia*, June 8, 1847.

" ' As a Member of the Committee of the American Ethnological Society, appointed to report on the Memoir on American Archæology, by Messrs. E. G. SQUIER and E. H. DAVIS, I have great pleasure in saying, that after a careful and repeated inspection of the materials in the hands of those gentlemen, I am convinced they constitute by far the most important contribution to the Archæology of the United States, that has ever been offered to the public. The number and accuracy of their plans, sketches, &c., have both interested and surprised me ; and it is gratifying to learn that the preliminary arrangements have been made for their publication under the honorable auspices of the Smithsonian Institution.
                              (Signed)   " SAMUEL GEORGE MORTON."

To ensure accuracy in the present volume, the plates and engravings have been prepared under the supervision of Mr. E. G. SQUIER, who has also had the general direction of the press. The sheets as they were printed, were also examined by Professor W. W. TURNER, of New York, and Mr. F. A. TEALL. The wood engravings were executed by Messrs. ORR & RICHARDSON, and Mr. J. W. ORR, from drawings on the blocks, chiefly by WM. WADE and Mr. HAMILTON BROWN. The Lithographic engraving was executed by Messrs. SARONY & MAJOR, and the printing by Mr. E. O. JENKINS.

REGENTS.

GEORGE M. DALLAS, ... *Vice President of the United States.*

ROGER B. TANEY, ... *Chief Justice* " "

WILLIAM W. SEATON, ... *Mayor of the City of Washington.*

JAMES A. PEARCE, ... *Member of the Senate of the United States*

SIDNEY BREESE, ... " " " " "

JEFFERSON DAVIS, ... " " " " "

HENRY W. HILLIARD, ... *Member of the House of Representatives*

GEORGE P. MARSH, ... " " "

ROBERT MCCLELLAND, ... " " "

RUFUS CHOATE, ... *Citizen of Massachusetts.*

GIDEON HAWLEY, ... " *New York.*

WILLIAM C. PRESTON, ... " *South Carolina.*

RICHARD RUSH, ... " *Pennsylvania.*

ALEXANDER D. BACHE, ... *Mem. of Nat. Inst., Washington.*

JOSEPH G. TOTTEN, ... " " "

MEMBERS EX OFFICIO OF THE INSTITUTION.

JAMES K. POLK, ... *President of the United States.*

GEORGE M. DALLAS, ... *Vice President of the United States.*

JAMES BUCHANAN, ... *Secretary of State of the United States.*

ROBERT J. WALKER, ... *Secretary of the Treasury* "

WILLIAM L. MARCY, ... *Secretary of War* "

JOHN Y. MASON, ... *Secretary of the Navy* "

CAVE JOHNSON, ... *Post Master General* "

ISAAC TOUCEY, ... *Attorney General* "

ROGER B. TANEY, ... *Chief Justice* "

EDMUND BURKE, ... *Commissioner of Patents* "

WILLIAM W. SEATON, ... *Mayor of the City of Washington.*

HONORARY MEMBERS OF THE INSTITUTION.

[No Honorary Members have yet been elected.]

ANCIENT MONUMENTS

OF

THE MISSISSIPPI VALLEY:

COMPRISING THE RESULTS OF

EXTENSIVE ORIGINAL SURVEYS AND EXPLORATIONS.

BY

E. G. SQUIER, A.M., AND E. H. DAVIS, M.D.

ACCEPTED FOR PUBLICATION
BY THE SMITHSONIAN INSTITUTION,
JUNE, 1847.

CONTENTS.

LIST OF PLATES.

LITHOGRAPHERS.—Sarony & Major, 117 Fulton street, New York.

WOOD ENGRAVERS.—Orr & Richardson, 90 Fulton street, do,

PRINTER.—Edward O. Jenkins, 114 Nassau street.   do.

LIST OF WOOD ENGRAVINGS.

PREFACE.

The fact of the existence, within the valley of the Mississippi river and its tributaries, of many ancient monuments of human labor and skill, seems to have escaped the notice of the adventurers who first made known to the world the extent and fertility of that vast region. Except some incidental allusions by La Vega, and the Portuguese chronicler of De Soto's unfortunate expedition, to structures bearing some analogy to those of the West, (and which seem to have been occupied, if they were not built, by the Indians of Florida,) we find no mention made of these monuments by any of the earlier explorers. No sooner, however, had trade been opened with the Indians beyond the Alleghanies, and the valley of the Mississippi begun to attract the attention of the rival nations that laid claim to this division of the continent, than the less prominent features of the country became subjects of observation and remark. Then, for the first time, we find these ancient monuments distinctly alluded to. It was not however until some time afterwards, when settlements had been established at various prominent points within the valley, and the tide of emigration began to flow thitherward, that any special attention was directed to them. Carver in 1776, and Hearte and others in 1791, were among the earliest of these observers at the North. Their accounts, however, served scarcely to make known the existence of these remains, and failed to convey any clear idea of their extent or character. But as the country became better known and more densely populated, notices of their exist-ence became more numerous, and some detailed accounts of particular groups were presented to the world, in the form of incidental notices in books of travel and local gazetteers, or in contributions to the pages of periodicals, and to the transactions of learned societies. HARRIS, in his "*Tour into the Territory north-west of the Ohio*," published in 1805, noticed at considerable length the ancient remains at Marietta on the Ohio river; and H. H. BRACKENRIDGE, one of the most accurate of the early explorers of the West, in his "*Views of Louisiana*," published in 1814, and in a paper in the first volume of the new series of the Transactions of the "American Philosophical Society," presented accounts of ancient remains at various points, together with some general remarks upon our antiquities, distinguished for their comprehensiveness and sound philosophical spirit. Bishop MADISON of Virginia, in 1803, addressed to Dr. Barton, then Vice President of the American Philosophical Society, a communication of considerable length "upon the supposed fortifications of the western country," which was published in the sixth volume of the old series of the Transactions of that institution. It contains some interesting facts relative to the ancient remains found within the valley of the great Kenhawa river, in Virginia, and is principally devoted to combating the popular notion that *all* the ancient earthworks were of defensive origin. BARTRAM, in his animated Journal of Travels in Florida, published in 1779, makes frequent mention of the ancient remains which fell under his notice. His accounts have been amply confirmed by later observations, and they may be regarded as presenting a very accurate view of their general character. Previous to Bartram's expedition, Adair, in his "Account of the American Indians," published in 1775, mentioned the existence of these remains, but gave no details respecting them.

In 1817, DE WITT CLINTON, whose active mind neglected no department of inquiry, read a paper before the "Literary and Philosophical Society of New York," (an institution no longer existing,) upon the "Antiquities of the western part of New York," which was subsequently published in a pamphlet form. It gave a connected view of these antiquities so far as then known, and indicated their character with such clearness, as to identify them at once as belonging to that imposing class of remains found in the valley of the Mississippi. McCAULEY, in his "*History of New York*," published at a later period, (1829,) added considerably to the number of facts presented by Mr. CLINTON.

Among the earliest and more important contributions to the general stock of information respecting the western monuments, is the chapter entitled "Antiquities," contained in "*The Natural and Statistical View of Cincinnati and the Miami country*," by DANIEL DRAKE, M. D., published in 1815. It not only embraces many facts, but is free from the tendency towards exaggeration which has been the prevailing fault of most that has been written upon the subject of American Antiquities. In connection with what was published by Mr. BRACKENRIDGE, and at a subsequent date by the late President HARRISON, (Address before the Historical Society of Ohio, 1832,) it presents a better view of the ancient remains of the region north of the Ohio, than can be obtained from any other source,—Mr. ATWATER's Memoir, in the Transactions of the American Antiquarian Society, alone excepted.

It would be impossible, as it is unnecessary, particularly to point out all that has been published upon this subject, chiefly consisting, as it does, of detached and incidental observations. In addition to the several authorities above named, we may mention LEWIS and CLARKE, Major LONG, Dr. EDWIN JAMES, HENRY R. SCHOOLCRAFT, TIMOTHY FLINT, HUGH WILLIAMSON, Dr. BARTON, Rev. JOSEPH DODDRIDGE, President JEFFERSON, Dr. LEWIS C. BECK, Dr. S. P. HILDRETH, KEATING, HAYWOOD, HOWE, NUTTALL, LATROBE, ROCHEFAUCAULT, SHORT, COLLINS, DICKESON, BROWN, FEATHERSTONHAUGH, Professors GERARD TROOST, JOHN LOCKE, and C. G. FORSHEY, R. C. and S. TAYLOR, Prince MAXIMILIAN, Prof. RAFINESQUE, CHARLES WHITTLESEY, etc., etc., as among those who have contributed to the general stock of information upon this subject.

The first attempt towards a general account of the ancient monuments of the West, was made by Mr. CALEB ATWATER, who deserves the credit of being the pioneer in this department. His Memoir, constituting 150 octavo pages, was published in the first volume of the "Archæologia Americana," in 1819. It contains plans and descriptions of a considerable number of ancient works,—embracing the imposing structures at Marietta, Newark, Portsmouth, Circleville, etc., etc.,—with accounts of a variety of ancient remains found in the mounds. It gives a better conception of the number, magnitude, and more obvious characteristics of the monuments treated of, than was before possessed, and for a time appeared to have satisfied public inquiry. It contains many errors, for which however we can find a ready apology in the unsettled state of the country, and the attendant difficulties of investigation at the time it was written,—errors which, under present advantages of research, would be inexcusable.

The facts presented by the earlier of the authorities above named, have been collected by various authors, either in support of a favorite hypothesis, or with a view of conveying to the world some conception of the antiquities of our country. These compilations, however, have proved eminently unsatisfactory, not less from the vague nature of the original accounts, than from the circumstance that they were in most instances mixed up with the crudest speculations and the wildest conjectures. Even when this was not the case, the fact that the original observations were made in a disconnected and casual manner, served still further to confuse the mind of the student and render generalization impossible. It was under an impression of existing deficiencies in these respects,—the paucity of facts, and the loose manner in which most of them had been presented,—that the investigations recorded in this memoir were commenced and prosecuted. At the outset, as indispensable to independent judgment, all preconceived notions were abandoned, and the work of research commenced *de novo*, as if nothing had been known or said concerning the remains to which attention was directed. It was concluded that if these monuments were capable of reflecting any certain light upon the grand archæological questions connected with the primitive history of the American Continent, the

E

origin, migrations and early state of the American race, that then they should be more carefully and minutely, and above all, more systematically investigated.

The locality chosen for the commencement of operations, is a section of the Scioto river and Paint creek valleys, of which the city of Chillicothe is the centre, and which possesses a deserved celebrity for its beauty, unexampled fertility, and the great number, size, and variety of its ancient remains. Situated in the middle of southern Ohio, and possessing a mild and salubrious climate, this seems to have been one of the centres of ancient population; and, probably, no other equal portion of the Mississippi basin furnishes so rich and interesting a field for the antiquarian. A glance at the "*Map of a Section of Twelve Miles of the Scioto Valley, with its Ancient Monuments*," Plate II, will fully illustrate this remark.

The plan of operations was agreed upon, and the field-work commenced, early in the spring of 1845. Subsequently, the plan was greatly extended, and the investigations were carried on, over Ohio and the adjacent States, with slight interruption, up to the summer of 1847.

The body of this memoir will indicate with sufficient clearness, the mode in which these investigations were conducted, and the extent to which they were prosecuted. It is perhaps enough here to say, that the surveys of ancient works were, for the most part, made by the authors in person, and that the excavations of mounds, etc., were all of them conducted under their personal direction and supervision. Care was exercised to note down, on the spot, every fact which it was thought might be of value, in the solution of the problems of the origin and purposes of the remains under notice; and particular attention was bestowed in observing the dependencies of the position, structure, and contents of the various works in respect to each other and the general features of the country. Indeed, no exertion was spared to ensure entire accuracy, and the compass, line, and rule were alone relied upon, in all matters where an approximate estimate might lead to erroneous conclusions.

The ancient enclosures and groups of works personally examined or surveyed, are upwards of one hundred in number. Some of these had before been noticed, but most are now for the first time presented to the world. About two hundred mounds, of all forms and sizes, and occupying every variety of position, have also been excavated. Several thousand remains of ancient art were collected in the course of these investigations, chiefly from the mounds themselves. These constitute a cabinet, as valuable in its extent, as it is interesting in the great variety and singular character of the illustrations which it furnishes of the condition of the minor arts, and the connections and communications of the people by whom these monuments were erected.

The prosecution of these researches naturally led to an acquaintance and correspondence with a large number of gentlemen in various parts of the Union, who felt interested in them, or who had devoted attention to the same subject. All of these have kindly rendered their services in cases where they could prove of value, or have freely contributed the results of their own labors to complete the design of the authors, in presenting as full and comprehensive a view of the ancient monuments of our country, as private means and limited facilities would allow.

First among these, it will not be invidious to name JAMES MCBRIDE, Esq., of Hamilton, Butler county, Ohio, whose valuable contributions constitute an important feature in the memoir herewith presented. This gentleman, residing for a long time in the centre of the fertile valley of the Great Miami river, amidst the numerous evidences of ancient population with which that valley abounds, has devoted a large proportion of his time to their attentive examination. Personally, and with the assistance of J. W. ERWIN, Esq., resident engineer on the Miami canal, he has made numerous surveys of ancient enclosures and groups of works in that valley, distinguished for their minute fidelity. He also, without however resorting very extensively to direct excavations, has collected an interesting cabinet of aboriginal relics. Anxious to contribute his share to whatever might elucidate the subject of American Archæology, Mr. MCBRIDE, with a generous liberality, placed in the hands of the authors his notes, plans, and drawings, without restriction, to be used as they deemed proper. This tender was accepted in the same spirit it was made, and the materials thus furnished have been freely used in the succeeding pages, where they rank second to none in interest and value.

Among the most zealous investigators in the field of American antiquarian research, is CHARLES WHITTLESEY, Esq., of Cleveland, formerly Topographic Engineer of Ohio. His surveys and observations, carried on for many years and over a wide field, have been both numerous and accurate, and are among the most valuable, in all respects, of any hitherto made. Although Mr. Whittlesey, in conjunction with JOSEPH SULLIVANT, Esq., of Columbus, Ohio, originally contemplated a joint work, in which the results of his investigations should be embodied, he has nevertheless, with a liberality which will be not less appreciated by the public than by the authors, contributed to this memoir about twenty plans of ancient works, which, with the accompanying explanations and general observations, will be found embodied in the following pages. Relating principally to the aboriginal monuments of northern Ohio, (as do those of Mr. McBride to the remains of western Ohio,) they contribute much to the interest and completeness of this memoir. It is to be hoped the public may yet be put in possession of the entire results of Mr. Whittlesey's labor, which could not fail of adding greatly to our stock of knowledge on this interesting subject.

Acknowledgment is also due to Rev. R. Morris, of Mount Sylvan, Lafayette county, Mississippi, for valuable facts relating to the monuments of the South. Although but recently commenced, Mr. Morris's investigations have been prosecuted in a manner which gives promise of important results.

It will be observed that several plans and notices of ancient works are presented in the succeeding chapters, upon the authority of the late Prof. C. S. Rafinesque. This gentleman, while living, devoted considerable attention to the antiquities of the Mississippi valley, and published several brief papers relating to them. His notes and plans, for the most part brief, crude, and imperfect, at his death found their way into the possession of Brantz Mayer, Esq., of Baltimore, late Secretary of the American Legation to Mexico. This gentleman placed them in the hands of the authors, with liberty to make use of the information which they contained. They, however, have chosen to avail themselves of this permission, only so far as to adopt Prof. Rafinesque's plans, etc., in cases where they have either been able to verify them in person, or to assure themselves by collateral evidence of their accuracy in all essential particulars. His notes are principally important, as indicating the localities of many interesting monuments, rather than as conveying any satisfactory information concerning them.

To Samuel George Morton, M.D., of Philadelphia, the eminent author of "Crania Americana," is acknowledgment especially due, not only for the warm interest manifested in these investigations from their commencement, but for the use of valuable manuscripts relating to our antiquities,—the collections of many years of laborious research in collateral departments. Among these is the brief account of the ancient remains on the Wateree river in South Carolina, by Dr. William Blanding; and also the highly important account of the monuments of the States bordering the Gulf of Mexico, by William Bartram, the first naturalist who penetrated the dense tropical forests of Florida. The history of the MSS. from which the latter account was taken, is unknown. It found its way by accident into the hands of its present possessor. It consists of answers to a series of questions, by a second person, (probably Dr. Barton,) relating to the history, religion, manners, institutions, etc., of the tribes which composed the Creek confederacy, and is undoubtedly the most complete and accurate account of those Indians in existence.

Dr. S. P. Hildreth, of Marietta, and Prof. John Locke, of Cincinnati, both of whom have devoted much attention to our antiquities, and whose observations upon the subject are distinguished for their accuracy, are also entitled to honorable mention for facts contributed, and assistance rendered. So also, for surveys of ancient works, drawings and descriptions of ancient relics, and facts of various kinds, is acknowledgment due to J. Dille, Esq., of Newark, Ohio; S. T. Oweins and W. B. FAIRCHILD, Esqs., of Xenia, Ohio; Col. B. L. C. WAILES, of Washington, Mississippi; J. H. BLAKE, Esq., of Boston; THOMAS REYNOLDS, M.D., of Brockville, Canada West; ARIUS NYE, Esq., and CHARLES SULLIVAN, Marietta, Ohio; HENRY HOWE, R. BUCHANAN, JOSEPH CLARKE, ERASMUS GEST, jr., and U. P. JAMES, Esqs., of Cincinnati; J. E. WHARTON, Esq., of Wheeling, Virginia; DANIEL MORTON, Esq., of New York; L. K. DILLE, M.D., of Cedarville, Ohio; CHARLES O. TRACY, of Portsmouth, Ohio; Prof. W. W. MATHER, Jackson, Ohio; Rev. W. B. STEVENS, Athens, Georgia; Hon. T. H. CLINGMAN, North Carolina; ASHEL AYLESWORTH, Granville, Ohio; P. N. WHITE, Esq., Circleville, Ohio; C. J. ORTON, Lower Sandusky, Ohio; Lieut. JOHN H. ALLEN, now of Easton, Md.; T. B. HUNT, Esq., of New Haven; WM. F. CLEMSON, Esq., of Chillicothe, Ohio; and JOSEPH SULLIVANT, Esq., Columbus, Ohio.

And while rendering these acknowledgments, it is but proper to express the obligations which the authors of these investigations feel themselves under to gentlemen in the various Atlantic cities, who, if they have not been able to add to the number of facts here presented, have nevertheless by their thorough appreciation of the subject, friendly encouragement, and disinterested aid, extended in various ways, facilitated this new attempt towards the elucidation of the antiquities of our own country. To the learned and venerable President of the American Ethnological Society, Hon. ALBERT GALLATIN, the closing years of whose long, active, and useful life have been closely and successfully devoted to researches in the wide field of American Ethnological Science, are our grateful acknowledgments especially due. His assistance and enlightened approbation have had a controlling influence in sustaining and carrying on these investigations. To JOHN R. BARTLETT, Esq., of New York, Foreign Corresponding Secretary of the Ethnological Society, distinguished for his zeal and energy in organizing and promoting historical and ethnological research, we cannot sufficiently express our obligations. His assistance, in a variety of ways, has been of value, especially in directing public attention to the importance of a subject, the extent and bearings of which were but imperfectly understood.

Hon. GEO. P. MARSH, of Burlington, Vermont, whose disinterested exertions have mainly contributed to the appearance of this memoir in its present form, has kindly examined the following chapters and given them the benefit of his sound and critical judgment. To Prof. EDWARD ROBINSON, D.D., and to Prof. W. W. TURNER, both of New York, and both officers of the American Ethnological Society, are we also indebted. The gentleman last named has supervised the memoir, and his suggestions have been deferred to with a readiness implying a confidence in his critical abilities, which is shared alike by the authors and by the public.

To Professors B. SILLIMAN and B. SILLIMAN, jr., of New Haven; Prof. JEFFRIES WYMAN, of Boston; Prof. LEWIS AGASSIZ, of Cambridge; S. F. HAVENS, Esq., Librarian of the American Antiquarian Society, Worcester; and to numerous other gentlemen in various parts of the Union, and particularly to GEO. R. GLIDDON, Esq., whose lectures and publications upon the subject of Egyptian Archæology have given a new and powerful impulse to cognate researches in America, and invested them with a popular interest indispensable to their successful prosecution,—to all of these are the warmest thanks of the investigators due.

It will not be improper here to mention, that the literary part of the present work, the responsible task of arranging and embodying for publication the original MSS. and other materials jointly got together in the course of these investigations, has devolved mostly upon the gentleman whose name stands first upon the title-page, who has also prepared the plans, drawings, and other illustrations. The other gentleman has been engaged for a number of years in researches connected with our ancient monuments, and in collecting relics of aboriginal art; and it is due to him to say, that the investigations here recorded, so far as they involve inquiries in natural science, have principally been made by him. He has also sustained the larger proportion of the expenses attending these explorations, and devoted considerable time to the restoration and arrangement of the relics recovered from the mounds.

Before concluding these prefatory remarks,—already extended beyond the original design,—we may be permitted to say that it has been a constant aim in the preparation of this memoir, to present facts in a clear and concise form, with such simple deductions and generalizations alone, as may follow from their careful consideration. With no hypothesis to combat or sustain, and with a desire only to arrive at truth, whatever its bearings upon received theories and current prejudices, everything like mere speculation has been avoided. Analogies, apparently capable of reflecting light upon many important questions connected with an enlarged view of the subject, have seldom been more than indicated. Their full consideration, as also that of the relations which the ancient monuments of the Mississippi valley bear to those of other portions of America and the world, has not been attempted here. To such an undertaking, involving long and careful research, as also a more comprehensive view of the monuments of the central parts of the continent, this memoir is only preliminary. It yet remains to be seen whether all the ancient monuments of the Mississippi valley were constructed upon similar principles; whether they denote a common origin, and whether they were probably contemporaneous or otherwise in their erection. It remains to be settled whether the singular and anomalous structures of Wisconsin and the North-west are part of the same grand system of defensive, religious, and sepulchral monuments found in the valley of the Ohio, and the more imposing, if not more regular remains which abound in the Southern States. The work of investigation has been just commenced; its future progress may, and no doubt will, result in new and perhaps more important disclosures than any hitherto made.

The importance of a complete and speedy examination of the whole field, cannot be over-estimated. The operations of the elements, the shifting channels of the streams, the levelling hand of public improvement, and most efficient of all, the slow but constant encroachments of agriculture, are fast destroying these monuments of ancient labor, breaking in upon their symmetry and obliterating their outlines. Thousands have already disappeared, or retain but slight and doubtful traces of their former proportions. Such an examination is, however, too great an undertaking for private enterprise to attempt. It must be left to local explorers, to learned associations, or to the Government. And if this memoir shall succeed in directing that attention to the subject which it merits, and thereby in some manner secure the thorough investigation of these monuments, that result will prove an ample recompense for labors performed in a field of absorbing interest, and one which holds out abundant attractions to the Antiquary and Archæologist.

CHILLICOTHE, OHIO, *June*, 1847.

ANCIENT MONUMENTS.

CHAPTER I.

GENERAL OBSERVATIONS.

THE ancient monuments of the Western United States consist, for the most part, of elevations and embankments of earth and stone, erected with great labor and manifest design. In connection with these, more or less intimate, are found various minor relics of art, consisting of ornaments and implements of many kinds, some of them composed of metal, but most of stone.

These remains are spread over a vast extent of country. They are found on the sources of the Alleghany, in the western part of the State of New-York, on the east; and extend thence westwardly along the southern shore of Lake Erie, and through Michigan and Wisconsin, to Iowa and the Nebraska territory, on the west.* We have no record of their occurrence above the great lakes. Carver mentions some on the shores of Lake Pepin, and some are said to occur near Lake Travers, under the 46th parallel of latitude. Lewis and Clarke saw them on the Missouri river, one thousand miles above its junction with the Mississippi; and they have been observed on the Kanzas and Platte, and on other remote western rivers. They are found all over the intermediate country, and spread over the valley of the Mississippi to the Gulf of Mexico. They line the shores of the Gulf from Texas to Florida, and extend, in diminished numbers, into South Carolina. They occur in great numbers in Ohio, Indiana, Illinois, Wisconsin, Missouri, Arkansas, Kentucky, Tennessee, Louisiana, Mississippi, Alabama, Georgia, Florida, and Texas. They are found, in less numbers, in the western portions of New-York, Pennsylvania, Virginia, and North and South Carolina; as also in Michigan, Iowa, and in the Mexican territory beyond the Rio Grande del Norte. In short,

---

* Some ancient works, probably belonging to the same system with those of the Mississippi valley, and erected by the same people, occur upon the Susquehanna river, as far down as the Valley of Wyoming, in Pennsylvania. The mound-builders seem to have skirted the southern border of Lake Erie, and spread themselves, in diminished numbers, over the western part of the State of New York, along the shores of Lake Ontario to the St. Lawrence river. They penetrated into the interior, eastward, as far as the county of Onondaga, where some slight vestiges of their works still exist. These seem to have been their limits at the north-east.

they occupy the entire basin of the Mississippi and its tributaries, as also the fertile plains along the Gulf.

It is a fact but recently made known, that there are an abundance of small mounds, or tumuli, in the territory of Oregon. We are not informed, however, whether there are any enclosures, or other works of like character with those usually accompanying the mounds of the Mississippi valley, nor whether the mounds of Oregon are generally disseminated over that territory.* That they are of frequent occurrence upon the river Gila, in California, and also upon the tributaries of the Colorado of the West, is also a fact but recently ascertained. Whether these mounds possess features identifying them with those of the Mississippi valley, or indicating a common origin, remains to be decided.

It is not to be understood that these works are dispersed equally over the area above indicated. They are mainly confined to the valleys of the rivers and large streams, and seldom occur very far back from them. Occasional works are found in the hill or broken country; but they are not frequent, and are always of small size.

Although possessing throughout certain general points of resemblance, going to establish a kindred origin, these works, nevertheless, resolve themselves into three grand geographical divisions, which present, in many respects, striking contrasts, yet so gradually merge into each other, that it is impossible to determine where one series terminates and the other begins. In the region bordering the upper lakes, to a certain extent in Michigan, Iowa, and Missouri, but particularly in Wisconsin, we find a succession of remains, entirely singular in their form, and presenting but slight analogy to any others of which we have an account, in any portion of the globe. The larger proportion of these are structures of earth, bearing the forms of beasts, birds, reptiles, and even of men; they are frequently of gigantic dimensions, constituting huge *basso-relievos* upon the face of the country. They are very numerous, and in most cases occur in long and apparently dependent ranges. In connection with them, are found many conical mounds and occasional short lines of embankment, in rare instances forming enclosures. These animal effigies are mainly confined to Wisconsin, and extend across that territory from Fond du Lac, in a south-western direction, ascending the Fox river, and following the general course of Rock and Wisconsin rivers to the Mississippi. They may be much more extensively disseminated; but it is here only that they have been observed in considerable numbers. In Michigan, as also in Iowa and Missouri, similar elevations, of more or less regular outline, are said to occur. They are represented as dis-

---

* The only reference we have to the mounds of Oregon is contained in a paragraph in the Narrative of the United States Exploring Expedition, vol: iv. p. 313 :

"We soon reached the Bute Prairies, which are extensive, and covered with tumuli, or small mounds, at regular distances asunder. As far as I can learn, there is no tradition among the natives concerning them. They are conical mounds, thirty feet in diameter, about six or seven feet above the level, and *many thousands in number.* Being anxious to ascertain if they contained any relics, I subsequently visited these prairies, and opened three of the mounds, but found nothing in them but a pavement of round stones."

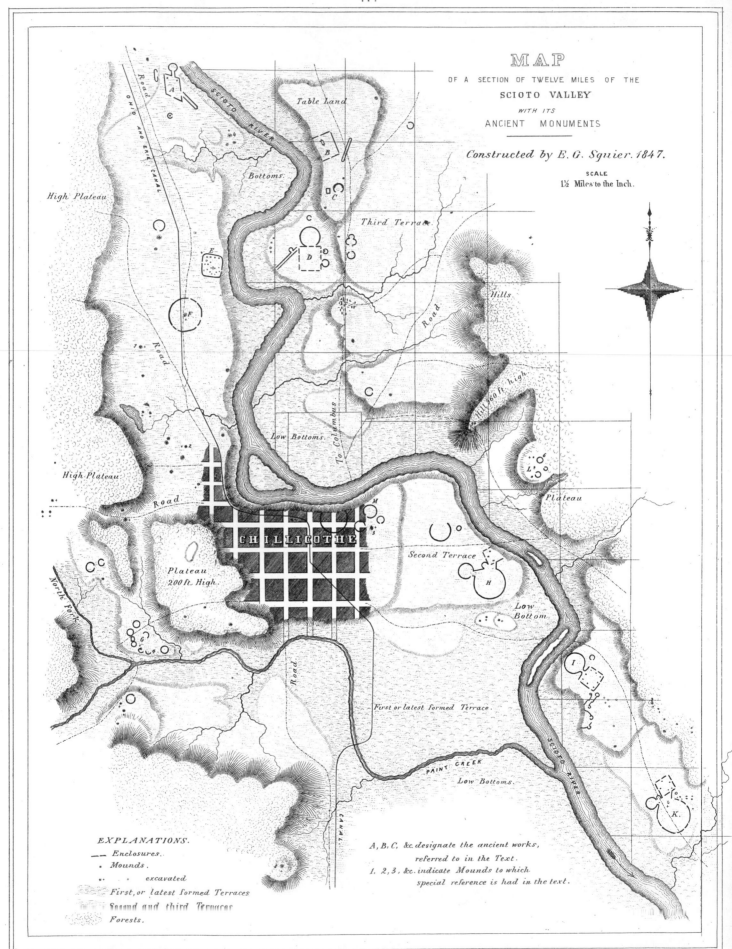

MAP
OF A SECTION OF TWELVE MILES OF THE
SCIOTO VALLEY
WITH ITS
ANCIENT MONUMENTS

Constructed by E. G. Squier. 1847.

SCALE
1½ Miles to the Inch.

EXPLANATIONS.
—— Enclosures.
• Mounds.
•• excavated
First, or latest formed Terraces
Second and third Terraces
Forests.

A, B, C, &c. designate the ancient works,
referred to in the Text.
1, 2, 3, &c. indicate Mounds to which
special reference is had in the text.

Table Land
Bottoms.
High Plateau
Third Terrace.
Hills
Hill 160 ft. high.
Low Bottoms.
To Columbus.
High Plateau
Plateau
North Fork.
CHILLICOTHE
Plateau 200 ft. High.
Second Terrace
Low Bottom
First or latest formed Terrace.
PAINT CREEK
Low Bottoms.
SCIOTO RIVER
OHIO AND ERIE CANAL
Road
Road
Road
Road
CANAL

Lith. of Sarony & Major 117 Fulton St. N.Y.

persed in ranges, like the buildings of a modern city, and covering sometimes an area of many acres.

Further to the southward, in the region watered by the Ohio and its tributaries, we find ancient works of greater magnitude and more manifest design. Among them are a few animal-shaped structures; but they seem to have been erected on different principles and for a different purpose from those just noticed. Here we find numberless mounds, most of them conical but many pyramidal in form, and often of great dimensions. The pyramidal structures are always truncated, sometimes terraced, and generally have graded ascents to their summits. They bear a close resemblance to the Teocallis of Mexico; and the known uses of the latter are suggestive of the probable purposes to which they were applied. Accompanying these, and in some instances sustaining an intimate relation to them, are numerous enclosures of earth and stone, frequently of vast size, and often of regular outline. These are by far the most imposing class of our aboriginal remains, and impress us most sensibly with the numbers and power of the people who built them. The purposes of many of these are quite obvious; and investigation has served to settle, pretty clearly, the character of most of the other works occurring in connection with them.

Proceeding still further southwards, we find, in the States bordering on the Gulf of Mexico, the mounds increasing in size and regularity of form, if not in numbers. Conical mounds become comparatively rare, and the Teocalli-shaped structures become larger and more numerous, and assume certain dependencies in respect to each other, not before observed. The enclosures, on the other hand, diminish in size and numbers; and lose many of the characteristic features of those of a higher latitude, though still sustaining towards them a strong general resemblance. Here, for the first time, we find traces of bricks in the mounds and in the walls of enclosures.

The peculiarities of these several divisions will be more particularly pointed out in the progress of this work; when the points of resemblance and difference will become more apparent. The succeeding observations relate more especially to the remains included in the central geographical section above indicated, where the investigations recorded in this volume were principally carried on, and which, in the extent, variety, and interesting nature of its ancient monuments, affords by far the richest and most important field for archæological research and inquiry.

The number of these ancient remains is well calculated to excite surprise, and has been adduced in support of the hypothesis that they are most, if not all of them, natural formations, " the results of diluvial action," modified perhaps in some instances, but never erected by man. Of course no such suggestion was ever made by individuals who had enjoyed the opportunity of seeing and investigating them. Simple structures of earth could not possibly bear more palpable evidences of an artificial origin, than do most of the western monuments. The evidences in support of this assertion, derived from the form, structure, position, and contents of these remains, will sufficiently appear in the progress of this work.

PLATE II, *exhibiting a section of twelve miles of the Scioto valley, with its ancient monuments*, will serve to give some general conception of the number of these remains. The enclosures are here indicated by dark lines, the mounds by simple dots. Within the section represented, it will be observed that there are not less than *ten* groups of large works, accompanied by a great number of mounds, of various sizes. Within the enclosure designated by the letter E are embraced twenty-four mounds. The enclosures D, H, I, K, have each about two and a half miles of embankment; and H and K enclose but little less than one hundred acres each. It is proper to observe, to prevent misconception, that there are few sections of country of equal extent which embrace so large a number of ancient works. The fertile valley of the Scioto river was a favorite resort of the ancient people, and was one of the seats of their densest population. The various works indicated in these maps, will be described at length in the subsequent pages. An enlarged plan of the enclosure designated by the letter A is given on Plate XXIII; B, on Plate XVIII; C, Plate XVIII; D, Plate XVII; E and F, Plate XIX; G, Plate XXII; H, Plate XXI; I, Plate XVI; K, Plate XX.

PLATE III, No. 1, *exhibits a section of six miles of the Valley of Paint Creek*, a tributary of the Scioto river. The village of Bourneville is ten miles west of Chillicothe. Within this limit are embraced three works of extraordinary size, besides several smaller ones. The works, designated by the letters A and B, have each upwards of two miles of heavy embankment, and contain not far from one hundred acres. The stone work C has an area of one hundred and forty acres, enclosed within a wall upwards of two and a fourth miles long. Enlarged plans of the various works here indicated are given in the following pages. A and B, Plate XXI; C, Plate IV; D and E, Plate XXX.

PLATE III, No. 2, *presents a section of six miles of the Great Miami valley*, included principally within the limits of Butler county, Ohio. Not less than seven enclosures, of considerable size, occur within these bounds. The work indicated by the letter G contains ninety-five acres. An enlarged plan of the work marked A, is given on Plate VI; of B, on Plate XI; C and F, on Plate XXX; D, Plate XXXI; and G, on Plate XIII.

Not far from one hundred enclosures of various sizes, and five hundred mounds, are found in Ross county, Ohio. The number of tumuli in the State may be safely estimated at ten thousand, and the number of enclosures at one thousand or fifteen hundred. Many of them are small, but cannot be omitted in an enumeration. They are scarcely less numerous on the Kenhawas in Virginia, than on the Scioto and Miamis; and are abundant on the White river and Wabash, as also upon the Kentucky, Cumberland, Tennessee, and the numerous other tributaries of the Ohio and Mississippi.

Nor is their magnitude less a matter of remark than their great number. Lines of embankment, varying in height from five to thirty feet, and enclosing areas of from one to fifty acres, are common; while enclosures of one or two hundred acres area are far from infrequent. Occasional works are found enclosing as many as

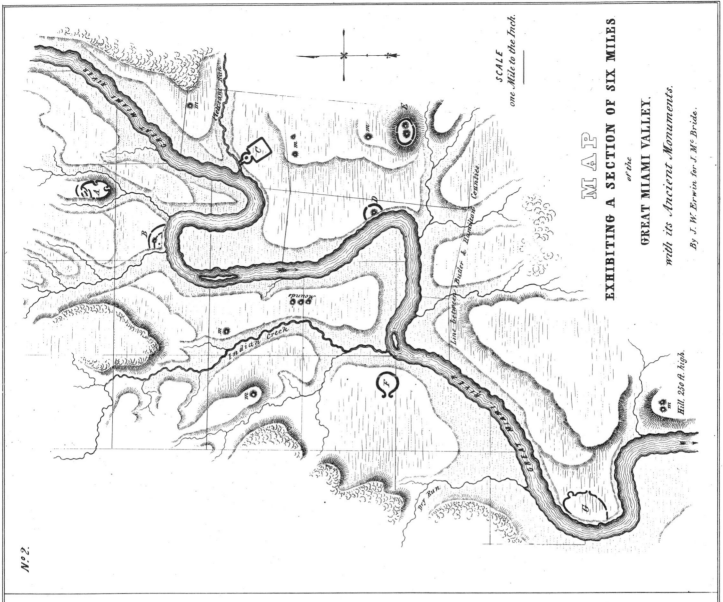

MAP

EXHIBITING A SECTION OF SIX MILES

of the

GREAT MIAMI VALLEY.

with its Ancient Monuments.

By J. W. Erwin. for J. Mc Bride.

SCALE
one Mile to the Inch.

Hill. 250 ft. high.

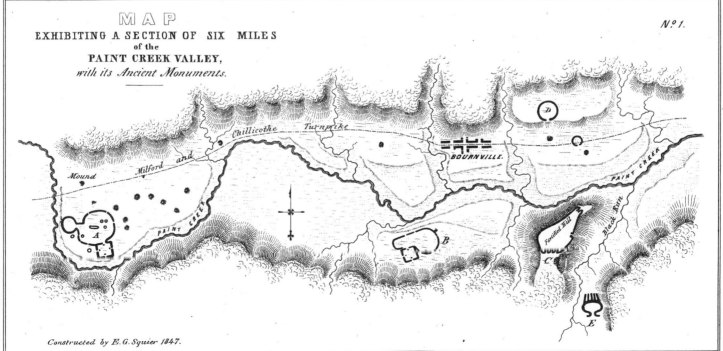

MAP

EXHIBITING A SECTION OF SIX MILES
of the
PAINT CREEK VALLEY,
with its Ancient Monuments.

N.º 1.

Chillicothe Turnpike

BOURNVILLE.

Milford and

Mound

PAINT CREEK

PAINT CREEK

Black Run

Fortified Hill

Constructed by E.G.Squier 1847.

four hundred acres.*   The magnitude of the area enclosed is not, however, always a correct index of the amount of labor expended in the erection of these works.   A fortified hill in Highland county, Ohio, has one mile and five-eighths of heavy embankment; yet it encloses an area of only about forty acres.   A similar work on the Little Miami river, in Warren county, Ohio, has upwards of four miles of embankment, yet encloses little more than one hundred acres.   The group of works at the mouth of the Scioto river has an aggregate of at least twenty miles of embankment; yet the entire amount of land embraced within the walls does not probably much exceed two hundred acres.

The mounds are of all dimensions, from those of but a few feet in height and a few yards in diameter, to those which, like the celebrated structure at the mouth of Grave Creek in Virginia, rise to the height of seventy feet, and measure one thousand feet in circumference at the base.   The great mound in the vicinity of Miamisburgh, Montgomery county, Ohio, is sixty-eight feet in perpendicular height, and eight hundred and fifty-two in circumference at the base, containing 311,353 cubic feet.

Fɪɢ. 1. GREAT MOUND AT MIAMISBURGH, OHIO.†

The truncated pyramid at Cahokia, Illinois, has an altitude of ninety feet, and is upwards of two thousand feet in circumference at the base.   It has a level summit of several acres area.   The great mound at Selserstown, Mississippi, is computed to cover six acres of ground.   Mounds of these extraordinary dimensions are most common at the south, though there are some of great size at the north.   The usual dimensions are, however, considerably less than in the examples here given.   The greater number range from six to thirty feet in perpendicular height, by forty to one hundred feet diameter at the base.‡

---

* Lewis and Clarke describe one on the Missouri river which they estimated to contain not far from six hundred acres.—*Travels*, p. 47.

† From a sketch by Henry Howe, Esq.

‡ "We have seen mounds which would require the labor of a thousand men employed upon our canals, with all their mechanical aids, and the improved implements of their labor, for months.   We have more than once hesitated, in view of one of these prodigious mounds, whether it were not really a natural hill. But they are uniformly so placed, in reference to the adjacent country, and their conformation is so unique and similar, that no eye hesitates long in referring them to the class of artificial erections."—*Flint's Geography*, p. 131.

All the above-mentioned constructions are composed of earth or stone; though a combination of these materials in the same work is by no means rare. When there are no ditches interior or exterior to the embankments, *pits* or "dug holes," from which the earth for their formation was taken, are generally visible near by. These are sometimes very broad and deep, and occasionally quite symmetrical in shape.* In the vicinity of large mounds such excavations are common. The earth and stone composing these works are sometimes foreign to the locality which they occupy, and must have been brought from considerable distances.

A large, perhaps the larger, portion of these enclosures are regular in outline, the square and the circle predominating. Some are parallelograms, some ellipses, others polygons, regular or irregular. The regular works are almost invariably erected on level river-terraces, great care having evidently been taken to select those least broken. The irregular works are those which partake most of the character of defences, and are usually made to conform to the nature of the ground upon which they are situated,—running along the brows of hills, or cutting off the approaches to strong natural positions. The square and the circle often occur in combination, frequently communicating with each other or with irregular works directly, or by avenues consisting of parallel lines of embankment. Detached parallels are numerous. The mounds are usually simple cones in form; but they are sometimes truncated, and occasionally terraced, with graded or winding ascents to their summits. Some are elliptical, others pear-shaped, and others squares or parallelograms, with flanking terraces. Besides these, there are others already alluded to, most common in the extreme north-west, which assume the forms of animals and reptiles. Another variety of remains are the causeways or "roads," and the graded descents to rivers and streams, or from one terrace to another. These several classes of works will be described at length, under appropriate heads.

As already remarked, these remains occur mainly in the valleys of the Western rivers and streams. The alluvial terraces, or "river-bottoms," as they are popularly termed, were the favorite sites of the builders. The principal monuments are found where these "bottoms" are most extended, and where the soil is most fertile and easy of cultivation. At the junction of streams, where the valleys are usually broadest and most favorable for their erection, some of the largest and most singular remains are found. The works at Marietta; at the junction of the Muskingum with the Ohio; at the mouth of Grave Creek; at Portsmouth, the mouth of the Scioto; and at the mouth of the Great Miami, are instances in point. Occasional works are found on the hill tops, overlooking the valleys, or at a little distance from them; but these are manifestly, in most instances, works of defence or last resort, or in some way connected with warlike purposes. And it is worthy of remark, that the sites selected for settlements, towns, and cities, by the invading Europeans, are often those which were the especial favorites of the mound-builders, and the seats of their heaviest population. Marietta, Newark, Portsmouth, Chillicothe, Circle-

---

* These are the "*wells*" of Mr. Atwater and other writers on American antiquities. It is barely possible that a few were really wells, or *secondarily* designed for reservoirs.

ville, and Cincinnati, in Ohio ; Frankfort in Kentucky ; and St. Louis in Missouri, may be mentioned in confirmation of this remark. The centres of population are now, where they were at the period when the mysterious race of the mounds flourished.*

The aboriginal monuments of the Mississippi valley, the general character of which has been thus briefly and imperfectly indicated, fall within two general divisions, namely, CONSTRUCTIONS OF EARTH OR STONE, comprising *Enclosures, Mounds, etc.;* and MINOR VESTIGES OF ART, including the *Implements, Ornaments, Sculptures, etc.* of the ancient people.

The Earth and Stone Works resolve themselves into two classes, viz : ENCLOSURES, bounded by embankments, circumvallations, or walls; and simple tumuli, or MOUNDS.† They constitute, together, a single system of works ; but, for reasons which will satisfactorily appear, it is preferred to classify them as above. These grand classes resolve themselves into other subordinate divisions : ENCLOSURES FOR DEFENCE, SACRED AND MISCELLANEOUS ENCLOSURES ; MOUNDS OF SACRIFICE, TEMPLE MOUNDS, MOUNDS OF SEPULTURE, etc.

---

* " The most dense ancient population existed in precisely the places where the most crowded future population will exist in ages to come. The appearance of a series of mounds generally indicates the contiguity of rich and level lands, easy communications, fish, game, and the most favorable adjacent positions."—*Flint.*

" The most numerous, as well as the most considerable of these remains are found precisely in any part of the country where the traces of a numerous population might be looked for."—*Brackenridge.*

† The term *Mound* is used in this work in a technical sense, as synonymous with *Tumulus* or *Barrow,* and in contradistinction to embankment, wall, &c.

CHAPTER II.

EARTHWORKS—ENCLOSURES.

THE Enclosures, or, as they are familiarly called throughout the West, " Forts," constitute a very important and interesting class of remains. Their dimensions, and the popular opinion as to their purposes, attract to them more particularly the attention of observers. As a consequence, most that has been written upon our antiquities relates to them. A considerable number have been surveyed and described by different individuals, at different times ; but no systematic examination of a sufficient number to justify any general conclusion as to their origin and purposes has heretofore been attempted. We have therefore had presented as many different hypotheses as there have been individual explorers ; one maintaining that all the enclosures were intended for defence, while another persists that none could possibly have been designed for any such purpose. Investigation has shown, however, that while certain works possess features demonstrating incontestibly a military origin, others were connected with the superstitions of the builders, or designed for other purposes not readily apparent in our present state of knowledge concerning them.

It has already been remarked that the square and the circle, separate or in combination, were favorite figures with the mound-builders ; and a large proportion of their works in the Scioto valley, and in Ohio generally, are of these forms. Most of the circular works are small, varying from two hundred and fifty to three hundred feet in diameter, while others are a mile or more in circuit. Some stand isolated, but most in connection with one or more mounds, of greater or less dimensions, or in connection with other more complicated works. Wherever the circles occur, if there be a fosse, or ditch, it is almost invariably *interior* to the parapet. Instances are frequent where no ditch is discernible, and where it is evident that the earth composing the embankment was brought from a distance, or taken up evenly from the surface. In the square and in the irregular works, if there be a fosse at all, it is *exterior* to the embankment ; except in the case of fortified hills, where the earth, for the best of reasons, is usually thrown from the interior. These facts are not without their importance in determining the character and purpose of these remains. Another fact, bearing directly upon the degree of knowledge possessed by the builders, is, that many, if not most, of the circular works are *perfect circles*, and that many of the rectangular works are *accurate squares*. This fact has been demonstrated, in numerous instances, by careful admeasurements ; and has been remarked in cases where the works embrace an area of many acres, and where the embankments, or circumvallations, are a mile and upwards in extent.

To facilitate description, and to bring something like system out of the disordered materials before us, the enclosures are, to as great a degree as practicable, divided into classes; that is to say, such as are esteemed to be works of defence are placed together, while those which are regarded as sacred, or of a doubtful character, come under another division.

WORKS OF DEFENCE.

Those works which are incontestibly defensive usually occupy strong natural positions; and to understand fully their character, their capability for defence, and the nature of their entrenchments, it is necessary to notice briefly the predominant features of the country in which they occur. The valley of the Mississippi river, from the Alleghanies to the ranges of the Rocky Mountains, is a vast sedimentary basin, and owes its general aspect to the powerful agency of water. Its rivers have worn their valleys deep into a vast original plain; leaving, in their gradual subsidence, broad terraces, which mark the eras of their history. The edges of the table-lands, bordering on the valleys, are cut by a thousand ravines, presenting bluff headlands and high hills with level summits, sometimes connected by narrow isthmuses with the original table, but occasionally entirely detached. The sides of these elevations are generally steep, and difficult of access; in some cases precipitous and absolutely inaccessible. The natural strength of such positions, and their susceptibility of defence, would certainly suggest them as the citadels of a people having hostile neighbors, or pressed by invaders. Accordingly we are not surprised at finding these heights occupied by strong and complicated works, the design of which is no less indicated by their position than by their construction. But in such cases, it is always to be observed, that they have been chosen with great care, and that they possess peculiar strength, and have a special adaptation for the purposes to which they were applied. They occupy the highest points of land, and are never commanded from neighboring positions. While rugged and steep on most sides, they have one or more points of comparatively easy approach, in the protection of which the utmost skill of the builders seems to have been exhausted. They are guarded by double, overlapping walls, or a series of them, having sometimes an accompanying mound, designed perhaps for a look-out, and corresponding to the barbican in the system of defence of the Britons of the middle era. The usual defence is a simple embankment, thrown up along and a little below the brow of the hill, varying in height and solidity, as the declivity is more or less steep and difficult of access.

Other defensive works occupy the peninsulas created by the rivers and large streams, or cut off the headlands formed by their junction with each other. In such cases a fosse and wall are thrown across the isthmus, or diagonally from the bank of one stream to the bank of the other. In some, the wall is double, and extends along the bank of the stream some distance inwardly, as if designed to prevent an enemy from turning the flanks of the defence.

To understand clearly the nature of the works last mentioned, it should be remembered that the banks of the western rivers are always steep, and where these works are located, invariably high. The banks of the various terraces are also steep, and vary from ten to thirty and more feet in height. The rivers are constantly shifting their channels; and they frequently cut their way through all the intermediate up to the earliest-formed, or highest terrace, presenting bold banks, inaccessibly steep, and from sixty to one hundred feet high. At such points, from which the river has, in some instances, receded to the distance of half a mile or more, works of this description are oftenest found.

And it is a fact of much importance, and worthy of special note, that within the scope of a pretty extended observation, no work of any kind has been found occupying the first, or latest-formed terrace. This terrace alone, except at periods of extraordinary freshets, is subject to overflow.* The formation of each terrace constitutes a sort of semi-geological era in the history of the valley; and the fact that none of the ancient works occur upon the lowest or latest-formed of these, while they are found indiscriminately upon all the others, bears directly upon the question of their antiquity.

In addition to the several descriptions of defensive works above enumerated, there are others presenting peculiar features, which will be sufficiently noticed in the plans and explanations that follow. These plans are all drawn from actual and minute, and in most instances personal survey, and are presented, unless otherwise specially noted, on a uniform scale of five hundred feet to the inch. When there are interesting features too minute to be satisfactorily indicated on so small a scale, enlarged plans have been adopted. This is the case with the very first plan presented. Sections and supplementary plans are given, whenever it is supposed they may illustrate the description, or assist the comprehension of the reader. To shorten the text, the admeasurements are often placed upon the plans, and the "Field Books" of survey wholly omitted. The greatest care has, in all cases, been taken to secure perfect fidelity in all essential particulars. In the sectional maps, in order to show something of the character as well as the positions of the works, it has been found necessary to exaggerate them beyond their proportionate size. Some of the minor features of a few works are also slightly exaggerated, but in no case where it would be apt to lead to misapprehension or wrong conceptions of their character.

---

* This observation is confirmed by all who have given attention to the subject, in the Ohio and Upper Mississippi valleys. Along the Gulf, and at points on the Lower Mississippi, where the entire country is low, and subject to inundation, and where the operation of natural causes is rather to elevate than depress the beds of the streams, some of the ancient works are invaded by water.

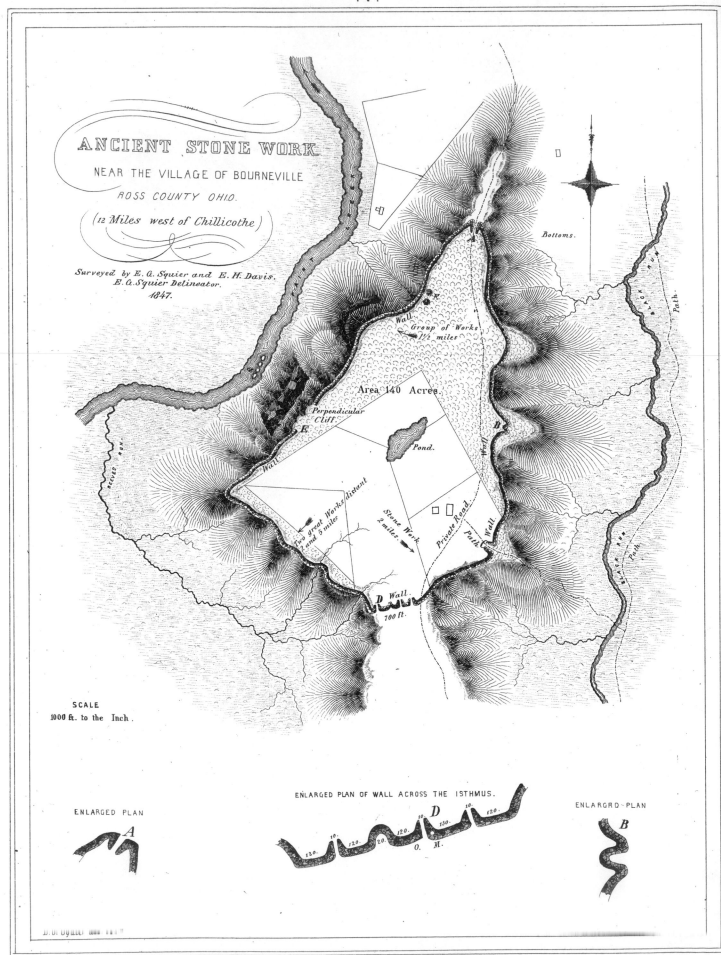

ANCIENT STONE WORK.

NEAR THE VILLAGE OF BOURNEVILLE

ROSS COUNTY OHIO.

(12 Miles west of Chillicothe)

Surveyed by E. G. Squier and E. H. Davis.
E. G. Squier Delineator.
1847.

Bottoms.

Wall

Group of Works
1½ miles

Area 140 Acres.

Perpendicular
Cliff.

E

Pond.

Wall

B

Wall

Two great Works distant
2 and 5 miles

Stone Work
2 miles

Private Road.

Path Wall

C

D Wall
700 ft.

BLACK RUN

Path

BLACK RUN
Path

SCALE
1000 ft. to the Inch.

ENLARGED PLAN OF WALL ACROSS THE ISTHMUS.

ENLARGED PLAN

A

10. 10.
10. 120.
120. 150.
10. 120.
120. 20.
O. M.

D

ENLARGED PLAN

B

Lith. by Sarony & Major. 117 Fulton St. N.Y.

PLATE IV.*

STONE WORK, NEAR BOURNEVILLE, ROSS COUNTY, OHIO.

THIS work occupies the summit of a lofty, detached hill, twelve miles westward from the city of Chillicothe, near the village of Bourneville. The hill is not far from four hundred feet in perpendicular height; and is remarkable, even among the steep hills of the West, for the general abruptness of its sides, which at some points are absolutely inaccessible. It is the advance point of a range of hills, situated between the narrow valleys of two small creeks; and projects midway into the broad valley of Paint creek, so as to constitute its most prominent natural feature. It is a conspicuous object from every point of view. Its summit is a wide and fertile plain, with occasional considerable depressions, some of which contain water during the entire year.

The defences consist of a wall of stone which is carried around the hill, a little below the brow; but at some places it rises, so as to cut off the narrow spurs, and extends across the neck that connects the hill with the range beyond. It should not be understood by the term *wall*, that, at this time, anything like a wall of stones regularly laid up exists; on the contrary, where the line is best preserved, there is little evidence that the stones were laid one upon the other so as to present vertical faces, much less that they were cemented in place. At a few points, however, more particularly at the isthmus D, there are some indications of arrangement in the stones, tending to the belief that the wall here may have been regularly faced on the exterior. The appearance of the line, for the most part, is just what might be expected from the *falling outwards* of a wall of stones placed, as this was, upon the declivity of a hill. Upon the western, or steepest face of the hill, the range of stones covers a space varying from thirty to fifty feet in width, closely resembling the "*protection walls*" carried along the embankments of rail-roads and canals, where exposed to the action of rivers or large streams. But for the amount of stones, it might be taken for a natural feature,—the *debris* of the out-cropping sand strata. Such, certainly, is the first impression which it produces upon the visitor; an impression, however, which is speedily corrected upon reaching the points where the supposed line of *debris*, rising upon the spurs, forms curved gateways, and then resumes its course as before.

Upon the eastern face of the hill, where the declivity is least abrupt, the wall is heavier and more distinct than upon the west, resembling a long stone-heap of fifteen or twenty feet base, and from three to four feet in height. Where it crosses the isthmus it is heaviest; and although stones enough have been removed from it,

---

* This work is marked C in the "*Map of a Section of Six Miles of the Paint Creek Valley,*" Plate III.

at that point, to build a stout division wall between the lands of two proprietors, their removal is not discoverable. This isthmus is seven hundred feet wide, and the wall is carried in a right line across it, at its narrowest point. Here are three gateways opening upon the continuous terrace beyond. These are formed by the curving inward of the ends of the wall for forty or fifty feet, leaving narrow passways between, not exceeding eight feet in width. At the other points, A and C of the plan, where there are jutting ridges, are similar gateways. It is at these points that the hill is most easy of access. At A is a modern roadway; at C is a pathway leading down into the valley of "Black Run." At B appears to have been a similar gateway, which for some reason was closed up; a like feature may be observed in the line D. At the gateways, the amount of stones is more than quadruple the quantity at other points, constituting broad, mound-shaped heaps. They also exhibit the marks of intense heat, which has in some instances vitrified their surfaces, and fused them together.   Light, porous scoriæ are abundant in the centres of some of these piles. Indeed, strong traces of fire are visible at many places on the line of the wall, particularly at F, the point commanding the broadest extent of country. Here are two or three small mounds of stone, which seem burned throughout.   Nothing is more certain than that powerful fires have been maintained, for considerable periods, at numerous prominent points on the hill; for what purposes, unless as alarm signals, it is impossible to conjecture.*

It will be observed that the wall is interrupted for some distance at E, where the hill is precipitous and inaccessible. There are, as has already been remarked, several depressions upon the hill which contain constant supplies of water. One of them covers about two acres, and furnishes a supply estimated by the proprietor as adequate to the wants of a thousand head of cattle. Water is obtained in abundance at the depth of twenty feet.

The area enclosed within this singular work is something over one hundred and forty acres, and the line of the wall measures upwards of *two and a quarter miles* in length.   Most of the wall, and a large portion of the area, are still covered with a heavy primitive forest. Trees of the largest size grow on the line, twisting their roots among the stones, some of which are firmly imbedded in their trunks.

That this work was designed for defence, will hardly admit of doubt; the fact is sufficiently established, not less by the natural strength of the position, than by the character of the defences. Of the original construction of the wall, now so completely in ruins, we can of course form no very clear conception. It is possible that it was once regularly laid up; but it seems that, if such were ever the case, some satisfactory evidence of the fact would still be discoverable.   We must consider, however, that it is situated upon a yielding and disintegrating declivity; and that successive forests, in their growth and prostration, aided by the action of the elements, in the long period which must certainly have elapsed since its con-

---

* It has been suggested that perhaps the walls of stone were sustained or surmounted by wooden structures of some sort, the destruction of which, in whole or in part, by fire, caused the appearances noticed in the text. The suggestion that these are the traces of "ancient furnaces," is not to be entertained for an instant.

struction, would have been adequate to the total demolition of structures more solid and enduring than we are justified in supposing any of the stone works of the ancient people to have been. The stones are of all sizes, and sufficiently abundant to have originally formed walls eight feet high, by perhaps an equal base. At some points, substantial fence-lines have been built from them, without sensibly diminishing their numbers. It can readily be perceived that, upon a steep declivity, such as this hill presents, so large an amount of stones, even though simply heaped together, must have proved an almost insurmountable impediment in the way of an assailant, especially if they were crowned by palisades.

In the magnitude of the area enclosed, this work exceeds any hill-work now known in the country; although the wall is considerably less in length than that of "Fort Ancient," on the Little Miami river. It evinces great labor, and bears the impress of a numerous people. The valley in which it is situated was a favorite one with the race of the mounds; and the hill overlooks a number of extensive groups of ancient works, the bearings of which are indicated by arrows on the plan.

Paint creek washes the base of the hill upon the left, and has for some distance worn away the argillaceous slate rock, so as to leave a mural front of from fifty to seventy-five feet in height. It has also uncovered a range of *septaria*, occurring near the base of the slate stratum; a number of which, of large size, are to be seen in the bed of the creek, at *a*. These, most unaccountably, have been mistaken for works of art,—"stone covers" for deep wells sunk in the rock. This notion has been gravely advanced in print; and the humble septaria, promoted to a high standing amongst the antiquities of America, now figure prominently in every work of speculations on the subject. The reason for sinking wells in the bed of a creek, was probably never very obvious to any mind. The supposed "wells" are simple casts of huge septaria, which have been dislodged from their beds; the cyclopean "covers" are septaria which have resisted the disintegrating action of the water, and still retain their places. Parallel ranges of these singular natural productions run through the slate strata of this region: they are of an oblate-spheroidal figure, some of them measuring from nine to twelve feet in circumference. They frequently have apertures or hollows in their middle, with radiating fissures, filled with crystalline spar or sulphate of baryta. These fissures sometimes extend beyond them, in the slate rock, constituting the "good joints" mentioned by some writers. The slate layers are not interrupted by these productions, but are bent or wrapped around them. The following cut illustrates their character.

A is a vertical section: *a* exhibiting the water, *b* the rock. At *c* the septarium has disintegrated, or has been removed, and its cavity or bed is filled with pebbles. At *d* the nodule still remains. B exhibits the appearance presented by *d* from above.

A stone work, somewhat similar in character to that here described, exists near the town of Somerset, Perry county, Ohio. It is described by Mr. Atwater in the Archæologia Americana, vol. i. p. 131.

Still another, of small size and irregular outline, is situated on Beaver creek, a branch of the Great Kenhawa, in Fayette county, Virginia, of which an account was published by Mr. I. Craig of Pittsburgh, in the "American Pioneer," vol. i. p. 199.

PLATE V.

"FORT HILL," HIGHLAND COUNTY, OHIO.*

THIS work occurs in the southern part of Highland county, Ohio; and is distant about thirty miles from Chillicothe, and twelve from Hillsborough. It is universally known as "Fort Hill," though no better entitled to the name than many others of similar character. The defences occupy the summit of a hill, which is elevated five hundred feet above the bed of Brush creek at its base, and eight hundred feet above the Ohio river at Cincinnati. Unlike the hills around it, this one stands detached and isolated, and forms a conspicuous object from every approach. Its sides are steep and precipitous; and, except at one or two points, if not absolutely inaccessible, extremely difficult of ascent. The points most easy of access are at the southern and northern angles, and may be reached on horseback. The top of the hill is level, and has an area of not far from fifty acres, which is covered with a heavy primitive forest of gigantic trees. One of these, a chestnut, standing on the embankment near the point indicated by the letter *e*, measures *twenty-one feet* in circumference; another, an oak, which also stood on the wall, at the point *f*, though now fallen and much decayed, still measures *twenty-three feet* in circumference. All around are scattered the trunks of immense trees, in every stage of decay; the entire forest presenting an appearance of the highest antiquity.

Thus much for its natural features. Running along the edge of the hill is an embankment of mingled earth and stone, interrupted at intervals by gateways. Interior to this is a ditch, from which the material composing the wall was taken. The length of the wall is eight thousand two hundred and twenty-four feet, or something over a mile and a half. In height, measuring from the bottom of the ditch, it varies from six to ten feet, though at some places it rises to the height of fifteen feet. Its average base is thirty-five or forty feet. It is thrown up somewhat below the brow of the hill, the level of the terrace being generally about even with the top of the wall; but in some places it rises considerably above, as shown in the sections. The outer slope of the wall is more abrupt than that of the hill; the earth and stones from the ditch, sliding down fifty or a hundred feet, have formed a

----

* This work was first described, though not first surveyed, by Professor LOCKE, of Cincinnati, in 1838. His description and plan—to the accuracy and fidelity of which every visitor can bear witness—were published in the "Second Annual Report of the Geological Survey of Ohio."

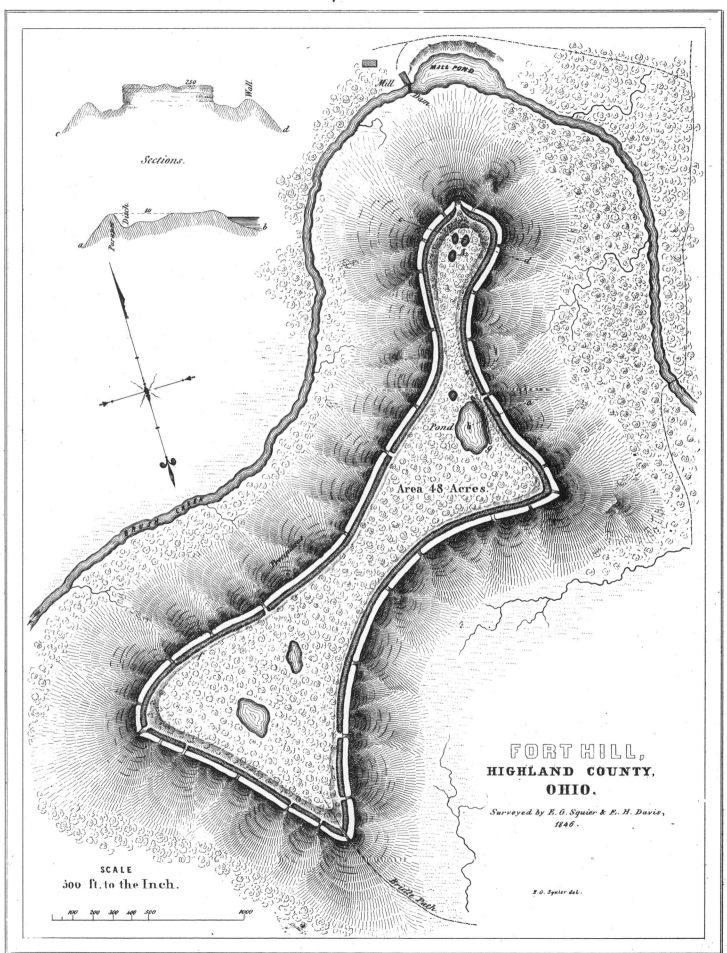

Sections.

250

Wall.

Parapet

Ditch.

80

a

b

c

d

MILL POND

Mill

Dam

d

a

Pond

b

g

Area 48 Acres.

Bridle Path

FORT HILL,

HIGHLAND COUNTY, OHIO.

Surveyed by E. G. Squier & E. H. Davis,
1846.

E. G. Squier del.

SCALE
500 ft. to the Inch.

100   200   300   400   500   1000

LITH. OF SARONY & MAJOR.

declivity for that distance, so steep as to be difficult of ascent, even with the aid which the trees and bushes afford. The ditch has an average width of not far from fifty feet; and, in many places, is dug through the sandstone layer upon which the soil of the terrace rests.* At the point A, the rock is quarried out, leaving a mural front about twenty feet high. The inner declivity of the ditch appears to have been terraced. It descends abruptly from the level for a few feet, then declines gently for some distance, and again dips suddenly, as it approaches the wall. The vertical section *a b* exhibits this feature.

There are *thirty-three* gateways or openings in the wall, most of them very narrow, not exceeding fifteen or twenty feet in width at the top: only eleven of these have corresponding causeways across the ditch. They occur at irregular intervals; and some of them appear to have been rather designed to let off the water which might otherwise accumulate in the ditch, than to serve as places of egress or ingress. Indeed, most of them cannot be supposed to have been used for the last named purposes, inasmuch as they occur upon the very steepest points of the hill, and where approach is almost impossible. At the northern and southern spurs or angles of the hill, the gateways are widest, and the parapet curves slightly outwards. The ditch is interrupted at these points.

There are three depressions or ponds within the enclosure; the largest of these, *g*, has a well-defined artificial embankment on its lower side, which has recently been cut through, and the water principally drawn off. When full, the water must have covered very nearly an acre. Bog-clumps are growing around its edges, and it is free from trees. It does not seem to have any perennial sources of supply. There are several other small circular depressions, a number of which occur together at the bluff A; there are also traces of other excavations, not clearly defined, at various points on the hill.

An inspection of the plan of the work, shows that it is naturally divided into three parts; that at A being, in many respects, the most remarkable. It is connected with the main body of the work by a narrow ridge but one hundred feet wide, and terminates at a bold, bluff ledge, the top of which is thirty feet above the bottom of the trench, and twenty feet above the wall. This bluff is two hundred feet wide. It is altogether the most prominent point of the hill, and commands a wide extent of country. Here are strong traces of the action of fire on the rocks and stones; though whether remote or recent, it is not easy to determine. The connection between the two principal divisions of the work is also narrow, being barely two hundred and fifty feet in width.

Such are the more striking features of this interesting work. Considered in a military point of view, as a work of defence, it is well chosen, well guarded, and, with an adequate force, impregnable to any mode of attack practised by a rude, or semi-civilized people. As a natural stronghold, it has few equals; and the

---

* This sandstone, it should be remarked, to prevent misapprehension, is the "Waverley sandstone," underlying the coal series, and which is found capping most of the hills in this region. It occurs in successive layers, of from a few inches to several feet in thickness. It is quite friable, and quarries readily.

degree of skill displayed and the amount of labor expended in constructing its artificial defences, challenge our admiration, and excite our surprise. With all the facilities and numerous mechanical appliances of the present day, the construction of a work of this magnitude would be no insignificant undertaking. And when we reflect how comparatively rude, at the best, must have been the means at the command of the people who raised this monument, we are prepared to estimate the value which they placed upon the objects sought in its erection, and also to form some conclusion respecting the number and character of the people themselves.

It is quite unnecessary to recapitulate the features which give to this the character of a military work; for they are too obvious to escape attention. The angles of the hill form natural bastions, enfilading the wall. The position of the wall, the structure of the ditch, the peculiarities of the gateways where ascent is practicable, the greater height of the wall where the declivity of the hill is least abrupt, the reservoirs of water, the look-out or citadel, all go to sustain the conclusion.

The evidence of antiquity afforded by the aspect of the forest, is worthy of more than a passing notice. Actual examination showed the existence of not far from *two hundred* annual rings or layers to the foot, in the large chestnut-tree already mentioned, now standing upon the entrenchments. This would give nearly *six hundred years* as the age of the tree. If to this we add the probable period intervening from the time of the building of the work to its abandonment, and the subsequent period up to its invasion by the forest, we are led irresistibly to the conclusion, that it has an antiquity of at least *one thousand years*.* But when we notice, all around us, the crumbling trunks of trees half hidden in the accumulating soil, we are induced to fix upon an antiquity still more remote.

It is worthy of note, that this work is in a broken country, with no other remains, except perhaps a few small, scattered mounds, in its vicinity. The nearest monuments of magnitude are in the Paint creek valley, sixteen miles distant, from which it is separated by elevated ridges. Lower down, on Brush creek, towards its junction with the Ohio, are some works; but none of importance occur within twelve miles in that direction.

———

PLATE VI.

FORTIFIED HILL, BUTLER COUNTY, OHIO.

THIS fine work is situated in Butler county, Ohio, on the west side of the Great Miami river, three miles below the town of Hamilton. The plan is from a

---

* "One of the mounds at Marietta must be more than eight hundred years old; for Dr. Hildreth counted eight hundred rings of annual growth in a tree which grew upon it."—*Lyell's Travels in North America*, vol. ii. p. 29. *See also Second Geological Report of the State of Ohio*, p. 268.

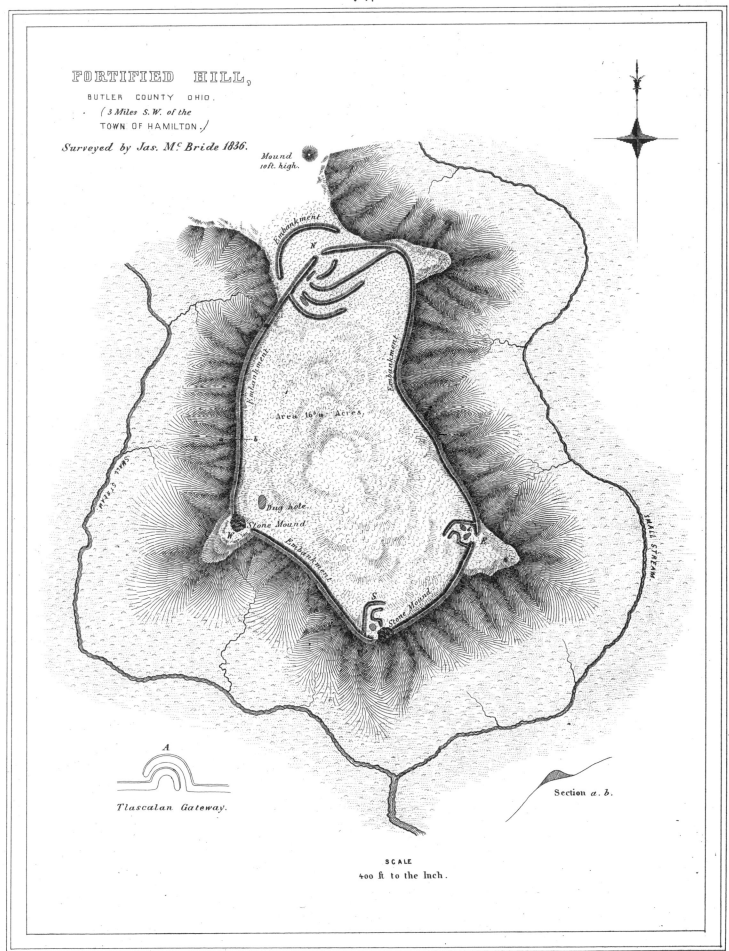

FORTIFIED HILL,

BUTLER COUNTY OHIO.

(3 Miles S.W. of the
TOWN OF HAMILTON.)

Surveyed by Jas. Mc. Bride 1836.

Mound
10ft. high.

Embankment

Embankment

Embankment

Area 16½ Acres,

Bug hole.

Stone Mound

Embankment

Stone Mound

Stone Mound

SMALL STREAM

SMALL STREAM

A

Tlascalan Gateway.

Section *a. b.*

SCALE
400 ft to the Inch.

Lith by Sarony & Major

survey by JAMES McBRIDE, Esq., and the description is made up from his notes. The hill, the summit of which it occupies, is about a half mile distant from the present bed of the river, and is not far from two hundred and fifty feet high, being considerably more elevated than any other in the vicinity. It is surrounded at all points, except a narrow space at the north, by deep ravines, presenting steep and almost inaccessible declivities. The descent towards the north is gradual; and from that direction, the hill is easy of access. It is covered with a primitive forest of oak, hickory, and locust, of the same character with the surrounding forests.

Skirting the brow of the hill, and generally conforming to its outline, is a wall of mingled earth and stone, having an average height of five feet by thirty-five feet base. It has no accompanying ditch; the earth composing it, which is a stiff clay, having been for the most part taken up from the surface, without leaving any marked excavation. There are a number of "dug holes," however, at various points, from which it is evident a portion of the material was obtained. The wall is interrupted by four gateways or passages, each twenty feet wide; one opening to the north, on the approach above mentioned, and the others occurring where the spurs of the hill are cut off by the parapet, and where the declivity is least abrupt. They are all, with one exception, protected by inner lines of embankment, of a most singular and intricate description. These are accurately delineated in the plan, which will best explain their character. It will be observed that the northern gateway, in addition to its inner maze of walls, has an exterior work of a crescent shape, the ends of which approach to within a few feet of the brow of the hill.

The excavations are uniformly near the gateways, or within the lines covering them. None of them are more than sixty feet over, nor have they any considerable depth. Nevertheless, they all, with the exception of the one nearest to gateway S, contain water for the greater portion, if not the whole of the year. A pole may be thrust eight or ten feet into the soft mud, at the bottom of those at E.

At S and W, terminating the parapet, are two mounds, each eight feet high, composed of stones thrown loosely together. Thirty rods distant from gateway N, and exterior to the work, is a mound ten feet high, on which trees of the largest size are growing. It was partially excavated a number of years ago, and a quantity of stones taken out, all of which seemed to have undergone the action of fire.

The ground in the interior of this work gradually rises, as indicated in the section, to the height of twenty-six feet above the base of the wall, and overlooks the entire adjacent country.

In the vicinity of this work, are a number of others occupying the valley; no less than six of large size occur within a distance of six miles down the river. [See Plate III. No. 2. This work is marked A on the map.]

The character of this structure is too obvious to admit of doubt. The position which it occupies is naturally strong, and no mean degree of skill is employed in its artificial defences. Every avenue is strongly guarded. The principal approach, the only point easy of access, or capable of successful assault, is rendered doubly secure. A mound, used perhaps as an alarm post, is placed at about one-fourth of the distance down the ascent; a crescent wall crosses the isthmus, leaving but

3

narrow passages between its ends and the steeps on either hand. Next comes the principal wall of the enclosure. In event of an attack, even though both these defences were carried, there still remains a series of walls so complicated as inevitably to distract and bewilder the assailants, thus giving a marked advantage to the defenders. This advantage may have been much greater than we, in our ignorance of the military system of this ancient people, can understand. But, from the manifest judgment with which their defensive positions were chosen, as well as from the character of their entrenchments, so far as we comprehend them, it is safe to conclude that all parts of this work were the best calculated to secure the objects proposed by the builders, under the modes of attack and defence then practised.

The coincidences between the guarded entrances of this and similar works throughout the West, and those of the Mexican defences, is singularly striking. The wall on the eastern side of the Tlascalan territories, mentioned by Cortez and Bernal Diaz, was six miles long, having a single entrance thirty feet wide, which was formed in the manner represented in the supplementary plan A. The ends of the wall overlapped each other, in the form of semicircles, having a common centre.*

PLATE VII.

"FORT ANCIENT," WARREN COUNTY, OHIO.†

ONE of the most extensive, if not the most extensive, work of this class, in the entire West, occurs on the banks of the Little Miami river, about thirty-five miles north-east from Cincinnati, in Warren county, Ohio. It has not far from four miles of embankment, for the most part very heavy, rising, at the more accessible points, to the height of eighteen and twenty feet. The accompanying map is from a faithful survey, made by Prof. LOCKE, of Cincinnati, and published by him amongst the papers of the American Association of Geologists and Naturalists, in

---

* De Solis describes this Tlascalan work as "a great wall which ran from one mountain to the other, entirely stopping up the way: a sumptuous and strong piece of building which showed the power and greatness of the owner. The outside was of hewn stone cemented with mortar of extraordinary strength. It was twenty feet thick and a fathom and a half high; and on the top was a parapet after the manner of our fortifications. The entrance was narrow and winding; the wall in that part dividing and making two walls, which circularly crossed each other for the space of ten paces."—*History of the Conquest of Mexico, p.* 139.

† An account of this work, accompanied by a very good plan, appeared in the "Portfolio," (a periodical published in Philadelphia,) for the year 1809. Both plan and description were copied by Mr. Atwater, in his memoir, in the first volume of the "Archæologia Americana." It was also briefly described by Dr. Drake, in the chapter on Antiquities contained in his "View of Cincinnati." Since that period, it has been the object of frequent visit and remark.

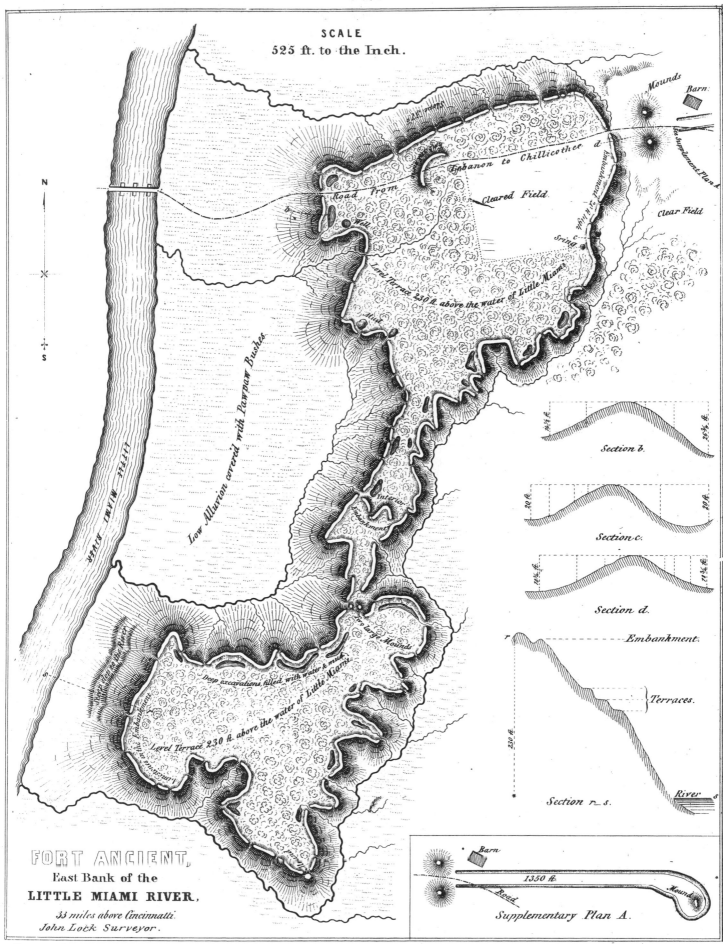

VII.

SCALE
525 ft. to the Inch.

Mounds   Barn

Road from Lebanon to Chillicothee

Cleared Field.

Clear Field

Spring c

Level Terrace 230 ft. above the water of Little Miami

Road from

Well

Mine

Low Alluvion covered with Pawpaw Bushes

LITTLE MIAMI RIVER

N

S

Interior Embankment

two large Mounds

Deep excavations filled with water & mud

Level Terrace 230 ft. above the water of Little Miami

Section b.

Section c.

Section d.

Embankment.

Terraces.

230 ft.

Section r_s.   River

FORT ANCIENT,
East Bank of the
LITTLE MIAMI RIVER,

33 miles above Cincinnatti.
John Lock Surveyor.

Barn
1350 ft.
Road   Mound
Supplementary Plan A.

Face P. 18.

1843. One or two slight additions have been made to his map, to indicate features which may be of some importance in a consideration of the work and its character. The description of Prof. Locke, accompanying the map, though brief, and written with a view to certain geological questions, may not be omitted in this connection.

"This work occupies a terrace on the left bank of the river, and two hundred and thirty feet above its waters. The place is naturally a strong one, being a peninsula, defended by two ravines, which, originating on the east side near to each other, diverging and sweeping around, enter the Miami, the one above, the other below the work. The Miami itself, with its precipitous bank of two hundred feet, defends the western side. The ravines are occupied by small streams. Quite around this peninsula, on the very verge of the ravines, has been raised an embankment of unusual height and perfection. Meandering around the spurs, and re-entering to pass the heads of the gullies, it is so winding in its course that it required one hundred and ninety-six stations to complete its survey. The whole circuit of the work is between four and five miles. The number of cubic yards of excavation may be approximately estimated at six hundred and twenty-eight thousand eight hundred. The embankment stands in many places twenty feet in perpendicular height; and although composed of a tough, diluvial clay, without stone, except in a few places, its outward slope is from thirty-five to forty-three degrees. This work presents no continuous ditch; but the earth for its construction has been dug from convenient pits, which are still quite deep, or filled with mud and water. Although I brought over a party of a dozen active young engineers, and we had encamped upon the ground to expedite our labors, we were still two days in completing our survey, which, with good instruments, was conducted with all possible accuracy. The work approaches nowhere within many feet of the river; but its embankment is, in several places, carried down into ravines from fifty to one hundred feet deep, and at an angle of thirty degrees, crossing a streamlet at the bottom, which, by showers, must often swell to a powerful torrent. But in all instances the embankment may be traced to within three to eight feet of the stream. Hence it appears, that although these little streams have cut their channels through fifty to one hundred feet of thin, horizontal layers of blue limestone, interstratified with indurated clay marl, not more than three feet of that excavation has been done since the construction of the earthworks. If the first portion of the denudation was not more rapid than the last, a period of at least thirty to fifty thousand years would be required for the present point of its progress. But the quantity of material removed from such a ravine is as the square of its depth, which would render the last part of its denudation much slower, in vertical descent, than the first part. That our streams have not yet reached their ultimate level, a point beyond which they cease to act upon their beds, is evident from the vast quantity of solid material transported annually by our rivers, to be added to the great delta of the Mississippi. Finally, I am astonished to see a work, simply of earth, after braving the storms of thousands of years, still so entire and well marked. Several circumstances have contributed to this. The clay of which it is built is not easily penetrated by water. The bank has been, and is still, mostly covered by a forest of beech trees, which have woven a strong web of their roots over its steep sides; and a fine bed of moss (*Polytrichum*) serves still further to afford protection."

Upon the steep slope of the hill, at the point where it approaches nearest to the river, are distinctly traceable three parallel terraces, which were not represented in the original map, but which are indicated here. It is not impossible that they are natural, and were formed by successive *slips* or slides of earth, a feature not uncommon at the West. They nevertheless, from their great regularity, appear to be artificial, and are so regarded by most persons. A very fine view of the valley, in both directions, is commanded from them; though, perhaps, no better than may be obtained from the brow of the hill along which the embankment runs. It has been suggested that they were designed as stations, from which to annoy an enemy passing in boats or canoes along the river. This feature is illustrated in the section *r s.*

From a point near the two large mounds on the neck of the peninsula, start off two parallel walls, which continue for about thirteen hundred and fifty feet, when they diverge suddenly, but soon close around a small mound. As this outwork is in cultivated grounds, it has been so much obliterated as to escape ordinary observation, and is now traceable with difficulty. These parallels are shown in the Supplementary Plan A. They are almost identical, in all their dimensions, with similar parallels attached to ancient works in the Scioto valley.

It is a feature no less worthy of remark in this than in other works of the same class, and one which bears directly upon the question of their design, that at all the more accessible points, the defences are of the greatest solidity and strength. Across the isthmus connecting this singular peninsula with the table land, the wall is nearly double the height that it possesses at those points where the conformation of the ground assisted the builders in securing their position. The average height of the embankment is between nine and ten feet; but, at the place mentioned, it is no less than *twenty*. At the spur where the State road ascends the hill, and where the declivity is most gentle, the embankment is also increased in height and solidity, being at this time not less than fourteen feet high by sixty feet base.

There are over seventy gateways or interruptions in the embankment, at irregular intervals along its line. For reasons heretofore given, it is difficult to believe they were all designed as places of ingress or egress. We can only account for their number, upon the hypothesis that they are places once occupied by block-houses or bastions composed of timber, and which have long since decayed. These openings appear to have been originally about ten or fifteen feet in width.

This work, it will be seen, consists of two grand divisions, the passage between which is long and narrow. Across this neck is carried a wall of the ordinary dimensions, as if to prevent the further progress of an enemy, in the event of either of the principal divisions being carried,—a feature which, while it goes to establish the military origin of the work, at the same time evinces the skill and foresight of the builders. This foresight is further shown, in so managing the excavations necessary for the erection of the walls, as to form numerous large reservoirs; sufficient, in

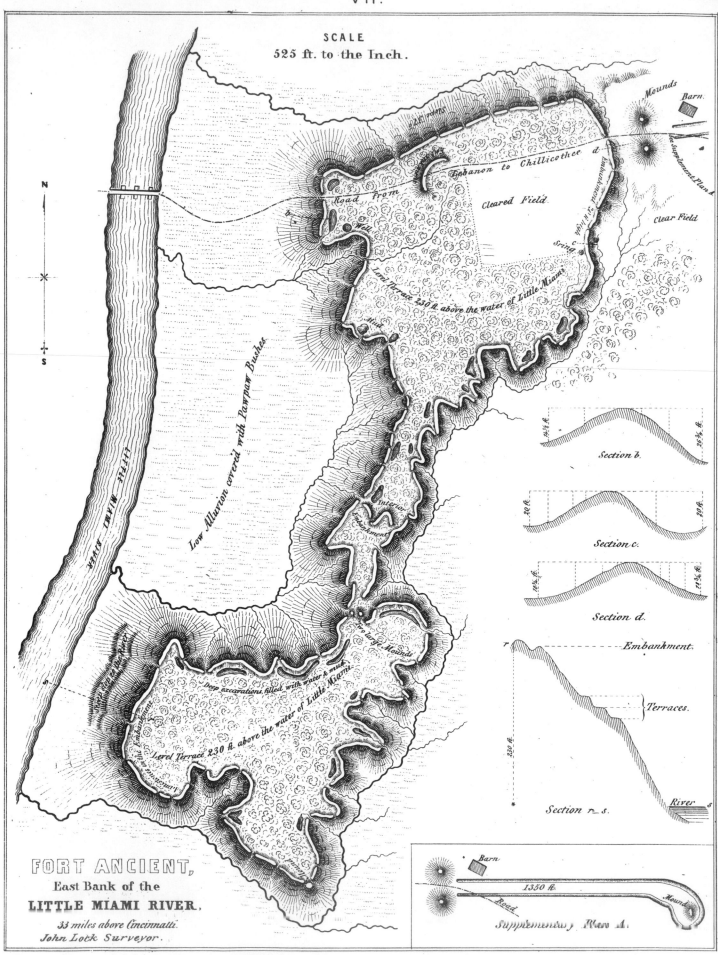

SCALE
525 ft. to the Inch.

Mounds

Barn

Supplement Plan A.

Clear Field

Road from

Lebanon to Chillicothe d.

Cleared Field.

Sring. c

Embankment

Well

Level Terrace 230 ft. above the water of Little Miami

Road

Low Alluvion covered with Pawpaw Bushes

LITTLE MIAMI RIVER

Mid

Interior Embankment

Section b.

Section c.

Section d.

Embankment.

Terraces.

230 ft.

Section r_s.

River

Deep excavations, filled with water & mud.

Level Terrace 230 ft. above the water of Little Miami

Mounds

FORT ANCIENT,
East Bank of the
LITTLE MIAMI RIVER,
33 miles above Cincinnati.
John Lock Surveyor.

Barn

1350 ft.

Road

Mound

Supplementary Plan A.

connection with the springs originating within the work, to supply with water any population which might here make a final stand before an invader. Even in the absence of these sources, surrounded as the work is on every hand by streams, it would be easy, in face of the most formidable investment, to procure an adequate supply.

At numerous points in the line of embankment, and where from position they would yield the most effective support, are found large quantities of stones. These are water-worn, and seem, for the most part, to have been taken from the river. If so, an incredible amount of labor has been expended in transporting them to the places which they now occupy,—especially will it appear incredible, when we reflect that all of them were doubtless transported by human hands.

A review of this magnificent monument cannot fail to impress us with admiration of the skill which selected, and the industry which secured this position. Under a military system, such as we feel warranted in ascribing to the people by whom this work was constructed, it must have been impregnable. In every point of view, it is certainly one of the most interesting remains of antiquity which the continent affords.

———

PLATE VIII. No. 1.

[From the Surveys and Notes of JAMES McBRIDE.]

THIS work occurs on the bank of the Great Miami river, four miles above the town of Hamilton, in Butler county, Ohio, and is one of the most interesting hill-works known. It corresponds in all essential particulars with those of the same class already described. It occupies the summit of a promontory cut from the table lands bordering the Miami river, which upon three sides presents high and steep natural banks, rendered more secure for purposes of defence by artificial embankments thrown up along their brows. The remaining side is defended by a wall and ditch, and it is from this side only that the work is easy of approach. The walls are low, measuring at this time but about four feet in height. The area enclosed is level, subsiding somewhat towards the north, so as to form a sort of natural terrace along the river. Previous to the construction of the Miami canal, this terrace was eight or ten rods wide, having a perpendicular bank next the river, some fifty or more feet high. Upon this terrace are situated several small mounds. The point indicated by c in the plan is the most elevated within the enclosure. The ground here was intermixed with large stones, most of which were removed in building the canal. Among them, it is said, were found several human skeletons, and also a variety of carved stone implements.

The most interesting feature in connection with this work is the entrance on the south, of which the enlarged plan can alone afford a fair conception. The ends of the wall curve inwardly as they approach each other, upon a radius of seventy-five feet, forming a true circle, interrupted only by the gateways. Within the space thus formed, is a small circle one hundred feet in diameter; outside of which and covering the gateway is a mound, e, forty feet in diameter and five feet high. The passage between the mound and the embankment, and between the walls of the circles, is now about six feet wide. The gateway or opening d is twenty feet wide. This singular entrance, it will be remarked, strongly resembles the gateways belonging to a work already described (*Plate VI.*), although much more regular in its construction.

The ditches, *f f*, which accompany the wall on the south, subside into the ravines upon either side. These ravines are not far from sixty feet deep, and have precipitous sides, rendering ascent almost impossible. The mound *h* is three feet high.

The area of the work is seventeen acres; the whole of which is yet covered with a dense primitive forest. The valley beyond the river is broad, and in it are many traces of a remote population, of which this work was probably the fortress or place of last resort, during turbulent periods.

PLATE VIII. No. 2.

THIS work is situated six miles south-west of the town of Hamilton, in Butler county, Ohio. It has no very remarkable features, although possessing the general characteristics of this class of works. It consists of a simple embankment of earth carried around the brow of a high, detached hill, overlooking a wide and beautiful section of the Miami valley. The side of the hill on the north, towards the river, is very abrupt, and rises to the height of one hundred and twenty feet above the valley. The remaining sides are steep, though comparatively easy of ascent. The walls are scarcely four feet high, and seem to have been much reduced by time. There are six gateways, two of which open upon natural bastions or look-outs, and the remaining four towards copious springs, as shown in the plan. The ground within the walls rises gradually to the centre, from which an extended view of the valley and surrounding country may be obtained. There are two mounds of earth placed near together on the highest point within the enclosure, measuring respectively ten feet in height.

South-east of the work, and nine hundred feet distant, is an eminence A, about fifty feet higher than the one occupied by the above mentioned work,—being much the highest point in the neighborhood. The area on the top is, however, inconsiderable. There are some traces of ancient occupation here, though they are far from being distinct or considerable.

PLATE VIII. No. 3.

The enclosure here represented is situated on the left bank of the Great Miami river, two and a half miles above the town of Piqua, Miami county, Ohio, upon the farm of Col. John Johnston, a prominent actor in the early history of Ohio. It occupies the third terrace, which here forms a bluff peninsula, bounded on three sides by streams. The banks of the terrace vary from fifty to seventy-five feet in height. The embankment is carried along the boundaries of the peninsula, enclosing an oval-shaped area of about eighteen acres. It is composed of earth intermixed with large quantities of stone, and is unaccompanied by a ditch. The stones that enter into the composition of the rampart are water-worn, and must have been brought from the bed of the river; which, according to Dr. Drake, for two miles opposite this work, does not at present afford a stone of ten pounds weight. A mound, five feet high and surrounded by a ditch, occurs within the work. There is also another, exterior to the walls, upon the second terrace, towards the river. This is classed as a defensive work, for very obvious reasons.*

Below this entrenchment, and on the present site of the town of Piqua, a group of works formerly existed, consisting of circles, ellipses, etc. These have been described at length, by Major Long.† There are also various small works on the opposite bank of the Miami. Indeed, the whole valley is here covered with traces of a former dense population.

———

PLATE VIII. No. 4.‡

This work resembles one already described, No. 2 of this Plate. It is situated on the bank of the Great Miami river, three miles below Dayton, Montgomery county, Ohio. The side of the hill towards the river is very steep, rising to the

---

* Dr. Drake, in the chapter on antiquities, in his "View of Cincinnati," has the following notice of this work:

"The adjacent hill, at the distance of half a mile, and at the greater elevation of about one hundred feet, is the site of a stone wall, mainly circular, and enclosing perhaps twenty acres. The valley of the river on one side, and a deep ravine on the other, render access to three-fourths of this fortification extremely difficult. The wall is carried generally along the brow of the hill, in one place descending a short distance, so as to include a spring. The silicious limestone of which it was built, must have been transported from the bed of the river, which, for two miles opposite these works, does not at present afford one of ten pounds weight. They exhibit no marks of the hammer or any other tool. The wall was laid up without mortar, and is now in ruins."

† Long's Second Expedition, vol. i. pp. 54—66.

‡ Surveyed by James McBride, Esq. and Samuel Forrer, Esq. of the Ohio Board of Public Works.

height of one hundred and sixty feet.   The remaining sides are less abrupt.   Upon
the south is the principal gateway, and here the declivity is gentle.   This gateway
is covered upon the interior by a ditch, *c c*, twenty feet wide, and seven hundred feet
long.   At *d d d* are dug holes, from which it is apparent a portion of the earth
composing the embankments was taken.   At *b* is a natural depression forty feet deep,
and covering not far from one and a half acres.   At the northern slope of the narrow
ridge which intersects the work, and within the line of the embankment of which
it forms a part, is a small mound.   From its top a full view of the surrounding
country, for a long distance up and down the river, may be obtained.   A terrace,
apparently artificial, skirts the north-west side of the hill, thirty feet below the
embankment.   As remarked in a former instance, this terrace may be natural; it
has, however, all the regularity of a work of art.

PLATE IX.   No. 1.

FORTIFIED HILL, NEAR GRANVILLE, LICKING COUNTY, OHIO.

THE work here represented is situated two miles below the town of Granville,
Licking county, Ohio.   It encloses the summit of a high hill, and embraces an area
of not far from eighteen acres.   The embankment is, for the most part, carried
around the hill at a considerable distance below its brow, and is completely overlooked from every portion of the enclosed area.   Unlike all other hill-works which
have fallen under notice, the ditch occurs *outside* of the wall; the earth in the construction of the latter having been thrown upwards and inwards.   This is observed
equally at the points where the hill is steepest; and the result has been, in the lapse
of time, that the ditch is almost obliterated, while the accumulating earth has filled
the space above the wall, so that the appearance of the defence, at these points, is
that of a high, steep terrace.   The height of the wall varies at different places;
where the declivity is gentle and the approach easy, it is highest,—perhaps eight
or ten feet from the bottom of the ditch; elsewhere it is considerably less.   The
embankment conforms generally to the shape of the hill.   It is interrupted by
three gateways, two of which open towards springs of water, and the other, or
principal one, upon a long narrow spur, which subsides gradually into the valley of
Raccoon creek, affording a comparatively easy ascent.
   Upon the highest part of the ground enclosed in this work, is a small circle, one
hundred feet in diameter, within which are two small mounds.   There is also
another truncated mound, a little distance to the northward of the circle.   The
mounds within the circle, upon excavation, were found, in common with all similar
structures occurring within enclosures, to contain *altars*.   No enduring remains
seem to have been deposited upon these altars, which were covered with ashes,
intermixed with small fragments of pottery.   This is the only hill-work which has

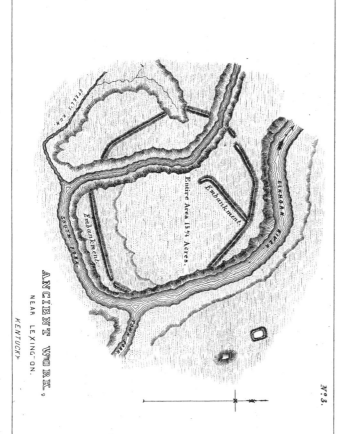

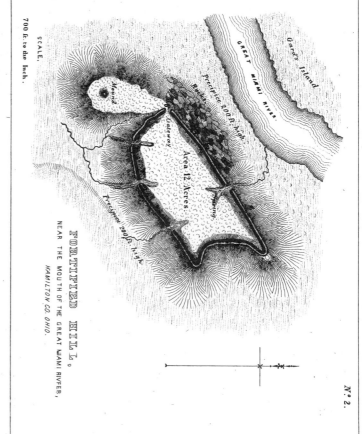

been observed to embrace a minor work of the description here represented. The character of the principal enclosure can hardly be mistaken; it is palpably a defensive work, although deficient in that grand essential, a supply of water. If we concede, what can hardly admit of doubt, that the minor structure had a sacred or superstitious origin, we must of necessity arrive at the conclusion that the altars of the ancient people sometimes accompanied their defences.

This work constitutes one of the Newark Group, and is indicated by the letter B in the "*Map of six miles of the Newark Valley*," presented upon a succeeding plate. This section of country was once densely populated, as is evidenced by the number and extent of the ancient remains which it includes; and it is probable that the work here noticed, together with one of like character upon the opposite side of the valley, three miles distant, constituted the places of last resort of the ancient inhabitants. The extensive works in the immediate vicinity of Newark, of which a full account is elsewhere given, can hardly be supposed to partake of a military character.

PLATE IX. No. 2.*

FORTIFIED HILL AT THE MOUTH OF THE GREAT MIAMI RIVER, HAMILTON COUNTY, OHIO.

THIS work is strictly analogous to the other hill-works already described, and is so well exhibited in the engraving as to need little explanation. It occupies the summit of a steep, insulated hill, and consists of a wall carried along its brow, composed of earth, thrown as usual in such cases from the interior. The wall conforms strictly to the outline of the hill, except at the west, where there is a considerable promontory, which is left unenclosed. Upon this promontory is a mound, corresponding doubtless in its purposes with the one on the principal avenue of approach to the remarkable fortified hill, higher up on the Miami, in Butler county (Plate VI.) The late President Harrison regarded this work as admirably designed for defence, and as evincing extraordinary military skill. He says:

"The work at the mouth of the Great Miami was a citadel, more elevated than the Acropolis of Athens, although easier of access, as it is not like the latter a solid rock, but upon three sides is as nearly perpendicular as could be, to be composed of earth. A large space of the low ground was, however, enclosed by walls uniting it with the Ohio. The foundation of that (being of stone as well as those of the citadel) which formed the western defence, is still visible where it crosses

---

* The above plan is copied from the map accompanying Harrison's published Address before the Historical Society of Ohio.— *Transactions,* vol. i. p. 217.

the Miami river, which, at the period of the erection of the work, must have discharged itself into the Ohio at a point much lower down than it now does. I have never been able to discover the eastern wall of the enclosure; but if its direction from the citadel to the Ohio was such as it should have been, to embrace the largest space with the least labor, there could not have been less than three hundred acres enclosed."*

———

PLATE IX. No. 3.

ANCIENT WORK NEAR LEXINGTON, KENTUCKY.

[From the RAFINESQUE MSS.]

THIS work is situated at the junction of the Town and South forks of the Elkhorn river, seven miles from the town of Lexington, Kentucky. Its character is sufficiently explained by the engraving. It is entirely singular in having a stream, of considerable size, running through it. The river has probably encroached upon its original proportions. About one hundred yards to the eastward of this work is a small, oblong enclosure, and a large, elliptical, truncated mound. Other mounds and enclosures occur in the vicinity.†

———

PLATE X.

CLARK'S WORK; NORTH FORK OF PAINT CREEK.‡

THE work here presented is one of the largest and most interesting in the Scioto valley. It has many of the characteristics of a work of defence, and is accordingly classified as such, although differing in position and some other respects from the entrenched hills just described. The minor works which it encloses, or which are in combination with it, are manifestly of a different character, probably religious

---

* Transactions Historical Society of Ohio, vol. i. p. 225.

† This work is not placed in the connection which it was designed to occupy. Its position in the text was determined by circumstances; and its character will be better understood in the progress of this chapter.

‡ This plan is from an original, minute survey by the authors. A plan and description of the same work were published by Mr. Atwater in the " Archæologia Americana." It will be found to differ in some important respects.

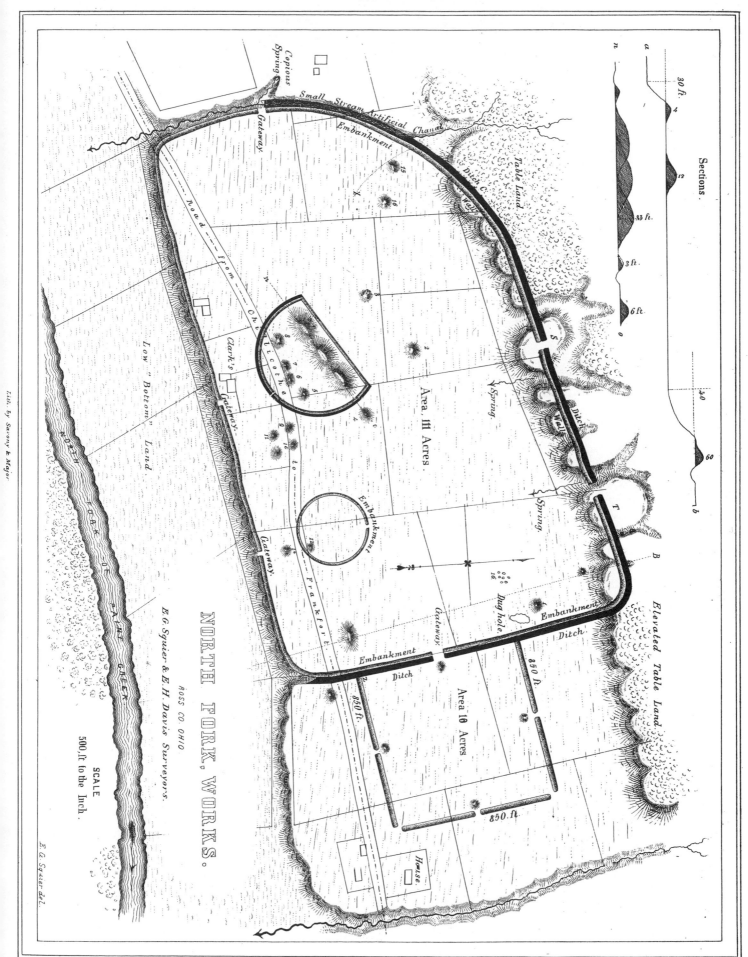

Sections.

30 ft.

NORTH FORK, WORKS.

ROSS CO. OHIO

E.G. Squier & E.H. Davis Surveyors.

SCALE
500 ft. to the Inch.

in their design, and would seem to point to the conclusion, that this was a fortified town, rather than a defensive work of last resort.

It is situated on the North fork of Paint creek, on the estate of W. C. CLARK, Esq. and occupies the entire width of the second terrace, which here presents a broad and level plain, of exceeding beauty and fertility. Its general form is that of a parallelogram, twenty-eight hundred feet by eighteen hundred, with one of its corners somewhat rounded. On the side next the creek, it is bounded by a wall four feet high, running along the very edge of the terrace-bank, and conforming to its irregularities; these however are slight. Its remaining sides are bounded by a wall and exterior ditch; the wall is six feet high by thirty-five feet base, and the ditch of corresponding dimensions. The lines ascend the declivity of the table land back of the terrace, and extend along its brow, dipping into the ravines and rising over the ridges into which it has been cut by the action of water. Wherever the ravines are of any considerable depth, the wall has been washed away; but in all cases leaving evidences that it once extended uninterruptedly through. The bank of the terrace is thirty, that of the table-land fifty feet in height.

The area thus enclosed is one hundred and eleven acres. To the right of the principal work, and connecting with it by a gateway at its centre, is a smaller work of *sixteen acres area*. It is a *perfect square;* its sides measuring respectively eight hundred and fifty feet. It has gateways at the middle of each side, thirty feet wide, and covered by small mounds, which are placed fifty feet interior to the walls. There are gateways also at the two outer corners, which are unaccompanied by mounds. The opening which leads to the principal enclosure is twice as wide as the others. The walls of the smaller work are much lighter than those of the large one, and have no attendant ditch.

Within the area of the great work, are two small ones: one of them is a perfect circle, three hundred and fifty feet in diameter, bounded by a single slight wall, with a gateway opening to the west; the other is a semi-circular enclosure, two thousand feet in circumference, bounded by a slight circumvallation and ditch as represented in

Fig. 3.

the plan. Within this last enclosure (of which Fig. 3 is a view) are seven mounds; three of which are joined together, forming a continuous elevation thirty feet high by five hundred feet long, and one hundred and eighty broad at the base. (See longitudinal section *n o.*) The ground within this work appears to be elevated above the general level of the plain, whether design- edly or by the wasting of the mounds it is im- possible to say. There are other mounds at the points indicated in the plan, most of which have been explored; with what results will appear in the chapter on mounds. It may nevertheless be proper to remark, that nearly all the mounds examined were places of sacrifice, containing altars; thus confirming the opinion already confidently expressed, respecting the character of the work.

Where the defences descend from the table lands to the left, is a gully or torrent-bed, which, before the construction of this work, kept the course indicated by the dotted line *x*. It was turned by the builders from its natural channel into the ditch, along which it still runs for a considerable distance; but at one place it has broken over the wall, obliterating it for nearly two hundred feet. It is dry at most seasons of the year; and, unless much swollen by the rains, keeps the course of the ditch, terminating in a deep gully, formed by the flow of water from a copious and unfailing spring. This gully is made to answer as a ditch, for the space yet intervening, to the edge of the terrace. It is fifteen feet deep, by sixty or seventy wide. In several other instances, this artificial change in water-courses has been observed.

The gateways of this work are six in number; one opening into the smaller enclosure to the east, two upon the table lands, one to the spring first mentioned, and two others towards the creek. Two considerable springs occur within the walls. It is not necessary, however, upon the hypothesis already advanced in respect to this work, to suppose its ancient population wholly dependent upon these sources for their supply of water; inasmuch as it is very evident that many centuries have not elapsed since the creek, now one hundred rods distant, washed the base of the terrace upon which it stands. Indeed, until recently, and until prevented by dykes above, the creek at its highest stages continued to send a portion of its waters along its ancient channel.

The slight wall along the terrace bank is composed chiefly of smooth, water-worn stones, taken from the creek, and cemented together by tough, clayey earth. The wall of the square is wholly of clay, and its outlines may be easily traced by the eye, from a distance, by its color. It appears, as do the embankments of many other works, to have been slightly burned. This appearance is so marked, as to induce some persons to suppose that the walls were, in certain instances, originally composed of bricks partially baked, but which have in process of time lost their form, and subsided into a homogeneous mass. That they have in some cases been subjected to the action of fire, is too obvious to admit of doubt. At the point *z* in the lower wall of the square, stones and large masses of pebbles and earth, much burned, and resembling a ferruginous conglomerate, are turned up by the plough. May not this feature be accounted for by supposing the walls to have been originally surmounted by palisades, which were destroyed by the action of fire? Such a cause, however, seems hardly adequate to produce so striking results.

The broken table land upon which the main work extends, forms natural bastions at *T* and *S*, which have gateways opening to them. At the point marked *C* in the embankment, a quantity of calcined human bones are observable.

Such are some of the features of this interesting work; and if their detail has been tedious, it may be urged in extenuation of such minuteness, that descriptions have hitherto been quite too vague and general. Minute circumstances are often of the first importance in arriving at correct conclusions. The comparative slightness of the wall and the absence of a ditch, at the points possessing natural defences,—the extension of the artificial defences upon the table lands overlooking and commanding the terrace,—the facilities afforded for an abundant supply of water, as well as the large area enclosed, with its mysterious circles and sacred

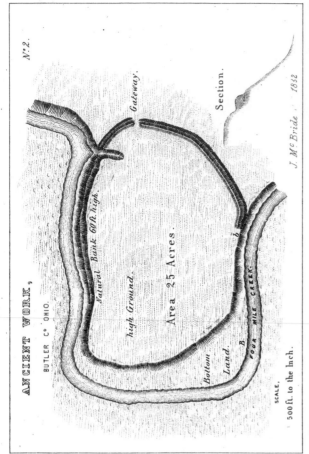

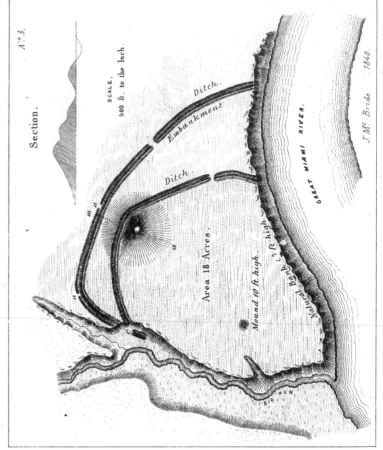

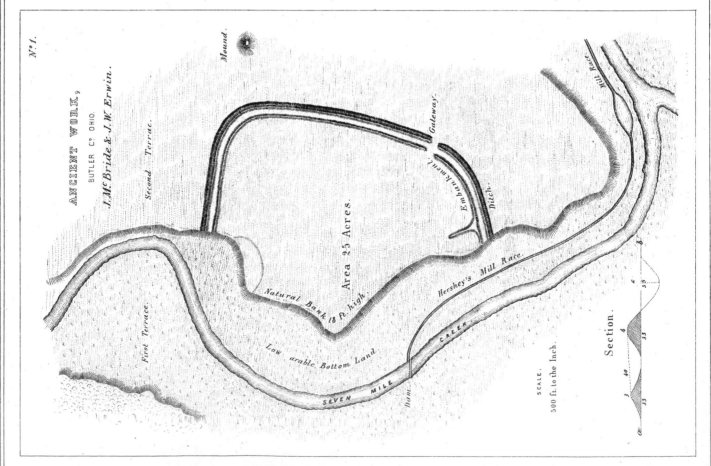

mounds,—*all* go to sustain the conclusion, that this was a fortified town or city of the ancient people. The history of its fall, if its strange monuments could speak, would perhaps tell of heroic defence of homes and altars, and of daring achievements in siege and assault.

The amount of labor expended in the construction of this work, in view of the imperfect means at the command of the builders, is immense. The embankments measure together nearly *three miles* in length; and a careful computation shows that, including mounds, not less than three millions cubic feet of earth were used in their composition.

Within this work, some of the most interesting discoveries recorded in this volume were made.

PLATE XI. No. 1.

[From the Surveys and Notes of JAMES McBRIDE.]

THIS highly interesting work is situated in Butler county, Ohio, on the banks of Seven Mile creek, five miles north of the town of Hamilton. It is formed by two irregular lines of embankment, and an exterior ditch, cutting off a jutting point of the second terrace; and has an area of twenty-five acres. These embankments are parallel throughout, and were evidently both made from the same ditch. The outer one has an average height of four, the inner one of three feet. The ditch is between five and six feet deep, by thirty-five feet wide. At the southern portion of the work, both walls and the ditch have their greatest dimensions. The side of the work next the stream is bounded by an abrupt natural bank, eighteen feet high. Distant a few rods from the north-eastern angle of the work, is an elliptical mound eleven feet high; its conjugate and transverse diameters are ninety-two and one hundred and eighteen feet respectively.

This work has a single gateway thirty feet wide. The inner wall, near its southern extremity, curves inward along the terrace-bank for a considerable distance. The first, or creek terrace, is a low alluvion, not subject to overflow. It is evident, however, that the creek once ran at the base of the natural bank (now bounding one side of this work), probably at the period of its construction and occupancy.

PLATE XI. No. 2.

THIS work affords a very fair illustration of one portion of the defensive structures of the West, already alluded to in the general remarks on the subject, at the beginning of this chapter. It occurs in Oxford township, Butler county, Ohio (Lot 6, Sec. 31, Tp. 5, Range 2, E. M.), at a point on Four Mile creek, where that stream forms a remarkable bend, constituting a peninsula one thousand and sixty feet across at its neck, and one thousand three hundred and twenty feet deep. This peninsula is, in fact, a bold head-land, with precipitous banks, rising sixty feet above the water in the creek, and overlooking the low bottoms that surround it. Across the neck of this peninsula is carried a crescent-shaped wall with an outer ditch. The wall is now but little over three feet in height, and the ditch of corresponding depth. Formerly it was much higher, precluding cultivation. It has been reduced by the present occupant, who has ploughed along it longitudinally, throwing the furrows into the ditch,—a common practice, which is fast reducing and obliterating these interesting monuments of antiquity. A single gateway twenty feet wide leads into the enclosure, which has an area of twenty acres. A terrace, apparently artificial, and thirty feet wide, occurs on the northern bank, at about midway from the water to the top. It may be a natural feature, and caused by the subsidence of the bank from the undermining of the stream. The creek, at one time, unquestionably ran close under the banks of the peninsula; whether or not the recession, leaving the intervening low bottom, B, took place subsequently to the erection of the work, it is of course impossible to determine.

In this work will be remarked the lapping round of the parapet, on the natural bank of the stream at *b*,—a feature heretofore mentioned, as probably designed to protect the flank of the defence.

PLATE XI. No. 3.

AMONG the works remarkable as possessing double walls, is the one here presented. It is situated on the Great Miami river, four miles south-west of the town of Hamilton, Butler county, Ohio. The plan obviates the necessity of a detailed description. The outer line of defence consists of a simple embankment five feet high, with an exterior ditch four feet deep. It has a single gateway fifteen feet wide. There are apparent gateways at *a a*, but the ditch only is interrupted.

Interior to this line of embankment, is another of less dimensions, having also but one opening. At *b* is a large broad mound, over which, and somewhat below the summit on the outer side, the inner line of embankment is carried. The ditch also continues uninterruptedly over the mound, which is thirty feet high. From its summit, a view of the entire work and surrounding country is commanded. Another mound, ten feet high, occurs at the point indicated in the plan. It is composed of stone and gravel, apparently taken from the river, and probably belongs to the class of mounds denominated " sacrificial," the characteristics of

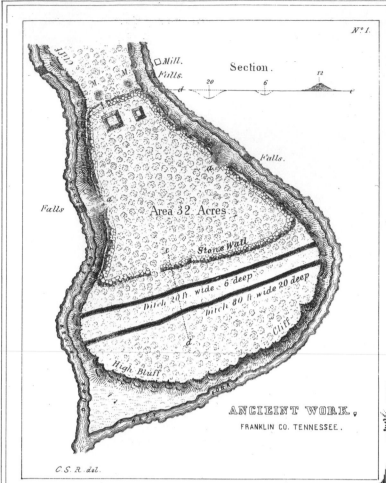

No. 1.

Section.

ANCIEINT WORK,

FRANKLIN CO. TENNESSEE.

Area 32 Acres.

Ditch 20 ft. wide 6 deep

Ditch 80 ft wide 20 deep

Stone Wall

High Bluff

Falls

Falls

Falls

Mill.

Cliff

C. S. R. del.

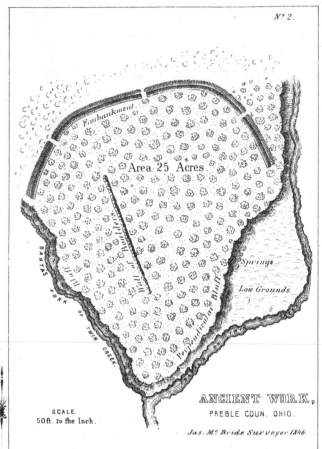

No. 2.

ANCIENT WORK,

PREBLE COUN. OHIO.

Area 25 Acres.

Embankment

Wall of Boulders

Perpendicular Bluff

Springs

Low Grounds.

BANTAS FORK OF TWIN CREEK.

SCALE
50 ft. to the Inch.

Jas. McBride Surveyor 1846.

No. 3.

ANCIENT WORK,

GREENE CO OHIO.

Area 12 Acres.

MASSIE'S CREEK.

Cliff.

Cliff.

Cliff, 15 to 30 ft. high.

Ancient Channel of the Creek.

Wall

Slope

SCALE,
330 ft. to the Inch.

S. P. Owens & J. R. Dille Surveyor.

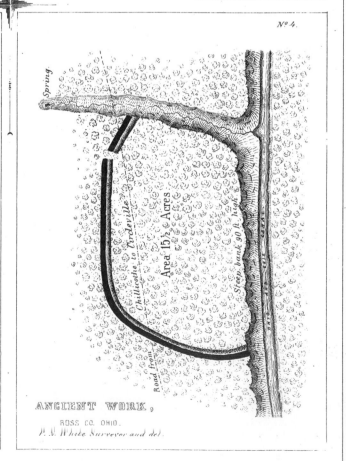

No. 4.

ANCIENT WORK,

ROSS CO. OHIO.

Area 15½ Acres.

Spring.

Chillicothe to Circleville

Road from

Steep bank 90 ft. high

J. N. White Surveyor and del.

which are explained in another chapter. At *c*, the outer wall appears to have formerly extended down to a lower level; but it has been much obliterated by the washing of the bank. The natural banks, on the side towards the river and next to Big Run, are inaccessibly steep, and between sixty and seventy feet high.

The area, embraced within the exterior lines, is a trifle less than eighteen acres. The defensive character of this work can hardly be doubted. It has been suggested that the large mound, over which the inner wall is carried, was designed as a look-out, or alarm post. This may not have been its primary, but it is not impossible that such was its secondary purpose.

———

PLATE XII. No. 1.

STONE WORK, ON DUCK RIVER, TENNESSEE.*

This work is situated in Franklin county, Tennessee, at the junction of the east and west branches of Duck river, and near the main road from Nashville to Winchester.

"It includes an area of about thirty-two acres. The walls are composed of stones of various sizes, collected from the surface of the surrounding country, and rudely thrown together; there is no appearance of their having been united by cement, nor do they exhibit any marks of the hammer. The wall on the south is covered with a layer of earth from one to two feet deep, and is about sixteen feet in thickness at the base, about five feet at the top, and from eight to ten feet high.

"At the northern extremity, near the front wall, are two conical mounds of stone, designated by M, M, in the plan. Each of these mounds is about six feet high, and ten feet in diameter at the base; originally they may have been of somewhat greater altitude, and being on the exterior of the wall, may have been intended as watch towers. In the rear of the mounds is the northern wall, extending to a high bank on either branch of Duck river, and opposite to a waterfall on each, of ten or twelve feet in height. In the northern wall is an entrance or gateway, and in the rear of the gateway are what appear to be the remains of two stone build-

———

* Two plans of this work exist among the MSS. of Rafinesque, which differ slightly from each other. One of them coincides, however, in all important particulars with a plan published some years ago in the "Western Messenger," and has therefore been adopted as probably essentially correct. The description in the "Messenger," which seems to have been written by an intelligent observer, is also adopted. It is amply sustained by the account of Judge Haywood, and by other evidence, and it is thought may be relied on in all respects.

ings (exaggerated in the plan), one about sixteen feet square, the other about ten feet; the stones are rough and unhewn. Stretching south, the walls are continued on both sides until they reach the points *a a*, at a bold limestone bluff, which forms a good natural defence. South of the bluff the walls are continued of the same height and thickness, until they reach the angles of the wall fronting the south which wall also extends from the bank of one river to the other, and has a gateway nearly opposite to that in the northern wall. At the points *a a*, it is supposed by many who have examined this work, there were formerly excavated passages leading to each branch of Duck river, with steps cut in the rock. There does not, however, appear to be sufficient evidence to sustain this conclusion. The ascent or descent is not very difficult; the steps appear to be formed by the projection of the rock strata; and it was no doubt by these passages that the occupants of the work gained access to the river, and were supplied with water.

" Near the base of the wall on the south side is a ditch, from sixteen to twenty feet wide, and six or eight deep. A short distance farther from the southern wall is another and much more extensive ditch or excavation. In some places it is seventy or eighty feet wide, and from twenty-five to thirty feet deep. The earth from these ditches was probably removed to cover the walls of the fort, or employed in the erection of the neighboring mounds, while the ditches themselves constituted an additional means of defence.

" About three quarters of a mile north of this work is a mound of an oblong form, about twenty-five feet high, one hundred feet long, and twenty broad. On the north-west, about half a mile distant, is another mound of similar form, twenty feet high, eighty long, and sixty wide. These mounds are constructed with the same regularity that distinguishes all the other works of similar character. On both these mounds, trees are growing as large as any in the surrounding forests.

" This work differs in its form, and in the material used in its construction, from all others in the vicinity; but it does not exhibit greater evidence of skill. The difference in form was probably owing to its location; it having evidently been made to conform in all respects to the nature of the ground. Stones were employed because they could be readily procured. Although the hammer had nothing to do with the preparation of the materials, it was nevertheless a work of great labor, and the place of location was selected with a military eye."

Numerous other defensive works are represented to exist in Tennessee; but very few of them have been surveyed and described. In Bedford county there is a stone work of considerable size, the walls of which are said to be from sixteen to twenty feet wide at the base, and four to five feet wide on the top. Other works adjoin it. It is generally believed to have been erected by De Soto; but in 1819 an oak-tree standing on the wall was cut down, which exhibited three hundred and fifty-seven annual layers, and must consequently have been seventy-eight years old when De Soto landed in Florida.*

A stone work, less in size, but of the same general character, occurs in Larue

---

* Haywood's Tenn. vol. ii.

county, Kentucky. It is situated on one of the bluffs of the Rolling Fork of Salt river, where the creek makes a sharp bend. A plan of it is published in Collins's History of Kentucky, p. 398. An account of another, of much the same character, in Allen county, is published in the same work, p. 167.

———

PLATE XII. No. 2.

THIS work is situated at the junction of the two principal forks of Twin creek, an affluent of the Great Miami river, six miles south-east of the town of Eaton, Preble county, Ohio, on S. E. corner of Sec. No. 10, Township 5, of Range 3, E. M. The plan is from a survey by Mr. McBride.

In position and mode of construction, this work does not differ materially from a number of others already described. The embankment has an average height of about four feet, and the ditch is not far from five feet deep. The bluff bordering upon the Franklin fork of the creek is for the most part precipitous, and has an average height of between fifty and sixty feet. At its base are several never-failing springs. The height of the bluff fronting upon the other fork varies from thirty feet near the end of the wall, to sixty feet at the junction of the two streams. At its highest part, the bluff consists of a conglomerate, composed of gravel and stones of considerable size. It is very porous, and overhangs about ten feet. There are a number of large cavities in it, which were once supposed to be artificial, and the entrances to subterranean chambers. They are formed by the disintegration of the materials composing the bluff.

Nearly in the centre of the work, in the position indicated in the plan, is a line of large stones. They occupy a space about seven hundred feet long, by twelve broad, and are laid compactly together. Though much sunk in the earth, they are yet distinctly traceable.

———

PLATE XII. No. 3.*

THE fortification here presented affords a fine illustration of the character of the ancient defences of the West. It is situated on Massie's creek, a tributary of the Little Miami river, seven miles east from the town of Xenia, Greene county,

---

* This work is laid down from surveys made by S. T. OWEINS, surveyor of Greene county, and by L. K. DILLE, M.D. The survey by Mr. Oweins was kindly communicated by W. B. Fairchild, Esq. of Xenia. The work has also been personally examined by the authors.

Ohio; and consists of a high promontory, bounded on all sides, excepting an interval at the west, by a precipitous limestone cliff. Across the isthmus, from which the ground gradually subsides towards the plain almost as regularly as an artificial glacis, is carried a wall of earth and stones. This wall is now about ten feet high by thirty feet base, and is continued for some distance along the edge of the cliff where it is least precipitous, on the north. It is interrupted by three narrow gateways, exterior to each of which was formerly a mound of stones, now mostly carried away. Still exterior to these are four short crescent walls, extending across the isthmus. These crescents are rather slight, not much exceeding, at the present time, three feet in height. The cliff has an average height of upwards of twenty-five feet, and is steep and almost inaccessible. At *d d* are breaks in the limestone, where the declivity is sufficiently gentle to admit of a passage on horseback. At E is a fissure in the cliff, where persons may ascend on foot. The valley, or rather ravine, C C, is three hundred feet broad. Massie's creek, a considerable stream, washes the base of the promontory on the north. The area bounded by the cliff and embankment is not far from twelve acres. The whole is now covered with the primitive forest.

The natural strength of this position is great, and no inconsiderable degree of skill has been expended in perfecting its defences. A palisade, if carried around the brow of the cliff and along the summit of the wall, would render it impregnable to savage assault. About one hundred rods above this work, on the opposite side of the creek, is a small circle, two hundred feet in diameter, enclosing a mound. About the same distance below, upon the same bank, is a large conical mound, thirty feet in height and one hundred and forty feet in diameter at the base. No other works of magnitude are known to exist, nearer than the great defensive structure on the Little Miami (Plate VII.), twenty-one miles distant.

———

PLATE XII. No. 4.

THIS work, unlike those just described, occurs upon the high table-land bordering the Scioto river bottoms, on the west bank of that stream, twelve miles above the city of Chillicothe. It consists of a single wall and ditch, cutting off a high promontory, formed by the declivity of the table land, and the bank of a wide and deep ravine. These banks are not far from one hundred feet in height, and at most points are absolutely inaccessible. It has a single gateway, opening towards a copious spring, at the head of the ravine just mentioned. The wall is four feet high, and the ditch of corresponding depth. There are no mounds within this enclosure, nor in its immediate vicinity; but a number of natural elevations are discernible, which an unpractised eye might mistake for works of art. In this instance, they may have subserved some of the purposes of the mounds.

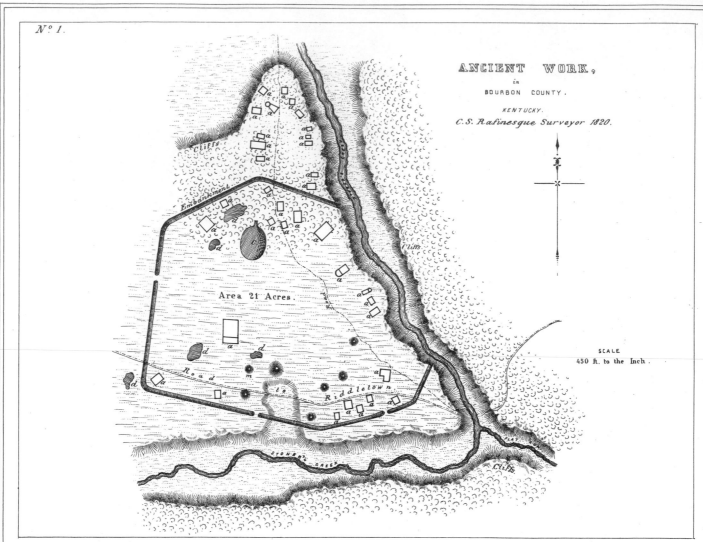

No. 1.

ANCIENT WORK,
in
BOURBON COUNTY.
KENTUCKY.
C. S. Rafinesque Surveyor 1820.

SCALE
450 ft. to the Inch.

Cliffs

Embankment

Area 21 Acres.

Cliffs

Road

Riddletown

STONER'S CREEK

Cliffs

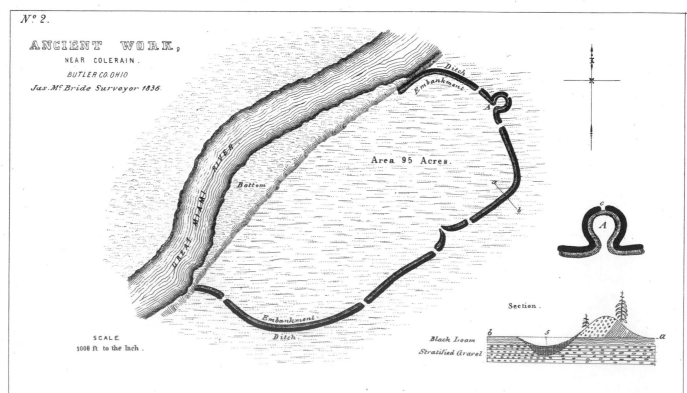

No. 2.

ANCIENT WORK,
NEAR COLERAIN.
BUTLER CO. OHIO.
Jas. McBride Surveyor 1836.

Ditch
Embankment

GREAT MIAMI RIVER

Bottom

Area 95 Acres.

Embankment
Ditch

SCALE
1000 ft. to the Inch.

Section.

Black Loam
Stratified Gravel

The water flowing through the ditch has formed deep gullies at the points where it terminates. The soil is here clayey and hard. The level at the foot of the promontory upon which this work stands, is the first or latest-formed terrace of the Scioto; indicating that the river, at one period, swept along where the Ohio canal now passes.

———

PLATE XIII. No. 1.

[From the RAFINESQUE MSS.]

THIS work, which seems incontestibly of a defensive character, is situated on Stoner's creek, at the mouth of Flat Run, in Bourbon county, Kentucky. The wall throughout is composed of earth, and is slight, not exceeding three or four feet in height. A number of mounds and excavations occur within the enclosure, together with other remains, consisting of raised outlines, two or three feet broad and one foot high. These are indicated by the letter *a*, and are denominated "remains of dwellings" by Rafinesque. Twenty of them are found within, and fourteen without the walls; the latter occupying the point of land to the north of the enclosure. The larger one is called "the palace" by our fanciful authority, and is represented to be eighty feet long by seventy-five broad. To the north of "the palace" is an elliptical, hollow area, fifteen feet deep; it is indicated by the letter *c*. A number of irregular excavations are marked by the letter *d*. The Lexington road passes through this work.

———

PLATE XIII. No. 2.*

[From the Surveys and Notes of JAMES McBRIDE.]

THIS work is one of the first magnitude; and in many respects bears a close resemblance to the great work on the North fork of Paint creek. (See Plate IX.) It is situated near the village of Coleraine, Hamilton county, Ohio, on the right bank of the Great Miami river, and encloses an area of ninety-five acres. The walls have an average height of nine feet, and have an exterior ditch of proportionate dimensions. The terrace upon which the work is located is thirty feet above the usual stage of water in the river.

———

* This work is marked C, in the map of a " *Section of six miles of the Miami valley,*" Plate III.

The outwork, of which A is an enlarged plan, possesses all the features of a bastion, and was perhaps designed as such. It could hardly have been intended as a gateway; for, although the ditch is interrupted for a narrow space at *c*, the embankment is unbroken.

The transverse section of the wall, *a b*, demonstrates the artificial origin of the work, which it is not probable any one would be disposed to deny. The upheaved gravel upon the exterior side of the wall, wherever it is under cultivation, supports dwarfed and sickly maize; while on the inner side, the grain is luxuriant. This feature and its cause are indicated in the section.

This work, which was undoubtedly defensive, commands a large peninsula, two miles in circumference, formed by a singular bend in the river. About two hundred paces distant from this enclosure, in a southern direction, is the site of old Fort Dunlap, somewhat celebrated in the early history of the Miami valley. It was invested by the notorious Simon Girty, with a force of six hundred Indians, in 1791, without success. Some distance from the fort, and still further to the south, is a hill three hundred feet in altitude, upon the top of which are two mounds, measuring five and ten feet in height, respectively. They are composed of earth and stones, considerably burned.

PLATE XIV.

NUMBER 1.—This work is situated near the north line of Pickaway county, Ohio, on the right bank of the Scioto river. It is entirely analogous to many of those already described; and is only remarkable as possessing three lines of embankment, with corresponding ditches, as shown by the section *a b*. " The ditches are here interior to the walls, which circumstance is adverse to the idea of a defensive origin. The situation, however, with a steep bank and deep water on one side, and deep ravines with precipitous banks on the others, is one of great natural strength and adaptation for defence. The walls are now very slight."

NUMBER 2.—This work is, in most respects, similar to the one last described. It is situated four and a half miles north of Worthington, Franklin county, Ohio, on the left bank of Olentangy creek. The artificial defences consist simply of an embankment of earth, three feet in height, with an exterior ditch of corresponding depth. The natural defences are sufficiently obvious. Both of these plans are from surveys by CHARLES WHITTLESEY, Esq.

NUMBERS 3 AND 4.—The character of these works is sufficiently explained by the engravings. From the position of the ditch and other obvious circumstances, they have been classed as of defensive origin. They are from the Rafinesque MSS.

ANCIENT WORK.
PICKAWAY Cº OHIO.
Chas Whittlesey S. & Del.

SCALE
250 ft. to the Inch.

Scioto Bottoms
Bayou River
Bluff
Section.

Nº 1.

ANCIENT WORK.
FAYETTE CO. KENTUCKY.

Area 25 Acres.

Elkhorn River ½ miles

SCALE
500 ft to the Inch

Nº 3.

ANCIENT WORK.
FRANKLIN CO. OHIO.
Chars. Whittlesey S. & del.

SCALE
500ft. to the Inch.

Slate Bluff 100ft

SCALE
500 ft to the Inch.

Nº 2.

ANCIENT WORK.
6 M. FROM LEXINGTON FAYETTE CO. KENTUCKY

Area 18 Acres.

Mill Road.
Morgan
Gally Ford Road

SCALE
500 Ft to the Inch.

Nº 4.

Place P. 56.

Lith. of Sarony & Major 117 Fulton S. N. Y.

C. Rafinesque del.

C. Rafinesque del.

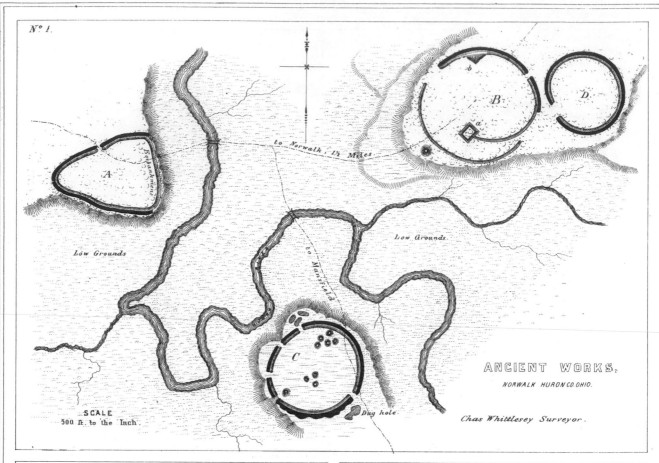

No 1.

to Norwalk 1½ Miles

to Mansfield

Low Grounds

Low Grounds

Embankment

A

B

D

C

Dug hole

SCALE
500 ft. to the Inch.

ANCIENT WORKS,

NORWALK HURON CO. OHIO.

Chas Whittlesey Surveyor.

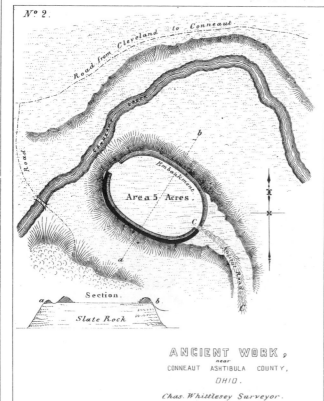

No 2.

Road from Cleveland to Conneaut

Road

Embankment

Area 5 Acres

b

c

a

Section.

Slate Rock

ANCIENT WORK,
near
CONNEAUT ASHTIBULA COUNTY,
OHIO.

Chas. Whittlesey Surveyor.

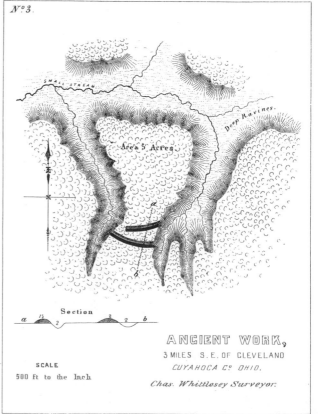

No 3.

SMALL STREAM

Deep Ravines.

Area 5 Acres

a

b

Section.

a   1½   2   2   b

SCALE
500 ft. to the Inch

ANCIENT WORK,
3 MILES S.E. OF CLEVELAND
CUYAHOCA CO OHIO.

Chas. Whittlesey Surveyor.

Lith. by Sarony & Major

PLATE XV.

ANCIENT WORKS IN NORTHERN OHIO.

The succeeding plans and descriptions, relating to aboriginal monuments of northern Ohio, were communicated by Charles Whittlesey, Esq., of Cleveland, whose archæological researches have been both extensive and accurate.

Number 1. *Ancient Works near Norwalk, Huron county, Ohio.*—" The relative positions of the various works composing this group are given by the eye; they are nevertheless sufficiently accurate. The individual works are laid down from actual survey.

" The enclosure A is principally in a field long cultivated, and is scarcely traceable. The ditch is exterior to the wall, and exists only upon the north-west and south-west sides. The walls were very much reduced: when first seen by the whites, they scarcely exceeded eighteen inches in height. The ditch was of corresponding depth.

" The enclosure B occupies a promontory of gravelly land, elevated about forty feet above the creek. The detached circular work D is nearly obliterated by the plough. It had a slight exterior ditch, as had also a part of the main work B. The present height of the wall is from one to two and a half feet; depth of ditch somewhat less. The breadth of the embankments, at the base, varies from fifteen to thirty feet. Within the enclosure B is an elevation of earth, *a*, of a rectangular form, about three feet high, from which a low embankment extends to the outer wall. At *b* is a similar elevation connected with the wall. Exterior to the work, and occupying the point of the headland on which it stands, is a small mound, from which a skull was taken some years since, and deposited in the museum of the Willoughby University of Lake Erie. In it were also found the two valves of what is described as a *clam shell*, each having three holes near the beak, suggesting the probability of a handle having been attached at that point, so as to constitute a spoon or ladle. Besides these were found two pipes of clay, and one of white marble, partly disintegrated, about two and a half inches high; also, a flat piece of a hard grayish slate, half an inch thick, wrought to an edge at the broad end, with a hole pierced obliquely through it, called by the finders ' a hoe.' A small earthen vessel, of coarse material and rude finish, holding about a pint, accompanied these relics. All these articles were taken from the vicinity of coals and ashes, and burned human bones. In the hands of one of the skeletons were pieces of clay, which had evidently been placed in them while in a plastic state, inasmuch as they still retained the impressions of the fingers, joints, and palms.*

---

* These relics, as also the skeletons found with them, were probably those of the more recent Indians, and constituted a second and comparatively late deposit. The burned remains, doubtless, resulted from the original burial by fire. Incremation was extensively practised by the mound-builders.

"The work C occupies a corresponding position with those already described, as belonging to this group. The peninsula upon which it is situated is approachable only from the south. Upon this side the ditch is irregular. The mounds of the central group have been opened; but it is not known with what results. They are quite low, not exceeding three feet in height. The wall of this work is very slight. At the south-west is a graded passage to the lower level of the river bottom.

"Huron river or creek, several branches of which join it at this point, is always fordable; and the bluffs which surround the enclosures are not very difficult of ascent. These works may have been designed for defence,—perhaps they were 'walled towns;' but they do not occupy positions of great natural strength. The grounds adjacent to the river are low, and in places swampy: the river evidently once ran at the base of the bluff occupied by the enclosure B."

NUMBER 2. *Ancient Work near Conneaut, Ashtabula county, Ohio.*—"This work is at present very slight, but distinctly traceable. The sketch is a mere *coup d'œil*, without measurements. The elevation of the bluff upon which it stands is about seventy feet; and the banks of aluminous slate are, upon the north, very precipitous. It would be entirely impracticable for a body of men to ascend upon this side, without ladders and scaling apparatus. Upon the south side it would be practicable for an assailant to ascend, unless prevented by some artificial obstacle. Upon this side, the wall which skirts the brow of the hill is accompanied by an outer ditch, while upon the north there is a simple embankment. The ascent, C C, is gradual and easy. Within the enclosure the earth is very black and rich; outside of the walls it is a stiff clay. The adjacent bottoms are very fertile, and the creek is everywhere fordable. There can be no doubt that this was a fortified position."

Near the village of Conneaut are a number of mounds, and other traces of an ancient population, among which is an aboriginal cemetery regularly laid out, and of great extent.

NUMBER 3. *Ancient Work three miles south-east of Cleveland, Cuyahoga county, Ohio.*—"This stronghold is on the great plain which extends some miles back from the shores of Lake Erie, gently declining towards it, and by many supposed to have been its ancient bed. Many portions of this plain are two hundred feet above the present surface of the lake. The marl, sand, and gravel deposits, of which this formation is made up, are from one hundred to three hundred feet thick.

"These materials are readily washed away by rains, springs, and rivulets; so that the flat region is intersected by numberless deep and narrow ravines, leaving bluff headlands, and furnishing the ancient people with numerous positions protected on nearly every side by deep gullies and high precipitous banks, and capable, with little artificial aid, of easy defence. These features of the country, and the manner in which they were made available for defensive purposes, are well illustrated in the example here presented. The isthmus connecting this promontory with the general table is but about two hundred feet wide, and is defended by parallel lines of embankments accompanied by exterior ditches. There seems to be no gateway or opening through the outer line; the inner one, however, terminates before reaching the bank of the ravine on the left, leaving a narrow passage-way upon that side. The natural banks have an angle of forty-five to sixty degrees with the horizon, and are in many places wet and slippery, and utterly inaccessible. About one-fourth of a mile to the eastward of this work, is a mound ten feet high, by sixty feet in diameter at the base."

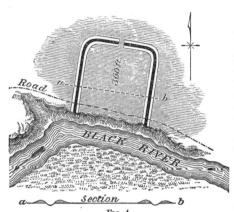

FIG. 4.

FIG. 4.—" This work is situated on the right bank of Black river, in Sheffield township, Lorain county, Ohio. The bank of the river is here nearly perpendicular and quite impossible of ascent, except by ropes or something equivalent, and is about sixty feet high. The water level of the lake reaches to this spot, and the river is in consequence too deep to be forded. The position seems to have been selected for the purpose of defence, although the land back of it is on the same level.

" The artificial defences consist of double embankments, with an intermediate ditch. The embankments are very slight, not much exceeding a foot in height. It is not improbable that the ditch was occupied by wooden pickets, supported by embankments on either side. The work could not have afforded any protection, except with additional defences,—palisades, or something of the sort. Within the enclosure the soil is very rich; but without, it is clayey and poor. The gateway, opening to the north, is forty feet wide."

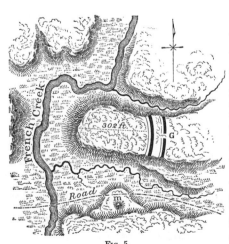

FIG. 5.

FIG. 5.—" This work is situated in the same township with that last described. It is bounded upon three sides by a vertical slate bluff, and defended upon the fourth by a double line of embankments, with accompanying exterior ditches. The height of the walls is about eight feet, measuring from the bottom of the ditches. There is an opening or passage-way through the outer line, but none through the inner. We may account for this circumstance by supposing the latter to have been thrown up after the commencement of a siege. As usual, the soil within this work is very rich compared with that without the walls. Under any mode of attack known to barbarians, this must have been an impregnable work. Upon the other side of the creek, are bluffs of equal height with that upon which this defence is located; but they are too far distant to afford positions of annoyance to besiegers."

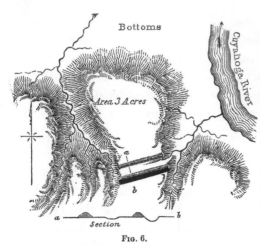

FIG. 6.

FIG. 6.—"This work is situated upon the Cuyahoga river, eight miles above Cleveland, Ohio. It corresponds, in all essential particulars, with the one on the same stream, five miles below, which has already been described. The ground has been so long under cultivation that the parallels are with difficulty traced; they are not more than a foot or eighteen inches high. The ditch is of corresponding depth. Between the lines there is a depression,—undoubtedly artificial in its origin, but now much deepened by rains. The soil is a clay-loam, and the area very difficult of access from all sides. The bluff is here from one hundred and fifty to two hundred feet high."

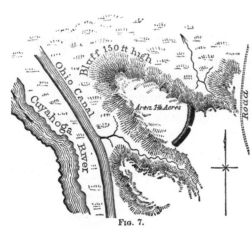

FIG. 7.

FIG. 7.—"This work is situated on the Cuyahoga river, two miles below that last described, with which it coincides in respect to position. It has, however, but a single wall and ditch; the latter is from two to four feet deep, the former of proportionate height. There is a gateway or unexcavated passage across the ditch, but no corresponding opening in the embankment. There is, however, a narrow, unprotected space between the left end of the defences and the bluff. The elevation of the ground is here about two hundred feet above the river, the soil sandy, and lately put under cultivation. The bluff is steep and difficult of ascent. Water is found in the adjacent ravines, which are narrow and deep."

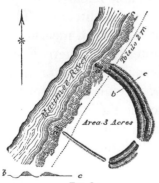

FIG. 8.

FIG. 8.—"This work is situated on the right bank of the Maumee river, two miles above Toledo, in Wood county, Ohio. The water of the river is here deep and still, and of the lake level; the bluff is about thirty-five feet high. Since the work was built, the current has undermined a portion, and parts of the embankment are to be seen on the slips at *a a*. The country for miles in all directions is flat and wet, though heavily timbered, as is the space in and around this enclosure. The walls, measuring from the bottoms of the ditches, are from three to four feet high. They are not of uniform dimensions throughout their extent; and as there is no ditch on the south-west side, while there is a double wall and ditch elsewhere, it is presumable that the work was abandoned before it was finished."

"Nothing can be more plain, than that most of the remains in northern Ohio, particularly those on the Cuyahoga river, are military works. There have not yet been found any remnants of timber in the walls; yet it is very safe to presume that palisades were planted on them, and that wooden posts and gates were erected at the passages left in the embankments and ditches.

"All the positions are contiguous to water; and none of them have higher land in their vicinity, from which they might in any degree be commanded. Of the works bordering on the shore of Lake Erie, through the State of Ohio, there are none but may have been intended for defence; although in some of them the design is not perfectly manifest. They form a line from Conneaut to Toledo, at a distance of from three to five miles from the lake; and all stand upon or near the principal rivers. There are probably five of them as yet unknown, to one that has been publicly noticed. In the interior of the State, so far as my observation has extended, this class of works is wanting. Their place is supplied by larger works, situated on low lands, their strength depending more on artifice than on position.* They are so different, that I am disposed to regard them, not only as designed for other purposes, but as the work of another and probably later people.

"The most natural inference in respect to the northern cordon of works is, that they formed a well-occupied line, constructed either to protect the advance of a nation landing from the lake and moving southward for conquest; or, a line of resistance for a people inhabiting these shores and pressed upon by their southern neighbors. The scarcity of mounds, the absence of pyramids of earth, which are so common on the Ohio, the want of rectangular and other regular works, at the north,—all these differences tend to the conclusion that the northern part of Ohio was occupied by a distinct people.

"At the north there is generally more than one wall of earth, and the ditches are invariably exterior. There are sometimes passages, or 'sally-ports,' through the outer parallel, and none through the inner one. There is also, in general, a space between the parallels sufficiently large to contain a considerable body of fighting men. By whatever people these works were built, they were much engaged in offensive or defensive wars. At the south, on the other hand, agriculture and religion seem to have chiefly occupied the attention of the ancient people.

"In view of the above facts, we may venture to suggest a hypothesis, without undertaking to assign to it any more than a basis of probability. Upon the assumption that two distinct nations occupied the State,—that the northern were warlike, and the southern peaceful and agricultural in their habits,—may we not suppose that the latter were overcome by their northern neighbors, who built the military works to be observed upon the Ohio and its tributaries, while the more regular structures are the remains of the conquered people?"

---

* "There is a small enclosure on the south line of Franklin county, and another in Pickaway county, which closely resemble those along the lake shore." See Plate XIV, Nos. 1 and 2.

6

The differences between the northern and southern earthworks, pointed out by Mr. Whittlesey, are not greater than would naturally be exhibited between the structures of a sparse frontier population, and those erected by more central and dense communities. Works, generally corresponding with those here described, are found still further to the northward and eastward; extending to the Genesee river and its tributaries in New-York, and even to the head waters of the Susquehanna in Pennsylvania,—which seems to have been the extreme limit to which the mound-builders penetrated in that direction. From plans previously presented, it will be seen that precisely analogous works occur in Kentucky and Tennessee. It will be seen also, in a succeeding chapter, on the "Antiquities of the Southern States," that similar structures are found in Mississippi, and elsewhere along the Gulf.

The examples of defensive works here presented will serve to give a very accurate conception of this class of structures. By a minute attention to their various details, we are prepared to estimate the judgment, skill, and industry of their builders. No one can rise from such an examination, except with the conviction that the race, by whom these works were erected, possessed no inconsiderable knowledge of the science of defence,—a degree of knowledge much superior to that known to have been possessed by the hunter tribes of North America previous to the discovery by Columbus, or indeed subsequent to that event. Their number and magnitude must also impress the inquirer with enlarged notions of the power of the people commanding the means for their construction, and whose numbers required such extensive works for their protection. It is not impossible that, like the defensive enclosures of the Polynesian Islanders, they were to a certain extent designed to embrace cultivated fields, so as to furnish the means of subsistence to their defenders, in the event of a protracted siege. There is no other foundation, however, for this suggestion, than that furnished by the great size of some of them. The population that found shelter within their walls must have been exceedingly large, if their dimensions may be taken as the basis of a calculation.

There is no positive evidence that the mound-builders fully understood the value of the bastion in their works of defence; although they seem, in some instances, to have secured the projecting points of the hills on which their defences are situated, with a view of enfilading the walls. The fortified hill near the mouth of the Great Miami, (Plate IX,) and Fort Hill, in Highland county, afford examples. These projecting points could however, from their wide distance apart, but very imperfectly answer the purpose of bastions; and the supposition that they were thus used is rendered less probable, from the fact that the walls oftener cut off these points than accommodate themselves to them. It is not improbable, notwithstanding the absence of direct evidence to that effect, that bastions of wood were erected at intervals along the walls. Such constructions would undeniably be the most simple and efficient for the purposes desired. The numerous openings in the walls of many of these works, although indiscriminately denominated gateways, were clearly not always designed as such. It is not unwarrantable to suppose that they mark the positions of wooden constructions, like the block-houses of later times, which projected beyond the walls, and answered the double purpose of bastions and watch-towers. The very regular intervals between these openings, particularly in the great work on the Little Miami, (Plate VII,) and the Fortified Hill in Highland county, just mentioned, (Plate V,) would seem to favor this hypothesis. Of course we cannot now expect to find any traces of wooden structures, even if such entered into the original defences.

The walls of earth and stone which constitute all that remains to us of these aboriginal fortifications, although often high and heavy, would nevertheless, in themselves, furnish very imperfect means of protection and resistance. Earth cannot be heaped up so as very much to impede an assailant; and the stone works, as far as noticed, do not appear to have been constructed of stone regularly laid, so as to present a vertical or inaccessible front to an enemy. These circumstances render it sufficiently obvious that the walls were surmounted by palisades, or by something equivalent. We are sustained in this conclusion by the concurrent practices of all nations, known to construct permanent works of this description. The ramparts of the Roman camps were strengthened by stakes fixed on the top; and to this day, the walls of *E'Pas*, or entrenched hills of the New Zealanders, are surmounted by palisades. Such also is the present practice of some of the tribes on the Missouri,—the Minatarees, Rickarees, and others. The walls of some works, which, from their position and other circumstances, are manifestly of defensive origin, are so slight that it would be absurd to suppose them designed for protection, unless crowned with palisades. Most of those of northern Ohio are subject to this remark. It has been asserted by certain writers on American antiquities, that traces of palisades are yet to be seen in some of them. Aside from the palpable improbability of anything of the sort, it is proper to remark that no such evidences have been observed in the course of our own investigations. A very few years of exposure would suffice to obliterate all traces of wood in these constructions.

We have already had occasion to remark the skill with which the gateways or entrances to these enclosures are sometimes protected by over-lapping or concentric walls, horn-works, etc. It is rational to conclude that means were made use of by the builders to close the entrances effectually, when desired. How this object was accomplished is, of course, entirely a matter of conjecture. The Australians, in case of alarm, completely close their entrenchments with stones or other obstructions. Entrance is effected only by a succession of posts of different lengths, like a stile, or by the aid of notched trees.

In connection with many of the defensive structures, mounds are occasionally to be found, so placed as to suggest the purposes of watch-towers, look-outs, or alarm-posts. They are sometimes exterior, and sometimes interior to the walls of the enclosures, and occasionally incorporated with them. Plate XI (Nos. 1 and 3) affords examples. It is possible that this was not the primary, perhaps not even the secondary purpose of these mounds. Proper excavations would settle the question. In the absence of these, we can only appeal to such light as analogy affords us in our inquiry. Such mounds were erected by the ancient Britons for purposes of observation, both in advance of their other defences and within them;

and the early Spanish writers speak of similar erections, for similar purposes, by the Floridian Indians. The New Zealanders compass the same ends by raising a tree, the branches of which have been lopped off within a few inches of the trunk, at some elevated point within their works.

The almost invariable presence of water within, or in immediate proximity to these enclosures, has been the occasion of frequent remark in the foregoing descriptions. In the absence of springs and streams, as also where, from position, access to such supplies of water is impracticable, we find their place supplied by reservoirs; an evidence of the forethought of the builders, as also an index to the true character of the works in which these features occur.

The vast amount of labor necessary to the erection of most of these works precludes the notion that they were hastily constructed to check a single or unexpected invasion. On the contrary, there seems to have existed a *System of Defences* extending from the sources of the Alleghany and Susquehanna in New York, diagonally across the country, through central and northern Ohio, to the Wabash. Within this range, the works which are regarded as defensive are largest and most numerous. If an inference may be drawn from this fact, it is that the pressure of hostilities was from the north-east; or that, if the tide of migration flowed from the south, it received its final check upon this line. On the other hypothesis, that in this region originated a semi-civilization which subsequently spread southward, constantly developing itself in its progress, until it attained its height in Mexico, we may suppose that from this direction came the hostile savage hordes, before whose incessant attacks the less warlike mound-builders gradually receded, or beneath whose exterminating cruelty those who occupied this frontier entirely disappeared, leaving these monuments alone to attest their existence, and the extraordinary skill with which they defended their altars and their homes. Upon either assumption, it is clear that the contest was a protracted one, and that the race of the mounds were for a long period constantly exposed to attack.* This conclusion finds its support in the fact that, in the vicinity of those localities, where, from the amount of remains, it appears the ancient population was most dense, we almost invariably find one or more works of a defensive character, furnishing ready places of resort in times of danger. We may suppose that a condition of things prevailed somewhat analogous to that which attended the advance of our pioneer population, when every settlement had its little fort, to which the people flocked in case of alarm or attack.

It may be suggested that there existed among the mound-builders a state of society something like that which prevailed among the Indians; that each tribe had its separate seat, maintaining, with its own independence, an almost constant warfare against its neighbors, and, as a consequence, possessing its own "castle," as a place of final resort when invaded by a powerful foe. Apart from the fact,

---

* "The Ohio fortresses were not erected for defence against a casual invasion. The size of the walls, and the solidity of their construction, show that the danger which they were designed to arrest was of constant recurrence."—*Harrison's Discourse, Transactions Ohio Historical Society*, vol. i. p. 263.

however, that the Indians were hunters averse to labor, and not known to have
constructed any works approaching in skilfulness of design or in magnitude those
under notice, there is almost positive evidence that the mound-builders were an
agricultural people, considerably advanced in the arts, possessing a great uniformity
throughout the whole territory which they occupied, in manners, habits, and
religion,—a uniformity sufficiently well marked to identify them as a single people,
having a common origin, common modes of life, and, as an almost necessary consequence, common sympathies, if not a common and consolidated government.

The question whether the North American Indians constructed defensive works
of this description, is one of much importance, but which cannot be fully discussed
in this connection. All the early writers concur in representing that the Indian
tribes, from Florida to Canada, possessed common modes of defending their villages
and protecting themselves from the attacks of their enemies. Their fortifications
consisted of rows of pickets firmly fixed in the ground, sometimes wattled together,
but occasionally placed so far apart, as to permit missiles of various kinds to be
discharged between them upon an assailant.* They seldom had more than a
single entrance, which, among the Floridians, was not direct, but circuitous.
Entrenchments of earth, consisting of an embankment and ditch, do not appear to
have been constructed by them. It seems, however, that of late years, the Indians
to the westward of the Mississippi, particularly the Mandans and Rickarees, have
constructed entrenchments of earth, surmounted by palisades.† But whether the
practice is of recent introduction or otherwise, it is difficult to say. It is stated
by Prince Maximilian, in his Travels in America, that the defences of the Mandan
village of Mih-tutta-hang-kush, which consisted of a wall and ditch, were built
by whites, who were employed by the Indians for that purpose.‡

The defences of the nations of the central portion of the Continent, and especially those of the Mexicans and Peruvians, so far as we are informed concerning
them, bore a close resemblance to those of the mound-builders, although exhibiting
a superiority entirely consonant with the further advance which we are justified in
supposing they had made in all the arts, including the art of defence.§ Some
reference has already been had to the actual identity which a few of the defences
of the West exhibit with those of Mexico, in some of their most interesting features. These resemblances might be pointed out in detail, but they will readily
suggest themselves to the Archæologist. The usual mode of fortification in
Peru consisted in throwing up a series of embankments around the summits of
isolated hills,—a practice which was common among the ancient Celts, and which
is still preserved among the Australian and Polynesian islanders.‖ Ulloa observes,

* Charlevoix, Canada, vol. ii. p. 128; Loskiel, p. 53; Du Pratz, Louisiana, p. 375; Herrara, History of America, vol. v. p. 324.

† Catlin's North American Indians, vol. i. p. 81; Lewis and Clark, *ubi supra.*

‡ Travels in North America, pp. 173, 243.

§ De Solis, History of Mexico, p. 54; Juarros, History Guatemala, p. 462; Stephens's Yucatan, vol i
pp. 165, 230; Molina, vol. ii. pp. 10, 68; Ulloa, vol. ii. p. 27.

‖ Ellis's Polynesian Res. vol. i. pp. 313, 314; Cook's Second Voyage, *ubi supra*; Pollack's New
Zealand, vol. ii. p. 26.

in respect to their numbers, that "one scarcely meets with a mountain without them." Precisely similar modes of defence prevailed among the savage South American tribes, who invariably crowned their entrenchments of earth with palisades of wood.*

The traces of ancient fortifications in the northern part of the State of New York, and upon the head waters of the Susquehanna in Pennsylvania, may, it is believed, be referred with entire safety to the same hands with those of the Mississippi valley. It will be seen that they have a close resemblance to those of northern Ohio, both in position and structure.

---

* Charlevoix, History of Paraguay, vol: i. p. 156.

CHAPTER III.

EARTHWORKS—SACRED ENCLOSURES.

THE structure not less than the form and position of a large number of the Earthworks of the West, and especially of the Scioto valley, render it clear that they were erected for other than defensive purposes. The small dimensions of most of the circles, the occurrence of the ditch interior to the embankments, and the fact that many of them are completely commanded by adjacent heights, are some of the circumstances which may be mentioned as sustaining this conclusion.* We must seek, therefore, in the connection in which these works are found, and in the character of the mounds, if such there be within their walls, for the secret of their origin. And it may be observed, that it is here we discover evidences still more satisfactory and conclusive than are furnished by their small dimensions and the other circumstances above mentioned, that they were not intended for defence. Thus, when we find an enclosure containing a number of mounds, all of which it is capable of demonstration were *religious* in their purposes, or in some way connected with the superstitions of the people who built them, the conclusion is irresistible, that the enclosure itself was also deemed sacred, and thus set apart as " *tabooed* " or consecrated ground,—especially where it is obvious, at the first glance, that it possesses none of the requisites of a military work. But it is not to be concluded that those enclosures alone, which contain mounds of the description here named, were designed for sacred purposes. We have reason to believe that the religious system of the mound-builders, like that of the Aztecs, exercised among them a great, if not a controlling influence. Their government may have been, for aught we know, a government of the priesthood; one in which the priestly and civil functions were jointly exercised, and one sufficiently powerful to have secured in the Mississippi valley, as it did in Mexico, the erection of many of those vast monuments, which for ages will continue to challenge the wonder of men. There may have been certain superstitious ceremonies, having no connection with the purposes of the mounds, carried on in enclosures specially dedicated to them. The purposes of the minor enclosures within and connected with the great defensive work already described on the banks of the North fork of Paint creek, (Plate X,) would scarcely admit of a doubt, even though the sacred mounds which they embrace were wanting. It is a conclusion which every day's

---

* " I have reason to agree with Stukely, that the circumstance of the ditch being *within* the vallum is a distinguishing mark between religious and military works."—*Sir R. C. Hoare on the Monuments of England.*

investigation and observation has tended to confirm, that most, perhaps all, of the earthworks not manifestly defensive in their character, were in some way connected with the superstitious rites of the builders,—though in what precise manner, it is, and perhaps ever will be, impossible satisfactorily to determine.

The general character of these works has already been briefly indicated.   They are mostly regular in their structure, and occupy the broad and level river bottoms, seldom occurring upon the table lands or where the surface of the ground is undulating or broken.   They are usually square or circular in form; sometimes they are slightly elliptical.   Occasionally we find them isolated, but more frequently in groups.   The greater number of the circles are of small size, with a nearly uniform diameter of two hundred and fifty or three hundred feet, and invariably have the ditch interior to the wall.   These have always a single gateway, opening oftenest to the east, though by no means observing a fixed rule in that respect. It frequently happens that they have one or more small mounds, of the class denominated sacrificial, within the walls.   These small circles occasionally occur within larger works of a different character.   Apart from these, numerous little circles, from thirty to fifty feet in diameter, are observed in the vicinity of large works.   They consist of very slight embankments of earth, and have no entrances or passage ways.   It has been suggested that these are the remains of ancient lodges or buildings.   The accounts which we have of the traces left of the huts of the Mandans and other Indians, at their deserted villages, render this supposition not improbable.   It sometimes happens that we find small circles embracing large mounds: these can hardly be regarded as of the same character with that numerous class already noticed.

The larger circles are oftenest found in combination with rectangular works, connected with them directly, or by avenues.   Some of these circles are of great extent, embracing fifty or more acres.   They seldom have a ditch; but whenever it occurs, it is interior to the wall.   As in the case of the square or rectangular works to which they are attached, (and which, it is believed, *never* have ditches, exterior or interior,) the walls are usually composed of earth taken up evenly from the surface, or from large pits in the neighborhood.   Evident care appears in all cases to have been exercised, in procuring the material, to preserve the surface of the adjacent plain smooth, and as far as possible unbroken.   This fact is in itself almost conclusive against the supposition of a defensive design, especially as we have abundant evidence that the mound-builders understood perfectly the value of the external fosse in their works of defence.   The walls of these works are, for the most part, comparatively slight, varying from three to seven feet in height.   Sometimes they are quite imposing; as in the case of the great circle at Newark, Licking county, Ohio; where, at the entrance, the wall from the bottom of the ditch has a vertical height of not far from thirty feet.   The square or rectangular works, attending these large circles, are of various dimensions.   It has been observed, however, that certain groups are marked by a great uniformity of size.   Five or six of these are noticed in the succeeding pages; they are *exact* squares, each measuring one thousand and eighty feet side,—a coincidence which could not possibly be accidental, and which must possess some significance.   It certainly establishes the existence of some standard of measurement among the ancient people, if not the possession of some means of determining angles. The rectangular works have almost invariably gateways at the angles and midway on each side, all of which are covered by small interior mounds or elevations. In some of the larger structures the openings are more numerous. A few of this description of remains have been discovered which are octagonal. One of these of large size, in the vicinity of Chillicothe, has its alternate angles coincident with each other, and its sides equal.

Another class of works, probably akin to those here noticed, are the parallels, consisting of slight embankments seven or eight hundred feet in length and sixty or eighty feet apart. Indeed, so various are these works, and so numerous their combinations, that it is impossible, through the medium of description alone, to convey an adequate conception of their character. If we are right in the assumption that they are of sacred origin, and were the temples and consecrated grounds of the ancient people, we can, from their number and extent, form some estimate of the devotional fervor or superstitious zeal which induced their erection, and the predominance of the religious sentiment among their builders.

Their magnitude is, perhaps, the strongest objection that can be urged against the purpose here assigned them. It is difficult to comprehend the existence of religious works, extending, with their attendant avenues, like those near Newark, over an area of little less than *four square miles !* We can find their parallels only in the great temples of Abury and Stonehenge in England, and Carnac in Brittany, and must associate them with sun worship and its kindred superstitions.

It was originally proposed to include within another division those structures which were regarded as anomalous, or to which it was impossible to assign a definite purpose. Reflection, however, has tended to strengthen the opinion, that those works not manifestly defensive were connected with the superstitions of the builders, and that all the enclosures of the West (except perhaps some of the petty circles to which allusion has been made) were either military or religious in their origin. Those only which are obviously defensive have been classed under the head of Defences, and all others have been thrown together into this chapter. It is not impossible, therefore, that some which follow should be included in the former division ; nor is it improbable that a few were designed to answer a double purpose.

7

PLATE XVI.*

HIGH BANK WORKS, ROSS COUNTY, OHIO.

THE beautiful group here represented is situated on the right bank of the Scioto river, five miles below the town of Chillicothe, near the road from that place to Jackson.   It occurs at a place where the river has cut its way up to the third terrace, which in consequence here presents a bold bank, rising seventy-five or eighty feet above the water.   This point is generally known as the "*High Bank*," and gives its name to these works.   The third terrace here spreads out into a beautiful, level plain of great extent.   The principal work consists of an octagon and a circle; the former measuring nine hundred and fifty feet, the latter ten hundred and fifty feet, in diameter.   The coincidences, in the dimensions, between this and the "Hopeton Works," (Plate XVII,) will be at once observed.   The octagon is not strictly regular; although its alternate angles are coincident, and its sides equal.   The circle is a perfect one.   In immediate connection with the work are two small circles, which are shown in the plan, each measuring two hundred and fifty feet in diameter.

The walls of the octagon are very bold; and, where they have been least subjected to cultivation, are now between eleven and twelve feet in height, by about fifty feet base.   The wall of the circle is much less, nowhere measuring over four or five feet in altitude.   In all these respects, as in the absence of a ditch and the presence of the two small circles, this work resembles the Hopeton Works already alluded to.   There are no mounds, except the small ones covering the gateways of the octagon.   About half a mile to the southward, and connected with this work by lines of embankment, much reduced but still traceable, is a small group of works, partially destroyed by the river.   A fourth of a mile below this subordinate group, on the bank of the terrace, is a large truncated mound, thirty feet in height.   It does not fall within the area exhibited on the map.

At various points around this work are the usual pits or dug holes, some of which are of large size.   To the left of the great circle, on the brow of the terrace, is an Indian burial place.   The construction of a farm road down the bank disclosed a large quantity of human bones, accompanied by a variety of rude implements.   A short distance below this point, on the same bank of the river, is the former site of an Indian town.

A number of small circles occur about a hundred rods distant from the octagon, in the forest land to the south-east.   They measure nearly fifty feet in diameter, and the walls are about two feet in height.   It has been suggested that they are

---

* Marked J in Map, Plate II.

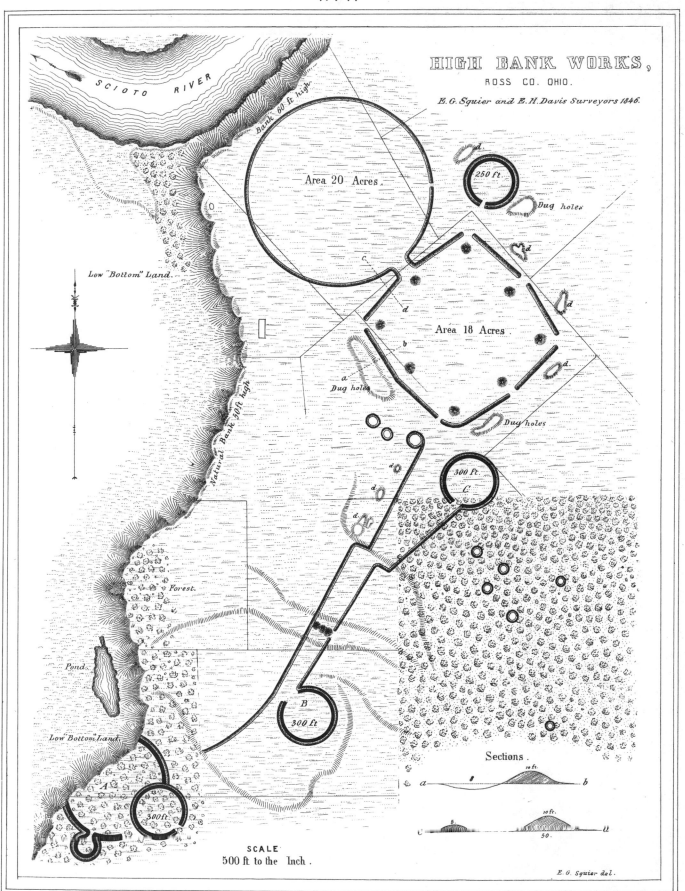

HIGH BANK WORKS,
ROSS CO. OHIO.

E. G. Squier and E. H. Davis Surveyors 1846.

SCIOTO RIVER

Bank 60 ft. high

Area 20 Acres

250 ft.

Dug holes

Low "Bottom" Land.

Area 18 Acres

Dug holes

Natural Bank 50 ft. high

Dug holes

300 ft.

C.

Forest.

Pond.

B
300 ft.

Low "Bottom" Land.

A
300 ft

Sections.

SCALE
500 ft to the Inch.

E. G. Squier del.

Lith. of Sarony & Major N. York.

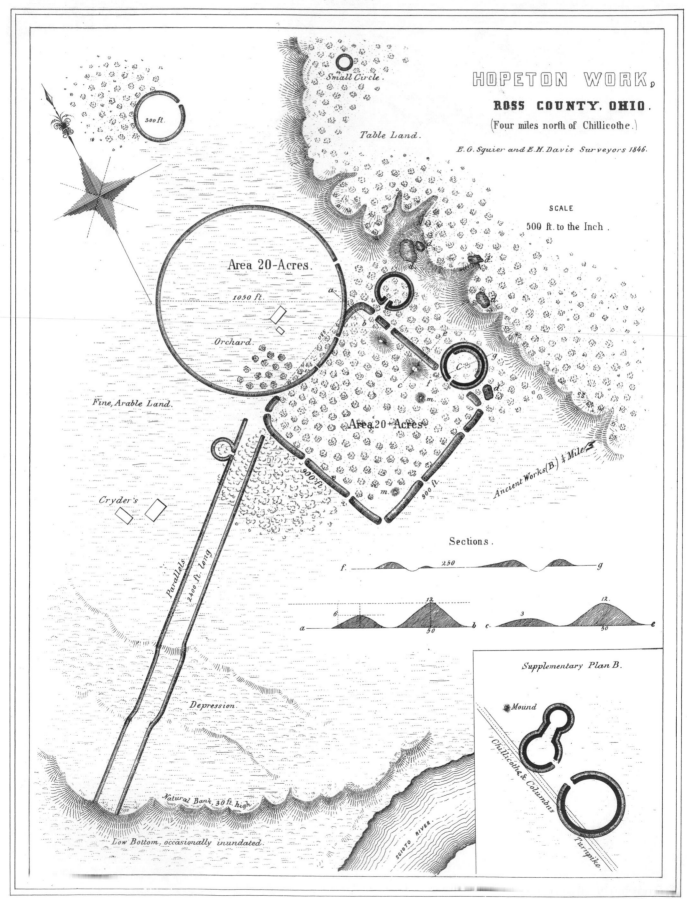

Small Circle.

300 ft.

Table Land.

HOPETON WORK,

ROSS COUNTY. OHIO.

(Four miles north of Chillicothe.)

E. G. Squier and E. H. Davis Surveyors 1846.

SCALE

500 ft. to the Inch.

Area 20-Acres.

1050 ft.

Orchard.

Fine, Arable Land.

Area 20 Acres.

900 ft.

900 ft.

Cryder's

Parallels. 2400 ft. long

Ancient Works (B.) ¼ Mile.

Sections.

250

12   12.

50   3   50

Depression

Natural Bank, 30 ft. high

Low Bottom, occasionally inundated.

SCIOTO RIVER.

Supplementary Plan B.

Mound

Chillicothe & Columbus Turnpike.

Lith. by Sarony & Major

Face P. 51.

the remains of structures of some kind, and also that they were the bases of unfinished mounds. There are no indications of entrances or passage ways, a circumstance which favors the latter hypothesis. Similar small circles occur within or in the immediate vicinity of several other large works.

———

PLATE XVII.*

HOPETON WORKS, ROSS COUNTY, OHIO.

Four miles above the city of Chillicothe, on the east bank of the Scioto river, is situated the singular group of works figured in the Plate. They are found upon the third "bottom" or terrace, just at the base of an elevated plain, upon which, five hundred paces distant, and to the right of the main works, the minor group B is situated. They consist of a rectangle, with an attached circle, the latter extending into the former, instead of being connected with it in the usual manner. The rectangle measures nine hundred and fifty by nine hundred feet, and the circle is ten hundred and fifty feet in diameter. The centre of the circle is somewhat to the right of a line drawn through the centre of the rectangle, parallel to its longest sides. The exterior gateways are twelve in number, and have an average width of about twenty-five feet. The chord of that part of the circle interior to the rectangle is five hundred and thirty feet. On the east side are two circles, measuring two hundred, and two hundred and fifty feet in diameter respectively; one covering a gateway, the other extending into, and opening within, the work. About two hundred paces north of the great circle is another smaller one, two hundred and fifty feet in diameter.

The walls of the rectangular work are composed of a clayey loam, twelve feet high by fifty feet base, and are destitute of a ditch on either side. They resemble the heavy grading of a railway, and are broad enough, on the top, to admit the passage of a coach. The wall of the great circle was never as high as that of the rectangle; yet, although it has been much reduced of late years by the plough, it is still about five feet in average height. It is also destitute of a ditch. It is built of clay, which differs strikingly in respect of color from the surrounding soil. The walls of the smaller circles are about three feet in height, with interior ditches of corresponding depth.

Parallel walls extend from the north-western corner of the rectangle, towards the river to the south-west. They are twenty-four hundred feet, or nearly half a mile

---

* This work is marked D in the Map, Plate II. Since this Plate was engraved, it has been ascertained that a plan of this work was published in the "Portfolio," in 1809. The two plans are substantially alike, except that the one in the "Portfolio" represents the parallels as terminating in a small circle, and as connected with the large circle,—both of which features are erroneous. The walls of the parallels are much obliterated, where they approach the bank of the terrace.

long, and are placed one hundred and fifty feet apart. They terminate at the edge of the terrace, at the foot of which, it is evident, the river once had its course; but between which and the present bed of the stream, a broad and fertile "bottom" now intervenes. They are carried in a straight line, and although very slight, (nowhere exceeding two and a half feet in height,) are uninterrupted throughout. They do not connect directly with the main work; at least, they are not traceable near it.

There is a dug hole, of considerable size, near the south-east angle of the rectangular portion of the work, exterior to the walls. In the bank of the table land, which approaches to within three or four hundred feet of the walls, are several excavations, *d d d*, from which large quantities of earth have been taken, though much less, apparently, than enters into the composition of the embankments.

There are no mounds of magnitude in connection with these works. There are two slight elevations of an oval form, and also one or two very small mounds, within the square, as shown in the plan. There is a large group, however, on the opposite bank of the river, in the direction pursued by the parallels above mentioned.

The truncated pyramid and accompanying circle, shown in the plan of the "Cedar Bank Works," (Plate XVIII,) are situated about one-fourth of a mile to the north-east, upon the superior plain. The coincidences between this circle and the small one C of the plan will be observed at once. The feature of an inner wall or platform, of the description here indicated, is of frequent occurrence. (See " *Newark Works,*" Plate XXV.)

From the height and solidity of the walls, it might be inferred that this was a work of defence. But its position, in respect to the third terrace which commands it, strongly opposes that conclusion. Still, this objection would not be insuperable, could we suppose that the walls were palisaded; for, in such a case, the interior of the work would be unassailable by any missiles known to barbarous or half-civilized nations,—in fact, proof against anything except artillery, and affording no mean protection against an assault of that description.

PLATE XVIII.*

CEDAR BANK WORKS, ROSS COUNTY, OHIO.

THIS work is situated upon the table lands bordering the Scioto river, at a point five miles above the town of Chillicothe, and about a mile above the works last

---

* Indicated by the letters B and C, in Map, Plate II.

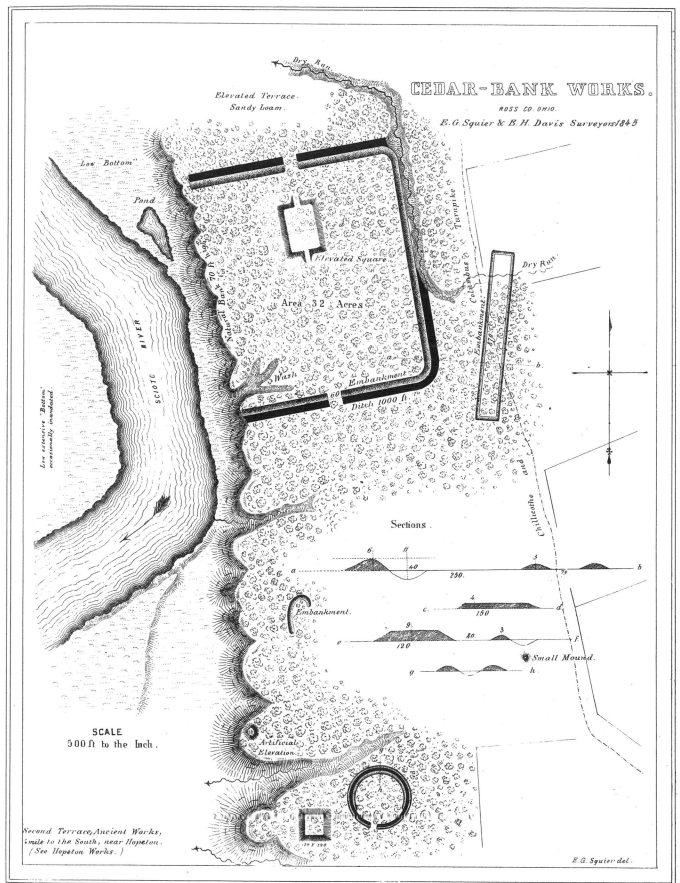

CEDAR-BANK WORKS.

ROSS CO. OHIO.

E. G. Squier & E. H. Davis Surveyors 1845

Dry Run

Elevated Terrace. Sandy Loam.

Low "Bottom"

Pond

Natural Bank 70 ft

Low extensive "Bottom" occasionally inundated.

SCIOTO RIVER

Elevated Square

Area 32 Acres

Wash

Embankment

60 Ditch 1000 ft

Turnpike

Columbus

Embankment 120

Dry Run

Chillicothe and

a

b

Sections.

Embankment.

Artificial Elevation.

SCALE
500 ft to the Inch.

Second Terrace, Ancient Works, ½ mile to the South, near Hopeton. (See Hopeton Works.)

120 x 120

Small Mound.

E. G. Squier del.

described. It consists of a wall and outer ditch, which constitute three sides of a parallelogram. The fourth side is protected by a natural bank or bluff, seventy feet high, and so steep as to admit of no ascent, except at one point where it has been gullied by the flow of water.

The walls of this work are about six feet high by forty feet base; the ditch five feet deep by forty wide. The ditch upon the longer or eastern side is formed, for two thirds of its length, by a "runway" or water-course. It is here from eight to ten feet deep. The wall upon this side is fourteen hundred feet long. The northern and southern walls are each ten hundred and fifty feet in length, and placed at right angles to the first; the southern extending to the very edge of the bluff, the northern terminating within twenty-five feet of it. It is possible that a fourth wall originally bounded the enclosure on the west, which has been destroyed by the river, in its encroachments. There are gateways, each sixty feet wide, at the centres of the northern and southern sides. Covering the northern gateway, and two hundred feet interior to it, is an elevated square, two hundred and fifty feet long by one hundred and fifty broad, and four feet high. It is ascended from the ends by graded ways, thirty feet broad, and in all respects resembles the truncated pyramids or " elevated squares " of the Marietta Works (Plate XXVI).

On the line of the southern embankment, and three hundred feet distant from the main work, are singular parallel walls, eight hundred and seventy feet long and seventy feet apart, connected at the ends. These walls have no ditch, and have been partially obliterated by the Chillicothe and Columbus turnpike, which passes through them. In the timbered land, where they are undisturbed, they are between two and three feet high.

About one third of a mile south of the principal work, is a truncated pyramid, 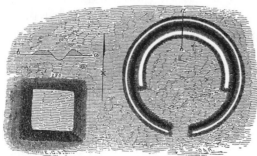 and a small circle, Fig. 9: the former is one hundred and twenty feet square at the base, and nine feet in height; the latter is two hundred and fifty feet in diameter, and has an entrance from the south, thirty feet wide. The sides of the pyramidal structure correspond to the cardinal points. The circle has a ditch interior to the embankment; and has also a broad embankment of about

FIG. 9.

the same height with the outer wall, interior to the ditch, upon the side opposite the entrance. This feature, which is found in many of the smaller circles, is illustrated by the plan, and by the section b a. This group is so disposed as to command a fine view of the river terraces below it; and the headland upon which it is situated seems to have been artificially smoothed and rounded. The spot is well chosen. The " elevated square " has been excavated, but was found to contain no remains. Upon the edge of the table land, both above and below this peculiar group, there are various inconsiderable remains, consisting of small, low terraces, and little mounds and circles.

It is difficult to determine the character of this group of works. The principal enclosure partakes of the nature of a defence; but the broad gateways and the regular terrace embraced in the walls, are features hardly consistent with the hypothesis of a military origin. The long parallel lines, found in connection with this and other works, are entirely inexplicable in their design and purposes. The most plausible suggestion concerning them is, that they were devoted to the celebration of certain games; they may, however, have been connected with religious observances. It has been suggested that the gully or "wash" towards the river was originally a graded way to the water, and that its present irregularity has been occasioned by the rains and storms of centuries.

It is a singular fact that there are no mounds of magnitude in connection with these works. Upon the opposite side of the river, however, there are a large number, as will be seen in the succeeding Plate.

———

PLATE XIX.*

MOUND CITY, ROSS COUNTY, OHIO.

THIS Plate presents a very interesting group of works. They are situated on the left bank of the Scioto river, four miles north of the town of Chillicothe. The enclosure, designated, from the great number of mounds within its walls, "*Mound City*," is in many respects the most remarkable in the Scioto valley. Through the generous kindness of HENRY SHRIVER, Esq., upon whose estate it is situated, the mounds were all permitted to be investigated; and the work will, in consequence, be often referred to in the course of this volume, particularly when we come to speak of "Mounds."

In outline it is nearly square, with rounded angles, and consists of a simple embankment, between three and four feet high, unaccompanied by a ditch. Its site is the beautiful level of the second terrace, and it is still covered with the primitive forest.

The first and most striking feature in connection with this work is the unusual number of mounds which it contains. There are no less than *twenty-four* within its walls. All of these, as above observed, have been excavated, and the principal ones found to contain *altars* and other remains, which put it beyond question that they were places of *sacrifice*, or of superstitious origin. [The evidence in support of this conclusion will appear in a subsequent chapter on the mounds and their purposes.]

These mounds seem placed generally without design in respect to each other, although there is a manifest dependence between those composing the central group, and between those numbered 4 and 5, and 12 and 13. From the principal

---

* These works are marked E and F respectively, in Map, Plate II.

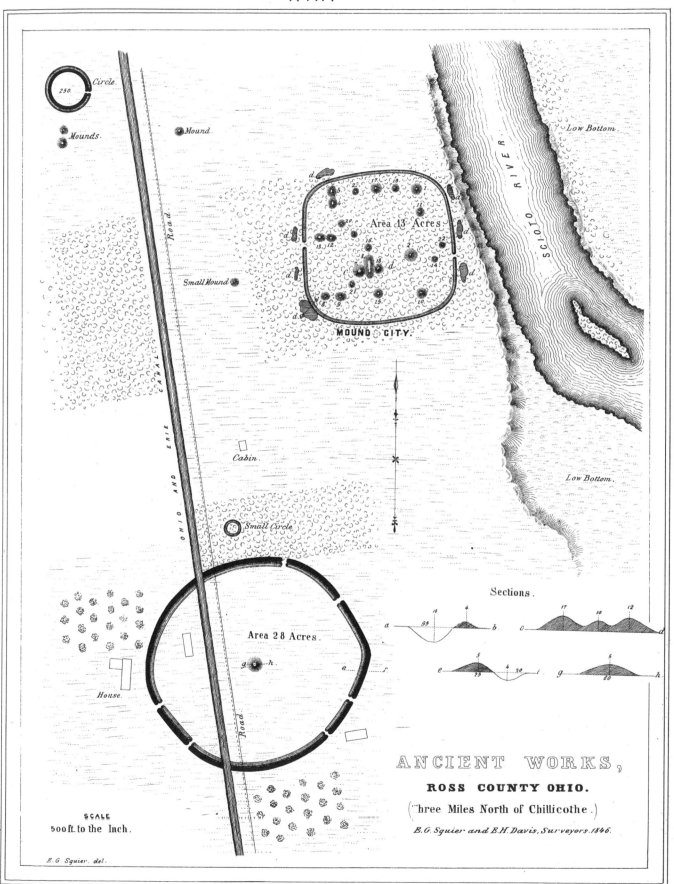

Circle.
250.
Mounds.
Mound.
Low Bottom.
d
d
5 23 17 19
4 11
20
Area 13 Acres.
d
13 12 16
2 22
7 18 d
C 14
d
21
18 9 15 10
MOUND CITY.
SCIOTO RIVER
Low Bottom.
Cabin.
Small Circle.
Sections.
a 93 18 4 b   c 17 10 12 d
e 5 4 20 f   g 5 60 h
Area 28 Acres.
House.
g h
e f
Road.
ROAD. OHIO AND ERIE CANAL.
Small Hound.

ANCIENT WORKS,

ROSS COUNTY OHIO.

(Three Miles North of Chillicothe.)

E. G. Squier and E. H. Davis, Surveyors. 1846.

SCALE
500 ft. to the Inch.

E. G. Squier. del.

mound, numbered 7 in the plan, after the fall of the leaves, a full view of every part of the work and of its enclosed mounds is commanded. This mound is seventeen feet high, with a broad base nearly one hundred feet in diameter. The long mound, No. 3, is one hundred and forty feet long, by eighty wide at the base, and ten feet in average height. Broad and deep pits, from which the earth for the construction of the mounds was taken, surround the work. The one occurring at the south-western angle, and of which *a b* exhibits a vertical section, is at this time eighteen feet deep, by one hundred and twenty feet in width, and over two hundred feet in length. The accumulation of vegetable deposit at the bottom is found, by excavation, to be not less than thirty inches,—a fact which may assist in an approximate estimate of the age of this monument.

The absence of an exterior ditch, as also the fact that the work is commanded from a slightly elevated terrace half a bow-shot to the left, seems sufficient to establish that it was not designed for defence. The skill, which the illustrations of a previous chapter convince us the mound-builders possessed in selecting and fortifying their military positions, is in no degree displayed in this instance. Taking in view also the character and purposes of the mounds as disclosed by excavation, we are certainly well warranted in classing this as a sacred work.

The custom of enclosing the Adoratorios or Teocallis, upon which their sacrifices and religious rites generally were practised, was universal among the Mexicans. The open temples of the ancient Britons were embraced within parapets of earth, usually, if not always, circular in form. The "tabooed" grounds or sacred places of the Pacific Islanders, are also surrounded, if not by earthen, by stone walls or by palisades.

One fourth of a mile to the north-west of this work is a small circle two hundred and fifty feet in diameter, accompanied by two large mounds.

About the same distance to the south is another work of somewhat similar outline, but of larger size. It is, moreover, surrounded by a ditch. Its position, in respect to "Mound City," requires that it should be noticed here. The plan and sections will convey a sufficiently accurate idea of its form and construction. Unlike the works obviously of sacred origin, which, if they possess a ditch at all, have it interior to the wall, this has an outer fosse; a circumstance which would seem to favor the suggestion of a defensive origin. On the other hand, it has a mound, very nearly if not exactly in its centre, which was clearly a place of sacrifice. It was found, upon excavation, to contain an altar singularly constructed of small stones, carefully imbedded in sand, forming a paved concavity, upon which were the usual traces of fire, and the remains of the sacrifice. This mound will be minutely noticed elsewhere.

PLATE XX.*

ANCIENT WORK, LIBERTY TOWNSHIP, ROSS COUNTY, OHIO.

THIS work is a very fair type of a singular series occurring in the Scioto valley,—all of which have the same figures in combination, although occupying different positions with respect to each other, viz. a square and two circles. These figures are not only accurate squares and perfect circles, but are in most cases of corresponding dimensions,—that is to say, the sides of each of the squares are each ten hundred and eighty feet in length; and the diameter of each of the large and small circles, a fraction over seventeen hundred and eight hundred feet, respectively. Such were the results of surveys made at different times, the measurements of which correspond within a few feet. Although in the progress of investigation singular coincidences were observed between these works, yet there was at the time no suspicion of the identity which subsequent comparison has shown to exist.

The first of the series here represented, is situated on the east bank of the Scioto river, and occupies the third bottom or terrace. The ground upon which it occurs is level. The walls of the entire work are unaccompanied by a ditch, and are slight, nowhere more than four feet in height. The embankment of the square is perceptibly heavier than that of the small circle, which is also heavier than that of the larger one. The square work measures ten hundred and eighty feet upon each side; and its walls are interrupted at the corners and at the middle of each side, by gateways thirty feet in width. The central gateways are each covered by a small mound, of about the same height with the embankment, and placed forty feet interior to it. The manner in which the circular works are connected with the square enclosure, and the relative position of each, are accurately shown in the plan, precluding the necessity of a long and intricate description. It will be observed, that while the wall of the larger circle is interrupted by numerous narrow gateways, that of the smaller one is entire throughout,—a feature for which it is, of course, impossible to assign a reason. Besides the small mounds at the gateways, there are three others within the work, two of which are inconsiderable, while the other is of the largest size, being one hundred and sixty feet long, by not far from twenty feet high. A section of this mound is given, illustrative of a detailed description, in a subsequent chapter. There are also a few other mounds outside of the walls, reference to which is had elsewhere. Numerous dug holes occur in the vicinity of the great mound. Most of these are interior to the work,—a very unusual circumstance. In fact, the whole work appears to have been but partially finished, or constructed in great haste. The mounds at the gateways, and those outside of

---

* Indicated by the letter K. in Map, Plate II.

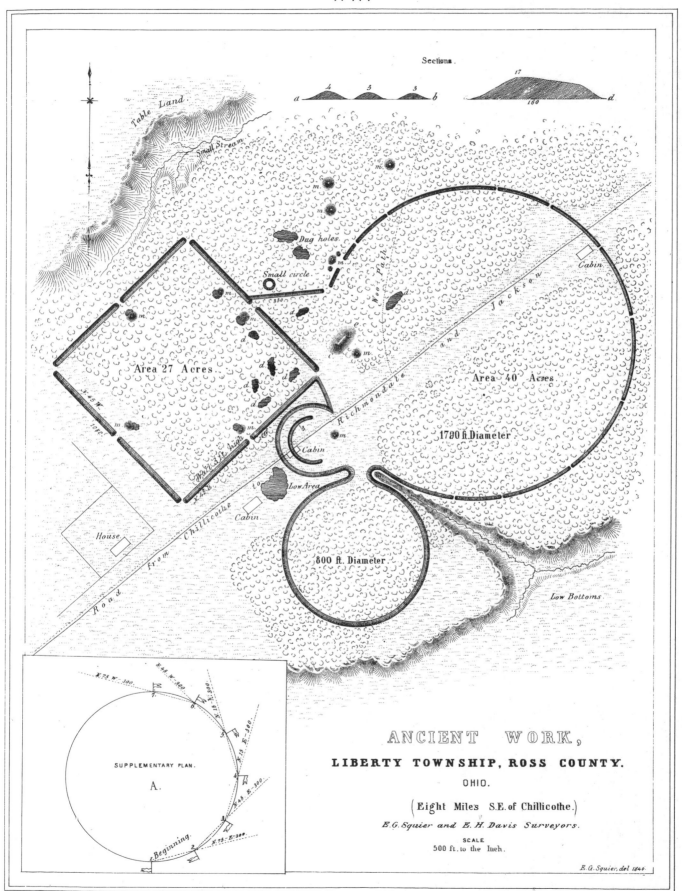

Sections.

Table Land.

Small Stream.

Dug holes.

Small circle

Woo Path

Cabin

Jackson

Area 27 Acres.

Area 40 Acres

1790 ft. Diameter

Richmondale

Cabin

Low Area

House

Cabin

800 ft. Diameter

Low Bottoms

Road from Chillicothe.

SUPPLEMENTARY PLAN.

A.

Beginning.

ANCIENT WORK,

LIBERTY TOWNSHIP, ROSS COUNTY.

OHIO.

(Eight Miles S.E. of Chillicothe.)

E.G. Squier and E.H. Davis Surveyors.

SCALE

500 ft. to the Inch.

E.G. Squier, del 1846.

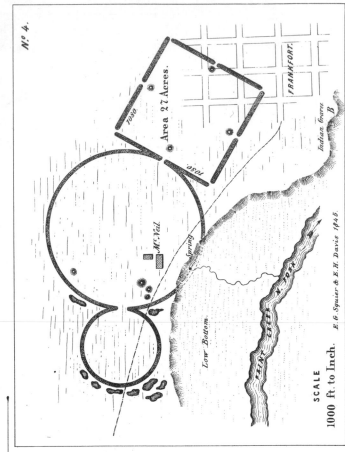

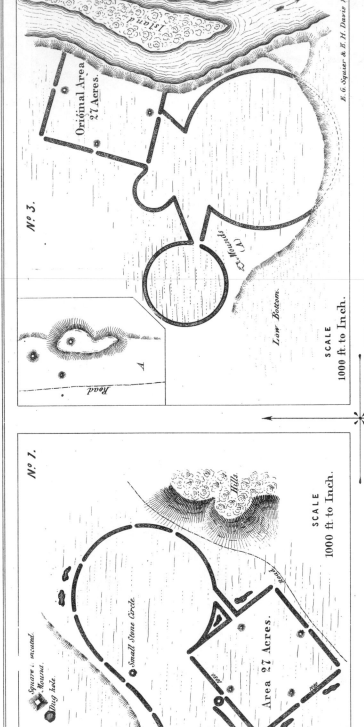

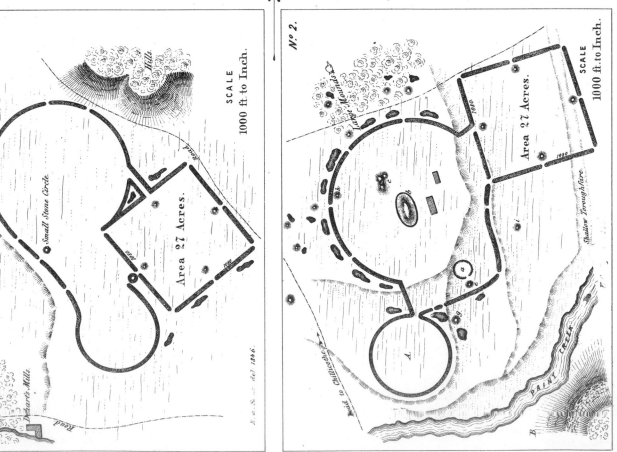

No. 3.

Original Area 27 Acres.

Island.

Mounds (A.)

Low Bottom.

SCALE
1000 ft. to Inch.

Road.

A

E. G. Squier & E. H. Davis 1846.

No. 4.

FRANKFORT.

Area 27 Acres.

1080

1080

Mc Veil.

Spring

Low Bottom.

Indian Graves

B

NORTH FORK PAINT

SCALE
1000 ft. to Inch.

E. G. Squier & E. H. Davis 1846.

No. 1.

Hills.

Road.

Square Vacated.
Mound.
Dug hole.

Small Stone Circle.

1080

Area 27 Acres.

PAINT CREEK

Stewarts Mills.

Road.

SCALE
1000 ft. to Inch.

E. G. Squier del. 1846.

No. 2.

Large Mounds

c
b
e
d

1080

Area 27 Acres.

1080

Road to Chillicothe.

g

Shallow Thoroughfare.

B

F

PAINT CREEK

SCALE
1000 ft. to Inch.

the walls, were formed by carelessly scooping up the earth at their base, leaving irregular pits near them. In most of the regular works, the material seems to have been taken up evenly and with care, or brought from a distance.

No one would be apt to ascribe a defensive origin to this work, yet it is difficult to conceive for what other purpose a structure of such dimensions, embracing nearly one hundred acres, could have been designed. The great mound is anomalous in its character, and throws no light on the question. That there is some hidden significance, in the first place in the regularity, and secondly in the arrangement of the various parts, can hardly be doubted. Nor can the coincidences observable between this and the other succeeding works of the same series be wholly accidental.*

PLATE XXI. No. 1.†

THIS work is situated on the right bank of Paint creek, fourteen miles distant from Chillicothe. It is but another combination of the figures composing the work belonging to this series, just described; from which, in structure, it differs in no material respect, except that the walls are higher and heavier. It is one of the best preserved works in the valley; the only portion which is much injured being

---

* To put, at once, all skepticism at rest, which might otherwise arise as to the *regularity* of these works, it should be stated that they were all carefully surveyed by the authors in person. Of course, no difficulty existed in determining the perfect regularity of the squares. The method of procedure, in respect to the circles, was as follows. Flags were raised at regular and convenient intervals, upon the embankments, representing stations. The compass was then placed alternately at these stations, and the bearing of the flag next beyond ascertained. If the angles thus determined proved to be coincident, the regularity of the work was placed beyond doubt. The supplementary plan A indicates the method of survey, the "Field Book" of which, the circle being thirty-six hundred feet in circumference, and the stations three hundred feet apart, is as follows:—

STATION.	BEARING.	DISTANCE.
1	N. 75° E.	300 feet.
2	N. 45° E.	" "
3	N. 15° E.	" "
4	N. 15° W.	" "
5	N. 45° W.	" "
6	N. 75° W.	" "
7	S. 75° W.	" "
8	S. 45° W.	" "
9	S. 15° W.	" "
10	S. 15° E.	" "
11	S. 45° E.	" "
12	S. 75° E.	" "

† Indicated by the letter B, in Map 1, Plate III. This and the succeeding work are represented by Mr. Atwater in the Archæologia Americana, vol. i. p. 146; with what fidelity, an inspection of the respective plans will show.

at that part of the great circle next the hill, where the flow of water has obliterated the wall for some distance. The gateways of the square are considerably wider than those of the other works,—being nearly seventy feet across. A large, square, truncated mound occurs at some distance to the north of this work. It is one hundred and twenty feet broad at the base, has an area fifty feet square on the top, and is fifteen feet high. Quantities of coarse, broken pottery are found on and around it. A deep pit, or dug hole, is near, denoting the spot whence the earth composing the mound was taken.

PLATE XXI. No. 2.*

FIVE miles above the work last described, at " the crossings of Paint creek," and on the opposite bank of the stream, occurs an equally singular and interesting work, situated upon the estate of JOHN WOODBRIDGE, Esq., of Chillicothe. The ground is here considerably broken, yet the work preserves its regularity throughout, although evidently constructed with some regard to the nature of the position. The square occupies the second terrace; while the main body of the work is placed upon the third, as shown in the plan.

Within the larger circle, and not far from its centre, is a large elliptical mound, two hundred and forty feet long by one hundred and sixty broad, and thirty in height. It is considerably larger than any other single mound in the valley, and covers a little more than two thirds of an acre. It seems to be composed, at least towards the surface, of stones and pebbles,—a feature peculiar to a certain class of mounds, of a highly interesting character. It is surrounded by a low, indistinct embankment, the space between which and the mound seems to have been raised by the wasting of the latter. Perhaps this was a low terrace. To the right of this fine mound is a group of three others in combination, as shown in the plan at c. There are several other small mounds in and around the work. Several very large and beautiful ones, composed entirely of clay, occur about one fourth of a mile distant, in the direction indicated in the plan.

The entire work is surrounded by deep pits or excavations, usually called " wells," from which the materials for the mounds and embankments were procured. So numerous are these, and such serious obstacles are the mounds and embankments to cultivation, that a deduction of several acres is allowed to the tenant in consequence, by the lease of the estate upon which they occur.

The small circle at a is two hundred and fifty feet in diameter. It has been so much reduced by the plough as to be traced with difficulty.†

----

* Indicated by the letter A, in Map 2, Plate III.

† Mr. Atwater (*Archæologia Americana*, vol. i. p. 143) describes the small mound at e, as composed " entirely of red ochre, which answers very well as a paint!" Its *present* composition is a clayey loam. It has been examined and found to contain an alton

Although the square enclosure connected with this work is situated on the second terrace, a portion of it, at periods of great freshets, is invaded by the water, which passes through a shallow thoroughfare indicated on the map. This singular circumstance is easily accounted for. The creek in its course strikes the base of a high hill at B, composed of shale, which readily undermines, occasioning great slips or slides. These fill the channel of the creek, damming it up and forcing it out of its usual course. It was probably at the period of one of these slides, that the creek, in its reaction on the opposite shore, broke through the embankment and formed the thoroughfare, or dry channel, above mentioned. The remark, therefore, that the earthworks of the West never occur upon the first, or latest-formed terrace, and are always above high-water mark, is not at all invalidated by this circumstance.

PLATE XXI. No. 3.*

THIS work very closely resembles the one last described. It is situated on the Scioto river, about one mile south of the town of Chillicothe. Near it was erected the first civilized habitation in the valley, and the ground has been in cultivation for more than forty years. As a consequence, the walls are much reduced, although distinctly traceable at this time. A portion of the square has been destroyed by the invasion of the river. The large circle has also been encroached upon at some period, if indeed it was ever completed. It extends to the terrace bank, which is here twelve or fifteen feet high. The low bottom, at the base of the terrace, was evidently at one time the bed of Paint creek, which has since changed its channel, and now runs more than a mile to the south-west, entering the river three or four miles below this point. If the encroachment upon the work was made by this stream, the fact would certainly assign to it a very high antiquity. There are no mounds in the immediate vicinity of this work, although there are several in the direction indicated in the plan, about one fourth of a mile distant, upon the corresponding terrace A. There is also an extensive and intricate series of works in the direction of Chillicothe, a portion of which once occupied the site of the city.†

One of the mounds at A is placed upon a singular ridge, some forty or fifty feet in height, which has resisted the encroachments of the water, and which itself somewhat resembles an artificial structure. This elevation commands the entire plain. There are several mounds at its base, one of which is of considerable size. All have been excavated: the larger one was found to be sepulchral in its character; the others are anomalous.

---

* This work is designated by the letter H on the Map, already several times referred to, Plate II.
† Their general character is indicated in Map, Plate II.

PLATE XXI. No. 4.

THIS work is sixteen miles distant from the one last described, and is situated on the left bank of the North fork of Paint creek. A portion of it is included in the town limits of Frankfort, better known as " Oldtown," or " Old Chillicothe."*

The combination of the great circle and the square, in this work, is identical with that which exists in the celebrated Circleville work,—which work, it may be observed, is no more remarkable than numbers of others, and owes its celebrity entirely to the fact, that it has been several times described with some minuteness.

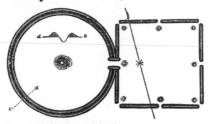

FIG. 10.

A reduced plan of the Circleville work, Fig. 10, is herewith presented, which will sufficiently illustrate this remark. Its dimensions were considerably less than those of the analogous structures already described. The sides of the square measured not far from nine hundred feet in length, and the diameter of the circle was a little more than one thousand feet. The work was peculiar in having a double embankment constituting the circle. It is now almost entirely destroyed, and its features are no longer traceable.†

The walls of the rectangular portion of the Frankfort work, where not obliterated by the improvements of the town, are still several feet high. They were, within the recollection of many people, much higher. They are composed of clay (while the embankment of the circle is composed of gravel and loam), which, as in the case of the square work described, Plate X, appears to have been very much burned.

The isolated mound near the upper boundary of the circle is composed entirely of clay, and is twelve feet high; the others are of gravel, the largest being no less than twenty feet in altitude. Various dug holes or pits, from which the material for the embankments and mounds was evidently taken, are indicated in the plan. Some of them are, at this time, fifteen or twenty feet deep. The subsoil at this locality, as shown by excavation, is clay. If there was no design, therefore, in constructing the walls of the square of that material, it follows that it was built last, and after the loam and gravel had been removed from the pits.

A portion of the large circle has been encroached upon and destroyed by the

---

* The site of the town of Frankfort was formerly that of a famous Shawnee town. The burial place of the Indian town is shown in the plan; from it numerous relics are obtained,—gun-barrels, copper kettles, silver crosses and brooches, and many other implements and ornaments which, in accordance with aboriginal custom, were buried with the dead. Some of them, from being found in close proximity to the work above described, have erroneously been supposed to appertain to the race of the mound-builders.

† Archæologia Americana, vol. i. p. 142.

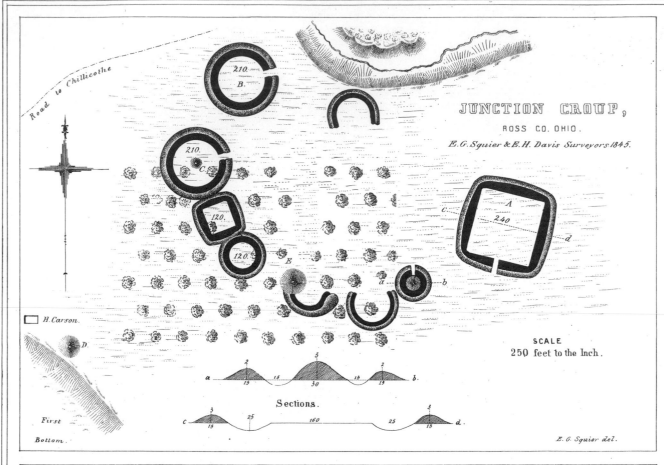

XXII

JUNCTION GROUP,
ROSS CO. OHIO.
E.G.Squier & E.H.Davis Surveyors 1845.

Road to Chillicothe

H.Carson.

First
Bottom.

Sections.

SCALE
250 feet to the Inch.

E. G. Squier del.

Lith. of Sarony & Major N.Y.

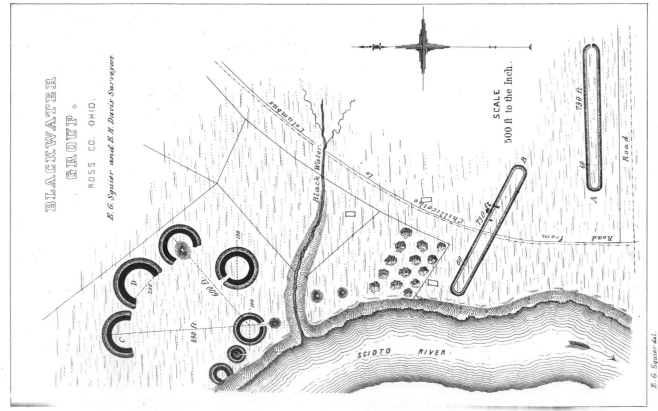

BLACKWATER
GROUP.
ROSS CO. OHIO.
E.G.Squier and E.H.Davis Surveyors.

Black Water.

Columbus

Road from Chillicothe

SCALE
500 ft to the Inch.

SCIOTO RIVER.

E. G. Squier del.

creek, which has since receded something over a fifth of a mile, leaving a low rich bottom intervening.

Such are the predominant features of this remarkable series of works. As already remarked, the coincidences observable between them could not have been the result of accident, and it is very manifest that they were erected for common purposes. What those purposes were, the reader must judge. Without entering into an argument upon the subject, we may content ourselves with the simple expression of opinion, that they were in some manner connected with the superstitions of the builders.

There is one deduction to be drawn from the fact, that the figures entering into these works are of uniform dimensions, which is of considerable importance in its bearing upon the state of knowledge among the people who erected them. It is that *the builders possessed a standard of measurement, and had some means of determining angles.* The most skilful engineer of the day would find it difficult, without the aid of instruments, to lay down an accurate square of the great dimensions of those above represented, measuring as they do more than *four fifths* of a mile in circumference. It would not, it is true, be impossible to construct circles of considerable size, without instruments; the difficulty of doing so, when we come to the construction of works five thousand four hundred feet, or *over a mile* in circumference, is nevertheless apparent. But we not only find accurate squares and perfect circles, but also, as we have seen, *octagons* of great dimensions. Other evidences tending to sustain the above conclusions will be adduced in the progress of this work.

PLATE XXII. No. 1.*

JUNCTION GROUP, ROSS COUNTY, OHIO.

THE singular group of works here represented is situated on Paint creek, two miles south-west of the town of Chillicothe. It consists of four circles, three crescents, two square works, and four mounds. The eastern enclosure is the principal one; and, in common with all the rest, consists of a wall three feet high, with an interior ditch. It is two hundred and forty feet square, the angles much curved, giving it very nearly the form of a circle. The area, bounded by the ditch, is an accurate square of one hundred and sixty feet side, and is entered from the south by a gateway twenty-five feet wide. To the south-west of this work, and one hundred and thirty feet distant, is a small mound enclosed by a ditch and wall, with

---

* This group is indicated by G in the Map, Plate II.

a gateway opening to it from the north. The ditch dips from the base of the mound, which is but three feet high by thirty feet base. Almost touching the circle enclosing the mound, is the horn of a crescent work, having a chord of one hundred and thirty-two feet. Sixty-six feet distant, in the same direction, is still another crescent, which terminates in a mound of sacrifice, seven feet high by forty-five feet base, which commands the entire group of works. This mound was carefully opened in October, 1845. The following passages, from the notes taken on the occasion, may not be out of place here. They will prove more intelligible to the reader, after an examination of the chapters on *Mounds*.

The mound is composed of clay. A simple shaft was sunk from the apex, five feet square. About three feet below the surface, upon the northern side of the excavation, was found a layer of wood coals, three or four inches in thickness, which extended within range of the excavation perhaps a foot, where it was broken up and intermixed with the clay composing the mound; some fragments were found within a few inches of the surface. From this fact it was inferred that the mound had been disturbed since its erection,—with what correctness will be seen in the sequel. In this layer of charcoal was found a human skeleton, much decayed, the skull and jaws crushed. Proceeding downwards, the earth below the unbroken charcoal was homogeneous, while towards the centre of the mound it was intermixed with detached coals. About seven feet beneath the surface of the mound, and probably a little below the surface of the adjacent plain, and in the centre of the excavation, were found three skeletons, in a very good state of preservation. The earth above them was mingled with coals, and also with fragments of hard-burned clay, which were immediately recognised as portions of the "altar" peculiar to a certain class of mounds devoted to religious purposes. It was clear that the mound had been opened, and its structure broken up, to afford the rite of sepulture to the skeletons here found; and it was concluded from this fact, as well as from their well-preserved condition, that the remains were those of the later Indians, who frequently buried in the mounds. The skeletons were placed side by side, with their heads towards the east. But one circumstance weighs against the above conclusion, and that is the depth at which the skeletons were deposited. The modern Indians bury in shallow graves.

Further examination disclosed the remains of the altar, about one third of which remained entire. Upon it were found a number of relics, clearly pertaining to the mound-builders.

The character of the remaining works is sufficiently apparent, without further explanation. That they were not designed for defence is obvious, and that they were devoted to religious rites is more than probable. They may have answered a double purpose, and may have been used for the celebration of games, of which we can have no definite conception. It has been suggested that the enclosure A, as also B and C, were occupied by structures, temples perhaps, which in the lapse of time have disappeared. Similar groups are frequent,—indeed, small circles, resembling those here represented, constitute, in the Scioto valley, by far the most numerous class of remains. They seldom occur singly, but generally in connection with several others of the same description, and accompanied by one or more

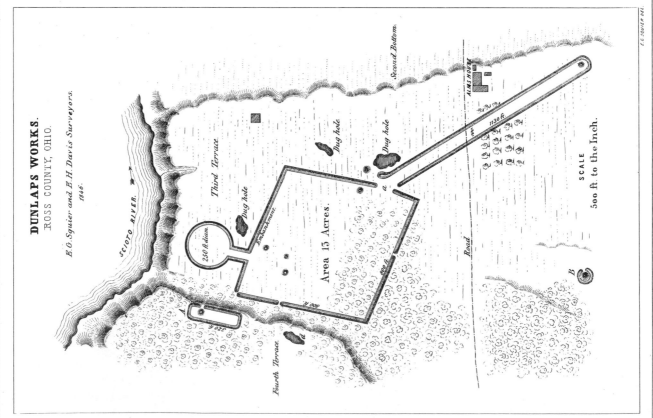

XXIII

ANCIENT WORKS
ATHENS C°. OHIO.
S. P. Hildreth. Surveyor.

SCALE.
2000 ft. to Inch.

CHAUNCEY

Salt Well

Broad level Plain.

Road from Athens to Chauncey

Hills.

Hills.

LITH. OF SARONY & MAJOR.

S. P. HILDRETH DEL.

REFERENCES.

1. Mound 18 ft. high.	8. Mound 18 ft. high.
2. „ 6 „ „	9. „ 15 „ „
3. „ 30 „ „	10. „ 10 „ „
4. „ 8 „ „	11. „ 11 „ „
5. „ 24 „ „	12. „ 15 „ „
6. „ 10 „ „	13. „ 6 „ „
7. „ 5 „ „	14. „ 10 „ „

REFERENCES.

A. Circle, 210 ft. in diameter.
B. „ 150 „ „ „
C. „ 150 „ „ „
D. „ 110 „ „ „
E. „ 110 „ „ „
F. „ 150 „ „ „
G. „ 200 „ „ „
H. „ 150 „ „ „

DUNLAPS WORKS.
ROSS COUNTY, OHIO.

E. G. Squier and E. H. Davis Surveyors.
1846.

SCIOTO RIVER.

Third Terrace

Dug hole

Embankment.

250 ft. diam.

Fourth Terrace.

Area 15 Acres.

Dug hole

Dug hole

Dug hole

Dug hole

Second Bottom.

ALMS HOUSE.

1130 ft.

Road

SCALE
500 ft. to the Inch.

E. G. SQUIER DEL.

Face P. 63.

mounds; sometimes they are connected with long parallel lines of embankments, of which more particular mention is elsewhere made.

This group occupies a beautiful plain forming the third terrace, upon the edge of which, at D, is a mound, formerly of considerable dimensions, but now much reduced in altitude. Upon the opposite bank of the creek, and occupying the corresponding terrace, are other works, consisting of a small circle and a number of small mounds.

PLATE XXII. No. 2.

BLACKWATER GROUP, ROSS COUNTY, OHIO.

THIS group, which very much resembles that last described, is situated on the right bank of the Scioto river, eight miles above Chillicothe, near the Columbus road. It is specially remarkable for its singular parallels, A and B of the plan. Each of these is seven hundred and fifty feet long by sixty broad, measuring from centre to centre of the embankments. They are in cleared ground, which has been cultivated for more than twenty years; consequently the walls are much reduced, being now scarcely two feet in height. A gateway opens into the southern parallel, from the east. A corresponding opening may have existed in the other parallel, though it is impossible to discern it now. The ground embraced in the semi-circular works C and D is reduced several feet below the level of the plain on which they are located. The mounds belonging to this group have never been investigated; hence their character is undetermined. The group is introduced in this connection, on account of its resemblance to the one just described. It is just to conclude that both were erected for a common or analogous purpose.

PLATE XXIII. No. 1.*

DUNLAP'S WORKS, ROSS COUNTY, OHIO.

THIS work, situated on the right bank of the Scioto river, six miles above Chillicothe, presents some remarkable features. It is rhomboidal in figure, with an avenue eleven hundred and thirty feet long extending to the south-east, and also a

---

* Indicated by A, in Map, Plate II.

short avenue, leading from a gateway to the north, connecting with a small circle. Along the western wall runs the bank of a plain, elevated a number of feet above the level of the work, upon the very brow of which is situated an outwork (A) eighty feet wide by two hundred and eighty in length. It overlooks the larger work, and has a wide gateway opening towards it. At this point the bank seems to have been graded to a more gentle descent. The great avenue approaches to within sixty feet of the gateway at a, which is one hundred and twenty feet wide; the walls closing, at the other extremity, upon a radius of half the width of the avenue. A low mound occupies the extreme point of the avenue. At some distance south of the main work, is a mound surrounded by a ditch and low embankment; and at the distance of about half a mile, very nearly in the course of the avenue, are a number of mounds,—one of which is fifteen feet high, truncated, and with a base of one hundred feet diameter. The diameter of the level area on the top is about fifty feet. These mounds stand on the lowest portion of the second terrace; the ground which they occupy being overflowed at periods of very high water in the river. These are the only monuments known which are reached by overflows. The top of the truncated mound was made a place of refuge, during the high water of 1832, by a family, with their cattle, horses, etc., numbering in all nearly a hundred. It was among the first opened, in the progress of these investigations, and before the characteristics of this class of works were clearly known. Hence, although a number of skeletons were disinterred, at depths of from two to five feet, together with a few rude instruments, the original deposit of the mound-builders was not reached. The skeletons were unquestionably those of the modern Indians. Upon the mound and around it, many fragments of rough pottery are found, and a number of entire vases of rude workmanship were exposed a few years since in ploughing over an adjacent small mound. Many decayed fresh-water shells are also found on and around the mound; and, as these when pulverized entered into the composition of the rude pottery of the more recent Indians, it seems highly probable that a sort of manufactory of this ware was established here. A number of large mounds also occur at some distance to the northward of the principal work.

———

PLATE XXIII. No. 2.

ANCIENT WORKS, ATHENS COUNTY, OHIO.

Four miles north of the town of Athens, Athens county, Ohio, is a broad and level plain, upon which is situated a large group of ancient earthworks. The accompanying plan and description were furnished by S. P. HILDRETH, M. D., of Marietta, Ohio.*

---

* The proportions of the circles, etc., are necessarily somewhat exaggerated in the plan: their relative positions are, however, very accurately preserved.

"The plain upon which these remains occur is not far from a mile and a half long, by a mile and a quarter broad, and contains upwards of one thousand acres. The soil is a sandy argillaceous earth, easily tilled and quite fertile. At the northern extremity of the plain is the village of Chauncey, where are located several salt factories, which are supplied by some of the most abundant saline waters in the State of Ohio. The plain has an elevation of sixty or seventy feet above the present bed of the Hocking river, and was evidently formed when its waters flowed at a higher level. This stream now runs from half a mile to a mile to the eastward of the plain, separated from it by low hills. All around the margin of the plain, where not bordered by hills, burst forth copious springs of fresh water, which are most abundant in the vicinity of the principal ancient works. Most of these works occupy the south-eastern portion of the plain. They consist of a number of small circles, accompanied by mounds, the several dimensions of which are given in the accompanying plan. The largest circle is situated upon a detached point of land, of the same level with the adjacent plain, from which it is cut off by a deep ravine, in which flows a small stream. This detached portion contains not far from six acres. The circle itself has a diameter of two hundred and ten feet; the diameter of the enclosed area is one hundred and thirty feet; the height of the wall is *seven* feet, and the depth of the ditch *six* feet. In all of these circles, the ditch is interior to the embankment.

"On the top of a hill, half a mile to the south of this plain, is a stone mound fifteen feet in height. It is built of stones of various sizes, none of which, however, are larger than one man could conveniently carry. They must have been collected from considerable distances, as there are very few lying upon the surface of the adjacent hills. Many of them are water-worn, and evidently came from the bed of some stream: some are limestone, some sandstone, and others quartz. About twenty years since a partial excavation was made, and the mound penetrated to about half its depth. Here were found three human skeletons, in tolerable preservation. From the appearance of ashes and charcoal beneath them, it was conjectured that the bodies had been burned. One of the skeletons had copper bracelets on its arms, and beads made of the tusks of the bear about its neck. These relics are now deposited in the Museum of the Ohio University, at Athens."

It has been suggested, that the work situated upon the detached portion of the plain above mentioned was designed for defence. There is nothing to favor the suggestion, except the fact of position, which is far from conclusive. On the other hand, the small size of the work, its form, and the occurrence of the ditch *interior* to the wall, may be taken to establish a different origin,—probably a religious one.

9

PLATE XXIV.

ANCIENT WORKS, PIKE COUNTY, OHIO.

THE plan so fully illustrates the character of this group of works, that little description is necessary. It consists principally of the constantly recurring figures, the square and the circle; the former measuring in this instance a little upwards of eight hundred feet upon each side, the latter ten hundred and fifty feet in diameter. They are connected by parallel walls, four hundred and seventy-five feet long, placed one hundred feet apart. These are intersected by a runway, which has here cut a passage in the terrace one hundred and twenty-five feet wide, by fifteen deep. This gully or ravine was undoubtedly in existence at the period of the construction of the works. The banks between the parallels appear to have an offset, as if they had been artificially graded; no further indications of a grade now exist.

The small works, in connection with the above, will attract special attention. The plan illustrates their forms, and the sections exhibit their dimensions. Nothing can surpass the symmetry of the small work A, of which an enlarged plan is herewith given, Fig. 11; B and C are also perfect figures of their kind. It will be remarked that we have here the square, the circle, and the ellipse, separate and in combination,—all of them constructed with geometric accuracy. The work D consists of a small circle, from which leads off a wall, extending along the brow of the terrace bank, until the latter turns, nearly at right angles, towards the north. It would seem that this line of embankment was constructed with specific reference to this natural feature. The fact, however, that a small circle, in the immediate vicinity, has been partially destroyed by the wasting of the bank, shows that it has receded since the construction of the works. The river now runs at a distance, although it is evident that it once washed the base of the terrace at this point. Its ancient bed is distinctly to be seen.

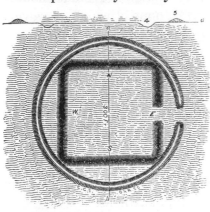

FIG. 11.

The walls of the square coincide very nearly with the cardinal points of the compass, varying therefrom but three degrees. This is, however, an accidental coincidence; as all the ancient works seem to have been made to conform to the position of the ground which they occupy. There is no evidence that any regard was had to the points of the compass, except that the gateways or openings of the small circles are oftenest towards the east.

About one mile to the northward of this group is the unique work shown in the

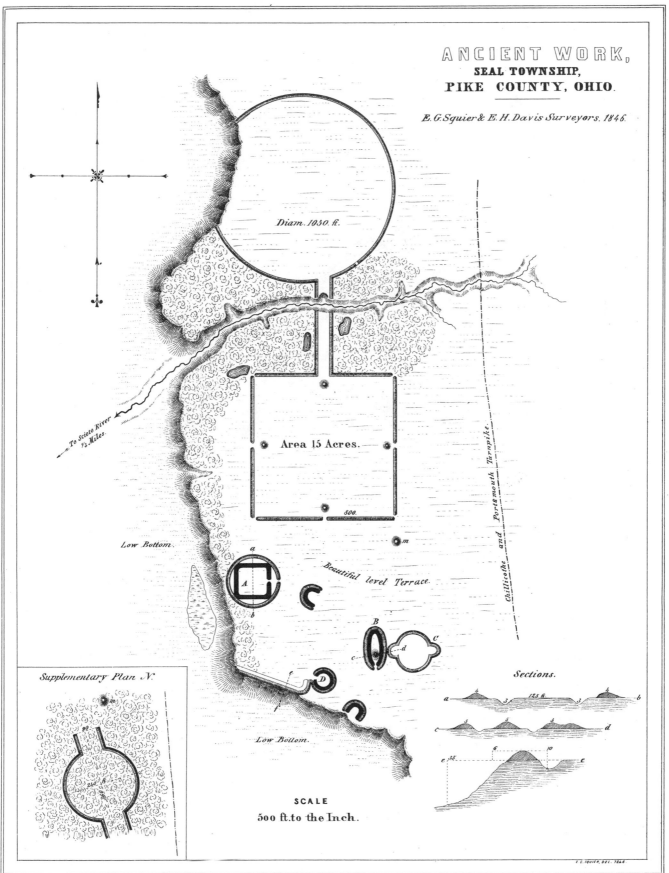

ANCIENT WORK,
SEAL TOWNSHIP,
PIKE COUNTY, OHIO.

E. G. Squier & E. H. Davis Surveyors. 1846.

Diam. 1030. ft.

To Scioto River ½ Miles.

Area 15 Acres.

800.

Low Bottom.

Beautiful level Terrace.

Chillicothe and Portsmouth Turnpike.

Low Bottom.

Sections.

Supplementary Plan N.

SCALE
500 ft. to the Inch.

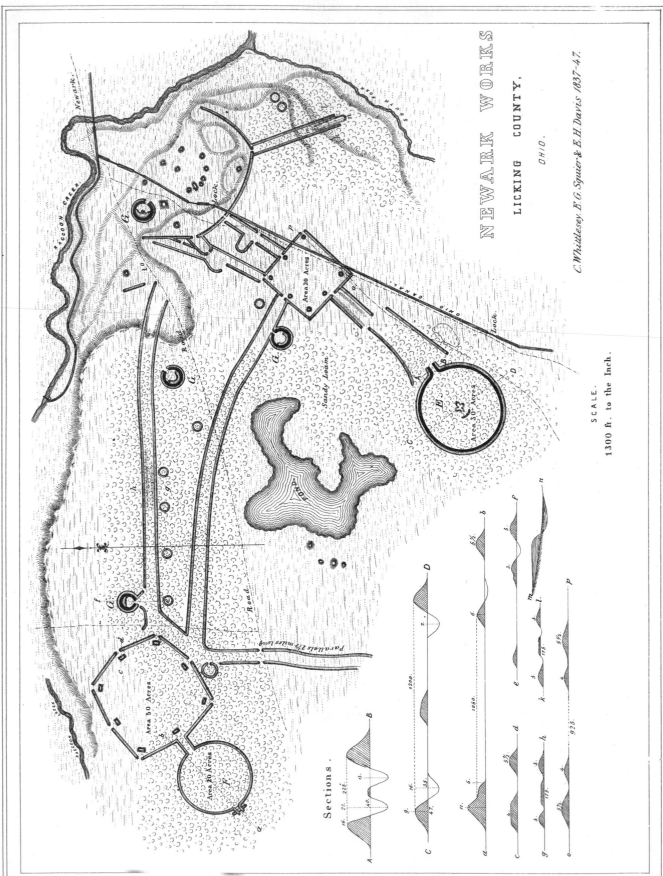

NEWARK WORKS,

LICKING COUNTY,

OHIO.

C. Whittlesey, E. G. Squier & E. H. Davis 1837–47.

SCALE.

1300 ft. to the Inch.

Sections.

Area 20 Acres

Area 50 Acres

Area 20 Acres

Area 30 Acres

Parallels 2½ miles long

Lith. by Sarony & Major.

supplementary plan N. Its walls are about four feet high, and its outlines beautifully distinct.*

It is impossible to resist the conviction that some significance attaches to these singular forms.

———

PLATE XXV.

THE NEWARK WORKS, LICKING COUNTY, OHIO.†

THE very extensive and complicated series of works here presented occur at the junction of the South and Raccoon forks of Licking river, one mile west of the town of Newark, Licking county, Ohio. Like those at Marietta, the works in question occupy a high fertile plain. This plain is here of great extent, and elevated from thirty to fifty feet above the alluvions bordering the streams: it is for the most part level, but in places broken and undulating.

These works are so complicated, that it is impossible to give anything like a comprehensible description of them. The plan, with the illustrative supplementary plans and sections, will furnish a better conception, as a whole and in detail, than could be afforded in any other way. It will be the object of the text to supply such information as cannot be obtained from the plan.

The group covers an extent of about two miles square, and consists, as will be observed, of three grand divisions, connected by parallels and works of a minor character. The walls of the parallels, and of the irregular portions of the works generally, as well as of the small circles, (of which there are a considerable number,) are very slight; for the most part not exceeding four feet in height.

---

* There are some singular structures in Sweden, which coincide very nearly with this remarkable little work. They are circles composed of upright stones, having short avenues of approach upon each side, opposite each other, in the manner here represented. See *Sjöborg's Samlingar för Nordens Fornälskare*, 1822.

† A number of plans of these works, as well as of those at Marietta, have been published; but they are all very defective, and fail to convey an accurate conception of the group. The map here given is from an original and very careful and minute survey made in 1836, by CHAS. WHITTLESEY, Esq., Topographical Engineer of the State of Ohio, corrected and verified by careful re-surveys and admeasurements by the authors. It may be relied upon as strictly correct. A large portion of the more complicated division of the group has, within the past few years, been almost completely demolished, so that the lines can no longer be satisfactorily traced. It is to be hoped that care may be taken to preserve the remainder from a like fate. The principal structures will always resist the reducing action of the plough; but, from present indications, the connecting lines and smaller works will soon be levelled to the surface, and leave but a scanty and doubtful trace of their former symmetry.

A sectional map of the Newark valley is given in a subsequent plate, on which the relative positions of this and other works of the vicinity are indicated with approximate accuracy.

The embankments of the principal, or regular portions of the works, are much heavier. Those of the larger circular work, E, are about twelve feet in perpendicular height by fifty feet base, and have an interior ditch seven feet deep by thirty-five wide. At the gateway or entrance, the walls are much higher than at any other point, being not less than *sixteen feet* in altitude, with a ditch *thirteen feet* deep, giving an absolute height of about *thirty feet* from the bottom of the ditch to the top of the embankment. The wall of the lesser circle, F, is six feet in height, and is unaccompanied by a ditch. The walls of the octagonal, as well as of the square work, are but five and a half feet high, and are also destitute of ditches, either exterior or interior.

The circular structure E is undoubtedly one of the best preserved and most imposing in the State. There are many enclosing larger areas, but none more clearly defined. At the entrance, which is towards the east, the ends of the walls curve outwards, for the distance of a hundred feet, leaving a passageway eighty feet wide, between the deep ditches on either hand. Here, covered with the gigantic trees of a primitive forest, the work presents a truly grand and impressive appearance; and, in entering the ancient avenue for the first time, the visitor does not fail to experience a sensation of awe, such as he might feel in passing the portals of an Egyptian temple, or in gazing upon the silent ruins of Petra of the desert. This work is not, as has been generally represented, a true circle; its form is that of an ellipse, its diameters being twelve hundred and fifty feet, and eleven hundred and fifty feet respectively. There are two or three slight irregularities in the outline, too trifling however to be indicated in the plan. The area of the enclosure is something over thirty acres. It is an almost perfect level, and is still covered with the original forest. Immediately in the centre of the area is a mound of singular shape, of which an enlarged plan, Fig.

FIG. 12.

12, is here given. It much resembles some of the "animal-shaped mounds" of Wisconsin, and was probably designed to represent a bird with expanded wings. It can hardly be called a mound, but is rather a group of four, so arranged and connected as to constitute an unbroken outline. Denominating the figure, for the sake of distinction, *a bird*, the dimensions are as follows: Length of body, one hundred and fifty-five feet; of each wing, one hundred and ten feet; between the tips of the wings, measuring in a right line, two hundred feet; width of body, sixty-three feet; of wings, in centre, forty-five feet; of same, next the body, forty feet; height of mounds composing the body, seven feet; of mounds composing the wings, five feet. The head of the bird points directly towards the entrance of the enclosure. The bearing of the body is S. 65° E. Immediately in the rear of the effigy, and one hundred feet distant, is a semi-circular embankment, about two hundred feet in length; it is but slightly elevated, and can hardly be traced; it is nevertheless exhibited in the plan. The long mound, constituting the body of the bird, has been opened. Upon examining the excavation, it was found that the structure had originally contained an *altar:* whether any relics were found upon it, is unknown. This feature, in conjunction with others, seems to point out a religious or superstitious design to this individual structure, if not to the whole group of works with which it is connected.

FIG. 13.—A GATEWAY OF OCTAGON, LOOKING INWARD.

Passing over the intermediate intricate works, of which it would be futile to attempt a description, we come to the octagon and its dependencies. The angles of this octagon, it will be observed, are not coincident, although its sides are very nearly equal.   At each of the angles is a gateway, which is covered upon the interior by a small, truncated pyramidal elevation, (Fig. 14,) five feet in height, and measuring eighty by one hundred feet at the base. These are placed about sixty feet interior to the walls.   The area of this work, which is a rich and beautiful level, is something over

FIG. 14.

fifty acres.   Connected with the octagon by parallels three hundred feet long, and placed sixty feet apart, is the smaller circle F.   Unlike the other circular work, *this is a true circle*, two thousand eight hundred and eighty feet, or upwards of half a mile in circumference.   It encloses no mounds, but possesses a remarkable feature in the line of the wall, at a point immediately opposite the entrance.   This consists of a crown work, (Fig. 15,) which is wholly unlike anything heretofore noticed.   It would almost seem that the builders had originally determined to carry out parallel lines from this point; but after proceeding one hundred feet, had suddenly changed their minds and finished the enclosure, by throwing an immense mound across the uncompleted parts.   This mound, which may be taken as constituting a part of the wall of the enclosure, is one hundred and seventy feet long, eight feet higher than the general line of the embankment, and overlooks the entire work.   It has been called the "Observatory," from this fact: it probably had some other purpose than that of a look-out, but what purpose, it is not undertaken to say.   It has been pretty thoroughly excavated, but the excavations seem to have disclosed nothing, except an abundance of rough stones, which must have been brought from the creek or some other remote locality, as none are scattered over the remarkable plain upon which these works are situated.

FIG. 16. VIEW OF "OBSERVATORY" FROM THE INTERIOR.

From the octagon lead off three lines of parallel walls : those extending towards the south have been traced for nearly two miles, and finally lose themselves in the plain ; the remaining parallels terminate as shown in the plan. They are upwards of a mile in length. The walls composing these singular lines are placed about two hundred feet apart, and are parallel throughout. A singular feature occurs in the northern one, which is exhibited by the transverse section *g h*. For the space of a quarter of a mile, advantage is taken of a slight natural ridge to construct between the walls a broad embankment, something higher than the parallels themselves. It is broad enough to permit fifty persons to walk abreast. A similar peculiarity is observed in the short parallel leading from the square enclosure towards the great circle E, and is exhibited by the section *i l*. A feature somewhat analogous occurs within the parallels extending from the irregular works on the extreme right of the plan. This parallel is carried down the bank of the third terrace, which is here fifteen or twenty feet high. Within the lines, the bank is cut down, and regularly graded to an easy ascent. The pathway or road, for a portion of its extent upon the alluvions, is elevated above the walls, as shown in longitudinal section *m n*. A similar grade is constructed at the extremity of the northern parallel, where the natural bank is much higher than at any other point. Here the bank is excavated inwardly, for upwards of one hundred and fifty feet ; and a portion of the earth is appropriated to form an elevated way over the low swampy ground immediately at the foot of the terrace. These excavations constitute quite imposing features, when viewed on the spot, but are hardly distinguishable upon the plan.

A number of small circles are found connected with the works, and are chiefly embraced in the area between the two principal parallels. They are about eighty feet in diameter, without gateways opening into them ; and it has been suggested that they probably mark the sites of ancient circular dwellings. The circles indicated by the letter G are of much larger dimensions, and are characterized by ditches interior to their walls. They each have a diameter of about two hundred feet, and have elevated embankments constructed interior to the ditch, as seen in the plan. This peculiarity has been already remarked, in some of the works of the Scioto valley.

Upon the lower terraces, towards the point of junction between the South and Raccoon forks, a great number of mounds of various sizes are situated. Some are large, but for the most part they are small. A small truncated pyramid once existed here, but the construction of the Ohio canal, and the subsequent establishment of the village of Lockport at this point, have obliterated this as well as numerous other mounds. Indeed, these causes have resulted in the almost total destruction of the singular maze of embankments, which communicates directly with the square enclosure. The ancient lines can now be traced only at intervals, among gardens and outhouses. At the period when the original survey, upon which this plan is constructed, was made, which is twelve years ago, the lines could all be made out. A few years hence, the residents upon the spot will be compelled to resort to this map, to ascertain the character of the works which occupied the very ground upon which they stand.

Within the area partially enclosed by this series of works, was formerly a large natural pond, covering upwards of one hundred acres. It has been drained, so that the greater portion is under cultivation. Previous to the earthquake of 1811, which resulted in the destruction of New Madrid on the Mississippi, it is said but little water was contained in the basin; after that event it rose to the depth of ten feet, and retained that level until the drainage took place. It has been suggested that it owed its origin to artificial excavation; but it is incontestibly natural, like several other smaller depressions in the vicinity, which still contain water. Excavations, denominated "wells," from which the materials for the construction of the wall were taken, are abundant in the neighborhood of these works.

Several extraordinary coincidences are exhibited between the details of these works and some of those already described. The smaller circle F is nearly identical in size with that belonging to the "Hopeton Works," and with the one attached to the octagon, in the "High Bank" group. (See Plates XVI and XVII.) The works last named are situated upon the Scioto, seventy miles distant. The square has also the same area with the rectangle belonging to the Hopeton, and with the octagon attached to the High Bank Works. The octagon, too, has the same area with the large, irregular square at Marietta. The small circles G, G, G, betray a coincidence with those in connection with the works above mentioned, which ought not to be overlooked. It is not to be supposed that these numerous coincidences are the result of accident.

It would be unprofitable to indulge in speculations as to the probable origin and purposes of this group of works. That it could not have been designed for defence, seems too obvious to admit of doubt.* The reasons urged against the

---

* " Great as some of these works are, and laborious as was their construction, particularly those of Circleville and *Newark*, I am persuaded *they were never intended for military defences*."—*General Harrison's Discourse.*

hypothesis of a defensive origin in the Marietta works apply with double force here. The structure which, from the height and solidity of its walls, would seem best adapted for defence, has its ditch *interior* to the embankment,—a blunder which no people possessing the skill and judgment displayed in the defensive works of the mound-builders, would be apt to commit.*

Hill works, incontestibly of a defensive origin, occur within four or five miles of this group, the relative positions of which are indicated by the "*Map of six miles of the Newark Valley.*" About four miles distant, and overlooking those works, is placed, upon the summit of a high hill, a gigantic effigy of some animal, probably the alligator. Of this remarkable structure a plan is presented on a subsequent page. Around these works, in the valley and crowning the hills bordering it, are numerous mounds, all of which, as compared with those of the Scioto, are singularly broad and flat. Many of them have been opened, but no account has been preserved of their character. So far as could be ascertained from diligent inquiry, they do not essentially differ in their contents from those found elsewhere in the State. Fifteen or twenty miles to the northward of these works, are others of an interesting character, which have never been investigated, and of which no public notice has yet been taken.

---

* The following passages, embodying some interesting facts respecting these works, were communicated by I. DILLE, Esq., now and for many years a resident of Newark:

"You are aware that the principal part of these remains are situated in the valley between the Raccoon creek and the South fork of Licking creek. The valley is here nearly two miles wide, from stream to stream. To the east of the lines of embankment and on the second bottom of the creek are numerous mounds. Some of these are very low,—so low, indeed, that a careless observer would hardly distinguish them from the common surface. Some of them are surrounded by a low circular wall of earth which, with a little attention, can be distinctly traced. In the year 1828, when constructing the canal, a lock was located on the site of one of these low mounds. In excavating the lock pit, *fourteen* human skeletons were found about four feet beneath the surface. These were very much decayed, and supposed by some to have been burnt. It was probably the natural appearance of decomposition which led to this opinion. On coming to the air they all mouldered into dust. Over these skeletons, and carefully and regularly disposed, was laid a large quantity of mica in sheets or plates. Some of these were eight and ten inches long by four and five wide, and all from half an inch to an inch thick. It was estimated that *fifteen or twenty bushels of this material* were thrown out to form the walls or supports of the lock. From a mound some four feet high, a few rods to the south of this, a large *volvaria* (sea-shell) was taken.

"On the opposite side of the creek I found, in one place, *twenty-four* flint axes, or imperfect arrowheads. These were found on the third bottom, on a promontory projecting towards the works in question. A very great quantity of broken flints were found here—enough to load a cart. They were of the same variety of flint, chert, or hornstone, which abounds on 'Flint Ridge.' On that ridge there is the appearance of a great deal of digging. Deep holes cover the ground for the extent of a mile. Many have supposed that these were mines of the precious metals, and no small amount of money and time has been expended in the search. I am of the opinion this place is the source of all the arrow-heads, flint axes, and other implements of that material, which have been used over a wide extent of territory.

"Separate from these valley works, and two miles to the west of them, is an irregular enclosure on a hill. The walls are of earth about three feet high, and enclose an area of some thirty or forty acres, extending from the top to the very foot of a high, long, and sloping hill. Again, two miles distant in a north-west direction, the summit of a high hill is surrounded by a similar embankment."

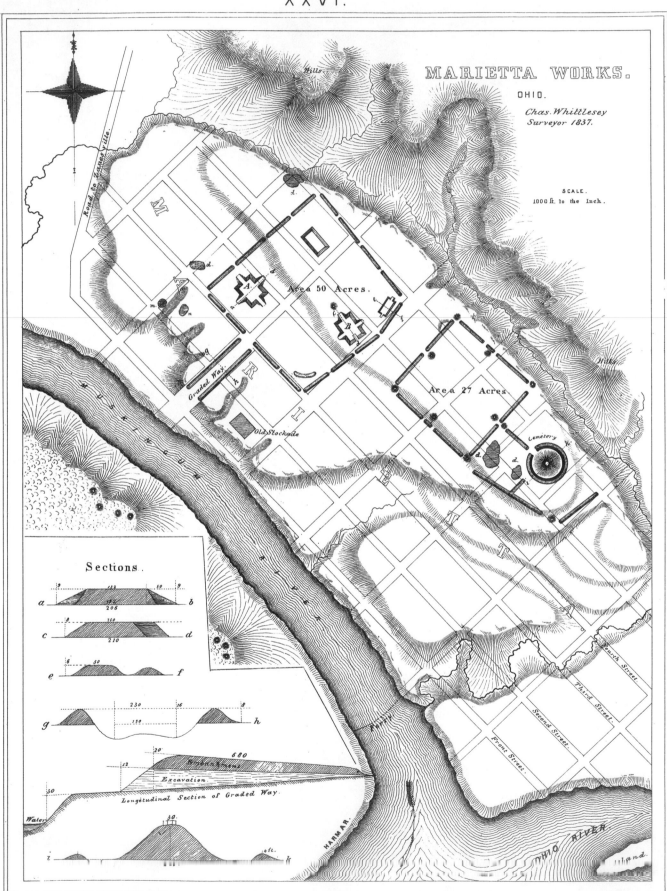

MARIETTA WORKS.

OHIO.

Chas. Whittlesey
Surveyor 1837.

SCALE.
1000 ft. to the Inch.

Area 50 Acres.

Area 27 Acres.

Cemetery

Graded Way.

Old Stockade.

Road to Barnesville.

Hills

Hills

MUSKINGUM RIVER

HARMAR.

OHIO RIVER

Island.

Front Street.

Second Street.

Third Street.

Fourth Street.

Ferry

Sections.

Embankment.

Excavation.

Longitudinal Section of Graded Way.

Water

Lith. by Sarony & Major

PLATE XXVI.

ANCIENT WORKS AT MARIETTA, OHIO.*

THIS remarkable group of works was among the earliest noticed by Western explorers. It was described by Harte as early as 1791; and a further account was presented in "Harris's Tour," published in 1805, in which an imperfect birds-eye view was also given. Since that period various descriptions have appeared in print; and a number of plans, differing materially in their details, have been published. It is of so much importance, however, and has been the basis of so much speculation, that it is time an *accurate* map and a careful description should be placed before the public. Such a map and such a description it is here aimed to present.

The works occupy the high, sandy plain, at the junction of the Muskingum and Ohio rivers. This plain is from eighty to one hundred feet above the bed of the river, and from forty to sixty above the bottom lands of the Muskingum. Its outlines are shown on the map. It is about three fourths of a mile long, by half a mile in width; is bounded on the side next the hills by ravines, formed by streams, and terminates on the side next the river in an abrupt bank, resting upon the recent alluvions. The topography of the plain and adjacent country is minutely represented on this map.

The works consist of two irregular squares, (one containing forty acres area, the other about twenty acres,) in connection with a graded or covered way and sundry mounds and truncated pyramids, the relative positions of which are shown in the plan. The town of Marietta is laid out over them; and, in the progress of improvement, the walls have been considerably reduced and otherwise much obliterated; yet the outlines of the entire works may still be traced. The walls of the principal square, where they remain undisturbed, are now between five and six feet high by twenty or thirty feet base; those of the smaller enclosure are somewhat less. The entrances or gateways at the sides of the latter are each covered by a small mound placed interior to the embankment; at the corners the gateways are in line with it. The larger work is destitute of this feature, unless we class as such an interior crescent wall covering the entrance at its southern angle.

---

* The map here presented is drawn from a careful survey of these works, made in 1837, by CHARLES WHITTLESEY, Esq., Topographical Engineer of the State, under the law authorizing a Geological and Topographical Survey of Ohio. It has never before been published; and its fidelity, in every respect, may be relied on. It will be seen that the supplementary or "small covert way" represented on the plan in the Archæologia Americana, does not appear. What was taken for a graded way is simply a gully, worn by the rains. The topography of the map, and the accompanying sections, are features which every intelligent inquirer will know how to appreciate.

Within the larger enclosure are four elevated squares or truncated pyramids of earth, which, from their resemblance to similar erections in Mexico and Central America, merit a particular notice.* Three of these have graded passages or avenues of ascent to their tops. The principal one is marked A in the plan, and an engraving more clearly illustrating its features is herewith presented, Fig. 17.

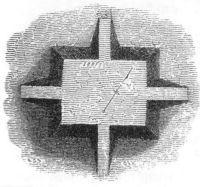

It is one hundred and eighty-eight feet long by one hundred and thirty-two wide, and ten high. Midway upon each of its sides are graded ascents, rendering easy the passage to its top. These grades are twenty-five feet wide and sixty feet long. The next in size is marked B in the plan, and is one hundred and fifty feet long by one hundred and twenty wide, and eight feet high. It has three graded passages to its top, viz. upon the north, west, and east. Those at the sides are placed somewhat to the north of the centre of the eleva-

FIG. 17.

tion. Upon the south side there is a recess or hollow way, instead of a glacis, fifty feet long by twenty wide. This elevation is placed upon an easy swell or ridge of land, and occupies the most conspicuous position within the enclosure, every part of which is commanded from its summit. A few feet distant from the northern glacis, is a small conical mound, surrounded with shallow excavations, from which the earth for its construction, and, perhaps, for the construction in part of the pyramidal structure, was taken. To the right of the elevation, and near the eastern angle of the enclosure, is a smaller elevation one hundred and twenty feet long, fifty broad, and six feet high. It had graded ascents at its ends, similar in all respects to those just described. It is now much obliterated. Near the northern angle of the work is another elevation, not distinctly marked. The two larger squares are covered with a close turf, and still preserve their symmetry. Indeed, no erections of earth alone could surpass them in regularity. They are perfectly level on the top, except where some uprooted tree has displaced the earth.

There is a passage or gateway one hundred and fifty feet wide, in the middle of the left wall of this enclosure, on the side next the Muskingum. Leading from it towards the river, and at right angles to the embankment, is the " *Sacra Via*," a *graded* or *covered way* of singular construction. It is six hundred and eighty feet long by one hundred and fifty wide between the banks, and consists of an excavated passage descending regularly from the plain, upon which the works just described are situated, to the alluvions of the river. The earth, in part at least, is thrown outward upon either side, forming embankments from eight to ten feet in height. The centre of the excavated way is slightly raised and rounded, after the manner of the paved streets of modern cities. The cross section *g h* exhibits this feature.

---

* The description of the two principal truncated pyramids embodies the substance of an account of the same, published by Dr. S. P. HILDRETH of Marietta, in the " American Pioneer " for June, 1843,— the entire fidelity of which has been attested by actual survey.

This section is constructed from measurements taken at a point midway between the top and base of the grade. Measured between the summits of the banks, the width of the way is two hundred and thirty feet. At the base of the grade, the walls upon the interior are twenty feet high. From this point there is a slight descent, for the distance of several hundred feet, to the bank of the river, which is here thirty-five or forty feet in height. It has been conjectured by some, that the river flowed immediately at the foot of this way at the time of its construction. This is, however, mere conjecture, unsupported by evidence. If admitted, it would give to this monument an antiquity greatly superior to that of the pyramids, unless the deepening of our river channels has been infinitely more rapid in times past, than at present. But one fact favors the conjecture, and that is the entire absence of remains of antiquity upon the beautiful terraces to which this graded passage leads. They may nevertheless have been once as thickly populated as they now are; and this passage may have been the grand avenue leading to the sacred plain above, through which assemblies and processions passed, in the solemn observances of a mysterious worship.

To the south of the smaller enclosure is a finely formed truncated mound, (a view of which is given in a subsequent Plate,) thirty feet high, and surrounded by a circular wall, constituting a perfect ellipse, the transverse and conjugate diameters of which are two hundred and thirty feet, and two hundred and fifteen feet respectively.* This beautiful monument is now enclosed in the public cemetery, and is carefully guarded from encroachment. A flight of steps ascends to its summit, on which seats are disposed, and from which a beautiful prospect is commanded.† In the vicinity occur several fragmentary walls, as shown in the map.

---

* Such is the result of careful admeasurements made by Dr. JOHN LOCKE, whose accuracy in matters of this kind, as in all others, is worthy of emulation.

† A very laudable disposition has been manifested, on the part of the citizens of Marietta, to preserve the interesting remains in their midst. The Directors of the Ohio Land Company, when they took possession of the country at the mouth of the Muskingum, in 1788, adopted immediate measures for the preservation of these monuments. To their credit be it said, one of their earliest official acts was the passage of a resolution, which is entered upon the journal of their proceedings, reserving the two truncated pyramids and the great mound, with a few acres attached to each, as public squares. They placed them under the care of the future corporation of Marietta, directing that they should be embellished with shade trees, when divested of the forest which then covered them, which trees, it was added, should be of *native* growth, and of the varieties named in the resolution. The great mound with its surrounding square was designated as a cemetery, and placed under the control of trustees. Ten years ago, these structures being yet unenclosed and much injured by the rains washing through the paths caused by the cattle that roamed over them, the citizens raised a sum of money adequate to the purpose, and fully restored them. The magnificent avenue named, not inappropriately, by the Directors, " *Sacra Via,*" or Sacred Way, but now generally known as the " Covered Way," was also preserved by a special resolution of the Company, "never to be disturbed or defaced, as common ground, not to be enclosed." One of the streets of Marietta, Warren street, passes through this avenue. It is, of course, impossible to resist encroachments upon the walls of the enclosures, which are rapidly disappearing.

Had a similar enlightened policy marked the proceedings of all the early companies and settlers of the West, we should not now have occasion to regret the entire obliteration of many interesting remains of antiquity. Or did a similar disposition exist generally, there would be less necessity for a careful, systematic, and *immediate* survey of our remaining monuments. The works at Chillicothe, Circleville,

Excavations, or "dug holes," are observable at various points around these works. Near the great mound are several of considerable size. Those indicated by *m* and *n* in the plan have been regarded and described as *wells*. Their regularity and former depth are the only reasons adduced in support of this belief. The circumstance of regularity is not at all remarkable, and is a common feature in excavations manifestly made for the purpose of procuring material for the construction of mounds, etc. Their present depth is small, though it is represented to have been formerly much greater. There is some reason for believing that they were dug in order to procure clay for the construction of pottery and for other purposes, inasmuch as a very fine variety of that material occurs at this point, some distance below the surface. The surface soil has recently been removed, and the manufacture of bricks commenced. The "clay lining" which has been mentioned as characterizing these "wells," is easily accounted for, by the fact that they are sunk in a clay bank!

Upon the opposite side of the Muskingum river are bold, precipitous bluffs, several hundred feet in height. Along their brows are a number of small stone mounds. They command an extensive view, and overlook the entire plain upon which the works here described are situated.*

Such are the principal facts connected with these interesting remains. The generally received opinion respecting them is, that they were erected for defensive purposes. Such was the belief of the late President HARRISON, who visited them in person, and whose opinion, in matters of this kind, is entitled to great weight. The reasons for this belief have never been presented, and they are not very obvious. The number and width of the gateways, the absence of a fosse, as well as the character of the enclosed and accompanying remains, present strong objections to the hypothesis which ascribes to them a warlike origin. And it may here be remarked, that the conjecture that the Muskingum ran at the base of the graded way already described, at the period of its erection, seems to have had its origin in the assumption of a military design in the entire group. Under this hypothesis, it was supposed that the way was designed to cover or secure access to the river,—an object which it would certainly not have required the construction of a passage-way one hundred and fifty feet wide to effect. The elevated squares were never designed for military purposes,—their very regularity of structure forbids the conclusion. They were most likely erected as the sites for structures which have long since passed away, or for the celebration of unknown rites,—corresponding in short, in purpose as they do in form, with those which they so much resemble in

---

Cincinnati, and St. Louis, might have been preserved with all ease; and would have constituted striking ornaments to those cities, to say nothing of the interest which would attach to them in other points of view. It is proper to observe, that the facts embraced in this note were kindly communicated by Dr. S. P. HILDRETH, of Marietta.

* The account of an English adventurer named *Ashe*, respecting some extraordinary remains which he professed to have discovered here, it is hardly necessary to say, is entitled to no credit whatever. The remark holds good of similar accounts, by the same hand, of some of the works at Newark, one hundred miles above, on the upper tributaries of the Muskingum.

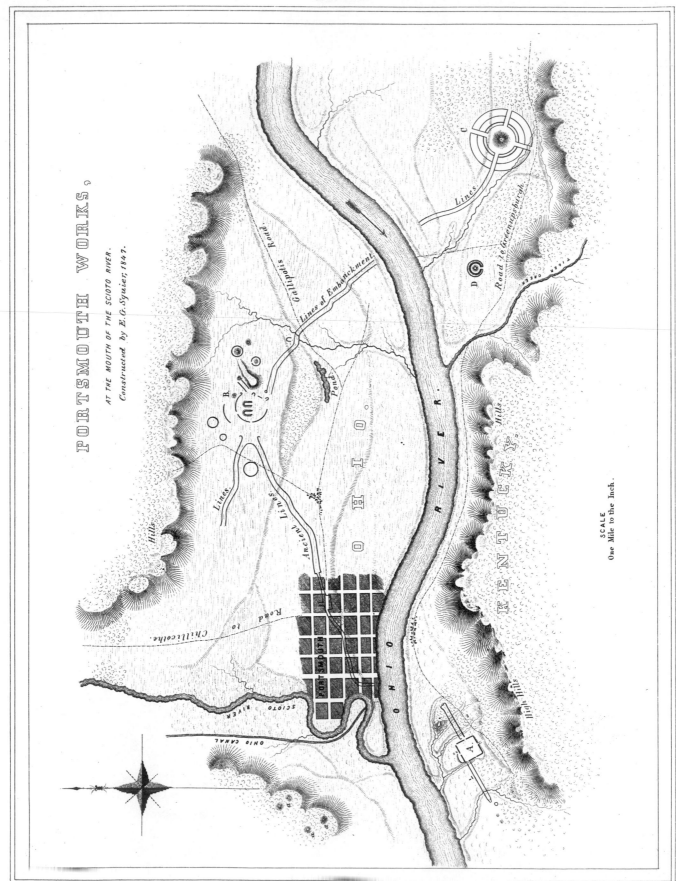

XXVII

PORTSMOUTH WORKS.

AT THE MOUTH OF THE SCIOTO RIVER.

Constructed by E. G. Squier, 1847.

SCALE
One Mile to the Inch.

Lith. by Sarony & Major 117 Fulton St.

Face P. 77.

Mexico and Central America. Do not these enclosed structures give us the clue to the purposes of the works with which they are connected? As heretofore remarked, the sacred grounds of almost every people are set apart or designated by enclosures of some kind.

The absolute identity in size between the smaller enclosure, (which varies a little from a true square,) and several of those which occur in the Scioto valley, should not be overlooked, in any attempt to educe the character and design of the group. That there is some significance in the fact is obvious. (See Plates XVI and XVII.) There are no other works in the immediate vicinity of Marietta. At Parkersburgh, Virginia, on the Ohio, twelve miles below, there is an enclosure of irregular form and considerable extent, a miniature plan of which, from the MSS. of Prof. Rafinesque, is herewith presented, Fig. 18. There are also some works at Belpre, opposite Parkersburgh.

Fig. 18.

The valley of the Muskingum is for the most part narrow, affording few of those broad, level, and fertile terraces, which appear to have been the especial favorites of the race of mound-builders, and upon which most of their monuments are found. As a consequence, we find few remains of magnitude in that valley, until it assumes a different aspect, in the vicinity of Zanesville, ninety miles from its mouth, where the interesting remains figured in the preceding Plate are situated.

PLATE XXVII.

THE PORTSMOUTH WORKS, SCIOTO COUNTY, OHIO.

The beautiful plain at the confluence of the Scioto and Ohio rivers, where now the flourishing town of Portsmouth is located, forms the site of a singular and interesting series of works. It has been preferred to present them together, as they seem to be intimately connected, leaving the reader to form his own conclusions respecting them.

The works consist of three divisions or groups, extending for eight miles along the Ohio river, and are connected by parallel lines of embankments. Two of these groups are on the Kentucky side of the river; the remaining one, together with the larger portion of the connecting embankment, on the Ohio shore. A reference to the accompanying map, exhibiting a section of eight miles of the Ohio valley, will show the relative positions and general plan, though not the exact proportions of the series. The avenues or "covered ways," extending from one work to the other, have induced many persons to assign them a military origin, and a design to protect communication between the groups. But unless the work at A be regarded as a work of defence, it is very certain that we must seek for some other explanation of their purposes. These avenues constitute a remarkable feature; and as enlarged plans and full descriptions of the several groups follow, it may be well to notice them more particularly here. It will be seen that from the central group B, three lines lead off: one to the south-east, to a point on the Ohio, nearly opposite to which, on the Kentucky side, it is resumed, leading to the circular work C; another bears south-west, to a point on the river, nearly opposite the large and regular work A. It does not appear to be resumed on the other side of the river. A third line runs north-west for a considerable distance, and loses itself in the broken grounds towards the Scioto. It may have communicated with other works in that direction, which have been obliterated by time, or, which is most likely, were destroyed in the manifest changes which the plain in that direction has undergone within a few centuries.

These lines consist of parallel embankments of earth, now measuring about four feet in height, by twenty feet base. They are not far from one hundred and sixty feet apart. The line leading towards the mouth of the Scioto, however, at about midway of the distance, suddenly contracts to seventy feet. It is said to have as suddenly widened further on, enclosing a square area, with a gateway opening to the north. The town of Portsmouth is built over this portion, and all traces of the parallelogram and the walls have disappeared. Near the point of contraction in this line are two or three mounds of medium size.

It is a fact to be observed in these as in similar lines at other places, that they are not interrupted by the inequalities of the ground, but conform to the undulations of the surface, running sometimes at right angles to the terrace banks, and sometimes diagonally up and down them. At some points these banks are very steep,—so steep, indeed, that in clambering up them the explorer is inclined to doubt that they were ever used or intended for purposes of communication. The only interruptions are those caused by the passage of streams, there being no gateways observable. The total length of the parallels now traceable may be estimated at eight miles, giving *sixteen miles* of embankment to the parallels alone. If we include the walls of the entire series, we have a grand total of upwards of *twenty* miles.

After this general view, the reader will be prepared to examine the groups forming the series A, B, and C, in the order of their succession.

———

PLATE XXVIII.

PORTSMOUTH WORKS—GROUP A.

THE singular work, a plan of which is here given, occurs on the Kentucky side of the Ohio river, opposite the old mouth of the Scioto, about two miles below the town of Portsmouth. The terrace on which it is situated is elevated some fifty feet above the first bottom, and extends back to the hills, which at this point

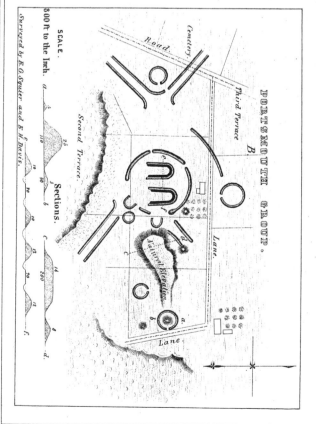

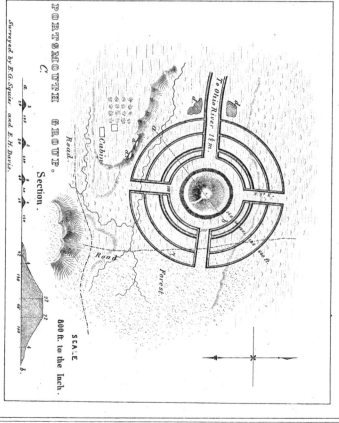

are at some distance from the river. It is much cut up by ravines, and is quite uneven.

The main body of the work is situated upon a very beautiful level, somewhat ascending to the east. The wings are on equally beautiful levels, except that they are broken at two or three points by ravines.

The principal work is an exact rectangle, eight hundred feet square. The walls are about twelve feet high, by thirty-five or forty feet base, except on the east, where advantage is taken of the rise of ground, so as to elevate them about fifty feet above the centre of the area. This feature is exhibited in the section *a b.*

The hollow way between the south-eastern wall and the terrace bank beyond seems artificial,—at any rate, it has been modified by art. The gateway on this side is entered by a slightly elevated causeway. At the southern angle is a bastion, probably natural but adapted by art, which commands the hollow way or ditch. The wall at this part is distinctly marked, but not more than three feet high. On the south-western side is a sort of runway, resembling a ditch, which loses itself in a deep gully towards the river. It is undoubtedly wholly or in part artificial. There are no traces of ditches elsewhere about the work. A narrow gateway thirty feet wide opens in the middle of each side, and at the northern and western angles, as represented in the plan.

The most singular features of this structure are its outworks, which consist of parallel walls leading to the north-east and south-west. They are exactly parallel to the sides of the main work, and are each two thousand one hundred feet long. Some measurements make them of unequal lengths; but after a careful calculation of the space occupied by the interrupting ravines, they are found to be very nearly, not exactly, of the same length.

The parallel to the south-west has its outer wall in line with the north-western wall of the main work, and starts at thirty feet distance from the same. It is broken by a deep ravine near its extremity, which is probably four or five hundred feet wide. Crossing the ravine, the walls, traces of which are seen on the declivity, continue to some distance, and then curve on a radius of one hundred feet, leaving a narrow gateway eight feet wide in the centre. Converging walls start from the point of curve, but lose themselves after running three hundred feet, without meeting. Just beyond and a little to the right, on the plain, are two clay mounds, also a small circle one hundred feet in diameter, the walls of which are two feet high.

The parallel to the north-east starts from the centre (nearly) of the main work, and is similar to the one already described, save that it is not terminated by converging walls, and has no mounds beyond. It is interrupted by two ravines, the walls running to their very edges. The left wall of the parallel bends to a right angle as it approaches the main work.

To the left of this parallel, four hundred and fifty feet from a point eight hundred feet distant from the main work, on a high peninsula or headland, is a singular redoubt, an enlarged view of which is given in the supplementary plan N. To the left of it is the bank of the second bottom, fifty feet high, and very steep. To the right is the hollow of a small stream with steep banks. The embankment of this work is heavy, and the ditch deep and wide, and interior to the wall. From the bottom of the ditch to the top of the wall, is perhaps twelve or fifteen feet. The enclosed oval area is only sixty feet wide by one hundred and ten long. It has a gateway to the north-east ten feet wide,—outside of which, in the deep forest, is the grave of one of the first settlers. The object of this enclosure it is difficult to divine. If a place of burial, as has been suggested, properly conducted excava- tions would disclose the fact.

A light wall of some hundred paces in extent runs from the left hand entrance of the main work, along the verge of a declivity terminating at the western angle. On this side are also three mounds, each about six feet high,—formerly much higher, having been greatly reduced by the plough. From the western angle a deep gully runs off to the river; it has been mistaken by some for a covered way.

The entire main work, the greater part of the lower parallel, and a portion of the upper one, are now in open cultivated grounds. The walls of the main work are so steep as to preclude cultivation, and now form the fence lines of the area, which is fifteen acres. The area of the parallels is ten acres each;—total, thirty- five acres.

Between this work and the river are traces of a modern Indian encampment or town,—shells, burned stones, fragments of rude pottery, etc., also some graves. This was a favorite spot with the Indians, for various reasons, one of which is its proximity to a noted saline spring or deer lick, known as " McArthur's Lick."

From the size of the walls, their position, and other circumstances, it has been supposed that this was a fortified place. If palisaded, it would certainly be impreg- nable to any savage attack. If designed as a sacred place, its sloping area would be most fit for the observance of sacrifices or ceremonies.

What may have been the purpose of the mysterious parallels, is more than we, at this period, can venture to say.

———

PLATE XXVIII.

PORTSMOUTH WORKS—GROUP B.

THIS group also occupies the third terrace, and, though not so imposing in magnitude as the one just described, seems to be the grand centre from which the parallel lines, characterizing this series of works, radiate. Its details are intricate, and can only be understood by the aid of the plan. The two crescent or horse-shoe- shaped walls constitute the first striking feature which presents itself. They are both of about the same size and shape, measuring eighty feet in length by seventy in breadth. The earth around them appears to have been considerably excavated. Enclosing these in part is a circular wall now about five feet high. The elevation to the right appears to be natural, although evidently much modified by art. It is eighteen feet high at the end next the principal division of the work, but gradually subsides into a low ridge towards the enclosed mound *a b.* A full view of the entire group may be had from its summit. The mound just mentioned is twenty-eight feet high, by one hundred and ten base; it is truncated and surrounded by a low circumvallation. There are several small circles, measuring from one hundred and fifty to two hundred and fifty feet in diameter; also a few mounds, in the positions indicated in the plan.

No one, after examining its details, would be apt to ascribe a military origin to this group. The most reasonable conjecture respecting it is, that it was in some way connected with the superstitions of the builders; in what manner, of course, it is impossible to determine. A thorough examination of the mounds might throw some light on the question. At any rate, it is entirely unique in many of its features, and furnishes an interesting study for the antiquary.

PLATE XXVIII.

PORTSMOUTH WORKS—GROUP C.

This group is on the Kentucky shore, and principally occupies the third terrace, or high level at the base of the hills bordering the valley. The ground is here considerably broken. The northern portion of the work is somewhat lower than the remainder, and a small brook cuts through the outer wall on the south. This work is in many respects novel, and for this reason, as well as from the connection in which it is found, is entitled to an attention not otherwise merited; for no person looking merely for what is striking from position, or imposing from magnitude, would be apt to pay it a second visit. It consists of four concentric circles, placed at irregular intervals in respect to each other, and cut at right angles by four broad avenues, which conform in bearing very nearly to the cardinal points. A large mound is placed in the centre; it is truncated and terraced, and has a graded way leading to its summit. A reference to the plan and sections will exhibit in one view the dimensions and general aspect of the work, obviating the necessity of a detailed description.

The mound in the centre, at first glance, would be taken for a natural elevation; and it is possible that it is a detached spur of a hill, modified and perhaps enlarged by art. A hillock in such a position is, however, a circumstance of very rare occurrence. From the level summit of this mound, a complete view of every part of the surrounding work is commanded. Were it not for the obstructing forests, it is believed the eye might obtain, from this position, a view of the river and intermediate plain, as also of the works beyond, and several miles distant. On the supposition that this work was in some way connected with the religious rites and ceremonies of the builders, this mound must have afforded a most conspicuous place for their observance and celebration. And it is easy, while standing on its summit, to people it with the strange priesthood of ancient superstition, and fill its avenues and line its walls with the thronging devotees of a mysterious worship. Whatever may have been the divinity of their belief, order, symmetry, and design were among his attributes; if, as appears most likely, the works that most strongly exhibit these features were dedicated to religious purposes, and were symbolical in their design.

About one mile to the west of this work are a number of mounds, some of considerable size, and also a small circular work, D, of exquisite symmetry and proportion. It consists of an embankment of earth five feet high by thirty feet base, with an interior ditch twenty-five feet across by six feet deep, enclosing an area ninety feet in diameter, in the centre of which rises a mound eight feet high by forty feet base. A narrow gateway through the parapet, and a causeway over the ditch, lead to the enclosed mound.

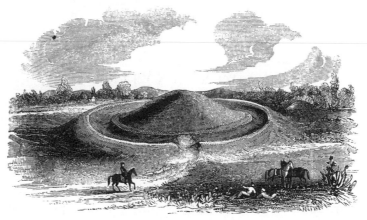

FIG. 19—CIRCLE AND MOUND, GREENUP COUNTY, KENTUCKY.

The above view, taken on the spot, will illustrate the appearance of this class of works. Nothing can exceed their regularity and beauty, when clothed with turf or covered with forest trees.

———

PLATE XXIX. No. 1.

ANCIENT WORKS, MONTGOMERY COUNTY, OHIO.*

THESE works are situated on the east bank of the Great Miami river, six miles below Dayton, Montgomery county, Ohio. They are built upon the second bottom or terrace, which is here nearly a mile broad, and elevated about twenty feet above the river. The plan of the group coincides very nearly with that of some of the

* From the Survey and Notes of James McBride, Esq.

Lith. of Sarony & Major.

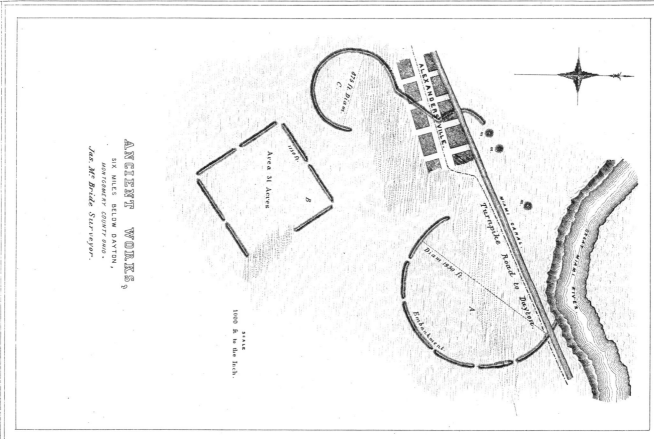

ANCIENT WORKS,

SIX MILES BELOW DAYTON,

MONTGOMERY COUNTY OHIO.

Jas. McBride Surveyor.

Area 31 Acres

875 ft. Diam.
C.

Diam. 1890 ft.
A.

Embankment

ALEXANDERSVILLE

Turnpike Road to Dayton.

MIAMI CANAL

GREAT MIAMI RIVER

SCALE
1000 ft. to the Inch.

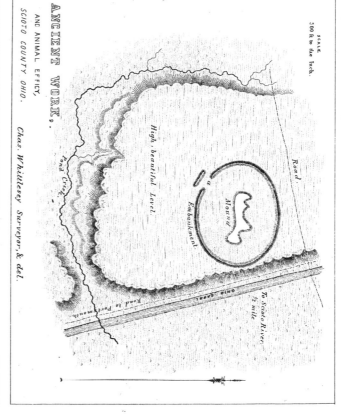

ANCIENT WORK,

AND ANIMAL EFFIGY,

SCIOTO COUNTY OHIO.

Chas. Whittlesey, Surveyor, & del.

High, beautiful Level.

Pond Creek.

Embankment

Mound

Road.

Road to Portsmouth.

To Scioto River.
½ mile

OHIO CANAL

SCALE
500 ft. to the Inch.

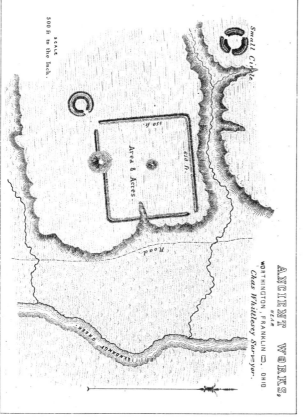

ANCIENT WORKS,

NEAR

WORTHINGTON, FRANKLIN ☐, OHIO.

Chas Whittlesey Surveyor.

Area 8 Acres.

550 ft.

630 ft.

Small Circle.

C

Road

SCALE
500 ft. to the Inch.

more regular works of the Scioto valley. (See Plates **XX** and **XXI**.) It seems never to have been completed; at any rate, the various parts were never connected. A portion of the great circle A has been washed away by the river, which here encroaches upon the second terrace. The diameter of this circle is one hundred feet greater than that of the corresponding large circle of the Scioto works; and the same proportionate increase in size is to be observed in the square and lower circle. The embankments are now between five and six feet high, and have a base fifty feet wide. They are composed of a tough, yellow clay, which is found to be superimposed on the loam of the original level. It must have been brought from a distance, as there are no excavations perceptible in the vicinity. The embankments, as in the case of several other works which have been noticed, appear to have been some time or other subjected to the action of fire. They are unaccompanied by a ditch.

The Miami canal extends through these works, and the little town of Alexandersville is laid out over a portion of the smaller circle. The clay composing the embankments is now much used in the manufacture of bricks, and but a little time will elapse before the work will be entirely obliterated.

We can only regard this structure as kindred in its purposes to those above alluded to in the Scioto valley, and associate it with the superstitions of the builders. It tends to confirm the impression produced by the other works, that some significance attaches to the combination of the two circles and the square.

PLATE XXIX. No. 2.

ANCIENT WORKS, SCIOTO COUNTY, OHIO.[*]

THIS singular work is situated five miles north of Portsmouth, Scioto county, Ohio, on the west bank of the Scioto river. It is not a true ellipse, but approaches very near it. Its longest axis is four hundred and eighty feet, its conjugate diameter four hundred and seven feet. It is built upon a high and beautiful level, elevated some sixty or seventy feet above the Scioto river, which flows about half a mile to the eastward. The embankment is unaccompanied by a ditch, and is about three feet in height, by thirty feet base. It has, as shown in the plan, a single gateway, ninety feet wide, opening to the south-east, which is covered by a long exterior mound, of about the same height with the embankment of the enclosure.

Within this enclosure is a large irregular mound, which, from its resemblance to the animal-shaped mounds of Wisconsin, of which notice will be taken in

---

[*] From the Survey and Notes of CHARLES WHITTLESEY, Esq.

another place, constitutes by far the most interesting feature of the work.   It is of the form and relative size indicated in the plan, and is composed of loose broken sandstone and earth, based upon dislocated and broken sand-rock.   It is from one to eight feet high, being lowest at the eastern end or head, and at the projecting points.   It is probably of the same design with those of Wisconsin, already alluded to, which occur in great numbers and in long and apparently dependent ranges. None of those, however, so far as known, are found enclosed after the manner of the one here presented.   (See " *Remains of the North-West.*")   No explanation of the probable design of this work will be attempted here : it is impossible, however, to disconnect it from the superstitions of the ancient people.   An interesting fact is communicated by F. Cleveland, Esq., of Portsmouth, who assisted Mr. Whittlesey in making the survey of this work, and who was engineer on the Ohio canal when it was in progress ; viz. that the workmen engaged in excavating found large quantities of mica, in sheets, in the immediate vicinity of this enclosure.   This mineral is found in great abundance in the mounds, and in the neighborhood of these ancient works.

PLATE XXIX. No. 3.

ANCIENT WORKS, FRANKLIN COUNTY, OHIO.[*]

THIS work occurs on the banks of Olentangy creek, a tributary of the Scioto river, about one mile west of the town of Worthington, Franklin county, Ohio. The plateau upon the edge of which it is situated is elevated about fifty feet above the bottoms of the Olentangy, and consists of a clayey soil resting on the black shale formation of Ohio.   The work is rectangular in form ; its sides correspond very nearly with the cardinal points, (varying but five degrees,) and measure six hundred and thirty, and five hundred and fifty feet respectively.   The walls are unaccompanied by a ditch, and are very slight, though distinctly trace-able.   In the line of the southern wall is a large truncated mound, C, twenty feet in height, and measuring one hundred and ninety-two feet in diameter at the base, and seventy-six feet in diameter at the summit.   It is covered with large trees.   The wall that leads from this mound to the left, is placed a little further outwards than that leading to the right.   The mound D, in the centre of the enclosure, is small and low.   Near the south-western corner of the work is a small circle, with an interior ditch and single entrance ; it is one hundred and twenty feet in diameter. Some distance to the north-west of the enclosure, and on the opposite side of a deep ravine, is another small circle, one hundred and forty feet in diameter, with three entrances.

----

[*] From the Plan and Notes of CHARLES WHITTLESEY, Esq.

Face P. 85.

PLATE XXX. No. 1.*

THIS work is situated four miles south-west of the town of Hamilton, Butler county, Ohio, on S. 10, T. 1, R. 2, between the Great and Little Miami rivers. It is indicated by the letter C, in the Map of a section of the Miami valley (Plate III, No. 2).

The ground upon which this unique work is built is the level bottom of the Miami river, at a distance from any high lands. The principal or square portion of the work is constructed of an embankment of earth, about four feet high by fifty feet base, unaccompanied by a ditch. The walls of the circular or irregular portion of the work, towards Pleasant run, are considerably heavier, and have an interior ditch. The work is not an exact square, nor are its gateways disposed with the usual degree of regularity. The walls, at the western angle, terminate in a large oblong mound, and a small mound occupies the centre of one of the attached circular works.

At a short distance from the enclosure, towards the south, are two large mounds, placed one hundred and thirty-five feet apart. They are each about two hundred and fifty feet in circumference, and fifteen feet in perpendicular height, and are in part composed of large stones. These mounds, as also the larger portion of the enclosure, are situated in timbered land, the forests presenting the usual primitive aspect. The trees growing upon the walls are of the largest size, and are surrounded by the fallen and decayed trunks of their predecessors. From this work to the Miami river, the distance is now about half a mile; the intervening bottom is low and of comparatively recent formation. It is probable that the river once washed the work, at the point now bounded by Pleasant run.

For reasons which it is here unnecessary to recapitulate, this work is deemed of religious origin.

——

PLATE XXX. No. 2.*

THIS work is indicated by the letter F, in the map of a section of the Miami valley, and is situated on the right bank of the Miami river, seven miles below the town of Hamilton, Butler county, Ohio, on S. 27 and 34, T. 3, R. 2, E. M.

Little can be said respecting it, except that it is a circle of considerable size,

* From the Survey and Notes of JAMES McBRIDE, Esq.

bounded by an embankment, at present about two feet high, composed of earth taken up evenly from the surface, or brought from a distance. It has an entrance to the left, two hundred and seventy-five feet wide; the embankment upon either hand terminating in a small mound, between four and five feet high. The area of the enclosure is level, and covered with forest: the trees are, however, small, owing probably to the nature of the soil, which is thin and gravelly. The plain is here fifty feet above the adjacent bottoms.

About a mile north-east of this work, on the opposite bank of Indian creek, are three large mounds, on a line with each other. On the lower bottom or terrace, opposite to each mound, is a corresponding hole or excavation, from which the earth composing them was doubtless obtained.

———

PLATE XXX. No. 3.

ANCIENT WORK NEAR BOURNEVILLE, ROSS COUNTY, OHIO.

THE small work here figured is one of the most beautiful in the State of Ohio. It is situated upon the highest terrace, directly facing, and about one mile distant from, the great stone hill-work of the Paint creek valley (Plate IV). It consists of a wall of earth, eight or ten feet in height, with a broad and shallow exterior ditch. In figure it is elliptical, with a transverse diameter of seven hundred and fifty, and a conjugate diameter of six hundred and seventy-five feet. It has a gateway one hundred and twenty feet wide, leading into it from the south-west. It opens upon a small spur of the terrace, which has been artificially rounded and graded, so as to make a regular and easy descent to the lower level. Upon either side of this grade, the banks of the terrace are steep and irregular. A very copious spring of water starts from the bank near the wall, a little to the right of the entrance. A small circle and a couple of mounds are situated on the next lower terrace, at the points indicated in the plan.

This work is admirably preserved, and is remarkable as being the only circular work at present known, which has its ditch exterior to the walls. The proprietor esteems the soil much richer within the enclosure, than upon the adjacent plain. We are unprepared to ascribe any other than a religious origin to this structure.

PLATE XXX. No. 4.

STONE WORK ON "BLACK RUN," ROSS COUNTY, OHIO.

THIS unique work is situated in the little valley of "Black run," a small tributary of Paint creek, and is distant about fifteen miles from Chillicothe. It is indicated by the letter E, in the "Map exhibiting a section of six miles of the Paint creek valley." The walls are composed of stones; but if ever regularly laid up, they are now thrown down, though not greatly scattered. The outlines are clearly defined, and can be exactly traced. The body of the work is elliptical in shape, its conjugate diameter being one hundred and seventy feet, its transverse two hundred and fifty feet. There is a single opening or gateway, fifty feet wide, on the south, where the walls curve outwards and lap back upon themselves for the space of sixty feet. The most remarkable feature of this singular work consists of five walls, starting within ten feet of the unbroken line of the elliptical enclosure, and extending thence northward, slightly converging, for the distance of one hundred feet. The lines of the outer walls, if prolonged, would intersect each other at the distance of two hundred and fifty feet. These walls are twenty feet broad at the ends nearest the enclosure, and ten feet apart. They diminish gradually, as they recede, to ten feet at their outer extremities. The western wall is nearly obliterated; the stones for the construction of all the "cabin" hearths and chimneys in the neighborhood having been taken from this spot. The western portion of the wall of the ellipse has also suffered from the same cause. The amount of stone embraced in the outer walls is considerable, probably sufficient to construct walls of equal length, six feet broad and eight feet high. They now exhibit but slight evidence of ever having been regularly laid up, and more resemble mounds of stones rudely thrown together. The stones have been removed from a section of the central wall, to the base; but we have been unable to ascertain that the operation disclosed relics of any kind. The wall of the body of the work appears considerably lighter than those last mentioned, and it is now quite impossible to determine whether it was ever regularly constructed. The stones cover a space fifteen or twenty feet broad, and are irregularly heaped together to the height of perhaps three feet. The work is overgrown with briers, bushes, and trees; which, when in leaf, completely hide its features from view, and render a satisfactory examination impossible. In the autumn or spring, the entire outline of the work is distinctly visible.

The purposes of this strange work are entirely inexplicable: its small size precludes the idea of a defensive origin. It is the only structure of the kind which has yet been discovered in the valleys, and it is totally unlike those found on the hills. The great "Stone Fort" on Paint creek (Plate IV) is but two miles distant, and overlooks this work; both may be regarded as belonging to the same era, and as probably in some way connected with each other.

PLATE XXXI.

GRADED WAY, NEAR PIKETON, PIKE COUNTY, OHIO.

THERE is a singular class of earthworks, occurring at various points at the West, which seem better to come up to the utilitarian standard of our day than any other, and the purposes of which to the popular mind, if not to that of the antiquarian, seem very clear. These are the *graded ways*, ascending sometimes from one terrace to another, and occasionally descending towards the banks of rivers or water-courses. The one already described, in connection with the works at Marietta, is of the latter description; as is also that at Piqua, Ohio, described by Maj. LONG.* One of the former character occurs near Richmondale, Ross county, Ohio; and another, and the most remarkable one, about one mile below Piketon, Pike county, in the same State. A plan and view of the latter is herewith presented.

FIG. 20.—VIEW OF GRADED WAY NEAR PIKETON, OHIO.

It consists of a graded ascent from the second to the third terrace, the level of which is here seventeen feet above that of the former. The way is ten hundred and eighty feet long, by two hundred and fifteen feet wide at one extremity, and two hundred and three feet wide at the other, measured between the bases of the banks.

---

* "It consists of a ditch dug down to the edge of the river, the earth from which has been thrown up principally upon the lower, or down-river side. The breadth between the parapets is much greater near the water than at any other point; so that it might have been used for the purpose of affording a safe passage to the river, or as a sort of harbor in which canoes may have been drawn up, or both. This water way resembles that found at Marietta, though smaller."—*Long's Second Expedition*, vol. i. p. 60.

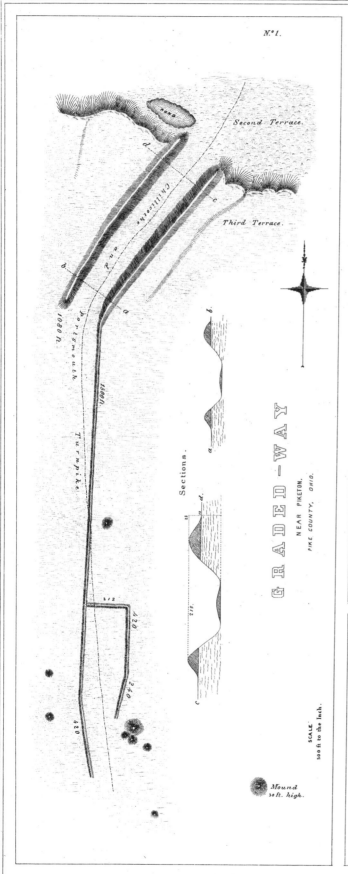

XXXI

No. 1.

Second Terrace.

Third Terrace.

GRADED-WAY

NEAR PIKETON.

PIKE COUNTY, OHIO.

Sections.

SCALE
500 ft. to the Inch.

Mound
30 ft. high.

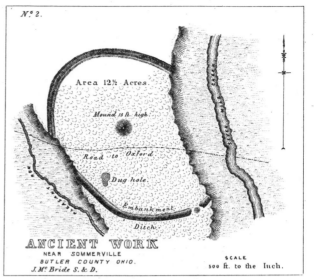

No. 2.

Area 12½ Acres

Mound 15 ft. high.

Road to Oxford

Dug hole.

Embankment.

Ditch.

ANCIENT WORK

NEAR SOMMERVILLE
BUTLER COUNTY OHIO.
J. Mc Bride S. & D.

SCALE
500 ft. to the Inch.

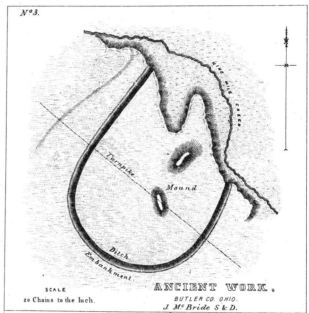

No. 3.

NINE MILE CREEK

Turnpike

Mound

Ditch.

Embankment.

SCALE
20 Chains to the Inch.

ANCIENT WORK.

BUTLER CO. OHIO.
J. Mc Bride S. & D.

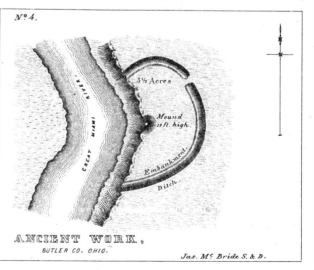

No. 4.

3½ Acres

Mound
15 ft. high.

GREAT MIAMI RIVER

Embankment.

Ditch.

ANCIENT WORK.

BUTLER CO. OHIO.

Jas. Mc Bride S. & D.

Lith. by Sarony & Major.

The earth is thrown outward on either hand, forming embankments varying upon the outer sides from five to eleven feet in height; yet it appears that much more earth has been excavated than enters into these walls. At the lower extremity of the grade, the walls upon the interior sides measure no less than *twenty-two* feet in perpendicular height. The easy ascent here afforded has been rendered available in the construction of the Chillicothe and Portsmouth turnpike, which passes through it. The walls are covered with trees and bushes, and resemble parallel natural hills, and probably would be regarded as such by the superficial observer. Indeed, hundreds pass along without suspecting that they are in the midst of one of the most interesting monuments which the country affords, and one which bears a marked resemblance to some of those works which are described to us in connection with the causeways and aqueducts of Mexico.

From the end of the right-hand wall, upon the third terrace, extends a low line of embankment, (now much obliterated by the construction of the turnpike,) two thousand five hundred and eighty feet long, leading towards a group of mounds, as shown in the plan. At the distance of fifteen hundred feet from the grade, a wall starts off at right angles, for the distance of two hundred and twelve feet, when it assumes a course parallel to the principal line for four hundred and twenty feet, and then curves inwardly, terminating near a group consisting of one large and three small mounds. A ground plan of the latter is elsewhere given. This group of mounds is now enclosed, and constitutes the cemetery of the neighborhood. Forty rods to the right of this group, is a large mound thirty feet in height. Several small mounds occur upon the adjacent plain, though no enclosures of magnitude are found nearer than five miles lower down, on the river.

The left-hand wall of the grade as we descend seems continued down upon the second terrace for some distance, terminating near a low spot of ground, usually containing water. Similar depressions are observed in the ancient beds of streams. It has been suggested that the Scioto river once flowed along the base of the terrace at this point, and that the way led down to it. Without expressing an opinion upon the probability of this conjecture, it is sufficient to observe that the river now flows more than half a mile to the left, and that two terraces, each twenty feet in height, intervene between the present and the supposed ancient level of the stream. To assent to the suggestion, would be to admit an almost immeasurable antiquity to the structure under consideration.

It is, of course, useless to speculate upon the probable purpose of this work. At first glance, it seems obvious; namely, that it was constructed simply to facilitate the ascent from one terrace to another. But the long line of embankment extending from it, and the manifest connection which exists between it and the mounds upon the plain, unsettle this conclusion. After all, we are obliged to leave this interesting work with the single remark, already several times made in respect to others equally interesting and inexplicable, that future investigations, carefully conducted, may solve alike the problem of their purposes and of their origin.*

---

* The reader is requested to compare the plan of this work given by Mr. ATWATER in the Archæologia Americana, with the one here presented.

A singular work of art occurs on the top of a high hill, standing in the rear of the town of Piketon, and overlooking it, which it may not be out of place to mention here. It consists of a perfectly circular excavation, thirty feet in diameter, and twelve feet deep, terminating in a point at the bottom. It contains water for the greater part of the year. A slight and regular wall is thrown up around its edge. A full and very distinct view of the graded way just described is commanded from this point.

———

PLATE XXXI. Nos. 2, 3, and 4.

THE works here presented possess few characteristics of works of defence, and yet have little of the regularity, and but few of the features, which distinguish the sacred enclosures.

NUMBER 2 is situated near Sommerville, Butler county, Ohio, on S. 3 and 10, T. 5, R. 2, E. M. It occupies the second terrace between Pleasant run and Seven Mile creek, and seems to have been encroached upon by both these streams. This terrace is about twenty-five feet higher than the first terrace, and is bounded by steep banks. The wall of the work is about four feet high, the ditch of proportionate depth. Near the centre is an exceedingly regular mound, one hundred feet in diameter at the base, and thirteen feet in altitude. It is now covered with a fine growth of maple-trees. At the north-east corner of the work, in the embankment, there is a quantity of stones placed with some degree of regularity,—probably originally constituting a sort of wall. At the opposite extremity of the work is a dug hole or "well."

NUMBER 3 is situated nine miles north of the town of Hamilton, Butler county, Ohio, on a rich alluvial bottom, between Seven Mile and Nine Mile creeks, the latter of which seems to have encroached upon the work. The large oblong mound in the centre was partially excavated in constructing the Hamilton and Eaton turnpike. A quantity of bones were discovered; but nothing is known of the position in which they were found.

NUMBER 4 is situated on the east bank of the Great Miami river, four miles below the town of Hamilton, Butler county, Ohio, and is indicated by the letter D, in the map of a section of the Miami valley. Probably not more than half the original work now exists, the remainder having been destroyed by the encroachments of the river. The wall and ditch are slight; the former not exceeding three feet in height, and the latter two feet in depth. At the bank of the river, however, the original depth of the ditch, as also the amount of the vegetable and other matter with which it is filled up, are distinctly visible. The ditch, which had been sunk into the

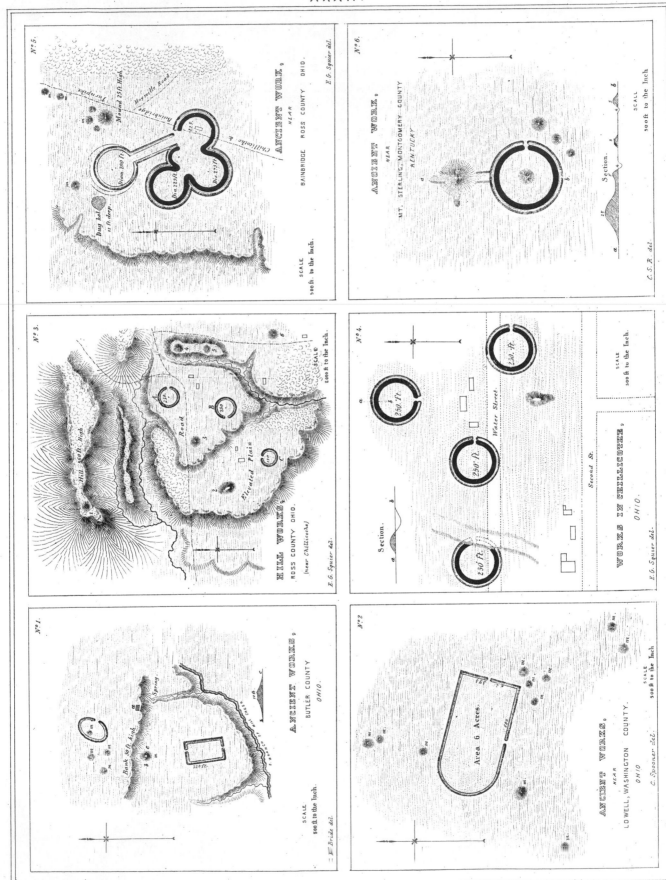

XXXII

N.º 5.

Maysville Road.

Mound 25 ft. High.

Turnpike.

Chillicothe &

Bainbridge.

Dug hole
11 ft. deep.

Diam 200 ft.

Dia 225 ft.

Dia 225 ft.

Dia 175 ft.

ANCIENT WORK,
NEAR
BAINBRIDGE ROSS COUNTY OHIO.

SCALE
500 ft. to the Inch.

E. G. Squier del.

N.º 6.

ANCIENT WORK,
NEAR
MT. STERLING, MONTGOMERY COUNTY
KENTUCKY

a

b

Section.

SCALE
500 ft. to the Inch

C. S. R. del.

N.º 3.

Hill 100 ft. High.

Road

A

B

250

C

Elevated Plain

HILL WORKS,
ROSS COUNTY OHIO.
(near Chillicothe)

SCALE
2000 ft to the Inch.

E. G. Squier del.

N.º 4.

a

250. Ft.

250. Ft.

250. Ft.

250 Ft.

Water Street.

Second St.

Section.
a

b

WORKS IN CHILLICOTHE,
OHIO.

SCALE
500 ft to the Inch.

E. G. Squier del.

Lith. by Sarony & Major.

N.º 1.

Spring

Bank 30 ft. high.

b c

a

220 ft.

ANCIENT WORKS,
NEAR
BUTLER COUNTY
OHIO.

SCALE
500 ft to the Inch.

W Bride del.

N.º 2.

161

692

Area 6 Acres.

ANCIENT WORKS,
NEAR
LOWELL, WASHINGTON COUNTY.
OHIO

SCALE
500 ft to the Inch

C. Spooner del.

gravel, was originally five feet eight inches in depth; the accumulation since its abandonment has been, therefore, three feet eight inches. Allowing the wall to have subsided to an equal extent, its original height from the bottom of the trench must have been upwards of twelve feet.

The rapidity with which the river encroaches upon its banks at this point may be inferred from the fact, that twenty years previous to the time of the survey of this work by Mr. McBride, in 1836, the river flowed not far from three hundred feet to the left of the central mound, which since that time has entirely disappeared. About thirty feet below this mound was found, some years ago, a number of flat stones set on edge, forming a kind of coffin, in which was a human skeleton, accompanied by a large marine shell and some rude implements. About a fourth of a mile below this work, appears to have been a general cemetery. The graves are indicated by small regular elevations.* The three works last described are laid down from the surveys of Mr. McBride, from whose notes the above facts are principally derived.

PLATE XXXII.

Upon this plate are placed a number of small works, and groups of works, arranged however with no view to any relationship, but as best served the purposes of the engraver.

Number 1 is a group of small works situated on a branch of Mill creek, near the south-east corner of Butler county, Ohio, on S. 14, T. 3, R. 2, M. R. The rectangular work is two hundred and twenty feet long, by one hundred and twenty feet broad. The walls are now about five feet high, and are unaccompanied by a ditch. There were standing upon the embankment, in 1842, a red-oak tree three and a half feet in diameter, and a white-oak tree three feet in diameter. Twenty rods north of this work is a truncated mound ten feet high; and a short distance

---

* Previous to the entire destruction of this mound, and at the time when about one half of it remained, it was examined by Mr. McBride, from whose original notes the following observations respecting it are taken:

"The mound was composed of rich surface mould, evidently scooped up from the surface; scattered through which were pebbles and some stones of considerable size, all of which had been burned. Upon excavation, we found a skeleton with its head to the east, resting upon the original surface of the ground, immediately under the apex of the mound. Some distance above this was a layer of ashes of considerable extent, and about four inches thick. The skeleton was of ordinary size; the skull was crushed, and all the bones in extreme decay. Near the surface were other skeletons. The inhabitants of the neighborhood tell of a copper band with strange devices, found around the brow of a skeleton in this mound; and also of a well carved representation of a tortoise of the same metal, twelve or fourteen inches in length, found with another skeleton."

beyond it, rises a steep bank, fifty feet high, ascending which we come to elevated ground. Here are the remains of another small elliptical work, and some mounds. Upon the brow of the bank, at *a*, is a pile of stones much burned, which is known in the vicinity as " *the furnace*." Immediately below, at the foot of the bank, is a copious spring. The survey of this group was made by Mr. McBride.

NUMBER 2 is situated near the town of Lowell, Washington county, Ohio, and consists of a slight embankment of earth, of exceedingly regular outline. Little can be said of it, except that it is accompanied by eleven mounds; all of which are, however, exterior to the walls.

NUMBER 3 is a group of small works, occupying the high lands on the east side of the Scioto river, opposite Chillicothe. They are indicated by the letter L, in the map of a section of the Scioto valley (Plate II). They are introduced on a very small scale, so as to exhibit the dependence which seems to exist between them. Of course the relative size of the circles and mounds is considerably exaggerated. The mound numbered 1 occupies the most conspicuous point in the valley; and from it is afforded the most extended view that can be obtained in that entire region. Whether this fact can be taken to establish its design as a beacon or observatory, it is not presumed to say. The mound numbered 2 is one of the finest known. It is elliptical, one hundred and sixty feet long, sixty broad, and fifteen high. It has never been investigated. The remaining mounds, 3, 4, 5, and 6, are all of large size. A fine view of the extensive ancient works in the vicinity of Chillicothe must have been afforded from these elevated plains.

NUMBER 4.—These works are included within the corporation limits of Chillicothe. They are already much obliterated, and will soon be no longer traceable. They consist of a series of small circles, of uniform size, each two hundred and fifty feet in diameter. More extensive works formerly existed in connection with them, but have now entirely disappeared. The mound represented in the plan is seventeen feet in height, and has what seems to be a graded ascent from the south. It has been excavated, and will be noticed at length elsewhere in this volume. The circles, it will be observed, appear to be disposed with some degree of regularity in respect to each other. The gateways of three of them open towards the east, that of the remaining one towards the south.

NUMBER 5.—This unique little work is situated in the valley of Paint creek, about one mile west of the village of Bainbridge, Ross county, Ohio, on the turnpike leading from Chillicothe to Cincinnati. Its character can only be understood from the plan. It affords but one of the thousand various combinations which the circular structures of the West assume. It can, of course, be regarded only as connected with the superstitions of the builders, for the reason that it could answer no good purpose for protection, nor subserve any of the

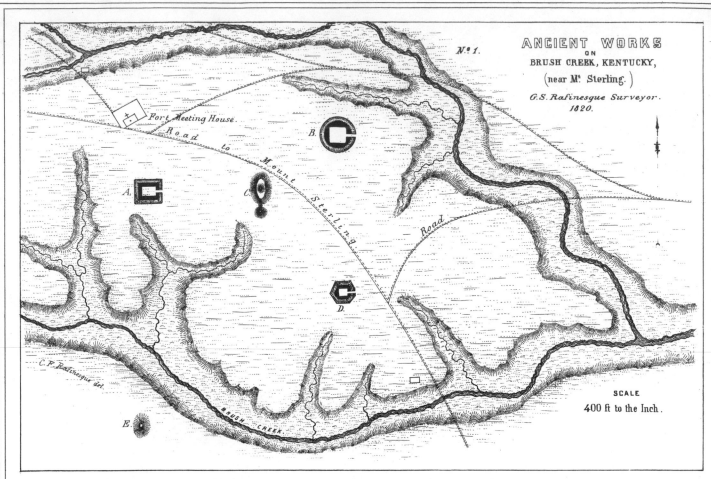

XXXIII

No. 1.

ANCIENT WORKS
ON
BRUSH CREEK, KENTUCKY,
(near Mt. Sterling.)
G. S. Rafinesque Surveyor.
1820.

Fort Meeting House.
Road to Mount Sterling Road

B.

A.

C.

D.

C. P. Rafinesque del.

E.

BRUSH CREEK.

SCALE
400 ft to the Inch.

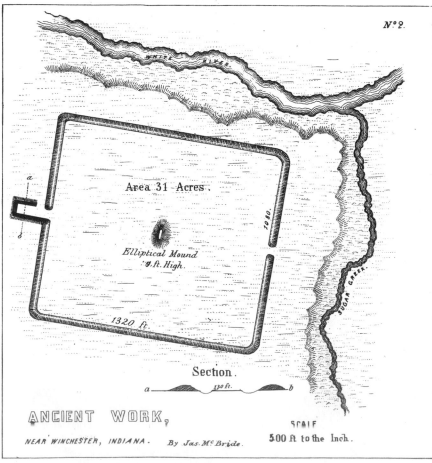

No. 2.

WHITE RIVER.

Area 31 Acres.

Elliptical Mound
9 ft. High.

1320 ft.

1080 ft.

a

b

SUGAR CREEK.

Section.

a 130 ft. b

ANCIENT WORK,

NEAR WINCHESTER, INDIANA.   By Jas. McBride.

SCALE
500 ft to the Inch.

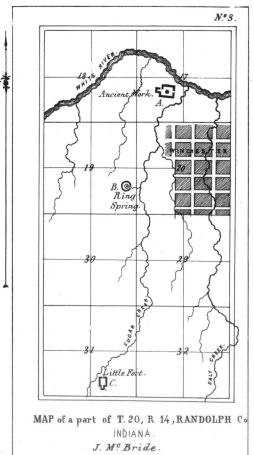

No. 3.

WHITE RIVER.

18   17

Ancient Work.
A.

19   20

WINCHESTER

B.
Ring
Spring.

30   29

SUGAR CREEK.

31   32

SALT CREEK.

Little Fort.
C.

MAP of a part of T. 20, R 14, RANDOLPH Co.
INDIANA.
J. McBride.

Face P. 93.

useful purposes for which enclosures are required, such as the limits of fields and possessions, or the boundaries of villages.

NUMBER 6.—This work is situated near Mount Sterling, Montgomery county, Kentucky; and consists of a large truncated mound, twenty-five feet in height, flanked on the north and west by narrow grades or slopes. It is connected with a circular work, three hundred and fifty feet in diameter, by an elevated way or terrace, one hundred feet long. The circle has a small mound in its centre, and a gateway opening to the east. Three small mounds occur in close connection with it. The plan is from the RAFINESQUE MSS.

Lest these comparatively little works should appear insignificant, from the small scale on which they are presented, it may be well enough to remark, that the circle formed by the stones composing the great temple of Stonehenge is but a little more than one hundred feet in diameter, and that most of the circular earth and stone structures of the British islands are considerably less in size than those here presented.

———

PLATE XXXIII. No. 1.*

THIS group of ancient works is situated on the west side of Brush creek, six miles south-east of Mount Sterling, Montgomery county, Kentucky. The work indicated by the letter A is one hundred feet square, and is composed of a slight embankment, with an interior ditch. There is an entrance from the east. The elliptical mound C is about two hundred yards distant from A, towards the east. It is nine feet high, two hundred and seventy feet in circumference, truncated, and surmounted by a smaller conical mound. Another small mound is connected with it, as shown in the plan. B is a circular work, five hundred and ten feet in circumference, with a ditch interior to the wall, and a gateway opening towards the east. The unexcavated ground in the interior is square in form, exhibiting an entire identity in this feature with various works in Ohio. (See Plates XXII, XXIV.) D is a hexagonal enclosure; whole circumference three hundred feet, each side fifty feet, with a gateway at the eastern corner. On the opposite side of Brush creek is a large elliptical mound, E. This group occupies a broad, elevated plain. Numerous other works occur in the same county.

---

* From the Rafinesque MSS.

PLATE XXXIII. No. 2.*

THE character of this work, which is situated in Randolph county, Indiana, is sufficiently well exhibited by the plan. In the same vicinity are other works of an interesting character, the relative positions of which are shown in the sectional map. The work of which the enlarged plan is here given is indicated by the letter A on the map. A precisely analogous work, of smaller size, is situated on Sugar creek at C. At B is a copious spring, surrounded by an embankment.

PLATE XXXIV. No. 1.

ANCIENT WORK, CLERMONT COUNTY, OHIO.

THE work here presented is situated near the western border of Clermont county, Ohio, about one mile east from the town of Milford, which is built near the junction of the East fork with the Little Miami river. It occupies the third terrace, which is here broad and fertile, and consists of those constantly recurring figures, the square and the circle. The plan will give a correct idea of its outline. In its form and combination, it closely resembles some of the more remarkable structures of the Scioto valley, and was doubtless erected for a common purpose with them. It has, however, one novel and interesting feature. The parallels which lead off from the large irregular circle extend upon an isolated hill to the left, which is elevated perhaps fifty feet above the plain, where they end in a small circle, not more than three hundred feet in diameter. From this circle diverging lines extend to the south-west, terminating in a maze of walls unlike any others which have yet fallen under notice. A portion of the parallels and the diverging lines just mentioned are much reduced, and when the crops are on the ground, are hardly traceable.

From the hill an extensive prospect is afforded, bringing in view the sites of several large groups of works in the vicinity. It has been suggested that the structures upon the hill were devoted to rites analogous to those attending the primitive hill or grove worship of the East.

An inspection of this work shows clearly that the irregularity of the great circle is due to the nature of the ground, and that the terrace bank bordering the old bed of the East fork existed at the period of the construction of the work. The river now flows a considerable distance to the southward.

---

* From the Survey of JAMES McBRIDE.

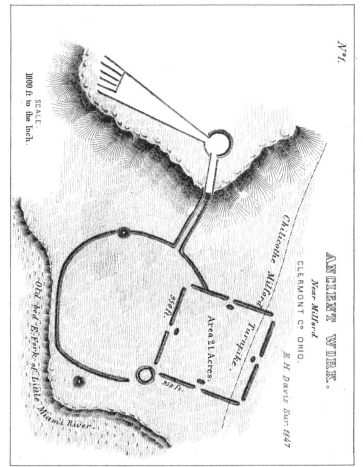

XXXIV

N° 1.

SCALE.
1000 ft to the Inch.

ANCIENT WORK.
Near Milford
CLERMONT C° OHIO.
E. H. Davis Sur. 1847

Chillicothe Milford Turnpike.

Area 21 Acres.

950 ft.

250 ft.

Old bed "E. Fork" of Little Miami River.

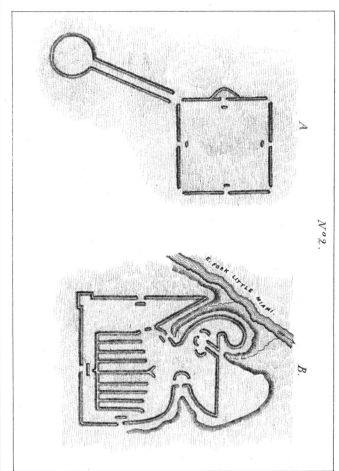

A.

N° 2.

B.

E. Fork Little Miami.

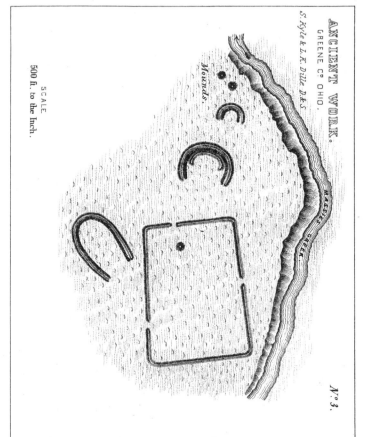

N° 3.

ANCIENT WORK.
GREENE C° OHIO.
S. Kyle & L. K. Dille D. & S.

SCALE
500 ft. to the Inch.

Mounds.

MASSIE CREEK.

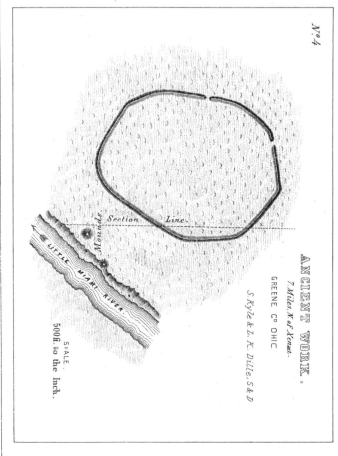

N° 4.

Section Line.

Mound.

LITTLE MIAMI RIVER.

SCALE
500 ft. to the Inch.

ANCIENT WORK.
7 Miles, N. of Xenia.
GREENE C° OHIO
S. Kyle & L. K. Dille, S & D

About four miles above the Milford work, on the East fork of the Little Miami, is a small rectangular work. It is entirely isolated. Its sides measure each seven hundred feet; and it has gateways at each corner and midway on each side.

A very good survey of this work was made many years ago by Gen. LYTLE of Cincinnati, and published in Worden's Appendix to Du Paix's work on the antiquities of Mexico.

PLATE XXXIV. No. 2.

THE work indicated by the letter A is situated upon the opposite side of the Little Miami, from that last described. The plan, which is also from a survey by Gen. LYTLE, sufficiently explains its character. Several mounds occur in the vicinity of this work, and a few miles below, at Newtown, there is a considerable group of large mounds.

About twenty miles above these remains, upon the East fork of the Little Miami, is a singular work, a plan of which, B, is here given. It was also surveyed by Gen. LYTLE, and a plan of it appears both in Du Paix's work, and in the appendix to Hugh Williamson's work on the climate of America. Whether both plans are from the same survey is unknown; they however coincide in all important particulars. Without vouching for the entire accuracy of the plan, we may be permitted to say that there can be no doubt of the existence of a work of this general and extraordinary outline, at the point indicated. Its thorough investigation is an object greatly to be desired.

PLATE XXXIV. Nos. 3 AND 4.

ANCIENT WORKS, GREENE COUNTY, OHIO.

NUMBER 3.—This group is situated on Massie's creek, about half a mile below the fortified promontory already described, Plate XII, No. 3. It has no features worthy of special notice. The walls of the semi-circles are about five feet in height.

NUMBER 4.—The polygon here presented is situated on the right bank of the Little Miami river, seven miles above Xenia, Greene county, Ohio. It lies chiefly in S. 24, T. 4, and R. 8, and closely resembles several of the Kentucky works, plans of which are given on Plate XIV. It was probably designed for defence. A number of other works occur in this vicinity. One of considerable size is found at Oldtown, near the former site of the "Old Miami towns," so famous in the history of our Indian wars.

———

AMONG the earthworks of the Ohio valley, there is a small but very interesting class, which has hitherto most unaccountably escaped observation. They are not enclosures, nor can we with propriety designate them as mounds, according to the technical application of the term in this work. They bear some resemblance to the "animal-shaped mounds" of Wisconsin, to which public attention has recently been several times directed; but from their position, dependencies, and other circumstances, they seem clearly of a different origin and dedicated to a different purpose. For reasons which cannot fail to be obvious to every mind, after an examination of the illustrations which follow, they have been classed as works of sacred origin. Their character, so far as known, will appear from the examples here presented. What may have been their mythological signification, it is perhaps hopeless for us to inquire. They possess some truly remarkable analogies to remains of other portions of the globe, which will furnish the studious inquirer with matter for deeply interesting speculation.

———

PLATE XXXV.

THE GREAT SERPENT, ADAMS COUNTY, OHIO.

PROBABLY the most extraordinary earthwork thus far discovered at the West, is the Great Serpent, of which a faithful delineation is given in the accompanying plan. It is situated on Brush creek, at a point known as the "Three Forks," on Entry 1014, near the north line of Adams county, Ohio. No plan or description has hitherto been published; nor does the fact of its existence appear to have been known beyond the secluded vicinity in which it occurs. The notice first received by the authors of these researches was exceedingly vague and indefinite, and led to the conclusion that it was a work of defence, with bastions at regular intervals, —a feature so extraordinary as to induce a visit, which resulted in the discovery here presented. The true character of the work was apparent on the first inspection.

It is situated upon a high, crescent-form hill or spur of land, rising one hundred and fifty feet above the level of Brush creek, which washes its base. The side of the hill next the stream presents a perpendicular wall of rock, while the other

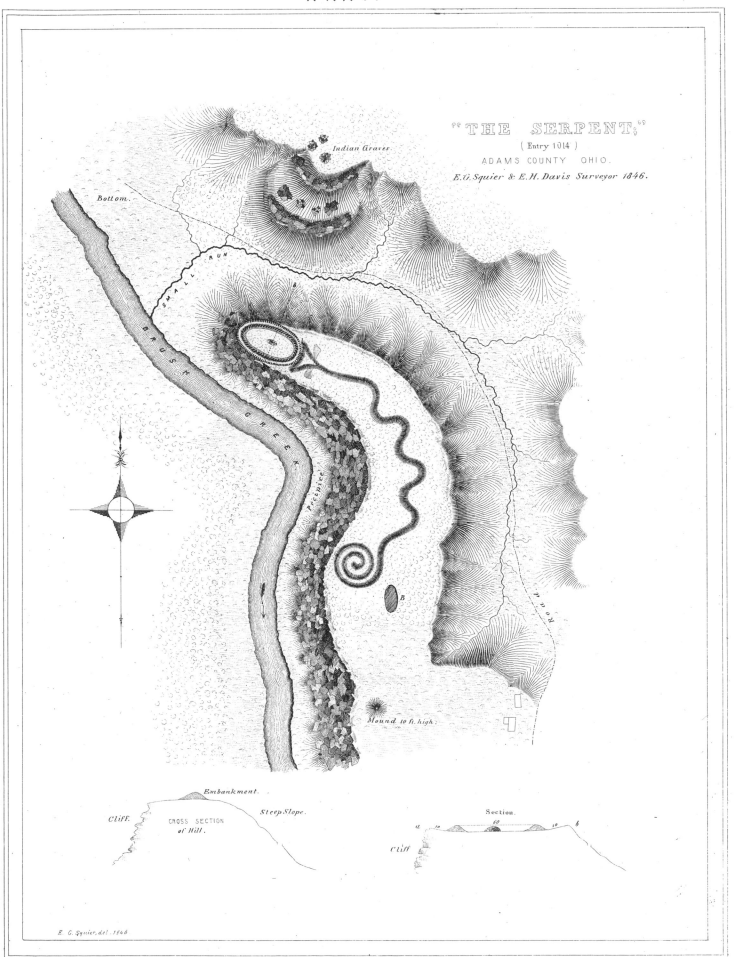

slopes rapidly, though it is not so steep as to preclude cultivation. The top of the hill is not level but slightly convex, and presents a very even surface, one hundred and fifty feet wide by one thousand long, measuring from its extremity to the point where it connects with the table land. Conforming to the curve of the hill, and occupying its very summit, is the serpent, its head resting near the point, and its body winding back for seven hundred feet, in graceful undulations, terminating in a triple coil at the tail. The entire length, if extended, would be not less than one thousand feet. The accompanying plan, laid down from accurate survey, can alone give an adequate conception of the outline of the work, which is clearly and boldly defined, the embankment being upwards of five feet in height by thirty feet base, at the centre of the body, but diminishing somewhat towards the head and tail. The neck of the serpent is stretched out and slightly curved, and its mouth is opened wide as if in the act of swallowing or ejecting an oval figure, which rests partially within the distended jaws. This oval is formed by an embankment of earth, without any perceptible opening, four feet in height, and is perfectly regular in outline, its transverse and conjugate diameters being one hundred and sixty and eighty feet respectively. The ground within the oval is slightly elevated: a small circular elevation of large stones much burned once existed in its centre; but they have been thrown down and scattered by some ignorant visitor, under the prevailing impression probably that gold was hidden beneath them. The point of the hill, within which this egg-shaped figure rests, seems to have been artificially cut to conform to its outline, leaving a smooth platform, ten feet wide, and somewhat inclining inwards, all around it. The section *a b* will illustrate this feature.

Upon either side of the serpent's head extend two small triangular elevations, ten or twelve feet over. They are not high, and although too distinct to be overlooked, are yet too much obliterated to be satisfactorily traced. Besides a platform, or level oval terrace, at B, and a large mound in the centre of the isthmus connecting the hill with the table land beyond, there are no other remains, excepting a few mounds, within six or eight miles,—none, perhaps, nearer than the entrenched hill in Highland county, (see Plate V,) thirteen miles distant. There are a number of works lower down on Brush creek, towards its mouth; but their character is not known. The point on which this effigy occurs commands an extensive prospect, overlooking the "bottoms" found at the junction of the three principal tributaries of the creek. The alluvial terraces are here quite extensive, and it is a matter of surprise that no works occur upon them.

The serpent, separate or in combination with the circle, egg, or globe, has been a predominant symbol among many primitive nations. It prevailed in Egypt, Greece, and Assyria, and entered widely into the superstitions of the Celts, the Hindoos, and the Chinese. It even penetrated into America; and was conspicuous in the mythology of the ancient Mexicans, among whom its significance does not seem to have differed materially from that which it possessed in the old world. The fact that the ancient Celts, and perhaps other nations of the old continent, erected sacred structures in the form of the serpent, is one of high interest. Of this description was the great temple of Abury, in England,—in many respects the most imposing ancient monument of the British islands.

13

It is impossible, in this connection, to trace the analogies which the Ohio structure exhibits to the serpent temples of England, or to point out the extent to which the symbol was applied in America,—an investigation fraught with the greatest interest both in respect to the light which it reflects upon the primitive superstitions of remotely separated people, and especially upon the origin of the American race.

———

PLATE XXXVI. No. 1.

" THE CROSS," PICKAWAY COUNTY, OHIO.

THE work here figured is found near the little town of Tarlton, Pickaway county, Ohio, in the narrow valley of " Salt creek," a tributary of the Scioto river, eighteen miles north-east from Chillicothe, on the great road to Zanesville. In position it corresponds generally with the remarkable work last described, though wholly unlike it in form. It occupies a narrow spur of land, at a prominent point of the valley; its form is that of a Greek cross, ninety feet between the ends, and elevated three feet above the adjacent surface. It is surrounded by a slight ditch, corresponding to the outline of the elevation; in the centre is a circular depression, twenty feet across and twenty inches deep. The sides of the cross correspond very nearly with the cardinal points. Immediately back of it, is a small circular elevation of stone and earth, resembling that in connection with the Granville effigy, (No. 2 of the Plate,) and denominated an altar in the description of that work. Several small mounds occur near by; and upon the high hill, a spur of which is occupied by the cross, are several large mounds. Mounds are quite numerous in this little valley, and on the hills bordering it; but it is not known to contain any enclosures.

———

PLATE XXXVI. No. 2.

" THE ALLIGATOR," LICKING COUNTY, OHIO.

THIS strange work occupies a position somewhat analogous to that of the great serpent already described. It occurs about one mile below the town of Granville, Licking county, Ohio, upon a high and beautifully rounded spur of land, which projects boldly into the delightful valley of " Raccoon creek," a stream which, in conjunction with the " South fork," forms Licking creek or river, the principal

XXXVI

Lith. of Sarony & Major.

"THE CROSS"
near
TARLTON PICKAWAY CO. OHIO.
E. G. Squier and E. H. Davis Surveyor's.

SCALE
100 ft to the Inch.

Section.
E. G. Squier del.

90 Ft.

Mounds.

Stones.

Nº 1.

"THE ALLIGATER"
near
GRANVILLE LICKING CO.
OHIO.
E. G. Squier and E. H. Davis Surveyors.

High Hill.

Section.
Curve of Hill.
E. G. Squier del.

Nº 2.

ROCK MILL WORK. FAIRFIELD CO. OHIO.
E. G. Squier & E. H. Davis Surveyors.

SCALE
500 ft. to the Inch.

Section.
E. G. Squier del.

420 Ft.
201.

Road from Lancaster to Co.

Nº 3.

MAP
of
SIX MILES OF THE NEWARK VALLEY
with its Ancient Monuments.
Constructed by E. G. Squier.

E. G. Squier del.

GRANVILLE.
Fortified Hill.
Circle
Branch Canal
Road
Fortified Hill.
Branch Canal.
Bread Plain
Newark Works
Ohio Canal
SOUTH FORK
NEWARK.

Nº 4.

tributary of the Muskingum. The hill or headland is one hundred and fifty or two hundred feet in height; and the effigy rests upon its very brow, conforming to its longitudinal as well as lateral curve. Its form is accurately indicated in the plan. It is known in the vicinity as "the Alligator;" which designation has been adopted, for want of a better, although the figure bears as close a resemblance to the lizard as any other reptile. It is placed transversely to the point of land on which it occurs, the head pointing to the south-west; its precise bearing is S. 67° W. The total length from the point of the nose following the curve of the tail to the tip, is about two hundred and fifty feet; the breadth of the body forty feet; and the length of the legs or paws, each thirty-six feet. The ends of the paws are a little broader than the remaining portions of the same, as if the spread of the toes had been originally indicated. The head, shoulders, and rump, are more elevated than the other parts of the body, an attempt having evidently been made to preserve the proportions of the object copied. The outline of the figure is clearly defined; its average height is not less than four feet; at the shoulders it is six feet in altitude. Upon the inner side of the effigy is an elevated circular space, covered with stones which have been much burned. This has been denominated an altar. Leading from it to the top of the effigy is a graded way, ten feet broad. The earth has been excavated at various points of the figure; but nothing was disclosed except the fact that the framework is composed of stones of considerable size. The superstructure is of fine clay, which seems to have been brought from a distance, as no signs of excavation are apparent in the vicinity.

The headland upon which this effigy occurs is so regular as almost to induce the belief that it has been artificially rounded. Its symmetry has lately been somewhat broken by the opening of a quarry in its face, the further working of which will inevitably result in the entire destruction of this interesting monument.* It commands a view of the entire valley for eight or ten miles, and is by far the most conspicuous point within that limit. Its prominence is, of necessity, somewhat exaggerated in the small map "exhibiting a section of six miles of the Newark valley," (No. 4 of the Plate,) in which it is indicated by the letter A. The extensive work E, in the vicinity of Newark, would be distinctly visible from this point, in the absence of the intervening forests. In the valley immediately opposite, and less than half a mile distant, is a large and beautiful circular work, C. To the right, three fourths of a mile distant, is a fortified hill B, (see Plate IX,) and upon the opposing side of the valley is another entrenched hill, D; all of which, together with numerous mounds upon the hill-tops and in the valley, are commanded from this position.

It seems more than probable that this singular effigy, like that last described, had its origin in the superstitions of its makers. It was perhaps the high place where sacrifices were made, on stated or extraordinary occasions, and where the

---

* The proprietor of this structure, ASHEL AYLESWORTH, Esq., we are happy to say, has determined to permit no further encroachment upon it. It is to be hoped that the citizens of Granville will adopt means to permanently and effectually secure it from invasion.

ancient people gathered to celebrate the rites of their unknown worship. Its position, and all the circumstances attending it, certainly favor such a conclusion. The valley which it overlooks abounds in traces of the remote people, and seems to have been one of the centres of ancient population.

PLATE XXXVI. No. 3.

ROCK MILL WORKS, FAIRFIELD COUNTY, OHIO.*

THIS work is remarkable as being the only one, entirely regular in its plan, which has yet been discovered occupying the summit of a hill. It is situated on the road from Lancaster, Fairfield county, Ohio, to Columbus, the capital of the State, seven miles distant from the former place, near a point known as the "Hocking river Upper Falls," or "Rock Mill." It consists of a small square measuring four hundred and twenty feet on each side, in combination with two small circles, one hundred and twenty-five and two hundred and ten feet in diameter respectively. The hill is nearly two hundred feet in height, with a slightly undulating plain of small extent at its summit. The works are so arranged that the small circle, enclosing the mound, overlooks every part and commands a wide prospect on every hand. Towards the brow of the hill, at prominent points, are two elliptical terraces or elevations of small size. The sides of the square enclosure correspond to the cardinal points. The walls, excepting those of the circular structures, are very slight, and unaccompanied by a ditch. The work is clearly not of a defensive origin, and must be classed with those of similar outline occupying the river terraces. At a short distance above this point, the champaign country commences, and no other remains are found. The erections of the mound-builders are almost exclusively confined to the borders of the water-courses.

There are very few enclosures, so far as known, in the Hocking river valley; there are, however, numerous mounds upon the narrow terraces and on the hills bordering them. In the vicinity of Athens are a number of the largest size, and also several enclosures. (See Plate XXIII.) Mounds are found upon the high bluffs in the neighborhood of Lancaster, at points commanding the widest range. An examination of the valley with a view of bringing to light its ancient monuments would, without doubt, be attended with very interesting results.

---

* This work should have been figured on a preceding plate. Its position, in connection with the effigies here described, was determined by accidental circumstances.

PLATE XXXVI. No. 4.

THIS little map exhibits a section of six miles of the Newark valley, showing the relative positions of the "Newark group" (Plate XXV); the "Fortified Hill" near Granville (Plate IX); and the "Alligator," just described. But a small proportion of the mounds occurring within this range are shown on the map.

––––

These comprise the only works in the form of animals which have fallen under notice. The singular mound occurring within the great circle near Newark may perhaps deserve to occupy a place with them: that, however, has the internal characteristics of the sacrificial mounds, while the others, so far as our knowledge extends, cover no remains. The mound found within the work in Scioto county, Ohio, (Plate XXIX,) and described on a preceding page, may also rank with them. From the information which we possess concerning the animal effigies of Wisconsin, it does not appear probable that they were constructed for a common purpose with those of Ohio. They occur usually in considerable numbers, in ranges, upon the level prairies; while the few which are found in Ohio occupy elevated and commanding positions,—"high places," as if designed to be set apart for sacred purposes. An "altar," if we may so term it, is distinctly to be observed in the oval enclosure connected with the "Great Serpent;" one is equally distinct near the Granville work, and another in connection with the lesser but equally interesting work near Tarlton. If we were to deduce a conclusion from these premises, it would certainly be, that these several effigies possessed a symbolical meaning, and were the objects of superstitious regard.

Whether any other works of this description occur in the State or valley is not known; it is extremely likely, however, that a systematic examination of the whole field would result in the discovery of others equally remarkable, and perhaps disclose a connection between them and the animal effigies of the North-west, already alluded to. The facts that none of these singular remains have been noticed, and that up to this time not a single intimation of their existence has been made public, show how little attention has been bestowed upon our antiquities, and how much remains to be accomplished before we can fully comprehend them.

––––

Such is the character of a large proportion of the ancient monuments of the Mississippi valley. How far a faithful attention to their details has tended to sustain the position assigned them at the commencement of this chapter, the intelligent reader must determine.

The great size of most of the foregoing structures precludes the idea that they were *temples* in the general acceptation of the term. As has already been intimated, they were probably, like the great circles of England, and the squares of India, Peru, and Mexico, the sacred enclosures, within which were erected the shrines of the gods of the ancient worship and the altars of the ancient religion. They may have embraced consecrated groves, and also, as they did in Mexico, the residences of the ancient priesthood. Like the sacred structures of the country last named, some of them may have been secondarily designed for protection in times of danger; "for," says Gomara, "the force and strength of every Mexican city is its temple." However that may be, we know that it has been a practice, common to almost every people in every time, to enclose their temples and altars with walls of various materials, so as to guard the sacred area around them from the desecration of animals or the intrusion of the profane. Spots consecrated by tradition, or rendered remarkable as the scene of some extraordinary event, or by whatever means connected with the superstitions, or invested with the reverence of men, have always been designated in this or some similar manner. The South Sea Islander, as did the ancient Sclavonian, encircles his *tabooed* or consecrated tree with a fence of woven branches; the pagoda of the Hindoo is enclosed by high and massive walls, within which the scoffer at his religion finds no admittance; the sacred square of the Caaba can only be entered in a posture of humiliation and with unshod feet; and the assurance that "this is holy ground" is impressed upon every one who, at this day, approaches the temples of the true God. The block idol of the poor Laplander has its sacred limit within which the devotee only ventures on bended knees and with face to the earth; the oak-crowned Druid taught the mysteries of his stern religion in temples of unhewn stones, open to the sun, in rude but gigantic structures, which in their form symbolized the God of his adoration; conquerors humbled themselves as they approached the precincts which the voice of the Pythoness had consecrated; no worshipper trod the avenues guarded by the silent, emblematic Sphynx, except with awe and reverence; and Christ indignantly thrust from the sacred area of the temple on Mount Zion the money-changers who had defiled it with their presence. "Thou shalt set bounds to the people round about,—set bounds to the mount and sanctify it," was the injunction of Jehovah from the holy mountain. Among the savage tribes of North America, none but the pure dared enter the place dedicated to the rude but significant rites of their religion. In Peru none except of the blood of the royal Incas, whose father was the sun, were permitted to pass the walls surrounding the gorgeous temples of their primitive worship; and the imperial Montezuma humbly sought the pardon of his insulted gods for venturing to introduce his unbelieving conqueror within the area consecrated by their shrines.

Analogy would therefore seem to indicate that the structures under consideration, or at least a large portion of them, were nothing more than sacred enclosures. If so, it may be inquired, what has become of the temples and shrines which they enclosed? It is very obvious that, unless composed of stone or other imperishable material, they must long since have completely disappeared, without leaving a trace of their existence. We find nevertheless, within these enclosures, the altars upon which the ancient people performed their sacrifices. We find also pyramidal structures, (as at Portsmouth, Marietta, and other places,) which correspond entirely with those of Mexico and Central America, except that, instead of being composed of stone, they are constructed of earth, and instead of broad flights of steps, have graded avenues and spiral pathways leading to their summits. If these pyramidal structures sustained edifices corresponding to those which crowned the Mexican and Central American *Teocalli*, they were doubtless, in keeping with the comparative rudeness of their builders, composed of wood; in which case, it would be in vain, at this day, to look for any positive traces of their existence.

CHAPTER IV.

MONUMENTS OF THE SOUTHERN STATES.

WE are in possession of very little authentic information respecting the monuments of the Southern United States.*   All accounts concur in representing them as very numerous and extensive, and as characterized by a regularity unknown, or known but to a limited degree, amongst those which occur further north, on the Ohio and its tributaries, and upon the Missouri and Upper Mississippi.   This extraordinary regularity, as well as their usually great dimensions, have induced many to regard them as the work not only of a different era, but of a different people.   Mounds of several stages, closely resembling the Mexican *Teocalli* in form and size; broad terraces of various heights; elevated passages and long avenues, are mentioned among the varieties of ancient structures which abound from Florida to Texas.   The mounds are often disposed with the utmost system in respect to each other.   Around some of the larger ones, others of smaller size are placed at regular intervals, and at fixed distances.   Some have spiral pathways leading to their tops, and others possess graded ascents like those at Marietta.†

It is to be observed, however, that while mounds are thus abundant, enclosures are comparatively few, especially those which seem to be of a military origin.   A few have been noticed in South Carolina, on the Wateree river, which partake of the character of military works, and of which some account will shortly be given.

The following plans from original and hitherto unpublished surveys will serve to illustrate, to a limited degree, the character of a portion of the Southern remains.

---

* The inability to add very largely to our stock of information respecting the monuments of the Southern United States, is less a matter of regret, since it is ascertained that Dr. M. W. DICKESON of Philadelphia, whose researches in natural science have created no little interest, has devoted much of his time to their investigation.   His inquiries have been conducted on a large scale, and will serve to reflect much new light upon our antiquities.   It is to be hoped the public will soon be put in possession of the results of his labors.

† Most of the accounts of the monuments of the South met with in various works, treating directly or incidentally of our antiquities, are derived from Bartram, whose animated descriptions of those which fell under his notice are not always easily recognised, in the various forms under which they are presented. Near the conclusion of his work, he sums up his observations in this department as follows:

"The pyramidal hills or artificial mounds, and high ways or avenues leading from them to artificial lakes or ponds, vast tetragon terraces, 'chunk yards,' and obelisks or pillars of wood, are the only monuments of labor, ingenuity and magnificence, that I have seen worthy of notice or remark.   The region lying between the Savannah river and Ockmulgee, east and west, and from the sea-coast to the Cherokee or

XXXVII.

LANCASTER. DISTRICT.

KERSHAW DISTRICT.

FAIRFIELD DISTRICT.

KERSHAW DISTRICT.

Old Indian Village.

Stone Mortar.

B

C

A

Ancient Work.

D

E

Old Indian Village.

Indian Grove.

F

G

White Oak Creek.

St. Louis.

CANAL.

Sawney Creek.

KERSHAW DISTRICT.

Rice Creek.

Camp Creek.

Mound.

H

I

J

K

O

L

M

N.

Nixon's Mound.

Town Creek.

Old Indian Village.

Pine Tree Creek.

Taylors Mounds.

Road to Columbia.

Road to Charleston.

ANCIENT WORKS,

on the

WATEREE RIVER, KERSHAW DISTRICT,

SOUTH CAROLINA.

Drawn by William Blanding M. D.

SCALE

2 Miles to the Inch.

PLATE XXXVII.

REMAINS ON THE WATEREE RIVER, KERSHAW DISTRICT, SOUTH CAROLINA.

IT is unquestionable that the race of the mounds occupied a portion of the State of South Carolina; and although the traces of their occupation are far from abundant, they are still sufficiently numerous to deserve notice. The only reliable information we have concerning them, is contained in a MS. letter from WILLIAM BLANDING, M. D., late of Camden, South Carolina, a gentleman distinguished for his researches in natural history, to SAMUEL GEORGE MORTON, M. D., of Philadelphia, the eminent author of " *Crania Americana*," by whose permission it is embodied in this connection. The observations of Dr. Blanding were confined to a section of the valley of the Wateree river, embracing about twenty-five miles in the immediate vicinity of Camden, and mainly included in the Kershaw district.

"The first monument deserving of notice is 'Harrison's Mound' (A in the Map). It is the highest in position of any on the river, and is situated on the west side of the same, in the Fairfield district. It is about four hundred and eighty feet in circumference at the base, fifteen feet high, and has a level area one hundred and twenty feet in circumference at its summit.

"The next relic of antiquity is the 'Indian Mortar,' (B in the Map,) in the Kershaw district. It is a regular bowl-shaped excavation in a solid block of granite, holding upwards of half a bushel, and is evidently the work of art. It

---

Apalachian mountains, north and south, is the most remarkable for these high conical hills, tetragon terraces, etc. This region was possessed by the Cherokees since the arrival of the Europeans, but they were afterwards dispossessed by the Muscogulges; and all that country was probably many ages preceding the Cherokee invasion inhabited by one nation or confederacy, who were ruled by the same system of laws, customs, and language, but so ancient that the Cherokees, Creeks, or the nation they conquered, could render no account for what purposes these monuments were raised. The mounts and cubical yards adjoining them seem to have been raised in part for ornament and recreation, and likewise to serve for some other public purpose, since they are always so situated as to command the most extensive prospect over the country adjacent. The tetragon terraces seem to be the foundations of fortresses; and perhaps the great pyramidal mounts served the purposes of look-out towers and high places for sacrifice. The sunken area called by white traders the 'chunk yard' very likely served the same conveniency that it has been appropriated to by the more modern and even present nations of Indians, that is, the place where they burnt or otherwise tortured their captives that were condemned to die; as the area is surrounded by a bank, and sometimes two of them, one behind and above the other, as seats to accommodate the spectators at such tragical scenes, as well as at the exhibition of shows, dances, and games. From the river St. Juan's, southwardly to the point of the peninsula of Florida, are to be seen high pyramidal mounts, with spacious and extensive avenues, leading from them out of the town, to an artificial lake or pond of water: these were evidently designed for ornament or monuments of magnificence to perpetuate the power and grandeur of the nation; and not inconsiderable neither, for they exhibit scenes of power and grandeur, and must have been public edifices."—*Travels in North America*, p. 518.

was used as a mortar by the early settlers, and is still devoted to the same purpose. The part of the rock projecting out of the ground is equivalent to eight or ten tons.

" Next is an old Indian town or camp near the mouth of Beaver creek (C in the Map). A little below the mouth of the creek is an old fortification, of oblong form, consisting of a wall and ditch (D in the Map). The embankment is now not more than three feet high above the level of the plain. The ditch is distinct. Nearly opposite this work, on the west side of the river, are the traces of an old Indian village, remarkable for its arrow-heads, fragments of pottery, etc.

" Proceeding down the river, we come to a point near the head of the canal, where the land rises to the extraordinary height of five hundred feet, forming a long, narrow hill. Upon the point of this hill nearest the river, stands what is called the 'Indian Grave' (F in the Map). It is composed of many tons of small round stones, weighing from one to four pounds each. The pile is thirty feet long from east to west, twelve feet broad, and five feet high, so situated as to command an extensive view of the adjacent country, stretching as far as Rocky Mount, twenty miles above, and for a long distance below on the river. It may be suggested that this is the elevated burial-place of some great chief, or that it was designed as some sort of an observatory. The Catawba Indians can give no account of it, nor will they venture a conjecture as to its purposes. A mound, G, is situated opposite this stone heap, on the other side of the river. The 'shoals' in the immediate vicinity seem to have been a favorite haunt of the ancient and more recent races. Here to this day is to be found an abundance of fish and game, and the vicinity is marked by numerous aboriginal relics. Here also is the highest boundary of the long-leaved pine, and the limit of the alluvial region. Below, the river becomes sluggish, and during high water leaves its banks and spreads over large tracts of land.

" The mound next below, H, was two hundred and fifty feet in circumference at the base, seventy-five feet at the top, and thirteen feet high. It was situated about a hundred yards from the river on lands subject to overflow. Three other small mounds surrounded it. In 1826 it was levelled, and the material used for manuring the adjacent lands. A part of the treasures which it contained were saved, but the rest are scattered or destroyed. The mound presented, upon excavation, a succession of strata, varying in thickness from six inches to one foot, from top to base. First vegetable loam, then human and animal bones, followed by charcoal of reeds, vessels of clay and fragments of the same, (some holding not more than one pint,) arrow-heads and stone axes, then earth, etc., alternately. In one small vessel was found a *tag* or needle made of bone, supposed to have been used in making dresses. Near it was found the skeleton of a female, tolerably entire, but which fell in pieces on exposure. A stratum of dark-colored mould was mixed with these articles; perhaps decomposed animal matter. The superstructure of the mound was the alluvial loam, and constituted tolerable manure. It was mixed with great quantities of mica, some pieces three or four inches square. Marine shells, much decomposed, were found in this as in other mounds, mixed with the bones, from top to bottom.

" Descending the river, near Mound creek, we come to a large mound, I, enclosed in a circle, and accompanied by a smaller one. It is perhaps the largest and most perfect on the river. It is five hundred feet in circumference at the base, two hundred and twenty-five feet in circumference at the summit, and thirty-four feet high,—slightly oblong. It is covered with stumps, briars, etc., having recently been brought under cultivation. In April last, while ploughing over the small mound, an urn was discovered, a sketch of which is enclosed. It holds forty-six quarts, or nearly twelve gallons. It had a cover fitting closely over the body for about six inches; this was broken by the plough. The vessel was curiously ornamented, and is probably the largest ever discovered in the valley. It contained a number of large shell beads, much decomposed, about the size and shape of nutmegs. It also contained another article of the same material, about the size of a man's palm, a quarter of an inch thick, and carved in open work; probably designed for suspension around the neck as a badge or ornament. The ditch around this mound is slight.

"Still further down the river, upon the opposite side, and some distance south of the road from Camden to Columbia, is the most remarkable ancient work in the valley (O). It is called the 'Indian Ditch.' It occurs at the great bend of the river, and consists of an embankment and ditch carried across the isthmus, cutting off, and, with the river, enclosing some hundreds of acres of fine alluvial land. It is about *one mile in length*, and the circuit of the river from one end to the other is between three and four miles. Twenty-one years ago, when I first visited it, this ditch was about eight feet deep and the wall of corresponding dimensions: a primitive forest was then growing upon its southern portion, but it is now all under the plough and fast disappearing. The bank is *exterior* to the ditch, which circumstance seems to conflict with the notion that the work was constructed for defence. It has been suggested, but with no good reason, that it was designed for a '*cut off*' or artificial channel for the river. Whatever its purpose, it was a great undertaking for a rude or savage people.

"On the opposite side of the river, about two hundred yards below the mouth of Pine-tree creek, is a group of mounds, surrounded by a low embankment (J). One of them has been nearly washed away by the river, and the others have been much reduced by cultivation. The largest is yet twelve or fifteen feet high, with a very wide base. From these mounds are disclosed arrow-heads, axes, urns, and other vestiges of art, accompanied by human bones and the bones of wild animals, and marine shells, all much decayed. As the water washes away the side of the mound on its bank, charcoal, urns, bones, etc., in successive strata, are exposed; as though it had constituted a cemetery, receiving deposits from time to time, from its commencement to its completion. The strata vary in thickness from six to eighteen inches, and are mixed with much mica, sometimes in large plates. It was long under cultivation in corn, then indigo, and in 1806, when I first saw it, in cotton, which is still cultivated on it. On the large mound stood the overseer's house; around it, on the smaller piles, were the negro quarters.

"In the bend of the river nearly opposite the south end of the 'Indian Ditch,' is a mound, perhaps fifteen feet high (K). Little is known respecting it, having been for many years the site of an overseer's house. I obtained a circular stone, with concave sides and finely polished, which had been found here, also two large urns, one holding twelve, the other twenty quarts, with a number of other aboriginal relics. At the mouth of Town creek, some distance below, there was formerly, no doubt, an Indian town or camp, (L,) judging from the quantity of relics found here. A very fine description of clay is found at this spot, which is resorted to by the Catawba Indians every spring and autumn, for the purpose of manufacturing pottery from it.

" Boykin's mound (M) is one mile lower down the river upon the same bank. It is now nearly washed away by the river. Twenty years ago, when I first saw it, large trees covered it, and it was entire. Four years afterwards I visited it, when only about one third remained, which on the side next the river beautifully exhibited the various strata composing it. It had the usual layers of earth, pottery, charred reeds, etc. Some few of the vases were entire, containing fragments of bones, and were well arranged in tiers, one above the other.

" Last of the series is Nixon's mound (N). It is much reduced, and is not now more than ten feet high. From this to the sea I know of no similar relics. Paint hill and Kirkwood, in the neighborhood of Pine-tree creek, must have been much frequented, judging from the numerous relics occurring on and around them; the former for its pure water, the latter for its fine clay. Hobkirk's hill, near Camden, abounds in aboriginal relics. I have procured several large pipes from these localities, all of which exhibit a skill in workmanship surpassing that of the present race. The entire section in which the above remains occur is exceedingly fertile, and capable of sustaining a large agricultural population."

————

PLATE XXXVIII. No. 1.*

ANCIENT WORKS ON THE ETOWAH RIVER, ALABAMA.

THIS work occurs within the present limits of the State of Alabama, upon the banks of Etowah river, a branch of the Coosa. It is situated upon an alluvial " bottom," at an angle or bend of the stream; and its defences consist of a semi-circular ditch, the flanks of which rest on the river. This ditch is twenty-five

---

* From the Rafinesque MSS. The scale on which the plan is drawn is not given. It is probably about five hundred feet to the inch. An account of this work, substantially the same with that given by Prof. RAFINESQUE, was published by Mr. E. CORNELIUS, in Silliman's Journal, vol. i. p. 223. Mr. Cornelius was accompanied in his visit by several Indian chiefs, who, he says, " gazed upon the remains with as much curiosity as any white man. I inquired," continues Mr. C., " of the oldest chief, if the natives had any tradition concerning them; to which he answered in the negative. I then requested each to say what he supposed was their origin. Neither could tell; but all agreed in saying, 'They were never put up by our people.' "

XXXVIII

Lith. by Sarony & Major.

C. S. Rafinesque del.

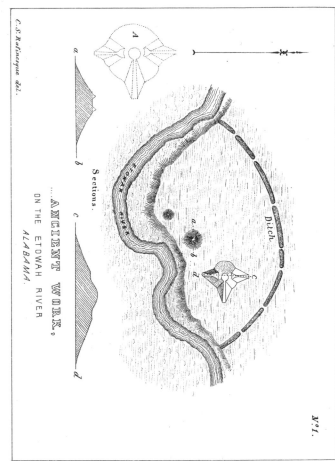

...ANCIENT WORK,
ON THE ETOWAH RIVER
ALABAMA.

Nº 1.

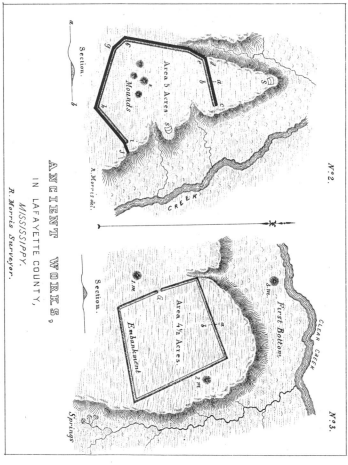

ANCIENT WORKS,
IN LAFAYETTE COUNTY,
MISSISSIPPY.
R. Morris Surveyor.

Nº 2.

Nº 3.

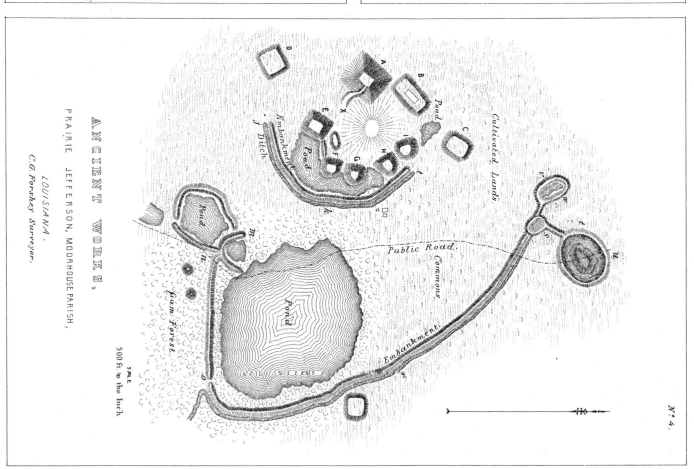

ANCIENT WORKS,
PRAIRIE JEFFERSON, MOORHOUSE PARISH,
LOUISIANA.
C. G. Forshey Surveyor.

Nº 4.

SCALE
500 ft. to the Inch

or thirty feet in width, by eight feet in depth; and is interrupted by no less than seven passage-ways, placed at irregular intervals, and formed by leaving the earth unexcavated at the points where they occur. It is a remarkable fact that no embankment accompanies the ditch; although the work is not entirely singular in that respect. Within the enclosure thus formed by the river on the one hand and the ditch on the other, are several mounds, one of which is of great size and extraordinary character. It measures upwards of seventy-five feet in height, and is twelve hundred feet in circumference at its base. It is truncated, the area at its summit having a diameter of one hundred and forty feet. A graded avenue, which may be ascended on horseback, leads to its top from the east. Upon its northern and southern sides, at the height of forty feet, are triangular platforms or terraces, which are also reached by graded ascents from the plain. The supplementary plan A exhibits the outlines of the monument. Upon its top, trees are growing, which, at the height of a man's head from the ground, measure little under eleven feet in circumference. A fallen oak measured by **Mr. Cornelius** in 1818 was found to be, at the distance of six feet from the branching of the roots, *twelve feet four inches in circumference*, exclusive of the bark. There are two other truncated mounds, to the south-west of the great mound, but of less dimensions. One of these has a perpendicular altitude of thirty feet; and its summit was fortified, with a parapet and palisades, by the Cherokees in their war with the Creeks. The earth taken from the ditch above mentioned was probably used in the construction of these mounds.

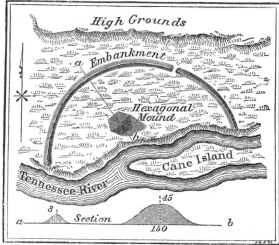

FIG. 21.

An analogous work of some interest, (Fig. 21,) but partially destroyed by the Tennessee river, upon the bank of which it stands, occurs near the town of Florence, in Alabama. "It consists of a large mound, hexagonal in form, truncated, and forty-five feet in height by four hundred and forty feet in circumference at the base. The level area at the summit is one hundred and fifty feet in circumference. It appears to be composed of the ordinary surface loam, and is carried up with great regularity. So far as it has yet been examined, no traces of bones or other foreign substances have been discovered.

"Partly surrounding the mound is a wall two hundred and seventy feet distant from its base, which extends from the main river below, to a branch formed by Cane island above, constituting a segment of a circle, the centre of which would be in the Tennessee river. The wall is about forty feet across the top, and, making allowances for the ravages of time, must have been originally from twelve to fifteen foot high; it is now about eight feet in height. The mound and wall bear the same marks of antiquity, both being covered with large timber of the same age and description with that found growing on the surrounding lands. The wall has what appears to be a ditch on the outside.

"These works are situated on the river bottom, and are half surrounded by a very high ridge, which runs parallel to the Tennessee river, about four hundred yards distant. This ridge, upon which the principal part of the town of Florence is situated, overlooks and entirely commands the whole. The mound, with its surrounding wall, thus situated and exposed to attack, could hardly have been designed as a place of defence. It must have been appropriated to another purpose."*

PLATE XXXVIII. Nos. 2 and 3.

THESE works are specially interesting from the fact that they partake more of the character of the works in the valley of the Ohio, than any other southern structures with which we are acquainted. The accompanying descriptions were furnished by Rev. R. MORRIS, of Mount Sylvan Academy, Lafayette county, Mississippi; the plans are from surveys by the same gentleman.

NUMBER 2.—"This work is situated in T. 4 S., R. 7 W., of the Chickasaw surveys, five miles south-east of the Tallahatchie river. It occupies a point of high land, overlooking the valley of a small creek, and consists of a simple embankment of earth, about three feet in height, with an exterior ditch of corresponding dimensions. It is a polygon in form, and at first glance appears entirely irregular. It will be observed, however, that the line $c\,d$ corresponds in length with $h\,i$, and also that $e\,f$ is exactly equal to $f\,h$,—coincidences which could not possibly be accidental. The side $c\,s\,j$, fronting on the creek, is not entrenched, being sufficiently protected by the high bluff bank. There are no interruptions in the embankment, the ends of which terminate within a short distance of the bluff on the right, leaving passage-ways fifteen or twenty feet wide. A ditch, however, extends from i to j, at the south-east angle; but it is a question whether it was not formed by the water overflowing the artificial ditch at i. The angles of this work are not rounded, but sharp as if newly dug. There are two points, (indicated by the letter s on the plan,) one on a spur of land within the enclosure, and the other at the extreme point of the headland on which the work is situated, where there are excavations from which the earth is thrown up on the outer side. They resemble short sections of the wall and ditch, and suggest the notion of sentry posts, or signal or alarm stations.

"Within the work are several low, irregular mounds, all of which are flat on the top, except k, which is basin-shaped, the concavity being about two feet deep by fifteen across. Excavations, at any point around these mounds, disclose ashes,

---

* Western Messenger.

charcoal, and sooty earth; the charcoal is of oak-wood and very bright. Abundant fragments of the black pottery, glazed inside, and so common in this region, are found in and around this work. At the time of my visit, I found several arrow-heads and a wedge-shaped stone. A few years ago a carved pipe was found here and a piece of heavy metal, which was tested for gold and afterwards mislaid. Inasmuch, however, as the Indians lately occupied this ground in great numbers for several years, these minor relics may be regarded as having pertained to them.

"The bluffs around this work are of extraordinary height for this region, and the whole position seems well designed for defence. The regularity and apparent *freshness* of the structure, and its correspondence, in some striking respects, to our modern system of defence, almost induce me to ascribe to it an European origin. This supposition is further favored by the well known fact that Hernando de Soto passed through here, and probably erected works at various points."

NUMBER 3.—"This work is situated on the left bank of Clear creek, near Mount Sylvan, Lafayette county, Mississippi. It occupies a high point of land, overlooking the creek bottom; upon the right is a bluff bank, forty feet high; towards the north the ground is somewhat broken, and upon the left it slopes gradually to a hollow. There are no hills or elevated points commanding the work within a mile or more. The ground within the enclosure is level.

"The structure itself is quadrangular in form, and consists of a slight embankment of earth, about three feet high by thirty feet broad at the base, and twelve feet broad on the top. It has no ditch, exterior or interior to the embankment, although upon *both sides* there are evidences of the removal of the earth, leaving slight depressions, as shown in the section. At the gateway G, the original level of the ground is preserved. Various forest-trees are growing upon the walls, consisting of black oak and hickory,—some of the oaks are upwards of eighteen inches in diameter. At the foot of the bluffs, to the right of the work, are numerous and copious springs of water.

"There are no mounds within the enclosure; although there are two a little way outside of the walls, occupying the positions indicated in the plan.* The one nearest the gateway, number 1, has trees growing upon it, twenty inches in diameter. Fragments of pottery are scattered in abundance upon and around it. Mound number 2 I have carefully examined. It is situated upon sloping ground, and is perhaps one foot high on the upper, and three feet on the lower side, by twenty feet base. In the centre is a regular concavity one foot deep and twelve feet across; and in this respect it is different from any I have elsewhere observed. The first excavation was made upon the lower side, where were found several

---

* The notices of these mounds, although falling with more propriety within the scope of the chapter on "*Mounds*," can hardly be omitted from the above connection. It will shortly be seen that the mound first described (number 2 of the plan) probably belongs to the class of altar or sacrificial mounds, or those which were connected with the superstitions of the builders. The human remains found in that, as in mound number 3, were, most likely, deposited subsequent to their erection. It is not impossible that the mound last named is of a later date than those upon the higher ground.

arrows, a human skeleton, (a mature subject,) and a large quantity, nearly a half bushel, of coarse pottery. It is of the same kind with that so abundant in the Clear creek valley, where it would be easy to fill a cart in a day. None of the vessels were whole; and I may here remark that I have not been able to recover any of the pottery entire,—all, not excepting the clay pipes, are invariably broken. Among the fragments of pottery was found a piece of hard-burned clay, resembling in form a sweet potato, split longitudinally. The next excavation was made in the centre or lowest part of the concavity above mentioned. The removal of the vegetable accumulation disclosed a layer of yellow clay, four inches thick; beneath which, and nearly upon the original level of the earth, was found a hard-burned stratum, perfectly black, and apparently mingled with ashes. It was with difficulty broken up. Beneath this hearth was a spongy unstratified mass, in which, to the depth of six inches, were mingled fragments of earthenware. Beyond this, nothing was discovered. There were no traces of bones upon the hearth, and but few fragments of pottery. Large trees are growing upon this mound.

"Mound number 3 is about four feet high, and is situated upon the creek bottom, not far from the stream. I opened it nearly a year since. About two feet from the surface was found the skeleton of a child, much decayed, and unaccompanied by remains of any sort. A little below the surface was found a stone tool, resembling a carver's flesh knife, and a leaden ounce bullet. There is much pottery upon and around this mound; but little, if any, within it. It was not thoroughly excavated; but so far as examined there were discovered no traces of fire,—it being, in this respect, peculiar. Every other mound which I have investigated has been found to contain ashes and charcoal."

Whether either of the works above described had a military origin is sufficiently doubtful; although the last named has some of the characteristics of a work of defence. There is nothing, however, in its position or structure so different from hundreds of other works as to warrant us in assigning to it a later date or a different origin. As a military work, it is vastly inferior to many with which we are acquainted, and its regularity is not sufficiently marked to entitle it to any special consideration on that account. It clearly belongs to that great family of remains, of which so many examples have already been presented. Throughout the entire field of their occurrence, these maintain certain characteristic features, some of which are well exhibited in the particular work here mentioned.

Had Hernando de Soto erected one tenth of the works which have been ascribed to him, in the States bordering the Gulf, in Tennessee, and even in Kentucky, he must have found ample demands on his time and exertions. It is most likely, however, that the intervals between his tedious and toilsome marches were occupied more profitably, if not less laboriously, than in the erection of vast earth structures of this description; which, when finished, could not possibly have served him any useful purpose. His handful of weary followers probably found in a small stockade of logs a better defence, and one more obviously within their capabilities of construction.

In addition to the above plans, Mr. Morris has kindly communicated accounts of several other interesting works; of none of which, however, he was able to make surveys. One of these is situated three miles east of Panola, Mississippi, and closely resembles No. 3, Plate XXXVIII. It is accompanied by several remarkable mounds. A few miles south-east of Delta there is a square enclosure of some twenty acres area. It contains several mounds, one of which is forty feet in height, truncated, and ascended by a graded way. Within this enclosure there is also a square excavation, fifteen feet deep, and one hundred feet in diameter. It is surrounded by a low embankment of earth, three feet in height.

———

PLATE XXXVIII. No. 4.

ANCIENT WORKS, PRAIRIE JEFFERSON, LOUISIANA.

THIS group of ancient works occurs on Prairie Jefferson, Moorhouse parish, Louisiana. They are minutely described by Prof. C. G. FORSHEY, in a letter to Prof. Silliman of New Haven, published, with the accompanying plan, in the American Journal of Science and Arts, vol. xlix. p. 38. For some interesting facts in addition to this account, acknowledgment is due to Dr. HARRISON, proprietor of the plantation upon which these remains are situated.

The works, consisting of a series of mounds and terraces, accompanied by lines of embankment and by excavations, are found near the south-western portion of the prairie, and partly in what is now woodland, though probably at no very remote date free from forests. The mounds are disposed with some degree of regularity in respect to each other, and are of the following dimensions:

A. base,	length 180 feet;	width, 135 feet;	height, 48 feet.
A. summit,	" 51 "	" 45 "	"
B. summit,	" 210 "	" 75 "	" 5 "
C. base,	" 132 "	" 132 "	" 4 "
D. summit,	" 120 "	" 120 "	" 4 "
E. summit,	" 60 "	" 42 "	" 10 "

F. on summit, length,	60 feet front;	78 feet rear;	42 feet wide;	12 feet high.
G. " " "	60 " "	39 " "	51 " "	12 " "
H. " " "	60 " "	60 " "	54 " "	7 " "
I. " " "	36 " "	27 " "	45 " "	10 " "

The embankment between E and F is one hundred and thirty-five feet long, fifteen feet broad at the base, and four high. The embankment _j k l_ is ten hundred and fifty feet long, twelve feet broad and from one to three feet high.

The great mound E has been denominated "the Temple." It has a level area on its summit fifty-one feet long and forty-five broad, which is reached from the west by the winding graded path X. All its angles are much rounded; still its four faces are very plainly marked. Since it has been cleared of trees, several slides have marred its symmetry. These slides, as also excavations made in it, have shown that it consists of a series of strata or tables, one above the other, each surmounted by a burned surface, resembling rude bricks. No bones have been found in it. Any extended examination of its contents is avoided, from a desire to preserve its proportions. From the summit a good view may be had of the surrounding works and country.

The mounds which face the "Temple" on the west have great uniformity of figure and dimensions, and are highest in the rear, except E and I, which are nearly level on top. E, F, H, and I, have terraces in front; and all incline gently to the plain, which exhibits marks of excavation. In the rear and on the sides they are for the most part very abrupt. The pond in the rear is evidently artificial, and formed by removing the earth for building purposes. Extending around this pond are an embankment and ditch, (*j k l,*) the latter produced by the excavation of the earth for the embankment, which seems to have constituted a sort of levée around the pond to the high grounds at *j* and *l*.

" The mounds C, D have great similarity in their magnitude, form, and general position in respect to the "Temple;" but situated, as they are, in cultivated fields, their definite outlines are fast disappearing. B, however, differs essentially from the other mounds of the system; it is perfectly level on its summit, of gentle declivity and moderate height, and has been fitly chosen as the site of a dwelling-house, which fronts the area surrounded by the mounds.

" The several ponds have outlets for the water at particular points, which were probably controlled as the mound-builders desired. The long embankment (*m n o*) is abruptly cut off at *o*, but is continued again towards *p*, diminishing in magnitude as the land grows higher, until it almost disappears at *s*. The swale or low strip of ground which borders this embankment on the left, continues up to very near the pond at *s*, but has no actual connection with it. It does not appear that the large pond, within this grand levée, is artificial. The smaller ones, however, were manifestly produced by throwing up the earth around them, as at *m n*; *s*; *t u,* and *v w*.

" The necessity for these artificial ponds is apparent from the fact, that there are no streams or supplies of water nearer this prairie than five miles. Hence the excavations, usually made without apparent design in constructing the mounds, are at this place so economized as to produce the ponds in the immediate neighborhood. Here the conformation of the ground, which is gently undulating, rendered it easy to construct large ponds or lakes, to contain a perennial supply of water. This has plainly been the object of the extensive levées or embankments traced in the map. The general inclination of the land is southward, and the drains in its surface were with some skill called into aid."

A similar mode of retaining a supply of water has already been remarked, in the case of a fortified hill, in Ohio. (See page 15.) The ancient inhabitants of Central America resorted to the same method. Their *aguadas*, lined with pavements and enclosed by embankments, are among the most interesting remains of ancient art.

XXXIX

ANCIENT MONUMENTS.

MADISON PARISH, LOUISIANA.

Surveyed by T. Hough for Jas. Mc Bride.

WALNUT BAYOU.

Elevated Way 2700 ft long 75 wide

Excavation

Excavation

Sections.

SCALE
500 ft to the Inch.

Lith. by Sarony & Major.

PLATE XXXIX.

ANCIENT MONUMENTS, MADISON PARISH, LOUISIANA.

THE accompanying plans are from original surveys made by JAMES HOUGH, Esq., of Hamilton, Ohio, for Mr. McBRIDE, and may, it is believed, be relied upon as entirely accurate, in every essential respect.*

The group here presented is situated upon the right bank of Walnut Bayou, in Madison Parish, Louisiana, seven miles from the Mississippi river. It consists of seven large and regular mounds, and a graded or elevated road-way half amile in length. The plan exhibits the relative positions of the remains and their predominating features, and obviates the necessity of a particular description, which at best would be intricate and obscure.

The largest mound of the group, A, is distant two hundred and fifty yards south from the *bayou*, which here extends in a direction nearly east and west. The principal structure is two hundred and twenty-five feet long, by one hundred and sixty-five feet broad at the base, and thirty feet in height. The summit is level, presenting an area of one hundred and twenty feet long, by seventy-five broad. On the side next the *bayou* towards the north, at the height of ten feet, is a terrace ten feet wide and extending the entire length of the mound. On the south side is a road-way twenty feet wide, commencing at a point sixty feet from the base of the mound, and leading with a regular grade to its top. At either end of the mound is an inclined platform or *apron*, seventy-five feet long by sixty wide. These are six feet in elevation at the point joining the mound, but decline gradually to three feet at the outer ends, where they terminate abruptly.

B is a mound similar to the one just described, but less in size. It is one hundred and eighty feet long, one hundred and twenty broad, and fifteen high. The level area on the top is one hundred and twenty feet long and sixty wide. A graded road leads to its summit from the north. At the east end is an inclined platform, seventy feet long by sixty broad, eight feet high where it joins the mound, and sloping to five feet at its outer extremity. At the west end is a similar elevation one hundred and twenty feet long by sixty broad.

C is a singular work, consisting of a central mound ninety-six feet square at the base, and ten feet high, with a level area forty-eight feet square on the top. Connected by elevated terraces with this mound, are two others of similar construction,

---

* The perfect regularity which the plans exhibit, it will readily be understood, does not actually exist. The angles of all these structures are more or less rounded. The predominant features, nevertheless,— the terraces, platforms, and graded ways,—are truly represented. All of these works seem to have been originally moulded with the utmost care, and possessed the highest degree of regularity of which the materials were capable. They were undoubtedly faced with turf, which seems better than solid masonry to resist the ravages of time and the elements.

each sixty feet square and eight feet high.   The terraces are forty feet broad, four high, and one hundred and twenty-five and seventy-five feet long respectively.

The character and dimensions of the remaining mounds are sufficiently indicated in the plan.   There is however another singular structure connected with the group, which deserves special notice.   It consists of a terrace extending due west from the principal mound above described, parallel to the *bayou*.   It is elevated three feet above the general level of the plain, and is seventy-five feet wide by two thousand seven hundred feet in length.   Upon either side of this terrace, and parallel to it, are broad excavations, at present about three feet deep. These excavations are not far from two thousand feet long, by from one hundred and fifty to three hundred feet wide.   There are no other perceptible excavations in the vicinity; and it is reasonable to conclude that most, if not all of the material for the construction of the works was taken from these points.

The ground occupied by these remains is for the most part under cultivation. It was originally covered with a heavy growth of the black walnut, a species of timber scarcely known on the alluvial lands of the Mississippi, so far south.   It was first cleared by a Mr. Harper, in 1827.   Broken pottery is found in abundance around these monuments; and fragments of human bones, much decomposed, are observed intermixed with the earth.   Upon the mounds, in many places, the earth is much burned.   There are no other remains of magnitude in the immediate vicinity.

FIG. 22.

The works here represented, Fig. 22, are situated in Bolivar county, Mississippi, near Williams's *bayou* in the Choctaw bend, one mile and a half from the Mississippi river.   They consist of two truncated pyramidal structures of the character already described, accompanied by two small conical mounds, the whole surrounded by a circular embankment of earth, without a ditch, two thousand three hundred feet in circumference, and four feet high.   A gateway opens into the enclosure from the east. Mound A is one hundred and fifty feet square at the base, seventy-five feet square on top, and twenty feet high, with a graded ascent from the east.   B is one hundred and thirty-five feet square at base, fifty feet at top, and fifteen feet high.   The ascent in this instance is from the north.   The two small conical mounds are about thirty feet in diameter, and five feet high.   The sides of the pyramidal structures do not vary two degrees from the cardinal points of the compass; a feature not observed in any of the others above noticed. They all, however, appear to have been placed with some reference to these points,— probably as near as they could be located without instruments.

At the junction of the Washita, Tenza, and Catahoola rivers in Louisiana, is a most remarkable group of ancient remains, of which no plan has yet been published. They have nevertheless been often referred to, and are described as consisting of a number of mounds, some rectangular and others round, embraced within a large enclosure of not far from two hundred acres area.* The principal mound is said to be circular, four hundred feet in diameter at the base, ninety feet in height, truncated, and having a level area at its summit, fifty feet in diameter. The summit is reached by a spiral pathway, which winds with an easy ascent around the mound, from its base to its top. This pathway is sufficiently broad to permit two horsemen to ride abreast. From the summit a wide prospect is commanded. Here, upon penetrating the earth to a slight depth, strong traces of fire are visible. The ground upon which the mound stands is somewhat elevated above the surrounding plain, which is low and marshy.†

The great mound at Seltzertown, near Washington, Mississippi, is one of very singular construction. It consists of a truncated pyramid six hundred feet long by about four hundred broad at its base, covering nearly six acres of ground. Its sides correspond very nearly with the four cardinal points, its greatest length being from east to west. It is forty feet in perpendicular height; and is surrounded

---

* Stoddard, in his History of Louisiana, p. 349, gives an account of some works near the junction of the Washita, Acatahoola, and Tenza, probably the very ones in question. His account is subjoined:

" Not less than five remarkable mounts are situated near the junction of the Washita, Acatahoola, and Tenza, in an alluvial soil. They are all enclosed in an embankment, or wall of earth, at this time ten feet high, which contains about two hundred acres of land. Four of these mounds are nearly of equal dimensions, about twenty feet high, one hundred broad, and three hundred long. The fifth seems to have been designed for a tower or turret; the base of it covers an acre of ground; it rises by two stages or steps; its circumference gradually diminishes as it ascends; its summit is crowned by a flattened cone. By admeasurement the height of this tower is found to be eighty feet. Perhaps these works were designed in part for defence, and in part for the reception of the dead."

There is a slight discrepancy in the dimensions of these works, as given by Prof. Rafinesque and Mr. Stoddard. Both agree, however, respecting their vast size, and general character.

† This monument is not singular. Mounds with spiral pathways are frequent at the South, and are occasionally found at the North. Bartram describes one on the Savannah river in Georgia:—" These wonderful labors of the ancients stand in a level plain near the bank of the river. They consist of conical mounds of earth and four square terraces, etc. The great mound is in form of a cone, about forty or fifty feet high, and the circumference of its base is two or three hundred yards; it is entirely composed of the loamy rich earth of the low grounds; the top or apex is flat; a spiral path or track leading from the ground up to the top is still visible: there appear four niches excavated out of the sides of this hill, at different heights from the base, fronting the four cardinal points; these niches or sentry-boxes are entered into from the winding path, and seem to have been meant for resting-places or look-outs."—Bartram's Travels in N. America, p. 323.

The niches here mentioned have been occasionally observed in Mississippi and Louisiana, placed at right angles in respect to each other, and not always, though sometimes, corresponding to the cardinal points. It has been suggested that they were designed as recesses for idols, or places where altars were erected. It seems likely that proper investigation would throw light upon this point.

by a ditch at its base, of variable dimensions, but averaging perhaps ten feet in depth. It is ascended by graded avenues. The area on the top embraces about four acres. Near each of the ends, and as nearly as may be in the longitudinal centre of the elevation, is placed a large conical mound. The one towards the west is represented to be not far from forty feet in height, and truncated, with a level area at its summit of thirty feet diameter. The opposite mound is somewhat less in size, and is also truncated. Eight other mounds are regularly placed at various points; they are of comparatively small size, measuring from eight to ten feet in height. The ground here is considerably broken; and it has been supposed by some, from the fact that it slopes in every direction from the base of the monument, that the structure is simply a natural elevation modified and fashioned into its present form by the hands of man.* Human bones have been exposed by the washing away of the sides of this structure.

The above examples, it is believed, may be taken as very fair illustrations of the general form and external characteristics of the Southern monuments. There are no perfect pyramids. With the exception of a portion, probably the larger portion, of the conical mounds, which are abundant, but overshadowed by the more remarkable structures which surround them, *all* appear to be truncated, and to have, in most instances, graded ascents to their tops. As already remarked, they do not seem to have been connected with any military system,—their form and structure, so far as developed, pointing to a religious origin. Some have been noticed as having parapets raised on their summits, as if to protect the area in case of assault; and hence it has been concluded that the larger elevations were "forts" or citadels. This feature was observed in many of the Teocalli of the Mexicans. It is possible that they may have been designed secondarily for defence. That the Mexicans fought with the greatest determination around the bases of their temples, from their terraces and their summits, we have abundant evidence in the records of the conquerors. However well these elevations may have served for places of retreat in case of sudden attack, it is obvious that they were in no wise adapted to resist anything like a regular siege or a continued investment. The absence of sources for procuring water, and the narrow compass to which the besieged must necessarily be limited, seem sufficient in themselves to

---

* Breckenridge's View of Louisiana, *Appendix*. Mr. J. R. BARTLETT, in a recent Memoir on the "Progress of Ethnology," presents, on the authority of Dr. M. W. DICKESON, some new facts respecting this mound. "On digging into it, vast quantities of human skeletons were found; also numerous specimens of pottery, including vases filled with pigments, ashes, ornaments, etc. The north side of the mound is supported by a wall of *sun-dried bricks,* two feet thick, filled with grass, rushes, and leaves. A shaft has been sunk in the mound to the depth of forty-two feet, without reaching the original soil." Dr. DICKESON also mentions angular tumuli, the corners of which "were quite perfect, formed of large bricks, bearing the impression of the human hand." We have the same authority for the fact that the great enclosure at the "Trinity" in Louisiana, which contains one hundred and fifty acres, "is partially faced with sun-dried bricks." Also that ditches and ponds are sometimes found, in the same State, "lined at the bottom and sides with bricks." These bricks are stated to be from sixteen to eighteen inches in length, and of proportionate breadth.

successfully combat this hypothesis. The defensive works on the Ohio, on the contrary, possess all the requisites for resisting an enemy and for sustaining a protracted defence.

We must seek therefore in the contents, as well as in the form and position of these works, for the secret of their origin and purposes. And it is at this stage of our inquiry, that the lack of a systematic and extended investigation, conducted on philosophical principles, is most sensibly felt. Some of these structures, it is stated, where their formation is disclosed by slides or the wasting action of the rivers, exhibit alternate layers or *platforms* of earth and burned clay, from base to summit. Others are represented as having alternate layers of earth and human bones in various stages of decomposition. And others still, we are assured, have various horizontal strata of earth and sand, upon which are deposited at various points human remains, implements, pottery, and ornaments. Many of the remains of art exhibit great skill in their construction, more especially the pottery and articles of similar composition. The conical mounds, so far as we are informed, have many features in common with those of a higher latitude. How far the coincidences between them may be traced can only be settled by future inquiries.

From what has been presented above, it will readily be seen that it is impossible, with our present limited knowledge concerning them, to form anything like a determinate or satisfactory conclusion respecting the numerous and remarkable remains of the South. The immense mounds that abound there may be vast sepulchres in which the remains of generations were deposited; they may have been the temples and "high places" of a superstitious people, where rites were celebrated and sacrifices performed; or, they may have answered as the places of last resort, where, when pursued by foes, the ancient people fled to receive the support of their gods and to defend the altars of their religion. Perhaps all of these purposes were subserved by them. What significance may attach to their form; whether there exists any dependence between their exterior features and their contents; the dates of the different deposits found in them; indeed, whatever of design and system which these works may have possessed, and how far they may serve to reflect light upon the character and customs of the people who built them, their religion, their modes of burial, and their arts,—*all* remain to be determined by careful and systematic investigation, conducted with a view to develop facts rather than to excite wonder. Such an investigation must also finally determine whether these are the remains of the same people whose works are scattered through the more northern States, and whether they were probably contemporaneous in their origin; and, if the works are of the same people, and not contemporaneous, whether the course of migration was southward or the reverse; whether the less imposing structures of the Ohio are the remains of a ruder and more warlike but progressive people, or the weaker efforts of a colony, pressed by foes and surrounded by difficulties. It may disclose the curious and important fact, that upon the Ohio and Mississippi first originated those elements which afterwards, in a regular course of progress, developed themselves in the gorgeous semi-civilization of Mexico and Peru. Or it may, on the contrary, make known the no less interesting fact, that from these centres radiated colonies, which sustained themselves for a period, and finally disappeared, leaving perhaps only a few modified remnants in the region bordering upon the Gulf.

———

Subsequent to the preparation of the foregoing pages for the press, and at too late a date to permit the introduction, in another connection, of the facts it embodies relating to the aboriginal monuments of the South, a manuscript work on the Southern Indians, by WILLIAM BARTRAM, was placed in the hands of the investigators, by Dr. Morton, of Philadelphia. The character and history of this MS. have been sufficiently explained in the Preface, to which the reader is referred.

As already observed, it relates principally to the manners, customs, government, and religion of the Muscogulges and other southern Indian tribes; but it also embraces many interesting and important facts respecting the remains under consideration. Taken in connection with those presented by the same author in his "Travels in North America," they serve very much to explain the character and illustrate the secondary if not the primary purposes to which the southern monuments were applied. The accompanying illustrations are reduced fac-similes of Bartram's original pen sketches. In introducing them he observes, in language somewhat quaint but forcible:

"The following rough drawings of the ancient Indian monuments, consisting of public buildings, areas, vestiges of towns, etc., will serve to illustrate what I have elsewhere said respecting them. They are, to the best of my remembrance, as near the truth as I could express. However, if I have in any respect erred, I hope my mistakes may be corrected by the observations of future and more accurate and industrious travellers. But as time changes the face of things, I wish they could be searched out and faithfully recorded, before the devastations of artificial refinements, ambition, and avarice, totally deface these simple and most ancient remains of the American aborigines."

"CHUNK YARDS.—The 'Chunk Yards' of the Muscogulges or Creeks are rectangular areas, generally occupying the centre of the town. The Public Square and Rotunda, or Great Winter Council House, stand at the two opposite corners of them. They are generally very extensive, especially in the large, old towns: some of them are from six hundred to nine hundred feet in length, and of proportionate breadth. The area is exactly level and sunk two, sometimes three, feet below the banks or terraces surrounding them, which are occasionally two in number, one behind and above the other, and composed of the earth taken from the area at the time of its formation. These banks or terraces serve the purpose of seats for spectators. In the centre of this yard or area, there is a low, circular mound or eminence, in the middle of which stands erect the 'Chunk Pole,' which is a high obelisk or four-square pillar declining upwards to an obtuse point. This is of wood, the heart or inward resinous part of a sound pine tree, which is very durable. It is generally from thirty to forty feet in height, and to the top is fastened some object which serves as a mark to shoot at, with arrows or the rifle, at certain appointed times. Near each corner of one end of the yard, stands erect a less pole or pillar, about twelve feet high, called a 'Slave Post,' for the reason that to them are bound the captives condemned to be burnt. These posts are usually decorated with the scalps of slain enemies, suspended by strings from the top. They are often crowned with the white dry skull of an enemy.

"It thus appears that this area is designed for a public place of exhibition, for shows, games, etc. Formerly, there is little doubt, most barbarous and tragical scenes were enacted within them, such as the torturing and burning of captives, who were here forced to run the gauntlet, bruised and beaten with sticks and burning chunks of wood. The Indians do not now practise these cruelties; but there are some old traders who have witnessed them in former times. I inquired of these traders for what reason these areas were called '*Chunk Yards;*' they were in general ignorant, yet, for the most part, concurred in a lame story that it originated in the circumstance of their having been places of torture, and that the name was but an interpretation of the Indian term designating them.

"I observed none of these yards in use in any of the Cherokee towns; and where I have mentioned them, in the Cherokee country, it must be understood that I saw only the remains or vestiges of them among the ruins of ancient towns. In the existing Cherokee towns which I visited, although there were ancient mounds and signs of the yard adjoining, yet the yard was either built upon or turned into a garden plat, or otherwise appropriated. Indeed I am convinced that the Chunk Yards now or lately in use among the Creeks are of very ancient date, and not the work of the present Indians; although they are now kept in repair by them, being swept very clean every day, and the poles kept up and decorated in the manner I have described.

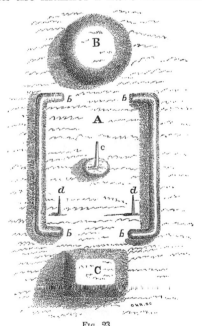

FIG. 23

"The following plan, (Fig. 23,) will illustrate the form and character of these yards.

"A. The great area, surrounded by terraces or banks.

"B. A circular eminence, at one end of the yard, commonly nine or ten feet higher than the ground round about. Upon this mound stands the great *Rotunda, Hot House,* or *Winter Council House* of the present Creeks. It was probably designed and used by the ancients who constructed it, for the same purpose.

"C. A square terrace or eminence, about the same height with the circular one just described, occupying a position at the other end of the yard. Upon this stands the *Public Square.*

"The banks enclosing the yard are indicated by the letters *b b b b; c* indicates the '*Chunk Pole,*' and *d d* the '*Slave Posts.*'

"Sometimes the square, instead of being open at the ends, as shown in the plan, is closed upon all sides by the banks. In the lately built or new Creek towns, they do not raise a mound for the foundation of their rotundas or public squares. The yard, however, is retained, and the public buildings occupy nearly the same position in respect to it. They also retain the central obelisk and the slave posts.

"In the Cherokee country, all over Carolina and the northern and eastern parts of Georgia, wherever the ruins of ancient Indian towns appear, we see always, besides these remains, one vast, conical, pointed mound. To mounds of this kind I refer, when I speak of *pyramidal mounds*. To the south and west of the Altamaha, I observed none of these, in any part of the Muscogulge country, but always flat circular or square structures. The vast mounds upon the St. John's, Alachua, and Musquito rivers, differ from those among the Cherokees, with respect to their adjuncts and appendages, particularly in respect to the great highway or avenue, sunk below the common level of the earth, extending from them, and terminating either in a vast savannah or natural plain, or an artificial pond or lake. A remarkable example occurs at Mount Royal, from whence opens a glorious view of Lake George and its environs.

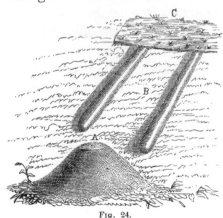

FIG. 24.

"Fig. 24 exhibits a view of the great mound last referred to. Fig. 25 is a plan of the same structure with its accompanying avenue, which leads off to an artificial lake or pond, on the verge of an expansive savannah or natural meadow. A, the mound, about forty feet in perpendicular height; B, the highway leading from the mound in a straight line to the pond C, about half a mile distant. What may have been the motive for making this pond I cannot conjecture, since the mound and other vestiges of the ancient town are situated close on the banks of the river St. Juan.* It could not therefore be for the conveniency of water. Perhaps they raised the mound with the earth taken out of the pond. The sketch of this mound also

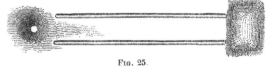

FIG. 25.

illustrates the character of the mounds in the Cherokee country; but the last have not the highway or avenue, and are always accompanied by vast square terraces

---

* The remains here described are referred to in Bartram's published travels, as follows: "They are situated upon an eminence, near the banks of the lake, and command an extensive and charming prospect of the waters, islands, east and west shores of the lake, the capes, the bay, and Mount Royal; and to the south the view is in like manner infinite, where the skies and waters seem to unite. On the site of this ancient town stands a very pompous Indian mount, or conical pyramid of earth, from which runs in a straight line a grand avenue or Indian highway, through a magnificent grove of magnolias, live oaks, palms, and orange trees, terminating at the verge of a large, green, level savannah."—*Travels*, p. 101.

placed upon one side or the other. On the other hand, we never see the square terraces accompanying the high mounds of East Florida."

From the above quotations it appears that, less than one century ago, a portion of the monuments of the South were in actual use by the Indians. It will be observed, however, that our authority ascribes their construction to an anterior race and assigns to them a high antiquity. In his Travels he remarks that the region in which they are most abundant, lying between the Savannah and Ock-mulgee rivers on the east and west, and between the sea-coast on the south and the Apalachian mountains on the north, was occupied subsequently to the arrival of Europeans, by the Cherokees, who were afterwards dispossessed by the Creeks; that "all this country was probably, many ages preceding the Cherokee invasion, inhabited by a single nation or confederacy governed by common laws, possessing like customs, and speaking the same language, but so ancient that neither the Creeks nor the Cherokees, nor the nations they conquered, could render any account by whom or for what purposes these monuments were erected." He nevertheless inclines to the belief, and not without reason, that the uses to which these structures were appropriated, by the existing Indian tribes, were not widely different from those for which they were originally constructed. Upon this point he adds: "The mounds and large areas adjoining them seem to have been raised in part for ornament and recreation, and likewise to serve some other public purpose, since they are always so situated as to command the most extensive pro-spect over the country adjacent. The square terraces may have served as the foundations of fortresses; and perhaps the great pyramidal mounds answered the purpose of look-outs, or were high places for sacrifice."*

Whatever date or origin we may ascribe to these monuments, we cannot over-look the singular attachment to the square and the circle exhibited by the Creeks in the public edifices known to have been constructed by themselves. That these forms had some significance at the outset can hardly be doubted, although their perpetuation may have depended upon custom. The circumstance that the eternal fire was only maintained in the circular structure, designated by Bartram as the "Rotunda," goes far to support the conclusion that its form was symbolical, and referred to the sun. That these tribes were sun worshippers is well known: the inferences drawn from analogy are therefore sustained by collateral facts. In their less imposing structures, may we not discern the type of the great circles and squares of Ohio,—the traces of a system of idolatry which has dotted the valleys of the West with giant temples, symbolizing in their form the nature of the worship to which they were dedicated?

---

* Travels in North America, p. 518.

CHAPTER V.

MONUMENTS OF THE NORTH-WEST.

IT has already been observed that the ancient monuments of the Southern United States, although partaking of the general character of those of the central region, are nevertheless in many respects peculiar. While enclosures are comparatively few, mounds are abundant and of great size and symmetry, and possess a regularity of arrangement which we look for in vain among the corresponding structures of a higher latitude. Proceeding to the North and North-west, we find the earthworks assuming a new form and character, in many respects so unlike those both of the central and southern divisions of the country, that we are almost induced to assign them a different origin. As at the South, there are few enclosures or works of defence; but, instead of regular pyramidal structures, the mounds generally assume the shape of animals, presenting a thousand singular forms and combinations. These effigies are situated upon the undulating prairies and level plains, and are accompanied by conical mounds and occasional lines of embankment; but the latter, except in a very few instances, have no obvious design, and enter into none of the combinations which we notice in the works of the Ohio valley. The interesting field occupied by these remains has not fallen within the range of the investigations of the authors, who are therefore unable to present much that is new respecting them; still, it will be necessary to embody the facts thus far disclosed in a general manner, in order to an adequate comprehension of the scope and character of our antiquities. And here, at the outset, we have again to regret the small amount of information respecting these works in possession of the public, as well as its unsatisfactory nature, resulting from the necessarily limited and disconnected observations of those who have paid any attention to the subject. These observations have been made by men of inquiring minds, in the scanty intervals of professional business, and are consequently too detached to justify or sustain any general conclusions. They have served rather to excite than to gratify curiosity, and in this way they may have the good effect of leading to a full and careful survey of the entire field.

The first public notice of the existence of these singular relics at the Northwest, was made by RICHARD C. TAYLOR, Esq., in the "American Journal of Science and Art," for the month of April, 1838. His paper, which was accompanied by several illustrations, attracted considerable attention, and was followed, in the same Journal for 1843, by a more extended account, very well illustrated, from the hand of S. TAYLOR, Esq. A later notice by Prof. JOHN LOCKE constituted a short chapter in the "Report on the Mineral Lands of the United

States," presented to Congress in 1840 and published in 1844. These, with a few unsatisfactory notices in the public prints, comprise the only sources of information which we possess; and from them the following facts are mainly derived.

The field in which these remains occur, so far as observed by the above authorities, is embraced within the lower counties of Wisconsin, and extends from Prairie du Chien on the Mississippi, by the way of the Wisconsin and Rock rivers, eastward towards Fond du Lac on Lake Winnebago, and Milwaukie on Lake Michigan. The country thus indicated is about one hundred and fifty miles in length by fifty in width. The great Indian trail or "war path," from Lake Michigan near Milwaukie to the Mississippi above Prairie du Chien, which has for the most part been adopted as the route of the United States military road, passes through this chain of earthworks. They are found in abundance by the sides of this great natural pathway, which has been for ages and must for ever remain the route of communication between the Great Lakes and the Great River. They occur principally in the vicinity of the large water-courses, observing in this respect a marked conformity with the remains of other sections, and are invariably placed above the influence of freshets or inundations. Like those of the Ohio valley, they are seldom found upon hilly or sterile lands, but mainly upon the rich undulating plains, or on the levels corresponding to the alluvions of the Ohio.

They consist of elevations of earth, of diversified outline and various size, for the most part constituting effigies of beasts, birds, reptiles, and of the human form; but often circular, quadrangular, and of oblong shape. The circular or conical tumuli differ from those scattered over the whole country in no outward respect, excepting that they are much smaller in their average dimensions; the largest seldom exceeding fifteen feet in height. Those in the form of parallelograms are sometimes upwards of five hundred feet in length, seldom less than one hundred; but in height they bear no proportion to their otherwise great dimensions, and may probably be better designated as walls, embankments, or terraces, than mounds. These works are seldom isolated, but generally occur in groups or ranges, sometimes, though not always, placed with apparent design in respect to each other. In these groups may be observed every variety of form,—the circular, quadrangular, and animal-shaped structures occurring in such connection with each other as to fully justify the belief that they are of contemporaneous origin. At first glance, these remains are said to resemble the sites or ground-plans and foundation-lines of buildings; and it is not until their entire outline is taken into view, that the impression of an effigy becomes decided. This is not surprising, in view of the fact that they are usually of inconsiderable height, varying from one to four feet; in a few cases, however, rising as high as six feet. Their outlines are, nevertheless, represented to be distinctly defined in all cases where they occupy favorable positions. Their small altitude should cause no doubt of the fidelity of the representations which have been made of these figures; since a regular elevation of six inches can be readily traced upon the level prairies and "bottom-lands" of the West, especially when it is covered with turf. The following illustrations, selected from those presented by the authorities above mentioned, will serve to explain the character of

these remains. It is to be regretted that explanatory sections do not accompany
the plans, so as to exhibit, at one view, the altitude as well as general outlines
and dimensions of the figures.

———

PLATE XL.

ANCIENT MONUMENTS, DADE COUNTY, WISCONSIN.

THIS group of mounds is figured and described from actual survey, by Mr. R. C.
TAYLOR.* It occurs about eighteen miles west of the " Four Lakes," and seven
miles east of the " Blue Mounds," in Dade county, Wisconsin. It is situated on
the Great Indian Trail already noticed, and consists; as will be observed, of effigies
of six quadrupeds, six mounds in the form of parallelograms, one circular tumulus,
one effigy of the human figure, and a small circle. The area comprehended in the
map is something less than half a mile in length. The dimensions of the figures
and their relative positions are indicated in the plan. It is not easy to make out,
from the effigies, the character of the animals intended to be represented. It has
been suggested that they were designed to represent the buffalo, which formerly
abounded in the vicinity; but the absence of a tail and of the characteristic hump
of that animal would seem to point to a different conclusion. They display a
closer resemblance to the bear than to any other animal with which we are
acquainted. These figures seem to be most prevalent; and, though preserving
about the same relative proportions, vary in size from ninety to one hundred and
twenty feet. In many other places, as at this point, they occur in ranges, one after
the other at irregular intervals. In the midst of this group is the representation
of a human figure, placed with its head towards the west, and having its arms
and legs extended. Its length is one hundred and twenty-five feet, and it is one
hundred and forty feet from the extremity of one arm to that of the other. The
body is thirty feet in breadth, the head twenty-five feet in diameter, and its elevation considerably greater than that of most of the others, being not much less than
six feet. The human figure is not uncommon among the effigies, and is always
characterized by the extraordinary and unnatural length of its arms. The conical
mound in the centre of this group is the most elevated work, and commands a view
of the entire series. These works are situated upon a high open prairie, on the
dividing ridge between the waters of the Rock and Wisconsin rivers. Half a mile
westward of this remarkable group, and on the same elevated prairie, occurs a
solitary mound, about ninety feet in length, representing an animal in all respects
like those just described, but lying with its head towards the south-west.

---

* From Silliman's Journal of Science and Art, vol. xxxiv. p. 91.

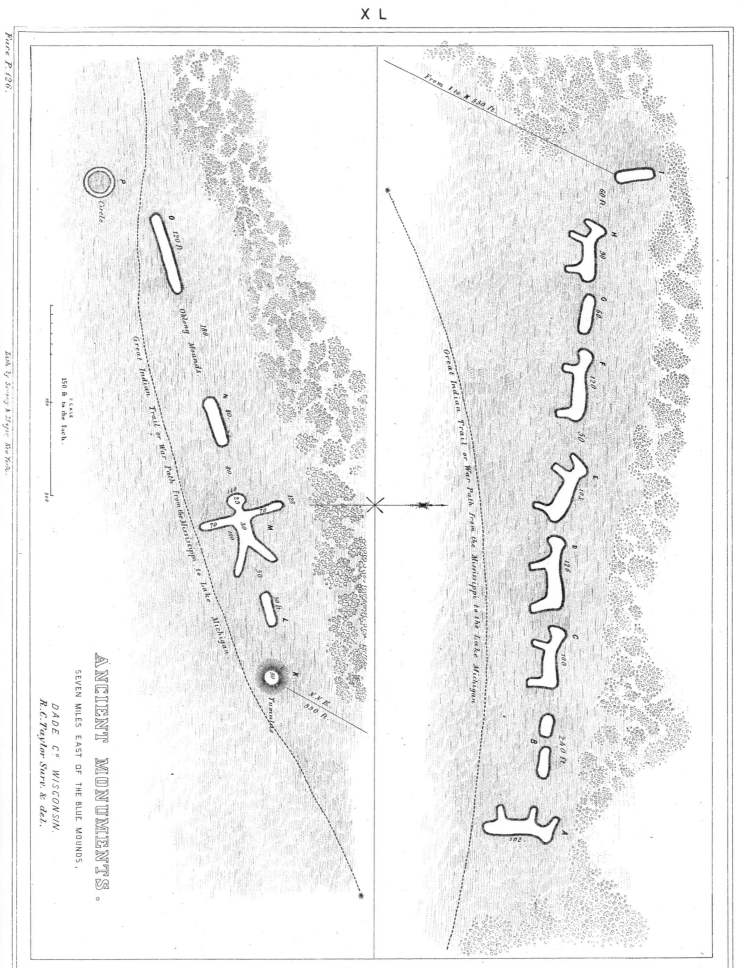

Lith. by Sarony & Major, New York.

SCALE

150 ft. to the Inch.

ANCIENT MONUMENTS.

SEVEN MILES EAST OF THE BLUE MOUNDS,

DADE C? WISCONSIN.

R. C. Taylor Surv. & del.

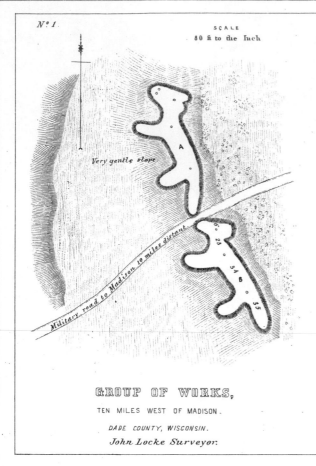

SCALE
80 ft to the Inch

Very gentle slope

Military road to Madison 10 miles distant.

GROUP OF WORKS,

TEN MILES WEST OF MADISON.

DADE COUNTY, WISCONSIN.

John Locke Surveyor.

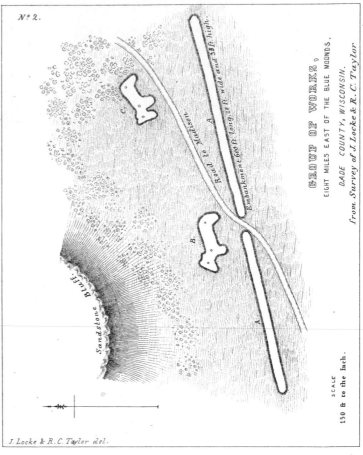

GROUP OF WORKS,
EIGHT MILES EAST OF THE BLUE MOUNDS.

DADE COUNTY, WISCONSIN.

From Survey of J. Locke & R. C. Taylor.

Face P. 127.

Road to Madison.

Embankment 600 ft. long, 20 ft. wide and 3⅓ ft. high.

Sandstone Bluff.

SCALE
150 ft to the Inch.

J. Locke & R. C. Taylor del.

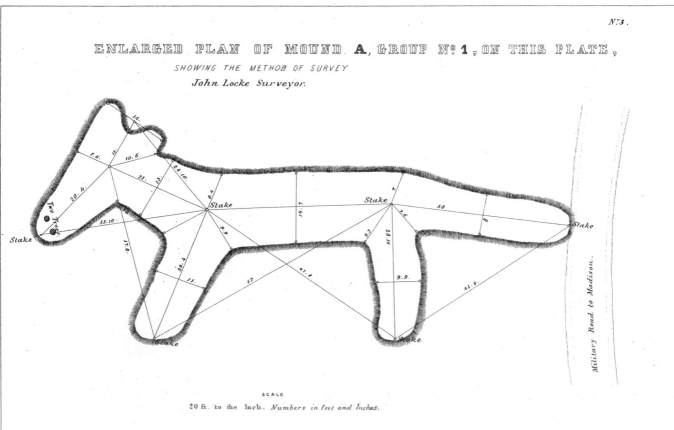

ENLARGED PLAN OF MOUND A, GROUP N.º 1, ON THIS PLATE,

SHOWING THE METHOD OF SURVEY

John Locke Surveyor.

Two Feet.

Stake *Stake* *Stake* *Stake* *Stake* *Stake*

Military Road to Madison.

SCALE

20 ft. to the Inch. *Numbers in feet and Inches.*

"Along the space of twenty miles from this position," observes Mr. R. S. Taylor, " extending to the Four Lakes eastward, similar monuments, intermixed with plain tumuli, are seen at almost every mile, in the lowest situations as well as crowning the highest swells of the prairies; and they are still more numerous all around those beautiful but almost unknown lakes. It would be a ceaseless repetition of similar forms to figure many of these."

PLATE XLI.

ANCIENT WORKS, DADE COUNTY, WISCONSIN.

NUMBER 1.—This group is figured both by Mr. R. C. TAYLOR and Prof. LOCKE, whose plans agree with great exactness. It occurs ten miles west of Madison, Dade county, Wisconsin. The old Indian trail, now the military road, runs between the nose of one animal and the tail of the other. They lie on the borders of an undulating prairie, at the edge of the woodland, upon a gentle slope. A short distance (five hundred or six hundred feet) to the west of them is a natural swell of ground, with an artificial circular tumulus on the top of it, overlooking the two figures. No. 3 on the same Plate illustrates the method of survey adopted by Prof. Locke, and also gives an enlarged plan of the more perfect figure of the group.* These effigies are the favorite resort of badgers, which, finding them raised and dry, have selected them for their burrows. Mr. Taylor suggests that these figures were intended to represent the fox. Prof. Locke, on the other hand, remarks that " they have an expression of agility and fleetness, and may have been intended to represent the cougar or American tiger, an animal still existing in that region."

NUMBER 2.—This group of works closely resembles that last described. One of the effigies (C) was opened by Prof. Locke. " It was composed of sand without any change to mark the original surface, although it is now overgrown with grass and covered with a thin black mould. The whole of the descent near the bottom of which the figure lies, has evidently been formed from the disintegration of the sandstone bluff contiguous; and at the time of the formation of this tumulus, it was most probably destitute of loam at this point, as it now is at a point nearer

---

* The measurements of this figure are given by Prof. Locke as follows, in feet and inches. *Triangles:* Eye to shoulder, 23 feet; shoulder to foot, 29,4; fore foot to eye, 37,8; eye to nose, 20,4; nose to shoulder, 35,10; eye to point half way between the ears, 11,0; shoulder to same point, 24,10; shoulder to hip, 38,4; fore foot to hip, 57,0; shoulder to hind foot, 47,8; hind foot to hip, 28,10; hip to tip of tail, 38; hind foot to tip of tail, 41,6. *Diameters:* Of neck, 13; fore leg, 11; body, 14,7; hind leg, 9,9; tail, 8. *Distances:* Eye to front, 7,6; ear to ear, 14; shoulder to armpit, 9,9; shoulder to back, 8,4; hip to rump, 7; hip to flank, 9,7; hip to insertion of tail, 7,6; length of throat, 12 feet.

the bluff. A section of the embankment, near the gap, exhibited a thin line of loam, even with what might be supposed to have been the surface of the ground. Alluvial stratification is positive proof that a formation is not artificial; but the absence of a base of mould is not proof of the same thing, for the surface of the earth may have been removed before the erection of the mound. In examining the tumuli of Wisconsin, I did not at any place discover a ditch or cavity from which the earth to construct them had been taken. They are uniformly raised from a smooth surface, always above inundation, and guarded from temporary currents produced by showers. The backs of the effigies are uniformly placed up hill."

PLATE XLII.

NUMBER 1.—This group of works is sufficiently well explained by the Plate itself. It is situated about two miles from the group last described, on the road to Madison. The large figure in the supplementary plan is about two thousand feet south-west of the embankment represented in the plan. "It appears to be solitary; lies on a low, level ground; and seems to be mutilated. If intended to represent an animal, the head is evidently too large, and the attitude stiff and rectangular."

NUMBER 2.—This singular group of works is situated upon section two, township eight, near the north bank of Wisconsin river, one and a half miles west of the principal meridian, Richland county, Wisconsin. It is minutely described by MR. S. TAYLOR. The figures composing the group are so arranged as to constitute a sort of enclosure of about half an acre area, which Mr. Taylor terms the "citadel." The ground is here prominent; to the north, south, and west of the embankments it has a graded descent; to the east it spreads into a broad plateau, upon which, as well as to the southward, are numerous other embankments of various forms and dimensions. From the top of the principal mound, occupying the centre of the group, and within four hundred yards to the westward, may be seen at least a hundred elevations similar to those forming the boundaries of the "citadel." "The elevation of these embankments generally is no more than *thirty inches,* and of the lesser mounds twenty inches, while the altitude of the large mound overlooking the whole group is ten feet. Exterior to the group, upon the east and north-east sides, excavations from which the earth had been removed are plainly indicated; and it was here, no doubt, that a portion of the material composing the structures was obtained. Notwithstanding the rank growth of vegetation upon these works, and the probability that they have been much reduced from their original height, the angles and terminations are quite visible. Near the north-east part of the group, part of the embankment appears to have been destroyed."

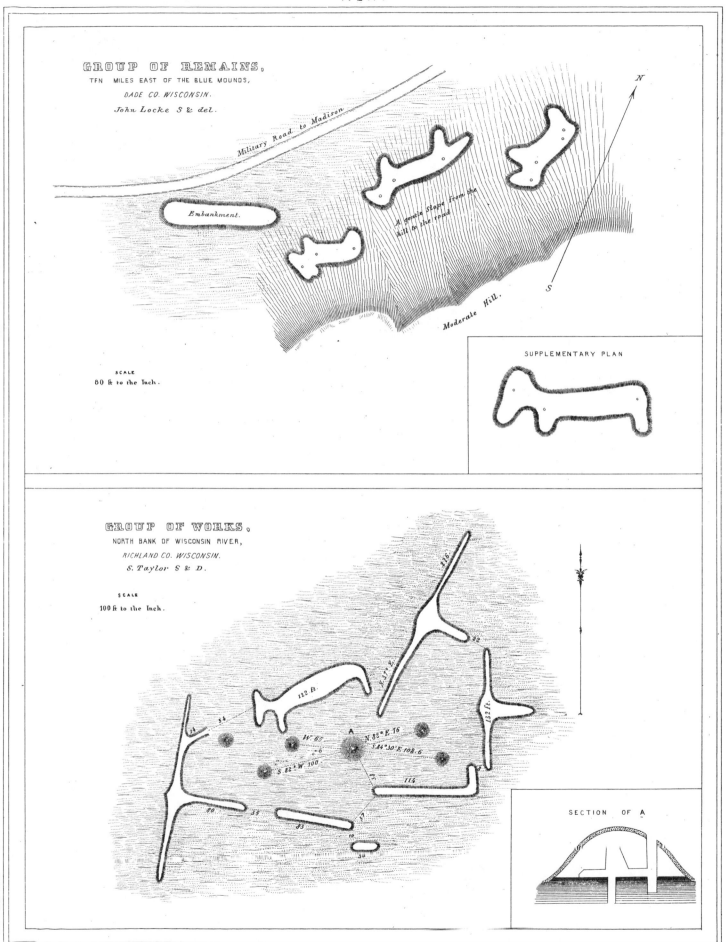

GROUP OF REMAINS,

TEN MILES EAST OF THE BLUE MOUNDS,

DADE CO. WISCONSIN.

John Locke S & del.

Military Road to Madison

Embankment.

A gentle Slope from the hill to the road

N

S

Moderate Hill.

SCALE
80 ft to the Inch.

SUPPLEMENTARY PLAN

GROUP OF WORKS,

NORTH BANK OF WISCONSIN RIVER,

RICHLAND CO. WISCONSIN.

S. Taylor S & D.

SCALE
100 ft to the Inch.

122 ft.

W. 65   A   N. 82° E. 76

S. 44° 30' E. 108.6

S. 82° W. 100

114

132 Ft.

80   55

93

SECTION OF A

Lith. by Sarony & Major

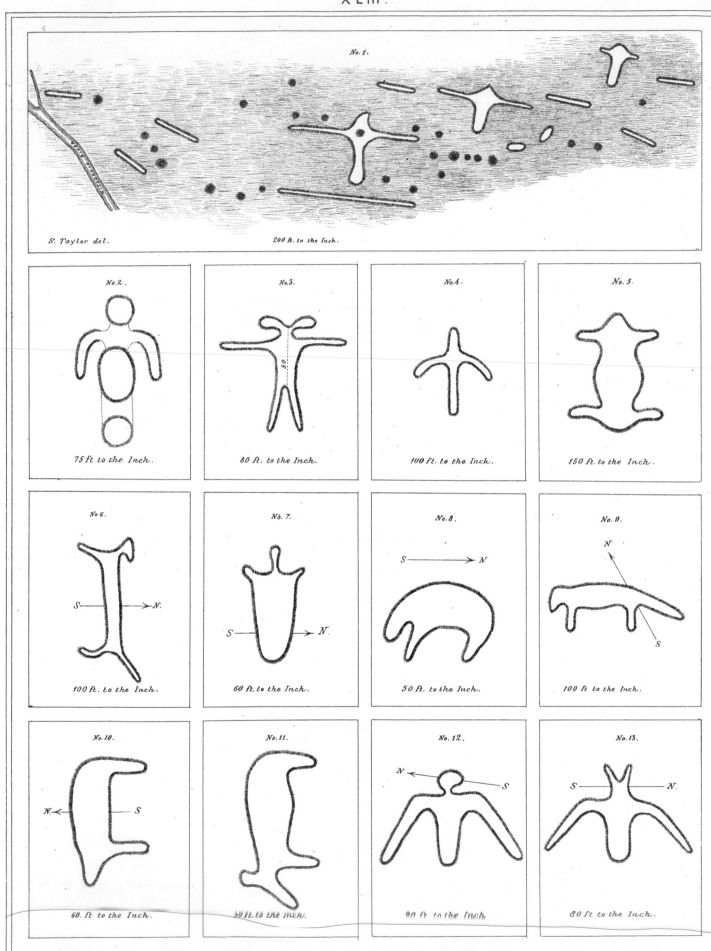

No. 1.

S. Taylor del.

200 ft. to the Inch.

No. 2.

75 ft. to the Inch.

No. 3.

50

80 ft. to the Inch.

No. 4.

100 ft. to the Inch.

No. 5.

150 ft. to the Inch.

No. 6.

S ⟶ N.

100 ft. to the Inch.

No. 7.

S ⟶ N.

60 ft. to the Inch.

No. 8.

S ⟶ N

50 ft. to the Inch.

No. 9.

N

S

100 ft. to the Inch.

No. 10.

N ⟵ S

60 ft. to the Inch.

No. 11.

50 ft. to the Inch.

No. 12.

N ⟵ S

80 ft. to the Inch.

No. 13.

S ⟶ N.

80 ft. to the Inch.

Lith by Sarony & Major.

The supplementary section, A, exhibits the excavation made by Mr. Taylor in the large central mound. " A shaft was sunk about midway from the top to the bottom of the mound. At the depth of eight feet the original sod was reached; it here assumes a different appearance from that which it possesses at the exposed surface, is hard and compact, resembling what is technically denominated 'hard pan,' caused perhaps by the pressure of the superincumbent earth. The mound is composed of ferruginous sand; and as it is free from any admixture, and is destitute of any appearance of stratification, it must have been built at one time, and not by contributions at intervals. The original sod is here about six inches thick; beneath it is the regular stratification of the plain. A shaft was carried along the original level for the space of fourteen feet, and some distance beyond the centre of the mound; but no remains of any kind were discovered."

———

PLATE XLIII.

NUMBER 1.—This interesting group of remains is situated in the village of Muscoda, (English Prairie,) Grant county, Wisconsin. It is described as follows, by Mr. S. TAYLOR: " The late cultivation of these grounds has in a measure obliterated these works, many of them being in the streets and commons; and the village in its future increase may destroy them entirely. In the group are three figures in the form of a cross [bird?]; in the centre of the largest of them is a depression, perhaps caused by an Indian *caché*. The outlines of the various figures are easily traced, although their elevation at this time does not exceed thirty inches. From the excavations around many of them, it is apparent that they must have been constructed with materials obtained adjacent to them. Some of these mounds however seem to have successfully resisted the abrasions of time; those towards the south-western portion of the group are six feet in height. The distance, from one to the other of the group here represented, is about four hundred and sixty yards. The site is a beautiful arenaceous loam, free from trees and shrubbery, so that a view of the entire group is commanded from the summit of some of the more prominent mounds. Human bones have been found in many of these."

NUMBER 2 is situated on the north-east part of Sec. 35 N., and is within a mile of the Wisconsin river. It occupies an eminence, and is the centre of a group of mounds, fifteen in number, extending the distance of three hundred yards, and placed at intervals of about twenty-five feet apart. " It appears to have been originally constructed as represented by the dotted lines, having at those points an elevation of about three feet. Additional earth seems then to have been heaped upon the head and breast, elevating those points to the height of six feet."

NUMBER 3 occurs about a mile to the westward of group No. 1, just described. "It represents a human figure having two heads, which gracefully recline over the shoulders. It is well preserved. The arms are disproportionately long; their full length is not exhibited in the plan for want of room. The various parts of the figure are gracefully rounded; the stomach and breast are full and well proportioned. DIMENSIONS.—*Widths:* from one arm-pit over the breast to the other, twenty-five feet; over arm at shoulders, twelve, and tapering to four feet at the extremities; over hips, twenty; over legs, near the body, eight, and tapering to five; over figure above the shoulders, fifteen; over each neck, eight; over the heads, ten. *Lengths:* of body, fifty feet; arms, one hundred and thirty; neck and heads, fifteen. *Elevations:* of breast, shoulders, and abdomen, thirty-six inches; arms at the junction of the shoulders, same height, diminishing towards their extremities to ten inches; the thighs near the trunk are twenty, at the feet but ten inches in height."

NUMBER 4 lies about four miles west of the village of Muscoda. It may have been intended to represent a bird, a bow and arrow, or the human figure. In the forest near this work are extensive groups of ancient monuments.

NUMBER 5 is situated on the Wisconsin river, east of the fourth principal meridian. The length of this figure is one hundred and fifty feet; elevation three feet. Mr. S. Taylor suggests that it is intended to represent the frog; it approaches nearer the form of a turtle. There are other works of a similar shape near by; also some in the form of a cross, mammillary mounds, and parallelograms.

NUMBER 6 occurs near group No. 1 of this plate. "It seems to have been intended to represent some fleet animal. It is one hundred feet in length, and eighteen inches high."

NUMBER 7 is found not far from that last described, and is supposed by Mr. Taylor to represent the turtle. It is seventy-six feet in length, and its greatest height is thirty inches. It is a common figure in Wisconsin.

NUMBER 8 was situated in Richland county, Wisconsin. Mr. Taylor thinks it was intended to represent a bear. It was fifty-six feet long, and twenty inches high. It has lately been destroyed by the passage of a road over it.

NUMBER 9 occurs in the vicinity of No. 2, and is the terminating figure of the series of which that is the centre. Earthworks of this form are common in Richland county.

NUMBER 10, near Blue river, English Prairie; length eighty-four feet, height six feet; supposed to represent a bear.

NUMBER 11 is found near No. 4. It is very perfect in outline; seventy-nine

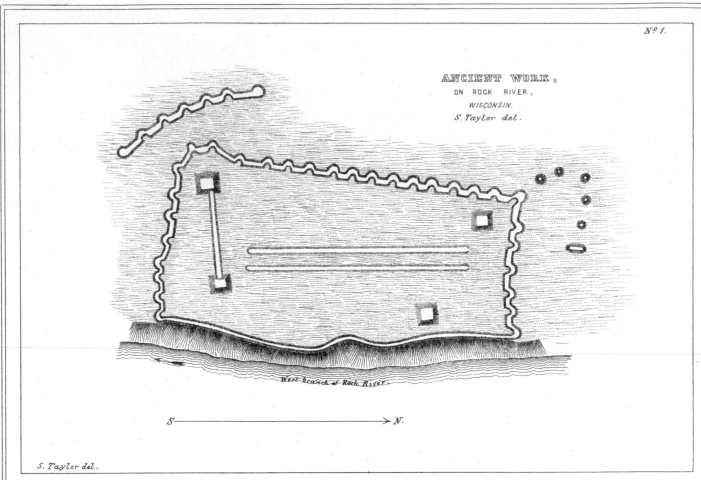

ANCIENT WORK,
ON ROCK RIVER,
WISCONSIN.
S. Taylor del.

S. Taylor del.

West branch of Rock River.

S —————————→ N.

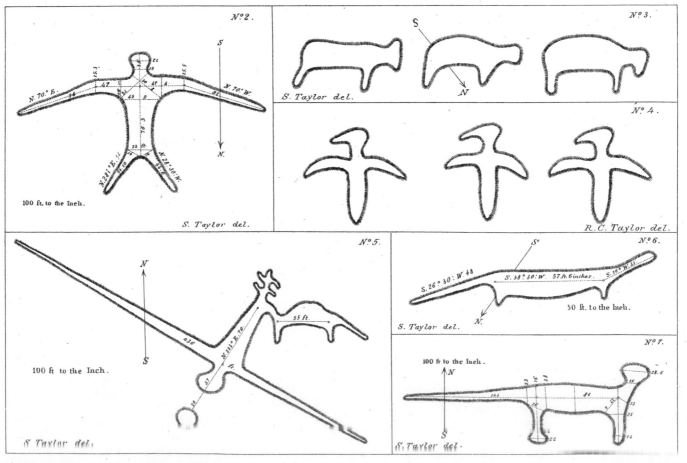

Nº 2.

N. 70° E. 84   N. 70° W.

N. 28° E. 51   N. 28° 30′ W.

100 ft. to the Inch.

S. Taylor del.

Nº 3.
S

S. Taylor del.
N

Nº 4.

R.C. Taylor del.

Nº 5.

55 ft.

100 ft to the Inch.

S. Taylor del.

Nº 6.
S

S. 26° 30′ W. 48   S. 38° 30′ W. 57 ft. 6 inches.   S. 76° W. 41

50 ft. to the Inch.

S. Taylor del.

Nº 7.

100 ft to the Inch.

S. Taylor del.

Face P. 131.   Lith. by Sarony & Major 177 Fulton St. N.Y.

feet long, and twenty-four broad. "Throughout this region," observes Mr. S. Taylor, "embankments of this form are very numerous: some have two parallel projections from the back of the head; in the present case they seem to be so blended as to represent but one."

NUMBER 12, one mile from the English Prairie, represents, according to Mr. S. Taylor, "a species of mounds which, under various modifications, are very numerous, comprising about one fifth of the embossed works of the region in which it occurs. The elevation of the figure, as well as of the group of which it forms a part, is about four feet. Between the base of the trunk and the southern wing, is a mound twenty-one feet in diameter, and five feet high." Supposed to represent a bird with wings partially expanded.

NUMBER 13, designated the "horned bird" by Mr. Taylor, is situated in the county of Grant, upon S. 16, T. 8, R. 1, W., where an extensive group of several hundreds may be seen.

———

PLATE XLIV.

NUMBER 1.—The only enclosure in Wisconsin at all resembling those of a lower latitude, or which seems to partake of a defensive character, is situated upon the west branch of Rock river, township seven, of range fourteen east, in the Milwaukie land district. It is known as the city or ruins of Aztalan. Several brief notices of this work have appeared in the public prints; the only account, however, which is at all satisfactory, was communicated, together with an illustrative map, by Mr. S. Taylor, to the American Journal of Science and Arts, in 1843.

This work, although possessing several features peculiar to itself, has others closely resembling those that characterize the works bordering the Gulf. It is described as situated in a beautiful rolling country, conveniently interspersed with timber, and watered by Rock river and its tributaries. It is said to consist of a "brick wall" five feet high by twenty-five feet base, enclosing an area of twenty acres, and having the general outline of an oblong square. Upon three sides the wall is interrupted, at intervals of from two to five rods, by *bastions* of the same height as the main wall, and extending seventeen feet beyond it. The inner wall, extending along the bank of the river, is much lighter than those upon the remaining sides, and is destitute of the singular feature last mentioned. Within this enclosure are a number of truncated pyramids, forty or fifty feet square upon the top, and between fifteen and twenty in height. Two of these are connected with each other by an elevated way, after the manner of some of the Mississippi and Louisiana structures. (See Plate XXXIX.) Two parallel ways or embankments are carried longitudinally, nearly the whole length of the enclosure. Several conical mounds are mentioned in the description as occurring within the enclosure, but do not appear in the plan. Quite a number occur just exterior to the walls, some of which are represented to be of large size. Covering the south-west angle is a crescent-form work of considerable extent, which also has bastions at intervals throughout its length. A cellar and stairway within one of the square mounds, and a subterranean passage *arched with stone*, are mentioned as existing here; but they lack confirmation and deserve little credit.

The walls, which are described as being built of *brick*, are composed of clay, probably burned on the spot. Whether they are burned throughout, has not yet been ascertained, and can only be determined by removing a section of the wall. It will doubtless be found that the burning is superficial, resulting from the combustion of some wooden superstructure, or from design. We shall be warranted in ascribing the use of burned bricks to the race which built these works, only upon the most conclusive evidence, and such we do not at present possess.* The walls of many of the enclosures in the Scioto valley appear to have been slightly burned. (See page 28.)

The plan of the work presented by Mr. Taylor is palpably an imperfect one. No gateways or entrances are represented, nor is the scale upon which the work is laid down exhibited,—omissions which would not be likely to occur in a plan made after accurate survey. A complete map and description of this work, such as its singular character merits, is a desideratum.

This is the only work with projections partaking of the character of bastions, which has fallen under notice, and is in this respect remarkable.

That these projections were designed to subserve the purposes to which bastions are applied in modern fortification is not clear. The object of the bastion is to enfilade the wall of the defence, so as to preclude an enemy from approaching it or carrying on his operations under its shelter. Hence they are placed at such intervals as may easily be swept or commanded by the weapons in use; the distance of a bow-shot apart would therefore be adequate to all the purposes for which their erection is required. So far from this being the case in the work under notice, it appears that they are placed at the short intervals of from thirty to eighty feet. This circumstance, though not conclusive on the point, would seem to indicate that they were not constructed for the purpose which we should be apt at first glance to assign to them.

NUMBER 2.—" Among the various works of antiquity in this region," observes Mr. S. Taylor, " those in the form of men are numerous. This figure forms one of an extensive series of these works, of various shapes, situated upon S. 35, T. 9, R. 1, W. of 4th M., in the margin of a forest, and is covered with large trees. It is truly a giant, measuring from the extremity of one arm to that of the other,

---

* The authors have the assurance of a gentleman for some time connected with the Milwaukie Land Office, and who is every way qualified to judge in the matter, that the walls are of clay, probably only superficially burned, and possess no indications of having been composed of bricks. The representations to the contrary have probably been the result of misapprehension.

two hundred and seventy-nine feet, and from the top of the head to the end of the trunk, one hundred and eleven feet. Its shoulders, head, and breast, are elevated four feet. In the centre of the breast is quite a depression, probably once used as a place of concealment for provisions by the French, called a *caché*. About a mile to the north of this figure is another of human shape and like magnitude, accompanied by a large group of works. Among them is a large mound two hundred feet in circumference, and fifteen in height."

NUMBER 3.—This group occurs upon the English Prairie, within the limits of Iowa county, Wisconsin. "In the vicinity of these are many other figures of various forms and dimensions. To the eastward commences a series of mammillary mounds, varying from one to two and a half feet in height. They are beautifully and with much regularity arranged at intervals, and extend to the distance of about fifteen hundred feet, terminating abruptly in a mound eighteen feet in height, and two hundred and twenty-five in circumference. To the north and south of the figures, and parallel with them, are numerous embankments with passage-ways through them."

NUMBER 4.—This group is also situated in the vicinity of English Prairie. But half of the figures are represented; the remainder are of the same forms, supposed to represent birds.

NUMBER 5.—"The site of this remarkable work is upon an eminence, near Eagle Mills, Richland county, Wisconsin. It seems to be a combination of two figures, one representing the buffalo, perhaps, and the other a man. Immediately to the south-west, and within twenty feet of the head of this figure, commences a series of mounds, mostly conical."

NUMBER 6 is near Blue river, English Prairie. Its outlines are very distinct; probably designed to represent the otter or a lizard. Figures of the kind are quite common.

NUMBER 7 is in the village of Muscoda, county of Grant. Its length is two hundred and sixty-four feet; height thirty inches.

There are many rectangular and some circular figures in addition to the animal-

Fig. 26.

shaped effigies of which so many examples have been given. Fig. 26 represents the manner in which they are often combined. This example is from the great group on the English Prairie. Individual figures might be multiplied, but enough have been presented to convey a general idea of the character of these singular monuments. A complete survey of the field of their occurrence might disclose a dependence between the various groups, and go far towards explaining the mystery of their origin and purposes.

Some of these mounds have been excavated and found to contain human remains in all parts, while the excavations in others have been attended with no such developments.   Those examined by Prof. Locke and Mr. S. Taylor revealed no deposits.   Mr. R. C. Taylor mentions that twelve mounds, near Red Bank on the Fox river, were opened in 1837, and found to contain human bones in a very advanced stage of decomposition.   One of the mounds was an animal-shaped structure, one hundred and fifty feet in length.   The position of the skeletons indicated that the bodies had been placed upon the original surface previous to being heaped over.   There were no appearances of excavation beneath the surface in any of the interments.   It may be suggested that the human remains found in these mounds were deposited by the existing tribes of Indians, a suggestion which derives great force from the fact that both the Messrs. Taylor concur in representing that many of the Indians to this day bury in these structures, conceiving that they were originally designed for that purpose, although they possess no tradition respecting their origin.   Some of the Indians, on the other hand, express the belief that the mounds in the form of animals were made by the " *Great Manitou*," and are indicative of a plentiful supply of game in the world of spirits.   At any rate, they are regarded with reverence by all the Indians, and are never disturbed by them, except for purposes of sepulture.

Proceeding upon the assumption that they were designed as burial-places, Mr. R. C. Taylor ingeniously suggests that their forms were intended to designate the cemeteries of the respective tribes or families to which they belonged: thus, the tribe, clan, or family possessing as its characteristic *totem*, blazon, or emblem, the Bear, constructed the burial-place of its members in the form of that animal; the clans having the Panther, Turtle, Eagle, or other animal or object for their *totems*, respectively conforming to the same practice.   Upon this hypothesis we can readily conceive the ancient inhabitant to have possessed the same anxiety to be buried in his family tomb which we see exhibited at this day, among our own people, " to rest in the sepulchres of their fathers."   Mr. Taylor discreetly remarks, however, that there is no evidence to show that any existing tribes of Indians ever erected such monuments, but that, on the contrary, they acknowledge the profoundest ignorance of their origin.   He advances the suggestion only as a plausible conjecture, in the absence of any satisfactory solution of the problem, which still remains unsolved.

What significance may attach to the fact that they occur mainly on the great lines of traverse between the Mississippi and Lake Michigan, or to the further fact that most if not all of these groups have one or more conical mounds so placed as to command a view of the remainder, it is not undertaken to say.*   That similar works are found in the central and western portions of Michigan, as

---

* "The choice, in selecting the sites of these monuments of ancient days, appears to have been influenced mainly by their contiguity to the lakes and principal rivers, and to those great lines of interior communication, which, from an unknown period, traversed this country.   *   *   *   These mounds are almost invariably contiguous to Indian paths, whose narrow but deeply-worn tracks attest their extreme antiquity and long use."—*R. C. Taylor.*

well as in Wisconsin, we have the assurance of witnesses whose statements are entitled to full credit. Whether they are identical with those noticed above is unknown; their character remains to be ascertained.* The few animal effigies found in Ohio, and of which an account has already been given, seem to have few features in common with those of the North-west, and probably, in their purposes, admit of less doubt. We cannot venture to assign a similar origin to the latter,— certainly not, until we are in possession of more facts concerning them, whereon to base our conclusions.

The absence of enclosures, or works of defence, (such as are found in great numbers in the Ohio valley,) in connection with these animal effigies, has been noticed in a preceding page. It appears that the effigies themselves, accompanied by short, low lines of embankment, are sometimes so arranged as nearly to enclose certain areas; whether the arrangement resulted from design or accident is not however very apparent.

Such is the extent of our knowledge respecting the monuments of Wisconsin. Carver mentions earthworks in the vicinity of Lake Pepin; and it is reasonable to conclude that they are scattered, in greater or less profusion, over the intervening territory. Of this, however, we are still uninformed. It would be an interesting point to determine the range of the mound effigies, and whether they merge gradually into the works of a lower latitude, or whether they occupy an exclusive field, and possess characteristics sufficiently striking to warrant us in ascribing them to a different race or era. Their purposes, in our present state of information concerning them, do not seem to be satisfactorily settled: it is still a matter of doubt whether they are sepulchral in their origin, connected with the superstitions of their builders, or erected as the monuments and memorials of migrations and events unrecorded by the pen of history. Certain it is that they are now invaded by a busy population, careless alike of their origin and of their future fate, before whose encroachments they are rapidly disappearing. Already the plough has broken in upon the outlines and symmetry of hundreds, and unless the present favorable moment is seized upon to secure their accurate admeasurement and delineation, these embossed illustrations of our ancient history will be obliterated forever. It is impossible to estimate their value in the elucidation of the grand ethnological problems involved in the past history of our country, until their extent and dependencies as well as their general character are better understood.

In the State of Missouri, and especially in the country lying between the Missouri and Arkansas rivers, various singular remains are represented to exist, which differ materially from those that have been noticed in the preceding pages.

---

* No accurate account of them has yet been published; and it is, consequently, uncertain whether any bear the form of animals. They are rather vaguely described as low elevations of considerable extent and well defined outline, somewhat resembling garden beds. Mr. Schoolcraft speaks of these remains as existing in considerable numbers on the Elkhart, St. Joseph's, Kalamazoo, and Grand rivers. According to the same authority, no large tumuli or *Teocalli* occur in connection with them. Similar monuments, it will be observed, are found in the State of Missouri.

These are said to consist of the ruins of towns, sometimes of great size, regularly laid out, in streets and squares. Dr. BECK mentions one of these ruined towns in Gasconade county, (probably now falling within the county of Crawford, erected out of Gasconade,) in which the sites of houses, possessing foundations of stone, are distinctly visible. Stone walls are said to occur in some parts of the area, covered by heaps of earth.* The same author describes several works of stone displaying, in his estimation, great architectural skill, which occur on Osage river and Buffalo creek, one of its tributaries. One said to exist on Noyer's creek, near the town of Louisiana, Pike county, has been particularly noticed. " It presents the dilapidated remains of a building constructed of rough, unhewn stones, fifty-six feet long and twenty-two broad, embracing several divisions and chambers. The walls are from two to five feet high. Eighty rods eastward of this structure is found a smaller one, of similar construction. The narrow apartments are said to be arched with stone, one course overlapping the other, after the manner of the edifices of Central America."† Nothing of this character has been observed elsewhere, and it is extremely probable that there is some mistake in the matter. If works answering to this description really exist, at the points mentioned, they deserve the careful attention of the archæologist. It is suspected that they will not bear a rigid scrutiny, such as is required to a proper substantiation. Our authority observes, that " these remains form a class of antiquities entirely distinct from the walled towns, fortifications, barriers, or mounds; and that the regularity and other peculiarities of structure which they display, favor the conclusion that they are the remains of a race different from those who erected the former, and who were familiar with the rules of architecture, and perhaps with a perfect system of warfare."‡

I. DILLE, Esq., of Newark, Ohio, in a communication addressed to the authors, presents the following facts respecting the remains of Missouri, which cannot fail to prove interesting in this connection: " I have been much interested in a singular kind of antiquities found in the State of Missouri. They have been mentioned, but not described, by various writers. They consist of small tumuli, generally raised about twelve or eighteen inches above the surface, and have the general form of an ellipse, measuring usually twenty-five by eighteen feet. They are very numerous, particularly upon the head waters of the St. Francis river, and are always near streams and water-courses. I have dug into several, but never succeeded in finding anything except coals and a few pieces of rude pottery. Hence I have concluded they are the remains of mud-houses. They are always arranged in straight lines, with broad streets intervening between them, crossing each other

---

* Beck's Gazetteer of Missouri, p. 234.   † Ibid. p. 306.

‡ Dr. BECK also mentions another stone work, described to him by Gen. Ashley, as situated upon a high cliff on the west side of the Gasconade river, from whence it commands an extensive prospect. It is represented to be from twenty-five to thirty feet square; and, although in ruins, exhibits an uncommon degree of regularity. From the monument leads a devious path, extending down the cliff to the entrance of a cave, in which was found a quantity of ashes.

at right angles. In different villages their distance apart varies, but is generally uniform in the same group. Sometimes they are as near as ten paces to each other, while in other instances they are separated twenty or thirty paces. These ruined villages are numerous in the vicinity of Mine la Motte.* The town of Frederickton stands upon one of these sites. I have noticed in them the usual prerogative of power,—the largest houses are always nearest the water, and the smallest most distant. It would appear that the selection of the site was governed by the convenience of water alone; the principals taking the nearest position to the stream. I have counted upwards of two hundred of these mounds in a single group. Arrow-heads of jasper and agate, and axes of sienite and porphyry, have been found in these vicinities. No other remains of a remarkable character have, so far as I am aware, been discovered."†

It may be conjectured, that the remains here mentioned are the traces of Indian villages. The Mandans, Minatarees, and some other tribes, built their huts of earth, resting on a framework of wood. Previous to their erection, however, the soil was excavated to the depth of about two feet, and the ruins of their towns are designated rather by depressions than elevations. It is also well known that their lodges were grouped without regularity, and close together, with just enough room between them to permit of moving about.‡ The sites of most of the Indian towns are only indicated by the graves in their vicinity, and by the bones and fragments of rude pottery scattered over the surface.

Besides these remains, there are numerous others in the valley of the Missouri, bearing a close resemblance to those upon the Ohio and its branches. Lewis and Clarke describe a very extensive series of works, one thousand miles up the Missouri, embracing an area of about four hundred acres. It is situated upon a peninsula formed by a bend of the river, and consists of two long walls, from six to fifteen feet in height, and from seventy-five to one hundred feet broad at the

---

* Remains, similar to those here described, are abundant in Peru, where they indicate the sites of ancient towns and cities. The streets are always easily traced, and cross each other at right angles with great regularity. "The sites of the houses or huts are generally marked by heaps of earth; though in some instances the walls of the larger structures remain, in part, standing. These walls are represented to be three feet in thickness. Some of these towns are enclosed by fortifications, which have now crumbled down so as to present the simple appearance of earth embankments. The remains of one of these ancient towns, occurring midway between Truxillo and Huanchuco, cover several miles in extent."—*Proctor*.

† It is probable the remains here described are similar to those observed by Lewis and Clarke, on the Missouri, some distance above the mouth of the Platte. "At ten miles above our encampment, we examined a curious collection of graves or mounds, on the south side of the river. Not far from a low piece of land and a pond, is a tract about two hundred acres in extent, which is covered with mounds of various shapes and sizes: some of sand, and some of both earth and sand; the largest being nearest the river. These mounds indicate the position of the ancient village of the Ottoes, before they retired to the protection of the Pawnees."—*Lewis and Clark*, p. 26.

‡ Catlin's North American Indians, vol. i. p. 82; Breckenridge's Voyage up the Missouri, (Views of Louisiana,) p. 248. "Imagine you see a heap of cabins without order or design, some like cart houses, others like tubs, built of bark, supported by posts, sometimes plastered on the outside with mud in a coarse manner; in a word built with less art, neatness, and solidity, than the cabins of the beaver; and you have an Indian village."—*Charlevoix's Travels in Canada*, vol. ii. p. 127.

base, one of which is six thousand feet long and extends across the isthmus, the other runs along the bank of the stream. The extremity of one of the long walls terminates in a species of citadel, of semi-circular shape, which has horn-works and curtains defending the gateways, and also protected ways to the river. Here are a number of mounds and excavations similar, in all respects, to those characterizing the defensive works generally. This work is not entire, having evidently been greatly encroached upon by the river, which is constantly under-mining the elevated terrace upon which it stands. Still beyond this point, upon the Platte, Kanzas, and the numerous other tributaries of the Missouri, many large and interesting works are said to occur.* They have been remarked high up the streams, in the valleys overlooked by the Rocky Mountains. But little more than the fact of their existence is known; of their character we are ignorant.

In the vicinity of the city of St. Louis formerly existed a very large and interesting group of works, consisting mainly of a series of mounds so arranged as to constitute the sides of a parallelogram. These mounds were generally square or oblong, with level summits. Some were terraced, bearing a close relationship to those in Mississippi and Louisiana. A few conical mounds occurred in connection with them, but there was neither embankment nor ditch. All were situated upon the second terrace.

The most interesting feature of the group is the singular work yet preserved, denominated the " Falling Garden." This, as described by James, consists of a succession of terraces, artificially formed from the bank of the natural terrace, which is here upwards of fifty feet in height. The lowest of these terraces is eighty-seven feet broad by one hundred and fourteen long; the second is fifty-one feet, and the third thirty feet wide. Their slopes are regular, and the aspect of the structure that of a Mexican teocalli of four stages.†

Structures of brick are mentioned as occurring both in Missouri and Arkansas, but their existence is not sufficiently well authenticated. There are, without doubt, numerous remains scattered over the territory embraced in Arkansas, Texas, and New Mexico; and it is not impossible that their investigation would result in developing the fact that there is a gradual transition, from the earth-works of the Mississippi to the more imposing structures of brick and stone of Mexico and Central America.‡

---

* Lewis and Clarke, p. 48.

† Views of Louisiana, p. 189 ; James, Expedition to Rocky Mountains, vol. i. p. 314.

‡ " The distance from the large mounds on the Red river to those in New Spain is not so great, but that they may be regarded as existing within the same country."—*Breckenridge.*

GREAT MOUND AT MARIETTA, OHIO.

Chas. Sullivan, del.

From an Original painting in possession of A. Nye Esq. Marietta.

LITH. BY SARONY & MAJOR NEW YORK.

CHAPTER VI.

EARTHWORKS—THE MOUNDS.

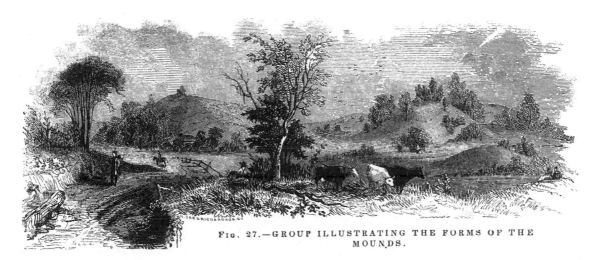

FIG. 27.—GROUP ILLUSTRATING THE FORMS OF THE
MOUNDS.

IN connection more or less intimate with the various earthworks already described, are the TUMULI or MOUNDS. Together, these two classes of remains constitute a single system of works, and are the monuments of the same people. And while the enclosures impress us with the number and power of the nations which built them, and enlighten us as to the amount of military knowledge and skill which they possessed, as well as, in some degree, in respect to the nature of their superstitions,—the mounds and their contents, as disclosed by the mattock and the spade, serve to reflect light more particularly upon their customs and the condition of the arts among them. Within these mounds we must look for the only authentic remains of their builders. They are the principal depositories of ancient art; they cover the bones of the distinguished dead of remote ages; and hide from the profane gaze of invading races the altars of the ancient people.

A simple heap of earth or stones seems to have been the first monument which suggested itself to man; the pyramid, the arch, and the obelisk are evidences of a more advanced state. But rude as are these primitive memorials, they have been but little impaired by time, while other more imposing structures have sunk into shapeless ruins. When covered with forests, and their surfaces interlaced with the roots of trees and bushes, or when protected by turf, the humble mound bids defiance to the elements which throw down the temple and crumble the marble into dust. We therefore find them, little changed from their original proportions, side by side with the ruins of those proud edifices which mark the advanced, as the former do the primitive state of the people who built them. They are scattered over

India; they dot the steppes of Siberia and the vast region north of the Black Sea; they line the shores of the Bosphorus and Mediterranean; they are found in old Scandinavia, and are singularly numerous in the British islands. In America, they prevail from the great lakes of the north, through the valley of the Mississippi, and the seats of semi-civilization in Mexico, Central America, and Peru, even to the waters of the La Plata on the south. We find them also on the shores of the Pacific ocean, near the mouth of the Columbia river, and on the Colorado of California. With the character of those abroad we have little, at present, to do, except perhaps to note some of the more striking features which they exhibit in common with those of our own valley.

Allusion has already been made to the number and dimensions of the mounds of the West. To say that they are innumerable in the ordinary use of the term would be no exaggeration. They may literally be numbered by thousands and tens of thousands. In form, as observed in a preceding chapter, they are generally simple cones, frequently truncated and sometimes terraced. They are also elliptical, pear-shaped, or of a square pyramidal form,—in the last case always truncated, and most usually having one or more graded ascents to their summits. These varieties are partially illustrated in the cut at the head of this chapter, and will be amply exhibited in the pages which follow. No doubt can be entertained that their forms were, in great part, determined by the purposes for which they were designed, and may therefore be of use to us in ascertaining their character. Thus, if any were designed to serve as the sites of temples, or as "high places" for the performance of religious rites and ceremonies, it is evident they would be constructed with special reference to these objects.

In common with the enclosures, the mounds are for the most part composed of earth, though stone mounds are by no means rare. They are sometimes composed entirely of clay, while the soil all around them, for a long distance, is gravel or loam. The object of this may perhaps be found in the fact that mounds composed of such materials better resist the action of the elements, and preserve their form. There is certainly no difference in their position or contents which would justify the supposition that any peculiar dependence existed between the material composing the mound and the purposes to which it was devoted. Whether any significance may attach to the predominance of stone, in some of the mounds, is a question difficult to answer. It occasionally happens that a mound of stone occurs in the midst of a group composed of earth. Such was the case with one which formerly stood within the limits of Chillicothe. As a general rule, however, the mound is composed of material found upon the spot or taken from pits near by; and stone mounds oftenest occur where, from the hardness of the soil or the abundance of stones, it would be easiest to construct the tumulus of the latter material.

In respect to the position of the mounds, it may be said that those of Ohio occur mostly within or near enclosures; sometimes in groups, but oftener detached and isolated, and seldom with any degree of regularity in respect to each other. Such is believed to be the case *generally* throughout the entire valley of the Mississippi. A section of the Ohio valley, however, embraced between the mouths of the Guyandotte and Scioto rivers, an extent of sixty miles, which was examined with special reference to this point, exhibited no works of magnitude in the form of enclosures; yet there was an abundance of mounds, though chiefly of small dimensions. Occasional groups of fifteen or twenty were noticed, sometimes occurring in lines, as if placed with design; a circumstance easily accounted for by the nature of the ground, which is here broken into long, low swells, or narrow ridges, with marshy intervals between them,—the mounds occupying the summits of the ridges.

On the tops of the hills, and on the jutting points of the table lands bordering the valleys in which the earthworks are found, mounds occur in considerable

FIG. 28.—HILL MOUNDS.

numbers. The most elevated and commanding positions are frequently crowned with them, suggesting at once the purposes to which some of the mounds or *cairns* of the ancient Celts were applied, that of signal or alarm posts. It is not unusual to find detached mounds among the hills back from the valleys and in secluded places, with no other monuments near. The hunter often encounters them in the depths of the forests, when least expected; perhaps overlooking some waterfall, or placed in some narrow valley where the foot of man seldom enters.

Thus much respecting the mounds could not escape observation, and has long been known; but beyond this our information has been extremely limited. And though partial excavations have been made at various times by different individuals, still nothing like a systematic exploration, sufficiently thorough and extensive to warrant any conclusion respecting them, has hitherto been attempted. The few detached observations which have met the light have been too vague, and in many cases too poorly authenticated, to enable the inquirer to make any satisfactory deductions from them.

The popular opinion, however, based in a great degree upon the well ascertained purposes of the barrows and tumuli occurring in certain parts of Europe and Asia, is that they are simple monuments, marking the last resting-place of some great chief or distinguished individual, among the tribes of the builders. Some have supposed them to be the cemeteries, in which were deposited the dead of a tribe or a village for a certain period, and that the size of the mound is an indication of the number inhumed; others, that they mark the sites of great battles, and contain the bones of the slain. On all hands the opinion has been entertained, that they were devoted to sepulture alone. This received opinion is not, however, sustained by the investigations here recorded. The conclusion to which these researches have led, is, that the mounds were constructed for several grand and dissimilar purposes; or rather, that they are of different classes. The conditions upon which the classification is founded are four in number,—namely: position, form, structure, and contents. In this classification, we distinguish—

1st. ALTAR MOUNDS, which occur either within, or in the immediate vicinity of enclosures; which are stratified, and contain altars of burned clay or stone; and which were places of sacrifice.

2d. MOUNDS OF SEPULTURE, which stand isolated or in groups more or less remote from the enclosures; which are not stratified; which contain human remains; and which were the burial places and monuments of the dead.

3d. TEMPLE MOUNDS, which occur most usually within, but sometimes without the walls of enclosures; which possess great regularity of form; which contain neither altars nor human remains; and which were "High Places" for the performance of religious rites and ceremonies, the sites of structures, or in some way connected with the superstitions of the builders.

4th. ANOMALOUS MOUNDS, including mounds of observation and such as were applied to a double purpose, or of which the design and objects are not apparent. This division includes all which do not clearly fall within the preceding three classes.

These classes are broadly marked in the aggregate, though in some instances it is difficult to determine the character of the mounds which fall under notice. Of one hundred mounds examined, sixty were altar or temple mounds; twenty sepulchral; and twenty either places of observation or anomalous in their character. Such, however, is not the proportion in which they occur. From the fact that the altar or sacrificial mounds are most interesting and productive in relics, the largest number excavated was of that class. Excluding the temple mounds, which are not numerous, the remaining mounds of the Scioto valley are distributed between the three other varieties in very nearly equal proportions.

These general observations will serve to introduce plans and sections with accompanying descriptions of each of the above classes of mounds. The sections, for obvious reasons, are not drawn upon a uniform scale, nor are the relative proportions of the mounds always preserved; this however will result in no misunderstanding in any essential particulars.

ALTAR OR SACRIFICIAL MOUNDS.

THE general characteristics of this class of mounds are:

1st. That they occur only within, or in the immediate vicinity of enclosures or sacred places.* Of the whole number of mounds of this class which were examined, *four* only were found to be exterior to the walls of enclosures, and these were but a few rods distant from them.

2d. That they are stratified.

3d. That they contain symmetrical altars of burned clay or stone; on which are deposited various remains, which in all cases have been more or less subjected to the action of fire.

The fact of stratification, in these mounds, is one of great interest and importance. This feature has heretofore been remarked, but not described with proper accuracy; and has consequently proved an impediment to the recognition of the artificial origin of the mounds, by those who have never seen them. The stratification, so far as observed, is not horizontal, but always conforms to the convex outline of the mound.† Nor does it resemble the stratification produced by the action of water, where the layers run into each other, but is defined with the utmost distinctness, and always terminates upon reaching the level of the surrounding earth. That it is artificial will however, be sufficiently apparent after an examination of one of the mounds in which the feature occurs; for it would be difficult to explain, by what singular combination of "igneous and aqueous" action, stratified mounds were always raised over symmetrical monuments of burned clay or of stone.

The altars, or basins, found in these mounds, are almost invariably of burned clay, though a few of stone have been discovered. They are symmetrical, but not of uniform size and shape. Some are round, others elliptical, and others square, or parallelograms. Some are small, measuring barely two feet across, while others are fifty feet long by twelve or fifteen feet wide. The usual dimensions are from five to eight feet. All appear to have been modelled of fine clay brought to the spot from a distance, and they rest upon the original surface of the

---

* It is not assumed to say that *all* the mounds occurring within enclosures are altar or sacrificial mounds. On the contrary, some are found which, to say the least, are *anomalous;* while others were clearly the *sites of structures,* or temple mounds.

† Some of the mounds on the lower Mississippi, as we have already seen in the chapter on the aboriginal monuments of the Southern States, are horizontally stratified, exhibiting numerous layers, from base to summit. These mounds differ in form from the conical structures here referred to, and were perhaps constructed for a different purpose. Some are represented as composed of layers of earth, two or three feet thick, each one of which is surmounted by a burned surface, which has been mistaken for a rude brick pavement. Others are composed of alternate layers of earth and human remains. The origin of the latter is doubtless to be found in the annual bone burials of the Cherokees and other southern Indians, of which accounts are given by Bartram and the early writers.

earth. In a few instances, a layer or small elevation of sand had been laid down, upon which the altar was formed. The height of the altars, nevertheless, seldom exceeds a foot or twenty inches above the adjacent level. The clay of which they are composed is usually burned hard, sometimes to the depth of ten, fifteen, and even twenty inches. This is hardly to be explained by any degree or continuance of heat, though it is manifest that in some cases the heat was intense. On the other hand, a number of these altars have been noticed, which are very slightly burned; and such, it is a remarkable fact, are destitute of remains.

The characteristics of this class of mounds will be best explained, by reference to the accompanying illustrations. It should be remarked, however, that no two are precisely alike in all their details.

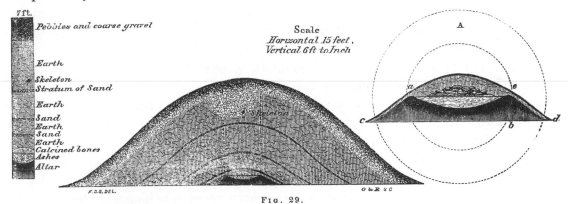

FIG. 29.

The mound, a section of which is here given, occurs in "Mound City," a name given to a group of *twenty-six* mounds, embraced in one enclosure, on the banks of the Scioto river, three miles above the town of Chillicothe. (See Plate **XIX**, mound No. 1.) It is seven feet high by fifty-five feet base. A shaft, five feet square, was sunk from its apex, with the following results:

1st. Occurred a layer of coarse gravel and pebbles, which appeared to have been taken from deep pits surrounding the enclosure, or from the bank of the river. This layer was one foot in thickness.

2d. Beneath this layer of gravel and pebbles, to the depth of two feet, the earth was homogeneous, though slightly mottled, as if taken up and deposited in small

FIG. 30.

loads, from different localities. In one place appeared a deposit of dark-colored surface loam, and by its side, or covering it, there was a mass of the clayey soil from a greater depth. The outlines of these various deposits could be distinctly traced, as shown in Fig. 30.

3d. Below this deposit of earth, occurred a thin and even layer of fine sand, a little over an inch in thickness.

4th. A deposit of earth, as above, eighteen inches in depth.

5th. Another stratum of sand, somewhat thinner than the one above mentioned.

6th. Another deposit of earth, one foot thick; then—

7th. A third stratum of sand; below which was—

8th. Still another layer of earth, a few inches in thickness; which rested on—

9th. An altar, or basin, of burned clay.

This altar was perfectly round. Its form and dimensions are best shown by the supplementary plan and section A. The altar, measured from *c* to *d*, is nine feet in diameter; from *a* to *e*, five feet; height from *b* to *e*, twenty inches; dip of curve *a r e*, nine inches. The sides *c a*, *e d*, slope regularly at a given angle. The body of the altar is burned throughout, though in a greater degree within the basin, where it is so hard as to resist the blows of a heavy hatchet,—the instrument rebounding as if struck upon a rock. The basin, or hollow of the altar, was filled up evenly with fine dry ashes, intermixed with which were some fragments of pottery, of an excellent finish, and ornamented with tasteful carvings on the exterior. One of the vases, of elegant model, taken in fragments from this mound, has been very nearly restored, and will be further noticed in the chapter on the Pottery of the Mounds. A few convex copper discs, much resembling the bosses used upon harnesses, were also found.

Above the deposit of ashes, and covering the entire basin, was a layer of silvery or opaque mica, in sheets, overlapping each other; upon which, immediately over the centre of the basin, was heaped a quantity of burned human bones, probably the amount of a single skeleton, in fragments. The position of these is indicated in the section. The layers of mica and calcined bones, it should be remarked, to prevent misapprehension, were peculiar to this individual mound, and were not found in any other of the class.

It will be seen, by the section, that at a point about two feet below the surface of the mound, a human skeleton was found. It was placed a little to the left of the centre, with the head to the east, and was so much decayed as to render it impossible to extract a single bone entire. Above the skeleton, as shown in the section, the layer of earth and the outer stratum of gravel and pebbles were broken up and intermixed. Thus, while on one side of the shaft the strata were clearly marked, on the other they were confused. And, as this was the first mound of the class excavated, it was supposed, from this circumstance, that it had previously been opened by some explorer; and it had been decided to abandon it, when the skeleton was discovered. Afterwards the matter came to be fully understood. No relics were found with this skeleton.

It is a fact well known, that the existing tribes of Indians, though possessing no knowledge of the origin or objects of the mounds, were accustomed to regard them with some degree of veneration. It is also known, that they sometimes buried their dead in them, in accordance with their almost invariable custom of selecting elevated points and the brows of hills as their cemeteries. That their remains should be found in the mounds, is therefore a matter of no surprise. They are never discovered at any great depth, not often more than eighteen inches or three feet below the surface. Their position varies in almost every case: most of them are extended at length, others have a sitting posture, while others again seem to have been rudely thrust into their shallow graves without care or arrangement. Rude implements of bone and stone, and coarse vessels of pottery, such as are known to have been in use among the Indians at the period of the earliest European intercourse, occur with some of them, particularly with those of a more ancient date; while modern implements and ornaments, in some cases of

European origin, are found with the recent burials. The necessity, therefore, of a careful and rigid discrimination, between these deposits and those of the mound-builders, will be apparent. From the lack of such discrimination, much misapprehension and confusion have resulted. Silver crosses, gun-barrels, and French dial-plates, have been found with skeletons in the mounds; yet it is not to be concluded that the mound-builders were Catholics, or used fire-arms, or understood French. Such a conclusion would, nevertheless, be quite as well warranted, as some which have been deduced from the absolute identity of certain relics taken from the mounds, with articles known to be common among the existing tribes of Indians. The fact of remains occurring in the mounds, is in itself hardly presumptive evidence that they pertained to the builders. The conditions attending them can alone determine their true character. As a general rule, to which there are few exceptions, the only authentic and undoubted remains of the mound-builders are found directly beneath the apex of the mound, on a level with the original surface of the earth; and it may be safely assumed, that whatever deposits occur near the surface of the mounds, are of a date subsequent to their erection.

The French maintained an intercourse, from a very early period, with the Indian tribes of the West. In the way of barter or as presents they distributed amongst them vast quantities of ornaments and implements of various kinds; which, in accordance with the Indian custom, were buried with the possessor at his death. Nothing is therefore more common, in invading the humble sepulchre of the Indian, than to find by the side of his skeleton the copper kettle, the gun, hatchet, and simple ornaments, so valued in his life-time. The latter consist chiefly of small silver crosses and brooches; several of which are sometimes found accompanying a single skeleton.*

In the class of mounds now under consideration we have data that will admit of no doubt, whereby to judge of the origin, as well as of the relative periods, of the various deposits found in them. If the stratification already mentioned as characterizing them is unbroken and undisturbed, if the strata are regular and entire, it

---

* In the construction of the Ohio canal, a mound was partially excavated, in which were found a dial-plate and other articles of European origin. The circumstances are detailed in a private letter from WILLIAM H. PRICE, Esq., of Chillicothe, late member of the Board of Public Works of Ohio, under whose direction the mound was removed :

"In the year 1827, during the excavation of a part of the Ohio canal in the township of Benton, Cuyahoga county, a short distance north of the mouth of Brandywine creek, it became necessary to remove part of a small mound, so situated in the valley of a small rivulet as, at first, to induce doubts as to its being artificial. However, in the process of excavation, the remains of one or more human skeletons were found, also a gun barrel, and perhaps some of the mountings of the stock. In relation to the last I am not positive, but distinctly remember a circular brass plate or disc perhaps one sixteenth of an inch in thickness, with (I think) *raised* letters and figures on one side, which exhibited a French calendar, so arranged as to serve for a century. I may mistake the duration for which it was intended, but give the above as my decided impression. I do not recollect the date, but think it was near the middle of the seventeenth century,—say 1640 or thereabouts."

Several silver crosses, a number of small bags of vermilion, and other relics, were discovered not long since by Mr. C. A. VAUGHN, of Cincinnati, in some mounds excavated by that gentleman in the vicinity of Beardstown, Ill. They were found with skeletons, a few feet below the surface.

is certain that whatever occurs beneath them was placed there at the period of the construction of the mound. But if, on the other hand, these strata are broken up, it is equally certain that the mound has been disturbed, and new deposits made, subsequent to its erection. It is in this view, that the fact of stratification is seen to be important, as well as interesting; for it will serve to fix, beyond all dispute, the origin of many singular relics, having a decisive bearing on some of the leading questions connected with American archæology. The thickness of the exterior layer of gravel, in mounds of this class, varies with the dimensions of the mound, from eight to twenty inches. In a very few instances, the layer, which may have been designed to protect the form of the mound, and which purpose it admirably subserves, is entirely wanting. The number and relative position of the sand strata are variable; in some of the larger mounds, there are as many as six of them, in no case less than one, most usually two or three.

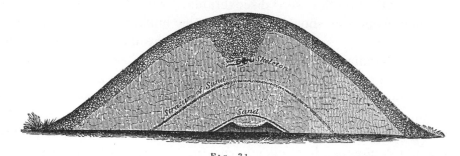

FIG. 31.

Fig. 31 exhibits a section of mound No. 2 in the plan of "Mound City." This mound is ninety feet in diameter at the base by seven and a half feet high, being remarkably broad and flat. A shaft six feet square was sunk from the apex with the following results :

1st. Occurred the usual layer of gravel and pebbles, one foot thick.

2d. A layer of earth, three feet thick.

3d. A thin stratum of sand.

4th. Another layer of earth two feet thick.

5th. Another stratum of sand, beneath which, and separated by a few inches of earth, was—

6th. The altar, Fig. 32.

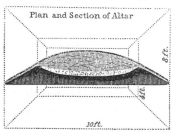

FIG. 32.

This altar was a parallelogram of the utmost regularity, as shown in the plan and section. At its base, it measures ten feet in length by eight in width; at the top, six feet by four. Its height was eighteen inches, and the dip of the basin nine inches. Within the basin was a deposit of fine ashes, unmixed with charcoal, three inches thick, much compacted by the weight of the superincumbent earth. Amongst the ashes were some fragments of pottery, also a few shell and pearl beads. Enough of the pottery was recovered to restore a beautiful vase, for a drawing and description of which the reader is referred to the paragraphs on *Pottery*. The second or lower sand stratum in this, as in several other instances, rested directly upon the outer sides of the altar.

In this mound, three feet below the surface, were found two very well preserved skeletons, the presence of which was indicated, at the commencement of the excavation, by the interruption of the layers, as above described. They were placed side by side, the head of one resting at the elbow of the other. Under and about the heads of both were deposited some large rough fragments of greenstone, identical with that of which most of the stone implements of the former Indian tribes of the valley were made. There were also deposited with the skeletons many implements of stone, horn, and bone; among which was a beautiful chip of hornstone, about the size of the palm of one's hand, which had manifestly been used for cutting purposes. There were several hand-axes and gouges of stone, and some articles made from the horns of the deer or elk, which resemble the handles of large knives; but no traces of iron or other metals were discoverable. Among the implements of bone was one formed from the shoulder-blade of the buffalo, in shape resembling a Turkish scimetar; also a singular notched instrument of bone, evidently intended for insertion in a handle, and designed, in common with similar articles in use by the Indians of the present day, for distributing the paint in lines and other ornamental figures on the faces of the warriors. Another instrument was also found, made by cutting off a section of the main stem of an elk's horn, leaving one of the principal prongs attached; used perhaps as a hammer or war-club. Besides these there were some gouges made of elk's horns, and a variety of similar relics; all of exceeding rudeness, and of no great antiquity. The skulls found in this mound possessed no marked features to distinguish them from the crania found in the known burial-places of the Shawanoes and other late Indian tribes.

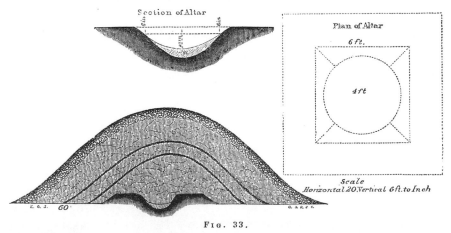

FIG. 33.

This mound, Fig. 33, is numbered 4 in the plan of " Mound City." It is oblong in shape, measuring ninety by sixty feet base, and six feet in height. It has two sand strata, as shown in the section. The altar in this mound is remarkable from its depth, which is twenty-two inches, the hollow of the basin sinking a foot or more below the original surface of the soil. Its form and dimensions are best explained by the plan and section. Nothing was contained in the basin, except a white mass or layer five inches thick, *a*, presenting all the appearances of sharp lime mortar. Mingled with this mass, which was hard and compact, were a few fragments of calcined shells; leading to the inference, that it was formed from the burning of shells. It was afterwards found upon analysis, that the mass was principally carbonate of lime, with a considerable portion of earthy particles, thus sustaining the inference already made. No fragments of bones, however small, were discoverable.

By the side of the mound just mentioned, the bases of the two running into each other, is another mound, No. 5 in the plan of "Mound City." It is of the same form and dimensions with the one just described, and like that has two sand strata. The altar however more resembles that of Fig. 31, though somewhat smaller in size. It contained a quantity, perhaps thirty pounds in all, of galena in pieces weighing from two ounces to three pounds; also several lumps of fine clay, possessing an unctuous feel. The latter appeared to have originally formed a model over which a vessel of some sort had been fashioned. Around this deposit there was considerable charcoal, apparently of a light wood, but very little ashes. The altar, although the galena was but slightly burned, bore marks of intense heat,—thus evincing that it had been previously subjected for a considerable period, or at frequent intervals, to the action of fire.

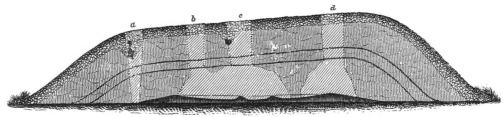

FIG. 34.

Fig. 34 is a section of the long mound, No. 3, in the plan of "Mound City." For several reasons,—its shape, the great dimensions of its enclosed altar, and the number and variety of its relics,—this mound was minutely investigated, and is worthy of a detailed description. It is egg-shaped in form, and measures one hundred and forty feet in length, by fifty and sixty respectively at its greater and smaller ends, and is eleven feet high.

Its longitudinal bearing is N. 20° W. Four shafts were sunk at as many different points; between three of which, for a distance of over forty feet, connecting drifts were carried, as indicated in the plan.

The shaft a was first sunk. At the commencement of the excavation the feature already mentioned, viz. the confusion of the layers, was remarked, and care was accordingly taken to uncover carefully the expected recent deposit. This proved to be a single human skeleton, placed in a sitting posture, the head resting on the knees. The top of the skull was eighteen inches below the surface. The skeleton was well preserved, still retaining a large portion of its animal matter. The lower jaw was broken, a circumstance observed in most of the skeletons thus found. No relics were deposited with this skeleton. The sand strata occurred low down, following the curvature of the mound, as represented in the section.

Shaft c was next sunk. On the left side of the excavation a disturbance was remarked; and at about two feet below the surface, a rude earthern vessel holding something over one quart, and the lower jaw of a human skeleton, were discovered. They were side by side, and seemed to have constituted the entire deposit.

Two sand strata occur in this mound, the first five feet below the surface, the second one foot deeper. The intermediate layers of earth presented the mottled appearance already explained, and were much compacted, rendering excavation exceedingly slow and laborious. The remaining shafts were afterwards sunk for the purpose of ascertaining the size and form of the altar, but disclosed nothing of importance in their course.

Although the altar in this mound was not fully exposed, yet enough was uncovered to ascertain very nearly its character and extent. Forty-five feet of its length was exposed, and in one place its entire width, which was eight feet across the top, by fifteen at the base. The portions in the section, extending beyond the line of the excavation, are supplied, giving an entire length to the altar of not far from sixty feet.

FIG. 35.—LONGITUDINAL SECTION OF ALTAR.

By attention to the longitudinal section of the altar B C B, it will be seen that it shelves gradually from the ends, forming a basin of not far from eighteen inches in depth. The outer slope is more gradual than the inner one. Near the centre of the altar, two partitions, A A, are carried across it transversely, forming a minor basin or compartment, C, eight feet square. Within this basin the relics deposited in the mound were placed. The outer compartments seemed to have been filled with earth, previous to the final heaping over, so as to present a perfectly level surface, which had been slightly burned. This feature is indicated in the section, which also illustrates another interesting and important peculiarity. Upon penetrating the altar (a task of no little difficulty in consequence of its extreme hardness) to ascertain its thickness, it was found to be burned to the depth of *twenty-two* inches. This could hardly be accounted for by the application or continuance of any degree of heat from above, and was therefore the occasion of some surprise. A more minute examination furnished the explanation. It was found that one altar had been built upon another; as if one had been used for a time, until, from defect or other causes, it was abandoned, when another was *recast* upon it. This process, as shown in the section F E, had been repeated

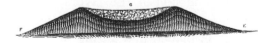

FIG. 36.—CROSS SECTION OF ALTAR.

three times, the outline of each successive layer being so distinct as to admit of no doubt as to its cause. The partitions A A were constructed subsequently to the erection of the altar, as is evidenced from the fact that they were scarcely burned through, while the altar immediately beneath them was burned to great hardness. Scattered upon the deposit of earth filling the compartments D D, and resting upon the slopes of the altar, were found the traces of a number of pieces of timber, four or five feet long, and six or eight inches thick. They had been somewhat burned, and the carbonized surface had preserved their casts in the hard earth, although the wood had entirely decayed. They had been heaped over while glowing, for the earth around them was slightly baked. In fact the entire hollow of the altar was covered with a thin layer of fine carbonaceous matter, much like that formed by the burning of leaves or straw. These pieces had been of nearly uniform length; and this circumstance, joined to the position in which they occurred in respect to each other and to the altar, would almost justify the inference that they had supported some funeral or sacrificial pile.

The remains found in this mound were, in their number and variety, commensurate with the labor and care bestowed on its construction. A quantity of pottery and many implements of copper and stone were deposited on the altar, intermixed with much coal and ashes. They had all been subjected to a strong heat, which had broken up most of those which could be thus affected by its action. A large number of spear-heads, as they have been termed, beautifully chipped out of quartz and manganese garnet, had been placed here; but, out of a bushel or two of fragments, four specimens only were recovered entire. One of them is faithfully figured under the head of "Implements." A quantity of the raw material, from which they were manufactured, was also found, consisting of large fragments of quartz and of crystals of garnet. Some of these crystals had been of large size, certainly not less than three or four inches in diameter. A single arrow-point of *obsidian* was found; also a number of fine arrow-heads of limpid quartz. One of these was four inches in length, and all were finely wrought. Judging from the quantity of fragments, some fifty or a hundred of these were originally deposited on the altar. Among the fragments were some large thin pieces of the same material, shaped like the blade of a knife. Two copper gravers or chisels, one measuring six, the other eight inches in length, (see "*Implements*,") also twenty or more tubes formed of thin strips of copper, an inch and a quarter long by three eighths of an inch diameter, (see "*Ornaments*,") were found among the remains. A large quantity of pottery, much broken up, enough perhaps to have formed originally a dozen vessels of moderate size, was also discovered. Two vases have been very nearly restored. They resemble, in material and form, those already mentioned, and have similar markings on their exterior. (See "*Pottery*.") Also a couple of carved pipes; one of which, of beautiful model and fine finish, is cut out of a stone closely resembling, if indeed not identical with, the Potomac marble, of which the columns of the hall of the House of Representatives at Washington are made. The other is a bold figure of a bird, resembling the toucan, cut in white limestone.

A portion of the contents of this mound were cemented together by a tufa-like substance of a gray color, resembling the scoriæ of a furnace, and of great hardness. It was at first supposed to be carbonate of lime gradually deposited, in the lapse of time, from the water percolating through the outer stratum of limestone gravel and pebbles. The quantity however, covering as it did a large part of the basin to the depth of an inch or two, weighed strongly against such a conclusion; and a subsequent analysis demonstrated that it was made up in part of *phosphates*. A single fragment of partially calcined bone was found on the altar. It was the *patella* of the human skeleton.

Such were the more important features of this interesting mound. It is evident that the enclosed altar had been often used, and several times remodelled, before it was finally heaped over. Why this was at last done, upon what occasion, and with what strange ceremonies, are questions which will probably forever remain unanswered.

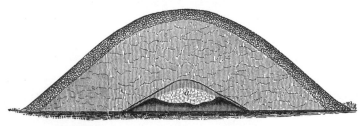

FIG. 37.

Fig. 37 is a section of mound No. 8 in "Mound City." In the number and value of its relics, this mound far exceeds any hitherto explored. It is small in size, and in its structure exhibits nothing remarkable. It had but one sand stratum,

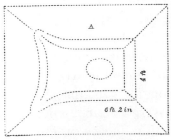

FIG. 38.—PLAN OF ALTAR.

the edges of which rested on the outer slopes of the altar, as shown in the section. Between this stratum and the deposit in the basin occurred a layer, a few inches thick, of burned loam. The altar itself (Fig. 38) was somewhat singular, though quite regular in shape. In length it was six feet two inches, in width four feet. At the point indicated in the section was a depression of perhaps six inches below the general level of the basin.

The deposit (*a*) in this altar was large. Intermixed with much ashes, were found not far from *two hundred* pipes, carved in stone, many pearl and shell beads, numerous discs, tubes, etc. of copper, and a number of other ornaments of copper, covered with silver, etc. etc. The pipes were much broken up,—some of them calcined by the heat, which had been sufficiently strong to melt copper, masses of which were found fused together in the centre of the basin. A large number have nevertheless been restored, at the expense of much labor and no small amount of patience. They are mostly composed of a red porphyritic stone, somewhat resembling the pipe stone of the *Coteau des Prairies*, excepting that it is of great hardness and interspersed with small variously colored granules. The fragments of this material which had been most exposed to the heat were changed to a brilliant black color, resembling Egyptian marble. Nearly all the articles carved in limestone, of which there had been a number, were calcined.

The bowls of most of the pipes are carved in miniature figures of animals, birds, reptiles, etc. All of them are executed with strict fidelity to nature, and with exquisite skill. Not only are the features of the various objects represented faithfully, but their peculiarities and habits are in some degree exhibited. The otter is shown in a characteristic attitude, holding a fish in his mouth; the heron also holds a fish; and the hawk grasps a small bird in its talons, which it tears with its beak. The panther, the bear, the wolf, the beaver, the otter, the squirrel, the raccoon, the hawk, the heron, crow, swallow, buzzard, *paroquet*, *toucan*, and other indigenous and southern birds,—the turtle, the frog, toad, rattlesnake, etc., are recognized at first glance. But the most interesting and valuable in the list, are a number of sculptured human heads, no doubt faithfully representing the predominant physical features of the ancient people by whom they were made. We have this assurance in the minute accuracy of the other sculptures of the same date. For engravings of these as well as of a large series of the other relics here mentioned, the reader is referred to the passages on "*Sculptures.*" Appropriate notices of the remaining articles discovered in this mound,—the copper discs and tubes, pearl, shell, and silver beads, etc.,—will be found under the head of "*Ornaments.*"

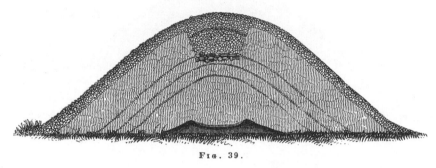

FIG. 39.

Fig. 39 is a section of mound No. 18 in "Mound City." It has three sand strata, and an altar of the usual form and dimensions. This altar contained no relics, but was thinly covered with a carbonaceous deposit, resembling burned leaves. The feature of this mound most worthy of remark was a singular burial by *incremation*, which had been made in it at some period subsequent to its erection. The indications (so often remarked as to need no further specification here) that the mound had been disturbed were observed at the commencement of the excavation. At the depth of four and a half feet, the deposit was reached (Fig. 41). A quantity of water-worn stones, about the size of common paving stones, and evidently taken from the river close by, had been laid down, forming a rude pavement six feet long by four broad. Lying diagonally upon this pavement, as shown in Fig. 40, with its head to the north-west, was a skeleton. It was remarkably well preserved, and retained much of its animal matter,—a fact attributable in some degree to the antiseptic qualities of the carbonaceous material surrounding it.* A fire had been built over the body after it was deposited, its traces being plainly visible on the stones, all of which were slightly burned. A quantity of carbonaceous matter, resembling

FIG. 40.

---

* The skull of this skeleton, which is singularly large and massive, is now in the possession of Samuel G. Morton, M.D., of Philadelphia. It is of the same conformation with those of the recent Indians which surround it, in his extensive collection.

that formed by the sudden covering up of burning twigs or other light materials, covered the pavement and the skeleton.   There were no relics with the skeleton; although around its head were disposed a number of large fragments of sienite, identical with that of which many of the instruments of the modern Indians are known to have been made, previous and for some time subsequent to the introduction of iron amongst them.   After the burial had been performed, and the hole partly filled, another fire had been kindled, burning the earth of a reddish color, and leaving a distinctly marked line, as indicated in the section.   The hole had then been completely filled up, so as to leave a scarcely perceptible depression in the mound.

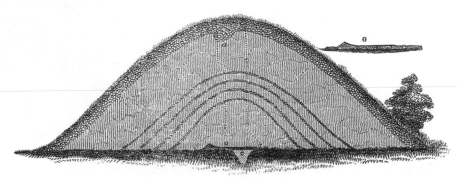

FIG. 41.

Fig. 41 is a section of mound No. 7 in "Mound City."   This mound is much the largest within the enclosure, measuring seventeen and a half feet in height by ninety feet base.   From its top a full view of the entire group is commanded.   A shaft nine feet square was sunk from the apex.   The outer layer of gravel, which in this case was twenty inches thick, was found to be broken up, and at the depth of three feet (at a point indicated by *a* in the section) were found two copper axes, weighing respectively two, and two and one fourth pounds.   At the depth of seven feet occurred the first sand stratum, below which, at intervals of little more than a foot, were three more,—*four* in all.   At the depth of nineteen feet was found a smooth level floor of clay, slightly burned, which was covered with a thin layer of sand an inch in thickness.   This sand had a marked ferruginous appearance, and seemed to be cemented together, breaking up into large fragments a foot or two square.   At one side of the shaft, and resting on the sand, was noticed a

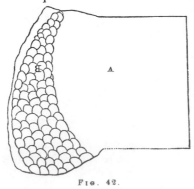

FIG. 42.

layer of silvery mica, as shown in the plan of the excavation, Fig. 42.   It was formed of round sheets, ten inches or a foot in diameter, overlapping each other like the scales of a fish.   Lateral excavations were made to determine its extent, with the result indicated in the plan.   The portion uncovered exhibited something over one half of a large and regular crescent, the outer edge of which rested on an elevation or ridge of sand six inches in height, as shown in the supplementary section *o*.   The entire length of the crescent from horn to horn could not have been less than twenty feet, and its greatest width five. The clay floor of this mound was but a few inches in thickness; a small shaft, c, was sunk three feet below it, but it disclosed only a mass of coarse ferruginous sand. The earth composing the mound was incredibly compact, rendering excavation exceedingly slow and laborious. Two active men were employed more than a week in making the excavation here indicated. It is not absolutely certain that the mound was raised over the simple deposit above mentioned, and it may yet be subjected to a more rigid investigation.

Although this mound is classed as a mound of sacrifice, it presents some features peculiar to itself. Were we to yield to the temptation to speculation which the presence of the mica crescent holds out, we might conclude that the mound-builders worshipped the moon, and that this mound was dedicated, with unknown rites and ceremonies, to that luminary. It may be remarked that some of the mica sheets were of that peculiar variety known as "hieroglyphic" or "graphic mica."

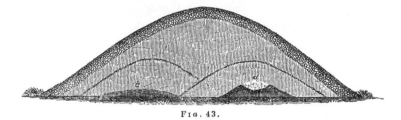

FIG. 43.

Fig. 43 is a section of mound No. 9, in the plan of the great work on the North fork of Paint creek (Plate X). It will be seen that this mound has several peculiar features. The altar, a, instead of occupying the centre, is placed considerably towards one side, and a layer of charcoal, c, fills the corresponding opposite side. Over the altar curves a stratum of sand, and over the layer of charcoal still another, as exhibited in the section. This altar was the smallest met with. It was round, not measuring more than two feet across the top. It was nevertheless rich in remains. Within it were found—

1st. Several instruments of *obsidian*. They were considerably broken up, but have been so much restored, as to exhibit pretty nearly their original form. Too large for arrow-heads, and too thin and slender for points of spears, they seem to have been designed for cutting purposes.

2d. Several scrolls tastefully cut from thin sheets of mica. They are perforated with small holes, as if they had been attached as ornaments to a robe of some description.

3d. Traces of cloth; small portions of which, though completely carbonized, were found, still retaining the structure of the thread. This appeared to have been made of some fine vegetable fibre. It was what is technically termed "doubled and twisted," and was about the size of fine pack-thread.

4th. A considerable number of ivory or bone needles, or graving-tools, about one tenth of an inch thick. Their original length is not known. Several fragments were found two and three inches long. Some have flat cutting points, the points of others were round and sharp; some were straight, others slightly bent.

5th. A quantity of pearl beads; an article resembling the cover of a small vessel, carved from stone; also some fragments of copper, in thin narrow slips.

There were no relics of any kind found amongst the charcoal. The layer of this material was not far from six feet square. It had been heaped over while burning.

F i g . 44.

Fig. 44 is a section of a large mound, No. 5, in the same enclosure. In this instance the altar was covered with stones; and instead of the usual sand stratum, there was found a layer of large flat stones, corresponding to it. The altar, A, was composed of earth elevated two and a half feet above the original level of the soil, and was five feet long by three feet four inches broad, the sides sloping at an angle of nearly thirty degrees. It was faced on the top and on the sides with slabs of stone, quite regular in form and thickness, and which, although not cut by any instrument, were closely fitted together, as shown in the supplementary section of the altar, A. The stone is the Waverley sandstone, underlying the coal series, thin strata of which cap the hills bordering these valleys. The altar bore the marks of fire; and a few fragments of the mound-builders' ornaments, a few pearl beads, etc., were found on and around it. The original deposit had probably been removed by the modern Indians, who had opened the mound and buried one of their dead on the slope of the altar. The stones composing the layer corresponding to the sand stratum were two or three deep, presenting the appearance of a wall which had fallen inwards.

F i g . 45.

In the centre of the large enclosure, Plate XIX, is a solitary mound, of which a section is here presented, Fig. 45. It is now, after many years of cultivation, about five feet high by forty feet base. Like that last described, it has some novel features, although its purposes can hardly admit of a doubt. It has the casing of pebbles and gravel which characterize the altar-mounds, but has no sand layer, except a thin stratum resting immediately on the deposit contained in the altar. This altar is entirely peculiar. It seems to have been formed, at different intervals of time, as follows: first, a circular space, thirteen feet in diameter and eight inches in depth, was excavated in the original level of the plain; this was filled with fine sand, carefully levelled, and compacted to the utmost degree. Upon the level thus formed, which was perfectly horizontal, offerings by fire were made; at any rate a continuous heat was kept up, and fatty matter of some sort burned, for the sand to the depth of two inches is discolored, and to the depth of one inch is burned hard and black and cemented together. The ashes, etc., resulting from this operation, were then removed, and another deposit of sand, of equal thickness with the former, was placed above it, and in like manner much compacted. This was moulded into the form represented in the plan, which is identical with that of the circular clay altars already described; the basin, in this instance, measuring seven feet in diameter by eight inches in depth. This basin was then carefully paved with small round stones, each a little larger than a hen's egg, which were laid with the utmost precision, fully rivalling the pavior's finest work. They were firmly bedded in the sand beneath them, so as to present a regular and uniform surface. Upon the altar thus constructed was found a burnt deposit, carefully covered with a layer of sand, above which was heaped the superstructure of the mound. The deposit consisted of a thin layer of carbonaceous matter, intermingled with which were some burned human bones, but so much calcined as to render recognition extremely difficult. Ten well wrought copper bracelets were also found, placed in two heaps, five in each, and encircling some calcined bones,—probably those of the arms upon which they were originally worn. Besides these were found a couple of thick plates of mica, placed upon the western slope of the altar.

Assuming, what must be very obvious from its form and other circumstances, that this was an altar and not a tomb, we are almost irresistibly led to the conclusion, that human sacrifices were practised by the race of the mounds. This conclusion is sustained by other facts, which have already been presented, and which need not be recapitulated here.

The two mounds last described are the only ones yet discovered possessing altars of stone; and, although it is likely there are others of similar construction, their occurrence must be very rare.

Such are the prevailing characteristics of this class of mounds. It will be remarked that while all have the same general features, no two are alike in their details. They differ in the number and relative position of their sand strata, as well as in the size and shape of their altars and the character of the deposits made on them. One mound covers a deposit made up almost entirely of pipes, another a deposit of spear-heads, or of galena or calcined shells or bones. In a few instances the symmetrical altar, of which so many examples have been given, is wanting, and its place is supplied by a level floor or platform of earth. Such was the case with mound No. 1, in the plan of the great work on the North fork of Paint creek, already referred to. This mound, although one of the richest in contents, was one of the smallest met with, being not over three feet in height. Its deposit was first disturbed by the plough, some years ago, and numerous singular articles were then taken from it. Upon investigation, in place of the altar, a level area ten or fifteen feet broad was found, much burned, on which the relics had been placed. These had been covered over with earth to perhaps the depth of a foot, followed by a stratum of small stones, and an outer layer of earth two feet in thickness. Hundreds of relics, and many of the most interesting and valuable hitherto found, were taken from this mound, among which may be mentioned several coiled serpents, carved in stone, and carefully enveloped in sheet mica and copper;

pottery; carved fragments of ivory; a large number of fossil teeth; numerous fine sculptures in stone, etc. Notice will be taken of some of the most remarkable of these, under the appropriate heads.

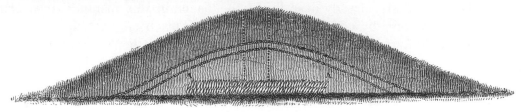

FIG. 46.

Another singular mound of somewhat anomalous character, of which a section is herewith given, (Fig. 46,) occurred in the same enclosure with the above. It is numbered 2 in Plate X, and is remarkable as being very broad and flat, measuring at least eighty feet in diameter by but six or seven in height. It has two sand strata; but instead of an altar, there are two layers of discs chipped out of horn-stone, (A A of the section,) some nearly round, others in the form of spear-heads. They are of various sizes, but are for the most part about six inches long, by four wide, and three quarters of an inch or an inch in thickness. They were placed side by side, a little inclining, and one layer resting immediately on the other. Out of an excavation six feet long by four wide, not far from six hundred were thrown. The deposit extends beyond the limits of the excavation on every side. Supposing it to be twelve feet square, (and it may be twenty or thirty,) we have not far from four thousand of these discs deposited here. If they were thus placed as an offering, we can form some estimate, in view of the facts that they must have been brought from a great distance, and fashioned with great toil, of the devotional fervor which induced the sacrifice, or the magnitude of the calamity which that sacrifice was per-haps intended to avert. The fact, that this description of stone chips most easily when newly quarried, has induced the suggestion that the discs were deposited here for the purpose of protecting them from the hardening influence of the atmosphere, and were intended to be withdrawn and manufactured as occasion warranted or necessity required. It is incredible, however, that so much care should be taken to fashion the mound and introduce the mysterious sand strata, if it was designed to be disturbed at any subsequent period. There is little doubt that the deposit was final, and was made in compliance with some religious requirement. An excavation below these layers discovered traces of fire, but too slight to be worthy of more than a passing remark.

A mound marked E in the plan of the great work, Plate XXI, No. 2, was found to enclose an altar of small dimensions, which contained only a few perforated wolf's teeth and some fifteen or twenty bones of the deer, all of them much burned. Six or eight inches above the deposit was a stratum of large pebbles.

It has been remarked that some of the mounds of this class contain altars which have been but slightly burned, and that such are destitute of remains. A few altars have been noticed, which have been much burned, but having no deposit upon them, except a thin layer of phosphate of lime, which seems to have incorporated itself with the clay of which they are composed, giving them the appearance of having been plastered with mortar. Nos. 6, 9, and 18, in "Mound City," are examples of this class. No coals or ashes were found on any of these; they appear to have been carefully cleaned out before being heaped over.

An explanation of this circumstance may probably be found in the character of a certain class of small mounds, occurring within enclosures and in connection with the altar mounds. In the plan of "Mound City" so often referred to are several of these, numbered 14, 15, 16, 19, 20, 21 and 23, respectively. They are very small, the largest not exceeding three feet in height, and are destitute of altars. In place thereof, on the original level of the earth, was found a quantity, in no case exceeding the amount of one skeleton, of burned human bones, in small fragments. That they were not burned on the spot is evident from the absence of all traces of fire, beyond those furnished by the remains themselves. They appear to have been collected from the pyre, wherever it was erected, and carefully deposited in a small heap, and then covered over. In one instance (mound No. 19) a small hole had been dug, in which the remains were found. A section of this mound is herewith given, Fig. 47. The deposit is indicated by the letter *a*. This feature is analogous to the *cists* of the British barrows. That the burning took place on some of the altars above mentioned is not only indicated by the presence of the deposit of phosphate of lime upon them, but is absolutely demonstrated by finding, inter-mixed with the calcined bones, *fragments of the altars themselves*, as if portions had been scaled up by the instrument used in scraping together and removing the burned remains.

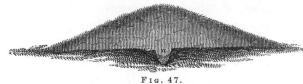

FIG. 47.

The inference that human sacrifices were made here, and the remains afterwards thus collected and deposited, or that a system of burial of this extraordinary character was practised in certain cases, seems to follow legitimately from the facts and circumstances here presented.*

That the stratified mounds are not burial places seems sufficiently well established by the fact that the greater number have no traces of human remains upon or around the altars. The suggestion that the various relics found upon these altars were the personal effects of deceased chiefs or priests, thus deposited in accordance with the practice common amongst rude people, of consigning the property of the dead to the tomb with them, is controverted by the fact that

---

* Amongst the Mexicans, burial by fire was generally practised. Clavigero mentions a fact, in connection with their funeral rites, which may serve to elucidate the point here raised, viz. that burial *in the vicinity of some altar or temple, or in the sacred places where sacrifices were made,* was often sought by the Mexicans:

"There was no fixed place for burials. Many ordered their ashes to be buried near some temple or altar, some in the fields, and others in their sacred places in the mountains where sacrifices used to be made. The ashes of the kings and lords were, for the most part, deposited in the towers of the temples, especially those of the greater temple."—*Clavigero, American Edition,* vol. ii. p. 108; *Acosta in Purchas,* vol. iii. p. 1029.

the deposits are generally homogeneous.   That is to say, instead of finding a large variety of relics, ornaments, weapons, and other articles, such as go to make up the possessions of a barbarian dignitary, we find upon one altar *pipes* only, upon another a simple mass of galena, while the next one has a quantity of pottery, or a collection of spear heads, or else is destitute of remains except perhaps a thin layer of carbonaceous material.   Such could not possibly be the case upon the above hypothesis, for the spear, the arrows, the pipe, and the other implements and personal ornaments of the dead, would then be found in connection with each other.   Besides the negative evidence here afforded in support of our classification, it is sustained by the circumstance that these mounds are almost invariably found within enclosures, which, for a variety of concurring reasons, we are induced to believe were sacred in their origin, and devoted primarily, if not exclusively, to religious purposes.   The circumstance of stratification, exhibiting as it does an extraordinary care and attention, can hardly be supposed to result from any but superstitious notions.   It certainly has no exact analogy in any of the monuments of the globe, of which we possess a knowledge, and its significance is beyond rational conjecture.   Why these altars, some of which, as we have already seen, had been used for considerable periods, were finally heaped over, is an embarrassing question, and one to which it is impossible to suggest a satisfactory answer.   That all were not covered by mounds is quite certain.   The "brick hearths," of which mention has occasionally been made by writers upon our antiquities, were doubtless none other than uncovered altars. Nothing is more likely than that, even though designed to be subsequently covered, some were left exposed by the builders, and afterwards hidden by natural accumulations, to be again exposed by the invading plough or the recession of the banks of streams.   The indentations occasioned by the growth of roots over their surfaces, or the cracks resulting from other causes, would naturally suggest the notion of rude brick hearths.   One of these " hearths " was discovered some years since near the town of Marietta in Ohio.   It was surrounded by a low bank, of about one hundred feet in circumference, which seemed to have been the ground plan or commencement of a mound.

FIG. 48.—ELLIPTICAL MOUND.

CHAPTER VII.

MOUNDS OF SEPULTURE

FIG. 49.—GROUP OF SEPULCHRAL MOUNDS.

MOUNDS of this class are very numerous. They are generally of considerable size, varying from six to eighty feet in height, but having an average altitude of from fifteen to twenty or twenty-five feet. They stand without the walls of enclosures, at a distance more or less remote from them. Many are isolated, with no other monuments near them; but they frequently occur in groups, sometimes in close connection with each other, and exhibiting a dependence which was probably not without its meaning. They are destitute of altars, nor do they possess that regularity which characterizes the "temple mounds." Their usual form is that of a simple cone; sometimes they are elliptical or pear-shaped.

These mounds invariably cover a skeleton, (in very rare instances more than one, as in the case of the Grave creek mound,) which at the time of its interment was enveloped in bark or coarse matting, or enclosed in a rude sarcophagus of timber,—the traces, in some instances the very casts of which remain. Occasionally the chamber of the dead is built of stone, rudely laid up, without cement of any kind. Burial by fire seems to have been frequently practised by the mound-builders. Urn burial also appears to have prevailed, to a considerable extent, in the Southern States.

With the skeletons in these mounds are found various remains of art, comprising

21

ornaments, utensils, and weapons.   The structure and contents of a few mounds of this class will sufficiently explain their general character.

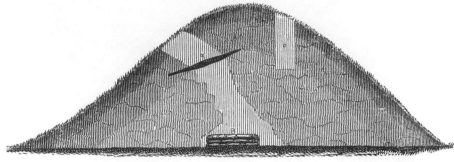

FIG. 50.

Fig. 50 exhibits a section of a large sepulchral mound situated on the third terrace, on the east bank of the Scioto river, about six miles below the city of Chillicothe.*   It is the largest of the group, represented in the cut (Fig. 49) at the head of this chapter.   There are no enclosures nearer than a mile ; though there are three or four other mounds of smaller size, on the same terrace, within a few hundred yards.   The mound is twenty-two feet high by ninety feet base.   The principal excavation was made (as represented in the section) from the west side, commencing at about one third of the height of the mound from the top, and was carried in a slanting direction towards the centre.   The soil of the mound is a sandy loam, entirely homogeneous throughout, though much compacted and slightly different in color towards the centre, where water cannot penetrate.   At ten feet below the surface occurred a layer of charcoal, *a*, not far from ten feet square, and from two to six inches in thickness, slightly inclined from the horizontal, and lying mostly to the left of the centre of the mound.   The coal was coarse and clear, and seemed to have been formed by the sudden covering up of the wood while burning, inasmuch as the trunks and branches perfectly retained their form, though entirely carbonized, and the earth immediately above as well as beneath was burned of a reddish color.   Below this layer, the earth became much more compact and difficult of excavation.   At the depth of twenty-two feet, and on a level with the original surface, immediately underneath the charcoal layer, and, like that, somewhat to one side of the centre of the mound, was a rude

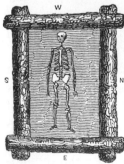

FIG. 51.

sarcophagus or framework of timber, Fig. 51, now reduced to an almost impalpable powder, but the *cast* of which was still retained in the hard earth.   This enclosure of timber, measuring from outside to outside, was nine feet long by seven wide, and twenty inches high.   It had been constructed of unhewn logs laid one upon the other, and had evidently been covered with other timbers, which had sunk under the superincumbent earth, as they decayed.   The bottom had also been covered with bark, matting, or thin slabs of wood,—at any rate, a whitish stratum of decomposed material remained, covering

---

* Numbered 1, in the "Map of a section of twelve miles of the Scioto valley," Plate II.

the bottom of the parallelogram. Within this rude coffin, with its head to the west, was found a human skeleton, or rather the remains of one; for scarcely a fragment as long as one's finger could be recovered. It was so much decayed that it crumbled to powder under the lightest touch. Of course, no portion of the cranium, of the slightest value for purposes of comparison, was recovered.

Around the neck of the skeleton, forming a triple row, and retaining their position as originally strung and deposited with the dead, were several hundred beads, made of the compact portion of marine shells and of the tusks of some animal. Several of these still retain their polish, and bear marks which seem to indicate that they were turned in some machine, instead of being carved or rubbed into shape by hand. A few laminæ of mica were also discovered; which completed the list of articles deposited with this skeleton, of which any traces remained. The feet of the skeleton were about in the centre of the mound; a drift beyond it disclosed nothing new, nor was a corresponding layer of charcoal found on the opposite side of the mound. It is clear, therefore, that the tumulus was raised over this single skeleton.

As a general rule, to which this mound furnished one of a very few exceptions, whatever occurs in the mounds, whether they be sepulchral or sacrificial in their purposes, is deposited immediately beneath the apex and on a level with the circumjacent plain.* The predominance of storms from a certain direction, and various other circumstances, may have contributed to alter the apparent centre of the mound. In the case of a mound of this kind which was opened at Gallipolis on the Ohio river, the skeleton was found in a *cist*, or chamber, excavated beneath the original surface. This can always be detected by a strongly marked line and the uniform drab color of the earth below it. The superstructure of the mounds is more or less mottled, as the materials entering into their composition are variant in character and color,—a circumstance which has elsewhere been sufficiently explained.

The charcoal layer is a frequent though by no means an invariable feature in mounds of this class, and would seem to indicate that sacrifices were made for the dead, or funeral rites of some description, in which fire performed a part, celebrated. This is further confirmed by the fact that fragments of bones and some few stone implements have been discovered in the layer of charcoal. The fire in every case was kept burning for a very little time, as is shown from the lack of ashes, and by the slight traces of its action left on the adjacent earth. That it was suddenly heaped over while glowing, is also certain.

A smaller mound, standing close by the one above described, was also excavated, but without any satisfactory results. It is probable the investigation was not sufficiently thorough.

---

* "In the investigation of barrows, marks of interment are frequently found near the surface; but investigation must not terminate upon such a discovery. Experience has convinced me that these were subsequent interments, and that the primary deposit was *always laid on the floor of the barrow, or within a cist in the native soil.*"—*Sir R. C. Hoare on the Barrows and Tumuli of Great Britain.*

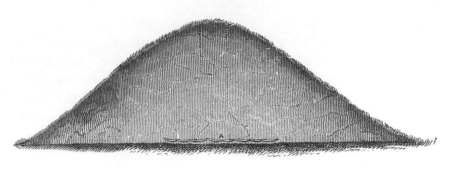

FIG. 52.

Fig. 52. This tumulus, selected as a type of the second description of sepulchral mounds, is situated upon the broad and beautiful terrace on which Chillicothe stands, about one mile to the north of that town.* It is fifteen feet in height by sixty-five or seventy feet base, and is composed of earth taken up from the surrounding plain. A shaft eight feet square was sunk from the apex. Nothing worthy of remark was observed in the progress of the excavation, until the skeleton at the base of the mound was reached. It was deposited with its head towards the south; and, unlike the one above described, had been simply enveloped in bark, instead of having been enclosed in a chamber of timbers. The course of preparation

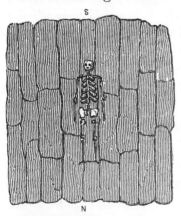

FIG. 53.

for the burial seemed to have been as follows : The surface of the ground was first carefully levelled and packed, over an area perhaps ten or fifteen feet square. This area was then covered with sheets of bark, on which, in the centre, the body of the dead was deposited, with a few articles of stone at its side, and a few small ornaments near the head. It was then covered over with another layer of bark, and the mound heaped above. This skeleton was better preserved than the one last mentioned, but not sufficiently well to be of much value for purposes of comparison. The skull was found broken into small fragments and completely flattened beneath the weight of the mound, which had been so great as to imbed the bones in the original level; so that, when the fragments were removed, a nearly perfect mould of the skeleton was exhibited. The subject had been a man of the ordinary size, not exceeding five feet ten inches in height. The lower maxillary or jaw-bone, wanting the *condyles*, was recovered. It exhibited some remarkable features, which will be noticed elsewhere. The articles found with the skeleton were few in number, and consisted of a stone tube and a stone implement or ornament, designed probably for suspension. The latter is three inches

* Numbered 2 in Map, Plate II.

long, one and a half broad, and three fourths of an inch in thickness, and weighs five ounces. Both articles are composed of a compact limestone, the surface of which was originally highly polished. Near the head of the skeleton were found a couple of bear's teeth which, from their position, were probably used as ear ornaments. Just at the head and also at the foot of the skeleton had been placed a small stick of timber, probably to retain the covering of bark in its place. That the envelope of the skeleton, in this case, was bark and not matting, was shown from the texture of the material, which was distinctly to be traced in the decomposed mass, as well as from other circumstances. From certain indications, it was, at first, thought the bark in the vicinity of the skeleton had been painted of a red color, as portions adhered to the bones, giving them a reddish tinge. This probably resulted from other and natural causes.

The charcoal layer was not observed in this mound, though it may have existed to one side or the other of the excavation. Several other large mounds occur on the plain in the vicinity of the one here described, a number of which were examined with similar results. It may be observed that in most instances, in mounds of this description, the skeleton is found enveloped in bark or matting, (it is difficult in some cases to decide which,) instead of being enclosed in a chamber of timber.

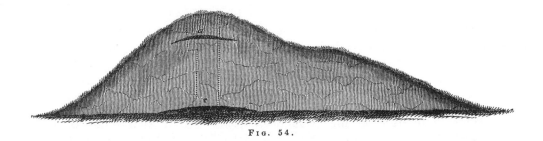

F I G. 54.

Fig. 54 exhibits a section of a mound in which burial by fire had been practised.* It is situated within the corporate limits of the city of Chillicothe, and was originally above twenty-five feet in height, though now reduced to about twenty. The customary shaft was sunk from its apex. At six feet below the surface a layer of charcoal, corresponding in all respects with that described in connection with the first example of mounds of this class, was found. It was placed a little to the eastern side of the mound, a circumstance not shown in the figure, which exhibits a section from north to south. Upon the original level of the earth was found a deposit or layer of charcoal and ashes six or eight feet square and from six inches to a foot in thickness. In this layer were discovered fragments of human bones; a stone hand-axe; several thin pieces of copper which had been worked into shape; and also a number of stones of the harder and less common kinds, fragments of sienite, gneiss, etc. The stone hand-axe here obtained, it is a remarkable fact, is the only one which has been recovered from the mounds, which incontestibly belonged to

---

* Numbered 3, in the Map, Plate II.

the builders.   Several of like character have nevertheless been found elsewhere. It is figured under the head of *Implements*.   The fire in this case had been a strong one, as is evidenced from the fact that the skeleton had here been almost entirely consumed.   That it had also been heaped over while burning, was shown by the charcoal, which was coarse and clear, and by the baking of the earth immediately above it.   In some instances, in which burial by incremation has been practised, the entire skeleton is traceable.   In such cases it has been observed that the charcoal occurs beneath as well as above the skeleton, demonstrating that the body had been placed upon a pyre of some sort before burning.   Remains of art, for obvious reasons, are not abundant in this description of sepulchral mounds; nor is the supplementary charcoal layer of frequent occurrence.

The gradual slope, resembling a graded way, upon the southern side of this mound, is a feature not easily explained.   It would seem at first glance to be designed as a passage to the top.   The more probable conclusion however is, that it is a supplementary mound, which by cultivation and the lapse of time has become so merged in the larger one at its side as not to be distinguishable from it.   Sepulchral mounds of various sizes, joining and running into each other, are common.   This mound is nearer to enclosures than any other of the class yet examined.

Mounds of this, as well as of the first class, were often disturbed by the later Indians.   Their remains are frequently found, in some cases in large quantities, as if the mound had been used for a long period as a general burial-place.   Such was the case with a large mound, situated six miles above the town of Chillicothe, in which a great number of burials had been made, at various depths, from eighteen inches to four feet.   The skeletons were, in places, two or three deep, and placed without arrangement in respect to each other.   Some were evidently of a more ancient date than others, showing, from their condition as well as position, that they had been deposited at different periods.   One or two were observed in which the skull had been fractured by blows from a hatchet or other instrument, establishing that the individual had met a violent death.   With some, rude vessels of pottery, and stone and bone implements, had been deposited; and, in a small mound close by, a *silver cross*, of French origin, was discovered,—all going to establish the comparatively recent date of these burials.   In sinking a shaft five feet square, no less than *seven* skeletons, the lowest about four feet from the surface, were exposed.   Beneath all of these, at the depth of fourteen feet and near the base of the mound, were found traces of the *original deposit* of the mound-builders.   In this case, had the investigation been less complete, it might have been concluded that this mound was a grand receptacle of the dead, and " contained many thousand human skeletons."   Another proof is here furnished of the necessity of thoroughness in explorations of this character, in order to arrive at correct conclusions.

The ceremonies of interment, so far as we are enabled to deduce them from these monuments, were conducted with great regularity and system.   None of those disturbances mentioned by various writers, where the remains seem to have been heaped together without order and without care, have been observed in the course of these investigations, except in cases where recent deposits had been made.

On the contrary, all the circumstances seem to indicate that burial was a solemn and deliberate rite, regulated by fixed customs of, perhaps, religious or superstitious origin. It is possible that in certain cases, a special practice was prescribed. We may thus account for the presence or absence of the charcoal layers, and also for the practice of incremation in some instances and simple inhumation in others.*

In a very few of the sepulchral mounds, a rude enclosure of stone was placed around the skeleton, corresponding to that of timber in others. No mounds possessing this peculiarity fell under notice during the investigations here recorded: there can, however, be no doubt of the fact. A mound within the limits of Chillicothe was removed a number of years since, in which a stone coffin, corresponding very nearly with the *kistvaen* of the English antiquaries, was discovered. The stones are said to have been laid up with great regularity.† In some instances a pile of stones seems to have been heaped carelessly over the skeleton ; in others it was heaped upon the timbers covering the sepulchral chamber, as in the mound at Grave creek.

Urn burial does not seem to have been practised in the valley of the Ohio. It is nevertheless undoubted that in some of the Southern States, by either the ancient races or the more modern Indians, burials of this character were frequent. This is sufficiently established by the discovery in the mounds and elsewhere, of earthen vessels containing human remains, generally but not always burned. In the mounds on the Wateree river, near Camden, South Carolina, ranges of vases, filled with human remains, were discovered. A detailed account of these is given by Dr. Blanding, in a preceding chapter. (See page 106.) When unburnt, the skeletons seem to have been packed in the vase, after the flesh had decomposed. Sometimes, when the mouth of the vase is small, the skull is placed, face downwards, in the opening, constituting a sort of cover. Entire cemeteries have been found, in which urn burial alone seems to have been practised. Such a one was accidentally discovered, not many years since, in St. Catharine's island, on the coast of Georgia. The vases were coarse in material, of rude workmanship, from eighteen to twenty inches in height, and filled with burned human bones. One of the vases from this locality is now deposited in the museum of the Georgia Historical Society.‡

---

* Among the ancient Mexicans the dead were burned, except in cases where death had been caused by leprosy or other incurable disease of that order. Boys under seventeen years of age were also denied that sacred rite. The Hurons, on the other hand, burned the bodies of those who had been drowned or killed by lightning.

† This feature was remarked by Mr. Lesueur, in some of the mounds opened by him, in the vicinity of New Harmony, Indiana. He found, at the base of several, a level space, upon which was a right-angled, oblong parallelogram, formed of flat stones, set edgewise and covered over with similar stones. Some decayed bones were found in them.—*Travels in North America by Prince Maximilian*, p. 80.

‡ Rev. Wm. B. Stevens, Athens, Ga.

The relics of art found in these mounds possess great uniformity of character. Personal ornaments are most common, such as bracelets, perforated plates of copper, and beads of bone, ivory, shell, or metal. Few weapons, such as spear or arrow points, are found; stone implements are more common. Many of these articles are identical with those found in mounds of the first class. Plates of mica are of frequent occurrence; they are sometimes of large size and considerable thickness. Instances are known in which this material has been found in vast quantities, dispersed over and sometimes completely covering the skeleton. It seems not unlikely that a degree of superstitious regard attached to it, or that it was sacred to certain purposes. The plates are often cut into regular figures, discs, ovals, etc. Vases of pottery are occasionally, but not often, found. Of all these varieties of relics appropriate notice will be taken in a subsequent chapter.

In all of the sepulchral mounds opened and examined in the course of these investigations, with a single exception, the human remains have been found so much decayed as to render any attempt to restore the skull, or indeed any portion of the skeleton, entirely hopeless. With this experience, it is considered extremely doubtful whether any of the numerous skulls which have been sent abroad and exhibited as undoubted remains of the mound-builders, were really such. A few are possibly genuine; this can only be determined by a full understanding of the circumstances under which they were obtained. The fact that they were found in the mounds, in view of the variety of deposits which have been made at different periods, is hardly presumptive evidence that they belonged to the builders.

Considering that the earth around these skeletons is wonderfully compact and dry, and that the conditions for their preservation are exceedingly favorable, while they are in fact so much decayed, we may form some approximate estimate of their remote antiquity. In the barrows of the ancient Britons, entire well-preserved skeletons are found, although possessing an undoubted antiquity of at least eighteen hundred years. Local causes may produce singular results, in particular instances, but we speak now of these remains in the aggregate.

It has already been observed, that, as a general rule, each mound was raised over a single individual. The mound at Grave creek furnishes the only exception to the remark within the range of our observation. The mounds of the Southern States are probably of different construction, and some of them may perhaps be regarded as general cemeteries.

The Grave creek mound, although it has often been described, deserves, from its size and singularity of construction, more than a passing notice. It is situated on the plain, at the junction of Grave creek and the Ohio river, twelve miles below Wheeling, in the State of Virginia. It occurs in connection with various works now much obliterated, but is not enclosed by circumvallations. It is one of the largest in the Ohio valley; measuring about seventy feet in height, by one thousand in circumference at the base. It was excavated by the proprietor in 1838. He sank a shaft from the apex of the mound to the base, ($b\ a$, Fig. 55,) intersecting it at that point by a horizontal drift ($a\ e\ e$). It was found to contain two sepulchral chambers, one at the base, (a,) and another thirty feet above (c). These chambers had been constructed of logs, and covered with stones, which had sunk under the superincumbent mass

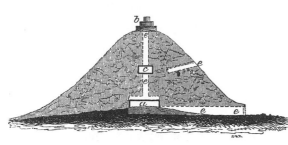

FIG. 55.

as the wood decayed, giving the summit of the mound a flat or rather dish-shaped form.* The lower chamber contained two human skeletons (one of which was thought to be that of a female); the upper chamber contained but one skeleton in an

FIG. 56.—GREAT MOUND AT GRAVE CREEK.

advanced stage of decay. With these were found between three and four thousand shell beads, a number of ornaments of mica, several bracelets of copper, and various articles carved in stone. After the excavation of the mound, a light three-story wooden structure was erected upon its summit. It is indicated by b in the section.

---

* In the construction of this mound the builders had availed themselves of a small natural elevation, above which the tumulus was raised. The vault a had been sunk in this elevation: it was an exact parallelogram, constructed by setting upright timbers around the sides, and covering these with logs

In respect to the number of sepulchral chambers and enclosed skeletons, this mound is quite extraordinary. It may be conjectured with some show of reason, that it contained the bones of the family of a chieftain, or distinguished individual among the tribes of the builders.

It is common to find two or three, sometimes four or five, sepulchral mounds in a group.   In such cases it is always to be remarked that one of the group is much the largest, twice or three times the dimensions of any of the others; and that the smaller ones, of various sizes, are arranged around its base, generally joining it, thus evincing a designed dependence and intimate relation between them.

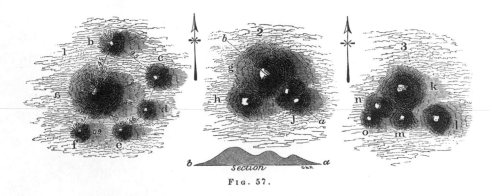

FIG. 57.

Plans of three groups of this description are herewith presented, Fig. 57.

NUMBER 1 is situated six miles below Hamilton, Butler county, Ohio. The relative sizes, positions, etc., of the mounds composing it, are indicated in the plan. The largest is twenty-seven feet high; the rest range from four to ten feet in height.

---

placed horizontally, above which were piled a quantity of loose stones. The second vault appears to have been smaller than the first, but corresponded with it in structure.

For detailed descriptions of this mound and its contents, see an account by Dr. CLEMENS, published in 1839, in *Morton's Crania Americana*, p. 221; by the proprietor of the mound, Mr. TOMLINSON, in the *American Pioneer* for 1843, vol. ii., pp. 195—203; and by HENRY R. SCHOOLCRAFT, Esq., in the first volume of the *Transactions of the American Ethnological Society*, 1846.

It should be remarked that some discrepancies exist between these several accounts. That of Dr. Clemens, which is the earliest, states that in carrying in the horizontal excavation, "at the distance of twelve or fifteen feet, were found numerous masses composed of charcoal and burnt bones. Before reaching the centre, a passage-way was discovered to a vault at the base; this passage had an inclination of ten or fifteen degrees, and had been covered with timbers, of which the impression in the earth alone remained. The vault itself appeared to have been covered with timbers and loose stones. After removing all the rubbish from the vault, two skeletons were found, one on the east, the other on the west side. The former was the smaller and more perfect of the two.   * * *   On reaching the lower vault from the top it was determined to enlarge it for the accommodation of visitors. In so doing ten more skeletons were discovered, all in a sitting posture, but in so fragile a state as to defy all attempts at preservation."

It may be suggested, that the smaller or female skeleton in the vault, as well as those surrounding it, were the remains of victims sacrificed, in accordance with barbarian practice, as attendants in the world of spirits upon the chieftain, in honor of whom this mound was erected.   This practice was common among the Natchez, Mexicans, Peruvians, and other aboriginal nations.

NUMBER 2 occurs upon the plain in the immediate vicinity of Chillicothe, and is numbered 4 in the Map of a section of the Scioto valley, Plate II. The small one indicated by the letter *j* was excavated, and found to contain the skeleton of a girl enveloped in bark, in the manner already described. The largest of the group is about thirty feet in height.

NUMBER 3 is situated in Pike county, Ohio, and is indicated in the plan of the " Graded Way " near Piketon, Plate XXXI.

FIG. 58.

Something like this arrangement was observed by Com. WILKES, in the mounds of Oregon. They occurred in groups of five, as shown in Fig. 58,—the largest occupying the centre.

May we not conclude that these groups are family tombs; the principal mound containing the head of the family, the smaller ones its various members? In the case of the Grave creek mound, it is possible that, instead of building an additional mound, a supplementary chamber was constructed upon a mound already raised,—a single mound being thus made to fill the place of a group. This suggestion derives some support from the fact that the second chamber is placed, above the lower vault, at about the usual height of the larger sepulchral mounds.*

It is not to be supposed that the mounds were the sole cemeteries of the race that built them. They were probably erected only over the bodies of the chieftains and priests, perhaps also over the ashes of distinguished families. The graves of the great mass of the ancient people who thronged our valleys, and the silent monuments of whose toil are seen on every hand, were not thus signalized. We scarcely know where to turn to find them. Every day the plough uncovers crumbling remains; but they elicit no remark,—are passed by and forgotten. The wasting banks of our rivers occasionally display extensive cemeteries, but sufficient attention has never been bestowed upon them to enable us to speak with any degree of certainty of their date, or to distinguish whether they belonged to the mound-builders or a subsequent race. These cemeteries are often of such extent, as to give a name to the locality in which they occur. Thus we hear, on the Wabash, of the " Big Bone Bank," and the " Little Bone Bank," from which, it is represented, the river annually washes many human skeletons, accompanied by numerous and singular remains of art, among which are more particularly mentioned vases and other vessels of pottery, of remarkable and often fantastic form. At various places in the States north of the Ohio, thousands of graves are said to occur, placed in ranges parallel to each other. The extensive cemeteries of Tennessee and Missouri have often been mentioned, and it has been conjectured that the caves of Kentucky and Ohio were grand depositories of the dead of the ancient people. We have, however, nothing at all satisfactory upon the subject,

---

* The barrows denominated the " Bell Barrows," of England, are thought, by English antiquarians, to be a modification of the " Bowl Barrow," formed by placing a new top upon the latter, and otherwise enlarging it, for the purpose of fresh interment. It is common in this description of barrows, to find one burial above the other, as at Grave creek.

which still continues to invite investigation. It is not improbable that many of the dead were burned, and that their ashes were heaped together, constituting mounds. Such an inference may not unreasonably be drawn from certain facts which will be presented when we come to speak of the anomalous or unclassified mounds. It may however be remarked in this connection, that no very distinct traces of the ancient burial-places can be expected to be found. If, from the mounds where, from their protection from the action of moisture and other decomposing causes, the enclosed remains would be most likely to be well preserved, it is found almost impossible to recover a single entire bone, it is not to be wondered at that the remains of the common dead are now nearly or quite undistinguishable from the mould which surrounds them. The apparent absence therefore of any general cemeteries of the era of the mounds, may be regarded as another and strong evidence of the remote antiquity of the monuments of the West.

It should be remarked before proceeding further, that the position of the mound-skeletons, in respect to the east or any other point of the compass, is never fixed. They are nearly always found disposed at length, with their arms carefully adjusted at their sides. None have been discovered in a sitting posture, except among the recent deposits ; and, even among these, no uniformity exists : some are extended at length, others lie upon their sides bent nearly double, others still in a sitting posture ; and in a few cases it seems that the bones, after the decomposition of the flesh, had been rudely huddled together in a narrow grave.*

---

* The North American Indians, in their burials by inhumation, very generally placed the body in a sitting posture. Their customs of burial were, however, extremely variant. Some of the tribes to this day, after enveloping the bodies of their dead, place them on scaffolds or in the forks of trees. Among some of the Southern Indians, they were exposed until the flesh parted from the bones, which were then gathered with various ceremonies and deposited in the huts of the relatives, the temples of the tribe, " the medicine house," or in buildings specially dedicated to the purpose. The Mexicans, in cases where burial by inhumation was practised, placed their dead in a sitting position: so too did the Central Americans and Peruvians, as is sufficiently evidenced by an examination of their tombs. It is a great mistake, however, to suppose that the custom was anything like universal either among the ancient inhabitants or more recent tribes.

CHAPTER VIII.

EARTHWORKS—TEMPLE MOUNDS.

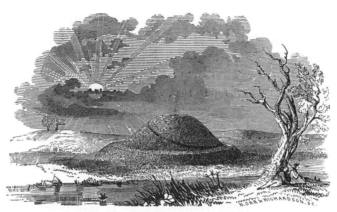

FIG. 59.—TERRACED MOUND.

THESE mounds are distinguished by their great regularity of form and general large dimensions. They occur most usually within, but sometimes without, the walls of enclosures. They consist chiefly of pyramidal structures, truncated, and generally having graded avenues to their tops. In some instances they are terraced, or have successive stages. But whatever their form, whether round, oval, octangular, square, or oblong, they have invariably flat or level tops, of greater or less area. Examples are known in which, although but a few feet in elevation, they cover several acres of ground; in which cases they are commonly called "platforms."

Mounds of this class are not numerous in Ohio, and it is believed are only found at Marietta, Newark, Portsmouth, and in the vicinity of Chillicothe. These are all described, and their predominant features illustrated, in the accounts of the works at the several points where they occur, to which attention is directed. (See Plates XVIII, XXV, XXVI.) Those at Marietta are situated within an enclosure; those at Newark and near Chillicothe, in close connection with small circles upon which they seem to have some degree of dependence. So far as ascertained, they cover no remains, and seem obviously designed as the sites of temples or of other structures which have passed away, or as "high places" for the performance of certain ceremonies. The likeness which they bear to the *Teocallis* of Mexico is striking, and suggestive of their probable purposes.

In addition to the pyramidal structures here noticed, there are others somewhat different in their forms, but which were undoubtedly appropriated to the same purpose. The mound embraced in the circular work connected with the Portsmouth group, is an example. (See Plate XXVIII.) Though much defaced, its original plan can easily be made out. It is circular, placed on a terrace, is truncated, and has a spiral pathway leading to its summit. The purpose already assigned to it, viz. that of a site for a temple, or a "high place" for the performance of ceremonies probably connected with the superstitions of the ancient people, is indicated not less by the peculiarities of its construction, than by the character of the enclosure in which it is situated.

The feature of truncation is not, however, peculiar to this class of mounds. It is frequently observed in those which, upon investigation, are found to be sepulchral in their character; in which cases it is to be attributed to the falling in of the sepulchral chambers. This circumstance gave the summit of the Grave creek Mound a hollow or dish-shaped form, which was a source of much conjecture, until the excavation of the mound explained the cause.

Along the Mississippi river, and especially as we approach the Gulf, these regular structures increase both in number and magnitude. In Kentucky they are more frequent than in the States north of the Ohio river; and in Tennessee and Mississippi they are still more abundant. Some of the largest, however, occur in pretty high latitudes. The great mound at Cahokia, Illinois, is one of the

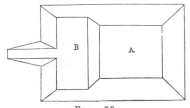

FIG. 60.

most remarkable. It has often been described, and all accounts concur in respect to its great size. The following approximate plan will serve to give an idea of its general outline. It is of course much rounded, and its regularity to a great degree destroyed, by the storms and changes of centuries; its original plan is, however, represented to be still sufficiently obvious. The form of the mound is that of a parallelogram, seven hundred feet long by five hundred wide at the base. It is ninety feet in height. Upon one side is a broad apron or terrace, which is reached by a graded ascent. At the time this mound was occupied by the monks of La Trappe, the terrace was used as a garden. It is one hundred and sixty feet wide and three hundred and fifty long; the summit or highest part of the mound (A) measures two hundred feet in width by four hundred and fifty in length. Here formerly stood a broad, low mound, which was disturbed in preparing the foundations of a dwelling house. Within it were found human bones, and various implements of stone and pottery, probably belonging to a recent deposit. This mound covers not far from eight acres of ground, and the area of its level summit is about five acres. Its solid contents may be roughly estimated at twenty millions of cubic feet.* A number of similar mounds, though of less size, occur in this

---

* Notes on the Antiquities of the Mississippi Valley, by H. H. Breckenridge, Trans. Am. Phil. Soc. 1813; Views of Louisiana, p. 172; Latrobe, vol. ii. p. 250; Featherstonhaugh's Travels in North America, p. 66.

vicinity, and others still exist near the city of St. Louis.* Mounds of this class 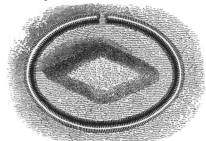 are sometimes surrounded by low embankments of earth. A fine example is furnished by the large conical mound at Marietta, of which a view is elsewhere given. Another occurs on the Virginia shore of the Ohio, nearly opposite the head of Blennerhassett's Island (Fig. 61). It is lozenge-shaped, and is surrounded by a wall and ditch.†

FIG. 61.

Some very remarkable mounds of this class occur in Kentucky, on the "Long Bottom" of Cumberland river, in Adair county; also near Cadiz, Trigg county; near Mount Sterling, and in Hickman and McCracken counties. In Whiteby county is one three hundred and sixty feet long, one hundred and fifty wide, and twelve high, with graded ascents; and at Hopkinsville, Christian county, is one of great size, upon which the court-house is built.

In Bradford county, Tennessee, several extensive terraces or platforms of earth are said to exist, one of which is represented to cover three acres. Six miles south-west of Paris, Henry county, is a terrace four or five feet high and two hundred feet square. It serves as the site of a dwelling. Similar ones are numerous on Old Town creek, nine or ten miles westward of Paris. There are others on the banks of the Cumberland river between Palmyra and Clarkesville, and a number occur in the vicinity of Knoxville. Some of large size are found in Missouri, at New Madrid, St. Genevieve and other places.

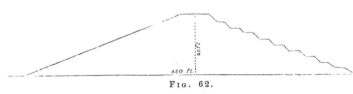

FIG. 62.

Fig. 62. A section from east to west of a large mound in Clarke county, Tennessee, not far from Claiborne. It is situated on a hill, and is fifty feet in height by four hundred and fifty in diameter at the base. It is truncated, and has a level area at its summit about one hundred feet in circumference. It is also terraced and has ten stages, each of which is not far from five feet above the other. The terraces are covered with turf; but the slopes exhibit the naked white clay of which the mound is composed. The stages are interrupted on the eastern side, where there is a graded ascent.‡

---

* There is an elevation of earth not far from Chicago, in the northern part of Illinois, which was supposed, for many years, to be of artificial origin. It is well known as Mount Joliet. It appears, however, from all direct information that can be gathered concerning it, that it is simply a natural eminence of regular outline. So far as we are informed, there are no traces of a great ancient population in that vicinity, such as we almost invariably find accompanying the more imposing aboriginal monuments.

† On the authority of Charles Sullivan, Esq., Marietta, Ohio.

‡ The description of this mound is from the RAFINESQUE MSS. The section purports to have been made by a Mr. Ewing.

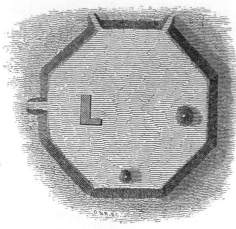

FIG. 63.

Fig. 63. This remarkable mound or terrace occurs near Lovedale, Woodford county, Kentucky. It is octagonal in form, measuring one hundred and fifty feet on each side. It has three graded ascents, one at each of the northern angles and one at the middle of the western side. It is but little more than five feet in height. Upon it are two conical mounds, as shown in the plan, and also the dwelling house of the proprietor. Some distance to the northward of this terrace are a number of large and deep pits, from which the material for its construction was probably taken.*

Fig. 64. The plan of this mound or terrace sufficiently explains its character. It is situated three miles from Washington, Mason county, Kentucky. Its height is ten feet.†

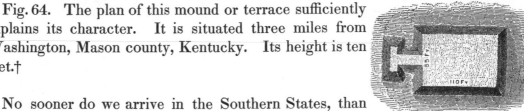

FIG. 64.

No sooner do we arrive in the Southern States, than we find these Teocalli-shaped structures constituting the most numerous and important portion of the ancient remains. They preserve very nearly the same form with those already described, but are generally of greater size, and enter into many new combinations. Examples of a considerable number have already been given in the chapter on the "Monuments of the Southern States." Here they often occur entirely separate from enclosures of any sort, and are frequently placed with a great deal of regularity in respect to each other. It sometimes happens that a large truncated mound is surrounded by a series of smaller ones, so as to form an ellipse, circle, square, or parallelogram.‡ In some instances the various mounds of a group are connected with each other by raised ways or terraces.

Many of the temple mounds of the South are circular; most have graded ascents, and a few have a low wall enclosing the level area at their tops. In Macon and Cherokee counties, North Carolina, quite a number, answering to this description, are said to exist. A very remarkable one occurs near the town of Franklin, on the Tennessee river, and another not far from the town of Murphy, on Valley

---

* RAFINESQUE MSS. The survey of this singular monument purports to have been made in 1820 The then proprietor was a Mr. Ship, the position of whose residence is shown in the plan.

† RAFINESQUE MSS., 1818

‡ Mounds placed in this manner are of occasional occurrence in the more northern States. Examples have been remarked in Illinois and Missouri. Twelve miles south-west of the town of Glasgow, Barren county, Kentucky, a group is found. The mounds are small, oval, and placed at intervals of about fifty yards, so as to constitute a circle of perhaps fifteen hundred feet in circumference. In the centre of the circular area is a large mound between twenty and thirty feet in height. These mounds appear to have sustained structures of some kind.—*Collins's Kentucky*, p. 176.

river. They are from twelve to fifteen feet high and of proportionate base. Their

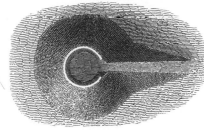

FIG. 65.

form is best illustrated by the accompanying engraving, Fig. 65. There are no enclosures in the vicinity of these works. It is said the Indians formerly built their council houses upon them.

Some of these circular mounds, as we have seen in a previous chapter, were ascended by spiral pathways, winding round them, as round a shaft, from base to summit. Indeed, it would be impossible to describe all the various forms which these structures assume; their general character is however sufficiently illustrated by the preceding examples.

It often happens that the temple mounds of the South have other mounds upon their summits. This is especially the case with the large pyramidal structures. An example is furnished in the great Seltzertown mound, which is covered with a number of smaller ones.

FIG. 66.—GROUP OF SEPULCHRAL MOUNDS.

CHAPTER IX.

ANOMALOUS MOUNDS.

BESIDES the mounds already described, the purposes of which seem pretty clearly indicated, there are many which will admit of no classification. Some of them possess features in common with all classes, and seem to have been appropriated to a double purpose; while others, in our present state of knowledge concerning them, are entirely inexplicable. As these mounds differ individually from each other, it is of course impossible to present anything like a general view of their character. We can therefore only describe a few of the more remarkable, dismissing the remainder with the single observation that their features do not indicate any specific design, and are not sufficiently distinct or uniform to justify or sustain a classification.

One of the most singular of these mounds, and one which best illustrates the remark that certain mounds were probably made to subserve a double purpose, is situated within a large enclosure on the east bank of the Scioto river. (Marked *c e*, Plate XX.) A plan and section of the mound are herewith presented (Fig. 67).

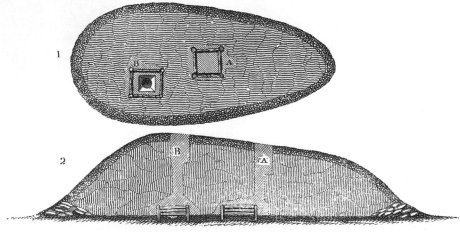

FIG. 67.

It is an irregular oval in form, and is one hundred and sixty feet long, ninety broad at its larger end, and twenty feet in height. Excavations were made at the points indicated in the section. The one towards the right or smaller end of the mound disclosed an enclosure of timber, eight feet square, and similar, in all respects, to those found in the sepulchral mounds, except that, in this instance, posts eight inches in diameter had been planted at the outer corners, as if to sustain the structure. These posts had been inserted eighteen inches in the original level or floor of the mound. The holes left by their decay were found filled with decomposed material; when this was removed, they exhibited perfect *casts* of the timbers. The casts also of the horizontal timbers were well retained in the compact earth, and one of the workmen, without much difficulty, was enabled to creep more than half the way around the enclosure which they had formed. Within this chamber the earth was as firm as in any portion of the mound. Upon removing a portion, a skeleton partly burned was found, and with it a thin copper plate seven inches long and four broad, perforated with two small holes; also a large pipe of bold outline, carved from a dark compact porphyry

Fig. 68. — Half size.

(Fig. 68). The bones seemed to have been enveloped in a species of matting, which was too much decayed to be distinctly made out. The floor of the mound, it should be mentioned, so far as explored, was composed of clay, was perfectly level, and had been burned to considerable hardness.

The second excavation (B) was made in the larger end of the mound, somewhat to one side of the centre, at a spot marked by a depression in the surface. At the depth of twenty feet was found an altar of clay of exceeding symmetry. This was sunk, as shown in the section, in the general level or floor of the mound, and had been surrounded by an enclosure in all respects similar to the one above described, except that the timbers had been less in size. A fine carbonaceous deposit, resembling burned leaves, was found within the altar. Amongst the decayed materials of the surrounding enclosure were found several *skewers*, if we may so term them, in lack of a better name, made of the bones (*ulna*) of the deer. They were finely tapered to a point, and had evidently been originally highly polished. Some were not less than nine or ten inches long. Though apparently sound, they were found to be exceedingly brittle, retaining little if any of their animal matter. Drifts were carried in the course shown in the section, and the evidences of another enclosure discovered. The excavation was suspended at this point, in consequence of heavy and continued rains. The holes soon became partly filled by the caving in of the loose earth near the surface; which discouraging circumstance, joined to the extreme difficulty of digging,* prevented a resumption of

---

* The difficulty of carrying on investigations in the large mounds cannot be readily appreciated. The earth is always so compact as to require, literally, to be *cut out*. It has then to be raised to the surface,— a task of great labor, and only accomplished by leaving stages in the descent and throwing the earth from one to the other, and finally to the surface. Four industrious men were employed not less than ten or twelve days in making the excavations in this mound alone.

the investigation. It is very certain that another, perhaps several other chambers are concealed by this mound.

The surface of this mound was covered with the layer of pebbles and coarse gravel already mentioned as characterizing the mounds of the first class; but the sand strata were absent. Around the base had been laid, with some degree of regularity, a large quantity of flat stones, constituting a sort of wall for the better support of the earth. These stones must have been brought from the hills, which are here nearly half a mile distant. Why the altar as well as the skeleton had been enclosed, and why the floor of the mound had been so carefully levelled, cast over with clay, and then hardened by fire, are questions which will probably remain unanswered and unexplained unless future investigations serve further to elucidate the mystery of the mounds. At any rate, this singular mound can prove no greater puzzle to the reader than it has to the authors of these inquiries.

A detached mound stands on the bank of Walnut creek, about three miles below the one just described, which is entirely anomalous in its character. It is about nine feet in height by forty base. The following section will best explain its construction.

FIG. 69.

Fig. 69. The principal portion of the mound, which is darkly shaded in the section, resembles long exposed and highly compacted ashes, and is intermingled with specks of charcoal, small bits of burned bones, and fragments of sandstone much burned. Beneath this, and forming the nucleus as it were of the entire mound, is a mass of very pure white clay, of somewhat regular outline; but whether this regularity was accidental or designed, it is not undertaken to say. The clay rested upon the original soil, and did not appear to have been subjected in any degree to the action of fire. The carbonaceous deposit, if we may so regard it, seems from this circumstance to have been brought here and not to have been produced by burning on the spot. The mound could not possibly have been designed for a *look-out*, inasmuch as it stands immediately at the base of the table lands, and commands but a very limited view.

Two other mounds, numbered 6 and 7 in the map, Plate II, exhibited some features in common with the one last mentioned, though neither had the clay deposit at the base. After penetrating a foot or twenty inches into these, traces of ashes and other carbonaceous matter, with here and there small quantities of burned bones in fine fragments, became abundant,—indeed the remainder of the mound seemed entirely constituted of such materials. In some instances, if not in all, the fragments of calcined bones were of the human skeleton. It has been suggested that these mounds were composed of the ashes of the dead, burned elsewhere, but finally thus heaped together. It is not impossible that such was the case in a few instances, though mounds possessing these features are too few in number and too small in size to justify the conclusion that such was the general custom.

A number of mounds, principally within enclosures, have been examined, which exhibited only a level, hard-packed area at their base, thinly covered with a fine-grained, carbonaceous material similar to that which is sometimes found on the altars, and which has several times been described as resembling burned leaves or straw. It has been suggested that sacrifices or offerings of vegetables or the "first fruits" of the year were sometimes made, of which these traces alone remain.

In one or two small mounds, deposits of arrow or spear points of flint have been found. The little mound No. 8 in the map, Plate II, contained a pile in its centre of twenty or more, each one broken into two or three pieces. They had not been exposed to the action of fire. In shape they are singular, differing materially from those usually found scattered over the fields, and are exceedingly thin and well wrought. It is fruitless to conjecture why they were thus broken up, or why indeed the simple deposit was made at all.

A few small mounds have been observed composed entirely of pebbles, of the average size of one's fist, unmixed with earth, excepting what had gradually accumulated over them. Several of those surrounding the great work on Paint creek (Plate XXI, No. 2) are of this description, and are supposed, by the residents of the vicinity, to be the missiles of the ancient people, thus conveniently deposited for use in case of an attack upon the supposed fortress! Unfortunately for this hypothesis, the magazines are outside of the walls.

It would prove an almost endless and perhaps an entirely unprofitable task to describe the peculiarities of individual mounds, not referable to either of the grand classes already noticed. Most of them appear inexplicable; not more so, however, than did the sacrificial or altar mounds when first noticed, and it is likely that more extended investigations may also serve to explain their purposes. The examples above presented are adduced to show that, while the leading purposes of the mounds (of Ohio at least) have been detected and settled, there is yet much left for future explorations to determine.

MOUNDS OF OBSERVATION.

It has already been several times remarked, that the most commanding positions on the hills bordering the valleys of the West, are often crowned with mounds, generally of intermediate, but sometimes of large size,—suggesting at once the purposes to which some of the *cairns* or hill-mounds of the Celts were applied, namely, that of signal or alarm posts.

Ranges of these mounds may be observed extending along the valleys for many miles. Between Chillicothe and Columbus, on the eastern border of the Scioto valley, not far from twenty may be selected, so placed in respect to each other, that it is believed, if the country were cleared of forests, signals of fire might be transmitted in a few minutes along the whole line. On a hill opposite Chillicothe, nearly six hundred feet in height, the loftiest in the entire region, one of these mounds is placed.   After the fall of the leaves in autumn, it is a conspicuous object from every work laid down on the Map of a section of twelve miles of the Scioto valley, to which such frequent reference has been made, as well as from other works not exhibited in the map.   It is indicated by the figure 5 in this map.   A fire built upon it would be distinctly visible for fifteen or twenty miles up, and an equal distance down the valley, (including in its range the Circleville works, twenty miles distant,) as also for a long way up the broad valleys of the two Paint creeks,—both of which abound in remains, and seem to have been especial favorites with the mound-builders.   In the Map of six miles of the Miami valley, (Plate III,) a similar feature will be observed.   Upon a hill three hundred feet in height, overlooking the Colerain work, and commanding an extensive view of the valley, are placed two mounds, which exhibit—in connection with other circumstances not entirely consistent with the conclusion that they were simple signal-stations—strong marks of fire on and around them.   Similar mounds occur, at intervals, along the Wabash and Illinois rivers, as also on the Upper Mississippi, the Ohio, the Miamis, and the Scioto.   On the high hills overlooking the Portsmouth and Marietta works, (Plates XXVI and XXVII,) mounds of stone are situated; those at the former place exhibit evident marks of fire.   On the heights around the works at Grave creek in Virginia, similar features have been observed.*   A trip of exploration, made with special reference to this and kindred points, disclosed the fact that, between the mouths of the Scioto and Guyandotte rivers, the hills upon both sides of the Ohio, for the entire distance, were studded with mounds.   Many of them, however, occurred in groups, their bases joining, and were placed so far back from the brow of the hills as to be entirely invisible from the valley,—facts wholly opposed to the hypothesis which ascribes a common purpose to all of the hill-mounds.   Indeed, for the distance above specified, these mounds, though less in size, seemed quite as numerous as those in the valley; in which, besides mounds and a few small circles, no works of magnitude were discovered,—another fact which may not be without its importance in this connection.

Some of the hill-mounds bordering on the Ohio have been opened by explorers, and found to contain human remains, but whether of an ancient or modern date, it is difficult, from the imperfect nature of the accounts, to determine.   The remarkable mound already mentioned, situated on the high hill near Chillicothe, was opened some twelve or fifteen years ago; and, it is said, human remains and a variety of relics were discovered in it.   Although the investigation of this class of mounds has, from a variety of causes, been comparatively limited, yet enough has been ascertained concerning them, to justify the belief that a large proportion contain human remains, undoubtedly those of the mound-builders.   And, although traces of fire are to be observed around very many, the marks are not sufficiently strong to sustain the inference that all were look-outs, and that fires were kindled upon them as signals.   It is not impossible that a portion were devoted to sepulture, another portion to observation, and that some answered a double purpose.

---

* Transactions of the American Ethnological Society, vol. i. p. 409.

This is a point which remains to be settled by the disclosures of the mattock and spade, and by a close and extended observation of the dependences which exist, not only between the hill-mounds themselves, but between them and the other monuments of the same people.

It may perhaps seem, from what has been adduced, that the classification of any portion of the hill-mounds as places of observation, is not sufficiently well authorized. The positions however which many of them occupy, are such as would most naturally be chosen for such purposes, though not necessarily for such only. The apparent dependence which exists between some of them and the larger earthworks would also seem to favor the idea that they were look-outs. But whether signal-stations or otherwise, there can be no doubt that the ancient people selected prominent and elevated positions upon which to build large fires, which were kept burning for long periods, or renewed at frequent intervals. For what purposes they were built, whether to communicate intelligence or to celebrate some religious rite, it is not undertaken to say.* The traces of these fires are only observed upon the brows of the hills: they appear to have been built generally upon heaps of stones, which are broken up and sometimes partially vitrified. In all cases they exhibit marks of intense and protracted heat. They are vulgarly supposed to be the remains of "*furnaces*," from the amount of scoriaceous material accompanying them, which often covers a large area, and is several feet in thickness. This popular error has led to some very extravagant conjectures as to the former mineral wealth of the vicinity in which they occur; an error which has been perpetuated in various works on American antiquities.

The dependence which exists between certain mounds, and the defensive structures within or near which they are located, is too evident to admit of doubt. It has already been made a subject of remark, (page 43,) and need only be referred to here. In the case of the fortified hill, Plate VI, we find a large mound commanding the only avenue leading to it, and so placed that no approach could be made unobserved from its summit. Similar dependences, perhaps still more marked, are perceived in other works, where mounds are placed on the approaches, or at such points within or without the walls as are best adapted for observation. (See Plate XI, Nos. 1 and 2.)

---

* When Lieut. Fremont penetrated into the fastnesses of Upper California, where his appearance created great alarm among the Indians, he observed this primitive telegraphic system in operation. "Columns of smoke rose over the country at scattered intervals,—signals by which the Indians, here as elsewhere, communicate to each other that enemies are in the country. It is a signal of ancient and very universal application among barbarians."—*Fremont's Second Expedition*, p. 220.

STONE HEAPS.

RUDE heaps of stone, occasionally displaying some degree of regularity, are not uncommon at the West, though by no means peculiar to that section of country. It is exceedingly questionable whether any of them belong to the same era with the other works here treated of, although they are usually ascribed to the mound-builders. The stone mounds, of which mention has already been made, are very different structures, and should not be confounded with these rude accumulations.

One of the most remarkable stone-heaps observed in the course of these investigations, is situated upon the dividing ridge between Indian and Crooked creeks, about ten miles south-west of Chillicothe, Ohio. It is immediately by the side of the old Indian trail which led from the Shawanoe towns, in the vicinity of Chillicothe, to the mouth of the Scioto river; and consists of a simple heap of stones, rectangular in form, and measuring one hundred and six feet in length by sixty in width, and between three and four in height. The stones are of all sizes, from those not larger than a man's head, to those which can hardly be lifted. They are such as are found in great abundance on the hill slopes,—the fragments or *debris* of the outcropping sandstone layers. Some are water-worn, showing that they were brought up from the creek, nearly half a mile distant; and although they were disposed with no regularity in respect to each other, the heap was originally quite symmetrical in outline. The stones have been thrown out from the centre, and an excavation of considerable depth made in the earth beneath, but without results. The heap is situated upon the highest point of land traversed by the Indian trail; upon the water-shed, or dividing ridge, between the streams which flow into Brush creek on the one side, and the Scioto river on the other.

Another heap of stones of like character, but somewhat less in size, is situated upon the top of a high, narrow hill, overlooking the small valley of Salt creek, near Tarlton, Pickaway county, Ohio. It is remarkable as having large numbers of crumbling human bones—to say nothing of living black snakes—intermingled, apparently without order, with the stones. A very extensive prospect is had from this point. Upon the slope of a lower hill near by, appears to have been formerly an Indian village. Many rude relics are uncovered on the spot, by the plough.

Smaller and very irregular heaps are frequent amongst the hills. They do not generally embrace more than a couple of cartloads of stone, and almost invariably cover a skeleton. Occasionally the amount of stones is much greater. Rude implements are sometimes found with the skeletons. A number of such graves have been observed near Sinking Springs, Highland county, Ohio; also in Adams county in the same State, and in Greenup county, Kentucky, at a point nearly opposite the town of Portsmouth on the Ohio.

Heaps of similar character are found in the Atlantic States, where they were raised by the Indians over the bodies of those who met their death by accident, or in the manner of whose death there was something unusual. Dwight, in his Travels, mentions a heap of stones of this description which was raised over the body of a warrior killed by accident, on the old Indian trail between Hartford and Farmington, the seat of the Tunxis Indians, in Connecticut. Traces of a similar heap still exist on the old trail between Schenectady and Cherry Valley in New York, with which a like tradition is connected. They were not raised at once, but were the accumulations of a long period, it being the custom for each warrior as he passed the spot to add a stone to the pile. Hence the general occurrence of these rude monuments near some frequented trail or path.

FIG. 70.—CONICAL MOUND.

24

CHAPTER X.

REMAINS OF ART FOUND IN THE MOUNDS.

THE condition of the ordinary arts of life amongst a people capable of constructing the singular and imposing monuments which we have been contemplating, furnishes a prominent and interesting subject of inquiry. The vast amount of labor expended upon these works, and the regularity and design which they exhibit, taken in connection with the circumstances under which they are found, denote a people advanced from the nomadic or radically savage state,—in short, a numerous agricultural people, spread at one time, or slowly migrating, over a vast extent of country, and having established habits, customs, and modes of life. How far this conclusion, for the present hypothetically advanced, is sustained by the character of the minor vestiges of art, of which we shall now speak, remains to be seen.

It has already been remarked, that the mounds are the principal depositories of ancient art, and that in them we must seek for the only authentic remains of the builders. In the observance of a practice almost universal among barbarous or semi-civilized nations, the mound-builders deposited various articles of use and ornament with their dead. They also, under the prescriptions of their religion, or in accordance with customs unknown to us, and to which perhaps no direct analogy is afforded by those of any other people, placed upon their altars numerous ornaments and implements,—probably those most valued by their possessors,—which remain there to this day, attesting at once the religious zeal of the depositors, and their skill in the simpler arts. From these original sources, the illustrations which follow have been chiefly derived.

The necessity of a careful discrimination between the various remains found in the mounds, resulting from the fact that the races succeeding the builders in the occupation of the country often buried their dead in them, has probably been dwelt upon with sufficient force, in another connection. Attention to the conditions under which they are discovered, and to the simple rules which seem to have governed the mound-builders in making their deposits, can hardly fail to fix with great certainty their date and origin.

Thus in the case of the stratified mounds, we well know, if the strata are entire, that whatever deposits are found beneath them were placed there at the period of the construction of the mounds themselves. On the other hand, if they are broken up, it follows with equal certainty that the mound in which the disturbance is observed, has been invaded since its erection.

It will therefore be seen that we have some certain means of determining, aside from the distinctive features of the articles themselves, which of the relics discovered in the mounds pertain to their builders, and which are of a later date. Hence results the importance of knowing the history of those relics which may fall under notice, and the circumstances attending their discovery, in order to feel authorized in drawing conclusions from them. Their true position satisfactorily ascertained, we proceed with confidence to comparisons and deductions, which otherwise, however ingenious and accurate they might appear, would necessarily be invested with painful uncertainty. From want of proper care in this respect, there is no doubt that articles of European origin, which, by a very natural train of events, found their way to the mounds, have been made the basis of speculations concerning the arts of the mound-builders. To this cause we may refer the existence of the popular errors, that the ancient people were acquainted with the uses of iron, and understood the arts of plating, gilding, etc.

Hence, too, the value of systematic investigations, conducted on the spot, if we would aim to throw any certain light upon this branch of inquiry, or do more than excite an ignorant wonder or gratify an idle curiosity.

The general character of this class of remains has already been indicated. They are such only as, from the nature of their material, have been able to resist the general course of decay :—articles of pottery, bone, ivory, shell, stone, and metal. We can, of course, expect to find no traces of instruments or utensils of wood, and but few and doubtful ones at best, of the materials which went to compose articles of dress. Such remains as are found, so far as their purposes are apparent, are classified; the remainder are so arranged as best to facilitate description.

POTTERY AND ARTICLES OF CLAY.

The art of the potter is hoary in its antiquity. It seems to have been the first domestic art practised by man, and the worker in clay may be esteemed the primitive artisan. Go where we will, from the hut of the roving Indian to the palace of the civilized prince, we everywhere find the products of his craft, rude and unpolished from the hand of the savage, or rivalling the marble from the manufactories of Wedgwood and Copeland.

The site of every Indian town throughout the West is marked by the fragments of pottery scattered around it; and the cemeteries of the various tribes abound with rude vessels of clay, piously deposited with the dead. Previous to the advent of Europeans, the art of the potter was much more important and its practice more general, than it afterwards became upon the introduction of metallic vessels. The mode of preparing and moulding the material is minutely described by the early observers, and seems to have been common to all the tribes, and not to have varied materially from that day to this. The work devolved almost exclusively upon the women, who kneaded the clay and formed the vessels.

Experience seems to have suggested the means of so tempering the material as to resist the action of fire; accordingly we find pounded shells, quartz, and sometimes simple coarse sand from the streams, mixed with the clay.   None of the pottery of the present races, found in the Ohio valley, is destitute of this feature; and it is not uncommon, in certain localities, where from the abundance of fragments, and from other circumstances, it is supposed the manufacture was specially carried on, to find quantities of the decayed shells of the fresh-water molluscs intermixed with the earth, which were probably brought to the spot to be used in the process. Among the Indians along the Gulf, a greater degree of skill was displayed than with those on the upper waters of the Mississippi and on the lakes.   Their vessels were generally larger and more symmetrical, and of a superior finish.   They moulded them over gourds and other models, and baked them in ovens.   In the construction of those of large size, it was customary to model them in baskets of willow or splints, which, at the proper period, were burned off, leaving the vessel perfect in form, and retaining the somewhat ornamental markings of their moulds.   Some of those found on the Ohio seem to have been modelled in bags or nettings of coarse thread or twisted bark.   These practices are still retained by some of the remote western tribes.   Of this description of pottery many specimens are found with the recent deposits in the mounds.   They are identical in every respect with those taken from the known burial-grounds of the Indians; and though generally of rude workmanship, they are not destitute of a certain symmetry of shape and proportion.

Among the mound-builders the art of pottery attained to a considerable degree of perfection.   Various though not abundant specimens of their skill have been recovered, which, in elegance of model, delicacy, and finish, as also in fineness of material, come fully up to the best Peruvian specimens, to which they bear, in many respects, a close resemblance.   They far exceed anything of which the existing tribes of Indians are known to have been capable.   It is to be regretted that none of these remains have been recovered entire in the course of our investigations: they have been found only in the altar or sacrificial mounds, and always in fragments.   The largest deposit was found in the long mound, No. 3, "Mound City," (see page 149,) from which were taken fragments enough to have originally composed a dozen vessels of medium size.   By the exercise of great care and patience in collecting and arranging the pieces, a few vessels have been very nearly restored,—so nearly, as not only to show with all desirable accuracy their shape, but also the character of their ornaments.   They exhibit a variety of graceful forms.

The material of which they are composed is a fine clay; which, in the more delicate specimens, appears to have been worked nearly pure, possessing a very slight silicious intermixture.   Some of the coarser specimens, though much superior in model, have something of the character of the Indian ware already described, pulverized quartz being intermixed with the clay.   Others are tempered with a salmon-colored mica in small flakes, which gives them a ruddy and rather brilliant appearance, and was perhaps introduced with some view to ornament as well as

2.

6.

utility.* None appear to have been glazed; although one or two, either from baking or the subsequent great heat to which they were subjected, exhibit a slightly vitrified surface. Their excellent finish seems to have been the result of the same process with that adopted by the Peruvians in their fictile manufactures.

——

PLATE XLVI.

EARTHEN VESSELS FROM THE MOUNDS.

THIS Plate exhibits drawings of eight vessels of pottery; of which Nos. 1, 2, 3, 4, were taken from the mounds of Ohio, and Nos. 6, 7, 8, 9, from the mounds of South Carolina and Florida. Nos. 3 and 4, although taken from the mounds, will readily be recognised as of comparatively modern manufacture. They were found with the recent deposits, and may be considered as fair specimens of Indian skill in this department. Unlike the older vessels with which they are placed in contrast, they are heavy and coarse, both in material and workmanship.

NUMBER 1 is a beautiful vase, moulded from pure clay, with a slight silicious intermixture. Its thickness is uniform throughout, not exceeding one sixth of an inch. Its outer as well as interior surface is smooth, except where it is dotted by way of ornament. Its finish resembles in all respects that of the finer Peruvian pottery, and, when held in certain positions towards the light, exhibits the same peculiarities of surface, as if it had been carefully shaved and smoothed with a sharp knife. It is highly polished, and has an unctuous feel. The exterior is ornamented as represented in the drawing. The lines are carved in, and appear to have been cut by some sharp *gouge-shaped* instrument, which entirely removed the detached material, leaving no ragged or raised edges. Nothing can exceed the uniformity and precision with which they are executed; and it seems almost impossible that the artist could have preserved so much regularity, with no other guide than the eye. There are four groups or festoons of lines, each of which occupies an equal division of the surface. A line is carried around the top of the vase near the edge, in which, at equal distances from each other, are pierced four small holes, a fifth of an inch in diameter. Between this line and the edge is a row of dots, formed with the same instrument used in carving the lines, held in an oblique direction to the surface. The spaces between some of the lines are

---

* " The present Chilenoes are good potters for common ware; they introduce a considerable quantity of earth and sand, containing abundance of yellow mica, and their vessels sometimes contain as much as seventy gallons or more. They are of great thinness, lightness, and strength."—*Schmidtmeyer's Chile,* p. 117.

roughened in a similar manner.   The color of this vase is a dark brown or umber. Its height is five and a half, its diameter six and a half inches.   The fragment, Fig. 5, exhibits the thickness of the ware, the size of the engraved lines, etc.

NUMBER 2 is a vase of coarser material but more elaborate outline than the one just described.   It is square, with slightly rounded angles, and has a singular offset or shoulder at the top.   Its exterior is divided into four compartments, within each of which is an ornamental figure, somewhat resembling a bird with extended wings.   This ornament is thrown in relief by the roughening of the remaining portions of the surface.   One or two other vases have been found, possessing the same shape and having identical ornaments, but lacking the offset or shoulder above mentioned.   The ornamental work, in all of these specimens, is executed in a free, bold style; and the figures differ just enough to show that they were not cut after a pattern.   This vase is burned hard; its thickness is but one eighth of an inch; its dimensions are, height five inches, greatest diameter the same.

From the delicacy of these specimens, and the amount of labor expended upon them, it is concluded that they were not used for ordinary purposes.   They were perhaps designed to contain articles valued by the possessor, or to be used only on certain important occasions.   It has been suggested that they were possibly the *censers* of the ancient priesthood, or, from the fact of their being found only in the altar mounds, appropriated to sacred purposes.   This supposition might be made with equal propriety in respect to the coarser varieties also found on the altars, and which, it is evident, were designed to be used for purposes requiring strength and the capability of withstanding fire.

NUMBERS 3 and 4 are drawn upon the same scale with the two above described; they contain between one and two quarts.   As before remarked, they may be regarded as in all respects very good specimens of the skill of the modern northern tribes in this description of manufacture.

In the mounds of the South, pottery exists in great abundance; but it differs very much in form and quality from the specimens found on the Ohio.   It is coarser in material, and seems to have been manufactured with less care.   The ornaments, although not without grace, are roughly executed.   Some of the vessels seem to have been burned to considerable hardness, and exhibit the consequent redness of color; but most are of a dark brown, and appear to have been hardened over fires, rather than burned in kilns.

NUMBERS 6, 7, 8, and 9, as already observed, are examples of this Southern ware.   Number 6 is from South Carolina; Nos. 7, 8, and 9, from Florida: they are all deposited in the cabinet of the Historical Society of New York.   No. 6 is about twelve inches in height, of rather elegant model, and ornamented with scrolls.   It contains upwards of a gallon.   Nos. 7 and 9 hold about a quart each; No. 8 perhaps three quarts.

Some of those found in the mounds of Carolina are of great size, and capable of holding from three to thirty gallons. These are seldom ornamented, but are extremely well formed. It may be remarked that the handles of the Southern vases are often neatly moulded into scrolls, or representations of the heads of animals and birds.

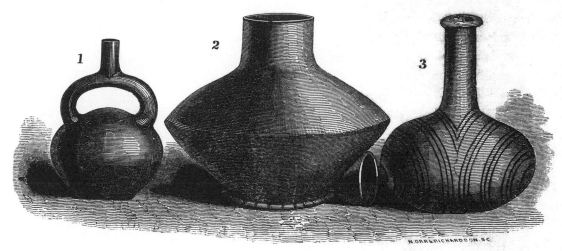

FIG. 71.

Fig. 71, Number 1, is a very good specimen of an ancient Peruvian vessel, now deposited in the museum of the Historical Society of Connecticut, at Hartford. The peculiar spout, answering the double purpose of use and ornament, has been observed in some of the vases of the Southern United States. Number 2 illustrates one variety of earthen ware, which is common from the mouth of the Ohio to the Gulf of Mexico. This specimen was taken from a mound at Ellis's Bluff, near Natchez. It contained burnt remains, though we are uninformed of what description. It is unbaked and composed of a singular kind of clay, which exhibits the appearance and has the feel of the softer varieties of " soap stone." The material is accurately described by Mr. Flint, in his account of certain articles of pottery found in Missouri. " The composition when fractured shows many white floccules in the clay, that resemble fine snow; and these I judge to be pulverized shells. The basis of the composition seems to be the alluvial clay, carried along in the waters of the Mississippi, and called by the French '*terre grasse,*' from its greasy feel." This specimen is seven inches high by eight inches in its greatest diameter. The neck is two and a half inches long, and a cover fits neatly over it, completely closing the vessel. It is very symmetrical, exhibiting but slight irregularities. Its thickness is not far from three eighths of an inch, but it is evidently not uniform throughout. It has no markings, except some irregular notches in the rim of the base.*

Many vessels of similar shape are found in Tennessee, Mississippi, and Louisiana, of which number 3 of the cut furnishes a very good example. They are of a great variety of sizes, and sometimes have the form of the human head, or of

---

* In the cabinet of Dr. S. P. HILDRETH, Marietta, Ohio.

animals.   The celebrated "Triune vessel," which has been made the basis of so much unprofitable speculation, was of the latter character, and represented three human heads joined at the back.   They are variously ornamented, and sometimes painted with red and brown colors.   Their form seems generally to have been suggested by that of the gourd.

FIG. 72.

Fig. 72, Number 1.   This vessel, clearly of modern workmanship, was found a few feet below the surface, near the town of Hamilton, Butler county, Ohio.   It was placed beside a human skeleton, and contained a single muscle-shell.   The material is a compound of clay and pounded shells; its height is seven inches, diameter five and a half.   Number 2 was found in the same vicinity, and under similar circumstances with that last described.   It is of like composition, thick, and of a dark black color.

Number 3 was found in Perry county, Indiana, at a locality known as the " Big Bone Bank."   It is composed of finer material than those just described.   The aperture at the mouth is two inches in diameter; the vase itself is five inches in height, and measures thirteen in circumference.   The " Big Bone Bank," to which we have alluded, occurs on the Wabash river, ten miles above its mouth, and is supposed by many to have been a cemetery of the mound-builders. Human remains are very abundant here, and are said to occur as deep as ten feet below the surface.   With these are deposited various relics, consisting for the most part of vessels of pottery, which are exposed from time to time by the wasting away of the bank.   The following specimens, obtained from this locality, together with those just described, are in the cabinet of JAMES McBRIDE, Esq., Hamilton, Ohio.

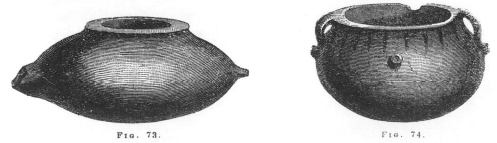

FIG. 73.   FIG. 74.

Fig. 70 measures three inches in height, by seventeen in circumference.   It is of fine clay, burned, and in model somewhat resembles the ancient pipkin. Before it was fractured, it probably terminated in a representation of the head of some animal.

Fig. 74 is of precisely the same material with that last described. Besides the two handles, it has four strong knobs at right angles to each other, by which it was probably designed the vessel might be suspended.

All the vessels from this locality are composed of clay, compounded as already described, and baked; they are of small size, the largest containing but little more than one quart. They fall far short of those from the mounds in fineness and elegance of finish, though superior to the general manufacture of the Indians. They resemble more closely the coarse but very well moulded pottery of Florida and the South-west.

A few *terra cottas* have been found in the mounds; they are said to be abundant at the South, where they are represented to possess a great variety of forms. In material they are identical with the finer specimens of pottery already described, and like them seem generally to have been baked.

Fig. 75. Half size.

Fig. 75. This unique relic was ploughed up, on the banks of the Yazoo river, in the State of Mississippi. It is composed of clay, smoothly moulded and burned, and represents some animal, *couchant*, lips corrugated and exhibiting its teeth as if in anger or defiance. It seems to have been used as a pipe. The attitude is alike natural and spirited.*

---

* In the cabinet of JAMES MCBRIDE, Esq.

FIG. 76. Half size.

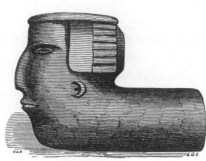

FIG. 77. Half size.

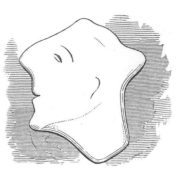

FIG. 78. Half size.

Figures 76 and 77 are both pipes of baked clay. They were ploughed up in Virginia at a point nearly opposite the mouth of the Hocking river, where there are abundant traces of an ancient people, in the form of mounds, embankments, etc. One represents a human head, with a singular head-dress, closely resembling some of those observed on the idols and sculptures of Mexico. The other represents some animal coiled together, and is executed with a good deal of spirit.

Fig. 78 is a reduced outline representation of an article of baked clay, found a number of years ago, in a mound near Nashville, Tennessee. It has the form of a human head, with a portentous nose and unprecedented phrenological developments. It is smooth and well polished, and contains six small balls of clay, which were discovered upon perforating the neck. They must necessarily have been introduced before the burning of the toy. Similar conceits were common in Mexico and Peru, and were observed by Kotzebue upon the North-west Coast. The Mexicans had also rude flutes of clay, upon which, with a little practice, not unmusical sounds may be produced.

FIG. 79.

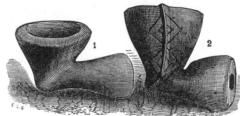

FIG 80.

Fig. 79 was taken from a mound in Butler county, Ohio. It represents the head of a bird, somewhat resembling the toucan, and is executed with much spirit. It seems originally to have been attached to some vessel, from which it was broken before being deposited in the mound.*

---

* In the cabinet of JAMES McBRIDE, Esq.

Fig. 80 presents greatly reduced sketches of a couple of clay pipes. The one indicated by the figure 1 was found in a mound in Florida, and is now in the museum of the Historical Society of New York; the other is from a mound in South Carolina, and is in the cabinet of Dr. S. G. Morton, of Philadelphia. Most of the ancient clay pipes that have been discovered have this form, which is not widely different from that adopted by the later Indians.

Notwithstanding the regularity of figure and uniformity of thickness which many of the specimens of aboriginal pottery exhibit, it is clear that they were all moulded by hand. There is no evidence that the potter's wheel was known, nor that the art of glazing, as now practised, was understood. It is not impossible, but on the contrary appears extremely probable, from a close inspection of the mound pottery, that the ancient people possessed the simple approximation towards the potter's wheel, consisting of a stick of wood grasped in the hand by the middle and turned round inside a wall of clay, formed by the other hand or by another workman. The polish, which some of the finer vessels possess, is due to other causes, and is not the result of vitrification. That a portion of the ancient pottery was not baked is very certain; but that another portion, including all vessels which were designed for common use, for cooking and similar purposes, was burned, is equally certain. In some of the Southern States, it is said, the kilns, in which the ancient pottery was baked, are now occasionally to be met with. Some are represented still to contain the ware, partially burned, and retaining the rinds of the gourds, etc., over which they were modelled, and which had not been entirely removed by the fire. "In Panola county," says Mr. R. Morris, in a private letter, " are found great numbers of what are termed '*pottery kilns;*' in which are masses of vitrified matter, frequently in the form of rude bricks, measuring twelve inches in length by ten in breadth." It seems most likely that these " kilns " are the remains of the manufactories of the later tribes, the Choctaws and Natchez, who, says Adair, " made a prodigious number of vessels of pottery, of such variety of forms as would be tedious to describe, and impossible to name."

CHAPTER XI.

IMPLEMENTS OF METAL.

THE first inquiry suggested by an inspection of the mounds and other earthworks of the West, relates to the means at the command of the builders in constructing them. However numerous we may suppose the ancient people to have been, we must regard these works as entirely beyond their capabilities, unless they had some artificial aids. As an agricultural people, they must have possessed some means of clearing the land of forests and of tilling the soil. We can hardly conceive, at this day, how these operations could be performed without the aid of iron; yet we know that the Peruvians and Mexicans, whose monuments emulate the proudest of the old world, were wholly unacquainted with the uses of that metal, and constructed their edifices and carried on their agricultural operations with implements of wood, stone, and copper. They possessed the secret of hardening the metal last named, so as to make it subserve most of the uses to which iron is applied. Of it they made axes, chisels, and knives.

The mound-builders were acquainted with several of the metals, although they do not seem to have possessed the art of reducing them from the ores. Implements and ornaments of copper are found in considerable abundance among their remains; silver is occasionally found in the form of ornaments, but only to a trifling amount; the ore of lead, galena, has been discovered in considerable quantities, but none of the metal has been found under such circumstances as to establish conclusively that they were acquainted with the art of smelting it. No iron or traces of iron, except with the recent deposits, have been discovered; nor is it believed that the race of the mounds had any knowledge of that metal. The copper and silver found in the mounds were doubtless obtained in their native state, and afterwards worked without the intervention of fire. The locality from which they were derived seems pretty clearly indicated by the peculiar mechanico-chemical combination existing, in some specimens, between the silver and copper, which combination characterizes only the native masses of Lake Superior. In none of the articles found is there evidence of welding, nor do any of them appear to have been cast in moulds. On the contrary, they seem to have been hammered out of rude masses, and gradually and with great labor brought into the required shape. The lamination, resulting from hammering the baser metals while cold, is to be observed in nearly all the articles. But, notwithstanding the disadvantages which they labored under, the mound-builders contrived to produce some very creditable specimens of workmanship, displaying both taste and skill.

No articles composed entirely of silver have been discovered: the extreme scarcity of that metal seems to have led to the utmost economy in its use. It is only found reduced to great thinness, and plated upon copper. By *plated*, it should not be understood that any chemical combination, or a union produced by heat, exists between the two metals, but simply that thin slips of silver were *wrapped* closely around the copper, their edges overlapping, so as to leave no portion exposed. This was done so neatly as, in many cases, almost to escape detection.

AXES.—Among the implements recovered from the mounds, are several copper axes, the general form of which is well exhibited in the engravings herewith pre-

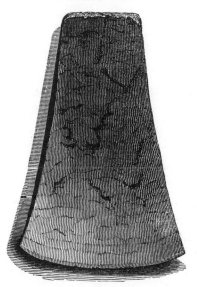

FIG. 81.

sented. They are well wrought, and each appears to have been made from a single piece,—showing that the metal was obtained in considerable masses. The largest of these, Fig. 81, weighs two pounds five ounces. It measures seven inches in length, by four in breadth at the cutting edge, and has an average thickness of

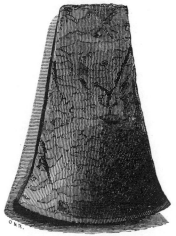

FIG. 82.

about four tenths of an inch. Its edge is slightly curved, somewhat after the manner of the axes of the present day, and is *bevelled* from both surfaces.

Fig. 82 is less in size, but of heavier proportions. It weighs two pounds, and measures six and one third inches in length, by three and one third in width on the edge. Unlike the other, it has a nearly straight cutting surface; the blade, however, is curved or *gouge-shaped*, closely resembling the adze at present used in hollowing timbers, and it was probably applied to a similar purpose with that instrument. Its head is slightly battered, as if it had sustained blows from a hammer, or had itself been used in pounding.

It may seem incomprehensible to many persons, how these axes, being destitute of an eye for the insertion of a handle, and not even possessing the groove of the Indian stone axe, for the reception of a withe, could have been used with any effect. They were doubtless fitted in the same manner with those of the ancient Mexicans and Peruvians, with which, from all accounts, they seem to be identical in form.

"The Mexicans," observes Clavigero, "made use of an axe to cut trees, which was also made of copper, and was of the same form with those of modern times, except that we put the handle in an eye of the axe, while they put the axe in an eye of the handle."*

The Pacific Islanders have a sort of adze, which is formed by firmly lashing a blade of stone, with its cutting edge at right angles, to a handle, having a sharp crook at its extremity. This mode of fastening would enable the axe with the curved blade to be used with the greatest efficiency as an adze. That it was designed to be so used, seems apparent from the fact that the edge is not formed by bevelling from both sides, but from the inner surface only, precisely in the

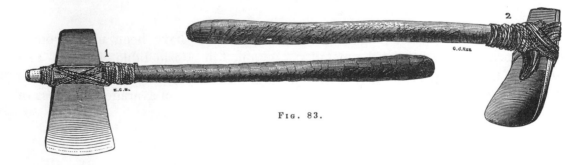

Fig. 83.

manner that the adze of the present day is ground. Fig. 83 exhibits the probable manner in which these instruments were fitted for use.

The circumstances under which these interesting relics were discovered, are detailed in the chapter on the Mounds. (See page 154.) It will be seen they were not found where, as a general and almost invariable rule, we must look for the only authentic remains of the mound-builders, viz. at the bottom of the mound. They are nevertheless classed as undoubted relics of the ancient race. The implements of the modern Indians are found, whenever they occur in the mounds, in

---

* "The copper axes of the Peruvians differ very little in shape from ours; and it appears that these were the implements with which they performed most of their works. They are of various shapes and sizes; the edge of some is more circular than others, and some have a concave edge."—*Ulloa*, vol. i. p. 483.

connection with human remains, in the position in which they were deposited with the dead. We have no evidence that the northern tribes of Indians possessed copper articles of this description, and but slender evidence at best that they were in use among the Indians along the Gulf.* A positive argument in favor of the origin imputed to them, is presented in the fact that many of the articles found both in the sepulchral and sacrificial mounds are of copper, and of similar workmanship, denoting that the mound-builders possessed the metal in considerable abundance, and were very well acquainted with its capabilities. That they have an antiquity higher than the date of the first European intercourse, is established by their form; but if this were insufficient, the evidence may be found in the fact that from immediately over them was removed the stump of a tree, originally of the largest size, which had long since fallen and decayed.

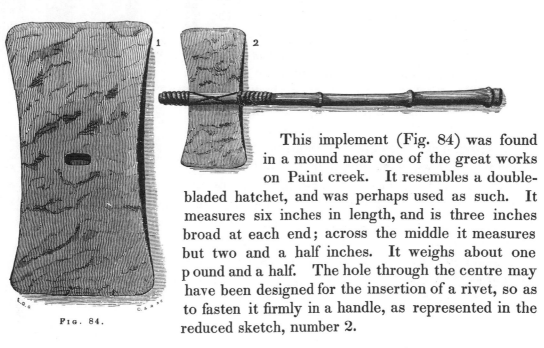

FIG. 84.

This implement (Fig. 84) was found in a mound near one of the great works on Paint creek. It resembles a double-bladed hatchet, and was perhaps used as such. It measures six inches in length, and is three inches broad at each end; across the middle it measures but two and a half inches. It weighs about one pound and a half. The hole through the centre may have been designed for the insertion of a rivet, so as to fasten it firmly in a handle, as represented in the reduced sketch, number 2.

---

* It is asserted by the Portuguese chronicler of De Soto's ill-fated expedition, that copper hatchets were found in possession of some of the Indian tribes along the Gulf, "which were said to have a mixture of gold." These, the Spaniards were told, were obtained in a province towards the north, called *Chisca*, "where there was a melting of copper, and of another metal of the same color, save that it was finer and far better to the sight, which they used not so much, because it was softer." The Spaniards did not visit the province of Chisca; as they were informed high mountains intervened, which could not be passed with horses. This, it is believed, is the only account of anything of the kind occurring north of Mexico.

Copper axes similar in all respects to those here described have been found at various places in Ohio. One of them, now in the possession of a gentleman of Hillsboro', is of the same shape with Fig. 82; it weighs two pounds. It was found near the great hill-work in Highland county (Plate V). Another, corresponding with the above, is in the possession of R. Buchanan, Esq., of Cincinnati. It was found, in connection with six others, a few miles north of Yellow Springs, in the valley of the Little Miami river. They were discovered in excavating a cellar, three or four feet beneath the surface. Large trees had been growing on the spot. Another axe, of different shape, was found not many years since, in a mound near Deerfield, on the Little Miami. It was worked up by the village blacksmith. Still another, of comparatively rude workmanship, is deposited in the Cincinnati Museum. The circumstances under which it was discovered are unknown.

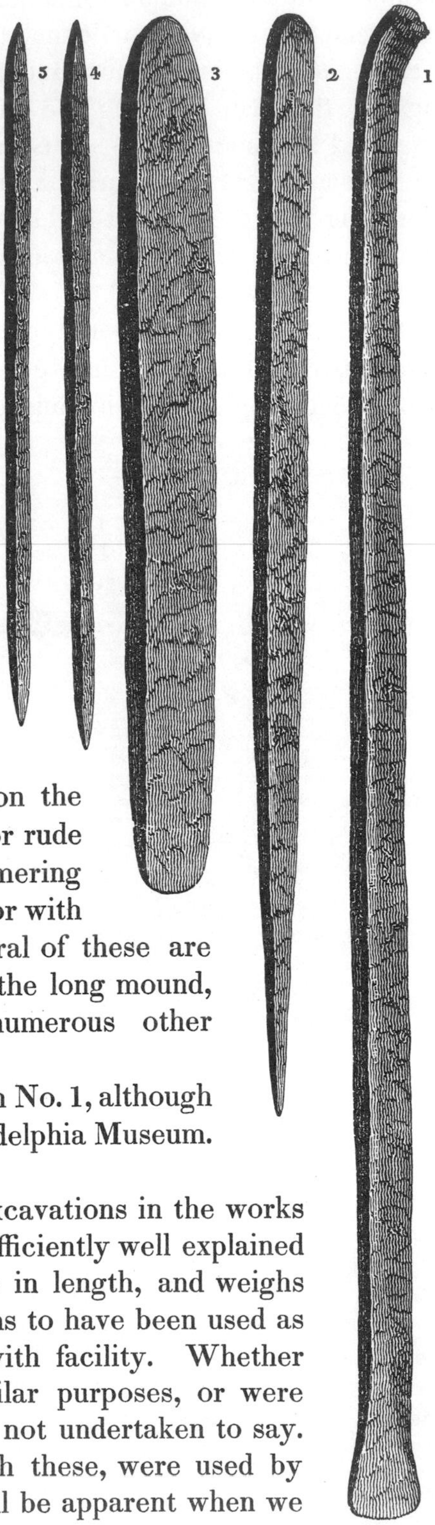

DRILLS OR GRAVERS.—Among the remains on the sacrificial altars, have been found graving tools or rude chisels of copper. These were formed by hammering the copper into rods, with sharp tapering points or with chisel-shaped edges. Full size sketches of several of these are presented, Fig. 85. Nos. 1 and 2 were found in the long mound, No. 3 "Mound City," in connection with numerous other remains.

An implement of copper, identical in shape with No. 1, although somewhat larger in size, is deposited in the Philadelphia Museum. It was taken from a mound in Alabama.

Nos. 3, 4, and 5, were discovered in making excavations in the works at Marietta. The character of each of these is sufficiently well explained by the engravings. No. 1 measures eight inches in length, and weighs about two ounces. No. 2 is less in size, and seems to have been used as a graver. It cuts the softer varieties of stone with facility. Whether those found at Marietta were designed for similar purposes, or were intended to be bent together for ornaments, it is not undertaken to say. That some instruments, of similar character with these, were used by the mound-builders, in their carvings in stone, will be apparent when we come to speak of their sculptures.

FIG. 85.

FIG. 86.

Fig. 86. No. 1 is a greatly reduced sketch of a copper spear or lance-head, found three miles north-west of Cincinnati, Ohio. It was discovered about two feet below the surface, at the base of a small hill, which was crowned by an Indian grave. The original is eight inches in length.*

No. 2 is a reduced sketch of a rude copper knife found in the summer of 1847, on Isle Royal, Lake Superior. It was discovered three feet below the surface, by the uprooting of a tree, which had grown above it. It has the lamination of surface already referred to, in a marked degree, and was evidently hammered from a single piece of native copper.

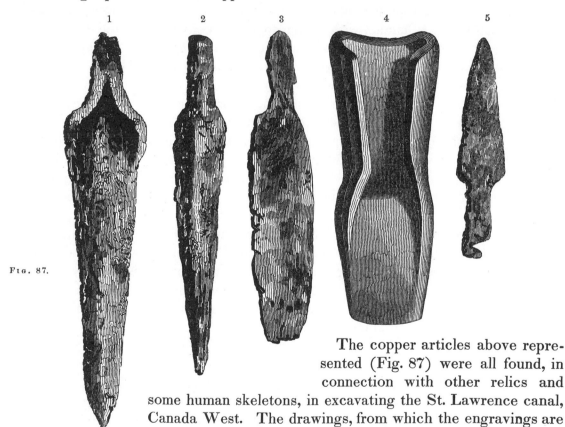

FIG. 87.

The copper articles above represented (Fig. 87) were all found, in connection with other relics and some human skeletons, in excavating the St. Lawrence canal, Canada West. The drawings, from which the engravings are reduced, were kindly furnished, together with a full description, by T. REYNOLDS, M. D., of Brockville, in whose possession the originals now are. "The spot where they were discovered, is a picturesque point on the banks of the river St. Lawrence, near the head of the first rapid or cascade met with in descending the river. They were found deposited fourteen feet below the surface, in a soil composed of blue clay and sand. A score of skeletons were found

---

* In the cabinet of R. BUCHANAN, Esq., Cincinnati.

arranged around them, their feet pointing to the spot where they were placed. The bones crumbled upon exposure to the air. A few yards from this place, and at about the same depth from the surface, another circular space was exposed to view; but strange to say, here the organic remains had been subjected to the action of fire, and the half-burned bones with the charcoal and ashes, evinced the fact that natural decomposition had been anticipated by the hand of man.

"Numbers 1 and 2 were evidently designed for spears, and intended to fit into handles. The blades are of considerable thickness, not much corroded, but of rude proportions. They are pointed, and have a double cutting edge, and were undoubtedly weapons of some service. No. 1 is a foot in length. No. 3 is a copper knife, engraved of half size. One edge is sharp, and has marks of considerable use. The point is broken off. No. 5 is also a knife, less in size, and has a hooked extremity, as shown in the engraving. It was probably designed to be used without a handle. No. 4 is an implement ten inches in length. It has a hollow or socket for the reception of a handle, with a corresponding convexity on the back. The chisel-shaped extremity is blunt, but capable of receiving a sharp edge. It may have been used as a chisel, or gouge,—perhaps as a sort of spade.

"With respect to the question whether these remains are of European origin or manufacture, I have merely to remark that their workmanship is very rude; that no traces of iron or of European implements were found with them, and that the copper corresponds exactly with the specimens of native metal obtained from Lake Superior. The nature of the soil at this spot is favorable for the preservation of organic remains; the fact, therefore, that the bones found with these relics were in so advanced a stage of decomposition, induces me to believe that they were deposited long before the discovery and occupation of Canada by Europeans. We might expect here to find relics bearing the stamp of French manufacture; but there is nothing in the form or composition of these which would lead one to suppose them to be of French origin. This spot was not the usual burying-place of the Indians. Their cemetery seems to have been some distance back from the river, upon a high sandy ridge, where their remains, apparently of very ancient deposit, are now found in abundance."

From what has been presented, it appears that the mound-builders were very well acquainted with the use of copper. They do not, however, seem to have possessed the secret of giving it any extraordinary degree of hardness. The axes above described were found, upon analysis, to be *pure copper*,—unalloyed, to any perceptible extent, by other metals. The hardness which they seem to possess, beyond the copper of commerce, is no doubt due to the hammering to which they were subjected in their manufacture. As already observed, the metal appears to have been worked, in all cases, in a cold state. This is somewhat remarkable, as the fires upon the altars were sufficiently strong, in some instances, to melt down the copper implements and ornaments deposited upon them, and the fact that the metal is fusible could hardly have escaped notice.

It has already been suggested, upon the strength of the fact that some of the specimens of copper obtained from the mounds have crystals of silver attached to them, that a part of the supply of the ancient people was obtained from the shores of Lake Superior, where alone this peculiar combination is known to exist. The circumstance that the mound axes are made of unalloyed copper, does not affect this conclusion; for a large proportion of the native metal found at this locality is pure. The conclusion is further sustained by the amount of the metal extracted from the mounds, implying a large original supply. Besides numerous small pieces, some large fragments are occasionally discovered. One of these, weighing twenty-three pounds, and from which portions had evidently been cut, was found a few years since near Chillicothe. Still, it does not appear that copper was sufficiently abundant to entirely supersede the use of bone and stone implements.

CHAPTER XII.

ORNAMENTS OF METAL.

NOTWITHSTANDING that it was often used for implements, copper seems to have been most highly valued by the mound-builders for purposes of ornament. The supposition is based upon the fact that ornaments of this metal are comparatively abundant. They are found of many varieties, comprising bracelets, pendants, beads, gorgets, etc., some of which display no inconsiderable degree of skill.

FIG. 88.

The *bracelets* are usually found encircling the arms of the skeletons, in the sepulchral mounds, but are not infrequent upon the altars. They consist of a simple rod of copper, hammered out with more or less skill, and so bent that the ends approach, or lap over, each other. Those which have been deposited under unfavorable circumstances are generally much corroded and appear ragged and rude. But some are found which are extremely well wrought. Such was the case with those obtained from a mound, within an enclosure, three miles above Chillicothe, (see page 156,) three of which of full size are shown in the engraving. These are smoothly and uniformly hammered, and seem to have been originally highly polished. They are bent with perfect regularity; and, it is a singular fact, are of uniform size and weight. They measure, between the outer surfaces, two inches and nine tenths,—between the inner surfaces, two and a half inches in diameter; and weigh four ounces each. They correspond exactly with some of the ruder ones, of the same metal, found in the tombs of the ancient Egyptians. They were but partially bent together before being placed upon the arm, after which they were closed as nearly as practicable.

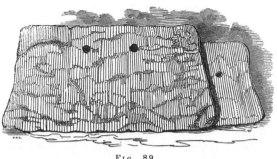

FIG. 89.

The ornaments denominated, for want of a better name, *gorgets*, are frequently found, but only, so far as observed, with skeletons, in the sepulchral mounds. An engraving of one of these is presented, (Fig. 89,) which exhibits their general form. The original, in this instance, measures eight and a half inches at the lower, and seven and a half at the upper edge, and is four and a quarter inches broad. It weighs five ounces. This is considerably above the average dimensions. They are usually about the thickness of ordinary sheet copper; and are always perforated with two holes, placed at equal distances from the ends and somewhat above the longitudinal centre, as shown in the engraving. This feature, and the fact that they are uniformly found with skeletons, suggest that they were suspended around the neck, resting upon the breast. There is one circumstance, however, that seems inconsistent with this conclusion, namely, that none of the holes exhibit the slightest elongation from wear. On the contrary, their edges are sharp as if newly cut. Such could not have been the case with articles of this soft material and extraordinary thinness, had they been suspended in the manner suggested. The holes in the little silver crosses, found in the graves of the modern Indians, are frequently worn so as to be nearly a fourth of an inch in length; and yet they weigh less than half an ounce, and are cut out of thicker plates of metal than the broad copper ornaments here mentioned. Either these plates were worn only on extraordinary occasions, or in such a manner that little or no friction was produced by the cords by which they were sustained or fastened.*

---

* RIBAULDE, who visited the shores of Florida in 1562, speaks of a chief who " had hanging about his neck a round plate of red copper well polished, with one other lesser one of silver, in the midst of it, and at his ear a little plate of copper wherewith they use to stripe the swete from theyer bodyes." Sir WALTER RALEIGH mentions, that the tribes, with which he held communication on the shores of North Carolina, wore copper plates on their heads, which were badges of authority and indicated the chiefs. These plates were so highly polished that they were, at first, mistaken for gold. It is not impossible that those found in the mounds were worn in a like manner by the ancient people. The one described in the text was found beneath the head of the skeleton with which it was buried.

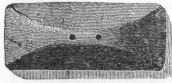

FIG. 90.

Fig. 90 represents an ornament, of something the same character with the above. It is formed of a copper plate of considerable thickness, which has been fashioned so as to present a convex surface. It is also perforated with two holes, and is identical in this respect, as well as in shape, with a large class of stone ornaments or implements found in the mounds, and of which notice will be taken in another place.

FIG. 91.

A large number of *discs* or medals of copper have been obtained from the mounds. They resemble, to use a familiar illustration, the *bosses* observed on harnesses. Some of these are not less than two inches, but most are about one inch and a half in diameter. They are formed of thin plates of copper, are perfectly round, and concavo-convex in shape. They are found only on the altar-mounds, where they seem to have been placed with their edges together, in pairs. Owing to the great heat to which they have been subjected, and subsequent oxydation, nearly all of them are so cemented together that they cannot be separated without breaking them into fragments. Their present appearance is very well exhibited by Fig. 91. Some of them, of more elaborate workmanship than the rest, and which have been more favorably situated for preservation, have been separated.*

These articles, it will be observed, display more skill in working the metal, than any of those previously noticed. They present every appearance of having been

FIG. 92.

pressed into shape, in the way in which similar articles are formed at this day. In opening one of the mounds, a block of compact sandstone was discovered, Fig.

---

* Dr. DRAKE, in his " *View of Cincinnati*," describes several ornaments or instruments found in a mound at Cincinnati, which are somewhat analogous to those described in the text, if not identical with them. " Several copper articles were discovered, each consisting of two sets of circular, concavo-convex plates ; the interior one of each set connected with the other by a hollow axis, around which had been wound some lint." Articles, answering to this description, were found, a few years since, in removing a mound on Paint creek, ten miles distant from Chillicothe. In this case, we are assured by the individual who discovered them, that the axis was wound round with a well-twisted and compact thread, resembling fine linen pack-thread, which was stained green by the salts of the copper, to which its preservation is entirely attributable. It is possible that some of the larger discs, above described, were originally thus connected.

92, in which were several circular depressions, in all respects resembling those in the work-blocks of copper-smiths, in which plates of metal are hammered to give them convexity. These depressions are of various dimensions, and are evidently artificial. It seems more than probable it was in such moulds that these articles were formed. This block weighs between thirty and forty pounds.

FIG. 93.

Small tubes of copper, formed by wrapping together thin slips of that metal, are often found. They are not soldered, and though the edges overlap each other very closely, they can easily be separated with the blade of a knife. They were doubtless strung as beads. Another variety of beads, made of coarse copper wire, closely wound and hammered together, are occasionally found.

FIG. 94.

Among the articles that exhibit the greatest degree of skill in their manufacture, may be mentioned a sort of *boss* or *button*, several of which are shown in the engraving. These present a convex and a plane surface, and are identical in form with some of the old-fashioned buttons which still linger on the small clothes of our grandfathers. They are hollow ; a portion of them are perforated from the sides, but most have the holes through which passed the thread, by which they were strung or attached, in the base. They bear a resemblance to some forms of the ancient *fibulæ*.

In addition to these, many small tubes, bands, and articles of wrought copper of various kinds have been found, the purposes of which are not apparent, and which it would be tedious to describe. Greatly reduced sketches of several of these are herewith presented.

FIG. 95.

The metal was sometimes very ingeniously used in repairing broken articles of stone, etc., as will shortly be seen. One or two stone pipes have been discovered which seem to have been completely encased, so as to present an unbroken metallic surface. The overlapping edges, in these cases, were so polished down as scarcely to be discoverable.

Silver, as has already been remarked, seems to have been possessed in very small quantities by the mound-builders. Indeed, within the entire range of these investigations, it has been discovered in but a single instance,—namely, in the remarkable " pipe mound," numbered 8 in the plan of " Mound City." It was here found, reduced to extreme thinness, (not exceeding in thickness ordinary foolscap paper,) and plated, or rather wrapped, over sundry copper beads and a few other ornaments of the same material. The whole amount discovered would probably not exceed an ounce in weight.

FIG. 96.

From the mound above mentioned were taken a number of large beads, the size and shape of which are accurately shown in the accompanying engraving. They are composed of shell, now completely calcined, and seem to have been carefully enveloped with sheet copper and afterwards with thin slips of silver, so as to completely cover the surface. Some of the beads exhibit both the copper and silver partially melted off. The heat of the fire, upon the altar where they were found, had been sufficiently intense, towards the centre, to melt considerable masses of copper.

Besides these beads, several star-shaped ornaments were found. They are also composed of shell, bound together by an envelope of sheet copper, over which the silver slips are carefully folded, so as to leave their overlapping edges scarcely perceptible. A small hole passed through the centre of these unique ornaments, by which they were fastened in such positions as the taste of the possessor suggested.

Silver crosses, it has several times been observed, have been discovered with the recent deposits in the mounds. The accompanying engraving illustrates their general form. Some are considerably larger and heavier than that here represented ; one found near Chillicothe weighed not less than one and a half ounces. They will readily be recognised as of European origin. The enterprising French passed frequently through the Mississippi valley, from a very early day, and maintained a constant intercourse with the natives, distributing amongst them vast numbers of these crosses, brooches, and other ornaments of silver ; which, in accordance with the aboriginal custom, were buried with the possessor at his death. Numbers of these relics have been found in the mounds and Indian graves of the South. They are perhaps oftener composed of brass than of silver.

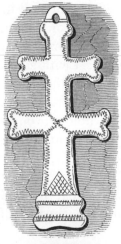

Fig. 97.

The instance first mentioned, it is believed, is the only one in which silver has been found in the mounds under such circumstances as to establish conclusively that it pertained to the builders. It is clear that, so far as the specimens here obtained are concerned, they did not understand the art of *plating*, in the proper meaning of the term. They had taken but the first step towards it. That art is certainly one which follows, instead of preceding, the knowledge of welding and of working metals through the assistance of fire, which knowledge does not seem to have been possessed by them. Their acquaintance with metallurgy appears to have been confined to working the native metals in a cold state ; in which, it must be admitted, they evinced considerable skill. Further than this, little can be claimed for them.

From the presence of *galena* in the mounds, it seems almost impossible that the builders could have been ignorant of the manufacture of lead. None of that metal has, however, been discovered under such circumstances as to place it beyond doubt that they were acquainted with it. A rude article, of pure lead, of the following form, and weighing about half a pound, was discovered, not long since, in sinking a well within the trench of the ancient works at Circleville. It was found about two feet

FIG. 98.

below the surface, and was thickly encrusted with a carbonate. We shall not undertake to ascribe a date to it. Upon one of the altars within a mound in "Mound City," (see page 149,) a quantity of galena was found. It had been exposed, in common with all articles found on the altars, to the action of fire, which had not, however, been sufficiently strong to reduce it, though some pieces seem to have been partially fused. Perhaps it may have been prized only for its brilliancy, and finally deposited, with other articles of use or ornament, as an offering.

27

CHAPTER XIII.

IMPLEMENTS OF STONE, ETC.

IN the absence of a knowledge of the metals, the ingenuity of man contrives to fashion from the different varieties of stone, from the tusks and bones of animals, and the harder kinds of wood, such rude implements as his necessities demand, and such ornaments as his fancy suggests. And even among nations who have a limited knowledge of the metals, we find these characteristic implements of a ruder state still adhered to. In Mexico and Peru, where the use of most of the metals, except iron, was well understood, the stone axe and flint-tipped arrow and lance were in common use, at the period of the discovery. The early explorers found all the American nations, from the squalid Esquimaux, who struck the morse with a lance pointed with its own tusks, to the haughty Aztec, rivalling in his barbaric splendor the magnificence of the East, in possession of them. We are not surprised, therefore, at their occurrence in the mounds. We find them with the original and with the recent deposits, and the plough turns them up to light on every hand. And so striking is the resemblance between them all, that we are almost ready to conclude they were the productions of the same people. This conclusion would be irresistible, did we not know that the wants of man have ever been the same, and have always suggested like forms to his implements, and similar modes of using them. The polished instrument with which the pioneer of civilization prostrates the forest, has its type in the stone axe of the Indian which his plough the next day exposes to his curious gaze. In the barrows of Denmark and Siberia, in the tumuli on the plains of Marathon, and even under the shadow of the pyramids themselves, the explorer finds relics, almost identical with those disclosed from the mounds, and closely resembling each other in material, form, and workmanship. We have consequently little whereby to distinguish the remains of the mound-builders, so far as their mere implements of stone are concerned, except the position in which they are found, and the not entirely imaginary superiority of their workmanship, from those of the succeeding races. We have, however, in the different varieties of stone of which they are composed, the evidences of a more extended intercourse than we are justified in ascribing to the more recent tribes.

The articles composed of stone and bone have a great variety of forms, which were probably suggested by the purposes for which they were designed. They will be classified, so far as their purposes seem apparent.

SPEAR OR LANCE HEADS.—Great numbers of flint points are found which, it is clear from their size and form, could not have been used for tipping arrows.

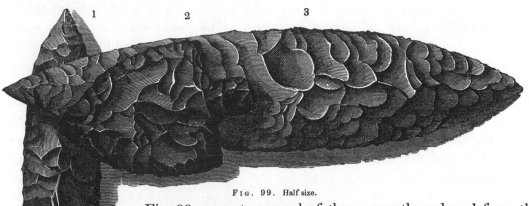

1   2   3

FIG. 99. Half size.

Fig. 99 presents several of these, greatly reduced from the original size. Nos. 1 and 2 were designed to be lashed to shafts, previously drilled or split to receive them. There are others, however, the manner of using which is not so obvious. No. 3 is an example. It measures eleven inches in length by two and a half in its greatest breadth. It has been suggested that it was fastened at right angles to a handle and used as a sort of battle-axe. In one of the mounds already several times referred to (page 149) were found, amongst large quantities of fragments, several perfect specimens of rather remarkable character; one of which, beautifully worked from milky quartz, is herewith presented of half size (Fig. 100). The difficulty of accounting for the manner in which they were used is scarcely less than in the instance last mentioned. It has been suggested that they were perhaps designed to be used in the construction of swords, or offensive weapons, on the plan of those made by the ancient Mexicans. These were formed by slitting a cane or other slender piece of tough wood, and inserting blades of stone, usually slips of obsidian, upon either side. These were retained in their place by firmly lashing the separated wood together, and filling the cavities with some hard variety of gum.* The implement was wielded with both hands, and, with its sharp serrated edges, constituted a very formidable

FIG. 100.

---

* The Spaniards entertained a strong dread of these weapons. Their historians tell some wonderful stories of their efficiency, and affirm that one stroke was sufficient to cut a man through the middle or decapitate a horse. The form of this sword, which was called *mahquahuitl* by the Mexicans, is represented in the accompanying engraving (Fig. 101).

FIG. 101.

FIG. 102.

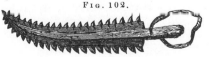

The Pacific islanders possess similar weapons, formed by inserting rows of shark's teeth on the opposite sides of a staff or sword-shaped piece of tough wood, and fastening the same with cords of native grass. One of this kind from the Aleutian Islands is here engraved (Fig. 102).

weapon. This notion is favored by the order in which some of the specimens, near the edges and least disturbed portions of the altar, were found.

Some spear-points of *obsidian* have been found, which, judging from the fragments, must have been of large dimensions. The ready fracture of this mineral, upon exposure to strong heat, has been exceedingly unfavorable to the recovery entire of any articles composed of it. This is the more to be regretted, from the fact that it is believed to be found *in place* only in Mexico and the volcanic regions of the South-west, and a comparison of the articles found here with those of the same material obtained from that direction, might serve to throw some degree of light upon the origin and connections of the race of the mounds. A further notice will be taken of the mineral when we come to speak of the minerals and fossils found in the mounds.

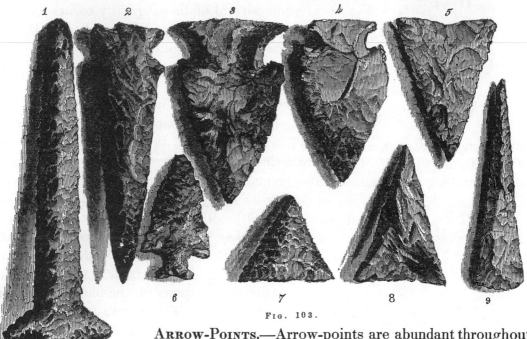

FIG. 103.

ARROW-POINTS.—Arrow-points are abundant throughout the West, especially in the valleys where the mounds occur; but although frequently found, they are not plentiful in the mounds themselves. They are much less numerous than the lance-heads just noticed. Sketches of a number, exhibiting their predominant forms, are given in the engraving. It will be noticed that they possess a great diversity of form. Some are barbed and have a serrated edge quite as sharp and ragged as the edge of a saw; some are so chipped that the line of their edges forms a large angle to their planes, as if to give them a revolving or *tearing* motion; and others are narrow and pointed, as if particularly designed for penetrating deeply. If anything were to be gained by it, a classification of these relics might be attempted. We might designate those having serrated edges and barbs, as the *war-arrow*, intended not only to penetrate the flesh, but retain their hold and rankle and fester in the wound; those destitute of this feature, as the *peace-arrow*, or *hunter-arrow*.

Many, as has already been remarked, and as will be perceived from the engravings, are delicately wrought, and from the richest materials within the reach of their makers. From one of the mounds in that, by this time, familiar locality, Mound City, (see page 149,) were taken a number of beautiful ones of transparent or hyaline quartz, which, from the brilliant play of colors upon their fractured surfaces, are real gems. It is not likely that these, and some others of like delicate material, were used for ordinary purposes, but rather for display and ornament.* From the same mound were also taken one or two arrow-points of *obsidian*.

Arrow-points, differing from each other only in the variety of stone of which they are composed, are discovered in all quarters of the globe. They have been found in the Scythian tumuli of Siberia, in the tombs of Egypt,† upon the plains of Greece,‡ and in the rude monuments of ancient Scandinavia. But whether obtained from Asia, from Europe, Africa, or America, they are almost identical in form and workmanship, and might readily be mistaken for the productions of the same people. Their prevalence seems to mark that stage of man's progress which the antiquaries of the north of Europe have denominated the " stone age," and which was followed by the " age of bronze," and the " age of iron." The manufacture of these arrow-points involves no inconsiderable degree of skill, as will be very apparent to any one who has the curiosity to attempt an imitation from the raw material. It has hence been inferred that it was anciently an art, like that of the potter, assigned to a class of armorers or makers of arrow-heads, whose skill was the result of long experience in the manufacture.

Arrow and lance heads, and cutting implements of the numerous varieties of quartz, embracing every shade of color and degree of transparency, from the dull blue of the ordinary hornstone to the brilliant opalescence of the chalcedonic varieties, are frequent in the mounds. Some are worked with great skill from pure, limpid crystals of quartz, others from crystals of manganesan garnet, and others still from *obsidian* (the *itzli* of the Mexicans, and *gallinazo stone* of the Peruvians). It is a singular fact, however, that few weapons of stone or other materials are discovered in the sepulchral mounds ; most of the remains found with the skeletons are such evidently as were deemed ornamental, or recognised as badges of distinction. Some of the altar or sacrificial mounds, on the other hand, have the deposits within them almost entirely made up of finished arrow and spear points, intermixed with masses of the unmanufactured material. From one altar were taken several bushels of finely worked lance-heads of milky quartz, nearly all of which had been broken up by the action of fire. (See page 149.) In another mound, an excavation six feet long and four broad disclosed upwards of six hundred spear-heads or discs of hornstone, rudely

---

* Lawson, in his account of the Carolina Indians, published in 1709, mentions having seen at an Indian town " very long arrows, headed with *pieces of glass*, which they had broken from bottles. They were shaped neatly, like the head of a dart, but the way they did it I can't tell " (p. 58). It is probable that these arrows were pointed with obsidian or quartz, which would be very liable to be mistaken for glass. Fremont (*Second Expedition,* p. 267) observed some Indians, of unusually fearless character, on the *Rio de los Angelos* of Upper California, who possessed arrows " barbed with a very clear, translucent stone, a species of opal, nearly as hard as a diamond."

† Wilkinson's Egypt, vol. iii. p. 261.　　　　　‡ Clarke's Travels, vol. iii. p. 22.

blocked out, and the deposit extended indefinitely on every side. (See page 158.) Some of these are represented in the accompanying engraving. They are neces-

Fig. 104

sarily much reduced. The originals are about six inches long and four broad, and weigh not far from two pounds each. Some specimens from this deposit are nearly round, but most are of the shape of those here figured. We are wholly at a loss respecting their purposes, unless they were designed to be worked into the more elaborate implements to which allusion has been made, and were thus roughly *blocked out* for greater ease of transportation from the quarries. With these relics, were found several large nodules of similar material, from which portions had been chipped off, exposing a nucleus, around which the accretion seems to have taken place. These nodules are covered to the depth of half an inch, with a calcario-silicious deposit, white, and of great hardness. Such nodules are found in the secondary limestone formations.

Several localities are known from which the material may have been obtained. One of these, named " Flint Ridge," exists in the counties of Muskingum and Licking, in Ohio. It extends for many miles, and countless pits are to be observed throughout its entire length, from which the stone was taken. These excavations are often ten or fourteen feet deep, and occupy acres in extent. It is possible that the late, as well as the more remote races worked these quarries. Like the red pipe-stone quarry of the *Coteau des Prairies*, this locality may have been the resort of numerous tribes,—a neutral ground, where the war-hatchet for the time was buried, and all rivalries and animosities forgotten.

KNIVES AND OTHER CUTTING INSTRUMENTS.—Knives of flint and obsidian have been taken from several of the mounds. Some are identical with those of Mexico, most if not all of which were made of obsidian. That material, as also some varieties of flint, breaks with a very clear, conchoidal fracture. With skill and experience in the art, the mound-builders, as well as the Mexicans, succeeded in striking off thin, narrow slips, with edges sharp as razors. Clavigero states that so skilful were the Mexicans in the manufacture of obsidian knives, that a single workman could produce a hundred per hour. These answered many of the purposes for which the more delicate cutting instruments of the present day are used, such as shaving, and incising in surgical operations, not to mention the part which they performed in the bloody observances of the Aztec ritual. Several knives of this description are represented in the following engraving, which also exhibits the absolute identity which sometimes exists between the remains of widely-separated people, and how, almost as it were by instinct, men hit upon common methods of meeting their wants.

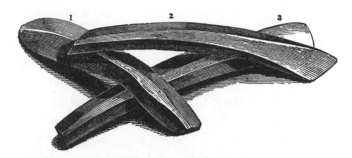

FIG. 105. Half size.

No. 1 is of flint from a Scandinavian barrow; No. 2 is of hornstone from a mound in Ohio; and No. 3 is obsidian from the pyramids of Teotihuacan in Mexico. Some of these are not less than six inches in length and three-fourths of an inch in breadth; others are not more than two inches long, and of exceeding delicacy. Besides these, and constituting a much larger class, are found cutting implements chipped with great neatness, so as to produce as clear and smooth a cutting edge as practicable. In shape they somewhat resemble an old-fashioned table-knife. Some are composed of the beautiful hyaline before mentioned, others of obsidian. Some irregular chips of flint have been found, with one or more sharp edges, which, it is presumed, were used for like purposes.

There is another variety of cutting instrument which it may not be out of place to notice here. These consist of hard compact minerals, worked into a chisel shape. Some have a very sharp, smooth edge, and form quite a good substitute for metal. Engravings of two, of full size, are herewith presented.

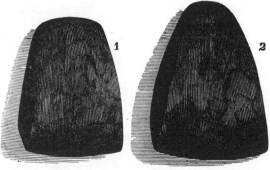

FIG. 106.

They are formed of very compact nodules of brown hematite, which have been ground into form and polished with great labor. They have a submetallic lustre, and very nearly the specific gravity of iron. A file produces a scarcely perceptible impression upon their rounded surfaces. Another variety is occasionally found in

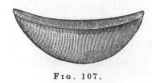

FIG. 107.

the Eastern States, of which Fig. 107 is an example. They are sometimes composed of slate, and are of various sizes, often measuring five or six inches in length. They are very well adapted for flaying animals, and other analogous purposes.

AXES.—The remark made in respect to the occurrence of the arrow-points, is equally true of the ancient axes. Although abundant in the valleys occupied by the mound-builders, they are not frequent in the mounds themselves. Those taken from the tumuli do not, however, differ materially from others found scattered over the surface of the earth from the St. Lawrence to Panama and the hills of Chili. They all have the same general features, and vary only in their materials and the style of their workmanship. Some of those found in the mounds and elsewhere at the West, are wrought with great skill, and from rare and beautiful materials, usually of the granitic or sienitic series of minerals. Amongst the Mexicans and Peruvians, axes of obsidian, and of basalt, greenstone, etc., were retained in common use, long after the discovery of the art of hardening copper.

The form of these relics seems to have been determined entirely by the manner in which they were designed to be used. Those intended for deadening trees or as war axes, have grooves for the adjustment of handles. There are many which are destitute of this feature, and which were probably designed to be used as chisels or *gouges*. Examples are given of each of these classes.

FIG. 108.

Fig. 108 is a fine specimen of the ancient axe. It was found within the large enclosure on Paint creek, noticed on page 58, and is regarded as a genuine relic of the mound-builders. Its form is almost identical with that of the forest axe of the present day. It is made of a very compact greenstone, and measures eight inches in length by five inches and a half in its greatest breadth, and weighs eight pounds. The marks of the pointed instrument with which it was chipped into form, are still discernible, notwithstanding the long use to which it has evidently been subjected.

The manner in which these instruments are mounted is apparent enough from their construction, and could hardly be mistaken even though the explanation were not furnished by the practice of the tribes still retaining their use.* A tough *withe*, or green slip of wood of proper size was bent into the groove and encircled the axe ; the ends were then firmly bound together with ligatures of hide or other material.

---

* LOSKIEL says of the axes of the Delaware Indians : " Their hatchets are wedges, made of hard stones, six or seven inches long, sharpened at the edge, and attached to a wooden handle. They are not used to fell trees, but only to peel them, and kill their enemies " (p. 54). ADAIR, speaking of the Southern tribes, observes : " They twisted two or three hickory slips, about two feet long, around the notched head of the axe, and by means of this simple and obvious invention they deadened the trees, by cutting through the bark and burned them when they became thoroughly dry " (p. 405).

Still further to fasten and render the instrument firm and immovable in the handle, it was *wedged* on the inner edge, which usually was slightly hollowed for that purpose.

It is clear, from the weight of many of these axes, that they were designed to be wielded with both hands. Some weigh not less than *fourteen* pounds, but most range from six to ten. The average weight of the ordinary wood-axe of the present day, is about six pounds.

Engravings of a number of axes analogous to that above described, but less symmetrical in form, are herewith presented, Fig. 109. The smaller varieties were

FIG. 109.

probably designed for war-axes or hatchets. They weigh from one to two and three pounds, and frequently have rounded heads, as if to serve the double purpose of hatchet and club. Occasionally one is found with a double blade, as shown in No. 1 of the engraving.

The *Hand-axes* are destitute of grooves, and, as already observed, seem designed to be used as chisels or gouges. They are more numerous than the other variety, and are of all sizes, from two inches to a foot in length. Some, like Fig. 110, are nearly cylindrical; others, like Fig. 111, are gouge-shaped. Fig. 110 is remarkable as being the only specimen of this kind of axe recovered from the mounds, under such circumstances as to establish conclusively that it pertained to the builders. It is composed of green-

FIG. 110.   FIG. 111.

stone, and the marks of the tool, by which it was *pecked* into shape, are distinctly visible upon it. The subjoined engraving (Fig. 112) presents examples of a number

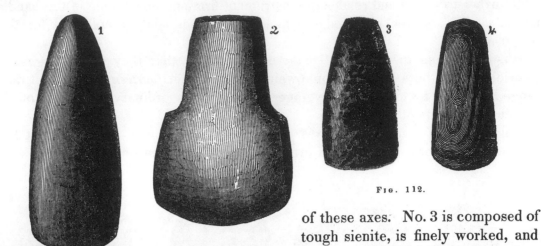

FIG. 112.

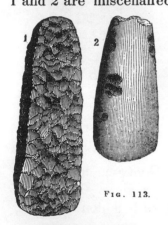

FIG. 113.

of these axes. No. 3 is composed of tough sienite, is finely worked, and highly polished. No. 4 is of a species of variegated slate, and was found near Middletown, Connecticut.* Nos. 1 and 2 are miscellaneous examples; both are composed of greenstone. This form of the stone axe is not peculiar to America. Numbers, differing only in material, are found in almost all parts of the globe. Fig. 113 represents two, composed of flint, which were brought from Denmark, by the late J. F. WOODSIDE, Esq., U. S. Consul at Copenhagen, and are now in possession of his family, at Chillicothe, Ohio. They were obtained from a Scandinavian barrow. No. 1 seems to have been simply chipped into shape, and never used; No. 2, on the other hand, is well polished, and has evidently seen much use. Except in respect to material, they are undistinguishable from thousands found in the United States.

It will be observed that the various kinds of axes above described, are imper-

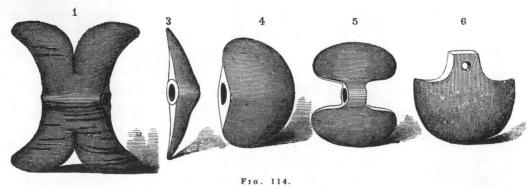

FIG. 114.

forate. A few implements have however been discovered, which are generally called hatchets, and which have holes for the reception of handles. Examples

---

* Presented by JOHN HALL, Esq., New York. Nos. 1 and 2 are in the cabinet of JAMES McBRIDE, Esq.

are given, Fig. 114.   It is clear nevertheless, both from their form and material, that they were not designed for use.   They may be regarded as having been intended simply for ornament or display.   No. 1 is composed of a beautiful talcose slate of a greenish brown color, slightly veined with dark lines.   It measures six inches in length, is two inches and a half broad at the centre, and five inches between the tips.

No. 4 was found in South Carolina, and is composed of a dark steatite.   The others were found in Mississippi, and are for the most part composed of soft and easily-worked stone.*

FIG. 115.   FIG. 116.   FIG. 117.

Fig. 115 is of similar material with No. 1, Fig. 114, is highly polished, and measures six inches in length.   The hole is half an inch in diameter at one end, but less at the other.†

Fig. 116 is an example of a kind of hammer or club-head of stone.   It weighs about two pounds.   Articles of this kind are not frequent; and none have been found in the mounds.   It is probable that a withe was passed around the groove in the middle, and the ends firmly bound together.   By this means the implement might be very efficiently used as a hammer or war-club.   Spherical stones are often found, weighing from half a pound to two pounds.   The manner in which they were used is, no doubt, correctly explained by Lewis and Clarke : " The Shoshonee Indians use an instrument which was formerly employed among the Chippeways, and called by them *pogamoggon*.   It consists of a handle, twenty-two inches long, made of wood, covered with leather, about the size of a whip-handle.   At one end is a thong two inches in length, which is tied to a stone weighing two pounds, enclosed in a cover of leather.   At the other end is a loop of the same material, which is passed around the wrist to secure the implement, with which they strike a powerful blow."   It is probable that the pear-shaped stones represented in the above engraving, Fig. 117, were used in like manner.   Carver describes a weapon, in use by the tribes beyond the Mississippi river, which consisted of a curiously wrought stone, enclosed in leather as above, and fastened, like the slung-shot of the present day, to a thong, a yard

---

* In the cabinets of B. L. C. WAILES, Esq., Washington, Miss. ; and of Rev. R. MORRIS, Mount Sylvan, in the same State.

† In the cabinet of JAMES McBRIDE, Hamilton, Ohio.

and a half long, which was also wound around the wrist.   These weapons were often used in battle.

FIG. 118.

PESTLES.—A large number of implements have been discovered, which have evidently been used for pounding and reducing maize. Fig. 118 presents examples.   These weigh generally not more than four or five pounds, though some are much heavier.   Occasionally they are elaborately worked, but most are rude. None of these have been found in the mounds. Similar articles were in common use among the modern Indians.   Rude mortars of various dimensions, composed of stone, were also frequent.

IMPLEMENTS OF BONE.—Pointed or sharpened bones of the deer and elk have been obtained from the ancient deposits in the mounds.   Several are here represented, Fig. 119.   They are reduced with entire regularity; and some of them,

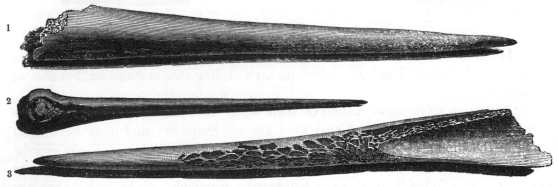

FIG. 119.

notwithstanding their decay, evince that they were originally highly polished.   Nos. 1 and 3 were obtained from a mound in Cincinnati, and are evidently formed from the tibia of the elk.*

No. 2 was taken, together with several others, from a mound near Chillicothe, (see page 178,) and measures eight inches in length.   It is formed from the ulna of the deer.

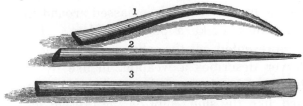

FIG. 120.

Some very delicate awl-shaped instruments have been found in the mounds, of which the above are full-sized sketches.   They have been burned, and it is

---

* In the cabinet of ERASMUS GEST Esq. and drawn by H. C. GROSVENOR, of Cincinnati.

impossible to tell of what description of bone they are made. They are as compact as ivory. Judging from the abundance of fragments, a considerable deposit must have been made where they were found. None were recovered entire; pieces were nevertheless found three inches in length. Some have round and tapering, others flat and chisel-shaped points; resembling in this, as in other respects, the different varieties of awls in use at the present day. They were probably used for similar purposes as needles and bodkins.*

Many implements made of elk and deer horns, and of the bones of the buffalo, have been found with the recent deposits in the mounds. These are all exceedingly rude.

DISCOIDAL STONES.—A few singular discs of stone have been discovered in the mounds, which seem related to a very numerous class of relics found scattered over the surface, from the valley of the Ohio to Peru. Those from the mounds

FIG. 121.

will claim our first attention. Fig. 121, Numbers 3 and 5, are examples. They were taken, in connection with numerous other remains, from a mound numbered 1 within the great enclosure on the North fork of Paint creek. (See Plate X,

---

* "The needles and thread they used formerly (and now at times) were fish-bones, or the horns or bones of deer rubbed sharp, and deer's sinews, and a sort of hemp that grows among them spontaneously."—*Adair's American Indians*, p. 6.

Mr. Stevens found a similar implement with the skeleton, in one of the ancient tombs near Ticul in Yucatan. "It was made of deer's horn, about two inches long, sharp at the point, with an eye at the other end. The Indians of the vicinity still use needles of the same material."—*Travels in Yucatan*, vol. i. p. 279.

and also page 157).   They are simple discs, (cut from plates of stone,) perfectly circular, but of variable thickness.   The largest measures three inches and three fourths in diameter, by one inch and one tenth in thickness; the smallest, two and eight tenths, by nine tenths.   They are of all intermediate sizes; a few have their edges slightly convex, but most are perfectly plane.   Those first found by individuals residing in the vicinity, were called "*weights*," from their resemblance to the iron weights in common use.   They are made of a very dense ferruginous stone, of a black or dark brown ground, thickly interspersed with minute and brilliant specks of yellow mica; it receives a remarkably high polish, displaying the mica flakes with great beauty.   The material was, not inaptly, termed "*gold stone*" by the persons who first discovered it.   Several delicately carved articles of this material have been taken from the same locality; but it is a singular fact, that none have been found except in this particular mound. Judging from the accounts of others, and the number of fragments of these discs disclosed upon a full investigation of the mound, the deposit must have been very considerable; probably not less than thirty or forty were originally placed there.

It has been suggested that these stones were used in certain games, analogous to those known to have been practised by the North American tribes.   The perfect polish of the edges of some of them weighs against this conclusion.   They are certainly enigmatical in their purposes.

The numerous class of discoidal stones already referred to, as being in some degree related to those above described, are composed of a large variety of hard materials,—granite, porphyry, greenstone, jasper, quartz, etc.

They are of all sizes from two to six inches in diameter, and of variable thickness, seldom, however, less than an inch and a half.   Some have concave sides, often perforated; others are solid or lenticular in shape, with oblique margins. Nos. 1, 2, 4, and 6, represent four varieties.

The sketches and accompanying sections will give a good idea of their character. Nos. 1 and 2 are the predominant forms, with sides more or less concave, and centre perforated.   Many of this kind are marked with radiating lines, resembling bird tracks, as exhibited in No. 1.   Occasionally both surfaces are thus marked.   Some of those possessing concave sides are imperforate.   No. 4 constitutes the simplest form, and approaches nearest to those found in the mounds; a very few are observed of the form represented by No. 6.

By far the larger proportion of these relics are worked with great symmetry, and are well polished; some, however, of manifestly similar purpose, are quite rude in workmanship and of coarse materials.   None have been discovered in the mounds examined by the authors; and it is doubtful whether any have been found in them elsewhere, except with the recent deposits.   We may safely set them down as of comparatively modern origin.   It is known that, among the Indian tribes on the Ohio, and along the Gulf, such stones were in common use, in certain favorite games.   Beyond the Mississippi their use is still retained.   They display considerable skill, but undoubtedly fall within the capabilities of a very rude people.   Their shape is that most easily obtained by attrition or grinding with other stones.

Adair describes them, and the game in which they were used, and remarks that they were " from time immemorial rubbed smooth on the rocks, and with prodigious labor," and furthermore were so highly valued, " that they were kept with the strictest religious care from one generation to another, and were exempted from being buried with the dead."

It is a singular fact that similar stones are found in Denmark, and Molina describes them as numerous in Chili. We may conclude that they everywhere had much the same use.*

---

* Rev. J. B. Finley (distinguished for his zealous efforts in christianizing the Indian tribes of Ohio) states that, among the tribes with which he was acquainted, stones identical with those above described were much used in a popular game resembling the modern game of " ten pins." The form of the stones suggests the manner in which they were held and thrown, or rather rolled. The concave sides received the thumb and second finger, the forefinger clasping the periphery. Adair, in his notice of the Southern Indians, gives a minute and graphic account of a game somewhat analogous to that described by Mr. Finley, in which stones of this description were used. Du Pratz notices the same game, and fully explains the purpose of the oblique-edged stones, Nos. 4 and 6 of the text. These, when rolled, would describe a convolute figure. The lines on the stones, resembling bird-tracks, were probably in some way connected with " counting" the game.

" The warriors have another favorite game, called *Chungke*; which, with propriety of language, may be called ' running hard labor.' They have near their state house a square piece of ground well cleaned; and fine sand is strewed over it, when requisite, to promote a swifter motion to what they throw along its surface. Only one or two on a side play at this ancient game. They have a stone about *two fingers broad at the edge and two spans round;* each party has a pole about eight feet long, smooth and tapering at each end, the points flat. They set off abreast of each other, at six yards from the edge of the play-ground; then one of them hurls the stone on its edge, in as direct a line as he can, a considerable distance towards the middle of the other end of the square; when they have run a few yards, each darts his pole, anointed with bear's grease, with a proper force, as near as he can guess, in proportion to the motion of the stone, that the end may lie close to the same;—when this is the case the person counts two of the game, and in proportion to the nearness of the poles to the mark, one is counted, unless by measurement both are found to be an equal distance from the stone. In this manner the players will keep moving most of the day at half speed, under the violent heat of the sun, staking their silver ornaments; their nose, finger, and ear rings; their breast, arm, and wrist plates; and all their wearing apparel, except that which barely covers their middle. *All the American Indians* are much addicted to this game, which appears to be a task of stupid drudgery; it seems, however, to be of early origin, when their forefathers used diversions as simple as their manners. (The hurling stones they use at present were, from time immemorial, rubbed smooth on the rocks, and with prodigious labor; they are kept with the strictest religious care from one generation to another, and are exempt from being buried with the dead.) They belong to the town where they are used, and are carefully preserved."—*Adair's History of American Indians*, p. 402.

" The warriors practise a diversion which they call the *game of the pole*, at which only two play at a time. Each pole is about eight feet long, resembling a Roman f, and the game consists in rolling a flat round stone, about three inches in diameter and one inch thick, *with the edges somewhat sloping*, and throwing the pole in such a manner that when the stone rests, the pole may be at or near it. Both antagonists throw their pole at the same time, and he whose pole is nearest the stone counts one, and has the right of rolling the stone."—*Du Pratz, History of Louisiana*, 1720, p. 366.

Mr. Breckenridge (Views of Louisiana, p. 256) mentions a game popular among the Arikara, (Riccarees,) played with a *ring of stone*. Lewis and Clarke also mention a game common among the Mandans, similar to the one above described, and which was also played with *rings of stone*. Mr. Catlin, (vol. i. p. 132) both describes and illustrates the game, which, among the Mandans as well as among the Creeks, was denominated " Tchung-kee."

Discoidal stones analogous, if not identical, with these, have been found in abundance in Chili. " In

RINGS.—Among the implements may be classed certain small grooved rings, beautifully worked from stone and bone. Some are composed of the micaceous stone, of which the mound discs already described are made, and are carved with the utmost delicacy, and highly polished. They measure about two inches and three fourths in diameter, and the thickness of the periphery is half an inch. They are deeply grooved upon the outer edge, and are pierced by eight small holes, at equal distances from each other, all radiating from the centre. Similar rings, of smaller size, have been found, cut from bone. They are pierced in the same manner with those above described. It is suggested that they formed part of a drilling apparatus, something like the "bow and drill" of the present day. Several of larger size than those here noticed were found, some years since, in a mound at Cincinnati. A variety of relics are found which resemble paint-mullers. Some of these are composed of brown hematite, and are very symmetrical in figure.

TUBES.—Not among the least remarkable and interesting relics, obtained from the mounds, are the stone tubes, of which several examples are given in the subjoined engraving, Fig. 122. They are all carved from fine-grained materials sus-

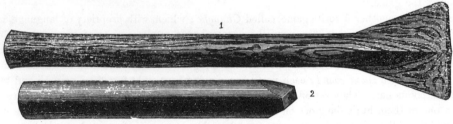

FIG. 122.

ceptible of receiving a polish and of being made ornamental, as well us useful. The finest specimen yet discovered, and which can scarcely be surpassed in the delicacy of its workmanship, was found in a mound in the immediate vicinity of Chillicothe. No. 1 is a greatly reduced sketch. It is composed of a compact variety of slate; the ground is brownish or leaden green, interstratified with veins of pure black, of variable thickness, from a line to the fourth of an inch. These, when worked obliquely to their planes, are decidedly ornamental. This stone cuts with great clearness, and receives a fine though not glaring polish. The tube under notice is thirteen inches long, by one and one tenth in diameter; one end swells slightly, and the other terminates in a broad, flattened, triangular *mouth-piece*, (so called for lack of a better designation,) of fine proportions, which is carved with mathematical precision. It is drilled throughout; the bore is seven tenths of an inch in diameter at the cylindrical end of the tube, and retains that

the plains and upon the mountains," says Molina, " are to be seen a great number of flat circular stones, of five or six inches in diameter, with a hole through the middle. These stones, which are either granite or porphyry, have doubtless received this form by artificial means, and I am induced to believe that they were the clubs or maces of the ancient Chilians, and that the holes were perforated to receive the handles."
—*Molina*, vol. i. p. 56.

calibre until it reaches the point where the cylinder subsides into the mouth-piece, when it contracts gradually to one tenth of an inch at the end. The inner surface of the tube is perfectly smooth, till within a short distance of the point of contraction. For the remaining distance the circular striæ, formed by the drill in boring, are distinctly marked. The mound in which this relic was found is sepulchral in its character, and the burial had been made by fire. One end of the tube is somewhat discolored by the heat to which it was exposed. The carving, in this instance, is very fine, and much superior to anything of which the Indians of this day are known to be capable.

No. 2 is a sketch of another tube, also found in one of the sepulchral mounds near Chillicothe (see page 164). It is made of different material, less beautiful and more destructible than the one just described,—a variety of limestone. It measures but six inches in length by three fourths of an inch in diameter; the bore is half an inch in diameter. The surface is much decomposed; the spots which have resisted corrosion are polished to the highest degree. The inner surface is smooth, and retains a uniform calibre to within a short distance of the reduced end, where it contracts, exhibiting the circular striæ before noticed. A qualification of the remark respecting the calibre is perhaps necessary: at a point one inch and a half from the smaller end is an offset in the bore. Whether this is the result of accident or design, it is not undertaken to say; probably the former, as the feature has not been observed in any others which have fallen under notice. As these tubes have been regarded with considerable interest, it is deemed proper to note every circumstance respecting them, even though not considered of much importance by the investigators themselves.

FIG. 123.

Fig. 123 represents a tube of somewhat different character.* It is carved from a dark, compact steatite, and measures ten inches in length by two inches in diameter at the larger, and one inch and a third at the smaller end. The bore is proportioned to the diameter, and is one and one tenth, and six tenths of an inch at the ends, respectively. Upon one side, as if to serve the double purpose of handle and ornament, is carved in high relief the figure of an owl, attached with its back to the tube. This carving is remarkably bold and spirited, and represents the bird with its claws contracted and drawn up, and head and beak elevated as if in an

---

* In the possession of J. VAN CLEVE, Esq., of Dayton, Ohio.

attitude of defence and defiance.   The *action* is very fine, but is imperfectly conveyed by the engraving.   The implement weighs little less than four pounds.   It was found in a mound on the Catawba river, Chester district, South Carolina.

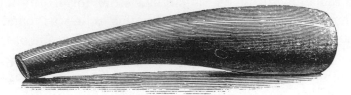

Fig. 124.

Fig. 124 is a tube of similar material with that last described.*   It is six inches long ; its greatest and least diameters being one inch and a quarter, and one inch and a half respectively, with a proportionate bore.   At a point about three inches from the larger end, is an oval hole or *stop*.   It was found while ploughing, near Marietta, Ohio.

It has been suggested that the last two articles were designed as wind instruments.   It is very certain that the skill of the present day succeeds in producing very indifferent music from them.   Either the art of playing upon them has sadly deteriorated, or the musical taste of the makers was not regulated by existing standards.   It has further been suggested that tubes of the character of those first described were designed as auxiliary to the eye in making distant observations.†   If it were deemed necessary to attempt an explanation of the probable purposes of every relic discovered, a *conjecture*, at least, might be based upon the peculiar mouth-pieces which many of these tubes possess,—namely, that they were used as *pipes* for smoking purposes.   The furthest advance towards designating their purposes, which it is here ventured to make, is to class them amongst implements.‡

---

* In the cabinet of Dr. S. P. HILDRETH, Marietta, Ohio.

† Several tubes, of very much the same character with those here referred to, have been found in the vicinity of the Grave creek mound.   Mr. SCHOOLCRAFT describes them as made out of a compact, blue and white mottled steatite, measuring from eight to twelve inches in length, by one inch and four tenths in diameter, and having a bore of four fifths of an inch, diminishing at one end to one fifth of an inch.   Our author observes :

" By placing the eye at the diminished point, the extraneous light is shut from the pupil, and distant objects more clearly discerned.   The effect is telescopic, and is the same which is known to be produced by directing the sight towards the heavens from the bottom of a well,—an object which we now understand to have been secured by the Aztec and Maya races in their astronomical observations, by constructing tubular chambers.   The quality of the stone, like most of the magnesian species, is soft enough to be cut with a knife.   It is evident that the circular lines observed in the calibre were produced by boring.   The circular striæ of this process are plainly apparent.   I learned by inquiry, that a quarry or locality of this species of rock exists on the banks of Grave creek, some four or five miles above the mound.   This establishes the fact, that they were made here and not brought from a distance.   The degree of skill evinced by these curious instruments is superior to that observed in the pipe-carvings and other evidences of North American Indian sculpture."—*Observations on the Grave creek Mound, Transactions of American Ethnological Society*, vol. i. p. 406.

‡ According to Vanegas, the " medicine men" of the Californian tribes of Indians, in their operations

There is another variety of tubes, which it may not be improper to notice in this connection, though partaking rather of the character of ornaments than

FIG. 125.

implements. Fig. 125, No. 1, represents one of these. It is in the form of a triangular prism, with sides slightly concave and angles rounded. It is three inches in length by one and three tenths in diameter at the ends, and is perforated longitudinally; the bore is half an inch in diameter. It is of the same variety of stone as the large tube first described, and of similar workmanship. No. 2 is, however, the prevailing form of articles of this description. It is a hollow cylinder, a little over four inches in length, swelling gently from the ends to the centre, where it measures an inch and a quarter in diameter; calibre, half an inch; material as above. Both these articles are highly polished. It is possible that they were worn as amulets, or as simple ornaments. This notion is favored by the fact, that none have been discovered which are not made of rare and beautiful stones.

PIPES.—The mound-builders were inveterate smokers, if the great number of pipes discovered in the mounds be admitted as evidence of the fact. These constitute not only a numerous but a singularly interesting class of remains. In their

FIG. 126.

construction, the skill of the makers seems to have been exhausted. Their general form, which may be regarded as the *primitive* form of the implement, is well exhibited in the accompanying sketch, Fig. 126.

---

for the cure of diseases, sometimes used tubes of stone. The operation in which they were used, was a kind of cautery.

"One mode was very remarkable, and the good effect it sometimes produced heightened the reputation of the physician. They applied to the suffering part of the patient's body the *chacuaco*, a tube formed out of a very hard black stone; and through this they sometimes sucked and at other times blew, but both as hard as they were able, supposing that the disease was either exhaled or dispersed. Sometimes the tube was filled with *cimarron* or wild tobacco lighted, and here they either sucked in or blew down the smoke, according to the physician's directions; and this powerful caustic sometimes, without any other remedy, has been known entirely to remove the disorder."— *Vanegas' California*, vol. i. p. 97.

They are always carved from a single piece, and consist of a flat curved base, of variable length and width, with the bowl rising from the centre of the convex side. From one of the ends, and communicating with the hollow of the bowl, is drilled a small hole, which answers the purpose of a tube ; the corresponding opposite division being left for the manifest purpose of holding the implement to the mouth. The specimen above represented is finely carved from a beautiful variety of brown porphyry, granulated with variously colored materials,—the whole much changed by the action of fire, and somewhat resembling porcelain. It is intensely hard, and successfully resists the edge of the finest tempered knife. The length of the base is five inches, breadth of the same one inch and a quarter. The bowl is one inch and a quarter high, slightly tapering upwards, but flaring near the top. The hollow of the bowl is six tenths of an inch in diameter. The perforation answering to the tube is one sixth of an inch in diameter, which is about the usual size. This circumstance places it beyond doubt that the mouth was applied directly to the implement, without the intervention of a tube of wood or metal. It will be observed that it is ornamented with cup-shaped holes, an eighth of an inch broad and about the same depth. Seven of these are placed in a circle upon each side of the bowl, which has a line of them extending spirally around it.

FIG. 127.

Fig. 127 is another pipe of a coarse-grained granite. It was not found in the mounds, but was turned up by the plough, in the vicinity of one of the large enclosures on the banks of Paint creek. It is quite unlike those figured above in shape, and perhaps belonged to a later race.

Such is the general form of these implements. The largest proportion of those which have been found in the mounds, however, are of much more elaborate workmanship. Their character has been briefly noticed on a previous page. (See page 152.) They are sculptured into singular devices— figures of the human head, and of various beasts, birds, and reptiles. These figures are all executed in miniature, but with a strict fidelity to nature. The attitudes of the animals are characteristic ; their very habits, in some cases, are indicated. Most are worked in porphyry ; and all display a truthfulness, delicacy, and finish, which we are unprepared to look for, except among the remains of a people considerably advanced in the arts. Some of them represent animals peculiar to the lower latitudes. Indeed, so remarkable in many respects are they regarded, in their bearing upon some of the more important questions connected with American archæology, particularly the migrations of the race of the mounds, that their full consideration is reserved for another place. They will be noticed at length, in connection with similar remains, under the more appropriate head of " Sculptures."

Besides these varieties of pipes, numerous others are found, most of which are probably referable to a comparatively recent era. They differ in style from those found in the mounds, and are for the greater part composed of steatites and other soft and easily worked varieties of stone. Some are of large size, and are boldly though not in general elegantly sculptured. They will also be noticed under the same head with those last mentioned.

From the appearance of these relics it is fairly inferable that, among the mound-builders as among the tribes of North American Indians, the practice of smoking was very general if not universal. The conjecture that it was also more or less interwoven with their civil and religious observances, is not without its support. The use of tobacco was known to nearly all the American nations, and the pipe was their grand diplomatist. In making war and in concluding peace it performed an important part. Their deliberations, domestic as well as public, were conducted under its influences; and no treaty was ever made unsignalized by the passage of the calumet. The transfer of the pipe from the lips of one individual to those of another was the token of amity and friendship, a gage of honor with the chivalry of the forest which was seldom violated. In their religious ceremonies it was also introduced, with various degrees of solemnity. A substitute for tobacco was sometimes furnished in the tender bark of the young willow; other substitutes were found among the Northern tribes in the leaves and roots of various pungent herbs. The custom extended to Mexico, where however it does not seem to have been invested with any of those singular conventionalities observed in the higher latitudes. It prevailed in South America and in the Caribbean islands. The form of the Indian pipe of North America is extremely variable, and very much the subject of individual taste. Some are excessively rude, but most are formed with great labor from the finest materials within reach. Along the Mississippi and among the tribes to the westward of that river, the material most valued for the purpose was, and still is, the red pipe-stone of the *Coteau des Prairies*, a beautiful mineral resembling steatite, easily worked and capable of a high finish. The spot whence it is obtained, and which is certainly one of the most interesting mineral localities of the whole country, is regarded with superstitious veneration by the Indians. It is esteemed to be under the special protection of the Great Spirit, and is connected with many of their most singular traditions. Until very recently it was the common resort of the tribes, where animosities and rivalries were forgotten, and where the most embittered foes met each other on terms of amity. In carving pipes from this material they expended their utmost skill, and we may regard them as the *chef d'œuvres* of modern Indian art. The following engraving, Fig. 128, from originals, will exhibit their predominant form, which it will be observed is radically different from that of the mound pipes. The larger of the two was once the favorite pipe of the eloquent KEOKUK, chief of the Sacs and Foxes, whose name occupies a conspicuous place in the Indian history of the North-west. These pipes were smoked with long tubes of wood, from twenty inches to three feet in length, fantastically ornamented with feathers and beads.

The sculpture of these articles, which is sometimes attempted in imitation of the human figure and of various animals, is often tasteful.   But they never display the nice observation, and true, artistic appreciation and skill exhibited

FIG. 128.

by those of the mounds, notwithstanding their makers have all the advantages resulting from steel implements for carving, and from the *suggestions* afforded by European art.   The only fair test of the relative degrees of skill possessed by the two races would be in a comparison of the remains of the mounds with the productions of the Indians before the commencement of European intercourse. A comparison with the works of the latter however, at any period, would not fail to exhibit in a striking light the greatly superior skill of the ancient people.

CHAPTER XIV.

ORNAMENTS OF STONE, BONE, ETC.

A **LARGE** proportion of the articles found in the mounds may be classed as ornaments. It is not undertaken to say, however, that all which follow under this head were really designed as such. The purposes of the remains of the mounds generally are so apparent, that little doubt can exist as to the place which they should occupy in the simple classification here attempted; but there are a few to which it is extremely difficult to assign a position. For all essential purposes, approximate conclusions are sufficiently exact; and although a good deal of ingenuity and much space might be expended in speculations upon the probable purposes of relics of doubtful use, it is not likely that the final result would be of much importance in its bearings upon archæological science.

BEADS.—The number of beads found in the mounds is truly surprising. They may be counted in some instances by hundreds and thousands,—each one the product of no inconsiderable amount of labor, unless our estimate of the means and facilities at the command of the makers is greatly underrated. The character of some of these beads, made of shell and enveloped in metal, has already been noticed. Others are composed of shell, worked into every variety of shape, round, oblong, and flattened; others still of animal bones and tusks, and many of *pearls* and small marine shells,—as the *marginella, natica, oliva*, etc. The perforated teeth of the wild cat, wolf, and shark, as well as the claws of animals and sections of the small bones of birds, were also used in the manner of beads, either for purposes of distinction and decoration, or as amulets. In all these we observe remarkable coincidences with the decorations of the existing tribes of Indians, who are extravagant in their use of beads and pendants.*

The beads found with the skeletons, so far as observation has extended, are composed of shell or tusks of animals,—those of shell greatly predominating. The surfaces of some of these are much discolored and corroded; many, however,

---

* Clavigero says of the ancient Mexicans: "It would be difficult to find a nation which accompanied so much simplicity of dress with so much variety and luxury in other ornaments of their persons. Besides feathers and jewels, with which they adorned their clothes, they wore ear-rings, pendants at the upper lip, and many likewise at their noses, necklaces, bracelets for the hands and arms, and also certain rings like collars around their legs. The ear-rings and pendants of the poor were shells, pieces of crystal, amber, or some other shining little stones; but the rich wore pearls, emeralds, amethysts, or other gems, set in gold."

retain their polish and appear quite sound.   They resemble sections cut from the ends of rods or small cylinders, and subsequently more or less rounded upon the edge : some are quite flat, and resemble the bone buttons of commerce ; others are perfectly round.   Their diameter varies from one fourth to three fourths of an inch ; the size of the perforation is also variable, usually, however, about one tenth of an inch.   Many exhibit circular striæ upon their surfaces, identical with those produced by turning in a lathe ; and it is possible they were formed by some such process, instead of being slowly and laboriously *worn* into shape by rubbing on stones, as was the practice of the modern Indians.   These are composed of the solid portion, the *columella*, of large marine shells.   In some of the mounds, the unworked columella has been found,—heavy and compact ; probably that of the *strombus gigas*, which shell is common upon the coasts of Florida.*

In the sacrificial or altar mounds a much greater variety of beads is found than in those devoted to sepulture ; a fact for which we cannot account, unless by supposing that the articles most valued for their rarity or beauty were those especially dedicated to their superstitions.   It is unfortunate, however, that those placed upon the altars, like everything else thus disposed of, are so much injured by the fire as to preserve but little of their former beauty.

FIG. 129.

The bead here represented is composed of shell, and is well wrought.   Some of this description have been obtained, which are not less than two inches in length by half an inch in diameter.   Abundance of others have been found of similar material but different shape : some are round, but most are oblong ; a few are lens-shaped.

But the most interesting and remarkable of the whole series are the *pearl beads*, of which a large number have been found in the altar or sacrificial mounds.   By exposure to the heat, they have lost their brilliancy and consequent value as ornaments ; most of them, indeed, are so much injured that they crumble under the touch.   The peculiarities of their form, and their concentric lamellæ, joined to the lingering lustre which some retain, place their character beyond dispute.   Several hundreds in number, and not far from a quart in quantity, are in our possession, which retain their structure sufficiently well to be strung and handled.   The largest of these measures two and a half inches in circumference, or upwards of three fourths of an inch in diameter.   They are of all intermediate sizes, down to one fourth of an inch in diameter.   Most are irregular in form, or pear-shaped ; yet there are many perfectly round.   They have been obtained from separate localities, several miles apart, and from five distinct groups of mounds.   Great numbers were so much calcined, that it was found impossible to recover them, and a large number crumbled in pieces after removal from the mounds.   It is no exaggeration to say

* Several thousands of these beads were found in the Grave creek mound.   They are much thinner than those discovered in the Scioto valley ; otherwise they closely resemble them.   They were for a long time supposed to be *ivory*.   Their true character was first detected by Mr. Schoolcraft.   See Transactions of American Ethnological Society, vol. i. p. 398.

that a number of quarts of pearls were originally deposited in the mounds referred to; probably nearly two quarts were contained in a single mound.

It may be inquired whence these pearls were obtained. Occasional specimens are found in the fresh water molluscs of this region, but they are exceedingly rare. They are very seldom discovered by our indefatigable naturalists on the Scioto, (some of whom annually collect thousands of the living shells,) and are never found of sizes at all comparable to those of the mounds. We know that among the natives of the West Indies, and the tribes of the Gulf, pearls were found in great abundance. Raleigh, Greenville, and others speak of them among the nations on the coasts of Virginia and the Carolinas; and Soto and Ribaulde observed large quantities among the tribes of Florida. It is a curious fact, that the Indians, observing the eagerness with which Soto's followers sought them, directed him, according to the chronicler, "to search certaine grauves that were in the town, and that he should find many; and that if he would send to the grauves of these dispeopled towns he might load all his horses; and they sought the grauves of the town, and there found fourteen *rooxes* of perles, [three hundred and ninety-two pounds,] and little babies and birds made of them." At another place the chronicler observes, they found "some perles of small valew, spoiled with the fire, which the Indians do string them like beads and weare them about their necks and hand wrists, and they esteem them very much." It is certainly not impossible that the "graves of the deserted towns" were the mounds themselves; for nothing could possibly be more in opposition to the Indian character, than to direct the hand of the invaders to the tombs of their own dead. An extreme and religious veneration and respect for the "graves of their fathers," universally characterizes the North American tribes.* They have been known to undertake long journeys to visit their ancient burial-places, and there perform the few simple rites enjoined by their superstitions. Such tributes were supposed to be grateful to the spirits of the dead.

FIG. 130.

Numerous beads composed of various small marine shells, of the genera *marginella, oliva,* and *natica,* pierced longitudinally, have been discovered. These are all found upon our Southern and South-western coasts, and in the West Indies.

Another species of beads found in the mounds, were made from some of the more beautiful varieties of the shells of the unios, so cut and strung as to exhibit

---

* "The tombs of the dead," says Charlevoix, "are held so sacred in this country, that to violate them is the greatest hostility that can be committed against a nation."—*Canada,* vol. 2, p. 153.

"Notwithstanding the North American Indians inter the whole riches of the deceased with him, and so make his corpse and the grave heirs to all, they never give them the least disturbance;—even a blood-thirsty enemy will not despoil or disturb the dead."—*Adair,* p. 178.

The Indians of the Columbia river, it seems, have less faith in the veneration of their race. They take care to bend the gun barrels, break holes in the vessels, and otherwise render valueless the various articles deposited with their dead; thereby removing the temptation to sacrilege.

the convex surface and pearly nacre of the shell. These must have formed very tasteful ornaments. Some neck ornaments identical in form and appearance with these were obtained by the Exploring Expedition, from Paumotou in the Pacific ; they are made of mother of pearl.

Other beads are composed of sections of the small bones of birds. Similar ornaments are common among the Indians to the west of the Mississippi, and have been observed among the natives of the Caribbean islands.

In addition to these several varieties of neck ornaments, may be enumerated the perforated canine teeth of certain animals, the wild cat, wolf, and bear ; also, the teeth of the shark and the alligator, and the claws of animals. The latter, separated from the foot at the first articulation, have been found in considerable numbers. Fig. 131 presents examples of these varieties. Some large imperforate

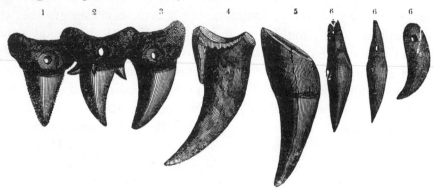

Fig. 131.

teeth of animals have been found with skeletons in such positions as to favor the conclusion that they were inserted into the lobes of the ear. No. 5 of the cut is an example. Several large *fossil* teeth of the shark, some of them perforated, have also been obtained from the mounds, and will be noticed, together with other singular remains of like character, under the head of " *Fossils and Minerals from the Mounds.*" These relics were perhaps worn as amulets or charms.*

A very tasteful variety of enamelled beads is frequently found upon the surface or with the recent deposits in the mounds. They are very erroneously supposed by some to have pertained to the race of the mounds ; so far is this from being the case, that they are all clearly of European origin. The early voyagers availed themselves, for purposes of traffic with the Indians, of their love of ornament,

---

* " Amulets and neck and ear ornaments constituted a very ancient and important department in the arcanum of the Indian's wardrobe. They were connected with his superstitions, and were part of the external system of his religion. The aboriginal man who had never laid aside his oriental notions of necromancy, and believed firmly in witchcraft, wore them as charms. They were among the most cherished and valued articles he could possibly possess. They were sought with great avidity, at high prices, and, after having served their purposes of warding off evil while he lived, were deposited in his grave at his death. Bones, shells, carved stones, gems, claws and hoofs of animals, feathers of carnivorous birds, and above all the skins of serpents, were cherished with the utmost care and regarded with the most superstitious veneration. To be decked with suitable amulets, was to him to be invested with a charmed life. They added to his feeling of security and satisfaction in his daily avocations, and gave him new courage in war."—*Schoolcraft's Notes on the Iroquois*, p. 226.

and "brought from the potteries and glass-houses of Europe various substitutes for the native wampum, in the shape of white, opaque, transparent, blue, black, and other variously colored beads, and of as many various forms as the genius of geometry could well devise. They also brought over a species of paste-mosaic, or curious oval or elongated beads of a kind of enamel or paste, skilfully arranged in layers of various colors, which, viewed at their poles, presented stars, radii, or other figures."*

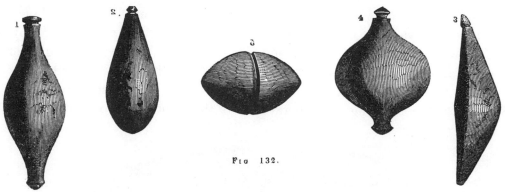

Fig. 132.

PENDANTS.—These ornaments are of frequent occurrence in the vicinity of the ancient works, though seldom found, if indeed found at all, in the ancient mounds themselves. They for the most part resemble the *plumbs* of the architect, and are usually made of rare and beautiful materials. No. 1 may be taken as the predominant form. It is symmetrically worked from a variety of greenstone, interspersed with large crystals of mica. It is drawn of half the dimensions of the original, which measures three and a half inches in length by one and a fourth in its greatest diameter, and weighs not far from four ounces. No. 2, also of half size, is well worked from a dark brown hematite, and is highly polished. No. 3 is also of hematite. It differs from the others in its shape, which is double conoid, and has the groove around the middle. Hematite seems to have been a favorite material for these ornaments. No. 5 is of quartz, and is much the rudest which has fallen under notice. These articles were all evidently designed for suspension. It has been suggested that they were used as ear ornaments; their weight, however, seems too considerable for such a purpose. To this day some of the savage tribes have the lobes of their ears greatly distended, in the language of the early writers, "like hoops," and the disfiguration is deemed a great improvement upon nature. "Some of the Indians," says Lawson, "wear great *bobs* in their ears, and sometimes in the holes thereof they put eagle's feathers, for a trophy."†

---

* SCHOOLCRAFT, "Notes on the Iroquois," p. 227. It is undoubted that some of the Indian tribes to the west of the Mississippi have the art, it is not presumed to say how or where acquired, of making a sort of enamelled beads, which they contrive to color of various shades. Some of these, of tolerable workmanship, are in the cabinet of the authors. They were obtained from the celebrated *Fond de Bœuf*, into which they were thrown under some superstitious impulse. Lewis and Clarke give an account of the manufacture of these ornaments, which is fully sustained by the peculiarities of the beads here mentioned.

† LAWSON's Carolina, p. 193. We have discovered none of these ornaments in the mounds, and it is difficult to say whether or not they are genuine relics of the mound-builders. It is possible they were

GORGETS.—Numerous relics of the description here presented are found in the mounds, generally with the skeletons. They seem to be identical in purpose, (differing only in respect of material,) with the articles of metal, described under this division (Figs. 89 and 90) in a previous page. They consist of plates or tablets of rare or beautiful stones, such as may easily be worked, and which admit of a high finish. In shape they are as diverse as fancy can suggest, but always of tasteful outline. Some are square, others oblong, oval, cruciform, or lozenge-shaped. Some are perforated with one, but most with two holes; the latter have always one, occasionally both, surfaces perfect planes.* Many have considerable thickness and display one face in relief; those with a single perforation often have both faces slightly convex. They exhibit, in general, much care and labor, and are elegantly finished. A few have been discovered which are quite rude, but possessing the general form of those more elaborately worked.

FIG. 133.

Fig. 133. No. 1 is composed of a very compact limestone. The surface is much corroded, but there are a few spots where it retains its original condition, and these exhibit a very high polish. Its form is sufficiently well indicated in the sketch. It measures, in length, three and a half inches; in width two inches; in thickness one inch and one tenth. It was found in a sepulchral mound near Chillicothe. (See page 164.) No. 2 is of the beautiful veined slate already described (page 224). Length, three inches; width, one and three fourths; thickness, three fourths of an inch. Found on the surface of the earth near Chillicothe.

---

used both by the earlier and later races. In the Museum of the East India Society at Salem, Mass., are a number of articles of similar character, which were found while making excavations in that city. They are larger and of much ruder workmanship than those of Ohio, but of the same shape, and grooved in like manner. It has been suggested that those of hematite, which are most numerous, were carried about the person for the purpose of supplying an ornamental paint. Rubbed upon any sharp grit with water, they furnish a dull red pigment,—much inferior, however, to the French preparations for the toilette. Irregular fragments of the same material are sometimes found bearing the marks of frequent trituration. Such may have been the secondary use of some of these articles; the frequent occurrence of those made from other materials establishes that they were primarily designed for other purposes. One composed of pieces of copper, rudely hammered together with little slips of silver inserted in the crevices, was found at Marietta, and is now in the cabinet of the Worcester Antiquarian Society; another, found at Cincinnati, and composed of quartz crystal, is in the Museum of the Philosophical Society at Philadelphia. Although found in mounds, it is exceedingly doubtful whether they were part of the original deposits.

* One of these articles, in the possession of Dr. Hildreth of Marietta, Ohio, is fourteen inches in length and is perforated with no less than *seven* holes. This seems to have been an exception to the general rule; perhaps it was designed for a different purpose.

Fig. 134 is of similar material with that last mentioned. It is three inches long, one and three fourths wide, and three fourths of an inch thick. Fig. 135 (half size) differs in material and shape from those above described. It is composed of a

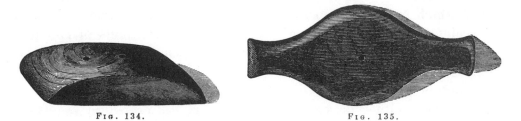

Fig. 134.   Fig. 135.

compact ferruginous stone, much altered by heat, and was found on the altar in the remarkable "Pipe Mound," in "Mound City" (page 152). It has but a single perforation.

It is a singular fact that the holes in the three specimens first noticed, as also in some of those which follow, are placed exactly four fifths of an inch apart. This could hardly have been the result of accident. These relics were found at different localities, several miles distant from each other.

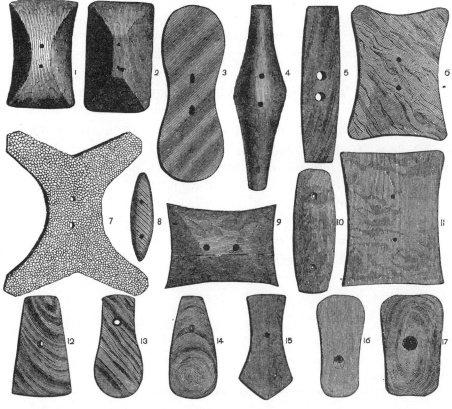

Fig. 136.

The above engraving presents at one view seventeen figures of as many different relics of this description,—all of which, with the exception of No. 7, and Nos. 12 to 17, are drawn of one fourth the size of the originals.

No. 1 is a vertical view of Fig. 133, No. 1, and is introduced here better to illustrate its form. No. 2 was found at Marietta, and is in the cabinet of Dr. Hildreth of that town. It measures: length, three inches and a half; width, one inch and nine tenths; thickness, three fourths of an inch. The material resembles that of which No. 1 is composed. No. 3 is of similar material, and was found beside a skeleton, in a mound formerly standing within the limits of Chillicothe.* Dimensions: length, six and a half inches; width at centre, two inches; thickness, four fifths. Nos. 4, 5, 6, 8, 9, 10, and 11, as also Nos. 15, 16, and 17, were found at various points in the Miami valley, and are in the possession of Mr. McBride. Most are of slate, either dark or variegated. No. 7 is cruciform in shape, and is composed of coralline limestone, of a very beautiful variety.

These illustrations might be indefinitely multiplied. The above will, however, give a very clear conception of the general character of this singular class of relics.

FIG. 137.

Fig. 137 illustrates the manner of the perforation. The holes are bevelled from one or both surfaces, and at the narrowest point are seldom more than one eighth of an inch in diameter. The circular striæ left in the process of boring, are to be observed with great distinctness in almost every instance.

These relics have been classed as *gorgets*, from their *apparent* purpose. It is not undertaken to say that such was their real purpose, for none of the many curious remains obtained from the mounds have more successfully baffled scrutiny. At first glance it seems obvious that they were designed for suspension, but there are many circumstances which it is not easy to reconcile with that conclusion. In common with the perforated copper plates, already described, they exhibit slight traces of friction upon the edges of the holes, which for the most part are as sharp as if newly cut. This could hardly be the case had they been worn suspended from the neck or upon any part of the person. Their material, shape, and style of workmanship, would seem to imply an ornamental purpose. It has been suggested that they were designed as implements, probably for condensing the raw hide or sinews used as bow-strings. This hypothesis is founded upon the character of the perforation, which is certainly such as would best subserve the purpose suggested; but the slight evidence of friction, already remarked, constitutes an objection to this conclusion which it is difficult to surmount.

---

* A relic, almost identical in shape with No. 4, was found in the great mound at Grave creek, and was supposed to be *ivory*, altered by long exposure in the earth. (*American Pioneer*, vol. ii. p. 200.) Mr. Schoolcraft, who examined it subsequently, describes it as " white, heavy, easily cut, moist, and possessing very much the appearance and feel of certain oxides," and suggests that a plate of some oxidable metal may still exist in the centre. (*Transactions of American Ethnological Society*, vol. i. p. 402.) This description would have applied to the articles described in the text, at the period of their removal from the earth. They, however, lost their moist feel and became quite hard upon exposure to the air. The material was a matter of speculation, until the fracture of one of the relics disclosed its character. The Grave creek relic measures six and a half inches in length.

The specimen dug up within the limits of Chillicothe, is said to have been found resting upon the breast of the skeleton with which it was deposited. The recollection of different individuals varies upon that point; hence no conclusion can be founded upon the position in which the relic was discovered. Those taken from the sepulchral mounds have uniformly been found by the side of the skeleton, near the bones of the hand.

Whatever their purposes, whether worn as ornaments or badges of authority and distinction, or designed as implements, it is certain they were in very general use. Not far from one hundred have been examined, which were procured from localities extending over the States of Virginia, Ohio, Kentucky, Tennessee, Illinois, and Indiana.*

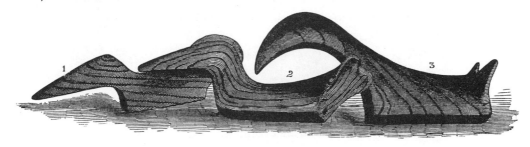

Fig. 138.

Fig. 138 (half size) also presents examples of a large class of remains probably of kindred character with those last described, and, like them, always composed of an ornamental kind of stone. The engravings will best illustrate their form, which, in almost every specimen, is slightly varied. They have holes perforated diagonally, at their lower corners, in which marks of wear from suspension or use are distinctly visible. The field of their occurrence is equally extensive with that of the relics last described.

It may reasonably be concluded from the uniform shape of these articles, and from their apparent unfitness as implements, as also from the wide range of their occurrence, that they were invested with a conventional significance as insignia or badges of distinction or as amulets. We know that the custom of wearing certain stones as preventives of disease, or as safeguards against accidents or the malice of evil spirits, has not been confined to one continent or a single age. It is not entirely obliterated among certain classes of our own people. Regal authority is still indicated by rich baubles of gold and gems. It matters little whether the

---

* ADAIR mentions ornaments worn by the "high priests" of the Southern tribes of Indians, which may have been identical with those here described. He says: "The American archi-magus wears a breast-plate, made of a white conch shell, with two holes bored in the middle of it, through which he puts the ends of an otter-skin strap, and fastens a buck-horn button to the outside of each." (*Adair's American Indians*, p. 84.) Our author does not fail to identify this badge with the sacred urim and thummim of the Jewish high priest, and draws a notable argument therefrom in support of his hypothesis of the Jewish origin of the American Indians. A similar ornament is mentioned by Beverly, as one of the principal decorations of the Indians of Virginia. He describes it as "a tablet of fine shell, smooth as polished marble." (*History of Virginia*, p. 141.)

index of royalty be a sceptre, or a simple carved and polished stone, so that it is sanctioned with general recognition.

F i g . 139.

Fig. 139 (half size) is made of a beautiful variety of quartz, of a white ground, clouded with green. It is smoothly wrought and polished, and is perforated from the ends. The shape is well shown by the engraving and supplementary section. It was probably designed for suspension, as an ornament.

F i g . 140.

Fig. 140 (quarter size) is wrought from the beautiful variegated slate so often referred to. It is marked upon its upper convex edge with notches, twenty-eight in number. Its purpose must remain entirely a matter of conjecture.

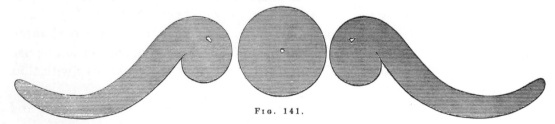

F i g . 141.

MICA ORNAMENTS.—Thin sheets of mica, cut in the form of scrolls, discs etc., have been occasionally found in the mounds. Fig. 141 presents examples. The scrolls, in this instance, measure six inches in length, and the discs are two inches in diameter. These are composed of the silvery or opaque mica, and are shaped with the utmost precision. The edges are perfectly smooth, as if cut with a very sharp instrument. They exhibit not the slightest irregularity, but are geometrically correct. Each piece is perforated with a small hole, such as would be formed by thrusting a blunt needle through it. They were probably in some way attached as ornaments to the dress.*

---

* Humboldt states that the *Guaynares* of the Rio Caura in South America are accustomed to stain themselves with arnotto, and to make broad transverse stripes on the body with some unctuous substance on which they stick spangles of silvery mica. Seen at a distance they appear to be dressed in lace clothes. (*Pers. Narration*, ch. xxiv.) Other nations, both of South and North America, used gold dust or other shining material, "with which they sprinkled their bodies and seemed to be gilt." (*Hackluyt*, vol. 2, p 57.)

In the Grave creek mound were found, with one of the skeletons, about one hundred and fifty bits of mica, an inch and a half or two inches square, each perforated with two or more small holes. These slips were about the thickness of ordinary writing paper, and it is supposed they were attached together, forming a sort of scarf or ornamental article of dress.* Many of the mounds, it may here be observed, contain mica, sometimes in plates of considerable thickness, but usually in simple folia, with ragged outlines.

In a mound excavated a year or two since near Lower Sandusky, Ohio, upwards of twenty oval plates of mica of great beauty were discovered, each perforated with a small hole at one end, evidently for the purpose of suspension. They were of the beautiful variety of the mineral known as "hieroglyphic" or "graphic" mica, and the natural markings were taken by the persons who discovered them to be veritable hieroglyphics—the records of an extinct people.

Most of the relics found in the mounds fall under the foregoing heads of classification. There are many, however, the purposes of which are entirely enigmatical. Whether designed as implements or ornaments, or whatever their particular purpose, it is not easy, and probably of not much importance, to determine. They are only valuable as illustrations of the skill of their makers, and can have but a slight bearing upon the more important questions connected with American archæology.

---

* Mr. Schoolcraft observes that some of the Algonquin bands, on the sources of the Mississippi, construct war-scarfs out of the brilliant-colored filaments of skins, ornamented with shells and the quills of the porcupine, and with the fine black points of deer's hoofs to produce a jingling sound. These are attached by strings to the breast, and are worn only by the warriors.—*Transactions of American Ethnological Society*, vol. i. p. 400.

CHAPTER XV.

MANY of the carvings in stone, already noticed, display no inconsiderable degree of taste and skill. There is, however, a large class of remains, comprising sculptural tablets, and heads and figures of animals, which belongs to a higher grade of art. Many of these exhibit a close observance of nature and a minute attention to details, such as we could only expect to find among a people considerably advanced in the minor arts, and to which the elaborate and laborious, but usually clumsy and ungraceful, not to say unmeaning, productions of the savage can claim but a slight approach. Savage taste in sculpture is generally exhibited in monstrosities,—caricatures of things rather than faithful copies. The dawn of art is marked by a purer taste; the result of an appreciation of the beauties of nature which only follows their close observance. The aim of the neophyte is to imitate, rather than distort, the objects which he sees before him. It is in this view that the sculptures taken from the mounds seem most remarkable; they exhibit not only the general form and features of the objects sought to be represented, but frequently, and to a surprising degree, their characteristic attitudes and expression.

It will, of course, be understood that nothing of the imposing character of many of the sculptured relics of Central America is found in the mounds. Aside from the stupendous earth structures, which deserve to be classed with the most wonderful remains of ancient power and greatness, there is nothing imposing in the monuments of the Mississippi valley. We have no sculptured façades of temples and palaces, invested with a symbolic meaning or commemorative of the exploits of chiefs and conquerors, nor have we ponderous statues of divinities and heroes, —nothing beyond the simplest form of stone structures. We must therefore estimate the minor sculptures which we discover here by other standards than those of Mexico and Peru, with which, from certain resemblances in other monuments, a comparison would be most likely to be suggested. They are simple in form as in design, and, as works of art, beyond a faithful observance of nature and great delicacy of execution, little can be claimed for them. In these respects they are certainly remarkable, and will be the more admired, the more closely they are inspected.

Some of these sculptures have a value, so far as ethnological research is concerned, much higher than they can claim as mere works of art. This value is derived from the fact that they faithfully represent animals and birds peculiar to other latitudes, thus establishing a migration, a very extensive intercommunication, or a contemporaneous existence of the same race over a vast extent of country.

The interesting inquiry here involved will be more appropriately made in another place, after an examination of the relics themselves.

It is a singular fact that no relics which were obviously designed as *idols* or objects of worship have been obtained from the mounds. Such are occasionally discovered on the surface, but none, so far as known, within the enclosures deemed sacred or defensive. Those which have been found are all of exceedingly rude workmanship, quite unlike any of the authenticated mound remains. They are more abundant in the region towards the Gulf than upon the Ohio, though not of frequent occurrence there. It is perhaps not to be wondered at that we discover none of these in the mounds, if our estimate of the purposes to which those structures were appropriated is a correct one.

In presenting the following illustrations of this branch of our subject, it will not be out of place to repeat the observation already once made, that, in the construction and ornament of their pipes, the mound-builders seem to have expended their utmost skill in sculpture. Accordingly most of the objects represented will be found to have subserved the purposes of pipes; but as the peculiarities of these implements have been sufficiently explained under the appropriate head, their bases and unessential parts have sometimes been omitted in the engravings. In many instances, the remains were so much broken up by the action of the fire, that it has been found impossible fully to restore them, although the utmost care was expended in collecting the fragments. This will account for the imperfect character of some of the illustrations. It would have been an easy matter to have restored many of these relics with the pencil, but it has been preferred to present an actual fragment rather than a fanciful whole. All the remains which follow, unless otherwise specially noted, were taken from the mounds by the authors in person, and are at present deposited in their collection. They comprise, however, but a limited selection from the whole number; no more being presented than are deemed sufficient to give the reader a clear conception of their general character and great variety. The scale upon which they are drawn is, generally, full size; when this is not the case, the dimensions are specially given.

SCULPTURES OF THE HUMAN HEAD.—Few sculptures of the human head have been found in the mounds, though several have been discovered under such circumstances as to leave little doubt that they belong to the mound era. Four specimens were taken from the remarkable altar mound, No. 8, " Mound City," three of which constitute the bowls of pipes. Front and profile views of each of these are herewith presented, of the size of the originals.

Fig. 142 is composed of a hard, compact, black stone, and is distinguished from the others by the hardness and severity of its outline. It has a singular head-dress, falling in a broad fold over the back of the head, as far down as the middle of the neck. Upon each side of the top of the head this head-dress, which may represent some particular style of platting the hair, rises into protuberances or knots,

Encircling the forehead, and coming down as low as the ears, is a row of small round holes, fifteen in number, placed as closely as possible together, which, when the head was found, were filled in part with pearls, completely calcined and only recognisable from their concentric lamination.   The holes were doubtless all originally filled in the same manner.   The ornamental lines upon the face are

Fig. 142.

rather deeply cut; their form is accurately indicated in the engravings.   Those radiating from around the mouth might readily be supposed to represent a curling moustache and beard.   The mouth of this miniature head is somewhat compressed, and the brow seems contracted, giving it an aspect of severity, which is not fully conveyed by the engraving.   The eyes are prominent and open.

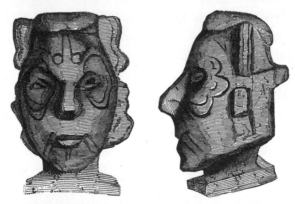

Fig. 143.

Fig. 143 resembles the one last described only in respect to the peculiar markings on the face, already noticed.   Its features are bolder, and the outline of the face quite different.   The nose is large and prominent, the eyes sunken and apparently closed, and the forehead high and narrow.   The head-dress is very remarkable.   A portion of the hair seems gathered in festoons upon either side of the head above the ears, the remainder centering in a kind of knot upon the back of the head.   The top of the head is covered with a sort of lappet or fold, which seems detached from the other portions of the head-dress, simply resting upon the crown.   The ears were each perforated; and from the strongly attached oxide of copper at those points, were probably ornamented with rings of that metal. This head, unlike the others, does not constitute a pipe bowl, but seems, from the fracture, to have been attached, at the lower and back part, to a rod carved from the same stone. The base, shown in the engraving, is simply an addition of plaster to sustain the head in a vertical position. The material, in this instance, is a compact yellowish stone, too much altered by the fire to be satisfactorily made out.

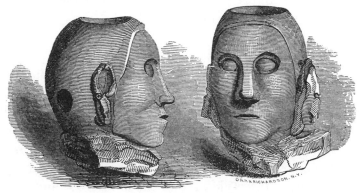

F ɪ ɢ . 1 4 4 .

Fig. 144 is composed of the same material with that last described. Its features are more regular than those of either of the preceding examples. The nose turns up slightly at the point, and the lips are prominent. The eyes seem closed, and the whole expression of the face is a repose like that of death. The head-dress is simple; and the ears, which are large, are each perforated with four small holes around their upper edges. At the lower and posterior portion of the head are drilled, in convergent directions, two holes, each one fifth of an inch in diameter and half an inch deep. Were they continued one fourth of an inch further in the same direction, they would intersect each other. This head is destitute of markings upon the face. It has been suggested, from the greater delicacy of the features, that this was designed to represent a female.

F ɪ ɢ . 1 4 5 .

Fig. 145. This is the most beautiful head of the series, and is evidently that of a female. It is carved from a compact stone, which is much altered, and in some places the color entirely changed, by the action of the fire. The muscles of the face are well exhibited, and the forehead finely moulded. The eyes are prominent and open, and the lips full and rounded. Whether the head is encased in a sort of hood, or whether the hair is platted across the forehead and down the sides of the face, it is not easy to say. The knots observable at the top of the forehead, and just back of the ears, may be designed to represent the manner in which the hair was gathered or wound. The workmanship of this head is unsurpassed by any specimen of ancient American art which has fallen under the notice of the authors, not excepting the best productions of Mexico and Peru. The whole is smooth and well polished.

These heads are valuable as being the only ones taken from the mounds, the ancient date of which is clearly established. In the same mounds in which they were found, it has already been observed, were also found upwards of a hundred miniature sculptures of animals, most of which are indigenous. The fidelity to nature observed in the latter fully warrant us in believing that the sculptures of the human heads discovered with them are also faithful copies from nature, and truly display not only the characteristic features of the ancient race, but also their method of wearing the hair, the style of their head-dresses, and the character and mode of adjustment of a portion of their ornaments. This conclusion will appear the more reasonable, when we come to observe the exactness displayed in the effigies of animals.

It is impossible to overlook the coincidence between the fillet of *real* pearls displayed upon the forehead of the head first described, and the similar range of sculptured pearls upon the brow of the small statue described by Humboldt, and denominated by him the "statue of an Aztec priestess."* The manner of its adjustment is in both instances substantially the same, and indicates a common mode of wearing those ornaments among both the mound-builders and the Mexicans. The markings upon the faces of two of these sculptures may be taken as representing paint lines or some description of tattooing. We know that, among the North American tribes, the custom of painting the face with every variety of color, and ornamenting it with fantastic figures, was wide-spread and common. The singular head-dresses observed in these figures bear little resemblance to those of the Indians, so far as we know anything of them. The North Americans usually allowed but a single tuft of hair to grow, which depended from the centre of the scalp; the hair of the women was allowed to fall loosely upon the shoulders, or was simply clubbed behind. Plumes of feathers, or the dried skins of the heads of certain animals, constituted about their only style of head-dress. That the practice of wearing rings and pendants in the ears existed among the race of the mounds may be inferred no less from these relics than from the character of some of the ornaments which have been occasionally discovered. The practice was almost universal among the hunter tribes and the Central American nations.

In respect to the physiological characteristics exhibited by these relics, it need only be observed that they do not differ essentially from those of the great Ameri-

---

* *Researches*, vol. i. p. 43.

can family, the type of which seems to have been radically the same through the extent of the continent, excluding, perhaps, a few of the tribes at the extremes.

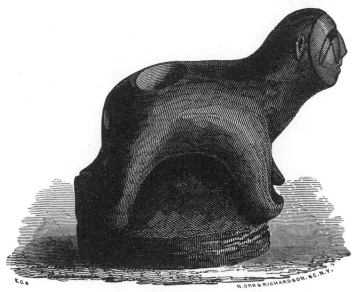

FIG. 146.

Fig. 146 is carved from a light-colored sandstone, and represents a human figure resting upon its knees and elbows, the soles of the feet and the palms of the hands being placed together. It is also adapted as a pipe. It has a singular, painful expression of countenance. A double set of converging lines start from the eye upon the right side of the face and extend diagonally across it. Upon the left side is a single set terminating in a point near the ear. This figure is boldly but not delicately carved, and was found while digging a mill race, three feet below the surface, on the west bank of the Miami river, near the village of Tippecanoe, Miami county, Ohio.* It measures six inches in length by about the same height.

FIG. 147.

Fig. 147 is a fine specimen of ancient sculpture. It was found within an ancient enclosure twelve miles below the city of Chillicothe, and, from the material and style of workmanship, may be regarded as a relic of the mound-builders. The

---

* In the possession of J. VAN CLEVE, Esq., Dayton, Ohio.

material is a fine porphyry of a greenish brown or lead-colored ground, interspersed with black and white granules of a harder nature, and is identical with the
material composing many similar articles taken from the mounds. It has the body
of a bird with the head of a man, and is delicately and symmetrically carved. It
is adapted as a pipe; the bowl rising from the centre of the back communicates
with a hole drilled for the insertion of a stem from the side. The attitude of the
entire figure is graceful, and the proportions of the different parts in admirable
harmony. The face displays less individuality than those already noticed, and is
distinguished for its greater width. The eyes are closed, and the general expression,
especially of the profile, is that of repose. The ears have been mutilated, but
display the usual marks of perforation. There is no head-dress distinguishable;
but there is a longitudinal band extending from the back of the head to the body
of the figure, the purpose of which is not obvious, unless designed to strengthen
the attachment of the parts. The wings are closely folded, and a waving line runs
along the centre. It measures five inches in extreme length.

Fig. 148.

Fig. 148 very closely resembles Fig. 146, above described. The posture is the
same, but the limbs are barely indicated. The head however is better carved and
is more characteristic. It will be observed that it is also distinguished by a line
bounding the face, and has similar markings extending from the eyes. A large
serpent is folded around the neck, the head and tail resting together upon the
breast of the figure. The head is surmounted by a knot, resembling the scalp
lock of the Indians. It is carved from a compact red sandstone, and is six inches
in greatest length by five inches in height, with a broad flat base. It was found
on the banks of Paint creek, one mile distant from the city of Chillicothe.
It is also adapted as a pipe. Several other articles, closely resembling these
two, have been found at various points on the surface, but none have been
taken from the mounds. Both in the character of their material and style of
workmanship they sustain a close relationship to certain " stone idols," as they

have been termed, found, for the most part, in the States of Tennessee and Mississippi. One of these "idols" was discovered some years since, in ploughing upon the Grave creek Flats in Virginia.* It represents a human figure in a squatting attitude, with its elbows drawn back and its hands resting upon its knees. It is thirteen inches high by six inches and a half broad. In material and workmanship it is identical with the articles last described, and, like Fig. 148, is distinguished by a crown-tuft or "scalp-lock." There are two orifices communicating with each other in its back. It was probably designed to serve as a pipe. A stone "idol," destitute however of orifices, was found not long since near the mouth of the Scioto river. It represents a human figure in a squatting attitude, the arms clasped around the knees, upon which the chin is resting. This is the common position of the North American Indians, when seated around the fires in their wigwams. It seems most likely that these rough sculptures have a comparatively recent date, and are the remains of the tribes found in possession of the country by the whites. As works of art they are immeasurably inferior to the relics from the mounds.

FIG. 149.

Fig. 149. This singular specimen of sculpture bears a close resemblance to those above described, but is of much superior workmanship. The features and style of ornament are peculiar. The material is a gray sandstone. It is now deposited in the museum of the Historical Society of New York; but its history is unknown. It is clearly the original from which the drawing published by Baron

---

* See memoir on the Grave creek mound by H. R. SCHOOLCRAFT, Esq., *Transactions of American Ethnological Society*, vol. i. p. 408. The original is regarded by that gentleman as furnishing tangible evidence of the existence of idol worship among the North American tribes. Its purposes, whatever they were, seem to differ but slightly from those to which the ruder articles noticed in the text were applied. The orifices in the back are supposed by Mr. Schoolcraft to be designed for the insertion of the thumb and finger in lifting the object, or for the introduction of a thong or cord in transporting or suspending it.

Humboldt was made.   This drawing was copied by Choris, in his " *Voyage Pittoresque*," where it is described as having been found in an ancient tumulus in the State of Connecticut, and presented to Baron Humboldt by Baron Hyde de Neuville, French ambassador to Rio Janeiro.   There must, of course, be some mistake as to the place of its discovery; for there are no ancient tumuli in the State of Connecticut.

Fig. 150.

Fig. 150 is a mask of the human face roughly carved from sandstone.   It is twelve inches long, seven and a half broad at the ears, and weighs nearly nine pounds.   It is slightly concave upon the back, the front being proportionally convex.   There is a hole underneath the chin, as if the object had been designed to be carried upon the point of a staff.   It was found, in ploughing, near Lawrenceburgh in the State of Indiana.*

Similar relics, some of which vary little from the above in size, are found in Mexico.   They are said to occur in the ancient Aztec tombs, covering the faces of skeletons.   Many of these are sculptured from *obsidian*, and are smooth and beautifully polished; others are of serpentine and a variety of ornamental stones.†

---

* In the collection of JAMES McBRIDE, Esq.

† Several of these masks are embraced in the collection of Mexican antiques, presented by Mr. POINSETT to the American Philosophical Society, at Philadelphia.

Figs. 151 and 152, are front and profile views of a relic found in Belmont county, Ohio, nearly opposite Wheeling, on the Ohio river. The original is six inches

FIG. 151. FIG. 152.

length. It is composed of sandstone. The back is deeply grooved, but it exhibits no marks of having ever been attached to any object.

SCULPTURES OF ANIMALS.—Sculptured figures of a considerable number of animals have been found in the mounds, including the lamantin, the beaver, otter, elk, bear, wolf, panther, wild cat, raccoon, oppossum, and squirrel.

Fig. 153. *The Lamantin, Manitus, or Sea-cow* is not found in this latitude, but is peculiar to tropical regions. Seven sculptured representations of this animal have been taken from the mounds, of which three are nearly perfect. When first

FIG. 153.

discovered, it was supposed they were monstrous creations of fancy; but subsequent investigation and comparison have shown that they are faithful representations of one of the most singular animal productions of the world. Naturalists assume to know but little of the lamantin, beyond its form and general characteristics. Its habits are involved in much obscurity. It is thus described by Godman:

" The general figure of the lamantin is rather elliptical and elongated. Its head is shaped like a simple truncated cone, and terminates in a thick fleshy snout, semi-circular at its extremity, and pierced at the upper part by two small semilunar nostrils directed forwards.   The edge of the upper lip is tumid, furrowed in the middle, and provided with thick and stiff whiskers.   The lower lip is narrower and shorter than the upper, and the opening of the mouth is small.   The eyes are situated towards the upper part of the head, at the same distance from the snout as the angle of the lips.   The ears are very small, scarcely perceptible, and placed at the same distance from the eyes that the latter are from the snout.

" The neck is not distinguished by any diminution or difference in size from the head and trunk, and the latter does not diminish except from the umbilicus, whence it rapidly decreases until it spreads out and becomes flattened, with a broad, thin, and seemingly truncated extremity.   The tail forms about a fourth of the length of the animal.

" The arm-bones which sustain the fins are more separated from the body than those of the delphinus, and have digits more distinguishable through the integuments.   The edges of the fin have four flat and rounded nails, which do not extend beyond the membrane, the nail of the thumb being deficient.   The skin is of a gray color, is slightly shagreened, and has upon it a few scattered hairs, which are more numerous than elsewhere about the angles of the lips and the palmar surface of the fins.

" The full-grown lamantin is from fifteen to twenty feet in length, by eight in circumference, and weighs several thousand pounds."*

" Head not distinct from the body; eyes very small; tongue oval; vestiges of nails on the margin of the pectoral fins; six cervical vertebræ; sixteen pair of thick ribs; *moustaches composed of a bundle of very strong hairs directed downwards and forming on each side a kind of corneous tusk.*"†

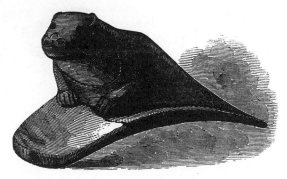

Fig. 154.

These external features are faithfully and minutely exhibited in the sculptures from the mounds.   The truncated head, small and scarcely distinguishable ears, thick, semi-circular snout, peculiar nostrils, tumid, furrowed upper lip, singular feet or fins, and remarkable moustaches, are all distinctly marked, and render the recognition of the animal complete.   Only one of the sculptures exhibits a flat, truncated tail; the others are round.   There is however a variety of the lamantin (*Manitus*

Senigalensis, **Desm.**) which has a round tail, and is distinguished as the " round-tailed manitus." It is smaller in size than the other variety.

The name of *Manati* was given to this animal by the Spaniards in consequence of the short anterior extremities, which were regarded as hands. It has been found difficult to assign a place to it in the animal creation, and it has been remarked that it " may be indiscriminately called the last of beasts or the first of fishes." It has two pectoral or abdominal mammæ, which from their position probably gave rise among mariners to the fable of the mermaid. Columbus, when he first saw these animals in the West Indies, called them *sirens*. They bring forth two young ones at a birth; in defence of which the manitus, though a peaceable and harmless animal, is insensible to pain or fear. Its habits are little understood. It is supposed never to leave the water, but frequents the shores to feed on the grass at the edge. Sea-grass or fucus and marine herbage are supposed to constitute its principal if not its only food; though this is a point upon which naturalists have not ventured to give a decision. The opinion, however, seems general, that it is an herbivorous animal.

As before observed, the manitus is found only in tropical waters, frequenting the mouths of rivers, but sometimes ascending them to great distances. They were seen by Humboldt in the Rio Meta, a branch of the Orinoco, one thousand miles above its mouth; and it is said they are found in the Amazon two thousand miles from the sea. They are also found among the Antilles on the southern coast of Mexico, and on the coast and in the rivers of Florida, in the United States. Excepting upon that peninsula, we have no account of their occurrence on our coasts. Bartram mentions a singular spring, a few miles below Tallahassee, Florida, which was frequented by the manitus; and its bones are found, and occasional living specimens observed, in the Manitee river, which enters Tampa bay.*

The flesh of this animal was used by the Indians for food, and its bones and thick tough hide employed in various manufactures. It was hunted for these purposes; and Oviedo, who seems to have been the first author who noticed it, gives a particular account of the manner in which it was captured. Bartram observes :

" The basin and stream were continually peopled with prodigious numbers and varieties of fish and other animals, such as the alligator, and, in the winter season, the manate or sea-cow. Parts of the skeleton of one which the Indians had killed last winter, lay upon the banks of the spring; the grinding teeth were about an inch in diameter, the ribs eighteen inches long and two and a half inches in thickness, bending with a gentle curve. This bone is esteemed equal to ivory. The flesh of this creature is counted wholesome and pleasant food; the Indians call them by a name which signifies ' the big beaver.' My companion, who was a trader, saw three of them at one time near this spring; they feed chiefly on aquatic grass and weeds."†

---

* Observations on the Geology of East Florida, by T. A. Conrad, Silliman's Journal of Arts and Sciences for July, 1846.

† Bartram's Travels in North America, p. 299.

Humboldt mentions a branch of the Apures river, itself a tributary of the Orinoco, " called the *Cano del Manati*, from the great number of manatees caught there." He states that their flesh is savory, resembling pork, and was in great request among the Indians during Lent, being classed by the monks among fishes. The fat was used in the lamps of the churches, and the hide cut into slips to supply the place of cordage.*

The flesh of this animal furnished formerly a large part of the subsistence of the inhabitants of St. Christophers, Guadaloupe, and Martinique. The fat was used at a late day for many of the purposes to which lard is applied, sometimes supplying the place of butter.†

The sculptures of this animal are in the same style and of like material with the others found in the mounds. One of them is of a red porphyry, filled with small white and light blue granules; the remainder are of sandstone, limestone, etc. Most of the mound sculptures are from these materials.

These singular relics have been thus minutely noticed, inasmuch as they have a direct bearing upon some of the questions connected with the origin of the mounds. That we find marine shells or articles composed from them, in the mounds, is not so much a matter of surprise, when we reflect that a sort of exchange was carried on even by the unsympathizing American tribes, and that articles from the mouth of the Columbia are known to have found their way, by a system of transfer, to the banks of the Mississippi; their occurrence does not necessarily establish anything more, than that an intercourse of some kind was kept up between the builders of the mounds on the banks of the Ohio, and the sea.‡ There is, however, something more involved in the discovery of these relics. They are undistinguishable, so far as material and workmanship are concerned, from an entire class of remains found in the mounds; and are evidently the work of the same hands with the other effigies of beasts and birds. And yet they faithfully represent animals found, (and only in small numbers,) a thousand miles distant, upon the shores of Florida. Either the same race, possessing throughout a like style of workmanship, and deriving their materials from a common source, existed contemporaneously over the whole range of intervening territory, and maintained a constant intercommunication; or else there was at some period a migration from the south, bringing with it characteristic remains of the land from which it emanated. The sculptures of the manitus are too exact to have been the production of those who were not well acquainted with the animal and its habits.

---

* Humboldt's Travels and Researches in South America.

† Godman's Natural History, vol. ii. p. 155.

‡ Mr. Schoolcraft mentions, in illustration of the extent of Indian exchanges in shells and ornaments, that he saw at the foot of Lake Superior, Indian articles ornamented with the shining white *Dentalium Elephanticum* from the mouth of the Columbia.

FIG. 155.

FIG. 156.

FIG. 157.

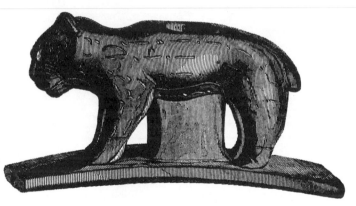

FIG. 158

FIG. 159.

FIG. 160.

Fig. 155. THE BEAVER.—Three sculptures of the beaver have been obtained from the mounds,—all in the characteristic attitudes of that animal. The engraving does not do justice to the original, which is better proportioned. These animals were frequent in the North-western States, but have now almost entirely disappeared. The large head, blunt snout, small ears and eyes, peculiar claws, and broad, oval, scaly tail, are all well characterized in the sculptures.

THE OTTER.—Two sculptures of the otter have been discovered, one of which represents the animal grasping a fish in its mouth; it is however much mutilated. That of which an imperfect engraving (Fig. 157) is given is composed of the peculiar porphyry already described, and displays in a striking manner the features of the animal. The flattened head, small mouth, almost imperceptible ears, rounded body, and short but strong and fin-like legs, no less than the attitude of the figure, enable us to recognise at once the most active, courageous, and voracious of the indigenous amphibious animals. The otter is still found, in limited numbers, about the waters of the North-western States. The eyes in this specimen were formed by drilling a narrow but deep hole, which was filled with a material of different color, resembling bone. In many instances small pearls were inserted for eyes, some of which have been found retaining their places, unreduced by the fire to which they have been exposed. This relic, in common with all the mound sculptures, is delicately carved and polished.

THE WILD CAT.—Figs. 158, 159, 160. Of this animal and others of the same genus a large number of sculptures have been obtained. One of these represents the female animal erect; the remainder are in characteristic positions. They are very minutely sculptured, the whiskers and variegated color of the hair around the head, as well as the general features of the animal,—strong jaws, short neck, and short thick tail,—are all well exhibited. Fig. 160 presents a head slightly different from most of the others. It bears a close resemblance to that of the cougar. Most of these are exquisitely carved from a red, granulated porphyry, of exceeding hardness,—so hard, indeed, as to turn the edge of the best tempered knife.

FIG. 161.

Fig. 161 is a very spirited representation of the head of the elk, although it is not minutely accurate.

Numerous other illustrations of these miniatures might be introduced; the above will, however, convey a very clear notion of the character of the sculptures and the fidelity of the representations.

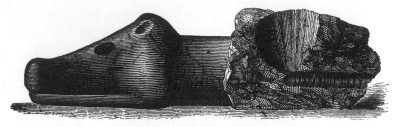

FIG. 162.

Fig. 162 is a fragment of a large and elaborately carved pipe representing the head of some animal. It is composed of the beautiful micaceous stone already several times noticed, and in respect of size is unlike any of the articles of this description which have been taken from the mounds. The circular striæ left by the instrument used in boring the tube are distinctly marked. At the termination of the bore, is what is technically termed "the *core*," showing that the drilling had been effected by some hollow instrument, probably a thin stem of cane. The cane is used at this day by the Indians for drilling, and with the aid of fine sand and water forms a very efficient instrument. It is probable that all the tubes, large and small, found in the mounds, were produced in this manner. This fragment of sculpture is nine inches long. The bowl was evidently carved in the form of some animal, but it is too much broken to be made out.

FIG. 163.

Fig. 163 is one of the most delicate specimens of ancient workmanship thus far discovered. It is of the same material with the article last noticed, and like that has the form of an animal's head. What animal it was intended to represent, it is not easy to determine; in the length of its ears it resembles the rabbit. A portion of the point of the nose is broken off. It is hollowed like a canoe upon the under side, leaving but a thin shell of material, not exceeding, for the most part, the tenth of an inch in thickness. It is perforated with small holes at the root of each ear, and has a hole, drilled from the interior, in the crown. It is impossible to conjecture the purpose to which this article was applied, unless that of ornament. It is elegantly and symmetrically carved, and highly polished.

SCULPTURES OF BIRDS.—The sculptures of birds are much more numerous than those of animals, and comprise between thirty and forty different kinds, and not far from one hundred specimens. We recognise the eagle, hawk, heron, owl, buzzard, toucan (?), raven, swallow, parroquet, duck, grouse, and numerous other land and water birds. There are several varieties of the same species; for instance, among the owls, we find the great owl, the horned owl, and the little owl; there are also several varieties of the rapacious birds. It is impossible to present examples of all these. The following specimens will, however, serve amply to illustrate the strict fidelity to nature which the sculptures display, as also the skill with which they are executed.

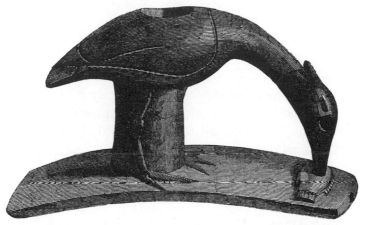

Fig. 164.

Fig. 164 will readily be recognised as the tufted heron, the most indefatigable and voracious of all the fisher varieties. The small body; long wings, extending to the extremity of the short tail; long, thin neck; sharp bill, and tufted head, are unmistakeable features. He is represented in the attitude of striking a fish, which is also faithfully executed. Nothing can surpass the truthfulness and delicacy of the sculpture. The minutest features are shown; the articulations of the legs of the bird, as also the gills, fins, and scales of the fish, are represented. It is carved from the red, speckled porphyry, already several times mentioned as constituting the material of many of these sculptures. As a work of art it is incomparably superior to any remains of the existing tribes of Indians. The engraving, in point of spirit, falls far short of the original.

Fig. 165.

Fig. 165 represents a rapacious bird, probably some variety of the eagle or hawk, in the attitude of tearing in pieces a small bird, which it grasps in its claws. The sculpture is spirited and life-like, as well as minute and delicate.   The wings are folded across each other; and the finer feathers upon their superior portions, and upon the thighs, are well represented.   The eyes of this bird were composed of small pearls, inserted about half their depth in the stone.   Pearls seem to have constituted the eyes of nearly all the birds.

Fig. 166.   This fragment also represents some variety of rapacious bird.   It is wrought with admirable skill and spirit, and it is to be regretted that the entire figure was not recovered.

THE SWALLOW.—Fig. 167.   This fine specimen cannot be too much admired for its fidelity to nature and its excellent finish.   The body is thrown forward, and the wings are apparently about to be expanded, as if the bird was just ready to dash off on its swift and erratic flight.   This attitude will readily be recognised as eminently characteristic, by those who have watched the graceful movements of this active, cheerful bird.   The engraving fails to convey the lightness and spirit of the original, which, it should be mentioned, is carved in red porphyry.

SUMMER or WOOD DUCK.—Fig. 168.   This bird is common throughout the United States.   The head is well characterized, and is admirably executed.   The engraving conveys but an imperfect notion of the original, which is lighter and of better proportions.

THE TOUCAN. (?)—Fig. 169.   The engraving very well represents the original, which is delicately carved from a compact limestone.   It is supposed to represent the toucan,—a tropical bird, and one not known to exist anywhere within the limits of the United States.   If we are not mistaken in supposing it to represent this bird, the remarks made respecting the sculptures of the manitus will here apply with double force.

Fig. 170.   This specimen will readily be recognised as intended to represent the head of the grouse.   It is exceedingly spirited, and in execution is inferior to none of the articles recovered from the mounds.   Birds of this species, though not abundant in the Scioto valley, are plentiful on the plains of Indiana and Illinois. The material is the red granulated porphyry so often mentioned.

Fig. 171.   This specimen, which is well exhibited in the engraving, is carved from a compact limestone.   It was probably intended to represent the turkey-buzzard.   This bird is common in southern Ohio.

Fig. 166.

Fig. 167.

Fig. 168.

Fig. 169.

Fig. 170.

Fig. 171.

Fig. 172.

Fig. 173.

Fig. 174.

Fig. 175.

Fig. 176.

Fig. 177.

THE PARROQUET.—Fig. 172.   Among the most spirited and delicately executed specimens of ancient art found in the mounds, is that of the parroquet here presented.   The fragment shown in the cut was alone recovered.   The engraving, though very good, fails to do justice to the original.   The parroquet is essentially a southern bird ; and, though common along the Gulf, is of rare occurrence above the Ohio river.   It is sometimes seen in the Scioto valley, fifty miles above its mouth.

Fig. 173.   The bird here represented much resembles the tufted " cherry bird." The head is somewhat disproportioned to the body,—a defect more common than any other in the mound sculptures.   It is carved from a brown, granulated porphyry, and is finished with great delicacy.   The bowl is ingeniously enlarged, below the opening, so as to admit a greater quantity of tobacco, or whatever article was smoked, without interfering with the symmetry of the bird, which a larger bore would have much impaired.

Fig. 174.   This specimen does not differ widely from that shown in the preceding figure, and was probably intended to represent the same bird.   The too great size of the head observed in the other is not so marked in this instance.   The material somewhat resembles, in color and substance, the red pipe-stone of the *Coteau des Prairies*, but has less of the talcose appearance and feel.   It receives a very good finish, but is not susceptible of a high polish.   The pearls which had been inserted in the cavities representing the eyes, were in this instance found retaining their places.   They had lost their brilliancy in consequence of exposure to the fire, but were yet easily recognisable.

Fig. 175.   The remarks made in respect to the relic last mentioned apply to the specimen here represented.   It is carved in the same material as Fig. 173, and is probably intended to represent a bird of the same variety.   Nothing can exceed the life-like expression of the original.

Fig. 176.   This specimen seems unfinished, and the features of the bird sought to be represented are not well made out.   It seems to have been rubbed or ground into its present shape, and is yet unpolished.

Fig. 177.   This is one of the least tasteful specimens recovered from the mounds, and, like the one last noticed, seems to be in an unfinished state.   The lines indicated in the cut are sharply graved in the stone.   It is not undertaken to say what bird is designed to be represented.

Fig. 178.   This carving is roughly executed, and represents a bird of some variety not easily recognisable.   The bill is broad and heavy, and the toes are long and wide-spread.   It is evidently intended to represent a bird in the act of picking up some articles of food, which are indicated by small circles on the palm of an extended hand.   On account of the convexity of the base of the pipe, these details are not shown in the engraving, which in all other respects is a faithful copy of the original.

From the size of its bill, and the circumstance of its having two toes before and two behind, the bird intended to be represented would seem to belong to the zygodactylous order—probably the toucan. The toucan (*Ramphastos* of Lin.) is found on this continent only in the tropical countries of South America.

Fig. 178

Pozzo, a distinguished naturalist, speaks of taming them very easily. Other travellers inform us that they are very highly prized by the Indians of Guiana and Brazil, principally on account of their brilliant plumage. They pluck off the skin from the breast, containing the most beautiful feathers, and glue it upon their cheeks by way of ornament. In those districts the toucan was almost the only bird the aborigines attempted to domesticate. The fact that it is represented receiving its food from a human hand, would, under these circumstances, favor the conclusion that the sculpture was designed to represent the toucan.

Fig. 179.

Fig. 179. This characteristic specimen is carved in limestone, and is well finished in every respect. It is uncertain what bird it is intended to represent. At the tail are two holes, evidently designed for the insertion of feathers or other ornaments.

Fig. 180. A great variety of fragments have been taken from the mounds, which it has been found impossible to match with others, so as to complete the originals. This is the more to be regretted, from the fact that many of them denote a degree of skill equalling, if not surpassing, that displayed in the most complete specimens. The two heads here presented, probably intended to repre-

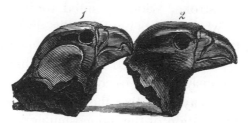

FIG. 180.

sent the eagle, are far superior in point of finish, spirit, and truthfulness, to any miniature carvings, ancient or modern, which have fallen under the notice of the authors. The engravings, though very accurate and spirited, still fail to do full justice to the originals. The peculiar defiant expression of the "king of birds" is admirably preserved in the carvings, which in this respect more than any other display the skill of the ancient artist.

FIG. 181.

Fig. 181. This engraving, which is half the size of the original, is introduced simply to illustrate the great variety of devices adopted by the mound-builders in the construction of their pipes. A number very much resembling the one here figured, have been recovered.

FIG. 182.

Fig. 182. This specimen is unfinished, and plainly exhibits the process adopted by the ancient artist in bringing it to its present state. None of the more minute details have as yet received any attention. The base and various parts of the figure exhibit fine striæ, resulting from rubbing or grinding; but the general outline seems to have been secured by cutting with some sharp instrument, the marks of which are plainly to be seen, especially at the parts where it would be difficult or impracticable to approach with a triturating substance. The lines indicating the feathers, grooves of the beak, and other more delicate features, are cut or graved in the surface at a single stroke. Some pointed tool seems to have been used, and the marks are visible where it has occasionally slipped beyond the control of the engraver. Indeed, the whole appearance of the specimen indicates that the work was done rapidly by an experienced hand, and that the various parts were brought forward simultaneously. The freedom of the strokes could only result from long practice; and we may infer that the manufacture of pipes had a distinct place in the industrial organization of the mound-builders.

MISCELLANEOUS SCULPTURES.—Sculptures of serpents, turtles, frogs, and other animals, have been discovered in abundance; all displaying a like faithful observance of nature.

Figs. 183 and 184. These sculptures of the toad are very truthful. The knotted, corrugated skin is well represented in one of them; which, if placed in the grass before an unsuspecting observer, would probably be mistaken for the natural object. Fig. 184 is in an unfinished state. It very well exhibits the mode of workmanship; while the general surface appears covered with striæ running in every direction, as if produced by rubbing. The folds and lines are clearly *cut* with some sort of graver. The marks of the implement *chipping* out portions a fourth of an inch in length, are too distinct to admit the slightest doubt that a cutting tool was used in the work. Those who deem expression in sculpture the grand essential, will find something to amuse as well as to admire in the lugubrious expression of the mouths of these specimens.

THE FROG.—Fig. 185. A large number of sculptures of the frog have been discovered; most, however, are much broken up by fire. This specimen is carved in white limestone.

Fig. 186 certainly represents the rattle-snake. Other sculptures of the serpent, coiled in like manner around the bowls of pipes, have been found. One represents a variety not recognised. It has a broad, flat head, and the body is singularly marked. All are carved in porphyry. Two sculptures of the alligator have also been found, but much broken up by the fire.

Figs. 187 and 188. Two views of a sculptured stone, representing, probably, the head of a goose; upon the back is carved a death's head. It is composed of a hard, black stone, and measures three and a half inches in length by two and a half in height. Found near Brookville, Indiana.

Fɪɢ. 183.   Fɪɢ. 184.

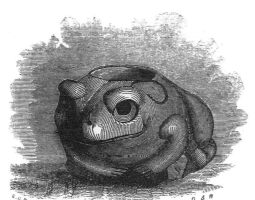

Fɪɢ. 185.

Fɪɢ. 186.

Fɪɢ. 187.

Fɪɢ. 188.

Figs. 189 and 190. These are fragments of sculptures, of which it was found

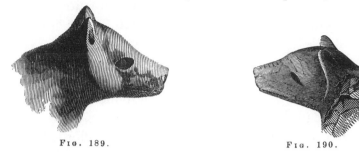

impossible to collect the various pieces. Fig. 189 is supposed to represent the head of the bear; Fig. 190 the head of the wolf.

FIG. 191.

Fig. 191. This is a reduced copy of a curious carving, representing some animal. Whether it is a " fancy piece," or whether the original counterpart exists in nature, it is not assumed to say.

FIG. 192.

Fig. 192. The remark last made holds good respecting this singular sculpture. It has been supposed to represent the head and shoulders of the morse.

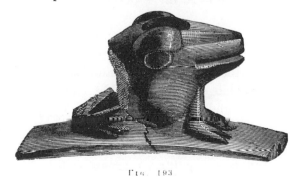

FIG. 193.

Fig. 193. This is probably a rude representation of the head of some kind of toad or frog. It is boldly cut, evidently with little attention to nature, and is chiefly interesting as illustrating the great variety of figures which these relics assume.

Such is the general character of the sculptures found in the mounds. It is unnecessary to say more than that as works of art, they are immeasurably beyond anything which the North American Indians are known to produce, even at this day, with all the suggestions of European art and the advantages afforded by steel instruments. The Chinooks, and the Indians of the North-western Coast, carve pipes, platters, and other articles, with much neatness, from slate. We see in their pipes, for instance, a heterogeneous collection of pulleys, cords, barrels, and rude human figures, evidently suggested by the tackling of the ships trading in those seas. Their platters, too, are copies of English ware, differing only in material and ornaments. The utmost that can be said of them is, that they are elaborate, unmeaning carvings, displaying some degree of ingenuity. A much higher rank can be claimed for the mound-sculptures; they combine taste in arrangement with skill in workmanship, and are faithful copies, not distorted caricatures, from nature. They display not only the figures and the characteristic attitudes, but in some cases, as we have seen, the very habits of the objects represented. So far as fidelity is concerned, many of them deserve to rank by the side of the best efforts of the artist-naturalists of our own day.

The Mexicans and Peruvians were very skilful in their representations of animals, and the early historians are profuse in praise of their workmanship, extolling it beyond that of the old world. Says La Vega of the Peruvians:

"They fashioned likewise all beasts and birds in gold and silver; namely, conies, rats, lizards, serpents, butterflies, foxes, mountain cats (for they have no tame cats in their houses); and they make sparrows and all sorts of lesser birds, some flying, some perching in trees; in short, no creature that was either wild or domestic, but was made and represented by them according to its exact and natural shape."*

Clavigero says of the exceeding skill of the Mexicans in the arts, that their works "were so admirably finished, that even the Spanish soldiers, all stung with the same wretched thirst for gold, valued the *workmanship* more than the materials." And Peter Martyr, noticing the works of the people along the coasts of the Caribbean sea and the Gulf of Mexico, exclaims,—"If man's art or invention ever got any honor in such like arts, these people may claim the chief sovereignty and commendation."†

The method practised by the makers of the articles above mentioned, in reducing them to shape, seems to have been the very obvious one resorted to by all rude nations unacquainted with the use of iron; namely, that of rubbing or grinding upon stones possessing a sharp grit. The Mexicans, it is said, used tools of obsidian in their sculptures; and the Peruvians, although possessing implements of

---

* Commentaries of Peru, Book vi. p. 187. † De Orbo Novo, Dec. 4, cap. 9.

hardened copper, according to La Vega, "rather wore out the stone by continued rubbing, than cutting." Most of the mound-sculptures have been so carefully smoothed and are so highly polished, as to show few marks of rubbing; but some have been found, as has already been shown, in an unfinished state, which exhibit fully the mode of workmanship. These show that the makers had also sharp cutting instruments, which were used in delineating the minor features. The lines indicating the folds in the skin of animals, and the feathers of birds, are not ground in, but *cut*, evidently to the entire depth, at a single stroke. Sometimes the tool has slipped by, indicating that it was held and used after the manner of the gravers of the present day. The time and labor expended in perfecting these elaborate works from obstinate materials, with no other than these rude aids, must have given them a high value when finished. Hence we find a great deal of ingenuity exhibited in restoring them when accidentally broken. This was accomplished by drilling holes diagonally to each other in the detached parts, so that by the insertion of wooden pegs or copper wire, they were, in technical phrase, "bound together." This attachment was further strengthened, in some cases, by bands of sheet copper; occasionally the entire pipe, when much injured, seems to have been plated over with that metal. When the fracture was such as materially to injure the tube, a small copper tube was inserted within it, restoring an unbroken communication. Many interesting facts of this kind, which perhaps may seem trivial and unimportant to most minds, might be presented. They illustrate how highly these remains were valued by their possessors. The manner in which the drilling was probably accomplished has already been indicated.

TABLETS.—A few small sculptured tablets have been found in the mounds. Some of these have been regarded as bearing hieroglyphical, others alphabetic inscriptions, and have been made the basis of much speculation at home and abroad. Nothing of this extraordinary character has been disclosed in the course of the investigations here recorded; nor is there any evidence that anything like an alphabetic or hieroglyphic system existed among the mound-builders. The earthworks, and the mounds and their contents, certainly indicate that, prior to the occupation of the Mississippi valley by the more recent tribes of Indians, there existed here a numerous population, agricultural in their habits, considerably advanced in the arts, and undoubtedly, in all respects, much superior to their successors. There is, however, no reason to believe that their condition was anything more than an approximation towards that attained by the semi-civilized nations of the central portions of the continent,—who themselves had not arrived at the construction of an alphabet. Whether the latter had progressed further than to a refinement upon the rude picture-writing of the savage tribes, is a question open to discussion. It would be unwarrantable therefore to assign to the race of the mounds a superiority in this respect over nations palpably so much in advance of them in all others. It would be a reversal of the teachings of history, an exception to the law of harmonious development, which it would require a large assemblage of well attested facts to sustain. Such an array of facts, it is scarcely necessary to add, we do not possess.

35

It is true, hardly a year passes unsignalized by the announcement of the discovery of tablets of stone or metal, bearing strange and mystical inscriptions,—generally reported to have a "marked resemblance to the Chinese characters." But they either fail to withstand an analysis of the alleged circumstances attending their discovery, or resolve themselves into very simple natural productions when subjected to scientific scrutiny. It will be remembered that some years ago it was announced that six inscribed copper plates had been found in a mound near Kinderhook, Pike county, Illinois. Engravings of them and a minute description were published at the time, and widely circulated. Subsequent inquiry has shown that the plates were a harmless imposition, got up for local effect; and that the village blacksmith, with no better suggestion to his antiquarian labors than the lid of a tea-chest, was chiefly responsible for them. Within the past two years an announcement was made of the discovery, in a mound near Lower Sandusky, Ohio, of a series of oval mica plates, inscribed with numberless unknown characters, which, in the language of the printed account, probably "contained the history of some former race that inhabited this country." These plates were found, upon examination, to be ornaments of that variety of mica known as "graphic" or "hieroglyphic mica,"—which is naturally marked with figures somewhat regular in their arrangement.

The Grave creek mound was also said to have contained a small stone, bearing an alphabetical inscription, which has attracted the attention of a number of learned men both in this country and in Europe. A critical examination of the circumstances attending the introduction of this relic to the world is calculated to throw great doubt upon its genuineness. The fact that it is not mentioned by intelligent observers writing from the spot at the time of the excavation of the mound, and that no notice of its existence was made public until after the opening of the mound for exhibition, joined to the strong presumptive evidence against the occurrence of anything of the kind, furnished by the antagonistic character of all the ancient remains of the continent, so far as they are known,—are insuperable objections to its reception. Until it is better authenticated, it should be entirely excluded from a place among the antiquities of our country.*

A small tablet was discovered, some years ago, in a mound at Cincinnati, of which Fig. 194 presents a front, and Fig. 195 a reverse view.

This relic is now in the possession of ERASMUS GEST, Esq., of Cincinnati. The circumstances under which it was discovered are thus detailed by Mr. Gest in a letter published at the time :

" I herewith send you what I deem to be a hieroglyphical stone, which was found buried with a skeleton in the ' old mound,' situated in the western part of the city, together with two pointed bones, each about seven inches long, taken from the same spot. (See page 220.)

" In the course of the excavation several skeletons were disinterred; and their being generally in a good state of preservation and near the surface, gave rise to

* For a critical examination of the question of the authenticity of this relic, see *Transactions of American Ethnological Society*, vol. ii.

the inference that they were deposited there since the mound was erected : but the one with which the sharpened bones and hieroglyphical stone were found, was in a decayed state. Being in the centre and rather below the level of the surrounding

FIG. 194.*   FIG. 195.

ground, it was no doubt the object over which the mound was erected. I have a part of the skull; the remainder of the skeleton was destroyed by the diggers."

The position of the skeleton with which it was found, as also the other circumstances attending the discovery of this relic, leave little doubt as to its authenticity. It was discovered in December, 1841. The material is a fine-grained, compact sandstone, of a light brown color. It measures five inches in length, three in breadth at the ends, two and six tenths at the middle, and is about half an inch in thickness. The sculptured face varies very slightly from a perfect plane. The figures are cut in low relief, (the lines being not more than one twentieth of an inch in depth,) and occupy a rectangular space four inches and two tenths long, by two and one tenth wide. The sides of the stone, it will be observed, are slightly concave. Right lines are drawn across the face near the ends. At right angles and exterior to these are notches, twenty-five at one end, and twenty-four at the other. Extending diagonally inward are fifteen longer lines, eight at one end and seven at the other. The back of the stone has three deep, longitudinal grooves, and several depressions, evidently caused by rubbing,—probably produced in sharpening the instrument used in the sculpture.

Without discussing the " singular resemblance which the relic bears to the Egyptian *cartouch*," it will be sufficient to direct attention to the reduplication of

---

* From a drawing by H. C. GROSVENOR.

the figures, those upon one side corresponding with those upon the other, and the two central ones being also alike. It will be observed that there are but three scrolls or figures, four of one description, and two of each of the others. Probably no serious discussion of the question whether or not these figures are hieroglyphical is needed. They more resemble the stalk and flowers of a plant than anything else in nature. What significance, if any, may attach to the peculiar markings or graduations at the ends, it is not undertaken to say. The sum of the products of the longer and shorter lines (24×7+25×8) is 368, three more than the number of days in the year; from which circumstance the suggestion has been advanced that the tablet had an astronomical origin, and constituted some sort of a calendar.

We may perhaps find the key to its purposes in a very humble but not therefore less interesting class of Southern remains. Both in Mexico and in the mounds of Mississippi have been found *stamps* of burned clay, the faces of which are covered with figures, fanciful or imitative, all in low relief, like the face of a stereotype plate. These were used in impressing ornaments upon the clothes or prepared skins of the people possessing them. They exhibit the concavity of the sides to be observed in the relic in question, intended doubtless for greater convenience in holding and using it, as also a similar reduplication of the ornamental figures,—all betraying a common purpose. This explanation is offered hypothetically as being entirely consistent with the general character of the mound remains; which, taken together, do not warrant us in looking for anything that might not well pertain to a very simple, not to say rude, people.*

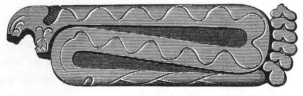

F I G . 1 9 6 .

Fig. 196. From one of the mounds, numbered 1 in the plan of the great enclosure on the North Fork of Paint creek, (Plate X,) were taken several singularly sculptured tablets, of one of which the figure here presented is a copy, so far as it has been found possible to restore it from the several fragments recovered. It represents a coiled rattlesnake; both faces of the tablet being identical in

---

* The following just observations are from the published notice of this relic, accompanying the communication of Mr. Gest, above quoted:

"The relic found here was with a skeleton, in the very centre of the mound, and all the external evidence favors the belief that it was placed there when the tumulus was raised. But the best evidence of its genuineness is this, that a person in our times could scarcely make so perfect an engraving as this stone, and not make it more perfect; the engraving represents something, whatever it is, the two sides of which are intended to be alike, and yet no two curves or lines are precisely alike, nor is there the least evidence of the use of our instruments to be discovered in the work. So difficult is it to imitate with our cultivated hands and eyes the peculiar imperfection of this cutting, that some excellent judges, who at first doubted the genuineness of the relic, have changed their opinion upon trying to imitate it. What the sculpture means is another matter."

sculpture, excepting that one is plane, the other slightly convex. The material is a very fine cinnamon-colored sandstone, and the style of the sculpture is identical with that displayed in the tablet from the Cincinnati mound already noticed. The original is six inches and a quarter long, one and three eighths broad, and one quarter of an inch thick. The workmanship is delicate, and the characteristic feature of the rattlesnake perfectly represented. It is to be regretted that it is impossible to restore the head, which, so far as it can be made out, has some peculiar and interesting features,—plumes or ornamental figures surmounting it. Previous to the investigation of the mound by the authors, an entire tablet was obtained from it by an individual residing near the spot, who represents it to have been carefully and closely enveloped in sheets of copper, which he had great difficulty in removing. Incited by a miserable curiosity he broke the specimen, to ascertain its composition; and the larger portion, including the head, was subsequently lost. The remaining fragment, from its exceedingly well preserved condition, confirms the statement of the finder respecting its envelopment. It seems that several of these tablets were originally deposited in the mound; the greater portions of four have been recovered, but none displaying the head entire. The person above mentioned affirms that the head, in the specimen which he discovered, was surrounded by ". feathers;" how far this is confirmed by the fragment, the reader must judge for himself. The tablets seem to have been originally painted of different colors: a dark red pigment is yet plainly to be seen in the depressions of some of the fragments; others had been painted of a dense black color.

It does not appear probable that these relics were designed for ornaments. On the contrary, the circumstances under which they were discovered render it likely that they had a superstitious origin, and were objects of high regard and perhaps of worship. It has already been observed, in connection with the account of the great serpentine structure in Adams county, Ohio, (Plate XXXV,) that the serpent entered widely into the superstitions of the American nations, savage and semi-civilized, and was conspicuous among their symbols as the emblem of the greatest gods of their mythology, both good and evil. And wherever it appears, whether among the carvings of the Natchez (who, according to Charlevoix, placed it upon their altars as an object of worship), among the paintings of the Aztecs, or upon the temples of Central America, it is worthy of remark, that it is invariably the *rattlesnake*. And as among the Egyptians the *cobra* was the sign of royalty, so among the Mexicans the rattlesnake was an emblem of kingly power and dominion. As such it appears in the crown of *Tezcatlipoca*, the Brahma of the Aztec pantheon, and in the helmets of the warrior priests of that divinity. The *feather-headed rattlesnake*, it should be observed, was in Mexico the peculiar symbol of *Tezcatlipoca*, otherwise symbolized as the sun.

CHAPTER XVI.

METALS, MINERALS, FOSSILS, SHELLS, ETC.

FREQUENT allusion has been made, in the preceding pages, to the numerous rare and beautiful varieties of minerals, fossils, and shells, disclosed from the mounds; but no opportunity has been afforded to speak of them with desirable fulness. The identification, accurate or approximate, of the localities from whence these were obtained, will serve, in a degree, to reflect light upon the grand archæological questions of the origin, migration, and intercommunication of the race of the mounds. In this respect they are of value; for, in the investigations here attempted, we are compelled to press into the work of elucidation, every fact and circumstance which can, in any way, affect the subject of our inquiries. The discovery of *obsidian*, a purely volcanic production, in the mounds, in a region entirely destitute of the evidences of immediate volcanic action, is, to the commonest apprehension, a remarkable fact, a subject of wonder; but neither marvels nor mysticism have aught to do with science. The fact, to the mind of the rational archæologist, is suggestive only of the inquiry, Whence was this singular product obtained? Its presence cannot be accounted for, in the quantities discovered, except upon the supposition that it was transported from a distance; which supposition involves, of necessity, intercommunication or migration. To measure the bounds of intercourse, casual or constant, or define the course of migration, it is necessary to ascertain the exact primitive locality of the product in question. So far as we are informed, the nearest point of its occurrence is Mexico, the ancient inhabitants of which country applied it extensively to the very purposes for which it was used by the race of the mounds.

In this process of investigation, there are many circumstances which must come under view and receive due consideration, before we venture upon the simplest conclusions. They are, however, entirely omitted in this connection; the object of the illustration being simply to show in what general manner facts of this kind may be made subservient, and of what importance they may become in a system of research, in which we have neither written record nor even the voice of tradition to give direction to our inquiries.

It so happens that it is difficult in every case to detect the true nature of the remains discovered, and often quite impossible to point out their original localities. Hence the necessity of presenting a comprehensive view of their extent and character, so that other laborers in the field of antiquarian research may be able to institute comparisons, and indicate localities, and thus gradually work out the grand problems involved in our aboriginal history. The process may appear tedious and intricate, and the results hardly worth the labor of their development; that is, however, a question open to discussion. The mode of investigation here indicated is, at any rate, the only one which philosophy sanctions, and which can ever lead to satisfactory results.

THE METALS.—Silver and copper are the only metals, pertaining to the race of the mounds, which have been taken from their depositories. The discovery of gold has been vaguely announced, but the fact is not well attested.* It is not unlikely that articles of gold have been found, with brass dial-plates, silver crosses, and other vestiges of European art, among the recent deposits in the mounds; and it is far from impossible that the metal may yet be disclosed, under such circumstances as to justify the conclusion that it was not, as from existing facts it seems to have been, an entire stranger to the ancient people. Its discovery will be no matter of surprise; as yet, however, we have no well authenticated instance of its occurrence. Mention is made, in a published work, of a silver cup, "finely gilded in the interior," which was said to have been found in a mound at Marietta. It will be early enough to ask for the verification of the statement, when any one shall be found to claim for the cup any other than a European origin, or assign it an antiquity beyond the period of the first European intercourse.

As has been already observed, considerable quantities of wrought, and some small fragments of unwrought native copper, have been extracted from the mounds. Axes, as we have seen, have been found, wrought from a single piece, weighing upwards of two pounds each. The metal appears, in all cases, to have been worked in a cold state. This is the more remarkable from the fact that, in some instances, the fires upon the altars were sufficiently intense to melt down the copper implements and ornaments deposited upon them. The hint thus afforded does not seem to have been seized upon. In consideration of the amount of the metal discovered, implying a large original supply, and the fact that it is occasionally found combined with silver in the peculiar manner characterizing the native deposits upon the shores of Lake Superior, we are led to conclude that it was principally, if not wholly, derived from that region. This conclusion is sustained by the recent investigations upon the shores of that lake. These have led to the discovery that the aborigines, from a very remote period, resorted there to obtain the metal. There is also evidence that some of the more productive veins were anciently worked to a considerable extent. "A few rods north of the present 'location' and works of the North-west Mining Company, and near the foot of the bluff, are excavations in the earth and rock, in which are found numerous rude implements of stone, such as hammers and wedges. Pieces of copper, partially wrought into shape, are to be found at various places around the works. Upon the earth and rocks thrown from the pits, large trees are now growing. One of these pits is sunk almost entirely in the rock, and is not far from seven feet deep.

---

* Archæologia Americana, vol. i. p. 176. The report here alluded to has been traced to its source. The ornament was not of gold but of copper.

To the north-west of this, an open cut mas made, twenty-four feet on the course of the vein, and from it was taken not less than a bushel of hammers and wedges of stone and pieces of copper. A few rods to the northward of the present works on the eastern vein of the ' Copper Falls Location,' and also at some distance to the south-east of the mines at the Eagle river, similar traces of ancient mining are to be observed."*

---

* These statements are confirmed by several observers. The subjoined passages are from a letter from the eminent geologist and mineralogist, Prof. W. W. MATHER.

" I am informed by gentlemen connected with the survey of the government mineral lands, that abundant traces of ancient mining are to be observed at the Copper Falls and Eagle river mines. It is stated that on the hill south of the Copper Falls mine, an excavation several feet in depth, and some rods in length, was discovered extending along the course of the vein. Fragments of rock, etc., thrown out of the excavation, were piled up along its sides, the whole covered with soil, and overgrown with bushes and trees. On removing the accumulations from the excavation, stone axes of large size, made of greenstone, and shaped to receive withe handles, were found. Some large, round, greenstone masses, that had apparently been used for sledges, were also found. They had round holes bored in them to the depth of several inches, which seemed to have been designed for wooden plugs, to which withe handles might be attached, so that several men could swing them with sufficient force to batter or break the rock and the projecting masses of copper. Some of them were broken ; and some of the projecting ends of rock exhibited distinct marks of having been battered in the manner here suggested."

The great Ontonagon mass of virgin copper, now deposited in Washington, when found, exhibited marks of having had considerable portions cut from it ; and the ground around was strewn with fragments of stone axes which had been broken in endeavors to detach portions of the mass. Henry (*Travels*, p. 195) observes that the Indians obtained much copper from the above localities, which they worked into spoons, bracelets, etc. He saw one piece in their possession, weighing twenty pounds.

The following additional information embraced in a private letter to a gentleman of Buffalo, under date of June 15, 1848, relating to ancient mining on the shores of Lake Superior, will prove highly interesting in this connection. The new discoveries which it records seem to establish that the mines were anciently extensively worked, and the copper extracted in large masses. Were it not for the abundance of stone implements in the excavations, it might be supposed that they were the traces of the later operations of the French.

" The gentlemen connected with Vulcan Mining Company have made some very singular discoveries in working one of the veins which has been lately found. They discovered an old cave, excavated centuries ago. This led them to look for other works of the same kind, and they have found a number of sinks in the earth which they have traced a long distance. By digging into those sinks, they find them to have been made by the hand of man. It appears that the ancient miners worked on a different principle from that adopted at the present time. The greatest depth yet found in these holes is thirty feet. After getting down to a certain depth, the ancient miners drifted along the vein, making an open cut. These cuts have been filled nearly to a level by the accumulation of soil, and we find trees of the largest growth standing in the depressions ; and also find that trees of a very large size have grown up and died, and decayed many years since : in the same places there are now standing others of over three hundred years' growth. Last week they dug down into a new place, and about twelve feet below the surface found a mass of copper weighing from eight to ten tons. This mass was buried in ashes, and it appears the ancient miners could not handle it, and having no means of cutting it, probably built fire around it to melt or separate the rock, which might be done by heating and then dashing on cold water. This piece of copper is pure and free from corrosion. The upper surface has been pounded smooth. It appears that this mass of copper was taken from the bottom of a shaft, at the depth of about thirty feet. In sinking this shaft from where the mass now lies, they followed the course of the vein, which dips considerably ; this enabled them to raise it as far as the hole came up with a slant. At the bottom of the shaft were found skids of black oak, from eight to twelve inches in diameter ; these sticks were charred through,

The tribes visited by De Soto indicated some portion of the South Appalachian chain as the locality whence they obtained the copper in their possession. We are ignorant of the sources whence the Indians on the Hudson procured the copper which was found among them; it probably reached their hands by a course of exchange with western tribes, and came from the north-west. Silver has been found in very small quantities, and was evidently exceedingly rare among the mound-builders. The specimens recovered are pure, and were undoubtedly derived from the same locality with the copper.

It is not certain, but nevertheless extremely probable, that the race of the mounds were acquainted with the art of reducing lead from its ores; the absence of the metal may be accounted for by the fact that, from its nature, it could not be applied by them to any useful purpose. Too soft for axes or knives, too fusible for vessels, and too soon tarnished to be valuable for ornament, there was little inducement for its manufacture. Still, unless we suppose that it was valued and used to a limited extent, we can hardly account for the amount of galena found in the mounds. The nearest locality, from which it can be obtained in quantities equal to those found, is the mineral region of Illinois.

Fossils.—A variety of fossils, selected for purposes of use or ornament, are obtained from the mounds. Among the more remarkable may be mentioned the fossil teeth of the shark, and some large teeth, probably cetacean. About one hundred of the latter were found in one mound; but they were too much burned to be recovered entire. One of the largest measures six inches in length, by about four inches in circumference at the largest part. They are destitute of enamel, and have a pulp cavity at the base, something like those of the whale, from which, however, they differ widely in shape. They have not yet been identified, although they have been examined by several eminent naturalists. The mound-builders evidently used them for various purposes, and some of the articles supposed to be ivory may have been made from them. Some of the specimens have been variously wrought, drilled, sawn, and polished. The striæ produced by sawing are distinctly visible. Accompanying these were found several beautifully carved cylinders of a compact substance resembling ivory. These were variously and tastefully ornamented. One of the rods was originally fourteen inches in length, and, when found, was closely enveloped in sheet copper. It has been suggested that these were carved from the ribs of the manitus; the bones of which animal,

---

as if burnt; large wooden wedges were also found in the same situation. In this shaft were discovered a miner's 'gad' and a narrow chisel made of copper. I do not know whether these copper tools are tempered or not, but they display good workmanship. There have been taken out of the excavations more than a ton of cobble-stones, which have been used as mallets. These stones were nearly round, with a groove cut round the centre, for the purpose of putting a withe around for a handle. The Chippewas all say that this work was never done by Indians. This discovery will lead to a new method of finding veins in this country, and may be of great benefit to explorers. I suppose the miners will continue to find new wonders for some time yet, as it is but a short time since they first found the old mine."

36

we are informed by Bartram, were much used by the Southern Indians for articles of use and ornament.

Several of the fossil teeth of the shark recovered from the mounds are represented in the cut, Fig. 197. It will be observed that they are of different species. They seem to have been used for various purposes. Some have holes drilled through them near the base; others are notched, as if designed to form spear or arrow-heads. Raleigh observed some used as such among the Indians of Carolina.

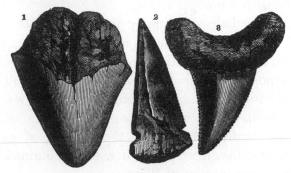

Fig. 197.—Half size.

It seems most probable that they were designed for cutting purposes. No. 2 is fragmentary; the remaining portion was not found. It will be seen that it had a hole drilled through it near the base, and was notched at the sides. We are of course ignorant of the locality from which they were obtained. It is a well known fact, however, that they are abundant in the tertiary formations of the Lower Mississippi.* From this direction must have come the teeth of the alligator, a number of which have been obtained from the mounds.

PEARLS.—Mention has been made, on a preceding page, of the great number of pearls found in the mounds. It is incredible to suppose that a hundredth part of these were obtained from the molluscs of our rivers. The question then arises, whence were they obtained? As has already been stated, the Indians of the South and South-west used them extensively as ornaments at the time of the Discovery, and at that time, it appears from the chroniclers, maintained regular fisheries for them.† If we may credit the early writers, they were abundant among all the nations inhabiting the shores and islands of the Gulf, and were found in considerable numbers on the Atlantic coast, as far north as Virginia. Raleigh saw them on the coast of North Carolina. Heriot, in his Voyage to the Shores of Virginia, says: "Sometimes in feeding on muscles we find pearls; but it was our hap to meet those which were ragged and of a pied color, not yet having discovered the country where we heard of better and more plenty. One of our company, a man of skill in such matters, had gathered from among the savage people about *five*

---

* B. L. C. WAILES, Esq., Proceedings of Sixth Annual Meeting of the American Association of Naturalists and Geologists, p. 80.—Also Prof. GIBBS, Jour. Acad. Nat. Sci. second series, vol. i

† De Soto's Expedition, Supplement to Hakluyt's Voyages, p. 715.

thousand; of which number he chose so many as made a fair chain, which for their likeness and uniformity in roundness, orientness, and piedness, of many excellent colors, with equality in greatness, had been presented to her majesty, had not a casualty by sea lost them."

Ribaulde, at an earlier day, (1562,) wrote in extravagant terms of the quantities of pearls which he saw on the coast of Florida. "They had also a great abundance of pearls; which they declared unto us they took out of oysters, and in so marvellous abundance, as is scant credible: and we perceive that there are as many and faire pearls found there, as in any country of the world. For we saw one man who had a pearl hanging at the end of a chain of gold and silver, as great as an acorn at the least."

The Decades of Peter Martyr teem with exclamations of surprise and wonder at their great number and beauty; they elicit both his praise and his philosophy.* We may therefore safely derive the pearls found in the mounds from the Gulf. Together with numerous other remains, they go to establish an extensive communication with southern and tropical regions, or a migration from that direction. At present it is believed no pearl-fisheries are maintained, except upon the coast of California.

MARINE SHELLS.—The *cassis* and *pyrula perversa* of Lamark; the *oliva, marginella,* and *natica;* as well as the columella of a shell, probably the *strombus,* have been found in the mounds. A *cassis* of large size, from which the inner whorls and columella had been removed to adapt it for use as a vessel, was found in mound No. 5, in the great enclosure, Plate X. It is doubtful whether this particular shell belongs to the era of the mounds, or is of a later date. Portions of these shells have nevertheless been found upon the altars, and they were consequently known to the mound-builders. This specimen is eleven inches and a half

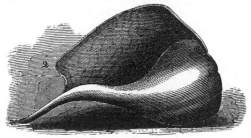

Fig. 198.

in length, by twenty-four in circumference at the largest part. Specimens have been found in the vicinity of Nashville, from which the inner whorls had been removed so as to give place to an idol of clay or stone.† Fragments only of the *pyrula,* Fig. 198, have been found in the mounds; although quite a number have been

---

* Peter Martyr, Supplement to Hakluyt's Voyages, pp. 415, 417, 419, 455, 469, 471, 475, 493, 500, 517, 520, 530, 539, 599; Oviedo, in Purchas, vol. iii. p. 972.

† Transactions of *American Ethnological Society,* vol. i. p. 361.

discovered entire in excavating at different points in the Scioto valley. In digging the Ohio and Erie canal, there was found near Portsmouth, its southern terminus on the Ohio river, a cluster of five or six, which appeared to have been thus carefully deposited by the hand of man. They were about three feet beneath the surface. The columellæ of some large shell, probably the *strombus gigas*, have also been discovered. Most of the shell beads and ornaments from the mounds appear to have been manufactured from them.

All these shells are found in the Gulf. The *strombus* is observed on the shores of the West Indies and Florida; the *cassis* occurs in the same localities, as do also the *pyrula* and the minor shells above mentioned. A very large number of the *marginella* were taken from the Grave creek mound.*

FLUVIATILE SHELLS.—Examples of the *unios* of the Western rivers also occur in the mounds, generally entire, but sometimes manufactured. The *unio ellipticus, crassus, rectus, verrucosus,* and *ovatus* have been identified, all existing, at the present time, in the neighboring streams. They occur side by side with the marine shells and other remains heretofore noticed.

MINERALS.—This department is very rich, and comprises some very interesting and beautiful varieties,—mica, transparent, opaque, silvery, and graphic; obsidian; quartz, many varieties; serpentine; porphyry, several beautiful kinds; manganesian garnet, in crystals; variegated slate, beautifully colored; catlinite or red pipe-stone (?); limestone, common and coralline, etc., etc.

MICA is abundant in the mounds and in the vicinity of ancient works, where it is often ploughed up. It seems to be extensively disseminated, south as well as north. The common, transparent, silvery or opaque, and graphic or hieroglyphical varieties, have been discovered; some specimens have a golden color, much resembling "Dutch leaf." It is in general neatly cut into ornamental figures, scrolls, discs, and oval plates. These plates are frequently a foot or more in diameter, and a fourth or half an inch in thickness. In a mound at Circleville, a plate is said to have been found, three feet in length, one foot and a half in breadth, and one inch and a half in thickness. It has been suggested that these plates were designed as mirrors; but there seems to be no good foundation for the supposition.† The opaque varieties, from their beauty, seem to have been uniformly applied to ornamental purposes, having often, as appears from the holes occasioned by the process, been worked into scarfs or attached to the martial or priestly robes of the ancient people. The mineral seems also to have been consecrated to some religious purpose. It appears at various points in the mounds, and is sometimes found resting on the breasts or above the heads of

---

* American Pioneer, vol. i. p. 200.

† Capt. LYON mentions finding among the Esquimaux, on the North-east coast, "a mirror composed of a broad plate of black mica, fitted into a leather frame, so as to be seen from either side."—*Narrative*, p. 68.

skeletons. It has also been found covering one sacrificial altar, and regularly disposed in the form of a crescent before another. (See pages 144 and 154.) The suggestion has been advanced that it was consecrated to some divinity, equivalent to the Mexican *Tezcatlipoca,* "Lord of the Light."

The mica of the mounds is often found fissile and fragile, perhaps the result of exposure to heat, but generally quite compact and possessing its original tenacity. Some very fine specimens of the graphic or discolored mica have been found in the mounds of the Scioto valley and elsewhere. Fifteen or twenty beautiful oval plates of this variety were taken recently from a low mound near Lower Sandusky, Ohio. They are beautiful specimens, stained with a solution of some of the oxides of iron or manganese, during the process of crystallization.

Mica, like many other substances, crystallizes in oblique rhombic prisms whose planes are 60° and 120°. When these planes are colored, they resemble many letters of the alphabet. The specimens in question are iridescent, exhibiting all the prismatic colors when the light falls upon them in a certain direction. These circumstances no doubt gave rise to the idea that they were painted hieroglyphics. Graphic mica occurs, in place, on the Schuylkill, some distance above Philadelphia, and probably in other localities. No original deposit of the mineral exists in the State of Ohio.

OBSIDIAN, the *itzli* of the Mexicans, and *gallinazo stone* of the Peruvians. Frequent reference has been had to this mineral, precluding the necessity of an extended notice here. It has been observed in five of the mounds excavated in the Scioto valley, from one of which a number of large and very fine specimens were obtained (page 155). It is only found in the form of implements, such as knives and spear and arrow-points. This mineral is a volcanic product, and occurs, so far as known, no nearer than Mexico, where it is found in abundance. It is also found in Peru, and was extensively used by the ancient inhabitants of both countries, for cutting and warlike implements. They also, notwithstanding its obstinacy and fragility, worked it elegantly into mirrors, ornamental rings, and masks.* Some specimens have been discovered in the mounds of Tennessee, which were doubtless obtained from the same source with those found on the Ohio.† All the specimens discovered are glassy black, subtranslucent, and break with a clear conchoidal fracture. According to Humboldt, the mountains of Jacul or Cerro Gordo, on the route between Vera Cruz and the city of Mexico, furnished the celebrated *itzli* quarries or mines of the ancient Mexicans; the locality is still known as *El Cerro de los Nabijas,* the Mountain of Knives.‡ This is believed to be the nearest point of its

---

* The Mexicans used blades of obsidian in the construction of their swords; their sacrificial knives and razors were of the same material; and, from practice, they became so perfect in their manufacture that, according to Clavigero, "in the space of one hour, an artist could finish more than a hundred."—*Clavigero,* vol. ii. p. 288.

† Transactions of *American Ethnological Society,* vol. i. p. 361.

‡ Researches, vol. ii. p. 204.

occurrence.   Lieut. Fremont observed some small nodules in the rocks of the *Sierra Nevada*, lying to the eastward of the valley of the Sacramento.   He also found numerous fragments on the hills bordering the Lewis fork of the Columbia river.

PORPHYRY.—Most of the sculptured pipes of the mounds are made of a very fine and beautiful description of porphyry.   It occurs of many shades of color.   Some varieties are of a greenish-brown base, with fine white and black granules ; others of a light brown base with white, purple, and violet-tinged specks ; but most are red, with white and purplish grains.   In some specimens the base scarcely exhibits any admixture either of grains or crystals, and strongly resembles the red pipe-stone of the *Coteau des Prairies*.   All are of intense hardness,—a natural characteristic, or in some degree the result of the great heat to which they have been subjected.   It generally breaks with a granular fracture, sometimes disengaging the grains of the foreign material.   Under heat it splinters, often on very nearly the same plane ; pieces partly fused into a porous, dull mass, have been remarked.   Heat has also the effect of giving a bright black color to the fragments more particularly exposed to its influence, and some of the restored sculptures present a striking contrast in the appearance of their parts.   It would seem incredible that the different fragments originally pertained to the same piece, did they not exactly fit to each other.   One or two of the varieties seem to have an argillaceous base, adhere slightly when applied to the tongue, and have a marked argillaceous odor ; these exhibit a rather dull surface, while the others are exquisitely polished.   It is difficult to tell how the ancient inhabitants worked this obstinate material with the elegance and finish which their sculptures display.   It resists the best tempered blade, and yields reluctantly to the finest grit stones. Yet it is clear from the markings on certain specimens that it was cut by some kind of implement.   We can only account for the fact by supposing that it was once much softer than it now is.   Under such a supposition, it is not improbable that it may have been derived from a locality mentioned by Du Pratz, on the Missouri.   So far as the external features of the stone are concerned, the description is very exact ; we are left in doubt, however, as to the size of the granules, which in the mound pipes are seldom larger than mustard seeds.

" In this journey of M. de Borgmont, mention is made only of what we meet with from Fort Orleans, from which we set out, in order to go to the Padoucas ; wherefore I ought to speak of a thing curious enough to be related, which is found on the banks of the Missouri ; and that is a pretty high cliff, upright from the water.   From the middle of the cliff juts out a mass of *red stone with white spots, like porphyry*, with this difference, that what we are now speaking of is almost soft and tender like sandstone.   It is covered with another sort of stone of no value ; the bottom is an earth like that on other rising grounds.   The stone is easily worked and bears the most violent fire.   The Indians of the country have contrived to strike off pieces thereof with their arrows, and after they fall in the water plunge in for them.   When they procure pieces large enough to make pipes, they fashion them with knives and awls.   This pipe has a socket two or three inches long, and on the opposite side the figure of a hatchet; in the middle of all is the bort or bowl to put the tobacco in."*

The fashion of the pipe here described is that adopted by the modern Indians; and the paragraph is introduced as suggestive, rather than as indicating the unknown locality of this singular stone. A description of red porphyry is said to occur upon the shores of Lake Superior; but in the absence of specimens for comparison, it is impossible to say how far it resembles that found in the mounds.

Many of the ancient carvings are executed in a description of compact slate, of a dull green ground, relieved with stripes of a dark black color, giving the stone a fibrous appearance, and leading many uninformed persons to suppose that it is petrified wood. It has a very fine grain, cuts clearly and readily, and receives a high finish. It seems to have been chiefly used for ornamental purposes. No one has, as yet, been able to identify its primitive locality. A single implement of this material was found a number of years ago, near Middletown, Connecticut. (See page 218.)

Another variety of stone, of a high specific gravity, dark ground, thickly interspersed with minute flakes of salmon-colored mica, is also found. It is not abundant. It has thus far defied scrutiny, and its primitive locality is unascertained. It is often very tastefully worked into rings, figures of animals, etc. It cuts without difficulty, and receives a very high polish.†

The axes, pestles, etc., of the mound-builders, like those formerly in use by the Indian tribes, are composed of tough sienitic rocks, greenstone, etc. The material must have been derived from primitive localities, or from boulders of primitive rocks.

Besides these varieties of stone, we find articles composed of every description of quartz; of brown hematite; steatite, black and mottled; slate; limestone, etc. Some very pretty articles are worked from coralline limestone.

---

* DU PRATZ, History of Louisiana, p. 179.

† A specimen of this mineral was submitted to JAMES T. HODGE, Esq., of New York, for examination, with the following results: "It resembles mica in appearance, in fine scales, cemented in one lump. Color, reddish brown. Before the blow-pipe it does not change. It fuses with soda, with difficulty, into a dark bead,—soluble in nitric acid, leaving a considerable residuum of *silicia*. The qualitative analysis gave *alumina*, *iron*, and *potash*, all of which are ingredients of mica."

CHAPTER XVII.

CRANIA FROM THE MOUNDS.

IT has already been several times observed that the human remains found in the mounds are of different eras. The superficial burials, it has been abundantly shown, are of comparatively late date, and are to be ascribed to the Indian tribes found in occupation of the country, at the period of its discovery in the fifteenth century. These skeletons are seldom deposited more than two or three feet below the surface, and are generally perfect; the crania rarely if ever crushed, and the bones still retaining a portion of their animal matter. In the ancient burials, on the other hand, the skeletons are almost invariably found at the base of the mounds, and in such a state of decay as to render all attempts to restore the skull, or indeed any part of the skeleton, entirely hopeless. The crania, when not so much decomposed as to crumble to powder beneath the touch, are crushed and flattened by the falling in of the sepulchral chambers, and by the weight of the superincumbent earth.

We are therefore unable to present much new light upon the cranial conformation of the race of the mounds. The only skull incontestibly belonging to an individual of that race, which has been recovered entire, or sufficiently well preserved to be of value for purposes of comparison, was taken from the hill-mound, numbered 8 in the Map of a section of twelve miles of the Scioto valley, Plate II. Plate XLVII is a full-sized side view, and Plate XLVIII presents reduced vertical and front views of the skull in question.

The circumstances under which this skull was found are altogether so extra-ordinary, as to merit a detailed account. It will be observed from the map, that the mound above indicated is situated upon the summit of a high hill, overlooking the valley of the Scioto, about four miles below the city of Chillicothe. It is one of the most prominent and commanding positions in that section of country. Upon the summit of this hill rises a conical knoll of so great regularity as almost to induce the belief that it is itself artificial. Upon the very apex of this knoll, and covered by the trees of the primitive forest, is the mound. It is about eight feet high by forty-five or fifty feet base. The superstructure is a tough yellow clay, which at the depth of three feet is intermixed with large rough stones, as shown in the accompanying section, Fig. 199.

These stones rest upon a dry carbonaceous deposit of burned earth and small stones, of a dark black color, and much compacted. This deposit is about two feet in thickness in the centre, and rests upon the original soil. In excavating the mound, a large plate of mica was discovered placed upon the stones, at the point indicated by the letter *a* in the section. Immediately underneath this plate of

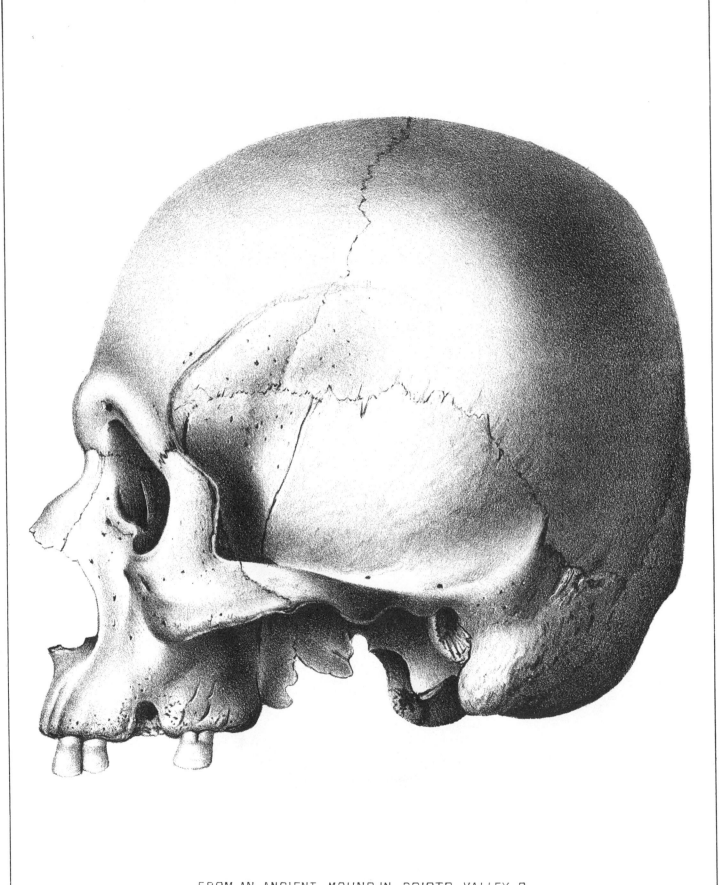

FROM AN ANCIENT MOUND IN SCIOTO VALLEY O.

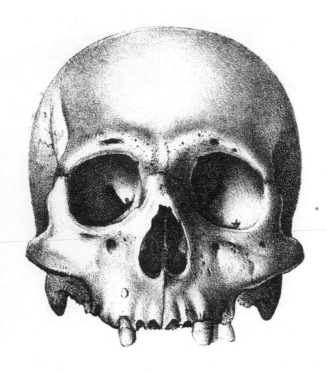

FRONT AND VERTICAL VIEW OF THE SAME

Face Page 289.

mica and in the centre of the burned deposit, was found the skull figured in the plates. It was discovered resting upon its face. The lower jaw, as indeed the

FIG. 199.

entire skeleton, excepting the clavicle, a few cervical vertebræ, and some of the bones of the feet, all of which were huddled around the skull, were wanting. No relics were found with the bones, except a few shells of the fresh-water molluscs from the neighboring river.

From the entire singularity of this burial it might be inferred that the deposit was a comparatively recent one; but the fact that the various layers of carbonaceous earth, stones, and clay were entirely undisturbed, and in no degree intermixed, settles the question beyond doubt, that the skull was placed where it was found at the time of the construction of the mound. Either, therefore, we must admit that the skull is a genuine relic of the mound-builders proper, or assume the improbable alternative that the mound in question does not belong to the grand system of earthworks of which we have been treating.

The skull is wonderfully well preserved; unaccountably so, unless the circumstances under which it was found may be regarded as most favorable to such a result. The imperviousness of the mound to water, from the nature of the material composing it, and its position on the summit of an eminence subsiding in every direction from its base, are circumstances which, joined to the antiseptic qualities of the carbonaceous deposit enveloping the skull, may satisfactorily account for its excellent preservation.

Of course no general conclusion as to the cranial characteristics of the ancient people can be based upon a single skull. It may nevertheless not be wholly unimportant or uninteresting to notice particularly the more prominent peculiarities of the specimen before us. The most striking feature is its extraordinary compactness or roundness. This will best be illustrated by the measurements, which show the vertical diameter to be 6.2 inches; longitudinal diameter 6.5 inches; inter-parietal diameter 6 inches. The vertical occiput, the prominent vertex, and great inter-parietal diameter, all of which are strongly marked in this skull, are, according to Dr. Morton, features characteristic of the American race, but more particularly of the family which he denominates the Toltecan, and of which the Peruvian head may be taken as the type. This skull was accurately measured by Dr. Morton, with the following results:

MEASUREMENTS.

Longitudinal diameter,	.	6.5 inches.	Inter-mastoid line,	. .	4.5 inches.
Inter-parietal, "	. .	6 "	Occipito-frontal arch, .	10.0 "
Vertical "	. .	6.2 "	Horizontal periphery,	.	19.8 "
Frontal "	. .	4.5 "	Facial angle, .	.	81 degrees.
Inter-mastoid arch, .	.	16 "	Internal capacity,	. .	90 cubic inches.

Dr. Morton, in his *Crania Americana*, has presented a number of examples of skulls from the mounds. Five of these are from mounds within the United States, and three are from the sepulchral tumuli of Peru. Those of the United States w ere obtained,—one from the Grave creek mound, one from a mound near the junction of the French Broad and Tennessee rivers in Tennessee, one from a mound on the Alabama river, one from a mound near Circleville in Ohio, and one from a mound on the Upper Mississippi. The first two may be regarded as genuine remains of the mound-builders; but it is more than probable, for reasons already advanced, that the rest are skulls of the recent Indians, who, as we have seen, often buried in the mounds. Numbers of these have been discovered by the authors in the mounds, and the measurements of four of them are introduced in the following comparative table, A, where they are indicated by an asterisk. This table exhibits the measurements of the mound skull discovered by the authors; of the eight skulls described by Dr. Morton; of four modern skulls recovered from the mounds; of a skull taken from the Mammoth Cave of Kentucky, three thousand yards from its mouth, and now in the possession of Messrs. FOWLERS & WELLS, of New York; and also of the skull of a mummy or desiccated body, taken from the same cave, and now in the Museum of the American Antiquarian Society, Worcester, Mass. It will be seen that the conclusion already adopted respecting three of the skulls noticed in the Crania Americana, are sustained by the general coincidence in measurements between them and those indubitably of recent date.

The comparatively large facial angle and great internal capacity of the skull figured in the plate cannot fail to attract attention. The mean internal capacity of the eight heads presented by Dr. Morton is but eighty-one cubic inches, while the facial angle does not exceed seventy-five degrees. The accompanying table, B, exhibiting the mean results of Dr. Morton's measurements of American aboriginal heads, as compared with the skull in question, and the mean measurements of the skulls supposed to pertain to the race of the mounds, may not prove unacceptable.

According to the same authority, the mean internal capacity of the Caucasian head is 87 cubic inches; of the Mongolian, 83; Malay, 81; American, 82; Ethiopian, 78.

From what has been presented, it will be seen that the skull here described exhibits, in a marked degree, the cranial characteristics of the American race, of which it may be regarded as a perfect type. Whether its peculiarities of form may not be, in part, artificial, it is not assumed to determine. It may nevertheless be observed, that the Natchez and Peruvians, as also many of the savage tribes, moulded the heads of their children in a variety of forms. The naturally vertical occiput was undoubtedly generally rendered the more marked by the almost universal practice of lashing the infant with its back against a board, by which it was suspended or carried about.

Several of the inferior maxillary bones of the mound skeletons have been recovered, nearly entire. They are remarkable for their massiveness, and seem to have been less projecting than those pertaining to the skeletons of a later date.

TABLE A.—COMPARATIVE MEASUREMENTS OF CRANIA.

	Mound-builder, from a mound in the Scioto Valley.	Mound-builder, from the Grave Creek Mound.	Mound-builder, from a mound in Tennessee.	From a tumulus near Santa in Peru (small).	From a tumulus in the valley of Rimac in Peru.	From a tumulus in the valley of Rimac in Peru (small).	From a mound on the Upper Mississippi. ?	From a mound near Circleville, Ohio. ?	From a mound in Alabama. ?	Recent Indian, from a mound in the Scioto Valley.*	Recent Indian, from a mound in the Scioto Valley.*	Recent Indian, from a mound in the Scioto Valley.*	Recent Indian, from a mound in the Scioto Valley.*	From the Mammoth Cave, Kentucky.	Skull of a mummy taken from the Great Cave in Kentucky, now in the Museum of Am. Antiquarian Society, Worcester, Mass.
Longitudinal diameter,	6.5	6.6	6.6	6.2	6.9	6.5	7.1	7.3	5.9	7.5	7.1	6.8	6.6	6.1	6.7
Inter-parietal "	6	6	5.6	5.4	5.6	5.6	5.3	5.8	6.6	5.3	5.6	5.7	5.2	5.4	5.5
Vertical "	6.2	5?	5.6	4.9	5.1	5	5.5	5.4	5.1	5.6	5.6	5.5	5.4	5.6	6.2
Frontal "	4.5	—	4.1	4.3	4.4	4.5	4.8	4.4	4.4	4.7	4.9	4.7	4.3	4.4	4.5
Inter-mastoid arch,	16	—	15.2	14.6	15.3	14.7	14.6	14.6	15.6	15.5	14.8	14.6	14.3	14.5	13.5
Inter-mastoid line,	4.5	—	4.4	3.8	4.3	3.8	4.2	4.2	4.4	4.3	4.4	4.4	3.8	4.4	5
Occipito-frontal arch,	13.8	—	14	13.3	14	13.2	14.6	14.1	12.4	15.4	14.2	14.3	13.7	13.6	—
Horizontal periphery,	19.8	—	19.5	18.5	19.7	19.2	20	20.3	19.6	21	20.3	20	18.6	18.4	19.7
Facial angle,	81°	78°	80°	71°	72°	74°	79°	76°	72°	76°	77°	—	70°	78°	61° 52'
Internal capacity,	90	—	80	74.5	79	76.5	85.5	86.5	80	—	—	—	—	75	

TABLE B.—COMPARATIVE VIEW OF MEAN CRANIAL MEASUREMENTS.

	MOUND SKULL FROM SCIOTO VALLEY.	MOUND-BUILDERS, FROM MISSISSIPPI VALLEY.		TOLTECAN NATIONS, INCLUDING SKULLS FROM THE MOUNDS.		BARBAROUS NATIONS, WITH SKULLS FROM OHIO VALLEY.		AMERICAN RACE, EMBRACING BARBAROUS AND TOLTECAN.		FLAT HEAD TRIBES OF OREGON.		ANCIENT PERUVIANS.	
		NO. OF SKULLS.	MEAN.	NO. OF SKULLS.	MEAN	NO. OF SKULLS.	MEAN.	NO. OF SKULLS.	MEAN.	NO. OF SKULLS.	MEAN.	NO. OF SKULLS.	MEAN.
Longitudinal diameter,	6.5	3	6.56	57	6.5	90	7	147	6.75	8	6.7	3	6.8
Inter-Parietal "	6	3	5.87	57	5.6	90	5.5	147	5.55	8	6	3	5
Vertical "	6.2	3	5.93	57	5.3	90	5.4	147	5.35	8	4.8	3	4.8
Frontal "	4.5	2	4.3	57	4.4	90	4.3	147	4.35	8	4.9	3	4.2
Inter-mastoid arch,	16	2	15.6	57	14.9	90	14.6	147	14.75	8	14.6	3	13.3
Inter-mastoid line,	4.5	2	4.45	57	4.1	90	4.2	147	4.15	8	4.1	3	4
Occipito-frontal arch,	13.8	2	13.9	57	13.6	90	14.2	147	13.9	8	13.1	3	14.3
Horizontal periphery,	19.8	2	19.65	57	19.4	90	19.9	147	19.65	8	20	3	18.8
Facial angle,	81°	3	79° 40'	55	75° 35'	83	76° 13'	138	75° 45'	8	69° 30'	3	67° 20'
Internal capacity,	90	2	85	57	76.8	87	82.4	144	79.6	8	79.25	3	73.2

CHAPTER XVIII.

SCULPTURED OR INSCRIBED ROCKS.

Rocks rudely inscribed with figures of men and animals, have been observed at various points within the United States, and have commanded no small share of attention. Their general character seems, however, but imperfectly understood; and for this reason care has been taken to preserve sketches and descriptions of such as fell under notice in the progress of the investigations recorded in this volume. In presenting the following illustrations, we are not to be understood as supposing that any of these rude monuments are referable to the era of the mounds, or that they have any extraordinary significance.

These illustrations comprise sketches of six sculptured rocks which occur upon the Guyandotte river in Virginia, and which have never before been noticed; together with a sketch of one occurring upon the Ohio river, never before figured, but to which distant allusion has several times been made. Notices of the locality and general character of several others, occurring chiefly within the valley of the Ohio, are also appended.

Proceeding upon a very vague intimation of the existence of certain rocks of this kind, upon the banks of the Guyandotte river, in Cabell county, Virginia, a visit was made to the locality in the autumn of 1846. The first of the series of rocks was found near the pathway, about eight miles above the town of Barbersville, or sixteen miles above the mouth of the river. It is a large detached block of weather-worn sandstone, of coarse texture, presenting above ground a flat but somewhat irregular surface. The edges are much rounded, and the rock closely resembles the water-worn boulders sometimes found on the alluvions. Immediately in the centre, which is slightly depressed, is cut in outline a rude effigy of a human figure, with arms extended and elevated, and apparently in the attitude of running. It is manifestly intended to represent a female, the breasts and other distinctive features being depicted. The action of the figure is well expressed, and the proportions are not materially wrong. It is four feet in height. Upon the edges of the rock are other outlines of the human figure, though too much obliterated to be traced with satisfaction or exactness. They are considerably less in size than the one just described. Besides these there are cut into the rock, at all angles to the plane of stratification, a number of tracks of various beasts and birds. Among them are those of the deer, bear, wolf, and turkey. They are very truthfully indicated, and it is no longer a matter of

surprise that similar sculptures have been mistaken by the uninformed for veritable impressions from the feet of the animals themselves.   They were cut at a later
date than the other figures, or have been cut deeper or subsequently retouched.
The turkey tracks are as distinct as if they had been left but yesterday in plastic
clay by the bird itself.   Among the tracks of the animals occurs the Roman
capital P, exactly formed.   This cannot be supposed to be anything more than an
accidental coincidence.   The lines are from one half to three fourths of an inch
deep, and for the most part appear to have been *pecked*, instead of chiselled, into

F I G . 2 0 0 .

the stone.   The rock measures about ten feet square.   It lies close by the side of
the road or bridle-path, upon the east bank, and about seventy-five yards from the
river.   Just below this point is quite a broad interval of level land, which is now
under cultivation.

From this place onward, the path winds under beetling cliffs of ragged sandstone, huge blocks of which, occasionally worn into fantastic shapes, are met at
every step.   At the distance of two miles, the traveller comes suddenly upon a confused mass of rocks, weighing many thousands of tons each, which have fallen from
the very brow of the cliff, crushing the puny forests in their course and bedding
themselves deep in the earth, which it has forced up in billows around them.   Here
occur the sculptured rocks of the Guyandotte.   Two only had been heard of
originally ; but after a careful examination, removing fallen trees and stones and
rubbish, three others were discovered, which, if not so large, nevertheless proved
quite as interesting as those which had at first attracted attention.   Drawings
were taken of these on the spot, which will give a better conception of the character of the sculptures, than any description can possibly afford.

Fig. 201.   The larger rock measures thirteen feet in length by an average of
ten feet in width.   Upon its horizontal face is cut, in deep outline, the figure of a
man, six feet three inches in height, by two feet in breadth at the shoulders.
There seems to have been no attempt at drapery.   The proportions of the figure,
the curve of the leg, etc., are very well represented.   The legs are placed near

together, the feet turned outwards, and the arms represented close by the side of the body. Something like a cocked hat, perhaps designed to represent the hair, covers the head. The face is triangular, and the eyes are represented by lines somewhat resembling an inverted **W**. The nose and mouth are indicated by simple lines. From the neck depends a singular figure, which rests upon the breast.

FIG. 201.

Perhaps it had a typical meaning, in common with similar representations among the wild Indians of the present day. The head of a deer or elk, with its branching antlers, is depicted upon the face of the rock below, and considerably to the right of the feet of the principal figure. There are also the tracks of certain animals, and two rows of round holes, numbering thirteen and fifteen respectively,—these last perhaps designed to indicate the number of achievements in war or chase of the chieftain whose effigy is beside them. There are many other lines; but the surface of the rock is so much worn and frayed by exposure to the elements, that it is quite impossible to make them out.

FIG. 202.

Fig. 202. Upon one of the vertical faces of this rock is cut, in bold and deep outline, the figure of an eagle, with wings extended as if just soaring upwards.

This is extremely spirited in design, and exhibits no small degree of artistic skill,—much more than is displayed in the engraving. A plume feather rises from the head of the bird. Immediately by its side is a rude outline of some bird with long neck and drooping wings. These figures are about two feet in length.

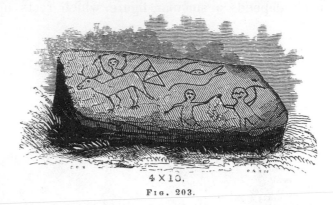

4 × 10.

FIG. 203.

Fig. 203. Upon another rock, close by the side of the one last mentioned, from which it appears to have been split off, is a sculptured group, manifestly representing a hunting scene. A deer or elk and several human figures, in attitudes of motion, are especially prominent. There is also a maze of lines which a fanciful mind might easily convert into an inscription in an ancient alphabet. Many of these lines are indistinct from exposure; those shown in the engraving are well marked. The rock measures four feet by ten.

FIG. 204.

Fig. 204. A third rock near by, almost entirely hidden by the ruins brought down by the rock avalanche from above, bears upon its face a figure of angular outline, resembling the outspread skin of some animal. The eyes and mouth are distinctly marked. By its side is the figure of a human head, and several wolf and deer tracks. There may be other sculptures on the rock; the portion exhibited in the engraving was exposed only by the expenditure of much severe labor, in the absence of tools for excavation.

Fig. 205. At the distance of a few rods from these is a small rock, four feet high by six in length. Upon its vertical face are cut the head and shoulders of an elk. The figure is faithfully executed, of full size, and in point of spirit can hardly be excelled by any outline representation. The savage artist who worked this head,

FIG. 205.

with his rude instruments, into the living rock, must have been a close observer of nature. He undoubtedly stood at the head of his profession—an Indian Landseer! Below this head is a rude representation of some object, probably a bow, an arrow from which is entering the neck of the elk.

There are unquestionably other rocks, in this immediate vicinity, covered over with earth and rubbish from the avalanche. The labors of the excavator would doubtless be rewarded with other discoveries; the employment however of some less primitive means than sharpened sticks and the naked hands can be feelingly recommended.

After leaving the vicinity of these rocks, it was ascertained that three miles higher up the stream, at a point known as the " Falls of the Guyandotte," there are others of a similar character. The figure of a man, with an upraised tomahawk, and that of a fox or other animal, are cut in the vertical face of the cliff, over which the river lately flowed, but which is now left exposed by some change in the channel of the stream.

The rocks above described occur in a sunny nook a short distance from the river, at a point where there is a small but beautiful interval of land. There is here a small earth circle and mound, showing that the race of the mounds penetrated thus far up the stream.

The rocks are weather-worn fragments of the coarse sandstone of the coal series, which breaks with a tolerably smooth and regular fracture, presenting surfaces well calculated for the kind of rude sculpture here exhibited. The lines upon the horizontal faces of the rocks are much less distinct than those upon their sides. They seem nevertheless to have been cut deeper, and are more elaborate. Those upon the vertical faces of the rocks seem to be little defaced, and probably are much in the same condition in which they were left by the sculptors. They are, for the most part, about three fourths of an inch wide by half an inch deep, sometimes a little wider and deeper: the outline of the principal figure on the large rock is not less than an inch wide and three fourths of an inch deep. Some of the round holes, which are very regular, will contain a gill of water each. The lines, as observed respecting the rock first noticed, do not appear to have been chiselled, but *pecked* into the stone. Where hard iron seams occur in the rock, a narrow ridge is left,—the rude instruments employed having evidently been inadequate to cut or break through them. That some of the tracks of animals, particularly those of the bear, were rubbed and smoothed with stones after having been chipped into shape, seems extremely probable, from the fact that they are not rough like the other lines, and exhibit the muscular developments of the foot with much accuracy. It is barely possible that they have been thus worn by the action of the elements.

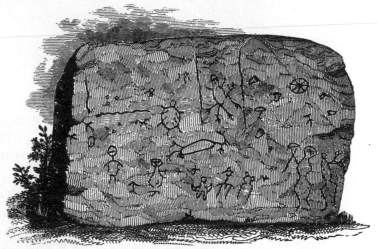

FIG. 206.

Fig. 206. A rock of similar character with those above described, occurs upon the Virginia shore of the Ohio river, four miles above the town of Steubenville in the State of Ohio, and about fifty miles below the city of Pittsburgh.* It is a detached block of sandstone, measuring seven feet by nine. The figures are cut in the same style with those before noticed, and are quite numerous. They comprise outlines of men and animals, including the tortoise and several serpents. There are also human footprints, and the tracks of animals, together with other emblematic figures, including the Indian symbol of the sun. The striking resemblance of the lower right-hand figures to those occupying a corresponding position on the Dighton rock, will not be overlooked.

A very interesting rock of this description lately existed at Catlettsburgh, on the Kentucky shore, at the confluence of the Big Sandy and Ohio rivers. It was

---

* These rocks are noticed by Dr. BARTON, *Transactions of American Philosophical Society*, vol. iv. p. 195. He regards them as " the work of a people acquainted with the use of iron instruments, or with hardened metallic instruments of some kind." The engraving in the text is from a sketch made for Mr. McBride, by J. W. Erwin, Esq.

entirely broken up about two years since, by a Vandal, to furnish the materials for building a chimney and walling a cellar! By a strange fatality this rock was selected for the purpose, although there were an abundance of others in the vicinity. It is represented to have been charged with numerous outline figures and emblematic devices. Efforts were made to recover some of the inscribed fragments, but without success. Nearly opposite this place, on the Ohio side, three miles below the village of Burlington, at a point where the Ohio sweeps

Fig. 207.—SITE OF THE SCULPTURED ROCKS OF THE GUYANDOTTE.

along the base of the sandstone cliffs, and where numerous fallen blocks line the shore, a similar inscribed rock once existed. It however has lately shared the fate of its neighbor on the other side of the stream. It was situated below the high-water mark; and its proximity to the water proved, in the end, the cause of its destruction, as the fragments quarried off could be easily placed on floats for transportation to the points required. Still another is said to have existed near the edge of the water, at a place known as the Hanging Rock, now the site of a furnace village, twenty-four miles above the mouth of the Scioto. It has probably been destroyed in like manner. There is however a very singular one still in existence a few miles above the town of Portsmouth, the southern terminus of the Ohio and Erie Canal, at the mouth of the Scioto. It consists of a colossal human head cut in outline, upon the vertical face of a large rock extending into the river. It is always under water, except when the river is at its very lowest stages, and is not exposed oftener than once in four or five years. It is familiarly known as the "Indian's Head," and is regarded as a sort of river guage or meter. When the water-line is at the top of the head, the river is considered very low.

Numerous other rocks of similar character are scattered over the West, occurring chiefly upon or near the banks of streams. They are not however confined to the westward of the Alleghanies, but are found in several of the Atlantic States. Those at Dighton and Tiverton in Massachusetts, and at Portsmouth in Rhode Island, are well known examples. They do not seem to differ materially in character from those already described.

From an inspection and comparison of these rocks, it must be very apparent that they are all the work of the same race: there is a family likeness in their style and workmanship, and a coincidence in position, which admits of no dispute, and seems to be conclusive upon this point. The further well known fact that the Indians possessed a system of representation, not inappropriately termed *picture-writing*, by which they conveyed intelligence and recorded events, serves still more clearly to indicate their probable origin,—especially as it is equally well known that they carved their rude pictures upon rocks as well as upon the bark of trees.

CHAPTER XIX.

CONCLUDING OBSERVATIONS.

WITH the facts presented in the foregoing chapters before him, the reader will be able to deduce his own conclusions, as to the probable character and condition of the ancient population of the Mississippi valley. That it was numerous and widely spread, is evident from the number and magnitude of the ancient monuments, and the extensive range of their occurrence. That it was essentially homogeneous , in customs, habits, religion, and government, seems very well sustained by the great uniformity which the ancient remains display, not only as regards position and form, but in respect also to those minor particulars, which, not less than more obvious and imposing features, assist us in arriving at correct conclusions. This opinion can be in no way affected, whether we assume that the ancient race was at one time diffused over the entire valley, or that it migrated slowly from one portion of it to the other, under the pressure of hostile neighbors or the attractions of a more genial climate. The differences which have already been pointed out between the monuments of the several portions of the valley, of the northern, central, and southern divisions, are not sufficiently marked to authorize the belief that they were the works of separate nations. The features common to all are elementary, and identify them as appertaining to a single grand system, owing its origin to a family of men, moving in the same general direction, acting under common impulses, and influenced by similar causes.

Without undertaking to point out the affinities, or to indicate the probable origin of the builders of the western monuments, and the cause of their final disappearance,—inquiries of deep interest and vast importance in an archæological and ethnological point of view, and in which it is believed the foregoing chapters may greatly assist,—we may venture to suggest that the facts thus far collected point to a connection more or less intimate between the race of the mounds and the semi-civilized nations which formerly had their seats among the sierras of Mexico, upon the plains of Central America and Peru, and who erected the imposing structures which from their number, vastness, and mysterious significance, invest the central portions of the continent with an interest not less absorbing than that which attaches to the valley of the Nile. These nations alone, of all those found in possession of the continent by the European discoverers, were essentially stationary and agricultural in their habits,—conditions indispensable to large population, to fixedness of institutions, and to any considerable advance in the economical or ennobling arts. That the mound-builders, although perhaps in a less degree, were also stationary and agricultural, clearly appears from a variety of facts and circumstances, most of which will no doubt recur to the mind of the reader, but which will bear recapitulation here.

It may safely be claimed, and will be admitted without dispute, that a large local population can only exist under an agricultural system. Dense commercial and manufacturing communities, the apparent exceptions to the remark, are themselves the offspring of a large agricultural population, with which nearly or remotely they are connected, and upon which they are dependent. Now it is evident that works of art, so numerous and vast as we have seen those of the Mississippi valley to be, could only have been erected by a numerous people,—and especially must we regard as numerous the population capable of constructing them, when we reflect how imperfect at the best must have been the artificial aids at their command, as compared with those of the present age. Implements of wood, stone, and copper, could hardly have proved very efficient auxiliaries to the builders, who must have depended mainly upon their own bare hands and weak powers of transportation, for excavating and collecting together the twenty millions of cubic feet of material which make up the solid contents of the great mound at Cahokia alone.

But the conclusion that the ancient population was exceedingly dense, follows not less from the capability which they possessed to erect, than from the circumstance that they required, works of the magnitude we have seen, to protect them in danger, or to indicate in a sufficiently imposing form their superstitious zeal, and their respect for the dead. As observed by an eminent archæologist, whose opinions upon this and collateral subjects are entitled to a weight second to those of no other author, "it is impossible that the population, for whose protection such extensive works were necessary, and which was able to defend them, should not have been eminently agricultural." The same author elsewhere observes, of the great mound at Grave creek, that " it indicates not only a dense agricultural population, but also a state of society essentially different from that of the modern race of Indians north of the tropic. There is not, and there was not in the sixteenth century, a single tribe of Indians (north of the semi-civilized nations) between the Atlantic and the Pacific, which had means of subsistence sufficient to enable them to apply, for such purposes, the unproductive labor necessary for the work ; nor was there any in such a social state as to compel the labor of the people to be thus applied."*

---

* GALLATIN's "Notes on the semi-civilized nations of Mexico," *Transactions of American Ethnological Society,* vol. i. p. 207.

Mr. Gallatin, in the memoir here quoted, has discussed at considerable length the question of the origin of agriculture among the American nations. His views, altogether the most philosophical of any hitherto presented on the subject, may not be without their interest in this connection. It should be observed, at the outset, that Mr. Gallatin is of the opinion, not only that agriculture on this continent was of domestic origin, but also that it originated between the tropics,—spreading thence in different directions to the north and south. The evidence in support of the latter conclusion is not presented in sufficient detail to enable us to judge how well sustained it may be. If we admit its correctness, we must derive the agriculture of the mound-builders from the south, and assign that race chronologically a comparatively low date. This we are not yet prepared to do ; on the contrary, there are many facts going to establish

Another evidence of the probable agricultural character of the mound-builders, is furnished in the fact already several times remarked, that these remains are almost entirely confined to the fertile valleys of streams, or to productive alluvions bordering on the lakes or on the Gulf of Mexico,—precisely the positions best adapted for agricultural purposes, and capable of sustaining the densest population, as also affording, in fish and game, the most efficient secondary aids of support.

If the mound-builders were a numerous, stationary, and an agricultural people, it follows of necessity that their customs, laws, and religion, had assumed a fixed and well defined form,—a result inseparable from that condition. The construction therefore of permanent fortifications for protection against hostile neighbors, and of vast and regular religious structures, under this hypothesis, fell clearly within their capabilities.

The modes of warfare which they practised, so far as they can be made out, and the probable state of the civil relations between them and their neighbors, and among themselves, have been noticed in the remarks on the Works of Defence, in a previous chapter. Little can, at present, be added upon these points.

---

for the mound-builders very high antiquity, and tending to the conclusion that the degree of civilization which they possessed was attained by a course of development in the Mississippi valley. It is not impossible that future investigations may show that the agriculture and civilization of the Mexicans, Central Americans, and Peruvians, had its origin among the builders of the ancient monuments on the banks of the great Mississippi river,—the Nile and the Ganges of North America.

"What was the first indispensable transition which withdrew a certain portion of the aborigines of America from the barbarism and ignorance in which all the other tribes are still found? That it was the transition from the hunter to the agricultural state, no one can doubt. It is true some of the tribes among whom agriculture was introduced, are still savages; but not an instance exists in America of a nation, either populous or to a certain extent civilized, which is not agricultural. * * * * We are then led to inquire how agriculture was introduced into America, and whether it was imported or of domestic origin.

"We have here two leading facts, one positively ascertained, and the other generally admitted by those who have inquired into the subject, the importance of which has not, it seems to me, been adverted to.

"The first is that all those nutritious plants cultivated in the other hemisphere, and which are usually distinguished by the name of cereals (millet, rice, wheat, rye, barley, oats), were entirely unknown to the Americans.

"The second is that maize, which was the great and almost sole foundation of American agriculture, is exclusively of American origin, and was not known in the other hemisphere till after the discovery of America, in the fifteenth century.

"If these two facts be admitted, it necessarily follows that the introduction of agriculture,—that first, difficult, and indispensable preliminary step before any advance whatever can be made towards civilization,—originated in America itself; that it was not imported from abroad; and that it was the result of the natural progress from barbarism to a more refined social state by the race of red men, insulated, left to themselves, and without any aid or communication from any foreign country. It is therefore highly important for a correct view of the history of man, that the presumed fact of maize being exclusively an American plant, should be thoroughly investigated. * * * If a domestic origin is admitted, it is quite natural that agriculture should have had its birth in the most genial climate, and in the native country of the maize."—*Transactions of American Ethnological Society*, vol. i. p. 100.

What climate more genial, and what soil better adapted to the cultivation of maize, in its perfection, than those portions of the Mississippi valley where the evidences of ancient civilization are most abundant and imposing?

If we are not mistaken in assigning a religious origin to that large portion of ancient monuments, which are clearly not defensive, nor designed to perpetuate the memory of the dead, then the superstitions of the ancient people must have exercised a controlling influence upon their character. If, again, as from reason and analogy we are warranted in supposing, many of these sacred structures are symbolical in their forms and combinations, they indicate the prevalence among their builders of religious beliefs and conceptions, corresponding with those which prevailed among the early nations of the other continent, and which in their elements seem to have been common to all nations, far back in the traditional period, before the dawn of written history. Their consideration under this aspect involves a preliminary analysis of the religious belief of the various aboriginal American families, an examination of their mythologies and superstitious rites, and a comparison between them and those of the primitive nations of the old world. It involves, also, an attention to the sacred monuments of the eastern continent, to the principles upon which they were constructed, and to the extent to which a symbolical design is apparent in their combinations and ornaments. But it is alike beyond the scope and design of this work to go into these inquiries, which in themselves, from their attractiveness and importance, deserve a full and separate consideration. We may, however, be permitted to express the belief, that researches in this department, philosophically conducted, must lead to results of the highest value, and greatly aid in the solution of the interesting problems connected with our aboriginal history. For, in the words of a writer of distinction, " of all researches that most effectually aid us to discover the origin of a nation or people, whose history is unknown or deeply involved in the obscurity of ancient times, none perhaps are attended with such important results, as the analysis of their theological dogmas, and their religious practices. In such matters mankind adhere with greatest tenacity, and though both modified and corrupted in the revolutions of ages, they still preserve features of their original construction, when language, arts, sciences, and political establishments no longer retain distinct lineaments of their ancient constitutions."*

The antiquity of the ancient monuments of the Mississippi valley has been made the subject of incidental remark in the foregoing chapters. It will not be out of place here to allude once more to some of the facts bearing upon this point. Of course no attempt to fix their date accurately can, from the circumstances of the case, be successful. The most that can be done is to arrive at approximate results. The fact that none of the ancient monuments occur upon the latest-formed terraces of the river valleys of Ohio, is one of much importance in its bearings upon this question. If, as we are amply warranted in believing, these terraces mark the degrees of subsidence of the streams, one of the four which may be traced has been formed since those streams have followed their present courses. There is no good reason for supposing that the mound-builders would have avoided building upon that terrace, while they erected their works promiscuously upon all the others.

---

* McCulloh *Philosophical and Antiquarian Researches*, p. 225.

And if they had built upon it, some slight traces of their works would yet be visible, however much influence we may assign to disturbing causes,—overflows, and shifting channels. Assuming, then, that the lowest terrace, on the Scioto river for example, has been formed since the era of the mounds, we must next consider that the excavating power of the Western rivers diminishes yearly, in proportion as they approximate towards a general level. On the lower Mississippi,—where alone the ancient monuments are sometimes invaded by the water,—the bed of the stream is rising, from the deposition of the materials brought down from the upper tributaries, where the excavating process is going on. This excavating power, it is calculated, is in an inverse ratio to the square of the depth, that is to say, diminishes as the square of the depth increases. Taken to be approximately correct, this rule establishes that the formation of the latest terrace, by the operation of the same causes, must have occupied much more time than the formation of any of the preceding three. Upon these premises, the time, since the streams have flowed in their present courses, may be divided into four periods, of different lengths,—of which the latest, supposed to have elapsed since the race of the mounds flourished, is much the longest.

The fact that the rivers, in shifting their channels, have in some instances encroached upon the superior terraces, so as in part to destroy works situated upon them, and afterwards receded to long distances of a fourth or half a mile or upwards, is one which should not be overlooked in this connection. (See pages 50, 60, and 89.) In the case of the "High Bank Works," Plate XVI, the recession has been nearly three fourths of a mile, and the intervening terrace or "bottom" was, at the period of the early settlement, covered with a dense forest. This recession, and subsequent forest growth, must of necessity have taken place since the river encroached upon the ancient works here alluded to.

Without doing more than to allude to the circumstance of the exceedingly decayed state of the skeletons found in the mounds, (see page 168,) and to the amount of vegetable accumulations in the ancient excavations, and around the ancient works, (see pages 55 and 90,) we pass to another fact, perhaps more important in its bearing upon the question of the antiquity of these works than any of those presented above. It is that they are covered with primitive forests, in no way distinguishable from those which surround them, in places where it is probable no clearings were ever made. Some of the trees of these forests have a positive antiquity of from six to eight hundred years (see pages 14 and 16). They are found surrounded with the mouldering remains of others, undoubtedly of equal original dimensions, but now fallen and almost incorporated with the soil. Allow a reasonable time for the encroachment of the forest, after the works were abandoned by their builders, and for the period intervening between that event and the date of their construction, and we are compelled to assign them no inconsiderable antiquity. But, as already observed, the forests covering these works correspond in all respects with the surrounding forests; the same varieties of trees are found, in the same proportions, and they have a like primitive aspect. This fact was remarked by the late President HARRISON, and was put forward by him as one of the strongest evidences of the high antiquity of these works. In an address before the Historical Society of Ohio, he said :

" The process by which nature restores the forest to its original state, after being once cleared, is extremely slow. The rich lands of the West are, indeed, soon covered again, but the character of the growth is entirely different, and continues so for a long period. In several places upon the Ohio, and upon the farm which I occupy, clearings were made in the first settlement of the country and subsequently abandoned and suffered to grow up. Some of these new forests are now sure of fifty years' growth, but they have made so little progress towards attaining the appearance of the immediately contiguous forest, as to induce any man of reflection to determine that at least ten times fifty years must elapse before their complete assimilation can be effected. We find in the ancient works all that variety of trees which give such unrivalled beauty to our forests, in natural proportions. The first growth on the same kind of land, once cleared and then abandoned to nature, on the contrary, is nearly homogeneous, often stinted to one or two, at most three kinds of timber. If the ground has been cultivated, the yellow locust will thickly spring up ; if not cultivated, the black and white walnut will be the prevailing growth.   *   *   *   Of what immense age then must be the works so often referred to, covered as they are by at least the second growth, after the primitive forest state was regained ? "

It is not undertaken to assign a period for the assimilation here indicated to take place. It must unquestionably, however, be measured by centuries.

In respect to the extent of territory occupied at one time, or at successive periods, by the race of the mounds, so far as indicated by the occurrence of their monuments, little need be said in addition to the observations presented in the first chapter. It cannot, however, have escaped notice, that the relics found in the mounds,—composed of materials peculiar to places separated as widely as the ranges of the Alleghanies on the east, and the Sierras of Mexico on the west, the waters of the great lakes on the north, and those of the Gulf of Mexico on the south,—denote the contemporaneous existence of communication between these extremes. For we find, side by side in the same mounds, native copper from Lake Superior, mica from the Alleghanies, shells from the Gulf, and obsidian (perhaps porphyry) from Mexico. This fact seems seriously to conflict with the hypothesis of a migration, either northward or southward. Further and more extended investigations and observations may, nevertheless, serve satisfactorily to settle not only this, but other equally interesting questions connected with the extinct race, whose name is lost to tradition itself, and whose very existence is left to the sole and silent attestation of the rude but often imposing monuments which throng the valleys of the West.

GUIDE TO
SQUIER AND DAVIS'S
REFERENCES.

Prepared by David J. Meltzer

There are nearly seventy-five bibliographic references in *Ancient Monuments*. Unfortunately—but in keeping with the custom of the time—Squier and Davis's citations were often little more than a name and/or a title (they were inconsistent in this regard), usually accompanied by a volume or page number but never a full bibliographic reference. Compounding the difficulties, they were often indifferent and inconsistent about their spelling of authors' names, dates of publication, abbreviations, and titles (for example, as best I can determine, neither Bartram nor Featherstonhaugh nor Prince Maximilian ever wrote a volume specifically titled *Travels in North America,* as they are so cited on pages 253, 174, and 167, respectively, but they did write about their travels in North America under different titles, and those are listed below with the assumption that these are the books Squier and Davis had in mind). These problems notwithstanding, all but five of their references could be identified and are listed below.

Where there was ambiguity, I have chosen what I believe to be the correct author and title. Where multiple editions existed, or where the edition they consulted is unknown, I generally list the edition closest to the time when they were writing. If a volume was published in the United States and overseas, I give the citation for the American edition, both for the sake of consistency and supposing that it would more likely have been the edition consulted by Squier and Davis.

Adair, J.
  1775 *The history of the American Indians; particularly those nations adjoining to the Mississippi, east and west Florida, Georgia, South and North Carolina, and Virginia; containing an account of their origins, languages, manners . . . and other particulars sufficient to render it a complete Indian system . . .* London: E. and C. Dilly.

Atwater, C.
  1820 Descriptions of the antiquities discovered in the state of Ohio and other western states. *Archaeologia Americana. Transactions and Collections of the American Antiquarian Society* 1:105–267.

Bartlett, J.
  1847 The progress of ethnology: An account of recent archaeological, philological and geographical researches in various parts of the globe, tending to elucidate the physical history of man. *Transactions of the American Ethnological Society* 2:appendix.

Bartram, W.
  1791 *Travels through North and South Carolina, Georgia, East and West Florida, the Cherokee country, the extensive territories of the Muscogulges, or Creek Confederacy, and the country of the Choctaws.* Philadelphia: James and Johnson. [Publication date is given as 1779 in *Ancient Monuments.*]

Beck, L. C.

1823   *A gazeteer of the states of Illinois and Missouri; containing a general view of each state—a general view of their counties—a particular description of their towns, villages, rivers . . .* Albany: C. R. and G. Webster.

Beverly, R.

1705   *The history and present state of Virginia.* London R. Parker.

Brackenridge, Henry M.

1813   On the population and tumuli of the aborigines of North America, in a letter to Thomas Jefferson. *Transactions of the American Philosophical Society*, 1:151–59.

1814   *Views of Louisiana; together with a Journal of a voyage up the Missouri River, in 1811.* Pittsburgh: Printed and published by Cramer, Spear, and Eichbaum, Franklin Head Office.

Carver, J.

1779   *Travels through the interior parts of North America in the years 1766, 1767, and 1768.* Dublin: S. Price and R. Cross.

Catlin, G.

1841   *Letters and notes on the manners, customs, and conditions of the North American Indians / written during eight years' travel, from 1832 to 1839, amongst the wildest tribes of Indians in North America.* New York: Wiley and Putnam.

Charlevoix, Pierre-François

1761   *Journal of a voyage to North-America. Undertaken by order the French king. Containing the geographical description natural history of that country, particularly Canada. Together with an account of the customs, characters, religion, manners, and traditions of the original inhabitants.* London: R. and J. Dodsley.

1769   *The history of Paraguay. Containing a full and authentic account of the establishments formed there by the Jesuits, from among the savage natives . . . establishments allowed to have realized the sublime ideas of Fenelon, Sir Thomas More, and Plato.* London: L. Davis.

Clavigero, Francesco Saverio

1787   *The history of Mexico. Collected from Spanish and Mexican historians, from manuscripts and ancient paintings of the Indians. Illustrated by Charts and other copper plates. To which are added, critical dissertations on the land, the animals, and inhabitants of Mexico.* Translated from the original Italian by Charles Cullen. London: G. G. J. and Robinson.

Clinton, DeWitt

1817   A memoir on the antiquities of the western part of the state of New York. *Transactions of the Literary and Philosophical Society of New York* 2:71–84.

Collins, Lewis

1847   *Historical sketches of Kentucky.* Cincinnati: J. A. and U. P. James.

Conrad, T. A.

1846   Observations on the geology of a part of east Florida, with a catalogue of recent shells of the coast. *American Journal of Science* 52:36–48.

Cook, James

1777   *A voyage towards the South Pole, and round the world: performed in His Majesty's ships the Resolution and Adventure, in the years 1772, 1773, 1774, and 1775.* London: Strahan and Cadell.

Cornelius, E.

1819   On the geology, mineralogy, scenery, and curiousities of parts of Virginia, Tennessee, and the Alabama and Mississippi territories, with miscellaneous remarks. *American Journal of Science* 1:214–26.

Drake, D.

1815   *Natural and statistical view; or, Picture of Cincinatti and the Miami country.* Cincinatti: Looker and Wallace.

Ellis, W.

1833   *Polynesian researches, during a residence of nearly eight years in the Society and Sandwich Islands.* New York: J. and J. Harper.

Featherstonhaugh, George W.

1844   *Excursion through the slave states: From Washington on the Potomac, to the frontier of Mexico; with sketches of popular manners and geological notices.* New York: Harper.

Flint, T.

1828 *A condensed geography and history of the western states, or the Mississippi Valley.* Cincinatti: E. H. Flint.

Forshey, C. G.

1845 Description of some artificial mounds on Prairie Jefferson, Louisiana. *American Journal of Science* 49:38–42.

Fremont, J. C.

1845 *Report of the exploring expedition to the Rocky Mountains in the year 1842 and to Oregon and North California in the years 1843–1844.* 28th Cong., 2d sess. S. Doc. 11, pp. 7–693.

Gibbes, R. W.

1847 New species of Myliobates from the Eocene of South Carolina, with other genera not heretofore observed in the United States. *Journal of the Academy of Natural Sciences of Philadelphia* 1:299–300.

Godman, J. D.

1826 *American natural history.* 2 vols. Philadelphia: H. C. Carey and I. Lea.

Harris, T.

1805 *The journal of a tour into the territory northwest of the Alleghany Mountains; made in the spring of the year 1805.* Boston: Manning and Loring.

Harrison, W. H.

1839 A discourse on the aborigines of the Ohio Valley. *Transactions of the Historical and Philosophical Society of Ohio.* Vol. 1, Part 2.

Haywood, John

1823 *The natural and aboriginal history of Tennessee, up to the first settlements therein by white people in the year 1768.* Nashville: George Wilson.

Hearte, J.

1787 Account of some remains of ancient work on the Muskingum, with a plan of these works. *Columbian Magazine* 1:425–27.

1792 Observations on the ancient mounds. In *Topographical description of the western territory,* edited by G. Imlay. London: Debrett.

Herrera y Tordesillas, Antonio de

1740 *The general history of the vast continent and islands of America, commonly call'd the West-Indies, from the first discovery thereof.* 2d ed. 6 vols. London: Wood and Woodward.

Hoare, R. C.

1812– *The ancient history of Wiltshire.* London: W. Miller.
1819

Humboldt, Alexander von.

1814– *Personal narrative of travels to the equinoctial regions of the New Continent, during the years*
1829 *1799–1804.* 7 vols. London: Longman, Hurst, Rees, Orme, and Brown.

1814 *Researches, concerning the institutions and monuments of the ancient inhabitants of America, with descriptions and views some of the most striking scenes in the Cordilleras.* London: Longman, Hurst, Rees, Orme, and Brown, J. Murray, H. Colburn.

James, E.

1823 *Account of an expedition from Pittsburgh to the Rocky Mountains, performed in the years 1819 and '20, by order of the Hon. J. C. Calhoun, Sec'y of War; under the command of Major Stephen H. Long, from the notes of Major Long, Mr. S. T. Say, and other gentlemen of the exploring party; compiled by Edwin James, botanist and geologist for the expedition.* Philadelphia: II. Carey and I. Lea.

Juarros, D.

1808– *Compendio de la historia de la ciudad de Guatemala.* Guatemala: I. Beteta.
1818

Keating, W. H. [Long's Second Expedition]

1824 *Narrative of an expedition to the source of St. Peter's River, Lake Winnepeek, Lake of the Woods, etc., performed in the year 1823, by order of the honorable J. C. Calhoun, Secretary of War, under the command of Major Stephen H. Long, U.S.T.E.; compiled from the notes of Major Long, Messrs Say, Keating, and Colhoun.* Philadelphia: H. Carey and I. Lea.

Latrobe, C. J.

1835   *The rambler in North America*. New York: Seeky.

Lawson, J.

1709   *A new voyage to Carolina, containing the exact description and natural history of that country, together with the present state thereof. And a journal of a thousand miles, travel'd thro' several nations of Indians, giving a particular account of their customs, manners*. London.

Le Page Du Pratz, A. S.

1758   *Histoire de la Louisiane, contenant la decouverte de ce vaste pays; sa description geographique; un voyage dans les terres; l'histoire naturelle, les moeurs, coutumes and etc.* Paris: De Bure.

Locke, J.

1844   Earthwork antiquities in Wisconsin Territory. In *Report of a geological exploration of part of Iowa, Wisconsin, and Illinois,* by David Dale Owen. *Mineral Lands of the United States.* Washington, D.C.: Government Printing Office.

Loskiel, G. H.

1838   *The history of the Moravian mission among the Indians in North America, from its commencement to the present time. With a preliminary account of the Indians.* London: T. Allman.

Lyell, C.

1845   *Travels in North America in 1841–42; with geological observations on the United States, Canada, and Nova Scotia.* New York: Wiley and Putnam.

Macauley, J.

1829   *The natural, statistical and civil history of the state of New York.* New York: Gould and Banks.

Madison, J.

1803   A letter on the supposed fortification of the western country from Bishop Madison of Virginia to Dr. Barton. *Transactions of the American Philosophical Society* 6:132–42.

Martyr, P. [d'Anghiera, Pietro Martire]

1555   *De Orbe Novo. The decades of the Newe Worlde or West India.* Translated by Richard Eden. London: Powell.

Molina, Giovanni Ignazio

1809   *The geographical, natural, and civil history of Chili.* London: Longman, Hurst, Rees, and Orme. [Christoval de Molina's *Narratives of the rites and laws of the Yncas* is a better fit in the context of the citation in *Ancient Monuments,* p. 45, but no printed edition appears to have been available until 1873.]

Morton, S. G.

1839   *Crania Americana; or, a comparative view of the skulls of various aboriginal nations of North and South America, to which is prefixed an essay on the varieties of the human species.* Philadelphia: J. Dobson.

Prince Maximilian [Wied-Neuwied, M. A.]

1843   *Reise in das innere Nord-America . . . in den jahren 1832 bis 1834, mit 49 kupfern, 33 vignetten, viele holzshnitten und einer charte* (Travels in the Interior of North America). Translated by H. E. Loyd. London: Ackermann and Company.

Proctor, R.

1825   *Narrative of a journey across the cordillera of the Andes, and of a residence in Lima, and other parts of Peru, in the years 1823 and 1824.* London: Hurst, Robinson, and Company.

Schmidtmeyer, P.

1824   *Travels into Chile, over the Andes, in the years 1820 and 1821, with some sketches of the productions and agriculture; mines and metallurgy; inhabitants, history, and other features of America; particularly of Chile, and Arauco.* London: Longman, Hurst, Rees, Orme, Brown, and Green.

Schoolcraft, H. R.

1845   Observations respecting the Grave Creek mound in western Virginia; the antique inscription discovered in its excavation; and the connected evidences of the occupancy of the Mississippi Valley during the Mound period and prior to the discovery of America by Columbus. *Transactions of the American Ethnological Society* 1:367–420.

1846   *Notes on the Iroquois; or, contributions to the statistics, aboriginal history, antiquities and general ethnology of western New York.* New York: Bartlett and Welford.

Solis, Antonio de
1783– *Historia de la conquista de Mexico, poblacion, y progressos de la America Septentrional cono-*
1784 *cida por el nombre de Nueva Espaóna.* Madrid: Antonio de Sancha.
Squier, E. G.
1847 Observations on the aboriginal monuments of the Mississippi Valley. *Transactions of the American Ethnological Society* 2:131–207.
Stephens, John L.
1842 *Incidents of travel in Central America, Chiapas, and Yucatan.* London: J. Murray.
Stoddard, A.
1812 *Sketches, historical and descriptive, of Louisiana.* Philadelphia: Mathew Carey.
Taylor, R. C.
1838 Notes respecting certain Indian mounds and earthworks, in the form of animal effigies, chiefly in the Wisconsin Territory. *American Journal of Science* 34:88–104.
Taylor, S.
1843 Description of ancient remains, animal mounds, and embankments, principally in the counties of Grant, Iowa, and Richmond, in Wisconsin. *American Journal of Science* 44:21–40.
Tomlinson, Abelard B.
1843 American antiquities at Grave Creek. Mr. Tomlinson's letter. *The American Pioneer* 2:196–203.
Ulloa, Antonio de, and J. Juan
1758 *A voyage to South-America : describing at large the Spanish cities, towns, provinces, &c. on that extensive continent : interspersed throughout with reflections on the genius, customs, manners and trade of the inhabitants : together with the natural history of the country and an account of their gold and silver mines : undertaken by command of His Majesty the King of Spain.* Translated by J. Adams. London: L. Davis and C. Reymers.
Vega, Garcilaso de la
1688 *The royal commentaries of Peru, in two parts : the first part : treating of the original of their Incas or kings, of their idolatry, of their laws and government both in peace and war, of the reigns and conquests of the Incas : the second part : describing the manner by which that new world was conquered by the Spaniards, also the civil wars between the Picarrists and the Almagrians and other particulars contained in that history : illustrated with sculptures.* Translated by Sir Paul Rycaut. London: M. Flesher for C. Wilkinson.
Venegas, Miguel
1757 *Noticia de la California y de su conquista temporal, y espiritual hasta el tiempo presente, sacada de la historia manuscita, formada en Mexico ano de 1739, por el Padre Miguel Venegas . . . y de otras noticias, y relaciones antiguas, y modernas.* Madrid: M. Fernandez.
Wailes, B. L.
1845 On the geology of the Mississippi. *Proceedings of the Association of American Geologists and Naturalists for 1845,* pp. 80–81.
Warden, D. B.
1834 Recherches sur les antiquities de l Amerique du nord. In *Antiquites Mexicans: Relations des trois expeditions du Capitaine DuPaix, ordonnees en 1805, 1806, et 1807,* edited by H. Baradere. Paris: Jules Didot.
Wilkes, C.
1844 *Narrative of the United States Exploring Expedition during the years 1838, 1839, 1840, 1841, 1842.* Vol. 4. Philadelphia: C. Sherman.
Wilkinson, J. G.
1837 *Manners and customs of the ancient Egyptians, including their private life, government, laws, arts, manufactures, religion, and early history.* 3 vols. London.
Williamson, H.
1811 *Observations on the climate in different parts of America, compared with the climate in corresponding parts of the other continent.* New York: T. and J. Swords.

INDEX.